Risk Detection and Cyber Security for the Success of Contemporary Computing

Raghvendra Kumar
GIET University, India

Prasant Kumar Pattnaik
KIIT Univeristy, India

A volume in the Advances in Information Security,
Privacy, and Ethics (AISPE) Book Series

Published in the United States of America by
  IGI Global
  Information Science Reference (an imprint of IGI Global)
  701 E. Chocolate Avenue
  Hershey PA, USA 17033
  Tel: 717-533-8845
  Fax: 717-533-8661
  E-mail: cust@igi-global.com
  Web site: http://www.igi-global.com

Library of Congress Cataloging-in-Publication Data

Names: Kumar, Raghvendra, 1987- editor. | Pattnaik, Prasant Kumar, 1969-
  editor.
Title: Risk detection and cyber security for the success of contemporary
  computing / edited Raghvendra Kumar, and Prasant Kumar Pattnaik.
Description: Hershey, PA : Information Science Reference, [2023] | Includes
  bibliographical references and index. | Summary: "Risk Detection and
  Cyber Security for the Success of Contemporary Computing presents the
  newest findings with technological advances that can be utilized for
  more effective prevention techniques to protect against cyber threats.
  This book is led by editors of best-selling and highly indexed
  publications, and together they have over two decades of experience in
  computer science and engineering. Featuring extensive coverage on
  authentication techniques, cloud security, and mobile robotics, this
  book is ideally designed for students, researchers, scientists, and
  engineers seeking current research on methods, models, and
  implementation of optimized security in digital contexts"-- Provided by
  publisher.
Identifiers: LCCN 2023016912 (print) | LCCN 2023016913 (ebook) | ISBN
  9781668493175 (h/c) | ISBN 9781668493182 (s/c) | ISBN 9781668493175
  (eISBN)
Subjects: LCSH: Computer security. | Robotics--Security measures. |
  Intrusion detection systems (Computer security)
Classification: LCC QA76.9.A25 .R4935 2023 (print) | LCC QA76.9.A25
  (ebook) | DDC 005.8--dc23/eng/20230824
LC record available at https://lccn.loc.gov/2023016912
LC ebook record available at https://lccn.loc.gov/2023016913

This book is published in the IGI Global book series Advances in Information Security, Privacy, and Ethics (AISPE) (ISSN: 1948-9730; eISSN: 1948-9749)

British Cataloguing in Publication Data
A Cataloguing in Publication record for this book is available from the British Library.

For electronic access to this publication, please contact: eresources@igi-global.com.

Advances in Information Security, Privacy, and Ethics (AISPE) Book Series

Manish Gupta
State University of New York, USA

ISSN:1948-9730
EISSN:1948-9749

MISSION

As digital technologies become more pervasive in everyday life and the Internet is utilized in ever increasing ways by both private and public entities, concern over digital threats becomes more prevalent.

The **Advances in Information Security, Privacy, & Ethics (AISPE) Book Series** provides cutting-edge research on the protection and misuse of information and technology across various industries and settings. Comprised of scholarly research on topics such as identity management, cryptography, system security, authentication, and data protection, this book series is ideal for reference by IT professionals, academicians, and upper-level students.

COVERAGE

- Computer ethics
- Privacy-Enhancing Technologies
- Privacy Issues of Social Networking
- Global Privacy Concerns
- Electronic Mail Security
- CIA Triad of Information Security
- Technoethics
- IT Risk
- Cookies
- Cyberethics

IGI Global is currently accepting manuscripts for publication within this series. To submit a proposal for a volume in this series, please contact our Acquisition Editors at Acquisitions@igi-global.com or visit: http://www.igi-global.com/publish/.

The Advances in Information Security, Privacy, and Ethics (AISPE) Book Series (ISSN 1948-9730) is published by IGI Global, 701 E. Chocolate Avenue, Hershey, PA 17033-1240, USA, www.igi-global.com. This series is composed of titles available for purchase individually; each title is edited to be contextually exclusive from any other title within the series. For pricing and ordering information please visit http://www.igi-global.com/book-series/advances-information-security-privacy-ethics/37157. Postmaster: Send all address changes to above address. Copyright © 2023 IGI Global. All rights, including translation in other languages reserved by the publisher. No part of this series may be reproduced or used in any form or by any means – graphics, electronic, or mechanical, including photocopying, recording, taping, or information and retrieval systems – without written permission from the publisher, except for non commercial, educational use, including classroom teaching purposes. The views expressed in this series are those of the authors, but not necessarily of IGI Global.

Titles in this Series

For a list of additional titles in this series, please visit: www.igi-global.com/book-series

Contemporary Challenges for Cyber Security and Data Privacy
Nuno Mateus-Coelho (Lusófona University, Portugal) and Maria Manuela Cruz-Cunha (Polytechnic Institute of Cávado and Ave, Porugal)
Information Science Reference • © 2023 • 308pp • H/C (ISBN: 9798369315286) • US $275.00

Privacy Preservation and Secured Data Storage in Cloud Computing
Lakshmi D. (VIT Bhopal University, India) and Amit Kumar Tyagi (National Institute of Fashion Technology, New Delhi, ndia)
Engineering Science Reference • © 2023 • 360pp • H/C (ISBN: 9798369305935) • US $265.00

Malware Analysis and Intrusion Detection in Cyber-Physical Systems
S.L. Shiva Darshan (Department of Information and Communication Technology, Manipal Institute of Technology, India) M.V. Manoj Kumar (Department of Information Science and Engineering, Nitte Meenakshi Institute of Technology, India) B.S. Prashanth (Department of Information Science and Engineering, Nitte Meenakshi Institute of Technology, India) and Y. Vishnu Srinivasa Murthy (Department of Computational Intelligence, Vellore Institute of Technology, India)
Information Science Reference • © 2023 • 415pp • H/C (ISBN: 9781668486665) • US $225.00

Handbook of Research on Data Science and Cybersecurity Innovations in Industry 4.0 Technologies
Thangavel Murugan (United Arab Emirates University, Al Ain, UAE) and Nirmala E. (VIT Bhopal University, India)
Information Science Reference • © 2023 • 620pp • H/C (ISBN: 9781668481455) • US $325.00

Perspectives on Ethical Hacking and Penetration Testing
Keshav Kaushik (University of Petroleum and Energy Studies, India) and Akashdeep Bhardwaj (University of Petroleum and Energy Studies, India)
Information Science Reference • © 2023 • 445pp • H/C (ISBN: 9781668482186) • US $225.00

AI Tools for Protecting and Preventing Sophisticated Cyber Attacks
Eduard Babulak (National Science Foundation, USA)
Information Science Reference • © 2023 • 233pp • H/C (ISBN: 9781668471104) • US $250.00

Cyber Trafficking, Threat Behavior, and Malicious Activity Monitoring for Healthcare Organizations
Dinesh C. Dobhal (Graphic Era University (Deemed), India) Sachin Sharma (Graphic Era University (Deemed), India) Kamlesh C. Purohit (Graphic Era University (Deemed), India) Lata Nautiyal (University of Bristol, UK) and Karan Singh (Jawaharlal Nehru University, India)
Medical Information Science Reference • © 2023 • 206pp • H/C (ISBN: 9781668466469) • US $315.00

701 East Chocolate Avenue, Hershey, PA 17033, USA
Tel: 717-533-8845 x100 • Fax: 717-533-8661
E-Mail: cust@igi-global.com • www.igi-global.com

Raghvendra Kumar dedicates this book to his son, Prakhar Pandey, and his wife, Priyanka Pandey.

Table of Contents

Preface xix

Chapter 1
A Comprehensive Review on Cyber Security and Online Banking Security Frameworks 1
    Suneeta Mohanty, KIIT University, India
    Sourav Sharma, KIIT University, India
    Prasant Kumar Pattnaik, KIIT University, India
    Ana Hol, Western Sydney University, Australia

Chapter 2
A Hybrid Reinforcement Learning and PSO Approach for Route Discovery of Flying Robots 23
    Ritu Maity, KIIT University, India
    Ruby Mishra, KIIT University, India
    Prasant Kumar Pattnaik, KIIT University, India
    Nguyen Thi Dieu Linh, Hanoi University of Industry, Vietnam

Chapter 3
A Review: Twitter Spam Detection Techniques 37
    S. Raja Ratna, SRM Institute of Science and Technology, India
    Sujatha Krishnamoorthy, Wenzhou-Kean University, China
    J. Jospin Jeya, SRM Institute of Science and Technology, India
    Ganga devi Ganesan, SRM Institute of Science and Technology, India
    M. Priya, SRM Institute of Science and Technology, India

Chapter 4
A Survey of Data Mining and Machine Learning-Based Intrusion Detection System for Cyber
Security 52
    Sangeetha Ganesan, R.M.K. College of Engineering and Technology, India
    G. Shanmugaraj, Velammal Institute of Technology, India
    A. Indumathi, Sri Venkateswara College of Engineering, India

Chapter 5
A Survey on Cyber Security Awareness 75
    G. Sangeetha, R.M.K. College of Engineering and Technology, India
    G. Logeshwari, R.M.K. College of Engineering and Technology, India
    Archana, R.M.K. College of Engineering and Technology, India
    L. Lavanya, R.M.K. College of Engineering and Technology, India
    Sai Harshitha, R.M.K. College of Engineering and Technology, India

Chapter 6
An Implemented Example of XKMS With Web Services 92
    Sumathi Pawar, Nitte Mahalinga Adyanthaya Memorial Institute of Technology, India
    Ankitha, Nitte Mahalinga Adyanthaya Memorial Institute of Technology, India
    V. Geetha, National Institute of Technology, Karnataka, India

Chapter 7
Artificial Intelligence and Machine Learning for Cybersecurity Applications and Challenges 109
    Aditya Roshan Sinha, Chandigarh University, India
    Kunal Singla, Chandigarh University, India
    Teresa Matoso Manguangua Victor, Instituto Superior Politécnico de Tecnologias e
        Ciências, Angola

Chapter 8
Assessing the Impact of GeoAI in the World of Spatial Data and Energy Revolution 147
    Shradha Chavan, Symbiosis International University, India
    Preeti Mulay, Symbiosis Institute of Technology, Symbiosis International University, India

Chapter 9
Cloud-Based Malware Detection Using Machine Learning Methods 171
    Pham Sy Nguyen, Government Office of Vietnam, Vietnam
    Nguyen Ngoc Cuong, University of Technology-Logistics of Public Security, Vietnam
    Hoang Viet Long, University of Technology-Logistics of Public Security, Vietnam

Chapter 10
Cyber Security Risk Assessment and Management Using Artificial Intelligence and Machine
Learning 198
    Sangeetha Ganesan, R.M.K. College of Engineering and Technology, India
    A. Indumathi, Sri Venkateswara College of Engineering, India
    Kumaravel Subramani, Sri Venkateswara College of Engineering, India
    N. Uma, Sri Venkateswara College of Engineering, India
    M. Sugacini, Sri Venkateswara College of Engineering, India
    S. Kavishree, Sri Venkateswara College of Engineering, India

Chapter 11
Fake News Detection With the Help of Computation Time to Increase Accuracy 218
    P. Umamaheswari, SASTRA University, India
    N. Umasankari, Sathyabama Institute of Science and Technology, India
    Selvakumar Samuel, Asia Pacific University of Technology and Innovation, Malaysia

Chapter 12
Hybrid Feature Selection Model for Detection of Android Malware and Family Classification 241
    Sandeep Sharma, The NorthCap University, India
    Prachi, The NorthCap University, India
    Rita Chhikara, The NorthCap University, India
    Kavita Khanna, Delhi Skill and Entrepreneurship University, India

Chapter 13
Identifying and Assessing Risk Factors to Lower Hazards in Cyber Security Penetration Testing ... 265
    Mayukha Selvaraj, Bharathiar University, India
    R. Vadivel, Bharathiar University, India

Chapter 14
Implementation of Image Steganography and Combination of Cryptography and Steganography ... 291
    S. Rashmi, Independent Researcher, India

Chapter 15
Managing Cyber Threats in the Age of Technology: The Role of Risk Detection and Cyber
Security 296
    R. Shobarani, Dr. M.G.R. Educational and Research Institute, India
    Chitrakala Muthuveerappan, Victoria University of Wellington, New Zealand
    I. Sujiban, Dr. M.G.R. Educational and Research Institute, India
    K. SuryaPrakhash, SRM University, India
    S. Pratheepa, J.H.A. Agarsen College, India
    M. J. Bharathi, St. Thomas College of Arts and Science, India

Chapter 16
Proactive DDoS Attacks Detection on the Cloud Computing Environment Using Machine
Learning Techniques 318
    Kishore Babu Dasari, Keshav Memorial Institute of Technology, India
    Srinivas Mekala, Keshav Memorial Institute of Technology, India

Chapter 17
Profile Clone Detection on Online Social Network Platforms 334
    Anthony Doe Eklah, University of Ghana, Ghana
    Winfred Yaokumah, University of Ghana, Ghana
    Justice Kwame Appati, University of Ghana, Ghana

Chapter 18
Risk Detection and Assessment in Digital Signature 361
    R. Hemalatha, PSG College of Arts and Science, India
    R. Amutha, PSG College of Arts and Science, India

Chapter 19
Securing the Future: The Vital Role of Risk Detection and Cyber Security in Modern Computing
Systems 383
    R. Shobarani, Dr. M.G.R. Educational and Research Institute, India
    Chitrakala Muthuveerappan, Victoria University of Wellington, New Zealand
    G. Aarthy Priscilla, St. Anne's Arts and Science College, India
    T. Suganthi, D.B. Jain College, India
    S. SriVidhya Santhi, Dr. M.G.R. Educational and Research Institute, India
    R. Surekha, St. Anne's Arts and Science College, India

Chapter 20
Vulnerability Assessment in Contemporary Computing 403
    Umamageswari, SRM Institute of Science and Technology, Ramapuram, India
    S. Deepa, SRM Institute of Science and Technology, Ramapuram, India

Compilation of References 431

About the Contributors 470

Index 477

Detailed Table of Contents

Preface... xix

Chapter 1

A Comprehensive Review on Cyber Security and Online Banking Security Frameworks 1

Suneeta Mohanty, KIIT University, India
Sourav Sharma, KIIT University, India
Prasant Kumar Pattnaik, KIIT University, India
Ana Hol, Western Sydney University, Australia

The rapid growth of online banking and financial transactions has increased the risk of cyber threats and attacks on financial institutions. Cyber security and online banking security frameworks are essential in mitigating these threats and securing sensitive information. This chapter provides a detailed examination of the cyber security and online banking security frameworks utilized by financial institutions to safeguard their assets and clients. The study identifies common threats to online banking systems and discusses the various security measures that can be implemented to prevent these threats. The chapter also evaluates the effectiveness of existing security frameworks and proposes a comprehensive security framework that combines multiple layers of protection to enhance the security of online banking transactions.

Chapter 2

A Hybrid Reinforcement Learning and PSO Approach for Route Discovery of Flying Robots 23

Ritu Maity, KIIT University, India
Ruby Mishra, KIIT University, India
Prasant Kumar Pattnaik, KIIT University, India
Nguyen Thi Dieu Linh, Hanoi University of Industry, Vietnam

Route discovery for flying robots is one of the major concerns while developing an autonomous aerial vehicle. Once a path planning algorithm is built and the flying robot reaches the destination point from the target point successfully, it is again important for the flying robot to come back to its original position and that is done through route discovery algorithms. Reinforcement learning is one of the popular machine learning methods in which the flying robot has to interact with the environment and learn by exploring the possibilities and maximum reward point method, without the requirement of a large amount of prior training data. Particle swarm optimization is an artificial intelligence inspired algorithm which finds optimal solution in a multi-dimensional space. This chapter has discussed a random exploration reinforcement learning approach combined with PSO algorithm that has been used to discover the optimum path for a flying robot to return from the destination point to the target point after it had traversed its best path from an already defined swarm intelligence technique. PSO+Reinforcement Learning (RL-PSO) is an optimization technique that combines the global search capability of PSO with the exploitation and exploration strategy of RL. Here higher reward points were assigned to the already defined best path obtained from the path planning technique, so that while returning from the destination point it will try to find the route with the highest reward point. With several iterations, it will optimize and find the best route for backpropagation. The algorithm is built using a python environment and the convergence result with the number of iterations has been validated.

Chapter 3
A Review: Twitter Spam Detection Techniques 37

S. Raja Ratna, SRM Institute of Science and Technology, India
Sujatha Krishnamoorthy, Wenzhou-Kean University, China
J. Jospin Jeya, SRM Institute of Science and Technology, India
Ganga devi Ganesan, SRM Institute of Science and Technology, India
M. Priya, SRM Institute of Science and Technology, India

One of the most well-liked social media is Twitter. Spam is one of the several issues that negatively affect users. The objective of this study is to provide an overview of different techniques used for detecting spam in twitter. The proposed framework mainly contains the comparison of four existing twitter spam detection techniques namely, machine learning, feature based detection, combinational algorithm, and deep learning. Machine learning detection uses techniques such as SVM, future engineering, machine learning framework, and semantic similarity function to assess spam. In feature based detection, metadata based, tweet based, user based, and graph based techniques are used to detect spammers. In combinatorial algorithm detection, Naive Bayes-SVM, K-nearest neighbour-SVM, random forest-SVM and RNN-Short term memory techniques are used to detect spam. Deep learning detection uses feature based, semantic cnn, convolution-short term memory nn, and deep learning convolution technique to identify spam. This paper covers relevant work and comparison of several anti spamming techniques.

Chapter 4
A Survey of Data Mining and Machine Learning-Based Intrusion Detection System for Cyber Security 52

Sangeetha Ganesan, R.M.K. College of Engineering and Technology, India
G. Shanmugaraj, Velammal Institute of Technology, India
A. Indumathi, Sri Venkateswara College of Engineering, India

With regard to intrusion detection systems (IDS), several research communities have shown interest in cyber security in recent years. IDS software keeps an eye out for malicious activity on a single computer or a network of computers. It is becoming increasingly important to detect intrusions and prevent them. Several methods to avoid or find intrusion in a network have been proposed in the past. However, the majority of the IDS detection methods currently in use are ineffective at solving this issue. Accuracy is the key factor in how well an intrusion detection system performs. In recent works, various techniques have been employed to enhance performance. In addition to this, machine learning (ML) has been used in many applications to produce results that are accurate in the relevant field. Determining how machine learning and data mining can be used to detect IDS in a network in the near future is the focus of this work. This literature review focuses on ML and data mining (DM) techniques for cyber analytics to support intrusion detection.

Chapter 5
A Survey on Cyber Security Awareness 75
    G. Sangeetha, R.M.K. College of Engineering and Technology, India
    G. Logeshwari, R.M.K. College of Engineering and Technology, India
    Archana, R.M.K. College of Engineering and Technology, India
    L. Lavanya, R.M.K. College of Engineering and Technology, India
    Sai Harshitha, R.M.K. College of Engineering and Technology, India

Nowadays, android phones are making a huge impact globally. According to the F-secure, the report says that 99% of current malwares are targeting the android OS. The main method of targeting the android is their permission system, where the software asks permission for the personal information of the users. The malware developers had two ways of attacking the android OS; one is reverse engineering technique, and another one is getting well-versed in the android permission system. Still, people are not aware of the real cyber security where the hackers are extracting our sensitive information without knowing. Since people are lacking knowledge about cyber security or social awareness, the hackers are gaining their success of getting our information and using it for incorrect purpose. This results in the threatening of the data and mitigation of the data. Now people have to be more conscious of keeping their data secure so that they can avoid this risky situation.

Chapter 6
An Implemented Example of XKMS With Web Services 92
    Sumathi Pawar, Nitte Mahalinga Adyanthaya Memorial Institute of Technology, India
    Ankitha, Nitte Mahalinga Adyanthaya Memorial Institute of Technology, India
    V. Geetha, National Institute of Technology, Karnataka, India

Web service is a loosely coupled system, which gets remote request for a particular service and returns results after executing that service. The data transfer of the web service is a request/response system which carries input parameters through request message and carries executed results of the web services. Both request and response messages are carried in the form of SOAP message which is XML based. XML signature and XML encryption are two methods of securing data transfer through simple access protocol (SOAP) messages from web services. The main goal of the XKMS initiative is to make it possible to create XML-based trust web services for handling and administration of PKI-based cryptographic keys. By making it possible to develop such web services, XKMS helps to simplify working with PKI and makes it simpler for web services to integrate security features into their programmes. This chapter provides a thorough working of the implemented draught of the W3C working group's XKMS specification.

Chapter 7
Artificial Intelligence and Machine Learning for Cybersecurity Applications and Challenges 109
    Aditya Roshan Sinha, Chandigarh University, India
    Kunal Singla, Chandigarh University, India
    Teresa Matoso Manguangua Victor, Instituto Superior Politécnico de Tecnologias e
        Ciências, Angola

This chapter discusses the potential of artificial intelligence (AI) and machine learning (ML) to revolutionize cybersecurity by automating threat detection and response. It reviews the key use cases for AI and ML in cybersecurity, such as network security, threat intelligence, and incident response, and the technical challenges involved in developing AI and ML-based cybersecurity solutions, such as data labeling and model interpretability. It also discusses the broader societal implications of the increasing use of AI and ML in cybersecurity, such as the potential for the creation of new security vulnerabilities and the need for ethical considerations in the development and deployment of these technologies. The chapter aims to provide practical insights and recommendations for organizations looking to implement AI and ML in their cybersecurity strategies, highlighting both the opportunities and challenges that arise when applying these technologies to the complex and rapidly evolving landscape of cybersecurity.

Chapter 8
Assessing the Impact of GeoAI in the World of Spatial Data and Energy Revolution...................... 147
Shradha Chavan, Symbiosis International University, India
Preeti Mulay, Symbiosis Institute of Technology, Symbiosis International University, India

Geospatial is going to be the absolute heart of making sense of trillions of bits of data that are going to be surveyed by big machines. The buzz word of the last 4-5 years has been artificial intelligence (AI) and is influencing every marketplace including GIS, healthcare, pollution, and the list is truly endless. It is the world of collaborative and multidisciplinary research where technology is applied in almost every domain and has proved extremely useful to end-users. The diversity of themes identified in this chapter can be grouped into the categories of renewable energy mapping: spatiotemporal analysis, and data mining. This chapter gives a comprehensive account of transformation from the classical ML clustering techniques with the potential of quantum clustering (QC) which can be applied or mapped to renewable energy solutions driven by use of GIS, or narrating the importance of GIS and quantum. This chapter highlights the relationship between GeoAI, cybersecurity, and quantum computing in the world of spatial data.

Chapter 9
Cloud-Based Malware Detection Using Machine Learning Methods 171
Pham Sy Nguyen, Government Office of Vietnam, Vietnam
Nguyen Ngoc Cuong, University of Technology-Logistics of Public Security, Vietnam
Hoang Viet Long, University of Technology-Logistics of Public Security, Vietnam

Malware in the cloud can affect many users on multiple platforms, while traditional malware typically only affects a system or a small number of users. In addition, malware in the cloud can hide in cloud services or user accounts, making it more difficult to detect and remove than traditional malware. Information security solutions installed on servers (such as anti-malware solutions) are not considered very effective as malware (especially sophisticated solutions) can bypass the detection capabilities of these solutions. Moreover, these solutions often cannot detect new and unknown malware patterns. To address this issue, machine learning (ML) methods have been used and proven effective in detecting malware in many different cases. This chapter per the authors focuses on introducing malware detection techniques in the cloud and evaluating the effectiveness of machine learning methods used, as well as proposing an effective model to support malware detection in the cloud.

Chapter 10
Cyber Security Risk Assessment and Management Using Artificial Intelligence and Machine
Learning 198
Sangeetha Ganesan, R.M.K. College of Engineering and Technology, India
A. Indumathi, Sri Venkateswara College of Engineering, India
Kumaravel Subramani, Sri Venkateswara College of Engineering, India
N. Uma, Sri Venkateswara College of Engineering, India
M. Sugacini, Sri Venkateswara College of Engineering, India
S. Kavishree, Sri Venkateswara College of Engineering, India

The threat of cyber-attacks and wireless communication technologies are now affecting a number of private and public organizations around the world. It is a challenge to protect today's data from cyber-attacks since it is highly dependent on electronic technology. It is possible to mitigate or reduce these risks by identifying them. Risk assessments can help to develop a plan for responding to and recovering from a cyber attack. It is crucial to continuously monitor and assess the risk environment to identify any changes in the organization's context and to keep track of the entire risk management process. Researchers from all around the world have proposed a number of methods to thwart cyber-attacks or minimize the harm they do. The aim of this chapter is to present in-depth analysis of the typical improvements achieved in the field of cyber security risk assessment and management and examines the impact of artificial intelligence and machine learning in cyber security risk assessment, and management.

Chapter 11
Fake News Detection With the Help of Computation Time to Increase Accuracy 218
P. Umamaheswari, SASTRA University, India
N. Umasankari, Sathyabama Institute of Science and Technology, India
Selvakumar Samuel, Asia Pacific University of Technology and Innovation, Malaysia

Newspapers were the primary source of receiving news. Though they were slow in getting us the news, they were reliable since almost every piece of an article printed in newspapers is proofread. But things are changing rapidly and we are reliant on other sources for news (such as Facebook, Twitter, YouTube, WhatsApp). This paved the way for information, whether it is fake or real, that has never been witnessed in human history before. However, ever since social media boomed and the spread of information became easy, it has been difficult to find and stop the spread of fake and fabricated news. Existing solutions identify fake news usage either or some of the machine learning algorithms. In this work, an ensemble machine learning model is developed using ensemble method and evaluate their performance for the computation time to increase the accuracy of fake news detection using datasets. The experimental evaluation confirms the superior performance of our proposed ensemble learner approach in comparison to individual learners.

Chapter 12

Hybrid Feature Selection Model for Detection of Android Malware and Family Classification 241
Sandeep Sharma, The NorthCap University, India
Prachi, The NorthCap University, India
Rita Chhikara, The NorthCap University, India
Kavita Khanna, Delhi Skill and Entrepreneurship University, India

Android OS based applications offer services in various aspects of our daily lives such as banking, personal, professional, social, etc. Increased usage of Android applications makes them extremely vulnerable to various malware threats. A resilient and attack resistant machine learning based Android malware detector is desired to achieve a safe working environment. This work employs feature selection on static and dynamic features and proposes a hybrid feature selection method that can identify most informative features while eliminating the irrelevant ones. Information gain from filter and recursive feature elimination from wrapper feature selection methods outperform other evaluated feature selection techniques. Thereafter, different classification algorithms are trained on the features selected through hybrid feature selection technique and experimental results showed that XGBoost obtained maximum accuracy i.e., 98% and 89% for binary and multiclass classification respectively using only 50 features.

Chapter 13

Identifying and Assessing Risk Factors to Lower Hazards in Cyber Security Penetration Testing ... 265
Mayukha Selvaraj, Bharathiar University, India
R. Vadivel, Bharathiar University, India

Penetration testing is a rapidly growing field. In today's technological exposure to cyber-attacks, there is a need for easily understandable metrics of cyber-attacks and the impact that it causes on enterprises. The measurement metrics are significant challenges in assessing a cyber-crime incident or a penetration testing audit. There are so many factors in the cyber security field that a penetration tester must consider determining the risk of a particular event or attack. Without any measurement or metrics, there is a chance that the pentesters or penetration testing can get stuck in a bottomless pit without arriving at a defined result. A tool called CVSS attempts to calculate risk based on specific parameters. There are complex technicalities involved in arriving at a risk index to be understood by the board members of an enterprise to make an informed decision about the enterprise's cyber security plan.

Chapter 14

Implementation of Image Steganography and Combination of Cryptography and Steganography ... 291
S. Rashmi, Independent Researcher, India

Information transmission over the net is a very common process and securing the information plays an important role. Cryptography and Steganography are the two important techniques that provides secure transmission of data over the internet medium. Cryptography converts the data into an unreadable format, steganography is used to hide the encrypted text into any file like an audio, video, image, etc. In this paper we have explained Cryptography and Steganography as well as combined cryptography and steganography.

Chapter 15
Managing Cyber Threats in the Age of Technology: The Role of Risk Detection and Cyber
Security 296

R. Shobarani, Dr. M.G.R. Educational and Research Institute, India
Chitrakala Muthuveerappan, Victoria University of Wellington, New Zealand
I. Sujiban, Dr. M.G.R. Educational and Research Institute, India
K. SuryaPrakhash, SRM University, India
S. Pratheepa, J.H.A. Agarsen College, India
M. J. Bharathi, St. Thomas College of Arts and Science, India

This chapter highlights the importance of risk detection and cybersecurity in modern computing systems. As technology continues to advance, these components become increasingly critical for ensuring the successful operation of these systems. The chapter suggests that failure to properly address these issues can result in serious consequences, including the compromise of sensitive information and the disruption of critical systems. Therefore, it is essential for organizations to prioritize risk detection and cybersecurity as a foundational element of their computing infrastructure.

Chapter 16
Proactive DDoS Attacks Detection on the Cloud Computing Environment Using Machine
Learning Techniques 318

Kishore Babu Dasari, Keshav Memorial Institute of Technology, India
Srinivas Mekala, Keshav Memorial Institute of Technology, India

Distributed Denial of Service (DDoS) is a cyber-attack targeted on availability principle of information security by disrupts the services to the users. Cloud computing is very demand service in internet to provide computing resources. DDoS attack is one of the severe cyber-attack to disrupt the resource unavailable to the legitimate users. So DDoS attack detection is more essential in cloud computing environment to reduce the effect of circumstances of the attack. This Chapter proposed DDoS attack detection with network flow features instead of conventional researchers use network type features in cloud computing environment. This study evaluate the DDoS attack detection in cloud computing environment using uncorrelated network type features selected by Pearson, Spearman and Kendall correlation methods. CIC-DDoS2019 dataset used for experiments this study which is collected from Canadian Institute for Cyber Security. Finally, Pearson uncorrelated feature subset produces .better results with KNN and MLP classification algorithms.

Chapter 17
Profile Clone Detection on Online Social Network Platforms 334

Anthony Doe Eklah, University of Ghana, Ghana
Winfred Yaokumah, University of Ghana, Ghana
Justice Kwame Appati, University of Ghana, Ghana

Successful profile cloning attacks have far-reaching consequences for the victims. People whose profiles are cloned suffer defamation, mistrust, loss of job, interdiction, public disgrace, dent of reputation, and defrauding. This chapter aims to identify and propose a model that detects profile cloning attacks on online social network platforms. The proposed model is based on unsupervised machine learning clustering and statistical similarity verification methods for the filtration of profiles. The model computes statistical values for attribute similarity measure (ASM) and friends network similarity measure (FNSM). The model has a precision score of 100%. The attribute weight and friends network similarity measures show percentile figures ranging from 0.45 to 1.00. Profile accounts that fall within this range for both ASM and FNSM measures are likely to turn out to be cloned. The higher the figures, the more the suspicion of being a fake account to the supposed original one. The strength of the model is that it exposes the actual clone using the outcome of the computation.

Chapter 18
Risk Detection and Assessment in Digital Signature 361
    R. Hemalatha, PSG College of Arts and Science, India
    R. Amutha, PSG College of Arts and Science, India

Nowadays people are living in a digital era in which all aspects of our lives depend on computers, networks, software applications and other electronic devices. Due to the technological development the security tasks and threat intelligence is a challenging task. Information theft is one of the most expensive segments of cybercrime. It is essential to protect information from cyber threats. In business, the digital signature plays an important role in authorizing the digital data. The receiver or some third party can verify this binding. In larger business, the signing process supports regulating the business. It uses asymmetric cryptography, which provides a layer of validation and security to the message communication through a non-secure channel. There are some risks in digital signature like forgery, fraud, and exclusions. This chapter discusses how to identify the risks and methods practices to mitigate the risks in adopting digital signature. Reasonable risk analysis can enhance the chance of successful electronic business.

Chapter 19
Securing the Future: The Vital Role of Risk Detection and Cyber Security in Modern Computing
Systems 383
    R. Shobarani, Dr. M.G.R. Educational and Research Institute, India
    Chitrakala Muthuveerappan, Victoria University of Wellington, New Zealand
    G. Aarthy Priscilla, St. Anne's Arts and Science College, India
    T. Suganthi, D.B. Jain College, India
    S. SriVidhya Santhi, Dr. M.G.R. Educational and Research Institute, India
    R. Surekha, St. Anne's Arts and Science College, India

Risk detection and cybersecurity are critical components for the success of contemporary computing systems. With the increasing reliance on technology and the Internet, cyber threats have become more complex and sophisticated, posing a significant challenge to the security of computer systems. In this chapter, the authors examine the importance of risk detection and cybersecurity measures in contemporary computing, highlighting the potential risks and threats that can impact system performance and integrity. They explore various techniques and tools used in risk detection and cybersecurity, including intrusion detection systems, firewalls, and encryption methods. Additionally, the authors discuss the role of risk management in identifying and mitigating potential threats to computing systems. They conclude that risk detection and cybersecurity measures are essential for the successful operation of contemporary computing systems and highlight the need for continued investment and innovation in this critical area.

Chapter 20
Vulnerability Assessment in Contemporary Computing 403
Umamageswari, SRM Institute of Science and Technology, Ramapuram, India
S. Deepa, SRM Institute of Science and Technology, Ramapuram, India

Vulnerability assessments are an important aspect of contemporary computing and cyber security. It is a process of distinguishing and assessing potential security weaknesses and vulnerabilities in a computing system or network. It involves using various tools and techniques to denote vulnerabilities and supply recommendations for mitigating them. The primary goal of a vulnerability assessment is to identify weaknesses that attackers could exploit to gain unauthorized access or cause damage to the system or network. By identifying vulnerabilities early, organizations can take proactive steps to address them and prevent attacks. Some of the key steps involved in vulnerability assessments include: It is important to note that vulnerability assessments should be conducted on a regular basis, as new vulnerabilities are constantly being discovered. Additionally, organizations should consider conducting penetration testing in addition to vulnerability assessments, which involves simulating real-world attacks to identify potential weaknesses.

Compilation of References 431

About the Contributors 470

Index 477

Preface

Risk Detection and Cyber Security for the Success of Contemporary Computing presents the newest findings with technological advances that can be utilized for more effective prevention techniques to protect against cyber threats. This book is led by editors of best-selling and highly indexed publications, and together they have over two decades of experience in computer science and engineering. Featuring extensive coverage on authentication techniques, cloud security, and mobile robotics, this book is ideally designed for students, researchers, scientists, and engineers seeking current research on methods, models, and implementation of optimized security in digital contexts.

Chapter 1 provides a detailed examination of the cyber security and online banking security frameworks utilized by financial institutions to safeguard their assets and clients. The study identifies common threats to online banking systems and discusses the various security measures that can be implemented to prevent these threats. The chapter also evaluates the effectiveness of existing security frameworks and proposes a comprehensive security framework that combines multiple layers of protection to enhance the security of online banking transactions.

Chapter 2 proposed DDoS attack detection with network flow features instead of conventional researchers use network type features in cloud computing environment. This study evaluate the DDoS attack detection in cloud computing environment using uncorrelated network type features selected by Pearson, Spearman and Kendall correlation methods. CIC-DDoS2019 dataset used for experiments this study which is collected from Canadian Institute for Cyber Security. Finally, Pearson uncorrelated feature subset produces .better results with KNN and MLP classification algorithms.

Chapter 3 discusses how to identify the risks and methods practices to mitigate the risks in adopting digital signature. The reasonable risk analysis can enhance the chance of successful electronic business.

Chapter 4 aims to identify and propose a model that detects profile cloning attacks on online social network platforms. The proposed model is based on unsupervised machine learning clustering and statistical similarity verification methods for the filtration of profiles. The model computes statistical values for Attribute Similarity Measure (ASM) and Friends Network Similarity Measure (FNSM).The model has a precision score of 100%. The Attribute Weight and Friends Network Similarity Measures show percentile figures ranging from 0.45 to 1.00. Profile Accounts that fall within this range for both ASM and FNSM measures are likely to turn out to be cloned. The higher the figures, the more the suspicion of being a fake account to the supposed original one. The strength of the model is that it exposes the actual clone using the outcome of the computation.

Chapter 5 main objective of targeting the android is that their permission system, where the software asks permission for the personal information of the users. So the malware developers had two ways of attacking the android OS, one is reverse engineering technique and another one is getting well-versed in the android permission system. Still people are not aware of the real cyber security where the hackers are extracting our sensitive information without knowing. Since people are lacking knowledge about the cyber security or social awareness, the hackers are gaining their success of getting our information and using it for incorrect purpose. So this results in the threatening of the data and mitigation of the data. Now people have to be more conscious of keeping their data securely so that they can avoid this risk situation.

Chapter 6 discussed the web application uses the SOAP (Simple Object Access Protocol) using communication protocols like HTTP, SMTP, or FTP to deliver a request message to a service at some URI.

Chapter 7 gives a comprehensive account of transformation from the classical ML clustering techniques with the potential of Quantum Clustering (QC) which can be applied or mapped to Renewable Energy solutions driven by use of GIS, or narrating the importance of GIS and quantum. This chapter highlights the relationship between GeoAI, cybersecurity, and quantum computing in the world of spatial.

Chapter 8 is to present in-depth analysis of the typical improvements achieved in the field of Cyber security risk assessment and management and examines the impact of Artificial Intelligence and Machine Learning in Cyber security Risk assessment and Management.

Chapter 9 employs feature selection on static and dynamic features and proposes a hybrid feature selection method that can identify the most informative features while eliminating the irrelevant ones. Information Gain from filter and Recursive Feature Elimination from wrapper feature selection methods outperform other evaluated feature selection techniques. Thereafter, different classification algorithms are trained on the features selected through hybrid feature selection technique and experimental results showed that XGBoost obtained maximum accuracy i.e. 98% and 89% for binary and multiclass classification respectively using only 50 features.

Chapter 10 discussed various techniques have been employed to enhance performance. In addition to this, Machine Learning (ML) has been used in many applications to produce results that are accurate in the relevant field. Determining "How machine learning and data mining can be used to detect IDS in a network" in the near future is the focus of this work. This literature review focuses on ML and data mining (DM) techniques for cyber analytics to support intrusion detection.

Chapter 11 provides a detailed assessment of cloud-based malware detection methods and makes the following contributions: Describe the role of cloud computing and the importance of protecting cloud infrastructure from malware. Explain malware generation trends and some cloaking techniques. Discuss current challenges and analyze malware detection techniques. Provides a summary of current academic research on cloud-based malware detection using machine learning. Propose a malware detection model in the cloud with the support of advanced techniques including machine learning/deep learning.

Chapter 12 suggests that failure to properly address these issues can result in serious consequences, including the compromise of sensitive information and the disruption of critical systems. Therefore, it is essential for organizations to prioritize risk detection and cybersecurity as a foundational element of their computing infrastructure.

Chapter 13 discussed Penetration Testing is one of the rapidly growing fields. In today's technological exposure to cyber-attacks, there is a need for easily understandable metrics of cyber-attacks and the impact that it causes on enterprises. The measurement metrics are significant challenges in assessing a cyber-crime incident or a penetration testing audit. There are so many factors in the cyber security field that a penetration tester must consider determining the risk of a particular event or attack. Without any measurement or metrics, there is a chance that the pentesters or penetration testing can get stuck in a bottomless pit without arriving at a defined result. A tool called CVSS attempts to calculate risk based on specific parameters. There are complex technicalities involved in arriving at a risk index to be understood by the board members of an enterprise to make an informed decision about the enterprise's cyber security plan.

Chapter 14 is to preserve impenetrability and improve invulnerability. The objectives of this chapter are to be recognized by enhancement of Blowfish which is believed as highly secure algorithm; the implementation of chaotic sequence-quantization method for audio samples. The proposed work's performance is contrasted with that of the existing blowfish method and standard audio LSB algorithm. The following criteria show the demonstration of analysis of the work done – Entropy values, Avalanche effect, Attack scenario, Execution time, PSNR value, Embedding capacity, Structural similarity index etc. The suggested system is the most effective method for intensifying protection and preserving the high caliber of the original entity.

Chapter 15 examines the importance of risk detection and cybersecurity measures in contemporary computing, highlighting the potential risks and threats that can impact system performance and integrity. We explore various techniques and tools used in risk detection and cybersecurity, including intrusion detection systems, firewalls, and encryption methods. Additionally, we discuss the role of risk management in identifying and mitigating potential threats to computing systems. We conclude that risk detection and cybersecurity measures are essential for the successful operation of contemporary computing systems and highlight the need for continued investment and innovation in this critical area.

Chapter 16 involves using various tools and techniques to denote vulnerabilities and supply recommendations for mitigating them. The primary goal of a vulnerability assessment is to identify weaknesses that attackers could exploit to gain unauthorized access or cause damage to the system or network. By identifying vulnerabilities early, organizations can take proactive steps to address them and prevent attacks. Some of the key steps involved in vulnerability assessments include: It is important to note that vulnerability assessments should be conducted on a regular basis, as new vulnerabilities are constantly being discovered. Additionally, organizations should consider conducting penetration testing in addition to vulnerability assessments, which involves simulating real-world attacks to identify potential weaknesses.

Chapter 17 proposed an ensemble machine learning model is developed using ensemble method and evaluate their performance for the computation time to increase the accuracy of fake news detection using datasets. The experimental evaluation confirms the superior performance of our proposed ensemble learner approach in comparison to individual learners.

Chapter 18 has discussed a random exploration reinforcement learning approach combined with PSO algorithm that has been used to discover the optimum path for a flying robot to return from the destination point to the target point after it had traversed its best path from an already defined swarm intelligence technique. Here we have assigned higher reward points to the already defined best path obtained from the path planning technique so that while returning from the destination point to the initial point it will try to find the route with the highest reward point and with several iterations, it will optimize for backpropagation.

Chapter 19 objective of this is to provide an overview of different techniques used for detecting spam in twitter. The proposed framework mainly contains the comparison of four existing twitter spam detection techniques namely, Machine Learning, Feature Based Detection, Combinational Algorithm and Deep Learning. Machine Learning Detection uses techniques such as SVM, Future Engineering, Machine Learning Framework and Semantic Similarity Function to assess spam. In Feature Based

Detection, Metadata Based, Tweet Based, User Based and Graph Based techniques are used to detect spammers. In Combinatorial Algorithm Detection, Naive Bayes-SVM, K-Nearest Neighbour-SVM, Random Forest-SVM and RNN-Short Term Memory techniques are used to detect spam. Deep Learning Detection uses Feature Based, Semantic CNN, Convolution-Short Term Memory NN and Deep Learning Convolution technique to identify spam. This paper covers relevant work and comparison of several anti spamming techniques.

Chapter 20 aims to provide practical insights and recommendations for organizations looking to implement AI and ML in their cybersecurity strategies, highlighting both the opportunities and challenges that arise when applying these technologies to the complex and rapidly evolving landscape of cybersecurity.

Raghvendra Kumar
GIET University, India

Prasant Kumar Pattnaik
KIIT University, India

Chapter 1
A Comprehensive Review on Cyber Security and Online Banking Security Frameworks

Suneeta Mohanty
https://orcid.org/0000-0001-7137-629X
KIIT University, India

Sourav Sharma
KIIT University, India

Prasant Kumar Pattnaik
https://orcid.org/0000-0002-4566-8077
KIIT University, India

Ana Hol
Western Sydney University, Australia

ABSTRACT

The rapid growth of online banking and financial transactions has increased the risk of cyber threats and attacks on financial institutions. Cyber security and online banking security frameworks are essential in mitigating these threats and securing sensitive information. This chapter provides a detailed examination of the cyber security and online banking security frameworks utilized by financial institutions to safeguard their assets and clients. The study identifies common threats to online banking systems and discusses the various security measures that can be implemented to prevent these threats. The chapter also evaluates the effectiveness of existing security frameworks and proposes a comprehensive security framework that combines multiple layers of protection to enhance the security of online banking transactions.

DOI: 10.4018/978-1-6684-9317-5.ch001

INTRODUCTION

The advent of digital technology has revolutionized the way banking services are delivered to customers. Today, customers can access their accounts, transfer funds, and make payments from the comfort of their homes, offices, or on-the-go. While online banking has brought about significant convenience to customers, it has also introduced new risks and vulnerabilities that can lead to security breaches and financial losses.

As financial transactions become increasingly digital, the need for robust cyber security measures has become paramount. Cyber criminals are becoming more sophisticated and are continuously developing new methods to exploit vulnerabilities in online banking systems. Financial institutions must, therefore, stay ahead of these threats by implementing effective security frameworks to protect their customers' data and financial assets.

Overview of Cyber Security and Online Banking Security

Cyber security is a complex and multifaceted field that encompasses a wide range of technologies, strategies, and best practices. Nanda etal.(2022) has listed some of the key components of cyber security as below:

1. Authentication and access control: ensuring that only authorized users can access sensitive information or carry out transactions.
2. Encryption is the use of encryption technologies to protect data while it is in transit and at rest.
3. Firewalls and intrusion detection/prevention systems: using hardware and software to detect and block unauthorized access attempts.
4. Incident response and disaster recovery: having plans and procedures in place to respond to cyber security incidents and minimize their impact.

In the context of online banking, cyber security is particularly important, as financial institutions and their customers are at risk from a wide range of cyber threats. These threats may include:

1. Phishing and social engineering attacks: Hackers engage in deceptive tactics with the intention of coaxing users into revealing confidential data, such as usernames, passwords, and account numbers
2. Malware and ransomware attacks: Malicious software is employed to illicitly infiltrate systems or data, or to encrypt data and demand payment in exchange for its restoration.
3. Distributed denial of service (DDoS) attacks: Attackers leverage a network of compromised computers to inundate a website or network with an overwhelming volume of traffic, rendering it inaccessible to genuine users.

To combat these threats, financial institutions must implement a range of security measures and best practices, including strong authentication and access controls, robust encryption technologies, and sophisticated intrusion detection and prevention systems.

Importance of Cyber Security and Online Banking Security

It is impossible to overstate the significance of online banking security and cyber security. A successful cyber-attack on a financial institution may lead to the theft of confidential data, money losses, and reputational harm. It can also have wider implications for the economy as a whole, as the failure of a major financial institution can have a ripple effect across the entire financial system.

This chapter aims to provide an overview of current cyber security and online banking security frameworks used by financial institutions. The chapter will review and analyze existing literature on the topic, providing insights into the current state of cyber security in online banking systems. The chapter will also identify common threats and attacks faced by financial institutions and evaluate the effectiveness of existing security frameworks in mitigating these risks.

Related Works in the Field of Cyber Security

Nazir, M. A., Ahmed, J., & Ahmad (2022) explored various techniques and challenges associated with cyber threat intelligence and discussed future research directions. The study looked at how CTI uses various techniques, including data mining, machine learning, and natural language processing, to gather useful information from a variety of sources. They also highlighted the challenges faced by CTI practitioners, including data quality, information overload, and the lack of standardization in the field.

Abid et al.(2022) discussed existing solutions and future research initiatives for different security concerns related with the Internet of Things (IoT). The writers begin by introducing the Internet of Things and addressing its advantages, such as enhanced efficiency and convenience. They do, however, point out that the increasing use of IoT technology has raised serious security issues, as the devices are subject to cyber-attacks. The authors then go into detail on the unique security difficulties that the IoT faces, such as data confidentiality, integrity, and availability; device authentication and authorization; network security; and privacy concerns.

Kaur, K., & Rana, H. K. (2022) explored various machine learning-based techniques for malware detection and discussed their benefits and limitations. The study looks into various ML algorithms for malware detection, such as decision trees, support vector machines, neural networks, and deep learning. This paper discusses the challenges in detecting new and unknown malware, and the potential for adversarial attacks on ML-based malware detection systems. Overall, the paper provides a thorough examination of the various ML-based malware detection techniques, as well as their limitations.

Gai, K., Tan, S., & Wang, L. (2021) investigated how machine learning can be applied to cyber security problems. The paper intends to give a thorough review of the existing research and development in this field, addressing issues such as threat detection, intrusion detection, malware analysis, and vulnerability assessment. The authors conducted a thorough review of the literature and examined the most common ML techniques used in cyber security, such as supervised, unsupervised, and semi-supervised learning.

Chen, L., Zhou, H., & Shang, X. (2021) explored various methods for privacy-preserving data sharing, secure computation, and differential privacy, among other topics, in the context of cyber security. The article emphasizes the need for privacy protection in machine learning models, especially in domains that involve sensitive data such as cyber security. The survey examines various PPML approaches such as differential privacy, homomorphic encryption, secure multi-party computation, and federated learning. The article compares the benefits and drawbacks of each strategy and gives examples of how they might be used in cyber security.

Xu et al.(2021) discussed the use of deep learning in various cyber security sectors. The authors conducted a literature study on the use of deep learning in cyber security, identifying the potential benefits and problems of employing deep learning in diverse security applications such as intrusion detection, malware analysis, and threat intelligence. The authors looked into the use of deep learning models for malware detection, intrusion detection, spam filtering, phishing detection, and network security, including Convolutional Neural Networks (CNNs), Recurrent Neural Networks (RNNs), and Auto encoders.

Li et al. (2021) examined various blockchain-based solutions proposed in recent years to address security challenges in IoT systems, including access control, data integrity, privacy, and trust management. Additionally, the authors covered the advantages and drawbacks of employing blockchain for IoT security as well as prospective future research topics. The authors first provide an overview of the IoT ecosystem and then highlight the various security challenges faced by IoT devices. They then explore how blockchain technology can be leveraged to enhance IoT security.

Dai, Y., Yang, Y., & Zou, C. (2021) explored the privacy-preserving technologies for cloud-based cyber security. They conducted a survey to explore the state-of-the-art privacy-preserving techniques used in cloud-based cyber security. In the context of cloud-based cyber security, the study examined the advantages and disadvantages of a wide range of strategies, including differential privacy, secure multi-party computation, homomorphic encryption, and blockchain-based solutions.

Goyal et al. (2021) explored a novel approach for detecting malicious Android applications using machine learning and compared its performance with other existing methods. The authors found that SVMs outperformed other machine learning algorithms with an accuracy of 98.05% in detecting malicious applications. They compared their approach to those already in use and found that it was superior in terms of recall, accuracy, and precision. The authors concluded that their proposed approach is effective in detecting malicious Android applications and can be used as a tool to aid in the security of mobile devices.

Jilani et al.(2021) explored various machine learning techniques for anomaly detection in online banking and compared their performance in terms of accuracy and efficiency. The study identified several machine learning algorithms commonly used in the literature, such as clustering, decision trees, and neural networks. The authors also discussed various types of anomalies that can occur in online banking, including fraudulent transactions, account takeover attacks, and phishing scams. The review highlighted the importance of anomaly detection in online banking and the potential of machine learning techniques to improve security and prevent financial losses.

Bahrami, F., & Vahedian, Z. (2021) explored the use of artificial intelligence-based approaches for predicting cyber-attacks in cloud computing and discussed their benefits and limitations. The study used a publicly available dataset that contained information about cloud computing systems and the types of cyber-attacks they had experienced. In order to maximize the predictive model's performance, the authors combined feature selection and hyper parameter tuning techniques.

Yang et al.(2021) compared the performance of different artificial intelligence-based phishing detection methods in terms of accuracy, precision, and recall. On a dataset of real emails and phishing emails, the authors tested various machine learning algorithms to determine how well they could identify phishing assaults. The techniques tested included artificial neural networks, support vector machines, decision trees, and random forests. Their results showed that artificial neural networks and random forests performed the best among the algorithms tested, achieving high accuracy rates in detecting phishing attacks.

Li et al.(2021) explored the use of a novel algorithm for credit card fraud detection using transaction data and compared its performance with other existing methods. The proposed algorithm first uses a supervised machine learning method, the Random Forest algorithm, to classify transactions as either legitimate or fraudulent. Then, an unsupervised machine learning method, the K-Means algorithm, is used to cluster the legitimate transactions into different groups based on their characteristics. This clustering helps to identify abnormal transactions that may not have been flagged by the Random Forest algorithm.

Alshahrani, M., & Zhang, X. (2021) examined a number of security issues and problems related to the Internet of Things (IoT), and talked about current remedies and potential future research initiatives. The authors identify the key security challenges facing IoT devices and propose various solutions and best practices to mitigate those challenges. The survey covers various topics related to IoT security, such as authentication, access control, confidentiality, integrity, and availability.

Wang et al. (2020) highlighted current solutions and next research areas as well as a variety of security challenges and issues with blockchain technology. The idea of blockchain technology and its numerous security aspects were initially described by the writers. The main security issues that affect blockchain systems were then covered, including 51% assaults, double-spending attacks, and Sybil attacks.

Arshad et al.(2020) discussed about the difficulties in protecting CPS and how blockchain technology can help. They examine various authentication and access control, data integrity and confidentiality, distributed consensus, and other blockchain-based security measures for CPS. The paper reviews existing literature on the use of blockchain in CPS security and identifies several potential benefits, including improved data integrity, accountability, and resilience against attacks.

Alharbi et al.(2020) discussed various applications of blockchain in cyber security, including securing data, identity management, secure communication, and secure supply chain management. The authors first provide an overview of the traditional cyber security landscape, highlighting its limitations and vulnerabilities. They then introduce blockchain technology and explain how it can address some of these limitations through its decentralized and immutable nature

Islam et al.(2020) discussed about how critical infrastructure, such as power plants, water treatment facilities, and transportation networks, is becoming more and more dependent on ICS and how this has increased the risks to these systems' cyber security. The authors discuss the importance of ICSs in critical infrastructure and how cyber threats to these systems can have serious consequences. They also examine the various types of cyber threats that ICSs face, such as malware, ransomware, and targeted attacks.

Al-Fuqaha, A., Alharbi, A., & Alsharif, M. (2020) discussed about blockchain technology and its uses, difficulties, and potential in the area of cyber security. The essential ideas behind blockchain technology, its architecture, and the different kinds of blockchain networks were covered by the authors. They also looked at how blockchain technology is used in a variety of fields, including energy, supply chain management, healthcare, and finance. Scalability, interoperability, and regulatory concerns are just a few of the challenges the authors identified in putting blockchain technology into practise.

Abubakar et al.(2020) explored entity of is the intersection of cyber security and digital banking. Given the rise in cyberattacks and data breaches in the financial industry, the article gives a general overview of the significance of cyber security in digital banking. The authors talk about the advantages of integrating machine learning and artificial intelligence (AI) methods in digital banking systems to strengthen cyber security measures.

The use of blockchain technology holds great promise for improving the security of digital systems. Blockchain is a distributed ledger technology that offers a secure, unchangeable record of transactions and is decentralized. The ability to store sensitive data securely and impenetrably is one of the main benefits of using blockchain in cyber security. Attackers find it challenging to manipulate or alter data stored on the ledger due to the decentralized and distributed nature of the blockchain. A high level of data integrity is also provided by the immutability of blockchain, which makes sure that once data is stored on the ledger, it cannot be changed or removed. By using blockchain-based authentication and authorization mechanisms, organizations can create a tamper-proof and transparent record of user identities and access permissions. By doing so, insider threats can be reduced and unauthorized access to sensitive data and systems can be prevented.As blockchain technology continues to evolve and become more widely adopted, there is a growing need for research into its use in cyber security. Researchers and practitioners need to develop new tools, protocols, and best practices for using blockchain to enhance cyber security. This will require collaboration across multiple disciplines including computer science, cryptography, and cyber security.

ONLINE BANKING SECURITY FRAMEWORKS

Definition of Online Banking Security Frameworks

The various techniques and technologies that financial institutions and other organizations use to guarantee the privacy, availability, and integrity of their online banking systems are referred to as online banking security frameworks. These systems aid in preventing unauthorized access, theft, and misuse of customers' financial and personal information.

Types of Online Banking Security Frameworks

1. **Two-factor authentication:** Due to the security measure known as two-factor authentication (2FA), users are unable to log into their online banking accounts without first providing two different forms of identification. A second factor, such as a fingerprint scan, a facial recognition scan, or a one-time code sent to the user's mobile device, is typically entered after the user enters their username and password as the first two factors. Even if hackers have the user's login information, it will be more challenging for them to access the account without authorization thanks to this additional layer of security.
2. **Encryption:** Sensitive data is encrypted, or changed into an unreadable format that can only be decoded by a person with the right decryption key, in order to protect it from unauthorized access. Online banking platforms use encryption to safeguard user data, including passwords, credit card numbers, and social security numbers, as it moves across the internet. Even if data is intercepted, encryption ensures that it cannot be read or used by hackers.
3. **Digital certificate:** Digital certificates are electronic documents that are used to validate the identity of a website or organization. When a user visits an online banking website, their browser validates the digital certificate to ensure that it is valid and issued by a reputable authority. The creation of fake websites by hackers to trick users into providing their login credentials or other sensitive information is thus prevented.
4. **Firewalls:** Firewalls are either hardware or software devices that monitor and control network traffic. Firewalls are used by online banking systems to prevent unauthorized access to their networks and the entry of malicious software. Firewalls also aid in data breach prevention by monitoring and filtering incoming and outgoing traffic.

5. **Intrusion detection and prevention systems (IDPS):** Systems for detecting and preventing intrusions on networks and systems are known as intrusion detection and prevention systems (IDPS). Potential security breaches can be recognized by IDPS, which can then take action to stop them as well as notify security personnel. Online banking systems use IDPS to detect and prevent attacks such as denial-of-service (DoS) and distributed denial-of-service (DDoS) attacks.

6. **Security information and event management (SIEM):** SIEM systems gather, examine, and manage security-related data from many different sources, such as firewalls, intrusion detection systems, and other security systems. Potential security threats can be identified with the aid of SIEM systems, and preventative measures can then be taken. SIEM is used by online banking systems to manage their security systems, monitor system activity, and take quick action in the event of a security incident.

7. **Security policies and procedures:** Security policies and procedures are the guidelines and rules that organizations use to govern their security practices. These guidelines and rules may include password specifications, access control regulations, incident response protocols, and disaster recovery strategies. Online banking systems use security policies and procedures to establish a framework for security and to make sure that all staff members and users are aware of their responsibilities for upholding security.

Advantages and Disadvantages of Online Banking Security Frameworks

The advantages of online banking security frameworks include:

1. **Improved security:** The confidentiality, integrity, and availability of user information are improved by the multiple layers of protection provided by online banking security frameworks against potential security threats.

2. **Increased user confidence:** By implementing strong security measures, online banking systems can boost user confidence and trust in their systems, resulting in increased usage and revenue.

3. **Compliance with regulatory requirements:** Financial institutions are required to comply with a variety of regulatory requirements related to security, and implementing online banking security frameworks can help to ensure compliance with these regulations.

4. **Improved detection and response capabilities: Online banking security frameworks like IDPS and SIEM can assist in quickly identifying and responding to potential security incidents, reducing the impact of any security breaches.**

However, there are also some potential disadvantages to online banking security frameworks, including:

1. **Increased complexity:** Implementing multiple security measures can increase the complexity of an online banking system, which can make it more difficult to manage and maintain.

2. **User inconvenience:** Some security measures, such as two-factor authentication, can be seen as inconvenient by users, which could lead to decreased usage of online banking systems.

3. **Cost:** Implementing robust security measures can be expensive, both in terms of hardware and software costs, as well as personnel costs for managing and maintaining the security systems.

4. **False positives:** Some security measures, such as IDPS, can generate false positives, which can lead to unnecessary alerts and potentially impact the usability of the system.

Overall, the advantages of implementing online banking security frameworks far outweigh the potential disadvantages. Online banking systems can ensure the confidentiality, integrity, and availability of user information by providing multiple layers of protection against potential security threats, while also increasing user confidence and trust in their systems.

CYBER SECURITY FRAMEWORKS

Definition of Cyber Security Frameworks

An organization can manage the risks related to information security by using a cyber security framework, which is a collection of policies, benchmarks, and best practices. These frameworks offer a methodical approach to identifying and assessing security risks, as well as guidance on how to manage and mitigate those risks.

Cybersecurity frameworks are made to be flexible, adaptable to various businesses and organizations, and they can be tailored to a company's particular requirements. They are typically developed by industry groups, government agencies, or standards organizations, and are based on a variety of sources, including industry best practices, legal and regulatory requirements, and expert analysis.

By offering a structured method for handling information security risks, a cyber-security framework seeks to assist organizations in enhancing their overall security posture. This entails determining and evaluating security risks, creating policies and practices to reduce those risks, and putting in place technical controls to defend against security threats.

Cybersecurity frameworks typically include a set of core functions or domains that may differ depending on the framework. Five essential tasks are included in the NIST Cybersecurity Framework, such as identify, protect, detect, respond, and recover. Each of these functions has a set of subcategories or activities that organizations can use to put the framework into action.

Aside from the core functions, cyber security frameworks may contain specific recommendations or controls that organizations can use to improve their security posture. These recommendations may be based on best practices in the industry, legal and regulatory requirements, or expert analysis.

Types of Cyber Security Frameworks

Organizations can manage information security risks more systematically with the help of cybersecurity frameworks. The NIST Cybersecurity Framework, ISO/IEC 27001, CIS Critical Security Controls, and SANS Top 20 Critical Security Controls are just a few examples of the cyber security frameworks that organizations can use to create their security programs. Each of these frameworks has its own set of advantages and disadvantages, and organizations should carefully evaluate each one to determine which one is best suited to their needs.

NIST Cybersecurity Framework

In order to help businesses manage and mitigate cybersecurity risks, the US government created the National Institute of Standards and Technology (NIST) Cybersecurity Framework. It is a non-mandatory framework for improving cybersecurity posture and protecting against cyber threats. The framework is applicable to organizations of all sizes and in all sectors, including the online banking industry.

Identification, protection, detection, response, and recovery are the five main divisions of the NIST Cybersecurity Framework. Each function has categories and subcategories that assist organizations in developing, implementing, and improving their cybersecurity programs. The framework is adaptable and flexible, allowing organizations to tailor it to their unique needs and risk profile.

The first function of the NIST Cybersecurity Framework is Identify. This function helps organizations understand their cybersecurity risks, determine the potential impact of a cyber attack, and establish a risk management strategy. Asset management, the business environment, and risk assessment are all subcategories of the Identify function.

The second feature is called Protect. This function assists organizations in implementing safeguards to protect against cyber threats. Access Control, Awareness and Training, and Data Security are all part of the Protect function.

The third function is Detect. This function assists organizations in identifying cybersecurity events and anomalies. The Detect function includes processes for detecting anomalies and events as well as security continuous monitoring.

The fourth function is Respond. This feature assists organizations in responding to cybersecurity incidents. Response Planning, Communications, and Analysis are all part of the Respond function.

The fifth and final function is Recover. After a cybersecurity incident, this function assists organizations in restoring services and operations. Recovery Planning, Improvements, and Communications are all part of the Recover function.

Some of the key benefits of using the NIST Cybersecurity Framework in online banking include:

- Establishing a common language and understanding of cybersecurity risks and controls
- Providing a systematic and structured approach to managing cybersecurity risks
- Improving the effectiveness and efficiency of cybersecurity programs
- Enhancing communication and collaboration among stakeholders
- Reducing cybersecurity risks and vulnerabilities
- Helping organizations comply with regulatory requirements
- Demonstrating cybersecurity due diligence to customers, regulators, and other stakeholders.

ISO/IEC 27001

A widely accepted standard for information security management is ISO/IEC 27001. It provides a framework for managing and protecting sensitive information in online banking, including financial data. Implementing ISO/IEC 27001 can help financial institutions ensure the confidentiality, integrity, and availability of their systems and data.

One of the most important advantages of implementing ISO/IEC 27001 in online banking is that it assists financial institutions in meeting regulatory requirements. Many countries have laws and regulations requiring financial institutions to put in place information security measures to protect customer data. By implementing ISO/IEC 27001, financial institutions can demonstrate their compliance with these regulations and avoid penalties for non-compliance.

Another benefit of ISO/IEC 27001 is that it helps financial institutions manage risks related to cyber threats. The standard establishes a methodical approach to risk management that can assist financial institutions in identifying, assessing, and mitigating potential security risks. This can assist financial institutions in preventing cyberattacks and mitigating the consequences of any incidents that do occur.

ISO/IEC 27001 implementation can also assist financial institutions in improving operational efficiency. The standard requires financial institutions to establish and maintain information security management policies and procedures. This can help financial institutions streamline their processes and reduce the risk of errors or delays that can impact customer service.

CIS Critical Security Controls

The CIS Critical Security Controls are a set of cybersecurity best practices developed by the Center for Internet Security (CIS). These controls are intended to assist organizations of all sizes and industries in improving their cybersecurity posture through the implementation of a prioritized set of security measures. In the context of online banking, implementing the CIS Critical Security Controls can significantly improve the security of financial institutions' systems and protect their customers' data.

The CIS Critical Security Controls consist of twenty controls that cover various areas of cybersecurity, including vulnerability management, access control, incident response, and network security. Financial institutions can adopt these controls to strengthen their cybersecurity defenses and mitigate cyber threats.

Some of the key benefits of implementing the CIS Critical Security Controls in online banking include:

- Prioritized approach: The CIS Critical Security Controls provide a prioritized list of security measures that financial institutions can implement to improve their cybersecurity posture. This approach ensures that financial institutions focus their resources on the most critical security measures that have the greatest impact on their security.
- Comprehensive coverage: The CIS Critical Security Controls cover a wide range of cybersecurity topics, such as vulnerability management, access control, network security, and incident response. This comprehensive coverage ensures that financial institutions address all critical security areas and safeguard their systems and data against a variety of cyber threats.
- Industry-standard best practices: The CIS Critical Security Controls are based on industry-standard best practices for cybersecurity. By implementing these controls, financial institutions can ensure that they are following industry-standard security measures and are in compliance with relevant regulations.
- Continuous improvement: The CIS Critical Security Controls are designed to be continuously updated to reflect the evolving cyber threat landscape. Financial institutions can ensure that their cybersecurity defenses are always up to date and effective against the latest cyber threats by implementing these controls.

Advantages and Disadvantages of Cyber Security Frameworks

Cybersecurity frameworks have become essential in the digital age to help organizations protect against cyber threats. Online banking is no exception, as it involves the handling of sensitive financial information that must be protected against unauthorized access, modification, or theft. The following are some of the benefits and drawbacks of implementing cybersecurity frameworks for online banking, along with relevant examples and case studies.

Advantages:

1. **Enhanced Security:** Cybersecurity frameworks provide a comprehensive approach to protecting online banking systems and data, ensuring that security measures are implemented throughout the organization. This helps to identify potential threats and vulnerabilities, and implement necessary security controls to mitigate them. For example, the NIST Cybersecurity Framework helps to prioritize and manage cybersecurity risks, while ISO/IEC 27001 provides a systematic approach to managing information security.

2. **Regulatory Compliance: Cybersecurity frameworks assist organizations in adhering to applicable regulations and standards.** In the banking sector, regulatory bodies such as the Federal Financial Institutions Examination Council (FFIEC) and the European Banking Authority (EBA) have issued guidelines on cybersecurity for financial institutions. Implementing cybersecurity frameworks helps organizations meet these regulatory requirements and avoid potential fines and legal action.

3. **Cost-Effective: Implementing cybersecurity frameworks can be cost-effective in the long run because it helps prevent security breaches that can result in financial losses and reputational damage.** According to a Ponemon Institute study, the average cost of a data breach for financial services companies in 2020 will be $5.85 million. Investing in cybersecurity frameworks can help mitigate these costs and improve the organization's overall financial performance.

4. **Improved Customer Trust:** Implementing cybersecurity frameworks can improve customer trust by ensuring that their financial information is secure. This can lead to increased customer loyalty and retention, which is critical for any online banking service's success. For example, JPMorgan Chase implemented a comprehensive cybersecurity framework, which helped to restore customer confidence after a major data breach in 2014.

Disadvantages:

1. **Implementation Challenges:** Implementing cybersecurity frameworks can be complex and challenging, requiring significant resources and expertise. It can be especially difficult for small and medium-sized businesses (SMEs) with limited resources and IT expertise. For instance, a survey by the UK's Federation of Small Businesses revealed that 66% of SMEs had been victims of cyberattacks, but only 15% had implemented cybersecurity frameworks.

2. **Implementing cybersecurity frameworks can create a false sense of security, leading organizations to become complacent and overlook other security measures.** Cybersecurity frameworks should be seen as a baseline for security, and organizations need to continually assess and improve their security posture. In spite of having a cybersecurity framework in place, Equifax, for instance, suffered a serious data breach in 2017 that exposed the personal data of over 143 million customers.

3. **Cost:** Implementing cybersecurity frameworks can be expensive, especially for SMEs with limited resources. The cost of implementing cybersecurity frameworks can vary depending on the organization's IT infrastructure's size and complexity. For example, implementing ISO/IEC 27001 can cost anywhere between $10,000 to $100,000 or more, depending on the scope of the implementation.

While there are some drawbacks to implementing cyber security frameworks in online banking, the benefits are significant. Frameworks provide a structured approach to security, reduce the likelihood of breaches, and demonstrate a commitment to protecting both the bank and its customers. As new technologies and threats emerge, it is important for financial institutions to continue to evolve and adapt their security measures to stay ahead of potential cyber-attacks.

CYBER THREATS TO ONLINE BANKING SECURITY

Types of Cyber Threats to Online Banking Security

The internet has become an indispensable part of our daily lives, and online banking has made financial transactions easier than ever. However, with the convenience of online banking comes the risk of cyber-attacks. Cybercriminals are constantly devising new and innovative ways to compromise online banking security and gain access to sensitive financial information. In this section, we will look at the various types of cyber threats to online banking security and how they can affect financial institutions and their customers.

Phishing

Phishing is a type of online fraud in which criminals employ social engineering strategies to acquire sensitive data, including login credentials, credit card numbers, and other personally identifiable information. It usually entails the use of fraudulent emails or websites that look like legitimate ones in order to trick users into providing their personal information.

Phishing attacks are a major concern in the online banking industry, as they can result in significant financial losses for individuals and banks alike. Attackers may use various tactics to make their phishing emails or websites appear legitimate, such as using logos, branding, and language that mimic those of the targeted organization.

To protect against phishing attacks, online banking customers should be vigilant in checking the legitimacy of emails and websites before providing any sensitive information. Banks can also implement various security measures to detect and prevent phishing attacks, such as email filters, website verification tools, and user education and awareness programs.

Malware

Any software that is intended to harm or exploit computer systems, networks, or devices is referred to as malware, or malicious software. Malware can be used by cybercriminals to steal sensitive data from unaware users, including login credentials, financial information, and personal details, when they are using online banking. Malware can infect a computer via a variety of methods, such as phishing attacks, email attachments, infected websites, and malicious software downloads.

One common type of malware used in online banking attacks is the banking Trojan. These Trojans are specifically designed to steal banking information by intercepting user credentials or redirecting transactions to attacker-controlled accounts. Banking Trojans can infect a computer through various means, including phishing emails, infected websites, and software downloads.

To protect against malware attacks, online banking customers can take various measures such as keeping their systems updated with the latest security patches, using antivirus software, avoiding suspicious email attachments and downloads, and using multi-factor authentication. To detect and prevent malware attacks, financial institutions can also implement various security measures such as intrusion detection systems, firewalls, and anti-malware software.

Denial of Service (DoS) Attacks

Cyberattacks of the DoS variety frequently target online banking platforms. An attacker who conducts a denial-of-service (DoS) attack tries to saturate the targeted system with traffic, making it difficult or impossible for legitimate users to access it. This is typically accomplished by flooding the system with traffic from a large number of sources, such as botnets, which are networks of compromised computers that an attacker can remotely control.

The attack on the US banking system in 2012 and 2013 was one of the most notable DoS attacks in online banking history. This attack was carried out by Iranian hackers and was directed at several major US banks, including Bank of America, JPMorgan Chase, and Wells Fargo. The attackers used botnets to flood the banks' websites with traffic, slowing them down or making them unavailable. The attack was thought to be in retaliation for US sanctions imposed on Iran.

The impact of a DoS attack on an online banking system can be significant. If the system becomes inaccessible, customers may not be able to access their accounts, make transactions, or perform other critical banking functions. This can result in financial losses for both the bank and its customers, as well as reputational damage.

Online banks use a variety of techniques to protect themselves from DoS attacks. Using traffic filtering tools to identify and block traffic from known malicious sources is a common approach. Banks may also use load balancing and redundancy techniques to distribute traffic across multiple servers and prevent any one server from becoming overloaded. Additionally, banks may work with their Internet service providers to detect and block traffic at the network level before it even reaches the bank's servers.

Despite these measures, DoS attacks remain a persistent threat to online banking security. To carry out these attacks, attackers continue to develop new techniques and exploit vulnerabilities in the banking system. As a result, banks must remain vigilant and up to date on the latest security measures to prevent and mitigate the impact of DoS attacks.

Man-in-the-Middle (MitM) Attacks

Man-in-the-Middle (MitM) attacks are a particular kind of cyberthreat in which an attacker listens in on communications between two parties with the intention of intercepting sensitive information, like login credentials or financial information. MitM attacks are a significant threat in the context of online banking because they allow attackers to gain access to sensitive information and manipulate transactions, potentially causing financial losses for customers and financial institutions.

There are several methods that attackers can use to carry out MitM attacks in online banking. One common method is to intercept data transmitted between a customer's device and the online banking website using public Wi-Fi networks, such as those found in coffee shops or airports. Another method is to use malware to install a backdoor on a customer's device, allowing the attacker to intercept data transmitted between the device and the online banking website.

Once the attacker has intercepted the data, they can then manipulate the data in various ways. For example, they may alter the transaction details, such as the amount or recipient, or redirect the transaction to a different account controlled by the attacker. The customer may be unaware of these manipulations, as the attacker may alter the display of the transaction details to appear legitimate.

To prevent MitM attacks in online banking, financial institutions can implement several security measures. One approach is to use end-to-end encryption to secure communications between the customer's device and the online banking website. This prevents attackers from intercepting and reading the information sent between the two parties. Additionally, financial institutions can implement multi-factor authentication to verify the customer's identity and prevent unauthorized access to their account.

Insider Threats

Insider threats are a subset of cyber threats that involve people who are given legitimate access to a financial institution's systems and data but abuse it for selfish or malicious reasons. Insider threats are particularly dangerous because they involve individuals who are familiar with the institution's systems and data, making it easier for them to circumvent security measures and cause significant harm.

There are several types of insider threats in online banking, including malicious insiders, careless or negligent insiders, and third-party contractors or partners. Malicious insiders are employees who intentionally use their access to cause harm to the financial institution, such as stealing customer data or disrupting services. Careless or negligent insiders are employees who inadvertently cause harm, such as accidentally sharing sensitive information. Third-party contractors or partners can also pose a risk as they may have access to the institution's systems and data but may not have the same level of security controls and oversight as regular employees.

Red Flag Rule

A written identity theft prevention program must be developed and implemented by financial institutions as per the Federal Trade Commission's (FTC) Red Flags Rule, which was enacted in 2010. All financial institutions that extend credit, including banks, credit unions, and other lending organizations, must abide by the rule. The purpose of the rule is to help financial institutions recognize and spot trends, behaviors, or particular actions that might be signs of fraud or identity theft.

The Red Flags Rule requires financial institutions to implement procedures to detect and respond to suspicious activity related to customer accounts when it comes to online banking. These procedures may include verifying the identity of customers, monitoring customer transactions for unusual activity, and responding promptly to any suspicious activity detected. The rule also requires financial institutions to train employees on how to detect and respond to suspicious activity on a regular basis.

Financial institutions must also appoint a Red Flags Program Administrator, who is in charge of overseeing the identity theft prevention program and ensuring that it is kept up to date with changes in risks and threats. The program must be reviewed and approved by the board of directors of the institution or an appropriate board committee.

Identification of "red flags" which are patterns, practices, or particular behaviors that may point to identity theft or fraud, is one of the Red Flags Rule's key components. Examples of red flags in online banking may include unusual account activity, requests for changes to account information, or attempts to access accounts from unfamiliar locations.

Financial institutions must establish procedures to respond to red flags, including notifying customers and law enforcement agencies of suspected identity theft or fraud, closing or freezing affected accounts, and taking other appropriate actions to prevent further harm.

Compliance with the Red Flags Rule is essential for financial institutions to maintain the trust of their customers and protect their reputation. Failure to comply with the rule can result in significant financial penalties as well as reputational harm to the institution. To maintain the security and integrity of their online banking services, financial institutions must be proactive in identifying and responding to red flags.

Red Whale Attacks

The term "Red whale" refers to a specific type of cyber attack that targets online banking systems. This is a type of social engineering attack in which cybercriminals use sophisticated techniques to trick bank employees into transferring large sums of money to fraudulent accounts. The name "Red whale" was coined by cybersecurity firm Secureworks, based on a reference made by a cybercriminal in a chat log.

Red whale attacks typically start with the cybercriminals researching and gathering information about the targeted bank and its employees. They then create a fake email address that appears to be from a senior executive at the bank, often the CEO or CFO. The email contains a sense of urgency and pressure, with a request to transfer a large amount of money to a specific account. The email often includes convincing details such as the name of the recipient and other relevant information, making it seem like a legitimate request.

To prevent Red whale attacks, banks need to take a multi-layered approach to cybersecurity. This includes employee education and training programs, email filtering and validation tools, and strong authentication procedures for financial transactions

Blue Whale Attacks

It is essential to note that the term "Blue Whale" is commonly associated with an online suicide game that originated in Russia in 2016. This game is not related to online banking or cybercrime. However, the term has been used in the context of cyber-attacks targeting financial institutions.

Blue Whale attacks are a type of cybercrime that involves compromising an individual employee's computer or mobile device within a financial institution in order to gain access to the institution's systems. This attack is named after the marine mammal known for breaching high walls, signifying the ability of attackers to overcome high security measures.

Employees are frequently duped into clicking on malicious links or downloading malware-filled attachments by phishing emails or other social engineering methods used in Blue Whale attacks. As soon as an attacker has access to a user's device, they can use a number of methods to elevate their privileges and gain access to systems and sensitive financial data.

Blue Whale attacks can have serious consequences, resulting in significant financial losses and reputational damage for the targeted institution. The stolen data can be used by attackers for a variety of malicious purposes, including fraudulent transactions, identity theft, and ransom demands.

To stop Blue Whale attacks, financial institutions must put in place thorough security measures like multi-factor authentication, encryption, and routine employee training. Multi-factor authentication can help prevent unauthorized access to financial institution systems, while encryption can keep attackers from accessing sensitive data. Regular employee training can help employees identify and respond to phishing attempts and social engineering tactics, reducing the likelihood of a successful attack.Furthermore, financial institutions should put in place robust incident response plans to lessen the impact of a Blue Whale attack.

Impact of Cyber Threats to Online Banking Security

Cyber threats to online banking security can have a significant and negative impact on both financial institutions and their customers. Financial loss, reputational harm, legal and compliance issues, operational disruption, and data breaches are among the consequences. To compromise online banking security, cybercriminals employ a variety of techniques such as phishing, malware, social engineering, denial of service attacks, man-in-the-middle attacks, and insider threats. Financial institutions and customers must be vigilant and take precautions to protect themselves from these threats, such as implementing effective security measures and monitoring financial accounts for suspicious activity.

In this section, we will look at how cyber threats affect online banking security:

1. **Financial Loss:** Financial loss is one of the most serious consequences of cyber threats to online banking security. Cyber criminals can steal money from online bank accounts using a variety of methods, including phishing attacks, malware infections, and man-in-the-middle attacks. These attacks can cause direct financial losses for customers as well as the bank in the event of liability issues.

2. **Reputational Damage:** Another effect of cyber threats to online banking security is harm to the financial institution's reputation. Customers may lose faith in the bank's ability to safeguard their financial information, resulting in lost business and revenue. This can be especially harmful to smaller banks or credit unions.

3. **Legal and Compliance Issues:** Cyber threats to online banking security can also cause financial institutions to face legal and compliance issues. Banks are required to abide by a number of laws, including the Gramm-Leach-Bliley Act (GLBA) and the Payment Card Industry Data Security Standard (PCI DSS), in order to protect the security and privacy of their customers' data. Heavy fines, legal repercussions, and client loss may follow noncompliance with these rules.

4. **Operational Disruption:** Cyber threats can also disrupt financial institutions' operations. A denial of service (DoS) attack, for example, can overwhelm a bank's servers and prevent customers from accessing their accounts. This can result in lost business and reputational damage.

5. **Data Breaches:** Data breaches brought on by online threats can make private customer data, including names, addresses, Social Security numbers, and financial account information, publicly available. Data breaches caused by cyber threats can expose sensitive customer information such as names, addresses, Social Security numbers, and financial account information. This could lead to other types of cybercrime like identity theft and financial fraud.

Financial loss, reputational harm, legal and compliance problems, operational disruption, and data breaches are just a few of the consequences that financial institutions and their customers may face. Banks must implement effective security measures to protect themselves from cyber threats, such as multi-factor authentication, encryption, and regular security audits. Additionally, customers should use security measures to safeguard their private data, such as creating strong passwords, updating software, and keeping an eye on their financial accounts for unusual activity.

Prevention and Mitigation Strategies for Cyber Threats to Online Banking Security

Cyber threat prevention and mitigation is a critical component of maintaining online banking security. To protect their systems and customers' information from cyber attacks, financial institutions must implement effective security measures. This section will go over strategies for preventing and mitigating cyber threats to online banking security.

1. **Multi-factor Authentication:** MFA is a security mechanism that requires users to provide two or more forms of authentication in order to access their accounts. A password, a security token, a fingerprint scan, or other forms of authentication can be used. Even if a cybercriminal obtains the customer's login credentials through phishing or other means, MFA can help prevent unauthorized access to customer accounts. A financial institution may require customers to enter their login credentials and then provide a code generated by an authentication app on their smartphone to access their account.

2. **Employee Training:** An important cyber threat prevention strategy is employee training. Employees at financial institutions must be trained to recognize and respond to cyber threats such as phishing and social engineering. Employees must also be trained on how to use security tools like firewalls and antivirus software to keep the institution's systems safe. A financial institution's employees may benefit from regular phishing attack detection and response training sessions.

3. **Encryption:** Encryption is the process of converting data into a coded language that is unreadable in the absence of a decryption key. Encryption can help protect customer data from cybercriminals who may intercept data while it is being transmitted. Encryption can be used by financial institutions to protect sensitive customer information such as login credentials and financial data. To protect customer data during transmission, a financial institution may use Transport Layer Security (TLS) encryption.

4. **Firewall:** A firewall is a type of network security system that keeps track of and regulates both incoming and outgoing network traffic in accordance with pre-established security rules. Firewalls can aid in preventing unauthorized access to financial institution systems by filtering out potentially harmful traffic. A financial institution may deploy a firewall to prevent cybercriminals from gaining access to its systems via a network connection.

5. **Continuous Monitoring:** Continuous monitoring of systems and networks is essential for detecting and responding to cyber threats. Financial institutions must implement monitoring tools to detect and alert administrators of any unusual activity on the institution's systems. Continuous monitoring can assist financial institutions in real-time detection and response to cyber threats. To monitor its systems for suspicious activity, a financial institution may employ a security information and event management (SIEM) system.

6. **Incident Response Plan:** An incident response plan is a written set of steps that financial institutions can use to react to a cyberattack. The plan should specify the actions to be taken in the event of a cyberattack, including the obligations of the incident response team. An incident response plan can assist financial institutions in mitigating the impact of a cyber-attack and restoring services as quickly as possible. In the event of a data breach, a financial institution may create an incident response plan that outlines the steps to be taken, including notifying customers and regulatory authorities.

7. **Regular Software Updates:** Regular software updates are required to keep financial institutions' systems secure. Security patches that address known vulnerabilities are frequently included in software updates. All software used in financial institutions' systems, including operating systems, applications, and security tools, must be kept up to date. To ensure that all security patches are applied in a timely manner, a financial institution may schedule regular software updates for its systems.

8. **Penetration Testing:** Penetration testing is the process of simulating a cyber-attack to test the security of financial institutions' systems. Penetration testing can assist financial institutions in identifying vulnerabilities in their systems and determining the effectiveness of their security measures. A financial institution may contract with a third-party cybersecurity firm to conduct penetration testing on its systems.

To summarize, preventing and mitigating cyber threats to online banking security necessitates a comprehensive approach that incorporates a variety of strategies, including multi-factor authentication, employee training, encryption, firewall, continuous monitoring, incident response plan, regular software updates, and penetration testing. Financial institutions must continuously evaluate and improve their security measures to keep up with evolving cyber threats.

These strategies can assist financial institutions in protecting their systems and customer data from cyber threats. For example, multi-factor authentication can prevent unauthorized access to customer accounts, while employee training can help employees identify and respond to phishing attacks. Encryption can protect sensitive data from cybercriminals who may intercept data during transmission, and firewalls can prevent unauthorized access to financial institution's systems. Continuous monitoring can detect and alert administrators to any unusual activity on the institution's systems, whereas incident response plans can help minimize the impact of a cyber attack and restore services as quickly as possible. Regular software updates can address known vulnerabilities, and penetration testing can assist in identifying and correcting any weaknesses in the institution's systems.

EMERGING TRENDS AND TECHNOLOGIES IN ONLINE BANKING SECURITY

Because of its convenience and accessibility, online banking has grown significantly in recent years. However, as usage grows, so does the need for robust security measures to protect against various cyber threats. As a result, there is increased interest in emerging trends and technologies in online banking security. We will look at some of these emerging trends and technologies in this section, such as artificial intelligence and machine learning for security analytics, blockchain technology for secure transactions, biometric authentication, quantum cryptography, and the future of online banking security.

1. **Artificial Intelligence and Machine Learning for Security Analytics**

AI and machine learning (ML) are becoming increasingly popular in a variety of industries, including online banking security. AI and machine learning can be used in security analytics to detect and prevent potential cyber threats. AI and ML can detect patterns and anomalies that may indicate malicious activity by analyzing large amounts of data.

For example, JPMorgan Chase, a leading financial institution, uses AI and ML to monitor and detect potential fraud in real-time. To detect potential fraud, the bank employs machine learning algorithms to analyze data from various sources, including transactions and account activity. This has led to a reduction in false positives and faster detection of potential fraud, improving the bank's overall security.

2.   Blockchain Technology for Secure Transactions

Blockchain technology has received a lot of attention in recent years because of its ability to provide secure and transparent transactions. Blockchain is a distributed ledger that is controlled by an interconnected system of computers as opposed to a single entity. Each block in the chain contains a record of transactions that the network verifies, making it difficult for a single party to manipulate the system. Online banking can benefit from blockchain technology by providing secure and transparent transactions for customers. By using blockchain technology, banks can reduce the risk of fraudulent activities such as double-spending and hacking attacks.For example, Ripple is a blockchain-based platform that allows banks to settle cross-border transactions in real-time. Ripple employs blockchain technology to provide secure and transparent transactions, lowering the risk of fraudulent activity and increasing the efficiency of cross-border transactions.

3.   Biometric Authentication

Biometric authentication is a technology that verifies a person's identity by using physical characteristics such as fingerprints or facial recognition. Because of its ability to provide strong authentication that cannot be easily duplicated or stolen, this technology is becoming increasingly popular in online banking security.For example, many smartphones now offer biometric authentication as a way to unlock the device or authenticate transactions. Banks can use this technology to provide secure authentication for online banking, improving the security of customer accounts.

4.   Quantum Cryptography

Quantum cryptography is a secure communication technology that makes use of quantum mechanics. Quantum cryptography uses the laws of physics to ensure that any attempt to intercept or eavesdrop on a communication will be immediately detected.

For example, Swiss Bank uses quantum cryptography to protect their online banking transactions. A quantum key distribution system is used by the bank to generate a unique key that is used to encrypt and decrypt transaction data. This ensures that the data is secure and that no unauthorized parties can intercept or decrypt it.

5.   The Future of Online Banking Security

Future developments in online banking security may be influenced by new technologies like blockchain, artificial intelligence, and biometric authentication. As cyber threats continue to evolve, banks will need to adapt and adopt new technologies to ensure the security of their customers' accounts.

Quantum computing is one potential technology that could shape the future of online banking security. Many of the existing encryption algorithms used to protect online transactions may be rendered ineffective by quantum computing. However, it also has the potential to provide new and stronger encryption algorithms that can better protect online transactions.

Another trend that could shape the future of online banking security is the use of big data analytics. By analyzing large amounts of data, banks can better identify potential threats and patterns of The use of quantum cryptography in online banking security is still in its early stages, but it has shown great potential for enhancing security. Quantum cryptography is based on quantum mechanics principles, allowing for the creation of a completely secure communication channel. Utilizing quantum bits, also known as qubits, which are particles that exist in a superposition of states up until they are measured, this is accomplished. One practical example of quantum cryptography in online banking security is the Quantum Key Distribution (QKD) protocol. QKD uses a physical layer of encryption that relies on the laws of physics, making it impossible to break the encryption without physically interfering with the communication channel. QKD can be used to securely distribute encryption keys between two parties, allowing them to communicate securely over an insecure channel.

Emerging technologies such as artificial intelligence, machine learning, and blockchain are likely to shape the future of online banking security. Both the security and user experience of online banking could be enhanced by these technologies. The adoption of blockchain technology in online banking faces challenges such as scalability, interoperability, and regulatory compliance.

CONCLUSION

In conclusion, online banking security is a critical issue that requires constant vigilance and adaptation to emerging threats and technologies. The use of online banking security frameworks, such as two-factor authentication, encryption, and intrusion detection systems, can help to mitigate risks and protect sensitive data. Emerging technologies like quantum cryptography, blockchain, artificial intelligence, and machine learning offer fresh possibilities for boosting security and enhancing the user experience in online banking. However, their adoption requires careful consideration of the potential benefits and drawbacks, as well as compliance with regulatory requirements and industry standards.

REFERENCES

Abid, M., Abbas, H., Hassan, S. A., & Afzal, M. K. (2022). Internet of things security challenges and solutions: A review. *Journal of Ambient Intelligence and Humanized Computing*. doi:10.100712652-022-03655-6

Abubakar, A. I., Sadiq, A. S., Dauda, M. D., & Garba, A. H. (2020). An overview of cyber security in digital banking and the role of machine learning and AI. *Procedia Computer Science*, *172*, 78–85. doi:10.1016/j.procs.2020.07.347

Al-Fuqaha, A., Alharbi, A., & Alsharif, M. (2020). A comprehensive review of blockchain technology: Applications, challenges, and opportunities in cyber security. *IEEE Internet of Things Journal*, *8*(1), 528–545. doi:10.1109/JIOT.2020.2971403

Alharbi, S., Qasim, S. M., & Alharbi, H. (2020). A Comprehensive Study on Blockchain-Based Cyber security: Applications, Opportunities, and Future Challenges. *IEEE Access : Practical Innovations, Open Solutions*, *8*, 82598–82615. doi:10.1109/ACCESS.2020.2992273

Alshahrani, A., & Zhang, X. (2020). Internet of things security: A survey. *Journal of Network and Computer Applications*, *150*, 102506. doi:10.1016/j.jnca.2019.102506

Arshad, M., Qaisar, S. B., & Choo, K. K. R. (2020). A review on blockchain security for cyber-physical systems. *IEEE Access : Practical Innovations, Open Solutions*, *8*, 167340–167362. doi:10.1109/AC-CESS.2020.3024662

Bahrami, F., & Vahedian, Z. (2021). Developing an artificial intelligence-based approach for predicting cyber-attacks in cloud computing. *Journal of Cloud Computing (Heidelberg, Germany)*, *10*(1), 16. doi:10.118613677-021-00241-x

Chen, L., Zhou, H., & Shang, X. (2021). A survey on privacy-preserving machine learning for cyber security. *Journal of Cybersecurity*, *7*(1), tyaa006. doi:10.1093/cybsec/tyaa006

Dai, Y., Yang, Y., & Zou, C. (2021). A survey on privacy-preserving technologies for cloud-based cyber security. *Journal of Network and Computer Applications*, *187*, 103027. doi:10.1016/j.jnca.2021.103027

Gai, K., Tan, S., & Wang, L. (2021). A survey of machine learning in cyber security. *Journal of Information Security and Applications*, *62*, 102893. doi:10.1016/j.jisa.2021.102893

Goyal, M., Ahuja, P., & Kaur, H. (2021). A novel approach for detecting malicious Android applications using machine learning. *Journal of Ambient Intelligence and Humanized Computing*, *12*(8), 8969–8980. doi:10.100712652-021-03548-0

Islam, M. H., Karmakar, G. C., Kamruzzaman, J., Al Mamun, S. A., & Shahjalal, M. (2020). A review of current trends and challenges in cyber security for industrial control systems. *IEEE Access : Practical Innovations, Open Solutions*, *8*, 49762–49785. doi:10.1109/ACCESS.2020.2982924

Jilani, F. A., Nazir, S., Khan, S. A., & Shah, S. A. (2021). Anomaly detection in online banking: A review of machine learning techniques. *Journal of King Saud University - Computer and Information Sciences*, *33*(1), 60-68. doi:10.1016/j.jksuci.2020.02.003

Kaur, A., & Rana, S. (2022). A review of machine learning-based techniques for malware detection. *Journal of Network and Computer Applications*, *193*, 103131. doi:10.1016/j.jnca.2021.103131

Li, J., Li, Y., Li, Z., & Li, L. (2021). Blockchain-based solutions for securing Internet of Things: A survey. *IEEE Internet of Things Journal*, *8*(2), 763–782. doi:10.1109/JIOT.2020.3025069

Li, K., Guo, Y., Wang, Z., Xie, X., & Wang, B. (2020). A novel algorithm for credit card fraud detection using transaction data. *International Journal of Information Management*, *52*, 102062. doi:10.1016/j.ijinfomgt.2019.09.011

Nanda, S. K., Mohanty, S., Pattnaik, P. K., & Sain, M. (2022). Throughput Optimized Reversible Cellular Automata Based Security Algorithm. *Electronics (Basel)*, *11*(19), 3190. doi:10.3390/electronics11193190

Nazir, S., Ahmad, F., & Ali, M. (2022). A survey of cyber threat intelligence: Techniques, challenges, and future directions. *Journal of Network and Computer Applications*, *200*, 103147. doi:10.1016/j.jnca.2021.103147

Wang, S., Chen, X., & Wu, Y. (2020). A comprehensive survey on blockchain security. *Journal of Information Security and Applications*, *50*, 102447. doi:10.1016/j.jisa.2019.102447

Xu, J., Huang, Z., Zhang, R., & Chen, Z. (2021). Deep learning in cyber security: A review. *IEEE Transactions on Neural Networks and Learning Systems*, *32*(6), 2333–2358. doi:10.1109/TNNLS.2020.3017571

Yang, Y., Zhang, Z., & Wang, L. (2021). A comparative study of artificial intelligence-based phishing detection techniques. *Journal of Ambient Intelligence and Humanized Computing*, *12*(8), 8943–8953. doi:10.100712652-021-03544-4

Chapter 2
A Hybrid Reinforcement Learning and PSO Approach for Route Discovery of Flying Robots

Ritu Maity
KIIT University, India

Prasant Kumar Pattnaik
KIIT University, India

Ruby Mishra
KIIT University, India

Nguyen Thi Dieu Linh
Hanoi University of Industry, Vietnam

ABSTRACT

Route discovery for flying robots is one of the major concerns while developing an autonomous aerial vehicle. Once a path planning algorithm is built and the flying robot reaches the destination point from the target point successfully, it is again important for the flying robot to come back to its original position and that is done through route discovery algorithms. Reinforcement learning is one of the popular machine learning methods in which the flying robot has to interact with the environment and learn by exploring the possibilities and maximum reward point method, without the requirement of a large amount of prior training data. Particle swarm optimization is an artificial intelligence inspired algorithm which finds optimal solution in a multi-dimensional space. This chapter has discussed a random exploration reinforcement learning approach combined with PSO algorithm that has been used to discover the optimum path for a flying robot to return from the destination point to the target point after it had traversed its best path from an already defined swarm intelligence technique. PSO+Reinforcement Learning (RL-PSO) is an optimization technique that combines the global search capability of PSO with the exploitation and exploration strategy of RL. Here higher reward points were assigned to the already defined best path obtained from the path planning technique, so that while returning from the destination point it will try to find the route with the highest reward point. With several iterations, it will optimize and find the best route for backpropagation. The algorithm is built using a python environment and the convergence result with the number of iterations has been validated.

DOI: 10.4018/978-1-6684-9317-5.ch002

1. INTRODUCTION

The domain of aerial vehicles is gaining importance in the last few years due to the wide range of applications of drones, and aerial vehicles in various sectors starting with the retail sector, agricultural sector, disaster management, industries, military, surveillance work, health care sectors, etc. Due to their wide range of applications, it is important to plan their path effectively for performing any kind of task. Flying robots are systems capable of vertical take-off and landing without any human intervention (Feron, 2008). While building an autonomous flying robot one of the key features is path planning for flying robots. We have been working on path planning of a hybrid type of fixed-wing flying robot which can be used in the healthcare sector for spraying disinfectant in operation theatres. There are numerous path-planning techniques proposed over years in the area of drones or flying robots. It is important to decide the optimum path planning technique as it takes into consideration various factors like obstacle avoidance, optimizing energy consumption, and minimizing the computational and flight time (Yang et al., 2016). Once a path planning technique is decided and the flying robot traverse from the source point to the destination point, after completing the assigned task the flying robot has to return to its initial position. To return flying robot has to use a route discovery technique to come back as the initial much amount of training data is not available to train it for traversing back autonomously. In this situation, we have tried to use a reinforcement learning approach where we have assigned higher reward points to the forward path traversed by the flying robot so that while returning the flying robot will try to randomly explore all possible paths to reach the initial point and with several iterations, it will try to optimize itself by choosing the path having the highest reward points. One of the major limitation of reinforcement learning algorithm is to establish a balance between exploration ie finding new action to gather information and exploitation ie which means using intelligence to maximize rewards and sometimes it gets stuck in local minima. To overcome this shortcoming we have used PSO along with reinforcement learning. PSO is a global optimization method which can find global optimal solution instead of getting confined in a local minima. Here we have tried to capture advantages of both PSO and reinforcement learning technique to come up with an efficient model.

2. LITERATURE REVIEW

In this section, we have tried to review different route discovery algorithms for flying robots and drones and their advantages and shortcomings. Path planning algorithms are of different types based on methods used for finding the optimal path. Some the sampling techniques like the RRT method, 3D Voronoi, Probabilistic Road Map, and Visibility Graphs are used to find the optimum path by setting random nodes in an environment and then searching for the optimal path by using sampling technique. Gai (Sheng et al., 2019) proposed six dof robotic obstacle avoidance using the artificial potential field method. Wei (Wei & Ren, 2018) proposed an improved RRT technique for path planning in a dynamic environment. Dijkstra's shortest path algorithm is one of the conventional routing methods which also uses a graph search method to find the shortest path (Wang, 2012). Numerous works were conducted using analytical techniques for path planning of aerial vehicles but these algorithms are mostly based on the graph search method which does not give accurate results in case of uncertain and dynamic conditions. The next categories of algorithms are numerical techniques in which Mixed integer linear programming, Binary integer linear programming, and Non-linear Branch and Bound optimization algorithm are used to determine the ideal solution for path planning of aerial vehicles (Chen et al., 2012; Kamal et al., 2005). A. Albert (Albert et al., 2017) proposes path planning algorithm for UAV using mixed integer linear programming. Further artificial intelligence-based techniques which are bio-inspired models are quite successful for path planning of autonomous flying robots. Anand Nayyar (Nayyar et al., 2019) proposed modified artificial bee colony optimization for the path planning of robots. The modified ABC algorithm showed exceptional results but the only concern was early convergence. Shikai Shao (Shao et al., 2020) used particle swarm optimization for the path planning of aerial vehicles. To strengthen the domain path planning these artificial intelligence-based algorithms were used one such algorithm was particle swarm optimization where acceleration coefficient and velocity parameters can be adjusted in such a manner that they can perform well in linearly varied patterns and environments. Stanislaw Konatowski (Konatowski & Pawlowski, 2019) used the PSO algorithm for path planning of aerial vehicles for obstacle, threat, and cost optimization. Ellips Masehian (Masehian & Sedighizadeh, 2010) had proposed a hybrid algorithm based on PSO and PRM algorithms. Different types of hybrid algorithms were also proposed which optimizes the path planning objective of flying robots. Some of the research papers has also proposed genetic algorithm with PSO to overcome to limitations of genetic algorithms (Sedeh et al., 2021). A fair amount of trade off can be marked between exploration and exploitation capabilities by including genetic operators into the hybrid algorithm structure. Similarly few more hybrid algorithms were proposed to have a adequate balance between exploration and exploitation capabilities like PSO and artificial bee colony optimization (Sharma et al., 2013). The hybrid algorithms also proved to be quite efficient as compared to individual algorithms when they are used in multi-dimensional and multi objective scenario. V. Roberge (Roberge & Tarbouchi, 2020) used a parallel evolutionary algorithm for the path planning of unmanned aerial vehicles. Quantum-based algorithms are transforming the state of optimization problems. Quantum-inspired models use quantum computing concepts for building algorithms that can work faster and can give better results. Lie Wang (Wang et al., 2020) performed an enhanced and improved quantum-inspired particle swarm optimization for path planning of UAVs. Zhangjie Fu (Fu, Yu, Xie, Chen, & Mao, 2018) proposed an evolutionary algorithm for the path planning of flying robots. Many research papers were using genetic algorithms (Aditya Gautam, 2014; Sonmez et al., 2015), ant colony optimization (De Santis et al., 2018; Yue & Chen, 2019), artificial bee colony optimization (Muntasha et al., 2021; Zhonghua, 2018), particle swarm optimization (Huang, 2018; Mesquita & Gaspar, 2020), and hybrid algorithms (Abhishek et al., 2020; Zhang et al., 2018) for performing path planning for intelligent flying robots. Reinforcement learning approaches are used to find the optimal path by trial and error method, learning by interacting with the environment. Yibing Li (Li et al., 2020) proposed a deep reinforcement learning-based method for UAV path planning. The algorithm automatically makes a decision taking into consideration the reward points concept. Hassan Ishtiaq Monhas (Minhas & Ahmad, 2021; Yan & Xiang, 2018) proposed a reinforcement learning-based routing protocol for unmanned aerial vehicles. Chao yan () proposed an improved Q-learning algorithm for the path planning of UAVs. The quality of the solutions obtained from RL depends heavily on the design of the reward function, which is used to guide the agent's behavior. Designing a good reward function that accurately represents the goals of the task can be difficult, and even small errors in the reward function can lead to poor solutions. To overcome the limitation deep reinforcement learning models were used for path planning. Kai Arulkumaran (Arulkumaran et al., 2017) had proposed deep reinforcement learning for optimization. Various hybrid reinforcement learning models were also developed (Liu & Zhang, 2021). To enhance the efficiency of algorithms hybrid algorithms are used. After reviewing various research papers we have used reinforcement learning techniques for path finding while returning from the destination point to the target point. As we had already used an artificial intelligence-based quantum-inspired algorithm for path planning of our developed hybrid type fixed wing flying robot. The main challenge was the backpropagation of our flying robot from the destination point to the target point. For this problem, we have identified the reinforcement learning method as we don't have much previous data for training the flying robot, and reinforcement learning work on the trial and error method, and it tries to discover the path by itself by reward point concept and we have tried to combine reinforcement learning with particle swarm optimization which is a global optimization technique so that the limitation of reinforcement learning ie getting stuck in local minima can be overcome by PSO technique.

3. TYPES OF PATH PLANNING ALGORITHMS

3.1 Reinforcement Learning

Reinforcement learning is a feedback-based machine learning model in which the agent interacts with the environment and learns to do the specific task by reward point concept in which positive action leads to a positive reward point and negative action leads to a negative point. (Gao et al., 2004; Watkins & Dayan, 1992) The goal of reinforcement learning is to find the best policy, which is a mapping from states to actions, that maximizes the cumulative reward over time. Reinforcement learning can be applied to a wide range of problems, from simple decision-making tasks to complex sequential decision problems in dynamic environments. It can also handle a variety of reward functions, which makes it a versatile tool for many applications. It can scale to high-dimensional state spaces, making it possible to tackle problems in complex real-world environments. They are sample-efficient, meaning they can learn from fewer examples than other machine learning techniques. This makes them suitable for situations where data is limited or expensive to acquire. In this project also we have limited information's available for which reinforcement learning can work best in this scenario. In reinforcement learning, an agent interacts with an environment by observing the current state of the environment and taking an action. The environment then transitions to a new state and provides the agent with a reward signal that indicates how good or bad the action was. The agent updates its policy based on the reward signal and the new state, and continues to interact with the environment in this way, learning from the feedback it receives. The agent chooses the path with the highest reward point as the best path. It is also knowns as Q learning as Q values of action taken can be stored in the Q matrix and with an increase in the number of iterations, the Q matrix is updated to get optimum results.

The state of a flying robot is firstly defined in terms of position and velocity(Ouahouah et al., 2022)

$$M_{t+1} = \begin{bmatrix} p1_{fr}^{t+1} \\ v1_{fr}^{t+1} \\ a1_{fr}^{t+1} \end{bmatrix} \tag{1}$$

Where $p1_{fr}^{t+1}$ denotes the position of the flying robot, $v1_{fr}^{t+1}$ denotes the velocity of the flying robot, $a1_{fr}^{t+1}$ denotes the acceleration of the flying robot, M_{t+1} denotes the state of the flying robot.

The action taken is expressed as

$$Ac = [\alpha_1, \alpha_2] \tag{2}$$

Where α_1 varies from $-\pi$ to π and α_2 varies from $-2/\pi$ to $2/\pi$ denotes the yaw and pitch angle of flying robots.

The main function of this algorithm is to make the flying robot discover the returning path from the destination point to the source point. The reward function concept follows the rule of the shortest distance transverse between one node to the neighbor node.

$$Q(k,l) = Q(k,l) + \beta \left(Q(k',l) - Q(k,l) \right) \tag{3}$$

Where k refers to the current state of the flying robot, l denotes the learning rate, k' denotes the next state of the flying robot, and β denotes normalization depending on the action taken.

The Q matrix is updated with each iteration and the Q matrix with the highest reward point will give the optimal path. The reward point will be calculated from the distance between the current state and the target point. The least distance will have a higher reward point. And the penalty will be given if encountered with obstacles. Let us consider obstacle is present at d1 distance from the flying robot then the obstacle function will be given as (Ouahouah et al., 2022):

$$Ob = \begin{cases} exp\left(1 - \dfrac{d_{min}^2}{d_{min}^2 - d_1^2} \right) \\ 0 \end{cases}$$

d1<dmin

d1>dmin

Ob is the obstacle function, the value of Ob is taken as a penalty if it is negative.

3.2 Particle Swarm Optimization

Particle Swarm Optimization (PSO) is a heuristic optimization technique used to find the global optimum solution in a search space. It is a population-based algorithm that is inspired by the behavior of birds flocking or swarming in search of food.

In PSO, a set of candidate solutions, called particles, are randomly initialized in the search space. Each particle has a position and velocity, which represents its current location in the search space and the direction of its movement. The fitness of each particle is evaluated based on a pre-defined objective function. At each iteration, the best position found so far by the particle (referred to as the personal best) and the best position found so far by the entire population (referred to as the global best) are used to update the velocity and position of each particle. This update process continues until a stopping criterion is met, such as a maximum number of iterations or a desired level of precision.

One of the advantages of PSO is that it does not require the gradient of the objective function, making it suitable for optimizing problems where the gradient is not easily computable. Additionally, PSO is computationally simple and can be implemented efficiently, making it a popular choice for solving optimization problems in a variety of fields, including machine learning, engineering, and finance.t is a swarm intelligence based technique for generating the best solution by iterating continuously for nonlinear problems. It is an evolutionary Meta heuristics algorithm that mimics the bird's behavior for food source identification. The equation below helps to revise velocity and position (Jun & Wei, 2012; Tung, 2017),

$$u^{m+1} = wu^m + t_1 * rand_1^m * \left(p_o^m - z^m \right) + t_2 * rand_2^m * \left(g_o^m - z^m \right)$$ (5)

$$z^{m+1} = z^m + u^{m+1}$$ (6)

m represents iterations, w represents weight function, t_1 represents position learning co-efficient and t_2 represents global learning co-efficient, $rand_1$ and $rand_2$ are random integer numbers that vary from (Feron, 2008):

u^{m+1} = velocity at m+1 iterations

z^m = position at m iterations

p_o^m = optimal position at mth iteration

g_o^m = global best solution at mth iteration

3.3 Hybrid Algorithm

A hybrid algorithm is a computational method that combines two or more algorithms to solve a problem. The idea behind hybrid algorithms is to leverage the strengths of multiple algorithms to overcome the limitations of any single algorithm and to achieve improved performance.

Reinforcement learning (RL) and Particle Swarm Optimization (PSO) are two different optimization algorithms, but they can be combined to form a hybrid optimization approach that combines the strengths of both methods. PSO+Reinforcement Learning (RL-PSO) is an optimization technique that combines the global search capability of PSO with the exploitation and exploration strategy of RL. In RL-PSO, each particle in the swarm is considered as an agent that interacts with the environment. The position of each particle represents the state of the agent, and the velocity of each particle represents the action taken by the agent. The objective of each particle is to maximize the cumulative reward obtained by interacting with the environment.

To achieve this, the particle updates its velocity based on the information obtained from the environment, such as the reward obtained from the previous interaction. The particle also updates its position based on the updated velocity. In this way, the particle can balance the exploration of new states and the exploitation of the states with higher rewards. The global best position in the swarm is considered as the best policy, which is updated as the particles interact with the environment and update their positions. The best policy can be used to guide the particles towards the optimal solution. The combination of RL and PSO can result in a more efficient and robust optimization algorithm compared to either method alone.

The steps followed for implementing reinforcement learning with Particle swarm optimization are:

i) In first step environment, state space, action space and reward system are defined.

ii) Initial particles are created in search space which represents a policy and assign random position and velocities to the particles.

iii) As per the highest reward point achieved the fitness function is calculated.

iv) For each particle update the local best position if its current position has better fitness than the previous one and the global best position also need to be updated according to fitness function.

v) The velocity and position are updated as per the equation 5 given above and the steps of updating the functions are repeated until desired level of accuracy is received.

vi) Finally the best policy with best fitness function is selected which will be used to control the agent in the desired environment

4. METHODOLOGY AND RESULTS

Our main focus is to build an optimal path for a flying robot to return from its destination point to the source point for which we have tried to implement the reinforcement learning method in combination with particle swarm optimization. In this section we have considered three cases. First one where we have only used reinforcement learning to find the sustainable path for flying robot for returning from destination point to target point. Then we have tried to implement only PSO technique and found the best path. And in third case we have taken hybrid mode ie reinforcement learning and PSO and found the best path and also for three cases we have recorded the time taken for execution and then we have compared the three results to come up with most efficient results.

First, we have built a random set of two points using libraries in python. And from the random points, we have marked the initial point and destination point. Then we implemented the reward system concept through python programming. With each iteration, the Q matrix is calculated and the flying robot will try to find the path and the path with the highest reward point will be considered the best path. The path with the shortest distance and zero obstacle function is given the highest reward points. Figure 1 shows the graph of random 2d points generated. Figure 2 given below shows the Q matrix generated by applying reinforcement learning and updating the reward points till it convergences by running 1000 iterations. The Q matrix shows the optimal path obtained is 0-1-3-9-10 as 1, 3 and 9 node points had the highest reward points as shown in the Q matrix.

Figure 3 shows the most efficient path obtained by applying reinforcement learning and using the reward point concept for optimizing the path. Figure 4 shows the graph between reward points achieved and the number of iterations.

The reinforcement learning takes computational run times of approximately 15 secs to reach the 600 iterations where our results converged. For the flying robot to traverse back to its original position reinforcement learning can be best model as it works on reward point concept and choose the path with highest reward point.

Initially, the starting point coordinates and threat points in a 2d closed room environment were assigned to the algorithm than using swarm intelligence it tries to discover the suitable path and keeps on updating outputs to get the best global optimal results. Figure 2 below shows the desired path obtained from the PSO. Our simulation results obtained had cost function which deals with distance parameter as 5.45 units and time traversed to arrive at the desired location using optimal path is 6.04 sec after 150 iterations.

Figure 1. The random set of 2d nodes generated for performing reinforcement learning algorithm

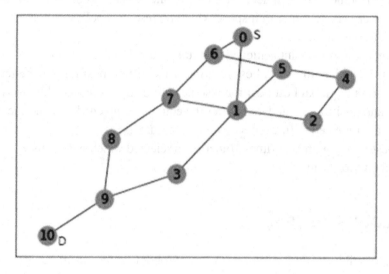

Figure 2. The Q matrix generated by performing the reinforcement learning algorithm

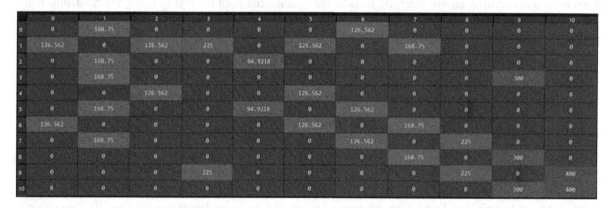

	0	1	2	3	4	5	6	7	8	9	10
0	0	168.75	0	0	0	0	126.562	0	0	0	0
1	126.562	0	126.562	225	0	126.562	0	168.75	0	0	0
2	0	168.75	0	0	94.9218	0	0	0	0	0	0
3	0	168.75	0	0	0	0	0	0	0	300	0
4	0	0	126.562	0	0	126.562	0	0	0	0	0
5	0	168.75	0	0	94.9218	0	126.562	0	0	0	0
6	126.562	0	0	0	0	126.562	0	168.75	0	0	0
7	0	168.75	0	0	0	0	126.562	0	225	0	0
8	0	0	0	0	0	0	0	168.75	0	300	0
9	0	0	0	225	0	0	0	0	225	0	400
10	0	0	0	0	0	0	0	0	0	300	400

Figure 3. The most efficient path achieved by applying reinforcement learning

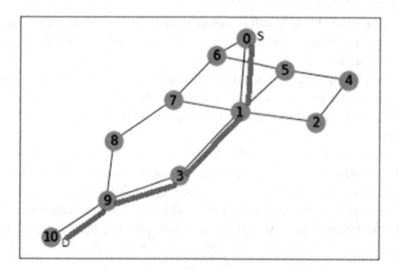

Figure 4. The graph between the number of iterations and reward point gained and the graph converges after 600 iterations

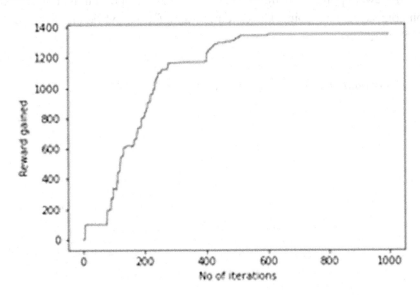

Figure 5. Figure shows the optimal path generated by applying particle swarm optimization

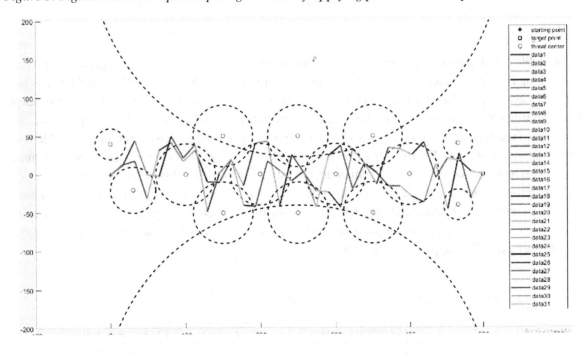

Then we have applied reinforcement learning in combination with particle swarm optimization where we have initialized the particle position randomly, defined the environment, state space and action space. We have created a particle class which will take initially random position and velocity but with number of iterations it will be updated to get the best position and velocity as we evaluate the fitness function based on reward point concept. The local best and global best were updated to reach to optimum solution with best policy and reward points. The diagram below shows the optimum path obtained for traversing from destination point to original point. The execution time for the hybrid algorithm was 5.05 secs and it converges at 150 iterations.

Figure 6. Figure shows optimal path generated by applying RL+PSO

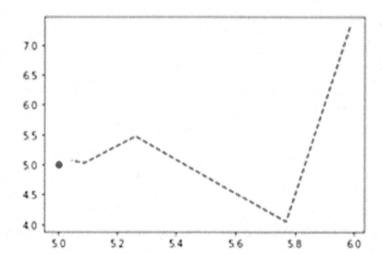

The table below shows the comparison of execution time for algorithms applied to generate best path for reaching from destination point to initial point. The reinforcement learning can be considered as best method when we plan for traversing back from a already travelled path by using reward point concept. When reinforcement learning was used we have found execution time was bit slower and it took 600 iterations to reach target point as it has tendency to stick in local minima. To overcome the problem we have combined PSO with RL technique. As previously we had used PSO algorithm for path planning which takes around 6.04secs to reach from target to destination point. PSO is a global optimization technique which can overcome the problem of local minima. So, we had combined PSO and reinforcement learning to overcome the limitation of individual algorithms. PSO+RL algorithm took 5.05 secs for execution and reached optimum solution with 100 iterations which was faster as compared to reinforcement learning and PSO applied individually.

Table 1. Table shows the comparison of execution time for three algorithms

SL NO	ALGORITHM TRAINED	EXECUTION TIME
1	Reinforcement Learning	15 Secs
2	PSO	6.04secs
3	Reinforcement learning+ PSO	5.05 secs

5. CONCLUSION

In this paper, we have used combination of reinforcement learning and PSO for our path-planning problem. Our main aim was to find the optimal path for our flying robot to return from the destination point to the source point as we had initially applied quantum-inspired particle swarm optimization to find the best path for the indoor application of the flying robot. Once it reaches the destination point and performs the task the challenge was again to return to its initial position autonomously. For the above-mentioned problem, we had chosen the reinforcement learning method in which the agent learns by itself by interacting with the environment and working on the reward point concept. As we did not have any previous data available for training the model so in our case reinforcement learning can be the best method to train the model to work autonomously. But during execution we observed reinforcement learning execution time higher and it requires more number of iterations to reach to its destination point, main reason can be the problem get stuck in local minima. To avoid this problem we have tried to combine PSO with reinforcement learning so that reward policy will be based on best position and velocity of the particle. It can have a well-marked tradeoff between exploration and exploitation stages. Here we applied the algorithm in a python environment and obtained the best path and made the comparison between reinforcement learning, PSO and hybrid PSO+RL execution time to conclude the suitable path for our problem. We have also checked the convergence of the model. Further work will be done to implement it in the hardware setup of the flying robot system.

REFERENCES

Abhishek, B., Ranjit, S., Shankar, T., Eappen, G., Sivasankar, P., & Rajesh, A. (2020). Hybrid PSO-HSA and PSO-GA algorithm for 3D path planning in autonomous UAVs. *SN Applied Sciences*, 2(11), 1805. doi:10.100742452-020-03498-0

Aditya Gautam, S. (2014). Path planning for unmanned aerial vehicle based on genetic algorithm & artificial neural network in 3D. *2014 International Conference on Data Mining and Intelligent Computing (ICDMIC)*. IEEE.

Albert, A., Leira, F. S., & Imsland, L. (2017). UAV Path Planning using MILP with Experiments. *Modeling, Identification and Control*, 38(1), 21–32. doi:10.4173/mic.2017.1.3

Arulkumaran, K., Deisenroth, M. P., Brundage, M., & Bharath, A. A. (2017). A Brief Survey of Deep Reinforcement Learning. *IEEE Signal Processing Magazine,* (Sept), 1–13. doi:10.1109/MSP.2017.2743240

Chen, Y., Han, J., & Zhao, X. (2012). Three-dimensional path planning for unmanned aerial vehicle based on linear programming. *Robotica*, 30(Sept), 773–781. doi:10.1017/S0263574711000993

De Santis, R., Montanari, R., Vignali, G., & Bottani, E. (2018, May 16). Roberto Montanari. Giuseppe Vignali, 'An adapted ant colony optimization algorithm for the minimization of the travel distance of pickers in manual warehouses'. *European Journal of Operational Research*, 267(1), 120–137. doi:10.1016/j.ejor.2017.11.017

Feron, E. (2008). *Aerial Robotics*. Springer Handbook of Robotics.

Fu, Z., Yu, J., Xie, G., Chen, Y., & Mao, Y. (2018). A Heuristic Evolutionary Algorithm of UAV Path Planning. *Wireless Communications and Mobile Computing, 2018*(Sept), 11. doi:10.1155/2018/2851964

Gao, Y., Chen, S. F., & Lu, X. (2004, January). Research on Reinforcement Learning Technology: A Review. *Acta Automatica Sinica, 30*. doi:10.16383/j.aas.2004.01.011

Huang, C., & Fei, J. (2018). UAV Path Planning Based on Particle Swarm Optimization with Global Best Path Competition. *International Journal of Pattern Recognition and Artificial Intelligence, 32*.

Jun, S., & Wei, F. (2012). Quantum behaved particle swarm optimization; analysis of individual particle behavior and parameter selection. *Evolutionary Computation*.

Kamal, W. A., Gu, D.-W., & Postlethwaite, I. (2005). Real Time Trajectory Planning for UAVs Using MILP. *Proceedings of the 44th IEEE Conference on Decision and Control*, (pp. 3381-3386). IEEE. 10.1109/CDC.2005.1582684

Konatowski, S., & Pawlowski, P. (2019). PSO algorithm for UAV autonomous path planning with threat and energy cost optimization. *XII Conference on Reconnaissance and Electronic Warfare Systems*, (pp. 1-6). IEEE. 10.1117/12.2524886

Li, Y., Zhang, S., Ye, F., Jiang, T., & Li, Y. (2020). A UAV Path Planning Method Based on Deep Reinforcement Learning. *2020 IEEE USNC-CNC-URSI North American Radio Science Meeting (Joint with AP-S Symposium)*, (pp. 93-94). IEEE. 10.23919/USNC/URSI49741.2020.9321625

Liu, X. & Zhang, D. (2021). Path planning method based on the particle swarm optimization trained fuzzy neural network algorithm. *Cluster Computing*, Springer.

Masehian, E., & Sedighizadeh, D. (2010). A Multi-Objective PSO-based Algorithm for Robot Path Planning. *IEEE Xplore*, (April), 465–470. doi:10.1109/ICIT.2010.5472755

Mesquita, R., & Gaspar, P. D. (2020). A Path Planning Optimization Algorithm Based on Particle Swarm Optimization for UAVs for Bird Monitoring and Repelling – Simulation Results. *2020 International Conference on Decision Aid Sciences and Application (DASA)*, (ppl 1144-1148). IEEE. 10.1109/DASA51403.2020.9317271

Minhas, HAhmad, R. (2021). A Reinforcement Learning Routing Protocol for UAV Aided Public Safety Networks. *Sensors, MDPI*, (June), 1–22.

Muntasha, G., Karna, N., & Shin, S. Y. (2021). Performance Analysis on Artificial Bee Colony Algorithm for Path Planning and Collision Avoidance in Swarm Unmanned Aerial Vehicle. *2021 International Conference on Artificial Intelligence and Mechatronics Systems (AIMS)*. IEEE. 10.1109/AIMS52415.2021.9466085

Nayyar, A., Nguyen, N., Kumari, R., & Kumar, S. (2019). Robot Path Planning Using Modified Artificial Bee Colony Algorithm. *Advances in Intelligent Systems and Computing*. Springer.

Ouahouah, S., Bagaa, M., Prados-Garzon, J., & Taleb, T. (2022). Deep-Reinforcement-Learning-Based Collision Avoidance in UAV Environment. IEEE Internet of Things Journal, 9(6), 4015-4030. doi:10.1109/JIOT.2021.3118949

Pehlivanoglu, Y. (2021, November). PerihanPehlivanoglu, "An enhanced genetic algorithm for path planning of autonomous UAV in target coverage problems". *Applied Soft Computing, 112*.

Roberge, V., & Tarbouchi, M. (2020). Parallel Algorithm for the Path Planning of Multiple Unmanned Aerial Vehicles. *2020 Fourth International Conference On Intelligent Computing in Data Sciences (ICDS)*, (pp. 1-6). 10.1109/ICDS50568.2020.9268775

Sedeh, O. M., Ostadi, B., & Zagia, F. (2021). A novel hybrid GA-PSO optimization technique for multi-location facility maintenance scheduling problem. *Journal of Building Engineering, 40*(August), 102348. doi:10.1016/j.jobe.2021.102348

Shao, S., Peng, Y., He, C., & Du, Y. (2020). *Efficient path planning for UAV formation via comprehensively improved particle swarm optimization*. Elsevier.

Sharma, T. K., Pant, M., & Abraham, A. (2013). Blend of local and global variant of PSO in ABC. *2013 World Congress on Nature and Biologically Inspired Computing*, Fargo, ND, USA. 10.1109/NaBIC.2013.6617848

Sheng, N. G., Sun, R., & Chen, S. (2019). 6-DOF Robotic Obstacle Avoidance Path Planning Based on Artificial Potential Field Method. *16th International Conference on Ubiquitous Robots (UR)*. IEEE.

Sonmez, A., Kocyigit, E., & Kugu, E. (2015). Optimal path planning for UAVs using Genetic Algorithm. *2015 International Conference on Unmanned Aircraft Systems (ICUAS)*. IEEE. 10.1109/ICUAS.2015.7152274

Tung, K. (2017). A novel hybrid PSO-ABC algorithm for effort estimation of software projects using agile methodologies. *Journal of intelligent systems*.

Wang, L., Liu, L., Qi, J., & Peng, W. (2020). *Improved Quantum Particle Swarm Optimization Algorithm for Offline Path Planning in AUVs* (Vol. 8). IEEE Access.

Wang, S. X. (2012). The Improved Dijkstra's Shortest Path Algorithm and Its Application. *Procedia Engineering, 29*, 1186–1190. doi:10.1016/j.proeng.2012.01.110

Watkins, C. J. C. H., & Dayan, P. (1992). Q-learning. *Machine Learning, 8*(May), 279–292. doi:10.1007/BF00992698

Wei, K., & Ren, B. (2018). A Method on Dynamic Path Planning for Robotic Manipulator Autonomous Obstacle Avoidance Based on an Improved RRT Algorithm. *Sensors (Basel), 18*(February), 571. doi:10.339018020571 PMID:29438320

Yan, C., & Xiang, X. (2018). A Path Planning Algorithm for UAV Based on Improved Q-Learning. *2018 2nd International Conference on Robotics and Automation Sciences*. IEEE. 10.1109/ICRAS.2018.8443226

Yang, L., Qi, J., Xiao, J., & Yong, X. (2016). *A Literature Review of UAV 3D Path Planning*.

Yue, L., & Chen, H. (2019, May). Unmanned vehicle path planning using a novel ant colony algorithm. *EURASIP Journal on Wireless Communications and Networking, 2019*(1), 136. doi:10.118613638-019-1474-5

Zhang, T., Huo, X., Chen, S., Yang, B., & Zhang, G. (2018). Hybrid Path Planning of A Quadrotor UAV Based on Q-Learning Algorithm. *37th Chinese Control Conference (CCC)*. IEEE Xplore.

Zhonghua, V. (2018). *Artificial bee colony constrained optimization algorithm with hybrid discrete variables and its application.* Acta Electronica Malaysia (AEM).

Chapter 3
A Review:
Twitter Spam Detection Techniques

S. Raja Ratna

(iD) https://orcid.org/0000-0002-3036-0993
SRM Institute of Science and Technology, India

Sujatha Krishnamoorthy
Wenzhou-Kean University, China

J. Jospin Jeya
SRM Institute of Science and Technology, India

Ganga devi Ganesan
SRM Institute of Science and Technology, India

M. Priya
SRM Institute of Science and Technology, India

ABSTRACT

One of the most well-liked social media is Twitter. Spam is one of the several issues that negatively affect users. The objective of this study is to provide an overview of different techniques used for detecting spam in twitter. The proposed framework mainly contains the comparison of four existing twitter spam detection techniques namely, machine learning, feature based detection, combinational algorithm, and deep learning. Machine learning detection uses techniques such as SVM, future engineering, machine learning framework, and semantic similarity function to assess spam. In feature based detection, metadata based, tweet based, user based, and graph based techniques are used to detect spammers. In combinatorial algorithm detection, Naive Bayes-SVM, K-nearest neighbour-SVM, random forest-SVM and RNN-Short term memory techniques are used to detect spam. Deep learning detection uses feature based, semantic cnn, convolution-short term memory nn, and deep learning convolution technique to identify spam. This paper covers relevant work and comparison of several anti spamming techniques.

DOI: 10.4018/978-1-6684-9317-5.ch003

1. INTRODUCTION

Twitter is one of the social media sites based on micro blogging, where users send and read tweets with a maximum of 140 characters. Twitters have been rapidly growing in recent years, and therefore have attracted unwanted attention from malicious users (Sun et al., 2020; Pierri et al., 2020; Chowdhury et al., 2020; Mendonca et al., 2020; Tajalizadeh et al., 2019). The majority of current studies on Twitter spam concentrate on blocking accounts, which is to recognise and block spam users. Alternatively, spammers may leverage a user's social network and tweets to their advantage and formulate spammer detection as an optimization problem. Similar to this, typical machine learning algorithms use features to identify spam users, including data from user tweets, demographics, shared URLs, and social connections (Ratna et al., 2015, 2016; Benisha et al., 2021, 2020). This paper discusses four different spam detection techniques on twitter.

More significantly, the twitter spam detectors employ two levels of categorization algorithms. The system begins with a limited number of labelled samples and then uses the confidently labelled tweets from the prior time window to update the detection models in a semi-supervised manner (Dutse et al., 2018; Alom et al., 2018; Benevenuto et al., 2015; Chen et al., 2015; Chhabra et al., 2011). The deep learning and machine learning approach aids in the learning of novel spamming techniques, strengthening the framework's ability to recognise spam tweets.

The proposed framework mainly contains the comparison between four different existing twitter spam detection techniques, namely, Machine Learning, Feature Based, Combinational Algorithm and Deep Learning (Ferrara et al., 2016; Gao et al., 2012; Adek et al., 2018).

The paper proceeds as follows. Section II describes the comparison of various twitter spam detection techniques. Section III describes detecting twitter spam using Machine Learning Detection Techniques (MLD). Section IV describes twitter spam detection using Feature Based Detection Techniques (FBD). Section V describes detecting twitter spam using the Combinational Algorithm Detection Technique (CAD). Section VI describes detecting twitter spam using Deep Learning Detection Techniques (DLD). Section VII describes the experimental evaluation of different detection techniques and finally section VIII concludes the paper.

2. COMPARISON OF TWITTER SPAM DETECTION TECHNIQUES

Recovery from spammers in twitter requires an efficient detection mechanism. Detection techniques are more important because an efficient detection technique can increase the twitter performance. This paper discusses four different existing twitter spam detection techniques namely, Machine Learning Detection (MLD), Feature Based Detection (FBD, Combinational Algorithm Detection (CAD) and Deep Learning Detection (DLD). The outline of various twitter spam detection techniques are presented in Figure 1

- In MLD techniques, Support Vector Machine, Future Engineering Based, Machine Learning Framework, Semantic Similarity Function are the following techniques used to detect whether the tweet is spam or non-spam.
- The FBD techniques, uses Metadata Based, Tweet Based, User Based and Graph Based techniques to detect spam in twitter.

Figure 1. Various twitter spam detection techniques

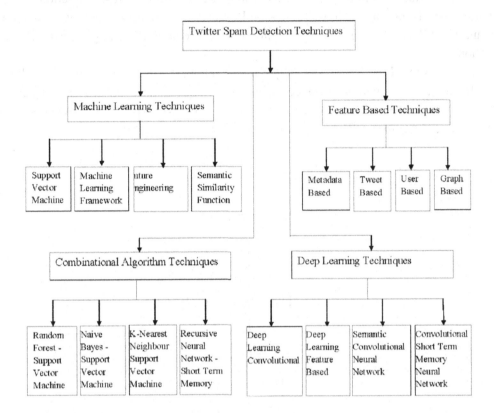

- In CAD techniques, Naive Bayes with Support Vector Machine, K-Nearest Neighbour with Support Vector Machine, Random Forest with Support Vector Machine and Recursive Neural Network with Short Term Memory are the detection techniques used to detect the spam tweet.
- The DLA technique uses, Feature-Based, Semantic Convolution Neural Network, Convolution with Short Term Memory Neural Network and Deep Learning Convolution Technique to detect twitter spam.

The twitter spam detection is the integration of three steps: a)Pre-processing, b)Spam Detection and c)Classification. The first step, Pre-processing, performs filtration and removal of stopwords and emoji's. Then after the removal of stopwords and emoji's, the twitter keywords are identified for detection.

The second step, Spam Detection discusses four different detection techniques namely, Machine Learning Detection, Feature Based Detection, Combinational Algorithm Detection and Deep Learning Detection to identify the spam twitter. Of the four different techniques, any one of the techniques can be used for detection.

i) In MLD, the Support Vector Machine Technique uses SVM Classifier; Machine Learning Framework Technique uses Metadata and Interaction Feature Extraction. The Future Engineering Technique uses Content Feature Extraction. Finally, the Semantic Similarity Function Technique uses Syntax and Feature Analysis Extraction schemes for spam detection.

ii) In FBD, the Metadata Based Technique uses Static and dynamic feature extraction, Tweet Based technique uses Hybrid algorithms. The Graph Based Technique uses Graph based feature extraction and User Based Technique uses Neighbour node prediction learning extraction schemes for detection.

iii) In CAD, the Naive Bayes-SVM Technique uses Lightweight Feature Extraction and K-Nearest SVM Technique uses a neural network classifier. The Random Forest SVM Technique uses Feature based, Content based and User behaviour extraction. The Recursive Neural Network Short Term Memory Technique uses URL based extraction schemes for detection.

Figure 2. System design of twitter spam detection

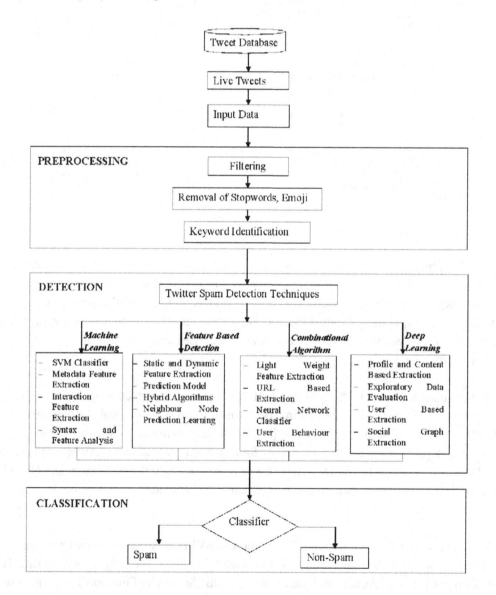

iv) In DLD, the Deep Learning Feature Based Technique uses Profile based extraction and exploratory data evaluation. Deep Learning Convolution Technique uses Lightweight features. The Semantic Convolution Neural Network Technique uses User based extraction, and the Convolution Short Term Memory Neural Network uses Social graph extraction schemes for spam detection.

The last step, Classification classifies whether twitter is spam or not spam. The outline system design of twitter spam detection is presented in Figure 2.

3. DETECTING TWITTER SPAM USING MACHINE LEARNING DETECTION TECHNIQUES

Four Machine Learning Detection techniques namely Support Vector Machine, Future Engineering Based, Machine Learning Framework, Semantic Similarity Function are used to assess spammers on Twitter (Beyt et al., 2021; Khaleel et al., 2019; Prakash et al., 2020; Mostafa et al., 2020; Falak, et al., 2021). For the four MLD techniques SVM Classifier, Metadata Feature Extraction, Interaction Feature Extraction and Syntax-Feature Analysis are the Extraction schemes used to detect whether the tweet is spam or non-spam. Different twitter spam detection using MDL techniques are listed in Table 1

(Beyt et al., 2021) discussed the extraction steps used to identify whether the tweets are spam or not spam; it uses the SVM classifier as the extraction scheme. The idea of using an automatic approach to identify whether the tweet is spam or non spam is presented here. This approach is based on feature extraction and pre-processing processes. The unique structure of tweets makes the pre-processing stage important. Only words from each tweet remain once the pre-processing step is completed, and these words could be crucial in deciding whether the tweet is spam or not. The key component of the suggested strategy is feature extraction. The features used in the suggested method were chosen to accurately represent the information included in tweets and to be useful in identifying spam from non-spam tweets. In the suggested method, there are nearly 28 groups of features like user profile features, account information features, user activity based features, user interaction based features, tweet content based features, and so on. An ideal subset of these features is picked during the feature selection step to aid in learning. Gaussian and polynomial kernels are used to learn along with support vector classifiers.

(Khaleel et al., 2019) presented a number of characteristics that Word2Vec extracts from twitter content. To achieve this, the author uses Wrod2Vec to convert each word in the data used in this work into a multidimensional vector and uses Content Feature Extraction as the extraction scheme. Three separate measures were used to assess the performance of the chosen method: precision, recall, and F-measure. The author chose MLP as one of the two classification methods in order to compare it against other classifiers, such as Random Forest (RF), Decision Tree (J48), and Naive Bayes (NB). This technique uses a neural network with two levels. The Huffman algorithm is used in the network as a SoftMax structure to determine the nature of repeated words. Consequently, the training model's effectiveness will increase when high-frequency words can be processed quickly or in real time. Using CBOW or Skip-Gram, the appropriate vectors for every single word are discovered. The classification technique used by this author was a multilayer perception (MLP) neural network. Ultimately, three alternative classifiers were used to compare the chosen technique.

(Prakash et al., 2020) discussed the detection of spam twitter using machine learning approaches. The author categories the discovered spam tweets based on Metadata and Interaction Feature Extraction. The strategies for detecting fraudulent users that are based on temporal features, content, structure, and users are contrasted. Two categorization modules were used in the datasets: SVM and Naive Bayes. Following a categorization of spam detection techniques, Twitter spams are categorized as URL-based and fake content-based. Using the dataset and a machine learning system, the spam is identified. Prior to classification, the prelabeled tweets should be used to train a classifier that comprises the knowledge structure. A new incoming tweet can be predicted using the classification model once it has assimilated the knowledge structure of the training data. There are only two steps in the entire process, learning and classifying. The first step will be to extract and vectorize the features of tweets. There are alternative methods that might be used to retrieve the class labels (spam or no spam).

(Mostafa et al., 2020) introduces a new detection model that depends on vector-based qualities to train sentence embedding. Syntax and Feature Analysis Extraction are the extraction schemes used for spam detection. The model depends on 3 steps: analyze the similarity of Twitter accounts, classify campaigns, and classify the detecting tweets as spam. To build the graph, the initial step is to determine how similar all accounts that tweet about related topics are to one another. Extracting cohesive graphs for a candidate campaign is the second phase. The classification of this effort as a legitimate or spam campaign comes in third. On datasets, a two-step semantic function is employed to examine Twitter account similarities. The first step is to group the tweets together by summarising their text. The second is to search for related tweets using the Siamese Recurrent Network.

Table 1. Twitter spam detection using machine learning detection (MID) techniques

Authors	Detection Technique	Extraction Scheme	Inference	Advantage	Disadvantage
Beyt, S. A. S., Rafie, M., Mojtaba, G. S.	Support Vector Machine	SVM Classifier	Extraction steps and pre-processing distinguish whether tweets were spam or not spam.	Uses real world datasets	Efficiency has to be improved.
Khaleel, A. A., Kaya, B.	Future Engineering	Content Feature Extraction	Learning process is obtained through polynomial kernels and Gaussians Support vectors.	Incorporate various dimensions of the problem.	Explained modules are not implemented.
Prakash, S. D., Gunjal. B. L.	Machine Learning Framework	Metadata and Interaction Feature Extraction	Four modules: Data Evaluation, Pre-handling, Feature engineering and Prediction module are used for detection.	Fake user based detection is also compared.	Accuracy is reduced.
Mostafa, M., Abdelwahab, A., Sayed, H. M.	Semantic Similarity Function	Syntax and Feature Analysis Extraction	The function classifies the campaigns and classifies the detecting tweets.	Uses a 3 day real life twitter dataset.	Spam drift problem is not solved.

4. DETECTING TWITTER SPAM USING FEATURE BASED DETECTION TECHNIQUES

Four Feature Based Detection techniques namely Metadata-based, Tweet-base, User-base and Graph based are used to detect spammers on Twitter (Fazil et al., 2018; Gupta et al., 2018; Murugan et al., 2019; Herzallah et al., 2017). For the four FBD techniques, Static and dynamic feature extraction, Prediction model, Hybrid algorithms and Neighbour node prediction learning are the extraction schemes used for detection. Different twitter spam detection using FBD techniques are listed in Table 2.

(Fazil et al., 2018) proposed a combinational feature based approach which combines features like content based, metadata based and interaction based features, and uses Static and Dynamic Feature Extraction as the extraction scheme. The basic idea of their approach is that the classification of user based is depending on their communications with their group. Three classifiers namely Random forest, Decision tree and Bayesian network algorithms are used to classify the real dataset. The focus of the study is on this description of the spammer, which is based on the interactions between its nearby nodes. They have introduced six new features in which content based is one, interaction based is three, and community based is two. Two existing features are redefined which are also content based. The result shows that metadata feature based provides least effective spam detection when compared to interaction- and community based features.

(Gupta et al., 2018) proposed a new framework for tweet classification that includes text-based characteristics, user-based features, and tweet-based features. With the use of user- based features and tweet-based features, text-based features may identify spam tweets using hybrid algorithms. The various issues addressed in this paper are time lag, exactness shortage and increased processing time. Based on a tweet that was taken from Twitter, the HSpam 14 dataset was created. Gradient Support, Support Vector Machine, Random Forests, and Neural Networks are machine learning train models. F-measure and Accuracy is calculated for various machine learning train models and compared. They have concluded that by including tweet based features along with user based features the spam is predicted well and the loss caused by it is reduced.

(Murugan et al., 2019) proposed the method for spam detection using intelligent Twitter spam technique and uses Neighbour Node Prediction Learning Extraction as the extraction scheme. Users will benefit from the security of their personal data. It uses a hybrid approach to provide information about the spammers #39;s profile, which does not have a single classifier. The hybrid approach uses a decision tree algorithm, Particle Swarm Optimization algorithm and Genetic Algorithms. Before receiving the tweets as samples, they secured it using Google security APIs. They divided the data from the tweets into two groups, namely, content-based features and user-based features.

(Herzallah et al., 2017) proposed a hybrid technique combining user graph, content-based features, and graph-based characteristics to detect spam profiles. Twitter API is used to collect the data set. Top 5 features are tested using various classifiers like Naive Bayes, Support vector machine and Random forest and K-Nearest Neighbour algorithms. These features are also used to construct the detection model. For trials, a Twitter dataset with 11,000 users and more 400,000 tweets were used. The findings revealed good classification accuracy and low false positive rates. The result shows that graph based features gave the highest performance ratio compared to user behaviours and content based features.

Table 2. Twitter spam detection using feature based detection (FBD) techniques

Authors	Detection Technique	Extraction Scheme	Inference	Advantage	Disadvantage
Fazil, M., Abulaish, M.	Metadata Based Features	Static and Dynamic Feature Extraction	The spam categorization is based upon its neighbouring nodes and their respective interactions.	Metadata-based analysis is effective for spam detection.	Spammers used various granularity levels to characterise some intriguing patterns.
Gupta, H., Jamal, M. S., Madisetty, S.	Tweet Based Features	Hybrid Algorithms	Tweets are classified based on tweet-based, feature-based and user-based.	Accuracy is increased to 91.65%.	Spam tweets of a bag of words are not updated.
Murugan, N. S., Devi, G. U.	User Based Features	Neighbour Node Prediction Learning Extraction	Tweets are classified-based on tweet-based and user based.	Google securities APIs are used.	Less Accuracy.
Herzallah, H., Faris, S., Adwan, O.	Graph Based Feature	Graph Based Feature Extraction	Uses twitter dataset with 11000 users and more than 400000 tweets.	High classification accuracy with low false positives.	Efficiency is reduced.

5. DETECTION OF TWITTER SPAM USING COMBINATIONAL ALGORITHM DETECTION TECHNIQUES

Four Combinational Algorithm Detection techniques namely, Naive Bayes with Support Vector Machine, K-Nearest Neighbour with Support Vector Machine, Random Forest with Support Vector Machine and Recursive Neural Network with Short Term Memory are used to detect spammers on Twitter (Sun et al., 2020; Gupta et al., 2018; Mateen, et al., 2017; Chen et al., 2016). The four CAD techniques uses, Lightweight feature extraction, URL based extraction; neural network classifier and User behaviour extraction schemes for detection. Different twitter spam detection using CAD techniques are listed in Table 3.

(Sun et al., 2020) proposed to create a training model using a vast volume of data for studies on detecting spam tweets and using Lightweight Feature Extraction as extraction scheme. After pre-processing, the tweets are collected, which enables the user to determine whether a tweet is spam or not. Features are extracted using a lightweight feature extraction method from the obtained dataset of ground truth data before using the aforementioned procedures. Machine learning algorithms used training data to determine whether tweets were spam or not. The neural network, K-Nearest Neighbour-based algorithm, decision tree based algorithm, Naive Bayes, deep learning, and the boosting technique are examples of supervised machine learning algorithms.

(Gupta et al., 2018) proposed a method which detects spam which spreads spamming in Twitter by sending unwanted advertisements and spreading infection. The detection model develops a strong and accurate model for detecting spam. Neural Network classifiers are used for the testing of data sets. The data sets are related to the characteristics of content-based, user behavior-based, and graph-based. To categorize the tweets, the author uses the user- and tweet-based capabilities as well as the tweet text function. The tweet text function has the advantage of making it feasible to identify spam tweets even if the spammer starts a new account, which was not achievable with just the user and tweet based features. The terms that can serve as strong indications are taken from tweets' text in order to categorize them into one of the following categories: either spam or not

(Mateen, et al., 2017) proposes a hybrid technique that uses the combination of three features namely, user based, content based and graph based to identify spammer and non-spammer users on Twitter. Conventional machine learning methods are used to analyze the value of spam detection features. It is analyzed on real Twitter dataset with an approximate of 11k uses and more than 400k tweets. After classification, the correlation between features is calculated and the correlated features are eliminated. User-based features are based on a user's connections and user account attributes. Users' written remarks or content provide the basis of content-based functionality. By using graph-based features, spammers' evasion techniques are defeated.

(Chen et al., 2016) proposed a hybrid method of URL based Extraction, Recursive Neural Networks and Long Short Term Memory for spam detection. Spam collected from SMS and Twitter datasets are used for experimental results. Before using the detection method the text has been changed into a meaning semantic word vector. For analysis ANN, Naive Bayes, K-NN, Random Forests and SVM are used. The first stage in statistical feature-based Twitter spam detection is to pinpoint the Spam Drift issue. The proposed method for spam detection is Lfun. When the classifiers in the Lfun approach are retrained using the modified spam tweets that are added and learned from unlabeled data, it can considerably lessen the effect of spam drift. In terms of Detection Rate and F-measure, the effectiveness of the Lfun method is assessed. According to experimental findings, the Lfun technique greatly improves both detection rate and F-measure. Four conventional machine learning methods are compared with Lfun, and it is discovered that Lfun performs better than all four in terms of overall accuracy, F-measure, and Detection Rate.

Table 3. Detecting twitter spam using combinational algorithm detection (CAD) techniques

Authors	Detection Technique	Extraction Scheme	Inference	Advantage	Disadvantage
Sun, N., Lin, G., Qiu, J., Rimba, P.	Naive Bayes with SVM	Lightweight Feature Extraction	Features are extracted using a lightweight feature extraction method.	Nine machine learning methods were used	Larger time delay.
Gupta, H., Jamal, M. S., Madisetty, S.	K-Nearest Neighbour, with SVM	Neural Network Classifier	Data sets are tested using classifiers such as neural network, random forest, decision trees, k-nearest neighbours', support vector machines and naive Bayes.	Strong and accurate model for spam detection.	Complexity is high.
Mateen, M., Aleem, M., Iqbal, M. A.	Random Forests with SVM	Feature, Content and User Behaviour Extraction	User-friendly features and content-based features are used to identify spammers.	High classification accuracy.	Doesn't work well for other social media platforms.
Chen, C., Wang, Y., Zhang, J., Xiang, Y., Zhou, W.	Recursive Neural Networks with Short Term Memory	URL Based Extraction	Spam collected from SMS and Twitter datasets are used for experimental results. By changing into semantic words the detection occurs.	Text has been changed into a meaning semantic word vectors	Incremental adjustment is not incorporated.

6. DETECTING OF TWITTER SPAM USING DEEP LEARNING DETECTION TECHNIQUES

Four Deep Learning Detection techniques namely Deep Learning with Feature-Based, Semantic Convolution Neural Network, Convolution with Short Term Memory Neural Network and Deep Learning Convolution Technique are used to detect spammers on Twitter (Svadasu et al., 2022; Wu et al., 2017; Ban et al., 2015; Jain et al., 2020). For the four DLD techniques Profile and content based extraction, exploratory data evaluation, User based Extraction and Social graph extraction are the extraction schemes used to detect whether the tweet is spam or non-spam. Different twitter spam detection using DLD techniques is listed in Table 4.

(Ban et al., 2015) discussed a new technique based on deep learning algorithms and uses Profile based extraction and exploratory data evaluation extraction scheme for spam detection. Word vector training method was used to learn the structure of a tweet. The data set is represented using a binary classifier. The data set is collected based on 10-day real tweet datasets which is not publicly available but was able to get only the interested objects. Also annotated data has been used around 1000000. This Hidden Markov Model predictive model which claims the work by statistically and it represents the hidden states using distribution probability. Two methods were adopted: Expectation Maximization which provides an optimal value for HMM parameter then there comes tuning the parameter based on the tuned parameters. Hence the proposed model found a first order HMM delivered an independent model for 98% of accuracy.

(Svadasu et al., 2022) proposed a technique by which the dataset is classified using deep learning neural network and spam detected using feature engineering method. To represent tweets, layers are removed from hidden features and use Lightweight Feature Extraction. This research compares the set features of deep learning with statistical features and word2vec features to estimate the performance of deep learning features. Word2vec characteristics and statistical features enable Deep Neural Networks to more correctly identify Twitter spam.

(Wu et al., 2017) Semantic Convolution Neural Networks have been made available by networks for the purpose of detecting spam from social media as its significance has grown. Convolution neural networks, which are also employed in NLP applications, were utilised for the processing. As a result of Word Net, Word2Vec, and CompetNet support, Word Vector is now semantically enhanced. Initially the twitter message is fed into the feature extraction phase which contains three stages like raw string identification which remove irrelevant phrases from the content. Then the word vector learning algorithm detects the semantic features of the contents and high dimension vector features generates the vector value of the user content. Then learning algorithms starts learning the features and classify based on the hyper parameter tuning. Here, Softmax Classification is involved with vector combination and the prediction is done. The experimental setting is Ground Truth Twitter database was collected from Twitter streaming API.

(Jain et al., 2020) proposed a Deep Learning technique based on Spam activity and uses Social graph extraction scheme for detection. Deep learning will be used to train Word Vector so that users may learn the syntax of each tweet. The performance of various classifiers, non-text-based detection techniques, and other text-based methods have all been discussed and compared. It was observed that the features used in this method were unique. This architecture provides a collaborative approach of CNN and LSTM for reliable and robust models. The keywords are identified using wordnet and concept net from the dataset. This system proposed a three level layer firstly, semantic CNN layer (SCNN) followed by semantic LSTM and the finalized using SSCL (Sequential stacked CNN LSTM). In the first layer wordtovec enhancement has been suggested in which counts and identifies the keywords using the function wordnet which are mapped in multi dimensional space. In the second layer variants of RNN have been employed for feature extraction it finds out that similar words attempt to compare the semantic nature. The tweets once collected were sent to wordvector phase for modularity for mapreduce function. Then the refined features are identified and fed to the CNN then followed by LSTM and Classification.

Table 4. Detecting Twitter spam using deep learning detection (DLD) techniques

Authors	Detection Technique	Extraction Scheme	Inference	Advantage	Disadvantage
Ban, X., Chen, C., Liu, S., Wang, Y., Zhang, J.	Deep Learning with Feature-Based	Profile based Extraction and Exploratory Data Evaluation	Word vector training method was used to learn the structure of a tweet. The data set is represented using a binary classifier.	The data set is collected based on a 10-day real tweet.	Training method is complex.
Svadasu, G., Adimoolam, M.	Deep Learning Convolutional Technique	Lightweight Features	Dataset is classified using deep learning neural network and spam detected using feature engineering method.	Accuracy is improved.	Larger time delay.
Wu, T., Wen, S., Liu, S., Zhang, J., Alrubaian, M.	Semantic Convolutional Neural Network	User Based Extraction	For detecting spam from social media semantic convolution neural networks have been used. An innovative technique based on deep learning techniques is used.	Features used were stronger than other features.	Minimum classifiers are used for comparison.
Jain, G., Sharma, G., Agarwal, M., Basant, P.	Convolutional with Short Term Memory Neural Network	Social Graph Extraction	Deep learning method is used to train word vectors so that users may easily learn the syntax of each tweet.	Accuracy has increased.	Doesn't work well for other social media platforms.

7. EXPERIMENTAL EVALUATION

The performance is measured by four metrics such as Precision, Accuracy, Recall and F-measure. Accuracy measurement reflects how close it is to the actual or acceptable value. Precision is the degree to which measurements of the same thing agree with one another. Recall measures how many correct class predictions were produced using all of the successful cases in the dataset. The accuracy of a test is gauged by the F-measure. It is derived from the test's recall and accuracy.

7.1 Metrics Value Analysis for Different Spam Detection Techniques

The metrics such as precision, Recall, Accuracy and F-measure which are used for detecting spam in various detection techniques such as Support Vector Machine, Machine Learning Framework, Random Forest, Semantic CNN and Naive Bayes are shown in Table 5. In the first set of experiments, it is observed that the Machine Learning Framework provides the lowest precision, recall and accuracy than other techniques, whereas its F-measure is higher than the semantic CNN. The Random Forest provides higher precision, recall, F-measure and accuracy than other techniques.

Table 5. Metrics values for five sam detection techniques

TECHNIQUES	PRECISION	RECALL	ACCURACY	F MEASURE
SVM	0.98	0.95	0.96	0.96
MACHINE LEARNING FRAMEWORK	0.92	0.89	0.92	0.91
RANDOM FOREST	0.98	0.99	0.98	0.98
SEMANTIC CNN	0.97	0.91	0.92	0.80
NAIVE BAYES	0.98	0.97	0.96	0.97

7.2 Precision and Accuracy on Different Spam Detection Techniques

Figure 3a and b shows the results of Precision and Accuracy for five different spam detection techniques; Support Vector Machine, Machine Learning Framework, Random Forest, Semantic CNN and Naive Bayes In the second set of experiments, it is observed that SVM, Naive Bayes and Random Forest provide the highest precision of 0.98, while Machine Learning Framework provides the lowest precision of 0.92. Similarly, it is also observed that Random Forest provides the highest accuracy of 0.98 than all other techniques, while Machine Learning Framework and Naive Bayes provide the lowest accuracy of 0.92.

Figure 3. With different spam detection techniques: (a) Precision (b) Accuracy

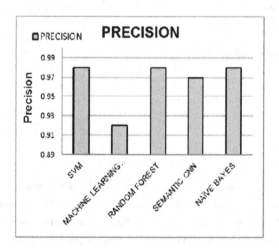 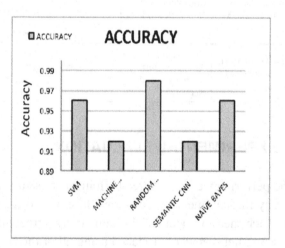

7.3 Recall and F-Measure on Different Spam Detection Techniques

Figure 4a and b shows the results of Recall and F-Measure for five different spam detection techniques; Support Vector Machine, Machine Learning Framework, Random Forest, Semantic CNN and Naive Bayes. In the third set of experiments, it is observed that Random Forest provides the highest Recall of 0.99 than other detection techniques, while Machine Learning Framework provides the lowest precision of 0.89. Similarly, it is also observed that Random Forest provides the highest F-measure of 0.98 than all other techniques, while Semantic CNN provides the lowest F-measure of 0.80.

Figure 4. With different spam detection techniques: (a) Recall (b) F-Measure

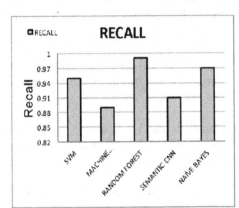
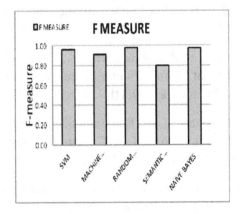

8. CONCLUSION

One of the social media platforms based on micro blogging is twitter, where anyone may send and read tweets. Twitter has experienced tremendous growth, which has drawn unwanted attention from malicious users. The paper has surveyed the main aspects of security against twitter and various spam detection techniques. Four different twitter spam detection techniques namely, Machine Learning Detection, Feature Based Detection, Combinational Algorithm Detection and Deep Learning detection are surveyed and their methodology, advantages, and disadvantages are also compared.

REFERENCES

Adek, R. T., & Nasution, S. (2018). Tweet Clustering in Indonesian Language Twitter Social Media using Naive Bayes Classifier Method. *Eurasian Journal of Analytical Chemistry*, *13*(6), 277–284.

Alom, Z., Carminati, B., & Ferrari, E. (2018). Detecting spam accounts on Twitter. *IEEE/ACM International Conference on Advances in Social Networks Analysis and Mining*. IEEE.

Ban, X., Chen, C., Liu, S., Wang, Y., & Zhang, J. (2015). A performance evaluation of machine learning-based streaming spam tweets detection. *IEEE Transactions on Computational Social Systems*, *2*(3), 65–76. doi:10.1109/TCSS.2016.2516039

Benevenuto, F., Magno, G., Rodrigues, T., & Almeida, V. (2015). Detecting spammers on Twitter. *ACM International Conference on Collaboration, Electronic messaging. Anti-Abuse and Spam*. ACM.

Benisha, R., & Ratna, S. R. (2020). Detection of Interruption Attack in the Wireless networked closed loop industrial control systems. *Telecommunication Systems*, *73*(3), 359–370. doi:10.100711235-019-00614-3

Benisha, R., & Ratna, S. R. (2021). Detection of interruption attack in the wireless networked closed loop industrial control systems. *Telecommunication Systems*, *73*(3), 359–370. doi:10.100711235-019-00614-3

Beyt, S. A. S., Rafie, M., & Mojtaba, G. S. (2021). Spam detection on Twitter using a support vector machine and users features by identifying their interactions. *Multimedia Tools and Applications*, 8(4), 11583–11605.

Chen, C., Wang, Y., Zhang, J., Xiang, Y., Zhou, W., & Min, G. (2016). Statistical Features Based Real-time Detection of Drifted Twitter Spam. *IEEE Transactions on Information Forensics and Security*, 12(4), 914–925. doi:10.1109/TIFS.2016.2621888

Chhabra, S., Aggarwal, A., Benevenuto, F., & Kumaraguru, P. (2011). Phishing social: The phishing landscape through short URLs. *ACM International Conference on Collaboration Electronic messaging Anti-Abuse and Spam,* (pp. 92–101). ACM. 10.1145/2030376.2030387

Chowdhury, R., Das, K. G., Saha, B., & Bandyopadhyay, S. K. (2020). A Method Based on NLP for Twitter Spam Detection. Preprints, 283-291

Dutse, I. I., Liptrott, M., & Korkontzelos, I. (2018). Detection of spam-posting accounts on Twitter. *Neurocomputing*, 315(13), 496–511. doi:10.1016/j.neucom.2018.07.044

Falak, A., Ghous, H., & Malik, M. (2021). Twitter Spam Detection Using Machine Learning. *International Journal of Scientific and Engineering Research*, 12(2), 792–815.

Fazil, M., & Abulaish, M. (2018). A Hybrid Approach for Detecting Automated Spammers in Twitter. *IEEE Transactions on Information Forensics and Security*, 13(11), 2707–2719. doi:10.1109/TIFS.2018.2825958

Ferrara, E., Varol, O., Davis, C., Menczer, F., & Flammini, A. (2016). The rise of social bots. *Communications of the ACM*, 59(7), 96–104. doi:10.1145/2818717

Gao, H., Chen, Y., Lee, K., Palsetia, D., & Choudhary, A. N. (2012). Towards online spam filtering in social networks. *Network Distributed System Security*, 15, 1–16.

Gupta, H., Jamal, M. S., & Madisetty, S. (2018). A Framework for Real-Time Spam Detection in Twitter. *International Conference on Communication Systems & Networks*. IEEE. 10.1109/COMS-NETS.2018.8328222

Herzallah, H., Faris, S., & Adwan, O. (2017). Feature engineering for detecting spammers on Twitter: Modelling and analysis. *Journal of Information Science*, 44(2), 1–19.

Jain, G., Sharma, G., Agarwal, M., & Basant, P. (2021). Spam Detection on Social Media Using Semantic Convolutional Neural Network. *International Journal of Knowledge Discovery in Bioinformatics*, 8(1), 12–26. doi:10.4018/IJKDB.2018010102

Jain, G., Sharma, M., & Agarwal, B. (2019). Spam detection in social media using convolutional and long short term memory neural network. *Annals of Mathematics and Artificial Intelligence*, 85(1), 21–44. doi:10.100710472-018-9612-z

Khaleel, A. A., & Kaya, B. (2019). *Spam detection in online social networks by deep learning*. IEEE Xplore.

Mateen, M., Aleem, M., & Iqbal, M. A. (2017). A Hybrid Approach for Spam Detection for Twitter. *International Conference on Applied Sciences and Technology*. IEEE. 10.1109/IBCAST.2017.7868095

Mendonca, R. R. D., Brito, D. F. D., Rosa, F. D. F., Reis, J. C. D., & Bonacin, R. (2020). A Framework for Detecting Intentions of Criminal Acts in Social Media: A Case Study on Twitter. *International Conference on Information Technology-New Generations, 11*(3). IEEE.

Mostafa, M., Abdelwahab, A., & Sayed, H. M. (2020). Detecting spam campaign in twitter with semantic similarity. *Journal of Physics: Conference Series, 1447*(2), 455–472. doi:10.1088/1742-6596/1447/1/012044

Murugan, N. S., & Devi, G. U. (2019). Detecting Streaming of Twitter Spam Using Hybrid Method. *Wireless Personal Communications, 103*(2), 1353–1374. doi:10.100711277-018-5513-z

Pierri, F., Piccardi, C., & Ceri, S. (2020). A multi-layer approach to disinformation detection on Twitter. *EPJ Data Science, 9*(35), 525–531.

Prakash, S. D., & Gunjal. B. L. (2020). New Approach for Detecting Spammers on Twitter using Machine Learning Framework. *International journal of Research and Analytical reviews, 7*(3), 794-798.

Ratna, S. R., & Ravi, R. (2016). Securing jammed network using reliability behavior value through neuro-fuzzy analysis. *Sadhana Academy Proceedings in Engineering Science, 40*(4), 1139–1153.

Ratna, S. R., Ravi, R., & Shekhar, B. (2015). An intelligent approach based on neuro-fuzzy detachment scheme for preventing jamming attack in wireless networks. *Journal of Intelligent & Fuzzy Systems, 28*(2), 801–820. doi:10.3233/IFS-141363

Sun, N., Lin, G., Qiu, J., & Rimba, P. (2020). Near real-time twitter spam detection with Machine learning techniques. *International Journal of Computers and Applications, 44*(4), 1–11.

Svadasu, G., & Adimoolam, M. (2022). Spam Detection in Social Media using Artificial Neural Network Algorithm and comparing Accuracy with Support Vector Machine Algorithm. *International Conference on Business Analytics for Technology and Security*. IEEE Xplore.

Tajalizadeh, H., & Boostani, R. (2019). A Novel Stream Clustering Framework for Spam Detection in Twitter. *IEEE Transactions on Computational Social Systems, 6*(3), 525–534. doi:10.1109/TCSS.2019.2910818

Vishwarupe, V., Bedekar, M., Pande, M., & Hiwale, A. (2018). Intelligent Twitter Spam Detection: A Hybrid Approach. *Smart Trends in Systems Security and Sustainability, 15*, 189–197. doi:10.1007/978-981-10-6916-1_17

Wu, T., Wen, S., Liu, S., Zhang, J., & Alrubaian, M. (2017). Detecting spamming activities in twitter based on deep-learning technique. *Concurrency and Computation, 29*(19), 1–11. doi:10.1002/cpe.4209

Chapter 4
A Survey of Data Mining and Machine Learning– Based Intrusion Detection System for Cyber Security

Sangeetha Ganesan
R.M.K. College of Engineering and Technology, India

G. Shanmugaraj
Velammal Institute of Technology, India

A. Indumathi
Sri Venkateswara College of Engineering, India

ABSTRACT

With regard to intrusion detection systems (IDS), several research communities have shown interest in cyber security in recent years. IDS software keeps an eye out for malicious activity on a single computer or a network of computers. It is becoming increasingly important to detect intrusions and prevent them. Several methods to avoid or find intrusion in a network have been proposed in the past. However, the majority of the IDS detection methods currently in use are ineffective at solving this issue. Accuracy is the key factor in how well an intrusion detection system performs. In recent works, various techniques have been employed to enhance performance. In addition to this, machine learning (ML) has been used in many applications to produce results that are accurate in the relevant field. Determining how machine learning and data mining can be used to detect IDS in a network in the near future is the focus of this work. This literature review focuses on ML and data mining (DM) techniques for cyber analytics to support intrusion detection.

DOI: 10.4018/978-1-6684-9317-5.ch004

1. INTRODUCTION

The demand for cyber security and defense against various types of cyber-attacks has been rising steadily in recent times. The prevalence of Internet-of-Things (IoT), the phenomenal expansion of computer networks, and the enormous number of pertinent applications that are used by individuals or groups for either personal or commercial use are the main causes. In large-scale networks, cyberattacks like the denial-of-service (DoS) attack (Sun N et. al.(2018)), malware (Dainotti et.al.(2007)), and unauthorised access (Sun N et. al.(2018)) caused irreparable harm and monetary losses. As an illustration, a single ransomware virus caused $8 billion in losses for a variety of businesses and industries, including finance, healthcare, energy, and universities (Qu et.al.(2017)). According to other statistics, a data breach typically costs an affected organisation 3.9 million USD and the US 8.19 million USD . Accordingly, the need for cyber security and defense against different types of cyberattacks is growing daily in line with the needs of the modern online environment. The practice of cyber security involves shielding computers, programs, etc. from intrusions, unauthorised access, modifications, destructions, etc. Every Cyber Security system should typically include a firewall, antivirus software, and an intrusion detection system (IDS). IDS are important because they aid in identifying any unwelcome and unwanted changes to the system (Sun N et. al.(2018)).

However, the following distinctions can be made in cyber analytics: I) based on signatures or misuse ii) based on peculiar encryptions iii) based on the hybrid nature. This technique is highly recommended because it can be used to identify novel attacks. To further ensure that intruders are unable to determine which activities can be carried out incognito, it customises the normal activity routine for each situation. But just as every coin has a flip side, this technique also has a drawback: it may cause false alarm rates (FARs). The final classification combines the misuse and anomaly detection techniques used in the first two classifications. They are primarily used to increase the rate of common attack detection and decrease the False Positive (FP) rate for minor attacks. IDSs can also be separated based on host or network. By monitoring the traffic passing through the network devices, an IDS that relies on the network can spot attacks. A host-based IDS monitors all software-related processes and file activities on the host.

a)Host-based IDS (HIDS): It primarily focuses on examining how a computer system operates internally. It might be able to tell which program is attempting to access which resource and whether any attempts at unauthorized access are being made. Suppose a word processor suddenly changes the system password database.

b) Network-based IDS (NIDS): It concentrates on examining and filtering network device traffic. It is frequently observed that intrusions follow ambiguous patterns. These are primarily brought on by attacks launched by outside intruders who want to enter the network to risk it and obliterate it.

- Signature-Based IDS; is used to find known attack types.
- Anomaly-Based IDS; is used to detect unauthorized attacks

IDSs typically have three key parts, as shown in Figure 1.

- To begin with, there needs to be a system for gathering data that tracks network flows.
- Finally, using this vector and a classification engine, the traced flow is classified as either not malicious or an intrusion based on prior knowledge.
- These data need to be used to identify the features and create a feature vector.

Figure 1. Main components of intrusion detection system

2. BACKGROUND AND RELATED WORK

An intrusion detection system is frequently used to spot malicious cyber-attack behaviour when a network is regularly monitored and assessed for security risks or threats (Milenkoski et.al.(2015; Xin et. al.(2018)). Numerous studies have been conducted in the field of cyber security to identify and prevent cyber attacks and intrusions. Signature-based network intrusion detection is one of the well-known systems used in the cyber industry (Seufert S et. al. (2007)). Recent years have seen widespread adoption of and commercial success with this system, which takes into account a known signature. But one advantage the anomaly-based approach has over the signature-based approach for detecting unknown or zero-day attacks (Buczak et. al.(2015); . Alazab A et.al.(2012)) is the ability to recognize them.

This approach looks at relevant security data to monitor network activity and spot attack behavior patterns. With the help of various data mining and machine learning approaches, such patterns of security event analysis are utilized to guide meaningful judgments (Sarker et al. (2019); Han et al. (2011)). The key drawback of the anomaly-based approach is that, according to Buczak et al. (2015), it may label previously unidentified system behaviors as anomalies, which could result in a high proportion of false alarms. Therefore, it must be a high goal to lower false positive rates for intrusion detection systems (Sommer et al., 2010). A machine learning-based effective detection solution is needed to lessen these issues. According to Han J et al. (2011) and Witten et al. (2005), machine learning is usually viewed as a branch of artificial intelligence that focuses on teaching computers to learn from data. Data mining, data science, and computational statistics are all strongly related to it.

It is closely related to mathematical theories, procedures, statistical analysis, optimization, and several relevant real-world application areas. As a result, machine learning is a type of data-driven methodology used in the field of cyber security where the first step in creating an intelligent security model for forecasting future incidents is to understand the raw security data. In this work, we primarily focus on classification learning techniques (Sarker et.al.(2019a,2019b), which are typically used to build a predictive model by utilizing a given training dataset. Association analysis is popular in machine learning techniques to build rule-based intelligent systems (Agrawal et.al.(1994); Sarker et.al.(2018,2019c);). For instance, several well-liked techniques have been used to create a data-driven predictive model, including the probability-based naive Bayes classifier, hyperplane-based support vector machines, instance-learning-based k-nearest neighbors, the logistic regression technique based on the sigmoid function, and rule-based classification techniques like decision trees (Sarker, I.H(2019); Han, J (2011)). The above-mentioned machine-learning classification techniques were employed by several researchers in the field of cyber security, specifically for the detection of intrusions or cyber-attacks. For instance, Li et al. (2012) presented a method for classifying predefined attack categories like DoS, Probe or Scan, U2R, R2L, as well as regular traffic using the most well-liked KDD'99 cup dataset by using the hyperplane-based support vector machine classifier with an RBF kernel. To build a quicker system, Amiri et al. 2011 trained the model using a least-squares support vector machine classifier. Hu et al. classified the anomalies in their study using a variant of the support vector machine classifier in Hu, W et. al. (2003).

In their study, Wagner et al. (2011) used a one-class support vector machine classifier to detect anomalies and various attacks, including NetBIOS scans, DoS attacks, POP spams, and Secure Shell (SSH) scans. This support vector machine classifier was employed by the authors of Wagner, C et al.(2011) to monitor the activity of unidentified computer worms. Similarly, support vector machine classifiers were employed in studies by Kotpalliwar et al. (2015), Saxena et al. (2014), Pervez et al. (2014), Li et al. (2012), Shon et al. (2005), Kokila et al. (2014) to develop intrusion detection systems.

Panda et al. (2007) employed the probability-based naive Bayes classifier to assess the KDD'99 cup data set, which comprises of four categories of attacks: Probe or Scan, U2R, DoS, and R2L. Koc et al. (2012) used the same naive Bayes classifier to build a multi-class intrusion detection system. The KNN instance-based learning algorithm, which categorizes a data point based on its k-nearest neighbors, is another well-liked machine learning method. In their studies for intrusion detection systems, Shapoorifard et al. (2017), Vishwakarma et al. (2017), and Sharifi et al. (2015) used the KNN classification technique. For the purpose of identifying malicious traffic and intrusions, the logistic regression model has also been utilized in a number of research papers (Bapat et al. (2018); Bapat (2019)). For the detection of anomalies, notably DoS assaults, writers Kumar, P.A.R et al. (2011) and Dainotti, A et al. (2009) investigated wavelet transform and neural classifiers in addition to these techniques.

To develop predictive models, the decision tree technique, which is based on trees, is one of the most widely used machine learning classification methods. The ID3 (Dainotti, A (1986)) and C4.5 (Quinlan, J.R (1993)) algorithms are the most well-known techniques for creating decision trees automatically. Sarker et al. (2019) recently proposed the behavioral decision tree algorithm Behav DT for examining behavioral patterns. Ingre et al. (2017), Malik et al. (2018), Relan et al. (2015), Rai et al. (2016), Puthran et al. (2016), Moon et al. (2017), Balogun et al. (2015), and Sangkatsanee et al. (2011) are just a few researchers who have used the decision tree classification approach in their studies to build intrusion detection systems. A decision tree model, however, may have a number of problems due to the high dimensions of security features, including high variance due to over-fitting, a long computation time, and poor prediction accuracy.

3. SYSTEM DESIGN FOR IDS

In addition to manually or automatically scanning the network and host-based traffic for malicious threats that are vulnerable, the IDS also generates false positive alerts. When firewalls encountered numerous network traffic threats in the early 2000s, Network Intrusion Detection Systems (NIDS) took their place as the industry standard for network security. The evolution of IDS for observing network traffic can be divided into four eras or generations. To begin with, the idea of intrusion detection was first introduced in 2000 for some small-scale networks in addition to firewalls because it gets around cross-site scripting threats and malicious SQL queries. The second era began in 2005 as the IPS grew and more vendors began to support the models of intrusion detection technology. Next-Generation Intrusion Prevention Systems (NGIPS), along with application and user control features, entered the market between 2011 and 2015. A conventional IPS examines network traffic in search of recognized attack signatures. It produces alerts for network traffic shutdown or traffic activity.

Figure 2. Intrusion detection system

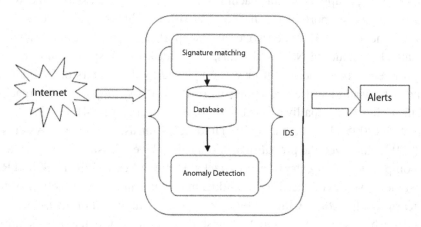

The intrusion detection system's system design is shown in Figure 2 and Figure 3. The main modules are as follows.

Phase 1: Preprocessing Internet-based (real-time) IDS: With the aid of packet sniffing tools (such as Wireshark and Capsa), packet features such as IP/TCP/ICMP headers are extracted from each packet during this phase of packet capturing and packet analysis. The packet header will then be divided into source addresses, destination addresses, etc. There are some techniques needed in this phase for the selection of key features. determining the packet's normality or intrusion, and so forth. Off-line IDS: During this phase, packets are captured from datasets (such as the KDD dataset/NLS KDD) to serve as the IDS's data source.

Phase 2: Classification Utilize the information from the previous phase during the classification phase to determine whether the packet is a normal packet or an attack packet. The corresponding algorithms will classify the packet into related groups based on the feature values. It involves two procedures: Data used for testing and training Answer classes and packet features are offered during the training phase to assist in the development of rules governing mapping domains. Depending on additional training, these guidelines might be replaced. Every algorithm has a unique classification strategy. Untrained data are provided to the system during the testing phase to sample whether or not true answers are obtained. Without specifying the answer class, the system process is carried out with input provided as packets.

Phase 3: Post-Processing

The preprocessing result is compared to the answer class, and system performance is calculated as the sum of correctness and false alarm rates. the True Positive, True Negative, False Positive, and False Negative categories.

Phase 4: Reducing False Alarms

More training is required if the system is still emitting some false alarms across all of the algorithms. The system will continue to learn on its own, free from human intervention, according to the machine learning mechanism. And hence there is no updating required.

Figure 3. System design for IDS

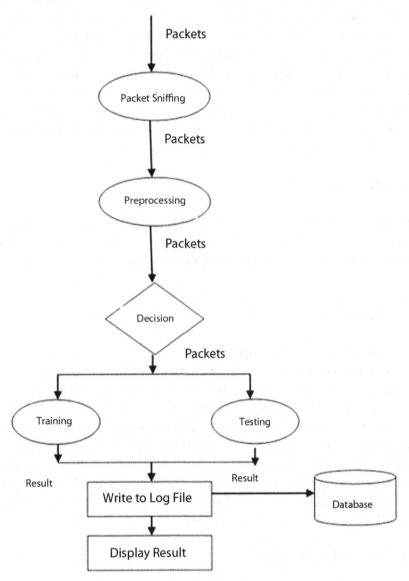

4. TAXONOMY OF ANOMALY DETECTION

In the past, a number of taxonomies for intrusion detection techniques have been put forth, but none of them are still widely accepted. The taxonomy presented here uses six criteria to categorize IDSs, as shown in Figure 1, and is based on the synthesis of several other taxonomies. At the moment, the two most common analytical methods of detection are signature-based and anomaly-based (Chebrolu et al.(2005); Lee et al.(2000)). The signature-based approach, also referred to as misuse detection, searches for a particular signature to match, which would indicate an intrusion. The shortcoming of signature-based intrusion detection systems is their inability to recognize novel attack types or novel variations of known attack patterns, even though they can detect most or all known attack patterns.

Anomaly detection is yet another helpful technique for intrusion detection. Since it was first suggested in Denning D (1987), anomaly detection applied to intrusion detection and computer security has been a focus of research. In anomaly-based IDSs, the typical system or network traffic behavior is represented, and any behavior that deviates over a predetermined threshold is recognized as an anomalous activity. Anomaly detection techniques can be divided into three main categories Lazarevic A et al.(2005): statistical-based, knowledge-based, and machine learning-based. These categories are based on the type of processing related to the "behavioral" model of the target system. The well-known intrusion detection methods and comparison of various methods are reviewed by Murali A and Rao M(2005), along with those methods' strengths and weaknesses.

4.1 IDS With a Statistical Anomaly

A statistical anomaly-based IDS learns about typical network activity, such as the bandwidth used, the protocols used, and the ports and devices that are typically connected. It then alerts the administrator or user when traffic is found that is anomalous (not typical). (Denning DE and Neumann PG(1985); Ye N (2002)).

4.2 Knowledge-Based Approaches

Knowledge-based databases contain subject-specific information. Knowledge-based information includes symbolic representations of expert judgment rules in a format that enables the inference engine to perform deduction on it. One of the most popular knowledge-based IDS strategies is the expert system approach. Frame-based models, rule-based models, and expert systems make up the three categories of knowledge-based techniques. The grammar-based production rules have been modified to become rule-based. A frame-based model localizes the entirety of the expected actions and knowledge into a single structure.

Three steps are involved in the expert system classification of the audit data by a set of rules. The training data is first used to identify various attributes and classes. Second, a set of parameters, rules, or processes for classification are inferred. Third, the audit data are appropriately categorized (Denning DE and Neumann PG (1985) ; Anderson D et al.(1995)).

4.3 Machine Learning-Based IDS

The foundation of machine learning techniques is the creation of an explicit or implicit model. The need for labeled data to train the behavioral model, a process that places heavy demands on resources, is a unique feature of these schemes. The applicability of statistical techniques and machine learning principles often coincides, despite the latter's emphasis on developing a model that enhances performance based on prior data. As a result, machine learning for IDS can modify its execution strategy. This characteristic might make it appealing to use such schemes in all circumstances. Pros: 1) Capturing interdependencies and being flexible and adaptable. Cons: 1) High depended on the behavior that was deemed acceptable by the system.

5. INTRUSION DETECTION AND MACHINE LEARNING

Applying machine learning techniques to intrusion detection entails creating a model automatically from training data. Each of the data instances in this set can be described by a set of attributes (features) and the labels that go along with them. The attributes may be continuous or categorical, for example. The suitability of anomaly detection techniques depends on the attributes' nature. For instance, distance-based approaches are typically unsatisfactory when applied to categorical attributes because they were initially designed to work with continuous features. Typically, labels for data instances take the form of binary values, such as normal and anomalous.

Instead of using the term "anomaly," some researchers have used other types of attacks like DoS, U2R, R2L, and Probe. Learning techniques can offer more details about the different kinds of anomalies in this way. However, experimental findings demonstrate that current learning methodologies are insufficiently precise to identify the specific types of anomalies. Obtaining an accurate labelled data set that is representative of all types of behaviors is quite expensive because labeling is frequently done manually by human experts. In light of this, three operating modes for anomaly detection techniques are defined: supervised learning, unsupervised learning, and semi-supervised learning.

Figure 4. Taxonomy of intrusion detection system

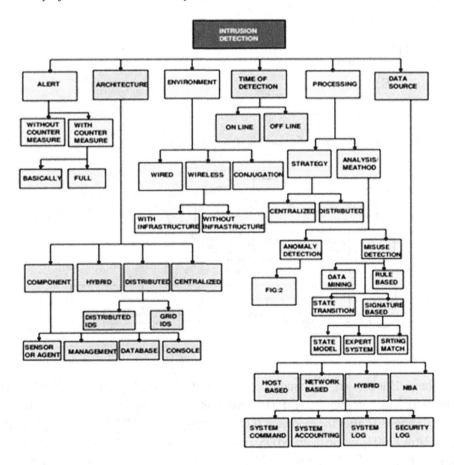

6. CLASSIFICATION OF ANOMALY DETECTION

IDS has been subjected to several machine learning-based schemes. The following subsections provide explanations of some of the most crucial techniques.

6.1 The Bayesian Network

A model called a Bayesian network encodes probabilistic connections between significant variables. This method is frequently applied for intrusion detection in conjunction with statistical schemes, a practice that has several benefits (Heckerman D (1995)), including the ability to encode interdependencies between variables, the ability to predict events, and the capacity to take into account both prior knowledge and data. The probability that condition B is met at once is determined using conditional probability P (A|B).

However, in applications in the real world. The conditional probability P (B|A) for B once its evidence A is present must be understood. The objective of this Bayes theory is to determine the likelihood that a given hypothesis H will hold given its sign or supporting evidence E.

The H can be assumed to be a sampled column feature vector and noted as x = {x1, x2, . . .}. In the following text the E (Evidence) and the C (Class) sign can be replaced (where C = {c1, c2, . . .}), if it makes it easier for the reader to understand the concept. The formula to calculate this probability is presented below

$$P\left(\frac{H}{E}\right) = \frac{P\left(H\right) * P\left(\frac{E}{H}\right)}{P\left(E\right)} \tag{1}$$

Figure 5. Hierarchical classification of anomaly detection

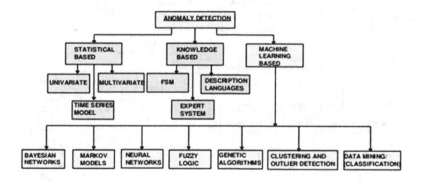

When hypothesis H is known, the conditional probability of evidence E is P (E |H). The likelihood of the hypothesis H is denoted by P(H). P (E) represents the likelihood of evidence E. The posterior probability of hypothesis H after the evidence E becomes available is P (H |E). Mrutyunjaya Panda, and Manas Ranjan Patra (2007) propose an NIDS framework based on the Naive Bayes algorithm. Over data sets that have been labeled by the network services, the framework constructs their usage patterns.

Using the built-in patterns and the naive Bayes Classifier algorithm, the framework finds attacks in the datasets. Their approach achieves a higher detection rate, takes less time, and is less expensive than the Neural network-based approach.

However, it produces more false positives. A naive Bayesian network is a constrained network with just two layers and total independence between the information nodes. This limits the study's potential application. Active platform or event-based classification may be thought of using a Bayesian network to minimize this issue and lower the false positives. In recent years, researchers have developed several systems to address the issue of false alarms. Y. Zhai et al. (2004), the author put forth the idea of using Bayesian networks to perform reasoning on additional security evidence, potentially lowering the rate of false alarms.

6.2 Markov Models

Markov chains and hidden Markov models are two of the Markov model subtypes. The topology and capabilities of the model are determined by the Markov chain, which is a collection of states connected by specific transition probabilities. The transition probabilities are estimated during the first training phase based on the target system's typical behavior. By comparing the anomaly score (associated probability) obtained for the observed sequences with a predetermined threshold, anomalies are then detected. When using a hidden Markov model, it is assumed that the system of interest is a Markov process in which states and transitions are concealed. It is only possible to observe the so-called productions.

Markov-based methods are frequently used in the context of host IDS and are typically applied to system calls. To reduce FAR, X.D. Hoang et al.(2009) propose a hybrid fuzzy-based anomaly IDS that combines a hidden Markov model (HMM) detection engine with a standard database detection engine. The study of the host-based anomaly IDS's development highlighted key areas of the system call-based HMM training described in Jiankun Hu (2009).

6.3 Neuronal Networks Artificial Neural Networks

Researchers in the field of artificial intelligence (AI) have created computational models with performance that is somewhat comparable to that of the brain, drawing inspiration from known facts about how the brain functions Naeem Seliya Taghi M. Khoshgoftaar (2010).Artificial neural networks (ANNs) are adaptive parallel distributed information processing models made up of (a) a collection of basic processing units (nodes, neurons), (b) a collection of synapses (connection weights), (c) the network architecture (pattern of connectivity), and (d) a learning procedure used to train the network(Li Xiangmei Qin Zhi (2011)). The Hybrid Neural Network Algorithm (HNNA) is presented in this paper based on the benefits and drawbacks of the enhanced GA and LM algorithms. First, the algorithms search for the global optimal point throughout the entire question domain by taking advantage of the improved GA's powerful whole searching capability. Then, it uses the fast local searching capability of the LM algorithm to refine the search process close to the global optimal point.

To modify the input and output parameters of the ANN model and adopt the theories of the fusion of the multi-classifiers to structure the Intrusion Detection System, the paper utilized respectively the three algorithms, namely the Improved GA, LM algorithm, and HNNA. Repeating an experiment reveals that the HNNA outperforms the LM algorithm in terms of stability and convergence precision, as well as improving GA based on the training data. The test results also demonstrate that the HNNA learning algorithm-based multiple classifier intrusion detection system has a higher detection rate than IDSs that use the LM and improved GA learning algorithms, including all attack categories with a few or many training samples, and a lower false negative rate.

By varying the assault categories, Xiangmei Li (2010) adjusted the 41-dimensional input features of the neural-network-based multiple classifier intrusion detection system. They discover that the 41-features multiple classifier intrusion detection system has a lower detection rate and a higher false negative rate than every adjusted sub-classifier, which also has a quicker training time and better convergence precision. The neural network-based multiple-classifier intrusion detection system has been shown to benefit from the idea of adjusting input features.

6.4 Fuzzy Logic Techniques

The predecessor of fuzzy logic, fuzzy set theory, uses approximate rather than precise deduction from classical predicate logic. Fuzzy techniques are applied in the field of anomaly detection because the required features can be viewed as fuzzy variables. (2000) Vaughn Bridges.

The first person to suggest using fuzzy logic for computer security was H.H. Hosmer in 1992. John E. (2000) claims that the anomaly-based IDS is implemented using fuzzy logic and data mining techniques and that the fuzzy intrusion recognition engine (FIRE) is advised for use in detecting intrusion activities. The system's fuzzy logic component is in charge of managing the complexity of the various input parameters as well as the imprecision of the input data.

The terms COUNT, UNIQUENESS, and fuzzy characteristics are used in this work. In this work, the three fuzzinesses of COUNT, UNIQUENESS, and VARIANCE are employed. Using the right fuzzy rules and five fuzzy sets (HIGH, MEDIUM-HIGH, MEDIUM, and MEDIUM-LOW) for each data element, the implemented fuzzy inference engine finds the intrusion. The study's authors left out a description of how they came to their fuzzy set in their report.

The fuzzy set is an important issue for the fuzzy inference engine, and in some cases, the optimal combination can be selected using a genetic algorithm. Using information gathered from the local area network of Iowa State University's College of Engineering, the proposed system is evaluated in this paper. It is difficult to judge how well the reported work was performed because the results are descriptive rather than numerical.

6.5 Genetic Algorithms

Genetic algorithms, which are categorized as global search heuristics, use evolutionary computation techniques like recombination, selection, inheritance, and mutation. Li W (2004)'s ability to derive classification rules and/or pick the ideal features or parameters for the detection process Genetic algorithms are added as a subset of machine learning-based techniques by Bridges and Vaughn (2000). To discover fresh network attacks, T.Lunt and I.Traore (2008) suggest a rule evolution strategy based on Genetic Programming (GP).

In their framework, new rules evolve through the use of four genetic operators: mutation, crossover, reproduction, and dropping condition operators. Whether they are obscure or well-known, network attacks are recognized using new rules. According to experimental findings, GPs created rules with low FPR, low FNR, and a high rate of identifying unidentified attacks using a portion of the KDD 1999 Cup data set. The paper does not, however, include an evaluation with complete KDD training and testing data.

In (Kamra, Bertino (2011); Lazarevic A (2005); Wenke Lee(2000)), which make additional attempts to use GA for intrusion detection, a linear representation scheme for evolving fuzzy rules is proposed. The concept of complete binary tree structures is used in this scheme. GA is used to generate genetic operators, which are useful and minimal structural modifications to the fuzzy expression tree represented by chromosomes. The training process for this approach, however, is computationally expensive in terms of time and money. Bridges and Vaughn employ GA to optimize the fuzzy membership functions and select the appropriate set of features for their intelligent intrusion detection system. Different IDS types have used GA as evolutionary algorithms with success. GA produced impressive results; the best fitness value was very close to the ideal fitness value. A popular randomization search method for optimization problems is GA. Suhail Owais (2008) reports that GA was successful in producing the desired characteristics of a high correct recognition rate and a low FPR for IDS.

6.6 Clustering and Identifying Outliers

The observed data are clustered using clustering techniques based on a defined similarity or distance measure. Selecting a representative point for each cluster is the approach that is most frequently used for this. the work involved in fine-tuning models of distributed information processing that include (a) a collection of basic processing units (nodes, neurons), (b) a collection of synapses (connection weights), (c) the network architecture (pattern of connectivity), and (d) a learning procedure used to train the network. Using clustering techniques, we can estimate the frequency of intrusion events solely from the audit data. Li Xiangmei Qin Zhi (2011) The Hybrid Neural Network Algorithm (HNNA) is presented in this paper based on the benefits and drawbacks of the enhanced LM and GM algorithms. First, the algorithm searches for the global optimal point throughout the entire question domain by taking advantage of the improved GA's powerful whole-searching capability. Then, it uses fast local searching, a strong point of the LM algorithm, to refine the search close to the global optimal point. To modify the input and output parameters of the ANN model and adopt the theories of the fusion of the multi-classifiers to structure the Intrusion Detection System, the paper utilised respectively the three algorithms, namely the Improved GA, LM algorithm, and HNNA. Repeating an experiment reveals that the HNNA outperforms the LM algorithm in terms of stability and convergence precision, as well as improving GA based on the training data.

The neural-network-based multiple classifier intrusion detection system's 41-dimensional input features are adjusted to account for differences in attack types (Xiangmei Li, 2010).

After conducting additional tests, they discover that the 41-features multiple classifier intrusion detection system outperforms every adjusted sub-classifier in terms of detection rate and false negative rate while also having a quicker training time and better convergence precision. The neural-network-based multiple classifier intrusion detection system can therefore be optimized by modifying the input features. This strategy has also been demonstrated to be practical.

6.7 Clustering and Outlier Detection

According to a specified similarity or distance measure, the observed data are grouped into clusters using clustering techniques. The method that is most frequently applied for this involves choosing a representative point for each cluster. Using clustering techniques, it is possible to estimate the amount of tuning work needed by calculating the frequency of intrusion events only from the raw audit data.

7. INTRODUCTION TO DATA MINING (DL) AND MACHINE LEARNING (ML) FOR CYBER SECURITY

There is a frequent conflation between the terms Knowledge Discovery in Databases (KDD), Data Mining (DM), and Machine Learning (ML). The KDD process is viewed as a whole and deals with obtaining significant, previously undiscovered knowledge/information from data, according to research. The implementation of algorithms for extracting sequences from data is the focus of the DM process, which has been specifically mentioned and described by Fayyad et al. (1996) as a step in KDD.

This suggests that they have characteristics in common with both ML and DM. The steps that make up the KDD process are data selection, data cleaning and pre-processing, data transformation, application of DM algorithms, and result interpretation/evaluation.

One of the steps, DM, applies algorithms to data to identify patterns. It should be noted that the process is viewed as DM by many publications, including Cross Industry Standard Process for Data Mining (CRISP-DM) (C. Shearer(2000)) and industry players.

These two expressions are frequently combined in conversations and used interchangeably. According to Arthur Samuel, the field of study known as machine learning (ML) enables computers to learn on their own without being explicitly programmed. The primary areas of focus for machine learning algorithms are classification and prediction techniques. The machine learning algorithms learn from training/previous data to find insights for future/unknown conditions. The various classification algorithms used in cyber security are discussed.

Decision Trees: A vital and well-liked classification method is decision trees. A decision tree is nothing more than a simple flowchart with a tree-like structure, where each leaf node is assigned a class label and each internal node represents a test for an attribute. The decision tree algorithm known as ID3 (Iterative Dichotomiser) was developed by Ross Quinlan. Then he represented the ID3-C4.5 replacement, which has become a benchmark for comprehending algorithms.

C4.5 algorithm: To account for ID3's flaws, this model adds additional traits while drawing inspiration from the ID3 algorithm. It is believed to take a greedy tack and employ a top-down recursive divide and conquer strategy.C4.5 uses the divide and conquer algorithm to build a tree from a set of data samples S, and the steps are as follows: If S is small or if all of the data samples in S belong to the same class, the leaf node is labeled with the most frequent class in S. b) As an alternative, the process of selecting attributes governs the splitting process's criterion.

The splitting criteria establish which attribute is to be tested at node S by identifying the most efficient way to divide the tuples into various classes. The process loops back on itself, producing a decision tree.

The Naive Bayes algorithm (NB) employs a condensed form of the Bayesian learning approach. Statistical classifiers are utilized. The probabilities of membership can be determined using these classifiers, which are based on the Bayes theorem. The assumption that a feature value from a specific class has no bearing on the values of other features is known as conditional independence. One of the best, most reliable, and most efficient ways to avoid noisy data is to use Naive-Bayes classifiers.

The key benefit is that it only needs a small amount of training data to roughly approximate the categorization strictures.

Table 1. The algorithm applied, data set, and metric used for anomaly and hybrid-based intrusion detection

S.No	Paper Details	Algorithm Applied	Data Set Used	Metric Used
1	R. P. Lippmann and R. K. Cunningham (2000)	ANN	Transcripts of telnet sessions	Accuracy and False alarm
2	C. Palagiri (2002)	ANN	DARPA	--
3	D. Apiletti et al.(2009)	NETMINE framework	Network capture software was created at Politecnico di Torino and is used to record network traffic packets.	Support
4	A. Tajbakhsh et al. (2009)	Fuzzy Association Based Classification (ABC)	KDD	Accuracy and FP rate
5	A. Ahmed, et al (2019)	Fuzzy Logic	Tcpdump	Accuracy
6	C. Kruegel et al.(2003)	Bayesian network	DARPA	Accuracy and False Alarm Rate (FAR)
7	S. Benferhat et al.(2008)	Naïve Bayes algorithm	DARPA	--
8	K. Sequeira et al.(2002)	sequence matching algorithms	shell commands	Accuracy and FAR
9	L. Bilge et al.(2011)	C4.5 Decision Tree algorithm	DSN	Accuracy and FAR
10	L. Bilge et al.(2012)	C4.5 Decision Tree algorithm	Real-World Network	Accuracy and FAR
11	M. S. A. Khan (2011)	Genetic algorithms	KDD	Accuracy and FAR
12	W. Lu et al.(2004)	Genetic algorithms	DARPA	Receiver's Operating Curve and FAR
13	S. S. Joshi et al.(2005)	Hidden Markov Network	KDD	False Positive(FP rate) and False Negative (FN rate)
14	W. Fan et al.(2004)	RIPPER	DARPA	FAR
15	N. B. Amor et al.(2004)	Bayesian network	KDD	Accuracy and FAR
16	Z. Li et al.(2007)	Apriori algorithm	DARPA	Support
17	W. Hu et al.(2003)	Robust Support Vector Machines	DARPA	Accuracy and FAR
18	C. Wagner et al.(2011)	SVM	NetFlow data	Accuracy and FP rate
19	T. Shon et al.(2007)	Self-Organizing Feature Map (SOFM), Genetic Algorithms (GA), and Support Vector Machine (SVM)	DARPA 1999	Accuracy, FP rate and FN rate

- K-Nearest-Neighbor (k-NN) is one of the most basic and straightforward classification methods. It is based on the learning by equivalence process and performs well even when there is little or no prior knowledge of the data distribution. 'm' dimensional numerical attributes are used for describing the training samples with each sample replicating a certain point in the m-dimensional space. Hence, we can see that all the points are stored in m-dimensional pattern space. In the case of an unknown data sample, a k-nearest neighbor classifier checks out the pattern space for the k training data modules which are quite close to that of an unknown sample. 'Closeness' refers to Euclidean distance. The new and unknown sample is designated with the most common class from it is nearest k neighbors.

- Static Vector Machine It primarily aids in the creation of a hyperplane by plotting the input vector into a space with extremely high dimensions. The data points can be divided into various classes by the hyperplane. Hyperplanes that have the largest functional margin—the distance from any class's closest training data point—achieve a high level of distinction. It has been found that as the margin increases, the classifier's generalization error decreases. For the two classes, the hyperplane serves as a decision boundary. The detection of a misclassification caused by a specific method is ensured by the persistence of a decision boundary. The SVM is used for regression analysis, classification, and other tasks.

- Repeated Incremental Pruning to Produce Error Reduction (RIPPER) RIPPER, is a generic methodology used for effectively applying separate-and -conquer rule learning. It helps in increasing the precision of protocols by replacing or re-enforcing the individual norms. Reduce Error Pruning was implemented to create the rule and the created rules are often restricted to a smaller number. It ensures the pruning of each rule right after the creation and removal of data samples. Reduced error pruning facilitates the handling of huge training sets, thus improving precision. The below-mentioned steps are carried out: Spot the characters/ features from the training data and identify the split of all attributes essential for categorization (i.e., feature/dimensionality reduction). The different machine learning and data mining methods applied for cyber security are mentioned in Table 1.

8. CONTRIBUTION OF ARTIFICIAL INTELLIGENCE, MACHINE LEARNING, AND DATA MINING TO CYBER SECURITY

Due to the internet's ability to draw in billions of users and the storage of data online (on the cloud side), cyber security today has put everything at risk. Every day, hostile nation launch serious attacks on a nation's computer labs, systems, or networks that have the potential to spark a third world war. As of right now, we detect cyber attackers or hackers using human labor; therefore, we need a sizable skilled labor force to monitor or defend against any cyber threats. But shortly, it's possible that artificial intelligence and machine learning will be used to detect intrusions or vulnerabilities.

Additionally, it will benefit society in many ways and prevent issues like weakened security, decreased efficiency, the disclosure of personal information by the Internet of Things, and growing vulnerabilities in cyber and physical systems.

Note that several countries have recently experienced numerous critical attacks from their rival nations on their nuclear programs or sites (Tyagi, Amit Kumar (2016, 2019); Sravanthi Reddy (2019); Meghna Manoj Nair(2019)). On the other hand, artificial intelligence (AI) will decrease workforce requirements, including the need for cyber security professionals and the speed of intrusion detection, among other things. Through its innovations, artificial intelligence can contribute to longer and better lives. These advantages of AI are outlined in the ways below.

- Managing voluminous security data
- Sifting through cyber haystacks to find threats
- A faster detection and response time
- Participating in the race against artificial intelligence
- A place where human cyber security teams can function.

Artificial intelligence, machine learning, and data mining are therefore essential elements for the 21st century generation. So, in the next 20 to 30 years, we will witness the enormous applications of artificial intelligence and machine learning, which will perform numerous daily tasks and benefit humanity evermore.

9. FUTURE DIRECTION

The difficulties we face with intrusion detection systems today are enormous, and they are as follows:

1. The inability to reduce the number of false positives, which lowers IDS effectiveness. High precision, high recall, a low false positive rate, and a low false negative rate are all characteristics of good IDS performance. A significant concern is how one can feel confident in the outcome.
2. It takes a very long time to process the enormous amount of data needed for training.
3. One of the main goals of IDS is to increase classification accuracy. focus on the multiple classifier systems.
4. A real-time intrusion detection system is required due to insufficient computing resources and a sharp rise in targeted attacks. Its application in the real world is difficult, though.
5. A standard evaluation dataset that simulates real-time IDS is required.
6. Feature reduction work - To reduce the computational complexity of data reduction, many studies use feature selection. To complete the data deduction task, you must pay closer attention.
7. A combination technique for misuse detection and anomaly detection must be implemented. By addressing these issues, the machine learning technique could be a very useful field for IDS.

10. CONCLUSION

There have been numerous attacks recorded or noticed in recent years or over several decades. This led to the creation of cyber security and intrusion detection in the modern, technological age. Due to the massive increase in internet usage over the past ten years, network security flaws must be fixed. Today, solving such a problem has become crucial. Generally speaking, intrusion detection systems are used to spot system flaws like unauthorized access and unusual attacks over secured networks. Therefore, many authors had discussed numerous studies to address this issue. We have a lot of data today (generated from internet use and web browsing), but the cyber-security industry is struggling to find talented workers. Machine learning is the only approach that can deliver effective results in the shortest amount of time. Therefore, to comprehend the significance of ML techniques for resolving IDS problems, they concentrate on the design of single, hybrid, and ensemble classifier models (while also discussing various algorithms and used datasets).

As a result, we discovered that using various classifier/ML techniques in IDS is a promising study in artificial intelligence and cyber security. It will continue to draw young scientists from the research communities. The removal of redundant data and irrelevant features for the training phase (which is important for system performance), i.e., consideration of the best feature selection algorithm, will play a significant role in the classification techniques shortly, there sare some valid points that this work has identified for future work. Additionally, using multiple or various featured selection algorithms will offer the best solutions for a variety of scenarios and intrusion detection in a network. Last but not least, when compared to single classification algorithms, ensemble classification algorithms perform better in terms of cyber security and intrusion detection systems.

REFERENCES

Agrawal, R., & Srikant, R. (1994). *Fast algorithms for mining association rules*. In *Proceedings of the 20th International Conference on Very Large Data Bases*, Santiago, Chile.

Ahmed. (2019). Modeling and Simulation of Office Desk Illumination Using ZEMAX. 2019 International Conference on Electrical, Communication, and Computer Engineering (ICECCE). IEEE. 10.1109/ICECCE47252.2019.8940756

Alazab, A., Hobbs, M., Abawajy, J., & Alazab, M. (2012). Using feature selection for intrusion detection system. In *Proceedings of the 2012 International Symposium on Communications and Information Technologies (ISCIT)*, Gold Coast, Australia. 10.1109/ISCIT.2012.6380910

Amiri, F., Yousefi, M. R., Lucas, C., Shakery, A., & Yazdani, N. (2011). Mutual information-based feature selection for intrusion detection systems. *Journal of Network and Computer Applications*, *34*(4), 1184–1199. doi:10.1016/j.jnca.2011.01.002

Amor, N. B., Benferhat, S., & Elouedi, Z. (2004). Naive bayesvs decision trees in intrusion detection systems. *Proceedings of the 2004 ACM symposium on Applied computing*, ACM. 10.1145/967900.967989

Anderson, D., Lunt, T. F., Javitz, H., Tamaru, A., & Valdes, A. (1995). *Detecting unusual program behavior using the statistical component of the next-generation intrusion detection expert system (NIDES)*. Computer Science Laboratory, SRI International.

Apiletti, E., Baralis, E., Cerquitelli, T., & D'Elia, V. (2009). Baralis, T. Cerquitelli, V. DElia, Characterizing network traffic by means of the netmine framework. *Computer Networks*, *53*(6), 774–789. doi:10.1016/j.comnet.2008.12.011

Balogun, A.O. & Jimoh, R.G. (2015). Anomaly intrusion detection using an hybrid of decision tree and K-nearest neighbor. J. *Adv. Sci. Res. Appl*.

Bapat, R., Mandya, A., Liu, X., Abraham, B., Brown, D. E., Kang, H., & Veeraraghavan, M. (2018). *Identifying malicious botnet traffic using logistic regression*. In *Proceedings of the 2018 Systems and Information Engineering Design Symposium (SIEDS)*, Charlottesville, VA, USA. 10.1109/SIEDS.2018.8374749

Benferhat, S., Kenaza, T., & Mokhtari, A. (2008). A naive bayes approach for detecting coordinated attacks. In *Proceedings of the 2008 32nd Annual IEEE International Computer Software and Applications*. IEEE. 10.1109/COMPSAC.2008.213

Benferhat, S., Kenaza, T., & Mokhtari, A. (2008). A naive bayes approach for detecting coordinated attacks. Computer Software and Applications. COMPSAC'08. 32nd Annual IEEE International. IEEE. doi:10.1109/COMPSAC.2008.213

Bilge, L., Balzarotti, D., Robertson, W., Kirda, E., & Kruegel, C. (2012). Disclosure: detecting botnet command and control servers through large-scale netflow analysis. In: *Proceedings of the 28thAnnual Computer Security Applications Conference.* ACM. 10.1145/2420950.2420969

Bilge, L., Kirda, E., Kruegel, C., & Balduzzi, M. (2011). Exposure: Finding malicious domains using passive dnsanalysis. NDSS.

Bridges, V. (2000). Fuzzy Data mining and genetic algorithms applied to intrusion detection. In: *Proceedings of the National Information Systems Security Conference.* IEEE.

Buczak, A. L., & Guven, E. (2015). A survey of data mining and machine learning methods for cyber security intrusion detection. *IEEE Communications Surveys and Tutorials, 18*(2), 1153–1176. doi:10.1109/COMST.2015.2494502

Chebrolu, S., Abraham, A., & Thomas, J. P. (2005, June). Feature deduction and ensemble design of intrusion detection systems. *Computers & Security, 24*(4), 295–307. doi:10.1016/j.cose.2004.09.008

Conference, T. Finland, 28 July–1 August 2008; pp. 704–709.

Dainotti, A., Pescapé, A., & Ventre, G. (2007). *Worm traffic analysis and characterization.* In *Proceedings of the 2007 IEEE International Conference on Communications,* Glasgow, UK. 10.1109/ICC.2007.241

Dainotti, A., Pescapé, A., & Ventre, G. (2009). A cascade architecture for DoS attacks detection based on the wavelet transform. *Journal of Computer Security, 17*(6), 945–968. doi:10.3233/JCS-2009-0350

Denning, D. (1987, February). An Intrusion-Detection Model. *IEEE Transactions on Software Engineering, SE-13*(2), 222–232. doi:10.1109/TSE.1987.232894

Denning, D. E., & Neumann, P. G. (1985). Requirements and model for IDES – a real-time intrusion detection system. *SRI International Technical Report #83F83- 01-00.* Computer Science Laboratory.

Fan, W., Miller, M., Stolfo, S., Lee, W., & Chan, P. (2004). Using artificial anomalies to detect unknown and known network intrusions. *Knowledge and Information Systems, 6*(5), 507–527. doi:10.100710115-003-0132-7

Fayyad, U., Piatetsky-Shapiro, G., & Smyth, P. (1996). The KDD process for extracting useful knowledge from volumes of data. *Communications of the ACM, 39*(11), 27–34. doi:10.1145/240455.240464

Han, J., Pei, J., & Kamber, M. (2011). *Data mining: Concepts and Techniques.* Elsevier.

Heckerman, D. (1995). *A tutorial on learning with Bayesian networks.* Microsoft Research.

Hoang, X. D., Hu, J., & Bertok, P. (2009). A program-based anomaly intrusion detection scheme using multiple detection engines and fuzzy inference. *Journal of Network and Computer Applications, 32*(6), 1219–1228. doi:10.1016/j.jnca.2009.05.004

Hosmer, H. H. (1993). *Security is fuzzy!: applying the fuzzy logic paradigm to the multipolicy paradigm.* Proceedings of the 1992-1993 workshop on New security paradigms, ACM.

Hu, J., Yu, X., Qiu, D., & Chen, H. (2009). A simple and efficient hidden Markov model scheme for host-based anomaly intrusion detection. *IEEE Transaction on Network.* IEEE. doi:10.1109/MNET.2009.4804323

Hu, W., Liao, Y., & Vemuri, V. R. (2003). Robust Support Vector Machines for Anomaly Detection in Computer Security. In *Proceedings of the International Conference on Machine Learning and Applications—ICMLA*. IEEE.

Hu, W., Liao, Y., & Vemuri, V. R. (2003). *Robust support vector machines for anomaly detection in computer security*. ICMLA.

Ingre, B., Yadav, A., & Soni, A. K. (2017). Decision tree based intrusion detection system for NSL-KDD dataset. In *Proceedings of the International Conference on Information and Communication Technology for Intelligent Systems*, Ahmedabad, India.

John, E. (2017). Dickerson and Julie A. Dickerson, Fuzzy network profiling for intrusion detection. *Proceedings of NAFIPS 19th International Conference of the North American Fuzzy Infor mation Processing Society,* Atlanta, USA).

Joshi, S. S., & Phoha, V. V. (2005). Investigating hidden markov models capabilities in anomaly detection. *Proceedings of the 43rd annual Southeast regional conference-*. ACM. 10.1145/1167350.1167387

Kamra, B., & Bertino, E. (2011). Design and Implementation of an Intrusion Response System for Relational Databases. *IEEE Transactions on Knowledge and Data Engineering, 23*(6), 875–888. doi:10.1109/TKDE.2010.151

Khan, M. S. A. (2011). Rule based network intrusion detection using genetic algorithm. *International Journal of Computer Applications, 18*(8), 26–29. doi:10.5120/2303-2914

Koc, L., Mazzuchi, T. A., & Sarkani, S. (2012). A network intrusion detection system based on a Hidden Naïve Bayes multiclass classifier. *Expert Systems with Applications, 39*(18), 13492–13500. doi:10.1016/j.eswa.2012.07.009

Kokila, R., Selvi, S. T., & Govindarajan, K. (2014). DDoS detection and analysis in SDN-based environment using support vector machine classifier. In *Proceedings of the 2014 Sixth International Conference on Advanced Computing (ICoAC)*, Chennai, India. 10.1109/ICoAC.2014.7229711

Kotpalliwar, M. V., & Wajgi, R. (2015). *Classification of Attacks Using Support Vector Machine (SVM) on KDDCUP'99 IDS Database*. In *Proceedings of the 2015 Fifth International Conference on Communication Systems and Network Technologies*, Gwalior, India. 10.1109/CSNT.2015.185

Kruegel, C., Mutz, D., Robertson, W., & Valeur, F. (2003). Bayesian event classification for intrusion detection. In: Computer Security Applications Conference. IEEE. doi:10.1109/CSAC.2003.1254306

Kruegel, C., Mutz, D., Robertson, W., & Valeur, F. (2003). Bayesian event classification for intrusion detection. In *Proceedings of the 19th Annual Computer Security Applications Conference*, Las Vegas, NV, USA.

Kumar, P. A. R., & Selvakumar, S. (2011). Distributed denial of service attack detection using an ensemble of neural classifier. *Computer Communications, 34*(11), 1328–1341. doi:10.1016/j.comcom.2011.01.012

Lazarevic, A., Kumar, V., & Srivastava, J. (2005). *Intrusion detection: "A survey, Managing cyber threats: issues, approaches, and challenges*. Springer Verlag.

Lee, W., & Stolfo, S. J. (2000). A framework for constructing features and models for intrusion detection systems. *ACM Transactions on Information and System Security, 3*(4), 227–261. doi:10.1145/382912.382914

Lee, W., & Stolfo, S. J. (2000, November). A framework for constructing features and models for intrusion detection systems. *ACM Transactions on Information and System Security, 3*(4), 227–261. doi:10.1145/382912.382914

Li, W. (2004). *Using genetic algorithm for network intrusion detection*. C.S.G. Department of Energy.

Xiangmei L. (2010). *Optimization of the Neural-NetworkBased Multiple Classifiers Intrusion Detection System*. IEEE

Li, Y., Xia, J., Zhang, S., Yan, J., Ai, X., & Dai, K. (2012). An efficient intrusion detection system based on support vector machines and gradually feature removal method. *Expert Systems with Applications, 39*(1), 424–430. doi:10.1016/j.eswa.2011.07.032

Li, Z., Zhang, A., Lei, J., & Wang, L. (2007). Real-time correlation of network security alerts. In: *e-Business Engineering*. IEEE. 10.1109/ICEBE.2007.69

Lippmann, R. P., & Cunningham, R. K. (2000). Improving intrusion detection performance using keyword selection and neural networks. *Computer Networks, 34*(4), 597–603. doi:10.1016/S1389-1286(00)00140-7

Lu, W., & Traore, I. (2004). Detecting new forms of network intrusion using genetic programming. *Computational Intelligence, 20*(3), 475–494. doi:10.1111/j.0824-7935.2004.00247.x

Lunt, T., & Traore, I. (2008, May). Unsupervised Anomaly Detection Using an Evolutionary Extension of K-means Algorithm, International Journal on Information and computer Science, 2, 107–139.

Malik, A. J., & Khan, F. A. (2018). A hybrid technique using binary particle swarm optimization and decision tree pruning for network intrusion detection. *Cluster Computing, 21*(1), 667–680. doi:10.100710586-017-0971-8

Milenkoski, A., Vieira, M., Kounev, S., Avritzer, A., & Payne, B. D. (2015). Evaluating computer intrusion detection systems: A survey of common practices. [CSUR]. *ACM Computing Surveys, 48*(1), 1–41. doi:10.1145/2808691

Moon, D., Im, H., Kim, I., & Park, J. H. (2017). Im, H.; Kim, I.; Park, J.H. DTB-IDS: An intrusion detection system based on decision tree using behavior analysis for preventing APT attacks. *The Journal of Supercomputing, 73*(7), 2881–2895. doi:10.100711227-015-1604-8

Moskovitch, R., Elovici, Y., & Rokach, L. (2008). Detection of unknown computer worms based on behavioral classification of the host. *Computational Statistics & Data Analysis, 52*(9), 4544–4566. doi:10.1016/j.csda.2008.01.028

Moskovitch, R., Nissim, N., Stopel, D., Feher, C., Englert, R., & Elovici, Y. (2007). *Improving the detection of unknown computer worms activity using active learning*. In *Proceedings of the Annual Conference on Artificial Intelligence*, Osnabrück, Germany. 10.1007/978-3-540-74565-5_47

Mukkamala, S., Sung, A., Abraham, A. (2005). *Cyber security challenges: Designing efficient intrusion detection systems and antivirus tools*. Vemuri, V.

Murali, A., & Rao, M. (2005). A Survey on Intrusion Detection Approaches. *Information and Communication Technologies. IEEE.* , 10.1109/ICICT.2005.1598592

Nair, M. M., Tyagi, A. K., & Goyal, R. (2019). Amit KumarTyagi, RichaGoyal, Medical Cyber Physical Systems and Its Issues. *Procedia Computer Science, 165,* 647–665. doi:10.1016/j.procs.2020.01.059

Owais, S., Snášel, P., & Krömer, A. (2008). Survey: Using Genetic Algorithm Approach in Intrusion Detection Systems Techniques. *Computer Information Systems and Industrial Management Applications. IEEE.*

Palagiri, C. (2002). Network-based intrusion detection using neural networks. Rensselaer Polytechnic Institute Troy.

Panda, M., & Patra, M. R. (2007). Network intrusion detection using naive bayes. *Int. J. Comput. Sci. Netw. Secur., 7,* 258–263.

Pervez, M. S., & Farid, D. M. (2014). *Feature selection and intrusion classification in NSL-KDD cup 99 dataset employing SVMs.* In *Proceedings of the 8th International Conference on Software, Knowledge, Information Management and Applications (SKIMA 2014),* Dhaka, Bangladesh. 10.1109/SKIMA.2014.7083539

Puthran, S., & Shah, K. (2016). *Intrusion detection using improved decision tree algorithm with binary and quad split.* In *Proceedings of the International Symposium on Security in Computing and Communication,* Jaipur, India. 10.1007/978-981-10-2738-3_37

Qu, X., Yang, L., Guo, K., Ma, L., Sun, M., Ke, M., & Li, M. (2019). A Survey on the Development of Self-Organizing Maps for Unsupervised Intrusion Detection. *Mobile Networks and Applications.*

Quinlan, J. R. (1986). Induction of decision trees. *Machine Learning, 1*(1), 81–106. doi:10.1007/BF00116251

Quinlan, J. R. (1993). *C4.5: Programs for Machine Learning.* Morgan Kaufmann Publishers, Inc.

Rai, K., Devi, M. S., & Guleria, A. (2016). Decision tree based algorithm for intrusion detection. *Int. J. Adv. Netw. Appl., 7,* 2828.

Relan, N. G., & Patil, D. R. (2015). Implementation of network intrusion detection system using variant of decision tree algorithm. In *Proceedings of the 2015 International Conference on Nascent Technologies in the Engineering Field (ICNTE),* Navi Mumbai, India. 10.1109/ICNTE.2015.7029925

Sangkatsanee, P., Wattanapongsakorn, N., & Charnsripinyo, C. (2011). Practical real-time intrusion detection using machine learning approaches. *Computer Communications, 34*(18), 2227–2235. doi:10.1016/j.comcom.2011.07.001

Sarker, C. (2019). I.H. Context-aware rule learning from smartphone data: Survey, challenges and future directions. *Journal of Big Data, 6*(1), 95. doi:10.118640537-019-0258-4

Sarker, I. H. (2019). A machine learning based robust prediction model for real-life mobile phone data. *Internet Things, 5,* 180–193. doi:10.1016/j.iot.2019.01.007

Sarker, I. H. (2019). Cybersecurity Data Science: An Overview from Machine Learning Perspective. *Journal of Big Data*, 6.

Sarker, I. H., Colman, A., Han, J., Khan, A. I., Abushark, Y. B., Salah, K., & Behav, D. T. (2019). A Behavioral Decision Tree Learning to Build User-Centric Context-Aware Predictive Model. *Mobile Networks and Applications*.

Sarker, I. H., Kayes, A., & Watters, P. (2019). Effectiveness Analysis of Machine Learning Classification Models for Predicting Personalized Context-Aware Smartphone Usage. *Journal of Big Data*, 6(1), 57. doi:10.118640537-019-0219-y

Sarker, I. H., & Salim, F. D. (2018). *Mining User Behavioral Rules from Smartphone Data through Association Analysis*. In *Proceedings of the 22nd Pacific-Asia Conference on Knowledge Discovery and Data Mining (PAKDD)*, Melbourne, Australia. 10.1007/978-3-319-93034-3_36

Saxena, H., & Richariya, V. (2014). Intrusion detection in KDD99 dataset using SVM-PSO and feature reduction with information gain. *International Journal of Computer Applications*, 98(6), 25–29. doi:10.5120/17188-7369

Sequeira, K., & Zaki, M. (2002). Admit: anomaly-based data mining for intrusions. In *Proceedings of the eighth ACM SIGKDD international conference on Knowledge discovery and data mining*. ACM. 10.1145/775047.775103

Seufert, S., & O'Brien, D. (2007). Machine learning for automatic defence against distributed denial of service attacks. In *Proceedings of the 2007 IEEE International Conference on Communications*, Glasgow, UK. 10.1109/ICC.2007.206

Shapoorifard, H., & Shamsinejad, P. (2017). Intrusion detection using a novel hybrid method incorporating an improved KNN. *International Journal of Computer Applications*, 173(1), 5–9. doi:10.5120/ijca2017914340

Sharifi, A. M., Amirgholipour, S. K., & Pourebrahimi, A. (2015). Intrusion detection based on joint of K-means and KNN. *J. Converg. Inf. Technol.*, 10, 42.

(2000). Shearer, The crisp-dm model: The new blueprint for data mining. *Journal of Data Warehousing*, 5(4), 13–22.

Shon, T., Kim, Y., Lee, C., & Moon, J. (2005). *A machine learning framework for network anomaly detection using SVM and GA*. In *Proceedings of the Sixth Annual IEEE SMC Information Assurance Workshop*, West Point, NY, USA. 10.1109/IAW.2005.1495950

Shon, T., & Moon, J. (2007). A hybrid machine learning approach to network anomaly detection. *Information Sciences*, 177(18), 3799–3821. doi:10.1016/j.ins.2007.03.025

Sinclair, C., Pierce, L., & Matzner, S. (1999). An application of machine learning to network intrusion detection. In *Proceedings of the 15th Annual Computer Security Applications Conference (ACSAC'99)*, Phoenix, AZ, USA. 10.1109/CSAC.1999.816048

Sommer, R., & Paxson, V. (2010). Outside the closed world: On using machine learning for network intrusion detection. In *Proceedings of the 2010 IEEE Symposium on Security and Privacy*, Berkeley/Oakland, CA, USA. 10.1109/SP.2010.25

Sommer, R., & Paxson, V. (2016). Outside the closed world: On using machine learning for network intrusion detection. In *Proceedings of the 2010 IEEE Symposium on Security and Privacy*, Berkeley/Oakland, CA, USA. 10.1109/SP.2010.25

Sravanthi, R. M. (2019). Cyber Physical Systems: The Role of Machine Learning and Cyber Security in Present and Future. Computer Reviews Journal, 5. PURKH.

Sun, N., Zhang, J., Rimba, P., Gao, S., Zhang, L. Y., & Xiang, Y. (2018). Data-driven cybersecurity incident prediction: A survey. *IEEE Communications Surveys and Tutorials*, *21*(2), 1744–1772. doi:10.1109/COMST.2018.2885561

Tajbakhsh, A., Rahmati, M., & Mirzaei, A. (2009). Intrusion detection using fuzzy association rules. *Applied Soft Computing*, *9*(2), 462–469. doi:10.1016/j.asoc.2008.06.001

Tyagi, A. K. (2019). *Building a Smart and Sustainable Environment using Internet of Things*. International Conference on Sustainable Computing in Science, Technology and Management (SUSCOM), Amity University Rajasthan, Jaipur – India. 10.2139srn.3356500

Vishwakarma, S., Sharma, V., & Tiwari, A. (2017). An intrusion detection system using KNN-ACO algorithm. *International Journal of Computer Applications*, *171*(10), 18–23. doi:10.5120/ijca2017914079

Wagner, C., François, J., & Engel, T. (2017). Machine learning approach for ip-flow record anomaly detection. In *Proceedings of the International Conference on Research in Networking*, Valencia, Spain. 10.1007/978-3-642-20757-0_3

Wagner, J. & Francois, T. (2011). Machine learning approach for ipflow record anomaly detection. *International Conference on Research in Networking*. Springer.

Witten, I. H., & Frank, E. (2005). *Data Mining: Practical Machine Learning Tools and Techniques*. Morgan Kaufmann.

Xiang, S. & Lim, L. (2005). Design of multiple-level hybrid classifier for intrusion detection system. *Workshop on Machine Learning for Signal Processing*. IEEE.

Xin, Y., Kong, L., Liu, Z., Chen, Y., Li, Y., Zhu, H., Gao, M., Hou, H., & Wang, C. (2018). *Machine learning and deep learning methods for cybersecurity*. IEEE Access.

Ye, N., Emran, S. M., Chen, Q., & Vilbert, S. (2002). Multivariate statistical analysis of audit trails for host-based intrusion detection. *IEEE Transactions on Computers*, *51*(7), 810–820. doi:10.1109/TC.2002.1017701

Zhai, Y., Ning, P., Iyer, P., & Reeves, D. S. (2004). Reasoning about complementary intrusion evidence. Proceedings of the 20th Annual Computer Security Applications Conference (ACSAC 04). IEEE. 10.1109/CSAC.2004.29

Chapter 5
A Survey on Cyber Security Awareness

G. Sangeetha
R.M.K. College of Engineering and Technology, India

G. Logeshwari
R.M.K. College of Engineering and Technology, India

Archana
R.M.K. College of Engineering and Technology, India

L. Lavanya
R.M.K. College of Engineering and Technology, India

Sai Harshitha
R.M.K. College of Engineering and Technology, India

ABSTRACT

Nowadays, android phones are making a huge impact globally. According to the F-secure, the report says that 99% of current malwares are targeting the android OS. The main method of targeting the android is their permission system, where the software asks permission for the personal information of the users. The malware developers had two ways of attacking the android OS; one is reverse engineering technique, and another one is getting well-versed in the android permission system. Still, people are not aware of the real cyber security where the hackers are extracting our sensitive information without knowing. Since people are lacking knowledge about cyber security or social awareness, the hackers are gaining their success of getting our information and using it for incorrect purpose. This results in the threatening of the data and mitigation of the data. Now people have to be more conscious of keeping their data secure so that they can avoid this risky situation.

DOI: 10.4018/978-1-6684-9317-5.ch005

1. INTRODUCTION

The Internet is one of the most important inventions of the twenty-first century that has had a significant impact on our lives (Lee, 2019). Today, the internet has broken down all barriers and transformed the way we communicate, play games, work, shop, make friends, listen to music, watch movies, order meals, pay bills, and greet pals on their birthdays and anniversaries. Our world is becoming increasingly networked, with digitized information underpinning key services and infrastructures (Atzori et. al.(2010)). Threats to the confidentiality, integrity, and accessibility of digital information worry nation states, organisations, and end users alike (Nurse, J.R.C. et al. 2017). Security is crucial in a digital age where it permeates every aspect of our daily lives, both public and private. Without security, everything in the world will crumble. Unprepared individuals, businesses, and organisations have been devastated by attacks like WannaCry, putting their operations in danger (Malik & Singh, 2019). Cybersecurity is important in the field of information technology. Cybersecurity has advanced over the past few decades (MarketsandMarkets, 2019). Cybersecurity is the first thing that comes to mind when we encounter a fraud. Our concern for online data security has grown significantly. In recent years, the number of connected devices has grown rapidly, and by 2020, that number will have surpassed 50 billion (PwC, 2020). The complexity of the cyber infrastructure increased due to the exponential growth in the number of connected devices, which led to an increase in the number of vulnerable devices (Irdeto, 2019. Data science is changing how businesses operate around the world (Aldmour et al. 2019). It is essential for the development of intelligent cyber security systems and services because "security is all about data." When attempting to identify cyber threats, we analyse security data that is present in the form of files, logs, network packets, and other pertinent sources (Rao et al. 2018). Without a focus on achieving effective cyber security in big data, hackers may be able to easily gain unauthorised access to information processed using big data technologies (Deloitte, 2018). Therefore, it is clear that big data (Hejazi et al. 2020) has both advantages and disadvantages. As a result, everyone in the world is concerned about cyber security. Examples include malicious software, phishing, password attacks, hyperlink drive-by downloads, virus attacks, and more. Cybersecurity is frequently confused in public discussions with other concepts like privacy, information exchange, gathering intelligence, and surveillance (Sha, K. 2018). Cybersecurity must be taken into account whenever cybercrime is present. Working in the field of cyber security are people from a variety of professions (Yu, R. (2018)). Because these are essential elements of cyber security, each profession works together to safeguard the availability, confidentiality, and integrity of information or data.

2. ABOUT CYBER SECURITY

The twenty-first century is characterised by the increasing need for computer safety as well as the trend towards cyberization, which is the continued use of the Internet or cyberspace by fanatic organisations, militias, or other similar groups engaged in conflicts to promote and disseminate their causes. A recent surge in global investment in new technology for computer security has coincided with the rise in cybercrime, digital currency, and e-governance. The concept of "cyber security" describes methods and practises for protecting digital data. The data is stored, transmitted, or used by an information system. After all, a criminal is interested in data. Computers, servers, and networks are merely data conduits.

Defending against attacks, unauthorised access, modification, and destruction is the goal of cyber security, which consists of a number of strategies and procedures. The advancement of information technology and Internet services can also greatly benefit from it. Cyber security is subject to a number of trends, with Web applications being the most prevalent. The delivery of information and services over the Internet using web applications is currently one of the most popular platforms. According to C. S. Kruse et al. (2017), "cyber security" refers to the methods, tools, and technologies used to guard against unauthorised access to networks, data, computers, programmes, and other digital assets. An increasing number of cyber threats are being handled in close to real-time by experts in forensics and cyber security.

Without the aid of threat intelligence, big data, and machine learning techniques, it is impossible to identify, evaluate, and counteract such threats in almost real-time. Cybersecurity is the practise of defending electronic systems, networks, computers, servers, mobile devices, and data from malicious attacks (Chang & Coppel, 2020). Information technology security and electronic information security are other names for it.

3. LITERATURE SURVEY ON CYBERCRIME

The study's objective is to examine college students in Tamil Nadu's awareness of cyber security by concentrating on various online security threats. Cybercrime has become a significant threat to public safety, personal privacy, and national security in recent years. Everyone needs to be aware of their own security and safety measures in order to protect themselves from becoming a victim of cybercrime. College students' knowledge of cyber security will be examined using a well-structured questionnaire survey method. This study will be carried out in Tamil Nadu's major cities with a focus on various online security threats, including spam, viruses, phishing, fake advertisements, pop-up windows, and other intrusions.

This survey looks at college students' awareness of security issues and their level of awareness of them, and it offers some solutions. In today's complex networked world, maintaining the integrity and confidentiality of the data is both crucial and difficult. Additionally, students make up the majority of those connected to these networks. Students may engage in cybercrime primarily out of curiosity or for retaliation. Students frequently aren't aware of the consequences of cybercrime. The majority of victims of cybercrime are female. Many accounts Colleges and universities display the prevalence of cyberattacks, including numerous attempts to hack into information systems. Education institutions face risks of losing priceless intellectual property, their research data, such as patents awarded to professors and students, as well as the personal information of the students, staff, and faculty. Social networks and bank account information are also at higher risk. The need for cyber awareness has grown as a result of the increased frequency of hacking attacks against institutions of higher education (X. Liu, 2013). Today, everyone uses the Internet for all facets of daily life. People use online services like video calls, virtual healthcare and education, business and banking transactions, and social networking to stay in touch with their loved ones. So, there are now more connections to technology. Continuous connectivity, however, raises the risks. Cyber threats to the economy and critical infrastructure are a concern for everyone. Individuals may face threats to their finances, identities, and privacy as a result of cyber security risks. There is a need for some cyber security-related awareness programmes to address the cyber security awareness among college students in higher education institutions. Computers and the Internet are now indispensable tools for both work and study (S. Kamara and K. Lauter, 2010). This survey will assist in analysing the level of cyber security awareness among Tamil Nadu college students and inform them of the threats and difficulties that are common in cyberspace.

3.1. Key Concepts Used to Frame the Understanding of User ID and Password

- periodic password changes
- Making use of outdated passwords.
- Making use of a universal password across all of their accounts.
- Disseminating passwords to all users.
- Click on No or Yes if their computer prompts them to save their password.

Making the password as long and secure as possible by using a minimum of eight characters and a maximum of eight characters, special characters, numbers, all uppercase letters, etc., and if they believe their password has been compromised, taking additional steps to recover it.

3.2. Key Points Taken Into Account When Framing the Survey Questions in Order to Gauge Awareness of Home Computer Protection

- When users are away from their PCs, computers should be turned off, locked with a password, or shut down.
- If users own a modem, they should make sure that the auto answer mode (which accepts incoming calls automatically) is disabled.
- Before sending the PC in for repair or replacement, if necessary, remove any sensitive or private data.

3.3. Some of the Questions to Analyse the Knowledge of Firewall Installation and the Requirement for Antivirus Software and Updating for the Same

- If the users are connected to a network, whether they store files in folders set aside for them.
- Whether data is saved to CDs or floppy disks regularly while the system is not connected to a network.
- Ensuring that backups reflect the most current information by copying the data on a regular basis after making all changes.
- Saving the original installation CDs/diskettes to use as their backup for their PC software.

3.4. Criteria Taken Into Account When Framing Survey Questions to Gauge Virus Awareness

At home, turning off the Internet connection and performing a thorough virus scan results in a virus-free system.

- Knowing that new, quickly spreading worms and viruses are released every day, people check their anti-virus software at least once a week or set it up for automatic updates.

- Use a current virus scanner to scan any software for viruses before implementing or using it. If students' computers do not already have a virus scanner installed, they should contact an organisation representative.
- Don't download free software from an unreliable source and install it on your computer.
- Taking into account file extensions like.bat,.cmd,.exe,.pif,.scr, or.zip using content filtering software.
- It may be necessary to reinstall the operating system depending on the severity of the infection.

4. SURVEY ON CYBERSECURITY IN DIGITAL SOCIETY

Sabrina Horovic et al (2021), created this paper to ensure the awareness about the cyber security and the crimes of the digital society. Now-a-days society has seen so much technological transformation in which new forms of digital crimes are also upgrading. As the society is developing with day to day technological facilities, it eventually increases the number of crimes digitally. One of the most upgrading crime is the technological crimes where people are not aware of those crimes. The misuse of the technologies will lead to the offensive crimes and people should know about the consequences of the cyber-crimes and all. So this paper creates the best social awareness and security essentials. Due to this the government policies should post many new laws according to the development of the new technologies. So the rules and the regulations should be strict and thorough so that people out there and the hackers will stick with the new laws. This paper will cover the analysis, some of solutions to the developing technologies, preventing the crime activities, the regulations of the cyber offenses and the origin of where these crimes have started. They have also mentioned about the cyberspace and its defining feature of the modern life and the digital society and their key process development. There are thousands of the cybercrimes that are recorded instantly on the daily basis. As well as the world's most leading countries have been constantly increasing their knowledge of the cyber-crimes and taking actions of those crimes. And cyber security mostly covers only the technical parts and it won't concentrate on the non-technical parts mostly.

Jesse schinilia (2023) had published this paper and the paper is all about the recent updates about the cyber activities in the United States. United Sates had created awareness about the state-sponsored cyber actors of network devices, mainly business and home office routers to support their campaign. They have conducted the quantitative analysis of the Internet Storm Center data and current Shodhan data for the exploration of the router attack surface compared to host devices. This analysis resulted that host devices are more often get attacked rather than routers on average even though it has been controlled for a relative number of devices. Whereas data has been depicting that routers are not often attacked while routers have to be observed with great care at the budding stages of the research and development through field deployment. They have also mentioned the recommendations for Device manufacturers, Internet Service Providers as well as Cyber Security Practitioners. This paper has been done many methods to prioritize not only the awareness of the cybercrimes but also they have changed and paved a way to look into the cyber security in a different way. Like Routers manufacturing and all people will not tend to look at, but the initiation of the cyber offenses can also start from the routers. This paper gives us a better way to understand the starting issue and most important issue of the cyber offenses.

Geoffrey Parker (2021) has been written this paper about the phishing campaigns and the procedures in the Phishing campaigns. The author has mentioned that these procedures has not changed since 2012 even in the security awareness era training platforms. Now-a-days they are using templates which is concluding that the level of difficulty is based on the template used and not the user. So the author has introduced new method, process and model for the Phishing procedures do that the level of difficulty will be based on the skill level of the user. This system has been evolved to scale the size of the enterprise through its intelligence, Automation, dynamic and platform-agnostic. The analysis has been made out and results are showing that it increases the user ability to detect phishing. So this ensures that it helps in many way in detecting the cybercrimes due to the improvement of the Phishing procedures. So this shows that this improvement is of great success. This system ensures the increase in users' skill to detect phishing. There is no evidence of this updates in this field. So this study is all about how the practitioners can make their move to improve the existing systems and enhance the users' skill and also embrace the system when used with User Behavior Analytics and Risk Scoring.

5. SURVEY ON CRIMINAL JUSTICE IN DIGITAL SOCIETY

Justin Store (2023) is significant that the attackers often "live off the land" with the help of tools that are built into the window operating system and other operating systems. These operating system tools are more powerful because they are likely to block less and are difficult to monitor. Even though evidences are available, these are difficult to get banned because of the legitimate uses that can earn some good things and create high potential numbers of false positive. Anyways defenders can use this in a positive approach to gain visibility of these attackers using the same built-in tools. Power shells can use the regular expression to define a baseline of normal activity flexibly. The use of regular expression is mainly because of that combination of fields extracted from event logs and they enable defenders to filter out the noise with the help of surgical precision. The illegal activities are being recorded for the further analysis. Actually the anomaly based detections allows defenders to build their very own customizable baselines to reduce the false positive rates efficiently. In conclusion these methods can be expanded beyond the monitoring of the other windows event types and structured log or tool output.

Reddy, G.N.; Reddy, G (2014) would like to share their thoughts on how important the role cyber security plays in our technological world. As we know cybercrime is rapidly increasing day to day, so the paper describes how the cybercrime issues are solved by the government by using the method of cyber security. It also gives a brief explanation on some of the different types of cybercrimes such as identity theft, stalking, bullying and terrorism which has become a major problem in this current era. Also the authors give the exact reports on the statistics of cybercrimes around the world. Then it provides some of the important current trends like web servers, cloud computing services, IPv6 and encryption of the code which are the most helpful in the world of cyber security.

The major area that cybercrimes take place is social media, which is the dangerous platform that encourages personal cyber threats and attacks, so why the authors discuss some important steps that will be useful in order to prevent oneself from the cyber-attacks. And some of the prevention methods that were discussed in the paper are access control and password security, authentication of data, malware scanners, firewalls, and anti-virus software. Finally the paper suggests some cyber ethics that are nothing but the code of the internet. So when we practice these cyber ethics there are very good chances of us using the internet in a much safer and proper way. This article (Perwej, Yusuf, et al (2021)) will contain the information like why cyber security is important, cyber security tools, cyber security framework, cyber security difficulties and so on. Through this article we can learn how to protect the organization data from cyber-attack and it is also used to defend and overcome from the life cycle of the cyber-attack.

This article tells about the internet in twenty first century like how internet is ruling our world. The statement about the internet is that "nowadays without network not even single work can't be done". Internet changed our life and fetched the method we interface, play games, jobs and listen to music etc. The earth will down fall aside if there is no safety. Over a preceding few decennary, cyber-security has proceeded.

When we come over trickery, cyber-security is the earliest object that comes to our mind. The major problem in today's world is giving protection to our personal data. So the world's business profession is converted to the data science. As we know that nowadays hackers are getting very smarter and they are learning new effective techniques to theft the important data from the organizations.

To overcome from these problems only cyber-security has been created. Cyber-security will give protection to our data from hacker attacks. So finally in this article they have explained the concepts of cyber-security. They have given the techniques that how to tackle the hacker's attack and they have thought the way for protecting the personal data. In this article, additionally they have given details about the block chain security, web security and so on. Technologies, procedures, and techniques used in cyber security shield networks, programs, computers, and data from harm, theft, and illegal access. Inappropriate comparisons are occasionally made between cyber security and other ideas like privacy, information sharing, intelligence collecting, and surveillance in public discourse. As we meet cybercrimes, cyber security enters the scene. It is crucial for individuals involved in the battle against cybercrime to attempt to foresee qualitative and quantitative changes in its underlying components so that they can construct their techniques appropriately. This will help prevent giving cybercriminals the upper hand. The significance of understanding the repercussions of cyber -crime while keeping in mind previous activities that have occurred and providing ways to shield a person or an organization(Perwej, Yusuf, et al (2021)).

The importance and value of cyber security has increased significantly on a global scale. A strategy paper containing more than 50 nations' official positions on cyberspace, cybercrime, and/or cyber security has previously been formally published. Most literary works refer to cyber security as an all-encompassing concept. There are various definitions for this term, such as "measures taken to guard a device or computer network from illegal access or attack," according to the Merriam Webster dictionary. For cyber security, the International Telecommunications Union (ITU) outlines the following. In order to secure the cyber environment as well as the assets of the business and the user, a variety of resources, protocols, security principles, safety measures, regulations, risk management techniques, activities, training, best practices, compliance, and technology can be employed. This is known as cyber-security.

6. INFORMATION AND COMMUNICATION TECHNOLOGY (ICT) AND INFORMATION SECURITY

This essay looked at the definitions of information and communication technology (ICT) and information security. Despite occasionally being used as a synonym for information security, cyber security is distinct from that idea. Information security is a benefit against potential damage known as information defense. On the other hand, cyber security encompasses not only the protection of the internet as a whole but also the security of everyone who uses it, including all of their properties that may be viewed online. This essay contends that although cyber security and information protection have many similarities, they are not exactly the same. The report also asserts that cyber security extends past the limitations(Pallavi Murghai Goel (2019)).

It is now necessary to define solutions to ensure the security and safety of data around the world due to the rapid development of ICT and its ongoing connection to the Internet. As a result, customer and business data are now at risk of electronic attacks. To safeguard the privacy and security of data against cyberattacks, it is now essential for nations and big businesses to implement cybersecurity technologies into their infrastructure. In order to understand this notion, its forms, and the tactics used to mitigate it, this study provides a comprehensive assessment of prior research on cyber-attacks. A systematic process is used to conduct the literature review, starting with data collection and ending with content. The open-access paper of Cyber-security publishes articles outlining novel, fundamentally interdisciplinary cyber research. The foundation of Journal of Cyber-security is the conviction that, while essential, methodologies based on computer science alone are insufficient to address cyber-security issues. Instead, in order to comprehend the various facets of cyber-security, scholarly contributions from a variety of fields are required.

The interdisciplinary cyber-security community can coalesce around the Journal of Cyber-security as a hub. The journal is dedicated to publishing high-caliber empirical research and scholarly work that is based on practical implications and solutions.

The following cybersecurity-related topics are encouraged for submission to the Journal of Cyber-security, widely construed and interpreted:

Studies of anthropology and culture, computer and security, crime and justice, cryptography and related subjects, security economics, human factors. By safeguarding IoT assets and user privacy, IoT cyber-security aims to lower cyber-security risk for businesses and users. Enhanced IoT security management may be possible with the help of new cyber-security technologies and tools. The frameworks for managing cyber risks and IoT cyber-security technologies are examined in this paper. The paper then presents a four-layer framework for managing IoT cyber risk. This study allocates financial resources to numerous IoT cyber-security projects using a linear programming method. As proof of concept, an example is given.

The potential security exposures increase exponentially as more connected devices of all types and sizes are additional to IoT networks. Intruders and hackers have more opportunities to access sensitive data and critical infrastructure when there is a lack of security in IoT systems. However, without a framework for managing IoT cyber-security risks, it is very challenging for organizations to invest in and manage IoT cyber-security risks effectively. This paper examined frameworks for managing cyber risks and IoT cyber-security technologies.

For instance, managers were not given any resource allocation techniques by existing frameworks. There are no methods for allocating resources, so any decisions regarding cyber investments were based solely on intuition and weak justification. This shortcoming was addressed by the IoT (four layer) cyber risk management framework that was proposed. Larger IoT systems with hundreds of decision variables, such as those used in smart manufacturing and smart transportation, can be easily scaled using the LP model. In order to react quickly to cyber-security breaches and attacks, organizations must continuously monitor the advancement of technologies. For instance, 5G's advancements and associated 5G-enabled IoT developments will lead to an increase in cyber-attacks. (Lee(2020))

Dan Craigen (2014), gave their literature search covered a wide variety of sources, including a wide variety of academic disciplines including: Computer Science, Engineering, Political Science, Psychology, Security Studies, Management, Education and Sociology. The most common disciplines covered in our literature review are engineering, technology, computer wisdom, and security and defense. But to a much lesser extent, there has also been reference to cybersecurity in journals on policy development, law, healthcare, public administration, accounting, management, sociology, psychology, and education.

7.CYBER-ATTACKS

Ghazizadeh-Ahsaee M (2019), has deconstructed the term cybersecurity, helps to stick the discussion within both disciplines of" cyber" and" security" and reveals some of the heritage issues. The prefix "cyber" refers to cyberspace and is used to describe electronic communication networks and virtual reality (Oxford, 2014). The term first appeared in the field of cybernetics, which is defined as the "field of control and communication proposition, whether in machine or in the beast." In his book Neuromancer from 1984, William Gibson first used the term "cyberspace" to describe his concept of a three-dimensional space made up entirely of information, in which people move between computer clusters and computers and serve as both its producers and consumers (Kizza, 2011).

Shiravi H, Tavallaee M, has said that cyberspace was intended and designed as an information terrain (Singer & Friedman, 2013), and there is an expanded appreciation of cyberspace. It's a global common where people are linked together to change ideas, services and fellowship.

"Cyberspace is not stationary; It's a dynamic, tiered ecosystem of physical structure, software, regulations, ideas, inventions, and relations, told by a growing inhabitants of contributors (Deibert & Rohozinski, 2010) representing the range of mortal intentions.

Kathleen M. Carley (2019), gave about the erecting a Social Media Community in Ukraine, there was a group of youthful men who were transferring instigative images of women. They did not know each other, they only posted filmland they liked. Bots were used in an influence crusade to shoot tweets mentioning each other and several of these youthful men. This urged the men to learn of others who, like them, were broadcasting these images. They formed a themed online group. Once formed, the bots sometimes twittered information about where to get ordnance and security and how to join the fight.

Papastergiou S (2022) has said that cyber geography is populated by issues of acquainted communities, groups of actors all communicating with each other about intriguing content. Each actor can be numerous themed communities. Actors can be people, bots, cyborgs (people with bot support), pixies (people who want to disrupt a company or government regard that uses a fake persona and frequently engages in hate speech and identity vilification), etc. The members of a themed community are approximately connected by interacting with each other. For illustration, they can friend, follow, retweet, cite, reply, quote, or like each other. Some actors will be opinion leaders, some will have a disproportionate capability to convey dispatches to the community (super spreaders), some will be heavily involved in the collective give and take of an ongoing discussion (super spreaders). The members of content acquainted communities are also approximately connected as they post or shoot or admit dispatches on the same motifs. For illustration, they're all agitating the Army- Navy game. Some actors will engage further laboriously and shoot further dispatches.

Khraisat A, Gondal I(2019), gave the thematic communities varying size and association. Eg. Aeroplane Gatekeepers is a huge community with little interconnectedness. Through new tools and exploration styles that measure the impact of social media communication, it's now possible to measure and fantasize data to show that issue driven communities that come exorbitantly connected come echo chambers.(Note an echo chamber is a pathological form of issue acquainted community where the position of connections is extremely thick and the issue is largely disunited and narrow.) dispatches transferred within echo chambers reach everyone snappily, and similar groups frequently can be willing to respond emotionally rather than rationally to outside information.

The term cybersecurity can be categorised into a number of typical areas, including mobile computing and enterprise settings. These include network security, which primarily focuses on defending a computer network from online attackers or intruders; application security, which considers how to ensure that devices and software are safe from risks and cyberthreats; and information security, which primarily focuses on the safety and protection of pertinent data.

Cyber security encompasses a wide range of measures that are implemented to safeguard an organization, its employees, and its valuable resources from the constantly evolving threats posed by cybercriminals. Cyberattack is when someone tries to gain access to your system. These results in letting unauthorized people access your system(Akram Junaid (2020))

It is essential to adopt a multifaceted approach to cyber security in order to effectively mitigate the risks associated with such attacks given the rising frequency and sophistication of cyber-attacks as well as the continuously growing complexity of corporate networks. Cybersecurity is essential for preventing unauthorised access to digital assets like networks, data, and computer systems. Cyberattacks of all kinds, such as malware, phishing, man-in-the-middle attacks, and password attacks, can jeopardise security.

One of the most frequent types of cyber-attacks is malware, which includes Trojan horses, adware, and spyware, to name a few. If users had downloaded any dubious attachments from the internet, the attachments may have contained malicious viruses that could have corrupted their systems. It is essential to adopt a multifaceted approach to cyber security in order to effectively mitigate the risks associated with such attacks given the rising frequency and sophistication of cyber-attacks as well as the continuously growing complexity of corporate networks. Cybersecurity is essential for preventing unauthorised access to digital assets like networks, data, and computer systems. Cyberattacks of all kinds, such as malware, phishing, man-in-the-middle attacks, and password attacks, can jeopardise security. One of the most frequent types of cyber-attacks is malware, which includes Trojan horses, adware, and spyware, to name a few. If users had downloaded any dubious attachments from the internet, the attachments may have contained malicious viruses that could have corrupted their systems.

To prevent future cyber-attacks the individual must be into implementing a few cyber security practices. First users have to install the firewall, it is a virtual wall between the user's computer and the internet. Firewall implementation is highly needed as it filters the incoming and outgoing traffic from your device to safeguard your network and they can either be software applications or hardware reinforcements. Secondly, the implementation of honeypots is mainly used to attract attackers. in addition, these users also decided to use unique alphanumeric passwords and antivirus software and started avoiding mail from unknown users. When there are many devices connected to the system many vulnerabilities can come into the picture (Akram Junaid (2020)) Cyber-attacks coffined both public and private organizations attackers use many tools to invade privacy.

Many large corporations and organisations in the public sector deal with the advanced persistent threat, wherein hackers continuously access the network for the purpose of obtaining sensitive information. Several customers are not aware of the flaws. An SQL injection attack is when a hacker manipulates a typical SQL query in the database and launches a Distributed Denial of Service (DDOS) attack using multiple systems. In this SQL injection hackers can view and delete tables from databases. There are many other factors that introduce vulnerability. it is a challenge for organizations with several networks and servers to ensure complete security. Bluetooth technology has safe sharing and browsing(Mohamed Abomhara and Geir M. Køien (2015)).

Ensuring security is a must these days especially when handling sensitive data. One of the important aspects is to prevent vulnerabilities. A simple vulnerability refers to the system's weakness that has been attacked to get the credentials and other information many software are not designed up to the security level. The cyber-attack runs malicious code and installs the necessary software to get sensitive data. The business should be from secured cyber threats (Mahesh Sharma and Seema Nath Jain(2022)).

These vulnerabilities are exploited by various methods such as SQL injections where its main objective is to get access to the database and steal data, also there are other vulnerabilities such as cross-site scripting which involves the addition of different malicious code which is used to access the information from a website there are also many chances of human errors such as maintaining a weak password, having unwanted or malicious software installed in the system or maybe even downloading files which contains vulnerabilities, in some cases sending information to a wrong recipient mainly causes trouble and the action can't be undone. Human weakness is one of the reasons vulnerabilities enter into the picture.

The vulnerabilities are classified into many categories such as hardware software networks, etc. Cyber security experts try to implement immediate remedies for data security. Cyber security protects us from vulnerabilities a flaw is typically defined as the irregular or poor design made by the cyber security specialist during implementation. Nowadays there are a lot of devices connected to the internet and network traffic is potentially high. Not only by internet attacks the machines such as printers and scanners even take up sensitive data these are even more vulnerable and can't be handled. It is one of the biggest crimes nowadays as it steals a lot of data. Hackers are using multiple exploits to see which gives the maximum reward. A threat means that there is some vulnerability in the machine and it uses the access in the machine without authorized permission.

There are two types of threats unstructured threats, and structured threats, unstructured threats consist of the individual who don't have much knowledge about the security protocols and vulnerabilities where they used hacking tools and got access, whereas in structured threats the individual will have good understanding about the security and breaks all the walls that are constructed and steal the important information. They are the ones who develop the vulnerable codes. Attacks are often taken in the system they are the ones who are a threat to the current digital world the attackers can be of many forms. Attack means the action that is taken to interrupt and steal information in a process.

The attacks are classified into many types such as physical, reconnaissance, denial of service, access attack, etc. the physical attack binds with the hardware components and operates in outdoor environments it changes the entire behavior of the device. In access attacks, some persons who are unauthorized somehow manage to come into the picture and attack. In order to solve these issues firewall, antivirus is introduced.

The concept of a firewall is it is a protective wall that manages incoming traffic and outgoing traffic this is considered the first line of security, firewalls are used in even cloud platforms such as software as a service, hardware as a service, and platform as a service. There are different types of firewalls such as proxy firewalls, stateful inspection firewalls, unified threat management firewalls, next-generation firewalls, threat-focused firewalls, virtual firewalls, and cloud-native firewalls.

The proxy firewall is the early type of firewall that involves providing different functionalities such as content caching and preventing direct connections. The stateful inspection firewall is a traditional firewall that allows or blocks traffic based on the state of the protocol this firewall monitors from the opening till the closing of a connection and many filters are done to regularly filter out the connections which are not up to connecting good resources unlike this the unified threat management firewall combines the stateful inspection firewall and antivirus and hence also provides cloud management protection. In the next-generation firewall has intelligence-based access and integrated intrusion which blocks harmful applications, even url filtering is done. Another type of firewall is the threat-focused firewall as the name states it mainly focuses on threats so that it can react to attacks quickly. Cloud-native firewalls are used to make secure applications so that they will not be under attack in the cloud and maintain the data without any leak.

There is another way called antivirus which is used to prevent the computer from virus attacks. Once it is installed as software it will ensure real-time protection. The antivirus thoroughly checks the files from the computer and constantly generates reports based on the analysis. The computers typically use three special detection devices namely specific detection, which is used to identify the known or visible malware, generic recognition which identifies the known parts of the malware and removes it, there are paid and free antivirus with limited features. The antivirus thoroughly checks all the files inside the machine and finds the vulnerable ones and deletes the file permanently or modifies it by removing the malicious code. The antivirus in phone or applet is not really needed as the play store provides real-time protection among different applications

This will alert the system security team to what needs to be changed or removed. Hardware vulnerabilities are harder to fix and diagnosed it takes a lot of effort to find the vulnerable code in the hardware, whereas the software mainly relies on either the operating system, application software, or communication software, the network security must be very good and precise as connections from the network to the internet will make your system be exposed into the cloud and it has high chances of stealing information's and other address connection may cause vulnerabilities

Thus, prevention of threat and vulnerabilities are very important and if attacked already, the virus recovery should be taken as soon as possible, we should be very cautious on being installing any software or connecting any external device to our system. Nowadays email is also adding vulnerabilities as we should be very cautious about downloading attachments without scanning the file thoroughly, we should be very cautious about spam messages. Safe browsing is highly recommended along with the evaluation of the browser security settings and while shopping we should be very cautious about the site as we are doing transactions online

8. TEST CASES

8.1. Case One: Virus Attack

From the response received, more than 70% of students from all the cities are conscious about the basic virus attacks and are using antivirus software (updating frequently) or Linux platforms to safeguard their system from virus attack. Remaining students are not utilizing antivirus and are the fatalities for virus attack. 11% of them are using antivirus but they are not updating the antivirus software. More than 97% of them don't know the source of the virus. The students using antivirus and updating that regular intervals are considered to be aware about the virus attacks and students not using antivirus software's or updating it at regular intervals are considered as unaware about virus attack.

8.2. Case Two

Phishing Phishing in email/message is taken into account. Almost more than 60% of students from all the cities received phishing emails/messages in any form. But the percentage of persons receiving phishing emails/messages varies between the cities.

Very less students only responded those E-mails/messages and those students claimed that they responded because for identifying the purpose of looking to which extent these mails will take and added that they all know that is fake E-mail/messages only. Other students simply marked that Email/Message as spam or simply ignored that mail/message. Only 10 students from overall 379 claimed that they will complain about this phishing mail/messages to Cyber Crime wing. The graphical representation of number of students received phishing mail/message is shown in Figure 3. So in the case of phishing attack all the students are aware in all the cities.

8.3. Case Three

Password strength Password strength depends upon the combination of alphanumeric characters, Special characters, length of the password and changing the passwords frequently. Students considering at least one of all these three categories for their password strength are considered to more aware about the misuse of passwords.

8.4. Case Four

Misuse of Social network Identity theft and publishing spam about a person is common is major threats in social networks. All students are in the part of any social networks. In order to determine how much personal information each student publishes on social networks, a survey is therefore carried out.

Accepting unknown persons in social network is considered to be the major threat in social network compared to any other identity outsourcing. After that, updating locations every time where ever they go is second major personal data of a person published in social networks. Compared to these two, career details and having original display picture has very less impact on publishing.

9. CONCLUSION

Cyber threats are one of the gravest national security, all are facing today. Visiting the websites which is already infected with malware, replying phishing e-mails, storing logging information in an third party location, or even sharing confidential information over the phone, exposing personal information to social networking are tend to steal personal information of common people. This survey result shows that the college students in Tamil Nadu are having above average level of awareness on Cyber related threat issues which can help them to protect themselves from the cyberattacks. Fully fledged cyber awareness will make students to protect themselves from hackers and hence the awareness has to be created in higher level.

REFERENCES

Ablon, L., Libicki, M. C., & Golay, A. A. (2014). Markets for Cybercnme Tools and Stolen Data. Hackers' Bazaar, 1-85.

Abomhara, M., & Køien, G. (2015). Cyber security and the internet of things: vulnerabilities, threats, intruders and attacks. *Journal of Cyber Security and Mobility,* 65-88.

Akhtar, N., Parwej, F., & Perwej, Y. (2017). A Perusal of Big Data Classification and Hadoop Technology. International Transaction of Electrical and Computer Engineers System (ITECES), USA. Doi:10.12691/iteces-4-1-4

Al-Fuhaidi, B. (2021). Literature Review on Cyber Attacks Detection and Prevention Schemes. *2021 International Conference on Intelligent Technology, System and Service for Internet of Everything (ITSS-IoE).* IEEE. 10.1109/ITSS-IoE53029.2021.9615288

Aldmour, R., Burnap, P., & Lakoju, M. (2019). Risk assessment methods for converged IoT and SCADA systems: Review and recommendations. In *Proceedings of the Living in the Internet of Things (IoT 2019),* London, UK. 10.1049/cp.2019.0130

Atzori, L., Iera, A., & Morabito, G. (2010). The internet of things: A survey. *Computer Networks, 54*(15), 2787–2805. doi:10.1016/j.comnet.2010.05.010

Barry, M. (2009, October). Leiner at. al., "A Brief History of the Internet,". *Computer Communication Review, 39*(5).

Bendavid, Y., Bagheri, N., Safkhani, M., & Rostampour, S. (2018). IoT Device Security: Challenging "A Lightweight RFID Mutual Authentication Protocol Based on Physical Unclonable Function". *Sensors (Basel), 18*(12), 4444. doi:10.339018124444 PMID:30558323

Beskow, D. M., & Carley, K. M. (2019). *Social cybersecurity: an emerging national security requirement.* Carnegie Mellon University Pittsburgh United States.

Chang, L. Y., & Coppel, N. (2020). Building cyber security awareness in a developing country: Lessons from Myanmar. *Computers & Security, 97,* 101959. doi:10.1016/j.cose.2020.101959

Craigen, D., Diakun-Thibault, N., & Purse, R. (2014). Defining cybersecurity. *Technology Innovation Management Review, 4*(10), 10. doi:10.22215/timreview/835

Dawson, J., & Thomson, R. (2018). The future cybersecurity workforce: Going beyond technical skills for successful cyber performance. *Frontiers in Psychology, 9*(JUN), 1–12. doi:10.3389/fpsyg.2018.00744 PMID:29946276

Deloitte. (2018). *Secure IoT by Design.* DeLoitte. https://www2.deloitte.com/us/en/pages/operations/articles/iot-platform-security.html

Gallaher, M., Link, A., & Rowe, B. (2008). *Cyber Security: Economic Strategies and Public Policy Alternatives.* Edward Elgar Publishing. doi:10.4337/9781781008140

Ghate, S., & Agrawal, P. K. (2017). A literature review on cyber security in indian context. *J. Comput. Inf. Technol*, 8(5), 30–36. doi:10.22147/jucit/080501

Hejazi, D., Liu, S., Farnoosh, A., Ostadabbas, S., & Kar, S. (2020). Development of use-specific high-performance cyber-nanomaterial optical detectors by effective choice of machine learning algorithms. *Machine Learning: Science and Technology*, 1(2), 025007. doi:10.1088/2632-2153/ab8967

Horovic, Sabrina, Marija Boban, and Ivana Stipanovic. "Cybersecurity and criminal justice in digital society." *Economic and Social Development: Book of Proceedings* (2021): 52-60.

Humayun, M., Niazi, M., Jhanjhi, N. Z., Alshayeb, M., & Mahmood, S. (2020). Cyber security threats and vulnerabilities: A systematic mapping study. *Arabian Journal for Science and Engineering*, 45(4), 3171–3189. doi:10.100713369-019-04319-2

Igor, S. (2018). Large-scale cyber-attacks monitoring using Evolving Cauchy Possibilistic Clustering. Applied Soft Computing (Vol. 62). Elsevier.

Irdeto. (2019). *New 2019 Global Survey: IoT-Focused Cyberattacks Are the New Normal*. IRDETO. https://resources.irdeto.com/global-connected-industries-cybersecurity-survey/new-2019-globalsurvey-iot-focused-cyberattacks-are-the-new-normal.

Junaid, A., & Ping, L. (2020). How to build a vulnerability benchmark to overcome cyber security attacks. *IET Information Security*, 14(1), 60–71. doi:10.1049/iet-ifs.2018.5647

Kamara, S., & Lauter, K. (2010). Cryptographic cloud storage. Proceedings of the 14th international conference on Financial crypto graphy and data security, (pp. 136-149). ACM.

Khraisat, A., Gondal, I., Vamplew, P., & Kamruzzaman, J. (2019). Survey of intrusion detection systems: Techniques, datasets and challenges. *Cybersecurity*, 2(1), 1–22. doi:10.118642400-019-0038-7

Kruse, C. S., Frederick, B., Jacobson, T., & Monticone, D. K. (2017). Cybersecurity in healthcare: A systematic review of modern threats and trends. *Technology and Health Care*, 25(1), 1–10. doi:10.3233/THC-161263 PMID:27689562

Lee, I. (2020). Internet of Things (IoT) cybersecurity: Literature review and IoT cyber risk management. *Future Internet, 12*, 157.

Liu, X., Zhang, Y., Wang, B., & Yang, J. (2013). Mona: Secure multi owner data sharing for dynamic groups in the cloud. *IEEE Transactions on Parallel and Distributed Systems*, 24(6), 1182–1191. doi:10.1109/TPDS.2012.331

Liu, X., Zhang, Y., Wang, B., & Yang, J. (2013). Mona: Secure multi owner data sharing for dynamic groups in the cloud. *IEEE Transactions on Parallel and Distributed Systems*, 24(6), 1182–1191. doi:10.1109/TPDS.2012.331

Malhotra, D. S. (2016). Cyber Crime-Its Types, Analysis and Prevention Techniques. *International Journal of Advanced Research in Computer Science and Software Engineering*, 6(5), 145–150.

Malik, V., & Singh, S. (2019). Security risk management in IoT environment. *J. Discret. Math. Sci. Cryptogr.*, 22(4), 697–709. doi:10.1080/09720529.2019.1642628

MarketsandMarkets. IoT Security Market Worth $35.2 Billion by 2023. 2019. Available online: https: // www.marketsandmarkets.com/PressReleases/iot-security.asp (accessed on 17 September 2020).

Mohammadi, S. (2019). Cyber intrusion detection by combined feature selection algorithm. *Journal of information security and applications, 44,* 80-88.

Mollah, M. B., Azad, M. A., & Vasilakos, A. (2017). Security and privacy challenges in mobile cloud computing: Survey and way ahead. *Journal of Network and Computer Applications, 84,* 38–54. doi:10.1016/j.jnca.2017.02.001

Nurse, J. R. C., Creese, S., & de Roure, D. (2017). Security risk assessment in Internet of Things systems. *IT Professional, 19*(5), 20–26. doi:10.1109/MITP.2017.3680959

Paliwal, (2016). *Cyber Crime.* Nations Congress on the Prevention of Crime and Treatment of Offenders.

Parker, G. (2021). *Building an Intelligent, Automated Tiered Phishing System: Matching the Message Level to User Ability.* SANAS Institute.

Parwej, F., Akhtar, N., & Perwej, Y. (2018). A Close-Up View About Spark in Big Data Jurisdiction. International Journal of Engineering Research and Application (IJERA) 8(1). doi:10.9790/9622-0801022641

Perwej, Y. (2017). An Experiential Study of the Big Data. International Transaction of Electrical and Computer Engineers System. *Science and Education Publishing, 4*(1), 14–25. doi:10.12691/iteces-4-1-3

Perwej, Y. (2019). The Hadoop Security in Big Data: A Technological Viewpoint and Analysis. *International Journal of Scientific Research in Computer Science and Engineering (IJSRCSE), 7*(3). doi:10.26438/ijsrcse/v7i3.1014

Perwej, Y. (2021). A systematic literature review on the cyber security. *International Journal of scientific research and management, 9,* 669-710.

Philip, C. L., Chen, Q., & Zhang, C. Y. (2014). Data-intensive applications challenges techniques and technologies: A survey on big data. *Information Sciences, 275,* 314–347. doi:10.1016/j.ins.2014.01.015

PwC. (2016). *Managing Emerging Risks from the Internet of Things.* PwC. https://www.pwc.com/ us/ en/services/consulting/cybersecurity/library/broader-perspectives/managing-iot-risks.html

Rao, A., Carreón, N., Lysecky, R., & Rozenblit, J. (2018). Probabilistic threat detection for risk management in cyber-physical medical systems. *IEEE Software, 35*(1), 38–43. doi:10.1109/MS.2017.4541031

Reddy, G. N., & Reddy, G. (2014). A study of cybersecurity challenges and its emerging trends on latest technologies. arXiv, arXiv:1402.1842.

Rid, T., & Buchanan, B. (2015). Attributing cyber-attacks. *The Journal of Strategic Studies, 38*(1-2), 4–37. doi:10.1080/01402390.2014.977382

Sarker, I. H., Kayes, A. S. M., Badsha, S., Alqahtani, H., Watters, P., & Ng, A. (2020). Cybersecurity data science: An overview from machine learning perspective. *Journal of Big Data, 7*(1), 1–29. doi:10.118640537-020-00318-5

Schibilia, J. (2023). *Really, How Bad Do Routers Have It?* SANS Institute.

Sha, K., Wei, W., Yang, T. A., Wang, Z., & Shi, W. (2018). On security challenges and open issues in Internet of Things. *Future Generation Computer Systems, 83*, 326–337. doi:10.1016/j.future.2018.01.059

Store, J. (2023). *Living Off the land as a defender: Detecting Attacks with Flexible Baselines*. SANS Institute.

Yu, R., Xue, G., Kilari, V. T., & Zhang, X. (2018). *Deploying Robust Security in Internet of Things*. In *Proceedings of the 2018 IEEE Conference on Communications and Network Security (CNS)*, Beijing, China. 10.1109/CNS.2018.8433219

Zhu, B., Joseph, A., & Sastry, S. (2011). A taxonomy of cyber-attacks on SCADA systems. *2011 International conference on internet of things and 4th international conference on cyber physical and social computing*. IEEE. 10.1109/iThings/CPSCom.2011.34

Chapter 6
An Implemented Example of XKMS With Web Services

Sumathi Pawar

Nitte Mahalinga Adyanthaya Memorial Institute of Technology, India

Ankitha

Nitte Mahalinga Adyanthaya Memorial Institute of Technology, India

V. Geetha

National Institute of Technology, Karnataka, India

ABSTRACT

Web service is a loosely coupled system, which gets remote request for a particular service and returns results after executing that service. The data transfer of the web service is a request/response system which carries input parameters through request message and carries executed results of the web services. Both request and response messages are carried in the form of SOAP message which is XML based. XML signature and XML encryption are two methods of securing data transfer through simple access protocol (SOAP) messages from web services. The main goal of the XKMS initiative is to make it possible to create XML-based trust web services for handling and administration of PKI-based cryptographic keys. By making it possible to develop such web services, XKMS helps to simplify working with PKI and makes it simpler for web services to integrate security features into their programmes. This chapter provides a thorough working of the implemented draught of the W3C working group's XKMS specification.

1. INTRODUCTION

Web services are loosely connected, self-contained software components that may be found and dynamically constructed to perform a particular function, solve a particular problem, or provide a specific solution to a consumer utilizing current Internet technologies (Beznosov, 2005). In a web services scenario, a web application uses the SOAP (Simple Object Access Protocol) using communication protocols like HTTP, SMTP, or FTP to deliver a request message to a service at some URI. The request message is received by the service, which then processes it and sends back a response message.

DOI: 10.4018/978-1-6684-9317-5.ch006

1.1 XKMS Overview

XKMS is an initiative by the W3C (https://www.w3.org/TR/2002/WD-skms2-2002318/) with the original input coming from an effort by Microsoft, VeriSign, and Web Methods. XKMS is designed to be implemented using standard XML tools (Bhatti et al., 2004). The message of XKMS is in XML and is designed to allow use of SOAP for communication between the XKMS client and the XKMS service. An XKMS request from the client or an XKMS response from the server typically embedded in the SOAP body. The XKMS services can be described using WSDL.

1.2 PKI Complexities

PKI is based on public-private (Huang, 2005) key pairs, where an organization owning the pair keeps the private key and distributes the public key to its partners. Partners wishing to communicate with an organization in a secured manner use the public key of the organization with which they wish to communicate to encrypt the message and send it through some transport mechanism. The target organization receives the message and decrypts it using its private key to get the plain text of the message.

In case of digital signatures, the organization sending the document signs the message using its private key and then sends the message to its partners. The partners use the public key of the organization that send the message to verify and validate the signature.

1.3 XKMS Services

XKMS-Specification supports three major services:

§ **Register Service**

The Register service is used for registering key pairs for escrow services. Once the key is registered, the XKMS service manages the revocation, re-issue, and recovery of registered keys. The registration service supports generation of public –private key pairs. Alternatively, client-generated key pairs also can be registered. A key–pair needs to be registered before a user can locate or validate keys.

§ **Locate Service**

The Locate service is used to retrieve a public key registered with the XKMS service. Location service accept <ds:KeyInfo> (Galbraith et al., 2001) as their input and provide the client with the required information. The recovered public key may be used for further processing, such as signature verification or encryption.

§ **Validate Service**

The Validate service provides all the functionality provided by the Locate service and in addition perform key validation. Applications can ensure that the public key registered with the XKMS service is valid and is not expired or revoked (OASIS, n.d.). The validation service also can assert the validity of the binding between different public key attributes.

2. RELATED WORK

The WS-Security specification (El-Aziz, 2013) defines a common format for securing SOAP messages using XML Encryption and XML Signatures to protect message confidentiality and integrity. It also provides a way of passing security tokens, such as X.509 certificates (El-Aziz, 2013) or Kerberos tickets (El-Aziz, 2013), through SOAP headers. Offering message-level security, WSSecurity is instrumental in providing end-to-end web services security as each message can be encrypted or signed independently, and thus self-protected. This is in contrast to transport-level security which provides point-to-point security through, for example, a secure channel established using the SSL/TLS protocol. Although message-level security provides finer granularity than transport-level security in terms of selective message protection, this fine granularity potentially causes significant performance issues, since each message needs to be processed separately and different security tokens may be used within the same message or from message to message. SAML defines methods for specifying trust assertions in XML (ALRassan, 2020). These methods enable portable trust in the sense that assertions applied to an individual are attached to a message and they can be transported from one point to another with the message. SAML assertions take the form of authentication, authorization or attributes of entities. One key benefit resulting from the use of SAML is web single sign-on. The SAML authorization assertion request/response protocol is usually run between a policy enforcement point (PEP) and a policy decision point (PDP), typically with the support of XACML (El-Aziz, 2013). It is also often used by a PEP to request attribute assertions from a policy information point (PIP).

XML Signatures provides integrity, message authentication, and/or signer authentication services to the data within the XML (Braith et al., 2002; W3, n.d.). Process of generating XML signature is shown in Figure 1.

In modern distributed systems, XML and Web services are frequently employed. The security of the Web services themselves as well as the XML-based communication is crucial to the overall security of these systems. Additionally, the security measures should ideally be based on recognized standards to promote interoperability. Authors offer a lesson on current security standards for XML and Web services in this document. The technologies that are covered include eXtensible Access Control Markup Language (XACML), Security Assertion Markup Language (SAML), XML Signature, XML Encryption, WS-Security, WS-Trust, WS-Secure Conversation, Web Services Policy, and XML Key Management Specification (XKMS) (Nordbotten, 2009).

ALRassan (2020) concentrated on the most difficult problem that Web Services face, namely how to safeguard their data. The major goal of this search is to find security standards that can be used to assure Web Services security. Every proposed model for security design should take the security's goals—integrity, secrecy, non-repudiation, authentication, and authorization—into consideration. The suggested paradigm explains how to secure SOAP messages' contents. This research has established a security model required to assure e-business security because the SOAP message is the primary means of transferring information in Web Services. In order to encrypt and sign SOAP messages, the core of our architecture depends on XML encryption and signature. The suggested methodology aims to provide fast transaction speeds and high levels of security without compromising the efficiency of information transfer.

Figure 1. Creation of XML signature

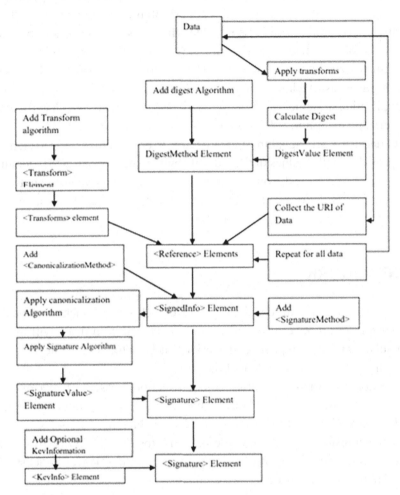

Due to its flexibility in offering a standard syntax for messaging systems, XML has been widely used for information transmission across numerous networks. Private information that cannot be shared by all user communities may be found in XML documents. In light of this, XML Security is crucial to the general security of distributed systems. We offer a thorough lesson on XML security standards in this document. XML encryption and XML signature are among the presented standards. We go through how to encrypt and decrypt XML data as well as how to establish and validate XML signatures. This article should act as a guide for future study and a starting point for additional investigation into pertinent standard specifications and scientific literature (El-Aziz, 2013).

Ramesh (2013) analyzed the value of XML encryption and XML signature for WS-Security. Organizations are devoting a significant portion of their resources to Web Services in the current e-business environment. Since SOAP and WSDL and other plain-text XML formats are used for the majority of Web Service Transactions, hacking them is not a difficult operation. It is simple to implement XML documents since XML Signature and XML Encryption guarantee their security while maintaining their structure. The criteria for authentication, authorization, integration, confidentiality, and non-repudiation are used to compare these two techniques.

The W3C's ongoing efforts to increase XML security have produced many positive outcomes. The terms "authentication," "integrity," and "privacy" are essential in the security industry (Kumar et al., 2017). Any security-related problems will be reduced when these three services become more widely used. The primary goal of this study is to describe several strategies for eliminating security threats. XML Signature (Sumathi, 2015), XML Encryption (Pawar, 2018), and XKMS (XML Key Management Specification) are the three basic techniques for establishing a secure environment in XML. In our article, we examined the application strategies for the aforementioned techniques, which will address problematic situations like forgery and unauthorized access to sensitive data, among others.

The IETF/W3C-defined XML signature standard refers to or recognizes signed elements by their distinctive identities provided by the values of the "id" attribute in the relevant XML document. Therefore, signed XML elements can be moved from one place in an XML document to another and still retain the capacity to be verified as authentic. This adaptability makes it possible for an attacker to alter the original XML message without the recipient noticing.

3. EXPERIMENTAL WORK

In the proposed work it is tasked with developing a travel web service such as Expedia.com which is named as MyTravel.com. As a travel reservation site, MyTravels.com deals with many partners that include airlines, hotels, car rental companies, and various package tour companies. The following shows a simple workflow that occurs between a few of the partners:

All of the reservation requests and reservation confirmation messages between the travel site and its partners are signed and encrypted. The body of message is first encrypted using XML Encryption and then is signed using XML Signature. This fact is identified by the <dcrpt:Except> element, which is based on the decrypt transform specification defined in https://www.w3.org/2002/07/decrypt#. This signature is applied to both the <EncryptedData> element and the <Travel:Request> header element as indicated by the URI of the two <Reference> elements.

3.1 Activities Involved

The key processing activities are occurred on both transmitting and receiving sides during this message exchange. As shown in Figure 2, the sender MyTravels.com has to get the public key of Marriott.com from somewhere in order to encrypt the message and use its private key to sign the message. To ensure it is keeping a valid key, MyTravels.com will need to constantly validate and update the database. Given the fact that a site such as MyTravels.com will be dealing with thousands of partners; does a database to maintain the key information sound like a good solution? This question is solved in this section.

On receipt of the message, Marriott.com has to validate the authentically and integrity of the sender. To do this, Marriott.com has to verify that the key sent via<KeyName> does in fact belong to MyTravels. com and is still valid. It'll probably need the help of a trust authority to do this verification. After authenticating, Marriott.com has to get the actual public key of MyTravels.com from somewhere to perform the signature validation. On successful validation, Marriott.com decrypts the message and act on it.

Figure 2. Key processing activities

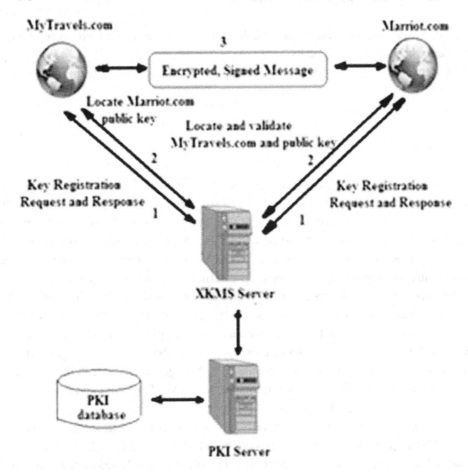

A simple message exchange involves key information of the partners, management of the obtained key information and trust authorities for key verification. Because all the partners are not going to use the same PKI implementation, to expand its reach, MyTravels.com has to work with most of the available PKI implementations, each having different syntax and semantics. Working with trust authorities involves dealing with their message exchange and communication mechanisms that may not be XML –based. This means MyTravels.com web service cannot be only based on SOAP, but must support various other protocols and data formats as well.

Management of keys is no longer a small problem for MyTravels.com. It forms a bulk part of the implementation, requires PKI expertise, is no longer pure XML based, and leads to a big footprint application.

Implementation of MyTravels.com web service will be much simpler if MyTravels.com can delegate the key processing activities to a third –party. It will be even easier if such a service is based on the web services protocol, and is aware of XML Signature and XML Encryption syntax and their key processing semantics. With such a service, MyTravels.com can just hand over the <ds:KeyInfo> element and have the key value retrieved and validated, enabling MyTravels.com to focus on its business logic.

XKMS is designed to make such services a reality.

3.2 Client Side Technologies and Options

Since the majority of the users of XKMS will be XKMS clients, therefore focus is on the technology options available to develop XKMS clients.

An XKMS Client would need, at the minimum, support for the following technologies:

- XML Parser
- SOAP
- XML Signature

Support for SOAP is strong and many interoperable implementations in many languages are readily available. Since XKMS requires a basic level of SOAP support, it could work with many of the SOAP implementations without detailed knowledge on SOAP. Support for XML Signature implementation is not widespread, but stable implementations in Java and NET environments do exist. Using these technologies and toolkits it is possible to hand code XKMS clients, since at the basic level we are only talking about creating and sending a SOAP message confirming to XKMS schema.

An alternative approach to hand-coding XKMS clients is to use the WSDL document published by the XKMS service implementations and generate clients using WSDL Code generators. WSDL code generators are available in Java, NET, C++, and various other platforms. Success on this approach requires proper WSDL documents form service providers and good WSDL code generators. There is some learning curve here, as it need to understand the API of the generated code to link it at applications. Also, it is unlikely that these WSDL code generators support XML Signature and it would mostly need to do XML Signature code using XML Signature implementation.

The other option is to use the client side toolkits provided by the XKMS service implementers and other third-party library providers. These toolkits are based on proprietary API and they provide some level of insulation form XKMS syntax and semantics. The last option is based on the fact that XKMS is not limited to a SOAP and WSDL based model. Other communication and transport protocols are possible.

3.3 Server Side Options

There are two options for working with XKMS server implementations. One option is to run own XKMS service implementation. The other option is to subscribe to an online XKMS service implementation run by trusted third party.

3.4 Example Using XKMS Service

This case study involves myTravels.com and marriott.com as 2 parties to exchange information. The process starts by both mytravels.com and marriott.com registering their key-pairs with the XKMS trust service using the register service.

As shown in Figure 3, after registering the keys, to encrypt the message to be sent to marriott.com, mytravels.com issues a locate request to the xkms server with the public key of marriott.com. The xkms server responds back with key since marriott.com already has registered its key with the service. My-travels.com uses this public key to encrypt the message, uses its own private key to sign the message, and sends it to marriott.com.

Figure 3. Before and after XKMS

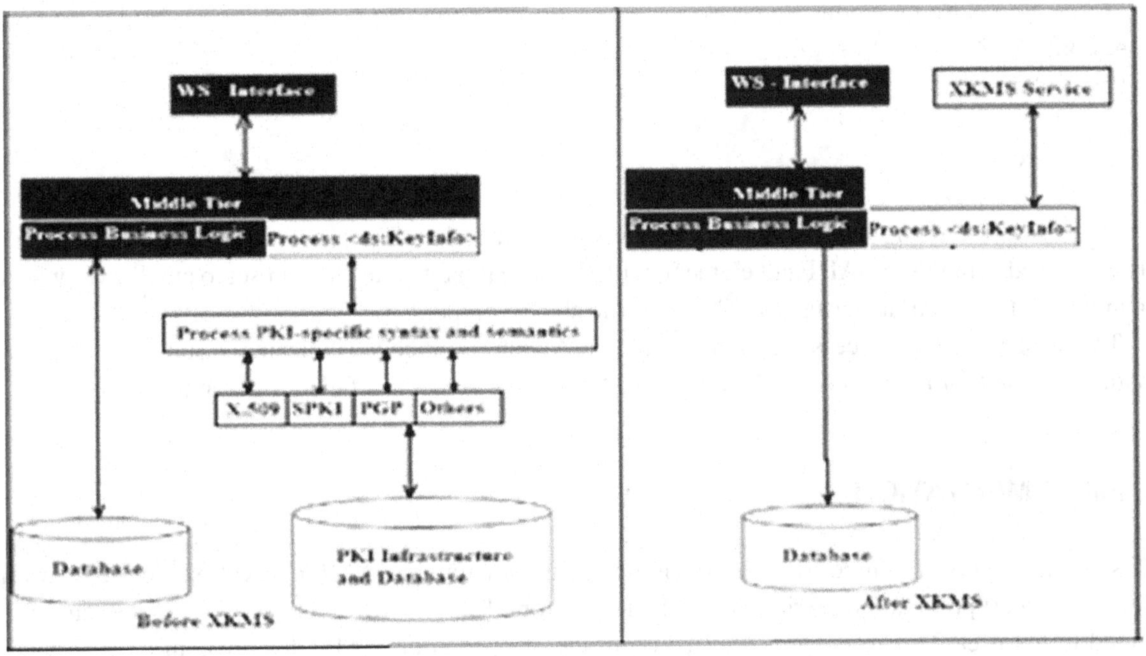

On receipt of the message, Marriott.com passes the <ds:KeyInfo> contained in the signed message to the XKMS service for validation. The XKMS service validates the key information and sends the status back along with the public key details of MyTravels.com. Marriott.com also uses the MyTravels.com public key to validate the signature.

Adding XKMS service to the MyTravels.com application simplifies the implementation, making it possible to delegate the PKI processing to the XKMS service.

3.5 SOAP Binding

When the XKMS messages are exchanged using the SOAP protocol, both the request and the response messages are encoded as an entry in the SOAP Body element. Here is an example of a SOAP encoded XKMS-request message.

```
<env:Envelope xmlns:env="https://www.w3.org/2002/06/soap- envelope"
Xmlns:xkms="http://www/w3.org/2002/03/xkms" Xmlns:ds="https://www.
w3.org/2000/09xmldsig#">
<env:Body>
<LocateRequest xmlns="https://www.w3.org/TR/2002/WD- xkms-2-20020318">
<KeyInfoQuery>
<ds:KeyName xmlns: ds ="https://www.w3.org/2000/09/xmldsig#">
http://marriott.com/key?company=Marriott&amp;department=OnLineReservation&amp;
CN=MarriottCourtyardGroup&am p;
Issuer_serial=8eacea76bcf3e46992493b42671bb9
```

```
<ds:KeyName><KeyInfoQuery>
<Respond>KeyName<Respond>
<Respond>KeyValue</Respond>
</LocateRequest>
</env:Body>
</env:Envelope>
```

When SOAP binding is used, all Result Code values other than Success, Incomplete, and No Match are expressed using the SOAP Fault element, with the SOAP fault code element set to env:Server where env maps to the SOAP namespace as shown in the above snippet.

This is because the Success, Incomplete, and No Match result codes indicate the status of the information returned for the request, and do not indicate that the server has failed to serve the request.

4. IMPLEMENTATION

This article used open source APIs for providing XML signature and XML encryption. At the receiver side, after decryption and integrity check, the required node from XML data set is extracted and presented to the user. This research is focused on usage of open source APIs for invoking web services as restful Web services, applying XML signature and XML encryption, parsing the XML result after reverse process at receiver side and extracting the required nodes according to the user given condition.

It is required to create public/private key pairs and an X.509 certificate by using Sun's keytool application with following command.

```
keytool -genkey -dname "cn=xxx, ou=xyz, o=yyy, c=India" -alias keyfield -key-
pass password -keystore filepath -storepass password
```

The above command generates the secured key with given password.

4.1 Applying XML Encryption Using Open Source API

It is necessary to generate a key to apply XML encryption to the signed XML message. J2SE via its Cryptographic Extension API is quite capable of generating keys for a wide variety of encryption algorithms. This paper uses the Triple DES key which is supported by a vendor – VeriSign for Encryptor object. Next step is to set the Encryptor object from the VeriSign TSIK API to encrypt the message. Here an XPath expression is used to select the element we wish to encrypt. In this case encrypting the entire signed XML message will take care of providing confidentiality to the message.

```
Encryptor e=new Encryptor(se.getAsDocument(), key, AlgorithmType.TRIPLEDES);
Document newD =e.encrypt(new XPath ("//*[name()='/']/*"));
```

4.2 Implementation of XML Decryption Using Open Source API

Decryptor is the VeriSign class used to decrypt the XML message. Here an XPath expression is used to select the element that we wish to decrypt:

```
Decryptor d=new Decryptor(se.getAsDocument(), key, new XPath("//*[name()='xen
c:EncryptedData']")); Document newD=d.decrypt();
```

At the receiver end, encrypted XML signature is decrypted and XML signature is validated as given in the above sections. The validated XML results are read as string, line by line and required nodes are extracted.

4.3 Register a Client Generated Key Pair

This example uses Verisign's API to register a client- generated key pair. The Versign 1.1 XKMS implementation does not support registration of server-generated key pair. The global variables raCert and raKey are the Certificate and key obtained from a Trust service using out-of-band communication for authenticating the sender. It is assume that values for these globals are set at some place prior to invoking the registerClient GeneratedKeyPair() method:

```
Public XKMSRegisterExample (X509Certificate raCert; PrivateKey raKey)
//Name of the key to be registered
String keyName = new String("http://www.mytravels.com/key?company=MyTravels.
com&amp;
Department = HotelReservation&amp;CN=MyTravels HotelGroup&amp");
//URL of the trust service String url=new String
("http://interopXkms.verisign.com/xkms/Acceptor.nano"); String passphrase =
new String ("MyFirstXKMSExample");
```

The certificate and the key used by the sender to sign the entire SOAP message.

Here the passphrase in plain text is used by the client for later revocation or recovery operations. This is sent as part of the

```
<RegisterRequest>element.
```

Collect the register parameters that contain the value and the name of the key to be registered using statement below:

```
XKMSKeyData keyData
=new XKMSKeyData (keyPair, new XKMSKeyName(keyName));
```

4.4 Create a Registration Request Using the Key Data

Here the authentication information is created at first using XKMSRegister request = new XKMSRegister (keyData, authInfo);

```
//Create a SOAP transport = new XmlTransport SOAP (new URL(url));
//This is to sign the whole transported message being sent for integrity.
transport.setSigningPrivateKey(msgSigningKey); transport.setSigningCertificate
(msgSigningCert);
//You can access the key information from the response returned
XKMSRegisterResponse response=request.sendRequest(transport);
}catch (XKMSException e) { If (e.getErrorCode()!=null) {System.out.
println("Code:"+e.getErrorCode());
}catch (Exception ignoreOtherExceptions) {
}//registerClientGeneratedKeyPair
}//XKMSRegisterExample
```

4.5 Locate a Key Using KeyName

In this code snippet it locates a key using a key name: public class LocateKeyUsingKeyName {

```
//This code snippet assumes that values for the following  global are  at some
place prior to invoking the locateKey()method
//URL of the trust service
String url=new String("http://interop -
Xkms.verisign.com/xkms/Acceptor.nano")_;
```

The above statement provides URL of trusted service as a paramenter.

4.6 Certificate and Key Used by Sender to Sign the Whole SOAP Message

```
<ds:KeyName> https://www.mytravels.com/key?company=MyTravels.co m&
amp:department
=
HotelReservation&amp;CN=MyTravelsHotelGroup&am p:
Issuer_serial=8e8934bcf3e469924936b42671bb9
</ds:KeyName>
</KeyInfo>
</Signature>
</SOAP:Body>
</SOAP:Envelope>
```

To provide XML signature, required key is used by the sender and that key is sent through above XML message in the form of encrypted SOAP envelop.

5. RESULT

The SOAP message exchanged between the travel site Mytravels.com and its hotel partner Marriott.com shown in Appendix A. It is found that size of signed SOAP envelop is more than normal SOAP envelop due to attributes of security information.

Figure 4. Result of comparison of normal SOAP message and signed SOAP message

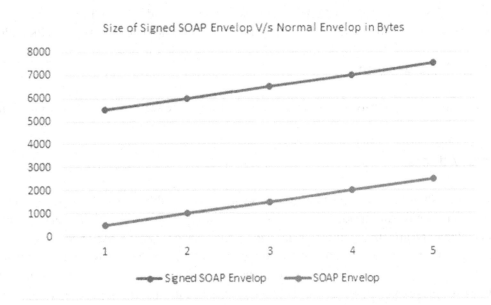

XKMS provides key management facility to the secured web services Mytravels.com. After signing, the signed message is given below in appendix-A is called as Signed SOAP message with XML signature and with XML Encryption. The size of signed SOAP envelope is more compared to unsigned soap message. The analysis of the size of the signed SOAP message with XML signature and XML encryption and unsigned SOAP message is given in the figure 4.

6. ANALYSIS

The XKMS initiative provides several benefits. Some of the most important benefits are:

§ XKMS simplifies usage of XML Signature and XML Encryption mechanisms in XML applications.
§ XKMS provides a simple, XML standards-based protocol for processing key information. This reduce the learning curve of understanding PKI semantics and eliminates the need to work directly with various, complex PKI syntax and semantics, enabling rapid development of trust features in XML applications and XML web services.

§ By moving the complexity of managing PKI out to the infrastructure level, individual applications become smaller and simpler and with their security easier to verify as a result. The use of common PKI infrastructure will make it easier to attain interoperability.

§ Use of XML vocabulary for representing PKI and support for WSDL and SOAP messages makes XKMS services to be platform, vendor, and transport –protocol neutral. XKMS fits into the developing web services environment smoothly.

§ Since much of the processing takes place on the server side, XKMS may make PKI more usable on small footprint devices.

§ Since XKMS builds a layer of abstraction between the application and PKI solutions, it makes it easier for the applications to support multiple PKI solutions and/or switch between different PKI solutions.

6.1 Security Considerations

In this section some of the security issues that could compromise the security of an XKMS implementation is given.

6.1.1 Replay Attacks

Replay of a previously-sent XKMS response is one such security problem that an XKMS server implementation needs to avoid. An intruder could store the messages sent by the XKMS server to play the messages back later and effectively impersonate the XKMS service. The XKMS specification does not mandate any specific mechanism to mitigate such replay attacks. However, XKMS recommends prevention of such attacks and leaves it to the server implementations to use a mechanism of their choice. A common way of preventing replay attacks is to embed a token in each message to demonstrate to the recipient that the message is fresh. The token may need to be signed to guarantee integrity of the token and the message.

Here are some "freshness" tokens that can be used for preventing replay attacks:

- A timestamp specifying the message origination time.
- A nonce, which is a random piece of data previously issued by the user.
- A message serial number could be added.

Such tokens may be encoded as XML Signature properties within the message.

6.1.2 Denial of Service

XKMS implementations need to take measures to prevent or mitigate DOS attacks. Operations such as URL resolution, Signature verification, and Key exchange are some examples of resource-intensive operations. XKMS implementations should avoid performing an unlimited number of resource- intensive operations prior to source authentication.

6.2 Recovery Policy

A key recovery operation may involve an unacceptable loss of confidence in the security of a private key component. This could lead to the possibility of repudiation of a signed document or of accountability of an encrypted document.

The XKMS specification does not mandate any specific recovery policy. XKMS implementations should exercise care in assessing the vulnerability of the recovery operations and accordingly apply sufficient controls, including revocation of the underlying key binding.

6.3 Limited Use of Shared Data

If a limited use shared data is used, care must be taken to ensure that the secret data is not revealed to an attacker. Encrypting the shared secret alone is not sufficient, as the PassPhraseAuth element is not cryptographically bound to the message. Any means employed must provide for both encryption and integrity, such as SSL.

7. CONCLUSION

The result shows that with the use of XML-based trusted web services transaction, the performance of the web transaction will be reduced in terms of speed. But it will be more secure because external signature and external encryption are applied to plain SOAP message. Also the size of the secured soap envelope is more compared to plain SOAP envelope. This reduces the speed of transmission. Mapping keys with PKI in XKMS gives delay to the SOAP envelope. The burden of the web services reduces and web service transaction will be more secured.

REFERENCES

ALRassan, I. (2020). XML Encryption and Signature for Securing Web Services. *International Journal of Computer Science & Information Technology (IJCSIT), 12*(4). https://ssrn.com/abstract=3688789

Beznosov, K., Flinn, S., Kawamoto, S., & Hartman, B. (2005). Introduction to Web services and their security. *Published in: Journal Information Security Tech., 10*(1).

Bhatti, R., Bertino, E., Ghafoor, A., & Joshi, J. B. D. (2004, April). XML- Based Specification for Web Services Document Security. *Journal of Computers, 37*(4).

Braith, B., Hankison, W., Hiotis, A., Galbraith, B., Janakiraman, M., Prasad, D., & Trivedi, R. (2002). *Professional Web Service Security*. Wrox Publication.

El-Aziz, A. & Arputharaj, K.A. (2013). Comprehensive presentation to XML signature and encryption. *2013 International Conference on Recent Trends in Information Technology*. IEEE. doi:10.1109/ICRTIT.2013.6844276

Galbraith, B., Hiotis, A., & Janakiraman, M. (2001). *Professional web services security*. Shroff Publishers & Distributors.

Huang, Y.-W. Tsai, C.H-., Lin, T.-P., Huang, S., Lee, D., & Kuo, S.-Y. (2005). A testing framework for Web application security assessment. *Journal Computer Networks: The International Journal of Computer and Telecommunications Networking - Web security, 48*(5).

Kumar, J., Rajendran, B., Bindhumadhava, B. S., & Chandra Babu, N. S. (2017). XML wrapping attack mitigation using positional token. *International Conference on Public Key Infrastructure and its Applications (PKIA)*, Bangalore, India. 10.1109/PKIA.2017.8278958

NewComer, E. (2022). Understanding Web Services. Addison-Wesley Professional.

Nordbotten, N. A. (2009). XML and Web Services Security Standards. IEEE Communications Surveys & Tutorials. IEEE. doi:10.1109/SURV.2009.090302

OASIS. (n.d.). *Oasis security services (SAML) TC*. OASIS. https://www.oasis-open.org/committees/tc/home.php/wg abbrev=security.

Pawar, S. & Chiplunkar, N. (2018). *Populating Parameters of Web Services by Automatic Composition Using Search Precision and WSDL Weight Matrix*. InderScience Publishers – Scopus indexed.

Ramesh, R. & Khandelwal, S. (2013). A Comprehensive Analysis Of Xml Digital Signature, Xml Encryption And Xkms, *International Journal Of Engineering Research & Technology (Ijert), 02*.

Stubblefield, A. (2005). *Managing the Performance Impact of Web Security*. Kluwer Academic Publishers.

Sumathi, N. (2015). Necessity of Dynamic Composition for Web Services. *IEEE Int. Conference on Applied and Theoretical Computing and Communication Technology*. IEEE.

Supporting Digital Signature by Brenda Coulson. (n.d.). *About*. DEVX. www.devx.com

XML Signature Syntax and Processing Version 1. (n.d.). W3.

APPENDIX A: SIGNED SOAP ENVELOP

```
<SOAP: Envelope
xmlns:SOAP="https://www.w3.org/2000/09/"
xmlns:Travel="http://www.myTravels.com">
<SOAP: Header>
<Travel: Request Type="Reservation" Transaction ID= "36ab70de"
Id="HeaderArulVigReservationRequestNov2002"
From= "MyTravels.com"/>
<SOAP: Header>
<SOAP: Body>
<EncryptedData
xmlns="https://www.w3.org/2001/04/xmlenc#" Type = "http://www.w3.org/2001/04/
xmlenc#Element"
Id=
"ArulVigReservationRequestNov2002">
<EncryptionMethod
Alogorithm="http://www.w3.org/2001/04xmlenc#tri
pledes-cbc"/>
<CipherData>
<CipherValue>jklekm=</CipherValue>
</CipherData>
</EncrypteData>
<Signature
Id="SignatureArulVigReservationRequestNov2002" Xmlns="https://www.
w3.org/2000/09/xmldsig#">
<SignedInfo>
<CanonicalizationMethod>
Algorithm="https://www.w3.org/TR/2001/REC-xml- c14n-20010315"/>
<SignatureMethod
Algorithm="http://www.w3.org/2000/09/xmldsig#ds
a-shal"/>
<Reference URI="#ArulVigReservationRequestNov2002">
<Transforms>
<Transform
Algorithm="https://www.w3.org/TR/2001/REC-xml- c14n-20010315"/>
<Transform>
<ds:Transform
Algorithm="https://www.w3.org/2002/07/decrypt"
```

```
xmlns:dcrpt="https://www.w3.org/2002/07/decrypt#">
<dcrpt:Except URI =
"#ArulVigReservationRequestNov2002"/>
<ds:Transform>
</Transforms>
<DigitMethodAlgorithm="http://www.w3.org/2000/09/xmldsig#shal"/>
<DigestValue>j61wx3rvEPOOvKtMup4NbeVu8nk=</Digest Value>
</DigestMethod>
</Reference>
<Reference
URI="#HeaderArulVigReservationRequestNov2002">
<Transforms>
<Transform
Algorithm="https://www.w3.org/TR/2001/REC-xml- c14n-20010315"/>
</Transform>
</Transforms>
<DigestMethodAlgorithm="http://www.w3.org/2000/09/xmldsig#shal"/>
<DigestValue>EPOOvKtuyMup4Nbe=</DigestValue>
</DigestMethod>
</Reference>
</SignedInfo>
<SignatureValue>MCOCFFrVLtRlk=</SignatureValue>
<KeyInfo>
<ds:KeyName>
http://www.mytravels.com/key?company=MyTravels.com& amp:department
=
HotelReservation&amp;CN=MyTravelsHotelGroup&amp: Issuer_serial=8e8934bcf3e4699
24936b42671bb9
</ds:KeyName>
</KeyInfo>
</Signature>
</SOAP:Body>
</SOAP:Envelope>
```

Chapter 7
Artificial Intelligence and Machine Learning for Cybersecurity Applications and Challenges

Aditya Roshan Sinha
Chandigarh University, India

Kunal Singla
Chandigarh University, India

Teresa Matoso Manguangua Victor
Instituto Superior Politécnico de Tecnologias e Ciências, Angola

ABSTRACT

This chapter discusses the potential of artificial intelligence (AI) and machine learning (ML) to revolutionize cybersecurity by automating threat detection and response. It reviews the key use cases for AI and ML in cybersecurity, such as network security, threat intelligence, and incident response, and the technical challenges involved in developing AI and ML-based cybersecurity solutions, such as data labeling and model interpretability. It also discusses the broader societal implications of the increasing use of AI and ML in cybersecurity, such as the potential for the creation of new security vulnerabilities and the need for ethical considerations in the development and deployment of these technologies. The chapter aims to provide practical insights and recommendations for organizations looking to implement AI and ML in their cybersecurity strategies, highlighting both the opportunities and challenges that arise when applying these technologies to the complex and rapidly evolving landscape of cybersecurity.

DOI: 10.4018/978-1-6684-9317-5.ch007

A BRIEF INTRODUCTION TO AI AND MACHINE LEARNING FOR CYBERSECURITY

As the world becomes increasingly reliant on technology, cybersecurity is more important than ever. With the rise of cyberattacks and cyber threats, organizations and individuals are seeking new and innovative ways to protect themselves from these threats. One solution that has gained popularity in the recent past the application of machine learning and artificial intelligence for cybersecurity. AI and ML can help identify threats, analyze them, and take appropriate action to mitigate or prevent them. We will examine the uses and difficulties of AI and ML for cybersecurity in this chapter.

What Is AI and Machine Learning?

The invention of computer systems that are capable of doing activities that traditionally require human intellect, such as perception, reasoning, learning, and problem-solving, is known as artificial intelligence (AI). Rule-based systems, expert systems, neural networks, and genetic algorithms are only a few of the numerous types of AI systems that may be divided into groups (Li et al., 2019).

On the other hand, machine learning is an subfield of artificial intelligence that focuses on creating algorithms and statistical models that enable computer systems that draw conclusions or judgements from data without being expressly programmed. To put it another way, machine learning algorithms are made to learn from examples, patterns, and correlations in data and then apply that information to create predictions or conclusions about fresh data.

Algorithms for machine learning can be classified into three categories: reinforcement learning, supervised learning and unsupervised learning (Al-Fuqaha, Guizani, Mohammadi, Aledhari, & Ayyash, 2015). In supervised learning, a model is trained using labelled data, while unsupervised learning involves discovering patterns and relationships in unlabeled data. Reinforcement learning, on the other hand, involves training a model to make decisions based on rewards or penalties received from the environment.

Overall, AI and machine learning are rapidly developing fields that are revolutionizing numerous areas, including transportation, entertainment, and the financial and healthcare sectors.

Why Use AI and ML for Cybersecurity?

Traditional cybersecurity solutions rely on rule-based systems that look for specific patterns of data or activity that indicate a threat. However, these systems can be limited in their effectiveness, as they may not be able to detect new or evolving threats. By examining vast volumes of data and finding patterns which could be suggestive of a threat, AI and ML can assist in resolving this issue.

There are several reasons why AI (Artificial Intelligence) and ML (Machine Learning) are being used in cybersecurity:

1. **Automation:** AI and ML can automate many cybersecurity tasks, such as threat detection, incident response, and vulnerability management. This automation can reduce the workload on security analysts and improve the speed and accuracy of security operations.
2. **Real-Time Analysis:** AI and ML algorithms can analyze large volumes of data in real-time, which is critical in detecting and responding to security threats quickly. Traditional security methods often

require time-consuming manual analysis, which can delay threat response and increase the risk of a successful attack.

3. **Detection of Advanced Threats:** Advanced threats, such as targeted attacks and zero-day attacks, are often difficult to detect using traditional security methods. AI and ML can help identify these threats by looking through a lot of data to find trends and abnormalities that could point to a security flaw.

4. **Improved Accuracy:** AI and ML algorithms can analyze data more accurately and consistently than humans, which can reduce the risk of false positives and false negatives in threat detection.

5. **Scalability:** AI and ML can scale to handle large amounts of data and rapidly evolving threat landscapes. This scalability is critical in today's cybersecurity environment, where the volume and complexity of data continue to increase.

Overall, AI and ML are being used in cybersecurity to make security operations more effective and efficient and to address the increasing complexity of the threat landscape.

Applications of AI and ML in Cybersecurity

There are many potential applications of AI and ML in cybersecurity. Some examples include:

1. **Threat detection:** ML algorithms can analyze network traffic, logs, and other data sources to identify patterns that may be indicative of a threat. Organizations may benefit from quicker and more effective threat detection and response thanks to this.

2. **Malware detection:** ML algorithms can learn to identify patterns in code that may be indicative of malware (Almgren et al., 2018). As a result, businesses may be able to identify malware more quickly and efficiently.

3. **Fraud detection:** ML algorithms can learn to identify patterns in financial data that may be indicative of fraud. This can make it easier for financial institutions to immediately identify and stop fraud.

4. **User behavior analysis:** ML algorithms can analyze user behavior to identify patterns that may be indicative of a threat. This may make it easier for businesses to identify insider dangers and take prompt, appropriate action.

5. **Vulnerability Management:** Prioritizing vulnerabilities is possible using AI and ML. based on their likelihood of being exploited and their potential impact on the organization. Algorithms for machine learning may also be used to make predictions, the likelihood of future vulnerabilities based on historical data.

6. **Incident Response:** Processes involved in incident response, such as disconnecting infected devices, can be automated using AI and ML. can be automated using AI and ML. and blocking malicious traffic. Machine learning algorithms can also be used to learn from previous incidents and improve the response to future incidents.

Challenges of AI and ML in Cybersecurity

While there are many potential benefits to using AI and ML in cybersecurity, there are also several challenges that must be addressed. Some of these challenges include:

1. **Data quality:** Large volumes of good-quality data are needed for ML systems to learn from. If the information is inadequate, the algorithm may not be able to learn effectively.
2. **Bias:** If ML algorithms are developed on data that is not representative of the society they are supposed to study, they may become biassed. This can lead to incorrect or unfair predictions.
3. **Adversarial attacks:** ML algorithms can be vulnerable to attacks that are designed to trick them into making incorrect predictions. This can be a serious problem in cybersecurity, as attackers may be able to exploit vulnerabilities in the algorithm to bypass security measures.
4. **Interpretability:** The interpretation of ML algorithms can be challenging, making it difficult to comprehend how predictions are being made. Because of this, it could be challenging to put your confidence in their forecasts and base your judgements on them.
5. **Data Privacy and Security:** AI and ML rely heavily on data, which can be a double-edged sword. While data can help train these systems, it can also be a target for cybercriminals (Amiri et al., 2020). Therefore, organizations must ensure that they collect and store data securely to prevent unauthorized access or misuse.
6. **Lack of Skilled Professionals:** As AI and ML continue to evolve, there is a shortage of skilled professionals with the skills and knowledge necessary to plan, create, and implement these technologies in the cybersecurity field.

Machine Learning Techniques for Cybersecurity

A subfield of artificial intelligence called machine learning is concerned with creating algorithms that can learn from data and generate predictions or judgements without being explicitly programmed. There are several machine learning techniques, each with its own strengths, weaknesses, and suitable use cases. Here's an overview of some of the most common techniques:

1. **Supervised Learning:** The machine learning algorithm is taught using the supervised learning method on a labelled dataset that contains input and related output data. By identifying patterns in the data, the algorithm learns how to translate inputs into outputs (Bhattacharya et al., 2019). This technique is commonly used for prediction problems, such as classification (e.g., distinguishing between different types of images) or regression (e.g., predicting the price of a house based on its characteristics).
2. **Unsupervised Learning:** Unsupervised learning uses an unlabeled dataset to train the machine learning algorithm, which means that there is no output variable associated with the input data. The algorithm learns to find patterns in the data, such as clustering similar data points or identifying unusual data points. This technique is commonly used for exploratory analysis, anomaly detection, or data compression.
3. **Reinforcement Learning:** The machine learning system learns to make decisions depending on rewards or penalties it gets from its environment using the reinforcement learning approach. Over time, the algorithm develops the ability to operate in a way that maximises its rewards. This method is frequently applied to robotics, gaming, and self-driving car navigation.
4. **Deep Learning:** Deep learning is a subset of machine learning that uses artificial neural networks, which are based on the design of the human brain, to learn from data. Deep learning is particularly useful for processing large and complex datasets, such as images, audio, and natural language, and has been used for jobs like speech recognition, language translation, and picture categorization.

These are only a handful of the numerous machine learning techniques that are available. Choosing the right technique depends on the specific problem you are trying to solve and the characteristics of your data.

Overview of AI and Machine Learning Techniques

Feature selection and engineering are crucial steps in developing effective cybersecurity applications. Here are some considerations for feature selection and engineering in this context:

1.1 Domain knowledge: Understanding the relevant domain is important for identifying the features that are most relevant for cybersecurity applications. This knowledge can come from experts in the field, security analysts, or security software developers.

1.2 Data collection: Collecting data from various sources is important for identifying features that are useful for cybersecurity applications. This data can be gathered from security logs, network traffic, and other sources that can provide information about the behavior of the system and its users.

1.3 Data preprocessing: Preprocessing data is essential for identifying relevant features. This can involve cleaning and transforming the data, identifying missing values, and dealing with outliers. Feature extraction techniques such as dimensionality reduction or feature scaling can also be used to reduce the amount of data needed for analysis.

1.4 Feature selection: Selecting the most important features from the available data is important for developing effective cybersecurity applications. This can be achieved using various techniques such as correlation analysis, statistical tests, or machine learning algorithms. The goal is to identify features that have the most significant impact on the security of the system and its users (Buczak & Guven, 2016).

1.5 Feature engineering: Feature engineering involves creating new features that are not present in the original dataset. This can involve combining existing features or creating new features based on domain knowledge. Feature engineering can help to identify complex relationships between features that may not be apparent from the original data.

1.6 Model selection: Once the features have been identified, it is important to select the appropriate model for the specific cybersecurity application. This may involve using classification, clustering, or anomaly detection algorithms, depending on the specific use case.

Overall, selecting and engineering features is an important part of developing effective cybersecurity applications. By combining domain knowledge, data collection, preprocessing, and modeling techniques, It is possible to decide which aspects are most important and create cybersecurity apps that work well (Buczak & Guven, 2018a).

Supervised Learning Algorithms for Cybersecurity

Supervised learning algorithms are commonly used in cybersecurity for various applications, such as intrusion detection, malware analysis, and anomaly detection. Here are some common supervised learning algorithms used in cybersecurity:

1   **Random Forest:** Several decision trees are used in Random Forest, an ensemble learning technique, to increase accuracy and decrease overfitting. It is often used for classifying malware and detecting intrusions.

2   **Support Vector Machines (SVM):** SVM is a binary classification algorithm that separates data points using a hyperplane. It is often used for detecting intrusions and classifying malware.

3   **Neural Networks:** Neural networks are powerful machine learning algorithms that can learn complex patterns from data. A broad spectrum of cybersecurity tasks such as detecting unauthorized access and identifying malicious software can be accomplished using them.

4   **Decision Trees:** Decision trees are simple algorithms that use a tree-like model to classify data. They are often used for intrusion detection and identifying anomalous behavior.

5   **Naive Bayes:** Naive Bayes is a statistical technique that utilizes Bayes' theorem to calculate probabilities. It is often used for classifying emails as spam or not spam.

6   **Logistic Regression:** Logistic regression is a binary classification algorithm that is used for predicting the probability of a certain event occurring. It can be used for detecting intrusions and identifying anomalous behavior.

7   **k-Nearest Neighbors (k-NN):** The k-NN algorithm is an uncomplicated technique that categorizes data by considering the classification of its nearest k neighbors. It is often used for intrusion detection and identifying anomalous behavior.

These are just a few examples of supervised learning algorithms that can be used in cybersecurity. The selection of an algorithm is determined by the particular problem being addressed and the attributes of the information involved.

Unsupervised Learning Algorithms for Cybersecurity

Unsupervised learning algorithms can be useful in the field of cybersecurity for detecting anomalies and potential threats (Buonocunto et al., 2019). Here are some examples of unsupervised learning algorithms that can be used:

1   **Clustering:** Clustering algorithms group similar data points together based on their similarity. In the context of cybersecurity, clustering can be used to group network traffic or user behavior patterns, and identify anomalies or potential threats.

2   **Principal component analysis (PCA):** PCA is a statistical method employed for reducing the number of dimensions in a dataset, while also preserving a significant amount of its variability. In cybersecurity, PCA can be used to identify patterns in network traffic that may be indicative of malicious activity.

3   **Autoencoders:** Autoencoders are a type of neural network that undergoes training to acquire the ability to generate a condensed version of the input data. In cybersecurity, autoencoders can be used to identify anomalies in network traffic or user behavior.

4   **Generative adversarial networks (GANs):** GANs refer to deep learning models that can produce novel data that shares characteristics with a specific dataset. In the realm of cybersecurity, GANs have the potential to generate artificial data that may be useful for training other models.

5   **Isolation Forests:** Isolation Forests are tree-based anomaly detection algorithms that can be used to detect outliers or anomalies in large datasets. In cybersecurity, Isolation Forests can be used to identify potential threats or malicious activity.

These unsupervised learning algorithms can help in identifying and preventing cyber attacks before they can cause harm to an organization or individual (Carlin et al., 2018). However, It's crucial to acknowledge that utilizing these algorithms alone may not provide comprehensive security measures. It's recommended to combine them with other cybersecurity measures, such as firewalls and intrusion detection systems, to achieve a more holistic approach to security.

Reinforcement Learning for Cybersecurity

Reinforcement learning (RL) is a machine learning subset that trains an agent to make decisions in a given environment based on rewards or penalties. Its versatility has demonstrated its potential in various domains such as gaming, robotics, and autonomous driving. However, there is a recent upswing in the use of RL in cybersecurity.

One of the main applications of RL in cybersecurity is intrusion detection. In this case, an RL agent is trained to detect and prevent attacks on a network. The agent is trained on a dataset of normal and abnormal network traffic, and it learns to detect abnormal traffic and trigger an alarm when an attack is detected. This can be particularly effective for detecting zero-day attacks, which are previously unknown attacks that do not match any existing signatures or patterns (Chandola et al., 2009).

Another application of RL in cybersecurity is malware analysis. In this case, an RL agent is trained to analyze malware behavior and detect malicious code. The agent is trained on a dataset of benign and malicious code, and it learns to identify the features that distinguish malicious code from benign code. This can be particularly effective for detecting new malware that has not been seen before.

A third application of RL in cybersecurity is network defense. In this case, an RL agent is trained to develop a defense system that can automatically respond to attacks on a network. The agent is trained to learn the optimal response to different types of attacks. The agent can then be used to automatically respond to attacks, for example by blocking traffic or quarantining infected devices.

Although RL presents promising advantages in cybersecurity, it also poses some difficulties that require attention. One of these challenges is the inadequacy of labeled data available for training RL agents. Collecting and labeling sufficient data to train an RL agent effectively can be a demanding task in numerous cases. This can be particularly true for new and emerging threats.

Another challenge is the complexity of the cybersecurity environment. The cybersecurity ecosystem is in a state of constant change, with novel threats and attacks arising frequently. This means that RL agents need to be able to adapt quickly to new threats and attacks. This can be particularly challenging for RL agents that are trained on static datasets.

In conclusion, RL has the potential to be a powerful tool in the fight against cyber threats. It can be used for intrusion detection, malware analysis, and network defense. HoweverThe performance of RL-based systems is reliant on the data quality used to train the agent, as well as the complexity of the attacks it intends to counter. As the cybersecurity ecosystem progresses, it's crucial to pursue the possibilities of applying RL in cybersecurity and establish novel methods to tackle the associated difficulties (Almukaynizi, 2020).

AI Techniques for Cybersecurity

Artificial Intelligence (AI) is playing an increasingly important role in cybersecurity, as traditional cybersecurity methods are no longer enough to protect against sophisticated cyber threats. AI techniques have the ability to analyze large amounts of data, identify patterns, and detect anomalies that are difficult for humans to identify. Here are some AI techniques used in cybersecurity:

Natural Language Processing (NLP)

NLP is a subset of artificial intelligence that concentrates on the interplay between computers and human language. This techniques can be used in cybersecurity to analyze text data, such as emails, chat messages, and social media posts. It can be used to detect phishing emails, which may use social engineering to trick users into revealing sensitive information. By analyzing the language used in the email, NLP can identify common patterns or keywords that are often used in phishing attacks.

Behavioral Analytics

Behavioral analytics is the process of using data to identify patterns of behavior. Behavioral analytics can be utilized in the realm of cybersecurity to identify irregularities in network traffic or user behavior. By analyzing data such as login times, file access patterns, and user locations, behavioral analytics can identify suspicious activity that may indicate a cyber attack.

Predictive Analytics

Predictive analytics refers to the practice of utilizing historical data, statistical algorithms, and machine learning methods to determine the probability of future results. In cybersecurity, predictive analytics can be employed to anticipate possible cyber threats before they materialize. By analyzing historical data on cyber attacks, predictive analytics can identify patterns or trends that may indicate a future attack.

Cybersecurity Automation

Cybersecurity automation uses AI and machine learning to automate security tasks, such as threat detection, incident response, and vulnerability management. By automating these tasks, cybersecurity professionals can respond to threats faster and more efficiently. By doing so, it's possible to decrease the duration required to discover and react to cyber assaults, thus lessening the destruction produced by the attack.

In conclusion, AI techniques are becoming increasingly important in cybersecurity, as cyber threats become more sophisticated and complex. By using machine learning, natural language processing, deep learning, behavioral analytics, predictive analytics, and cybersecurity automation, cybersecurity professionals can quickly identify and respond to cyber threats, helping to protect against potential data breaches and cyber attacks.

Neural Networks for Cybersecurity

Neural networks are an AI algorithm variety that has proven successful in several fields, including cybersecurity. Their capacity to learn from massive amounts of data and identify intricate patterns that may signify a cyber threat makes them a potent instrument for identifying and addressing such risks.

In cybersecurity, neural networks have been used for tasks such as intrusion detection, malware classification, and network traffic analysis. The ability of neural networks to automatically learn features from data makes them particularly useful for detecting unknown or zero-day attacks, which traditional security systems may not be able to detect (Akintoye & Alaba, 2020).

One of the most common applications of neural networks in cybersecurity is intrusion detection. Intrusion detection systems (IDS) are crafted to supervise network traffic and recognize trends that might denote an assault. IDS can be classified into two types: signature-based and anomaly-based. Signature-based IDS employ a collection of established attack signatures to detect cyber attacks, whereas anomaly-based IDS detect traffic that deviates from normal behavior. Neural networks can be applied to enhance both types of IDS.

For example, a neural network can be trained on a dataset of normal and abnormal network traffic. The network can learn to identify patterns that are associated with a cyber attack, such as unusual traffic spikes or unusual combinations of protocols. Once the neural network has been trained, it can be used to classify new network traffic and alert security professionals when an attack is detected (Alvarez & Vaisman, 2020).

Another common application of neural networks in cybersecurity is malware classification. Malware is a major threat to cybersecurity, and traditional signature-based antivirus software may not be able to detect new or unknown malware. Neural networks can be trained to classify malware based on its behavior, such as the actions it takes on a system or the files it modifies. Once the neural network has been trained, it can be used to identify new or unknown malware and respond to the threat accordingly.

Neural networks can also be used for network traffic analysis. The practice of network traffic analysis encompasses scrutinizing network traffic with the intention of identifying behavior patterns that might signify a cyber attack. Neural networks can be trained to identify patterns of traffic that are associated with different types of cyber attacks, such as denial-of-service attacks or port scans. Once the neural network has been trained, It has the potential to be utilized in real-time to automatically detect and counter cyber attacks.

One of the difficulties in implementing neural networks in cybersecurity is the necessity for substantial amounts of training data that are of excellent quality. Neural networks require a significant amount of training data to accurately learn the features of a dataset, Moreover, the caliber of the training data is crucial as it can significantly affect the performance of the neural network. Additionally, neural networks can be vulnerable to adversarial attacks in which an attacker deliberately alters the input data to cause the network to make inaccurate forecasts.

Despite these challenges, neural networks have the potential to significantly improve the state of cybersecurity. By automatically learning from large volumes of data and identifying complex patterns that may indicate a cyber attack, Neural networks can assist cybersecurity experts in promptly and efficiently recognizing and responding to security threats.

Deep Learning for Cybersecurity

Deep learning has become a potent asset for cybersecurity as it can quickly and accurately identify and react to intricate and changing security hazards. In this article, we'll explore how deep learning is being used in cybersecurity and its potential benefits and limitations.

Deep learning is a type of machine learning that employs neural networks to acquire knowledge and generate predictions based on data. When applied to cybersecurity, deep learning techniques have a broad range of uses, such as identifying malware, detecting intrusions, enhancing network security, and assessing system vulnerabilities.

Deep learning is advantageous in its capability to detect patterns and irregularities in massive data sets, making it a useful tool in cybersecurity where threats can be subtle and hard to identify. By training deep learning models on extensive amounts of data, they can identify patterns and anomalies that may go undetected by conventional signature-based methods (Arora & Kapoor, 2019).

One application of deep learning in cybersecurity is malware detectionMalware refers to malicious software that is specifically designed to cause harm or exploit vulnerabilities in computer systems. Deep learning models can be trained to identify patterns in malware code, behavior, or network traffic, allowing them to detect and block new and unknown malware in real time.

Deep learning has found another application in cybersecurity, which is intrusion detection. Intrusion detection systems (IDS) are designed to monitor network traffic and identify any unauthorized access or malicious activity. Deep learning models can be trained to analyze network traffic and detect suspicious patterns that may indicate an intrusion. They can also learn from past attacks to improve their accuracy and speed in detecting future attacks.

Deep learning can also be used to improve network security by identifying and mitigating vulnerabilities. Vulnerability assessment involves identifying weaknesses in a network that could be exploited by an attacker. Deep learning models can be used to scan a network for vulnerabilities and prioritize them based on the likelihood and severity of an attack (Bhowmik et al., 2020).

While deep learning has many potential benefits for cybersecurity, it also has some limitations. One major obstacle is the requirement of significant amounts of annotated data to effectively train deep learning models. In cybersecurity, this can be particularly challenging, as data sets may be limited, and labeling may be time-consuming and costly.

Deep learning in cybersecurity has a limitation of false positives and false negatives, where false positives refer to the incorrect identification of a threat that is not actually present, and false negatives refer to the failure of a model to identify a threat that actually exists. This can be particularly problematic in cybersecurity, as false positives can lead to unnecessary alerts and wasted resources, while false negatives can result in undetected threats.

In addition, deep learning models can be vulnerable to attacks themselves. Adversaries can attempt to manipulate the data used to train a model or manipulate the model's outputs to evade detection. This highlights the need for robust and secure deep learning models that are resistant to adversarial attacks.

Despite these challenges, deep learning has the potential to revolutionize cybersecurity by enabling faster, more accurate, and more scalable threat detection and responseAs the domain of cybersecurity progresses, it is expected that more developments will emerge in tools and techniques for cybersecurity that rely on deep learning.

In conclusion, Deep learning is a robust and effective tool for cybersecurity that provides a variety of applications for network security, vulnerability assessment, and detecting threats. However, it also has limitations and challenges that must be addressed to ensure its effectiveness and security. As cybersecurity threats continue to evolve, deep learning is expected to have a growing significance in safeguarding our digital assets and infrastructure.

Natural Language Processing for Cybersecurity

Natural Language Processing (NLP) is a specialized area within the field of Artificial Intelligence (AI) that focuses on enabling machines to communicate and understand human language in a natural way. With the proliferation of the internet and the rise of connected devices, the importance of cybersecurity has increased. NLP has the potential to significantly improve cybersecurity by processing natural language data and detecting possible security threats. In this article, we will explore the applications of NLP in cybersecurity.

Threat Intelligence

NLP can aid in the collection and analysis of massive quantities of unstructured data from various sources, including social media, blogs, forums, and news sites. By using machine learning algorithms, NLP can identify patterns and extract relevant information from this data to identify potential security threats. This can help security analysts to stay ahead of potential cyber-attacks (Bishop, 2019).

Malware Detection

Malware can be disguised in many ways, and it can be difficult to detect. NLP can help in identifying malicious code by analyzing the natural language content in email messages and social media posts. NLP algorithms can detect suspicious language patterns that are commonly associated with malware and flag them for further analysis.

Identity Verification

Identity verification is a crucial component of cybersecurity. NLP algorithms can help in verifying the identity of a user by analyzing their natural language content. By comparing the user's writing style and language patterns with their previous interactions, NLP can detect potential fraud or impersonation attempts.

Cyber Threat Hunting

Cyber threat hunting involves proactively searching for potential threats within an organization's network. NLP can be used to identify suspicious patterns in the natural language content of emails and other communication channels. By analyzing language patterns, NLP can detect potential phishing attempts and other social engineering attacks (Bouzeghoub & Zeghidour, 2021).

Incident Response

In the event of a cyber-attack, NLP can help in analyzing the language content of emails and other communication channels to identify the source of the attack. NLP algorithms can also be used to generate automated responses to contain the attack and prevent further damage.

Compliance Monitoring

Many industries have strict regulations that require companies to monitor their communication channels to ensure compliance. NLP can be used to monitor the natural language content of emails and other communication channels to ensure that they comply with regulatory requirements. NLP algorithms can detect potential violations and flag them for further review.

In conclusion, NLP can play a crucial role in enhancing cybersecurity by analyzing natural language data and identifying potential threats. With the rise of connected devices and the proliferation of data, the importance of NLP in cybersecurity is only going to increase in the future. By leveraging NLP algorithms, organizations can proactively identify potential security threats and take preventive measures to secure their networks.

Genetic Algorithms for Cybersecurity

Genetic algorithms (GAs) are an optimization technique that mimics the process of natural selection to find the best possible solution to a problem. This is done by creating a population of candidate solutions and repeatedly selecting, breeding, and mutating them to generate increasingly better solutions. GAs have been successfully applied in various fields, including cybersecurity. In this article, we will explore the applications of genetic algorithms in cybersecurity.

Password Cracking

Password cracking is a common method of cyber-attack. Hackers can use brute force methods or password lists to crack passwords. GAs can be used to generate candidate passwords and evolve them through successive generations until the correct password is found. By incorporating heuristics that mimic human password creation patterns, GAs can improve the success rate of password cracking attacks.

Malware Detection

Malware detection is a challenging problem due to the rapid evolution of malware. GAs can be used to evolve malware samples and generate new strains of malware that are not detected by current antivirus software. By repeatedly testing and refining these samples, attackers can create malware that can evade detection and compromise systems.

Intrusion Detection

The function of intrusion detection systems (IDS) is to observe network traffic and recognize possible security risks. Genetic algorithms (GAs) can be employed to enhance the detection of potential attacks by optimizing the rules used by IDS (Chen et al., 2020). By evolving the rules through successive generations, GAs can improve the accuracy and speed of intrusion detection.

Vulnerability Analysis

Vulnerability analysis is the process of identifying and mitigating security weaknesses in software systems. GAs can be used to generate inputs that cause software to fail or reveal security vulnerabilities. By evolving these inputs through successive generations, GAs can identify previously unknown vulnerabilities and help developers to fix them.

Network Security

Network security is critical to protect against cyber-attacks. GAs can be used to optimize the configuration of network security parameters, such as firewall rules and access controls. By evolving the configuration through successive generations, GAs can identify the most effective set of parameters to protect against potential threats (Chhetri & Singh, 2020).

Cryptography

Cryptography is the science of securing communication using mathematical algorithms. The optimization process of genetic algorithms can be utilized to enhance the security of cryptographic algorithms by fine-tuning their parameters. By evolving the parameters through successive generations, GAs can identify the optimal set of parameters that provide the best balance of security and performance.

In conclusion, genetic algorithms have been successfully applied in various fields, including cybersecurity. By evolving candidate solutions through successive generations, GAs can help attackers to find optimal solutions to cyber-attacks, or help defenders to optimize security parameters and identify vulnerabilities. However, GAs can also be used by attackers to create new strains of malware and evade detection. Therefore, Defenders need to be conscious of the potential threats posed by GAs-based attacks and create measures to protect against them (Chu & Chen, 2019).

Cyber Threat Detection and Prevention With AI and Machine Learning

The rising number and complexity of cyber threats have made cybersecurity a crucial concern for both businesses and individuals. To address this issue, AI and machine learning techniques can be utilized for detecting and preventing cyber threats. This article will examine the various ways in which AI and machine learning can be applied to cyber threat detection and prevention.

Anomaly Detection

To detect patterns in data that deviate from the expected norms, anomaly detection is used. In cybersecurity, anomaly detection helps to detect abnormal behavior that could be a sign of a cyber-attack. Machine learning algorithms can be taught using past data to recognize usual behavior patterns and identify anomalies that could indicate a potential threat. By continuously monitoring network traffic and system logs, these algorithms can detect and alert security teams to potential threats.

Predictive Analytics

Predictive analytics involves using historical data and machine learning algorithms to predict future events. In cybersecurity, predictive analytics can be used to identify potential threats before they occur. By analyzing data from multiple sources, including user behavior, system logs, and network traffic, predictive analytics algorithms can identify patterns that may indicate a future threat. This enables security teams to proactively take steps to prevent the threat before it materializes.

Malware Detection

Malware is a significant threat to cybersecurityMachine learning techniques have the capability to analyze codes and behavioral patterns to identify novel types of malware. By training on large datasets of known malware and legitimate software, these algorithms can accurately identify potential threats and alert security teams to take action (Cosgrave et al., 2021).

Behavior-Based Detection

Behavior-based detection involves monitoring system and user behavior to identify potential threats. Machine learning algorithms can be trained to identify patterns of behavior that may indicate a cyber-attack. By monitoring system logs and network traffic, these algorithms can detect unusual patterns of behavior and alert security teams to investigate potential threats.

Continuous Learning

As cyber threats continue to evolve and new ones arise frequently, machine learning algorithms can be trained to learn and adapt to these new threats on a continuous basis. By updating their algorithms and training on new data, these algorithms can identify and prevent new threats as they emerge.

In conclusion, AI and machine learning can be powerful tools in the fight against cyber threats. By using advanced algorithms to analyze data and identify potential threats, Although security teams can utilize machine learning algorithms to anticipate and thwart potential cyber-attacks, it is important to acknowledge that these algorithms are not completely infallible and may be vulnerable to evasion tactics employed by advanced attackers (Debar et al., 2020). Therefore, it is critical for security teams to continuously monitor and update their systems to stay ahead of potential threats.

Overview of Cyber Threats

Cyber threats refer to any form of malicious activity that seeks to damage, disrupt, or steal data and information from digital devices or networks. As our world becomes increasingly digitized, cyber threats have become more frequent, sophisticated, and costly. In this article, We will present a summary of some of the frequently occurring types of cyber threats (Dougan, 2019).

Malware: Malware refers to a category of software created with the intention of causing damage or exploiting vulnerabilities on devices, networks, or applications. This can take many forms, including viruses, trojans, ransomware, and spyware. Malware is often spread through malicious email attachments, phishing links, or fake software downloads.

Phishing: Phishing is a kind of manipulation tactic used by hackers to deceive a user into giving away confidential information, such as login details or financial data. These attacks usually employ bogus emails or websites that seem genuine but are specifically intended to obtain information illicitly.

DDoS Attacks: A DDoS attack is when an effort is made to flood a website or network with traffic in order to overwhelm it and make it inaccessible to users. This can be done by infecting devices with malware and using them to launch the attack, or by utilizing a botnet, which is a group of infected devices working together. The result is a website or network that crashes or becomes unavailable to its intended audience.

Man-in-the-Middle (MitM) Attacks: A man-in-the-middle attack is a situation where a cyber attacker intercepts the communication between two parties and tries to steal or alter the information that is being transmitted. MitM attacks can be carried out by intercepting Wi-Fi signals or by using malware to intercept communication.

Insider Threats: Insider threats refer to attacks that are carried out by individuals within an organization, such as employees or contractors. Insider threats can be intentional, where the individual intends to harm the organization, or unintentional, where the individual accidentally causes harm through negligence or lack of training.

Advanced Persistent Threats (APTs): APTs refer to advanced persistent threats which are prolonged and focused cyber attacks that aim to collect confidential data from a specific target without being discovered. APTs often involve sophisticated techniques, such as custom malware and social engineering. Usually, APTs are perpetrated by either government-sponsored organizations or criminal groups involved in cybercrime.

Ransomware: Ransomware refers to a form of malicious software that encodes the files of its target and seeks payment in return for the key to decode them. Cybercriminals may use phishing messages or exploit software weaknesses to execute ransomware attacks (Adadi & Berrada, 2018).

Zero-Day Exploits: A zero-day exploit is a form of cyber-attack that capitalizes on a weakness in software before it is identified or fixed. Zero-day exploits can be used to infect devices with malware or to steal sensitive data.

In conclusion, cyber threats are a significant risk for individuals, businesses, and governments. In light of our increasing dependence on digital technology, it is crucial to recognize potential risks and take measures to safeguard against them. These precautions encompass creating robust passwords, regularly updating software, and exercising vigilance when encountering dubious emails and websites. Furthermore, organizations and governing bodies should allocate resources towards cybersecurity measures such as firewalls, intrusion detection systems, and employee education to avert and react to cyber-attacks (Alom et al., 2019).

Use of AI and Machine Learning in Cyber Threat Detection

The application of artificial intelligence (AI) and machine learning (ML) techniques has grown in popularity within the field of cybersecurity, particularly in the area of threat detection. AI and ML techniques have the potential to detect and prevent cyber threats in real-time, allowing for a proactive and dynamic response to emerging threats. This article will examine several methods by which AI and ML are currently employed to detect cyber threats (Arpaci-Dusseau & Arpaci-Dusseau, 2018).

Anomaly Detection: Anomaly detection refers to the identification of uncommon or unforeseen activity within a system. To this end, AI and ML algorithms can scrutinize extensive datasets and pinpoint patterns of behavior that deviate from the standard. This can help to identify potential threats, such as unusual network activity or unauthorized access attempts.

Behavior-Based Detection: Behavior-based detection is an AI and ML methodology that involves utilizing machine learning algorithms to evaluate the conduct of networks, devices, and users. By monitoring and analyzing patterns of behavior, behavior-based detection can identify potential threats, such as a user accessing data they shouldn't, or a device attempting to connect to an unauthorized network (Buczak & Guven, 2018b).

Threat Intelligence: Threat intelligence pertains to utilizing information and data to recognize possible threats. AI and ML algorithms can assess extensive datasets from various origins, including social media, dark web forums, and prior attacks, to identify potential threats. This data can be used to identify potential threats, such as new malware or hacking techniques.

Predictive Analysis: Predictive analysis involves AI and ML techniques that leverage machine learning algorithms to scrutinize historical data, detecting patterns that suggest a possible future threat. This strategy can be utilized to foresee and preempt cyber attacks before they materialize.

Natural Language Processing (NLP): Natural language processing is a subdomain of AI that concentrates on examining and comprehending human language. NLP can be employed to evaluate text-based data, such as social media posts or email messages, to detect potential threats, such as phishing attacks.

Adaptive Security: Adaptive security is a type of AI and ML technique that uses machine learning algorithms to monitor and adjust security policies in real-time. By analyzing network and user behavior, adaptive security can adjust security policies to prevent potential threats and limit the impact of attacks.

In conclusion, AI and ML are powerful tools that have the potential to revolutionize the way we detect and prevent cyber threats. By implementing these methodologies, companies can take a proactive approach towards recognizing and addressing possible threats, thus decreasing the likelihood of data breaches and other types of cyber attacks. However, it is important to note that AI and ML are not a silver bullet for cybersecurity. To establish a comprehensive and effective cybersecurity plan, these approaches should be utilized alongside other security measures, including firewalls, intrusion detection systems, and employee education.

Use of AI and Machine Learning in Cyber Threat Prevention

In addition to detecting cyber threats, artificial intelligence (AI) and machine learning (ML) have the potential to prevent them as well. In fact, with the increasing sophistication and frequency of cyber attacks, it is becoming more and more important to implement AI and ML technologies for effective cybersecurity.

Here are some ways AI and ML can be used for cyber threat prevention:

Predictive Analytics: Predictive analytics employs machine learning algorithms to examine vast quantities of data and detect trends that may suggest the likelihood of a cyber assault. This technique can be employed to anticipate and forestall attacks before they happen.

Behavioral Analytics: Behavioral analytics uses ML algorithms to identify anomalous behavior on a network or device, such as unusual data transfers, unauthorized access attempts, and unusual user activity. This can help to identify potential threats before they become a problem.

Security Automation: AI and ML can automate many security tasks, such as monitoring network traffic, detecting and blocking malicious traffic, and identifying vulnerabilities. This reduces the risk of human error and allows for faster, more efficient threat prevention (Cai & Vasconcelos, 2018).

Natural Language Processing (NLP): Natural Language Processing (NLP) is employed to examine textual information, such as emails or social media messages, to identify potential threats, such as phishing attacks. This can be particularly useful for preventing social engineering attacks.

Adversarial Machine Learning: Adversarial machine learning refers to a category of machine learning which is intended to recognize and avert cybersecurity breaches. It leverages a blend of supervised and unsupervised machine learning approaches to gain insights from prior attacks and recognize novel risks.

Cloud Security: The task of securing cloud is intricate and can be enhanced through the implementation of AI and ML. AI and ML can be utilized to observe cloud infrastructure, recognize potential hazards, and refine security measures.

Cybersecurity Orchestration: Cybersecurity orchestration refers to the automation and integration of security tasks and technologies. AI and ML can be used to automate the orchestration of security tasks, reducing the risk of errors and enabling faster response times to threats (Cao et al., 2019).

In conclusion, AI and ML are powerful tools that can be used for cyber threat prevention. By using these technologies, organizations can predict and prevent potential threats, reduce the risk of cyber attacks, and improve overall cybersecurity posture. However, it is important to note that AI and ML are not a silver bullet for cybersecurity. For a thorough and efficient cybersecurity plan, it is important to incorporate other security measures such as firewalls, intrusion detection systems, and employee training in conjunction with their use.

Challenges and Limitations of Using AI and Machine Learning in Cyber Threat Detection and Prevention

Although artificial intelligence (AI) and machine learning (ML) have immense potential to transform the way we detect and prevent cyber threats, there are certain difficulties and restrictions that organizations need to take into account while incorporating these technologies. This piece aims to explore some of the primary obstacles and constraints associated with utilizing AI and ML for the purpose of cyber threat detection and prevention.

Adversarial Attacks: Adversarial attacks are designed to fool AI and ML algorithms by manipulating input data. For example, attackers can create a targeted attack that is designed to evade detection by an AI and ML-based security system. Organizations must be aware of these types of attacks and develop countermeasures to detect and prevent them.

Data Quality: AI and ML algorithms require large amounts of high-quality data to be effective. The quality of the data used to train AI and ML algorithms can impact the accuracy of the results. Organizations must ensure that the data used to train these algorithms is accurate, representative, and up-to-date.

Complexity: AI and ML-based security systems can be complex, requiring specialized expertise to develop, implement, and maintain. Organizations must have access to the right expertise to be able to implement these technologies effectively (Chen et al., 2016).

Explainability: AI and ML-based security systems can be difficult to interpret, making it difficult to explain how a decision was made. This lack of explainability can make it difficult to justify security decisions to management or regulators.

False Positives: AI and ML algorithms can generate false positives, flagging benign activity as malicious. This can lead to unnecessary investigation and potentially divert resources away from other critical tasks.

False Negatives: AI and ML algorithms can also generate false negatives, failing to identify actual threats. This can result in missed opportunities for prevention and increased risk of a successful attack (Chollet, 2017).

Lack of Context: AI and ML algorithms can be limited in their ability to understand the context of a situation. For example, an algorithm may identify a user as suspicious based on their behavior, but fail to take into account that the user is authorized to access the system.

Bias: Artificial intelligence (AI) and machine learning (ML) algorithms may exhibit bias due to the training data used to develop them. As a result, these biases can lead to discriminatory results and possibly perpetuate pre-existing biases.

Cost: Implementing AI and ML-based security systems can be expensive, particularly for smaller organizations. These costs can include hardware, software, and specialized expertise.

Ethical Concerns: AI and ML-based security systems can raise ethical concerns, particularly when it comes to the collection, storage, and use of personal data. It is crucial for organizations to practice transparency in regards to their data collection and usage methods, while also ensuring that their systems are being utilized ethically.

To sum up, while the use of AI and ML for cyber threat detection and prevention has significant potential, there are also challenges and limitations that organizations must be aware of. These challenges include adversarial attacks, data quality, complexity, explainability, false positives and negatives, lack of context, bias, cost, and ethical concerns. Organizations must carefully consider these challenges when developing and implementing AI and ML-based security systems to ensure their effectiveness and reliability (Cui et al., 2019).

Vulnerability Management With AI and Machine Learning

Vulnerability management refers to the systematic process of recognizing, evaluating, ranking, and reducing weaknesses or flaws in the systems and software of a company or institutionThe utilization of AI and machine learning (ML) can enhance vulnerability management by automating specific duties and presenting observations that might not be immediately discernible to human analysts.

Here are a few ways AI and machine learning can be used in vulnerability management:

Automated vulnerability detection: AI and ML can be used to scan a large number of systems and applications for vulnerabilities, detecting potential security weaknesses that may have been missed by human analysts. This can save time and resources, allowing security teams to focus on the most critical vulnerabilities.

Prioritization of vulnerabilities: AI and ML can help prioritize vulnerabilities by analyzing factors such as severity, likelihood of exploitation, and potential impact on the organization. This can help security teams focus their efforts on the most critical vulnerabilities first.

Threat intelligence analysis: With the ability to scrutinize extensive quantities of threat intelligence data, AI and ML can recognize developing threats and possible methods of attack. This can help organizations stay ahead of attackers by proactively addressing vulnerabilities before they can be exploited.

Behavioral analysis: AI and ML can analyze user and system behavior to detect potential security threats, such as suspicious login attempts or unauthorized access attempts This can assist security teams in detecting potential dangers that conventional security methods may have overlooked.

Automated response: AI and ML can be used to automate the response to security threats, such as blocking malicious traffic or isolating compromised systems. This can help organizations respond quickly to threats, minimizing the impact of an attack (Dal Pozzolo et al., 2018).

Overall, AI and machine learning can help improve vulnerability management by automating certain tasks, providing insights that may not be immediately apparent, and enabling organizations to respond more quickly to security threats. However, it's important to note that AI and machine learning are not a silver bullet for security and It is recommended to utilize this in combination with other security measures, such as periodic security evaluations, penetration testing, and training of employees (Dang et al., 2019).

Overview of Vulnerabilities

Vulnerabilities denote shortcomings or defects in software, networks, or systems that can be taken advantage of by malicious individuals to illicitly access, take confidential data, or interfere with normal functioning. In the context of cybersecurity, identifying and mitigating vulnerabilities is critical to maintaining the security and integrity of digital assets.

There are several types of vulnerabilities that can occur in different areas of a system, including:

Software vulnerabilities: These are deficiencies in the structure or execution of software that can be manipulated by attackers to gain illegal entry, confiscate information, or run harmful commands. Frequently occurring software vulnerabilities include buffer overflows, cross-site scripting (XSS), SQL injection, and remote code execution.

Network vulnerabilities: These are frailties in network infrastructure that can be utilized to obtain unlawful entry, intercept data, or launch a denial-of-service (DoS) attack. Common network vulnerabilities include misconfigured firewalls, open ports, weak encryption, and unsecured wireless networks.

Human vulnerabilities: These are weaknesses related to human behavior, such as poor password hygiene, social engineering, or phishing attacks. Humans are often the weakest link in the security chain, and attackers often use psychological tactics to trick users into divulging sensitive information or downloading malware.

Physical vulnerabilities: These are weaknesses related to physical security, such as unsecured facilities or improperly disposed of hardware. Physical vulnerabilities can allow attackers to gain unauthorized access to physical assets or data, steal equipment or data, or install malicious software or hardware.

Supply chain vulnerabilities: These are weaknesses in the supply chain that can allow attackers to compromise products or services before they reach the end user. For example, attackers can inject malicious code into a software package before it is distributed to users, or tamper with hardware during manufacturing.

To identify and mitigate vulnerabilities, organizations can use a variety of techniques, such as vulnerability scanning, penetration testing, and threat modeling. Vulnerability scanning is the process of using automated tools to examine a system or network for established vulnerabilities, whereas penetration testing involves imitating an attack on a system to discover weaknesses. Threat modeling involves analyzing a system to identify potential vulnerabilities and the impact they could have on the system if exploited (Demertzis et al., 2019).

In addition to technical solutions, organizations can also implement best practices to reduce the risk of vulnerabilities, such as implementing strong passwords, regularly patching software, and providing security awareness training to employees. Organizations can enhance their cybersecurity stance and decrease the likelihood of a successful attack by adopting a proactive approach to recognizing and resolving vulnerabilities.

Use of AI and Machine Learning in Vulnerability Management

The cybersecurity industry, along with other fields, has been considerably influenced by the utilization of Artificial Intelligence (AI) and Machine Learning (ML) in recent years. Vulnerability management, which involves identifying and mitigating security vulnerabilities, is one area where AI and ML are increasingly being used to improve efficiency and effectiveness (Elgamal & Rizk, 2020).

AI and ML technologies can automate several aspects of vulnerability management, such as vulnerability scanning, identification, prioritization, and remediation. This automation enables organizations to quickly and accurately identify vulnerabilities and prioritize them for remediation based on their potential impact on the organization's security.

One way AI and ML can be used in vulnerability management is through automated vulnerability scanning. By using AI and ML algorithms, vulnerability scanners can analyze vast amounts of data and identify potential vulnerabilities in an organization's IT infrastructure. These algorithms can learn from past scans to improve their accuracy and reduce the likelihood of false positives or false negatives.

Another area where AI and ML can be useful is in vulnerability identification and prioritization. These technologies can analyze data from multiple sources, including threat intelligence feeds and security event logs, to identify new vulnerabilities and determine their potential impact on an organization's security. By prioritizing vulnerabilities based on their severity, an organization can focus its resources on addressing the most critical issues first, reducing the risk of a successful attack.

AI and ML can also help automate the remediation process. By learning from past remediation efforts, these technologies can suggest the most effective remediation strategies for each vulnerability, reducing the time and effort required to address security issues. This automation can also free up security personnel to focus on more critical issues that require human intervention.

Another area where AI and ML can be beneficial in vulnerability management is in predicting future threats. These technologies have the capability to examine immense volumes of data to detect patterns and tendencies that indicate the possibility of upcoming attacks. By providing early warnings, organizations can take proactive measures to prevent attacks before they occur.

One significant benefit of using AI and ML in vulnerability management is their ability to learn and improve over time. By analyzing past data and outcomes, these technologies can continuously improve their accuracy and effectiveness. This capability can significantly reduce the risk of security breaches and make vulnerability management more efficient and effective (Farahmandi et al., 2019).

Despite the benefits, there are difficulties related to employing AI and ML in vulnerability management. Among the primary obstacles is the risk of false positives and false negatives. The precision of AI and ML algorithms is solely dependent on the quality of data they analyze, and if the data is deficient or incorrect, it can result in erroneous outcomes. Additionally, because AI and ML algorithms are trained on past data, they may not be effective in identifying new, previously unknown vulnerabilities.

To conclude, integrating AI and ML into vulnerability management can substantially enhance the productivity and potency of vulnerability management. By automating various aspects of the process, these technologies can quickly and accurately identify vulnerabilities, prioritize them for remediation, and predict future threats. While there are challenges associated with using these technologies, their ability to learn and improve over time makes them an invaluable tool for organizations looking to improve their security posture (Al-Fuqaha, Guizani, Mohammadi, Aledhari, & Ayyash, 2015).

Challenges and Limitations of Using AI and Machine Learning in Vulnerability Management

AI and machine learning have shown great potential in helping organizations manage vulnerabilities and improve their overall security posture. However, there are also several challenges and limitations that need to be addressed to ensure the effectiveness of these technologies in vulnerability management (Amin et al., 2019).

The deficiency of high-quality data is among the major hurdles in utilizing AI and machine learning in vulnerability management. AI and machine learning algorithms require large amounts of high-quality data to effectively detect vulnerabilities and prioritize them based on their severity. However, the data used to train these algorithms may be incomplete or biased, leading to inaccurate or incomplete results. Additionally, some vulnerabilities may be unknown or difficult to detect, making it challenging to train algorithms to detect them.

Another challenge is the lack of explainability in AI and machine learning algorithms. In many cases, it can be difficult to understand how these algorithms arrived at their conclusions, which can make it challenging for security professionals to assess the accuracy and effectiveness of their results. Additionally, the absence of transparency can make it challenging to recognize and resolve problems or partialities in the algorithm, which can result in inaccurate outputs like false positives or false negatives (Appelbaum et al., 2014).

There is also a concern about the potential for AI and machine learning algorithms to be manipulated by threat actors. Adversaries could attempt to manipulate data to bias the algorithm towards overlooking certain vulnerabilities or prioritizing others. Additionally, threat actors could attempt to trick the algorithm by intentionally introducing false positives or other deceptive inputs.

Furthermore, the efficacy of AI and machine learning algorithms is solely dependent on the quality of data used to train them. If the training data is inadequate or partial, the algorithm might not be proficient at detecting all categories of vulnerabilities. Additionally, the algorithms may struggle to adapt to new or unknown vulnerabilities, as they may not have sufficient training data to accurately identify them (Arashloo & Rabiee, 2019).

Another challenge is the cost and complexity of implementing AI and machine learning in vulnerability management. These technologies require significant resources and expertise to implement and maintain, which can be a barrier for many organizations. Additionally, the cost and complexity of implementing these technologies may be disproportionate to the benefits they provide, particularly for smaller organizations with limited resources.

Furthermore, the effectiveness of AI and machine learning in vulnerability management has certain limitations. While these technologies can help to detect and prioritize vulnerabilities, they cannot replace the need for human expertise and judgment. Security professionals must still be involved in the vulnerability management process to assess the accuracy of the results and make decisions about how to remediate vulnerabilities.

Moreover, AI and machine learning algorithms are not infallible and can generate inaccurate results such as false positives or false negatives. False positives can lead to wasted resources as security professionals investigate non-existent vulnerabilities, while false negatives can leave organizations vulnerable to attack.

Lastly, there is apprehension about the likelihood of AI and machine learning algorithms being exploited to automate attacks. Adversaries could potentially use these technologies to scan networks and systems for vulnerabilities and automatically launch attacks, potentially at a scale and speed that would be difficult for humans to detect and mitigate.

To conclude, although AI and machine learning have the potential to substantially enhance vulnerability management, there are still challenges and limitations that need to be addressed, there are also several challenges and limitations that need to be addressed. These include the need for high-quality data, explainability, the potential for manipulation by threat actors, and the cost and complexity of implementation. Additionally, these technologies cannot replace the need for human expertise and judgment, and there is a risk that they could be used to automate attacks. To address these challenges and limitations, It is advisable for organizations to thoughtfully assess the advantages and disadvantages of integrating AI and machine learning in vulnerability management and guarantee that they possess the essential resources and proficiency to efficiently adopt and sustain these technologies (Arias-Oliva et al., 2020).

Malware Detection and Analysis With AI and Machine Learning

Malware detection and analysis is an important area of cybersecurity that has traditionally relied on signature-based techniques, which can only identify known threats. The identification of unidentified and previously undetected threats can be made possible with the help of Artificial Intelligence (AI) and Machine Learning (ML), which has the potential to substantially enhance malware detection and analysis.

Here are some ways AI/ML is used in malware detection and analysis:

Behavioral analysis: The algorithms of AI/ML can scrutinize the conduct of malware to detect irregularities and patterns that may indicate a fresh or unidentified threat. The algorithms are capable of observing system calls, network traffic, and other indicators to pinpoint malevolent activity that could be typical of malware.

Dynamic analysis: The behavior of malware can also be assessed in a confined environment like a sandbox or virtual machine, with the help of AI/ML algorithms. This allows the algorithms to identify malicious behavior that may not be evident in a static analysis of the malware.

Feature engineering: AI/ML algorithms can be used to automatically identify the features of malware that are most indicative of malicious behavior. For example, the algorithms can identify specific types of system calls, network traffic, or file characteristics that are most commonly associated with malware.

Classification: With proper training, AI/ML algorithms can categorize malware into distinct groups according to its features, conduct, and other properties. This can aid analysts in recognizing certain forms of threats and in prioritizing their response based on the severity and consequences of the threat.

Threat intelligence: Large datasets of threat intelligence can be used to train AI/ML algorithms, which can identify correlations and patterns that may indicate emerging threats. This can enable organizations to stay ahead of the evolving threat landscape and take proactive measures to respond to new threats.

While AI/ML has the potential to significantly improve malware detection and analysis, there are also some limitations and challenges that must be taken into account. For example, AI/ML algorithms can be vulnerable to adversarial attacks, where attackers manipulate the data used to train the algorithms to produce incorrect results. In addition, AI/ML algorithms may also be biased based on the data used to train them, which can lead to incorrect or unfair outcomes.

To sum up, AI/ML has the potential to transform the way malware is detected and analyzed, allowing organizations to respond to threats with greater speed and precision. However, it is crucial to assess the limitations and difficulties associated with implementing these technologies in this area, and to ensure that they are utilized in a secure and responsible manner (Baker & Wilson, 2020).

Overview of Malware

Malware, which is an abbreviation for malicious software, refers to any software that is intentionally designed to cause harm or damage to a computer system, network, or device. There are various types of malware, such as viruses, worms, Trojans, ransomware, spyware, adware, and many others (Banerjee & Gupta, 2020). The use of malware by cybercriminals is prevalent in gaining unauthorized access to systems, stealing data, launching attacks, and causing disruption and destruction.

Viruses are one of the oldest and most well-known forms of malware. They are designed to replicate themselves and spread to other computers or devices. Malware usually spreads through various means such as email attachments, infected files, or websites that contain malicious content. Once it infects a system, it can cause harm by corrupting files, stealing sensitive data, or launching attacks.

Worms are similar to viruses in that they are designed to replicate and spread. However, unlike viruses, worms do not need a host program or file to spread and can propagate autonomously across networks and devices (Bhattacharyya et al., 2020). Worms can be used to carry out a wide range of malicious activities, such as launching distributed denial-of-service (DDoS) attacks, stealing data, or installing other types of malware.

Trojans are a form of malicious software that pretends to be a genuine application or file. They are frequently distributed using social engineering tactics like phishing emails and can be utilized to steal data, launch attacks, or create a backdoor into a system.

Ransomware refers to a category of malicious software that encrypts data belonging to a victim and then demands payment in exchange for the decryption key (Buczak & Guven, 2016). It can be propagated via email attachments, vulnerable software or malicious websites. Ransomware attacks can cause severe disruptions and financial losses for both individuals and organizations.

Spyware is a form of malware that is intended to monitor a victim's computer usage and online activities in order to collect information. It can be used for surveillance, identity theft, or other malicious purposes.

Adware is a form of malware that exhibits undesired advertising in the form of pop-ups or banners on a victim's computer or device. While not necessarily harmful, adware can be intrusive and annoying, and may slow down a victim's computer.

Malware is a constantly evolving threat, and new types of malware are emerging all the time. Cybercriminals are always looking for new ways to exploit vulnerabilities and gain unauthorized access to systems and data. Staying informed and current about the most recent threats and vulnerabilities poses a major challenge in the fight against malware (Bukhari & Awad, 2019).

In order to safeguard against malware, it is crucial to adhere to cybersecurity best practices, which include maintaining up-to-date software and systems, using strong passwords, and avoiding links and attachments that seem suspicious. Additionally, anti-malware software can assist in identifying and eliminating malware from a system.

Furthermore, companies can deploy various security measures such as firewalls, intrusion detection systems, and Security Information and Event Management (SIEM) solutions to identify and prevent malware attacks. User education and training can also help to raise awareness about the risks of malware and how to avoid falling victim to an attack.

In conclusion, malware is a significant threat to computer systems, networks, and devices. There are many different types of malware, each with its own specific characteristics and behaviors. To protect against malware, keeping abreast of the latest threats and vulnerabilities is crucial, and to follow best practices for cybersecurity. Organizations can also implement security measures to detect and prevent malware attacks, and to educate users about the risks of malware and how to avoid falling victim to an attack.

Use of AI and Machine Learning in Malware Detection

The field of cybersecurity is utilizing artificial intelligence (AI) and machine learning (ML) more and more for the purpose of malware detection and analysis. This is due to their ability to identify patterns and anomalies, learn from historical data, and adapt to new threats in real-time. The focus of this article is on the utilization of AI and machine learning in cybersecurity, specifically in the context of malware detection, and how these technologies can enhance cybersecurity measures.

AI and ML-based malware detection systems work by analyzing large volumes of data, such as network traffic, system logs, and application behavior, to identify potential malware activity. These systems use advanced algorithms and machine learning models to analyze this data and identify patterns that are indicative of malware activity (Calderon & Zeadally, 2020).

One of the key benefits of using AI and ML in malware detection is their ability to detect and respond to previously unknown or zero-day threats. Traditional signature-based detection systems rely on known patterns of malware to identify threats, and are often ineffective against new and unknown threats. In contrast, AI and ML-based detection systems can learn from historical data and adapt to new and emerging threats, This can significantly enhance their ability to identify and stop attacks.

AI and ML-based malware detection have the advantage of being able to detect advanced threats, such as fileless malware and polymorphic malware, which can evade traditional detection methods. These types of threats are designed to change their behavior and evade detection, making them very difficult to identify. AI and ML-based detection systems can analyze multiple factors to identify these types of threats, such as network traffic, system logs, and application behavior, and provide a more comprehensive view of the threat landscape (Carlini & Wagner, 2017).

In addition, AI and ML-based malware detection can help to reduce the workload for security teams by automating the process of recognizing and reacting to potential dangers. This could help to free up valuable resources and allow security teams to focus on more strategic tasks, such as threat hunting and incident response.

Despite these benefits, there are also some challenges and limitations to using AI and ML in malware detection. One of the key challenges is the need for high-quality data to train the algorithms. Machine learning models require large amounts of high-quality data to effectively detect malware, If the data used to train AI and ML algorithms is incomplete or biased, it can result in inaccurate detections. Additionally, there is a risk of false positives or false negatives, which can lead to wasted resources or missed threats.

Another challenge is the potential for adversaries to manipulate the data or the algorithms themselves to evade detection. Threat actors can attempt to train malware to evade detection by AI and ML-based detection systems, or they can manipulate data to bias the algorithms and avoid detection.

Finally, there is also a risk of over-reliance on AI and ML in malware detection, which can lead to a false sense of security. While these technologies can significantly improve malware detection and response, they cannot replace the need for human expertise and judgment. The involvement of security teams is still necessary in the process of recognizing and reacting to potential security threats, and use AI and ML as a tool to support their decision-making.

In conclusion, AI and ML are increasingly being used in the field of cybersecurity for malware detection and analysis. These technologies can help to detect and respond to previously unknown or advanced threats, and reduce the workload for security teams. However, there are also challenges and limitations to their use, such as the need for high-quality data, the potential for manipulation by threat actors, and the risk of over-reliance on these technologies. To effectively use AI and ML in malware detection, organizations must carefully consider the benefits and drawbacks, and ensure that they have the necessary resources and expertise to implement and maintain these technologies.

Use of AI and Machine Learning in Malware Analysis

AI and ML are gaining significance in the cybersecurity industry, particularly in the realm of malware analysis. Malware analysis is the process of analyzing malicious code to understand its behavior, purpose, and potential impact. AI and ML can play a key role in this process by automating certain tasks and providing greater insights into the behavior of malware. In this piece, we will examine how AI and machine learning are utilized in the analysis of malware.

Machine learning and AI can be utilized in various methods for malware analysis. A common technique is to use machine learning algorithms to detect and categorize malware by its behavior. These algorithms can examine vast amounts of data, including system logs and network traffic, to identify abnormal patterns and characteristics that signify malicious activity. They can then classify the malware based on its behavior, such as whether it is a Trojan, worm, or virus.

Another use of AI and ML in malware analysis is to automatically extract features from malware samples. These features can include things like strings, function calls, and file paths. Machine learning algorithms can then use these features to identify similarities and differences between malware samples, and help to identify families of malware and potential relationships between them.

AI and ML can also be used to identify malicious code within a larger application. For example, a machine learning algorithm can analyze an application's code and identify any code that is behaving suspiciously or that is similar to known malicious code. Using AI and ML in malware analysis can aid in identifying potential vulnerabilities and decreasing the probability of a successful attack.

Using AI and ML in malware analysis offers a significant advantage in identifying new and emerging threats. Traditional methods of malware analysis, which rely on human analysts to identify patterns and behavior, can be time-consuming and error-prone. In contrast, AI and ML algorithms can rapidly and accurately analyze large amounts of data, identifying patterns and anomalies that suggest the presence of new or previously unknown threats.

Another advantage of AI and ML in malware analysis is their ability to automate certain tasks, such as feature extraction and classification. This can help to reduce the workload for analysts and free up resources for more strategic tasks, such as threat hunting and incident response.

Despite these benefits, there are also some challenges and limitations to using AI and ML in malware analysis. One of the key challenges is the need for high-quality data to train the algorithms. Machine learning models require large amounts of high-quality data to effectively identify and analyze malware, the accuracy of AI and ML algorithms in malware analysis may be compromised if the data they use is biased or incomplete.

Another challenge is the potential for adversaries to manipulate the data or the algorithms themselves to evade detection. Threat actors can attempt to train malware to evade detection by AI and ML-based detection systems, or they can manipulate data to bias the algorithms and avoid detection.

Finally, there is a risk of over-reliance on AI and ML in malware analysis, which can lead to a false sense of security. While these technologies can significantly improve malware analysis, they cannot replace the need for human expertise and judgment. The involvement of analysts is still necessary in identifying and responding to threats, and the role of AI and ML is to serve as a tool to assist and enhance their decision-making process.

In conclusion, AI and ML are increasingly being used in the field of cybersecurity for malware analysis. These technologies can help to identify new and emerging threats, automate certain tasks, and reduce the workload for analysts. However, there are also challenges and limitations to their use, such as the need for high-quality data, the potential for manipulation by threat actors, and the risk of over-reliance on these technologies. To effectively use AI and ML in malware analysis, organizations must carefully consider the benefits and drawbacks, and ensure that they have the necessary resources and expertise to implement and maintain these technologies (Carrara et al., 2020).

Challenges and Limitations of Using AI and Machine Learning in Malware Detection and Analysis

AI and ML are gaining popularity in the realm of cybersecurity, with an increasing focus on malware detection and analysis. These technologies offer significant benefits in terms of automating certain tasks, identifying new and emerging threats, and improving the accuracy of malware analysis. However, there are also challenges and limitations to their use, which must be carefully considered in order to ensure effective and reliable cybersecurity.

A major obstacle in utilizing AI and ML for malware detection and analysis is the requirement of abundant, high-quality data. Machine learning algorithms rely on copious amounts of data to accurately detect patterns and irregularities that are representative of malware. The effectiveness of the algorithms can be compromised if the data is incomplete or biased, leading to the possibility of false positives or false negatives. This means that organizations must ensure they have access to sufficient, high-quality data to train their models effectively.

Another challenge is the potential for adversaries to manipulate the data or algorithms in order to evade detection. Threat actors can attempt to train malware to avoid detection by AI and ML-based detection systems, or manipulate the data used to train the algorithms in order to bias them and avoid detection. This means that organizations must be aware of the potential for these attacks, and develop strategies to detect and respond to them effectively (Cavoukian, 2015).

A further challenge is the speed of technological change in the cybersecurity landscape. The development of new types of malware and new attack techniques is rapid, and organizations must be able to keep up with these changes in order to protect themselves effectively. However, developing and deploying new AI and ML-based detection and analysis systems can be time-consuming and expensive, meaning that organizations may struggle to keep pace with the changing threat landscape (Alqurashi & Mahmoud, 2019).

Another challenge of using AI and ML in malware detection and analysis is the issue of explainability. Machine learning algorithms can be highly complex, and It can be challenging to comprehend how AI and ML algorithms arrive at their decisions, which makes it difficult for analysts to justify to senior management or stakeholders why a specific decision was made, or to identify any potential biases in the algorithms. This lack of transparency can be a significant obstacle to the adoption of AI and ML-based systems in some organizations.

There are also some limitations to the use of AI and ML in malware detection and analysis. One of the key limitations is the risk of false positives and false negatives. While AI and ML algorithms can be highly effective at identifying patterns and anomalies, they can also make mistakes. False positives can lead to unnecessary alerts and wasted resources, while false negatives can result in successful attacks.

Another limitation is the difficulty of dealing with encrypted data. Encrypted data is becoming increasingly common in the cybersecurity landscape, and it can be challenging to analyze it effectively using AI and ML algorithms. This means that organizations must develop strategies to deal with encrypted data, and ensure that their AI and ML-based systems are capable of analyzing this data effectively.

Finally, there is a risk of over-reliance on AI and ML in malware detection and analysis. While these technologies can significantly improve the accuracy and efficiency of malware analysis, they cannot replace the need for human expertise and judgment. Analysts should remain an integral part of the threat detection and response process and use AI and ML as an aid to enhance their decision-making capabilities.

In summary, although AI and machine learning offer great potential for enhancing malware detection and analysis, there are numerous challenges and limitations to consider. The requirement for vast amounts of high-quality data and the possibility of bias in that data are major challenges that can impact the precision and efficiency of AI and ML algorithms. Additionally, the lack of transparency in the decision-making process of these algorithms can make it hard for analysts to justify their decisions to stakeholders. Therefore, it is vital to treat the use of AI and ML in malware detection and analysis as a tool to support human decision-making rather than a replacement for it. Ultimately, cybersecurity professionals need to strike a balance between leveraging the benefits of AI and ML while being mindful of their limitations.

Case Studies: Real-World Applications of AI and Machine Learning in Cybersecurity

Cybersecurity is a rapidly evolving field, and organizations are constantly seeking new ways to stay ahead of potential threats. In the past few years, there has been notable interest in the field of artificial intelligence (AI) and machine learning as a technology domain. These technologies have the potential to revolutionize the way organizations approach cybersecurity by providing automated and intelligent tools for detecting, responding to, and preventing cyber threats. This article will explore actual instances of how AI and machine learning are being applied in cybersecurity.

Palo Alto Networks - Cortex XDR: Palo Alto Networks is a cybersecurity company that offers a range of products and services to help organizations protect their networks and systems. One of their products is Cortex XDR, an AI-powered extended detection and response platform that integrates endpoint protection, network security, and cloud security. Cortex XDR uses machine learning to identify patterns in endpoint and network data that indicate potential threats, and provides real-time alerts and automated response actions.

In a case study with a large US healthcare provider, Cortex XDR was able to detect and contain a ransomware attack in just 30 minutes, preventing the spread of the attack to other endpoints. This quick response time was made possible by the use of machine learning algorithms that continuously analyze endpoint data for patterns that may indicate an attack. The algorithms were able to identify the ransomware attack based on patterns in the data, and Cortex XDR automatically quarantined the infected endpoint to prevent the attack from spreading.

Darktrace - Enterprise Immune System: Darktrace is another cybersecurity company that offers an AI-powered platform for detecting and responding to threats in real time. Their product, the Enterprise Immune System, uses unsupervised machine learning to detect anomalous activity on a network that may indicate a potential attack. The platform learns the normal patterns of activity on a network and identifies anomalies that could indicate a potential attack.

In a case study with a global food and beverage manufacturer, Darktrace's platform was able to detect and respond to a malware attack in just 15 minutes, preventing the attack from causing any damage to the organization. The malware had evaded traditional signature-based antivirus solutions, but was identified by Darktrace's machine learning algorithms. Once the malware was detected, the Enterprise Immune System automatically blocked the attack and prevented it from causing any damage to the organization.

IBM Watson for Cybersecurity: IBM Watson is a platform that uses artificial intelligence to examine security data and offer security analysts valuable insights by utilizing natural language processing and machine learning techniques. In a case study with a large financial services company, IBM Watson was able to reduce the time taken to investigate security incidents from hours to just minutes, allowing the organization to respond to potential threats more quickly.

The system uses machine learning algorithms to examine security information from various origins and detect trends that could signify a possible assault. The algorithms also have the ability to learn from the decisions made by security analysts, allowing them to become more accurate over time. By automating the analysis of security data, IBM Watson for Cybersecurity enables security analysts to focus on more complex tasks, such as investigating and responding to potential threats (Chen et al., 2014).

McAfee - MVISION Endpoint: McAfee is a well-known cybersecurity company that offers a range of products and services to protect organizations from cyber threats. MVISION Endpoint is a product offered by them, which is a safeguard platform for endpoints, powered by artificial intelligence. The platform utilizes machine learning techniques to detect and avert malware and various other hazards. By examining endpoint data, the system can identify patterns that could potentially signal an impending danger and use this data to prevent the threat from causing any harm.

In a case study with a large US energy company, MVISION Endpoint was able to detect and block a malware attack that had evaded traditional signature-based antivirus solutions. The platform identified the malware based on its behavior, rather than its signature, and was able to prevent the attack from causing any damage to the organization. The use of machine learning in MVISION Endpoint allowed the platform to detect and prevent previously unknown threats, providing a higher level of protection for the organization.

Fortinet - FortiAI: Fortinet is a cybersecurity company that offers a range of products and services to protect organizations from cyber threats. Their product range includes FortiAI, a security platform that employs artificial intelligence and machine learning to swiftly recognize and counteract potential hazards. By seamlessly integrating with Fortinet's suite of security products, it provides a comprehensive and robust solution for safeguarding organizations from cyber threats. The system operates in real-time, quickly detecting and responding to potential risks to prevent any damage.

In a case study with a large US healthcare provider, FortiAI was able to detect and contain a ransomware attack in just 15 minutes. The platform used machine learning algorithms to identify the ransomware attack based on patterns in the network data. Once the attack was detected, FortiAI automatically quarantined the infected endpoint and prevented the attack from spreading to other endpoints. The use of machine learning in FortiAI allowed the platform to quickly detect and respond to the ransomware attack, preventing any damage to the organization (Cohen & Toubiana, 2018).

Splunk - User and Entity Behavior Analytics (UEBA): Splunk is a well-known cybersecurity company that offers a range of products and services for analyzing and managing security data. One of their products is User and Entity Behavior Analytics (UEBA), an AI-powered platform that uses machine learning to identify potential threats based on user and entity behavior. The platform employs machine learning techniques to scrutinize the behavior of users, network information, and other security-related data in order to detect any regularities that could suggest a possible security risk.

In a case study with a large US bank, UEBA was able to detect and prevent a phishing attack that had evaded other security solutions. The platform identified the attack based on patterns in user behavior, and was able to prevent the attack from causing any damage to the organization. The use of machine learning in UEBA allowed the platform to detect and prevent previously unknown threats, providing a higher level of protection for the organization.

CONCLUSION

AI and machine learning have the potential to revolutionize the way organizations approach cybersecurity. These technologies provide automated and intelligent tools for detecting, responding to, and preventing cyber threats. Real-world examples have demonstrated that AI and machine learning are capable of identifying and thwarting various types of cybersecurity threats, including malware and phishing attacks.

Nevertheless, there exist obstacles and restrictions regarding the implementation of AI and machine learning in cybersecurity. Among the most significant challenges is the absence of transparency in machine learning algorithms, which can complicate the comprehension of how these algorithms arrive at their decisions. There is also a risk of false positives and false negatives, which can lead to security teams becoming overwhelmed with alerts or missing important threats.

Notwithstanding these challenges, the advantages of utilizing AI and machine learning in cybersecurity surpass the potential risks. By offering automated and intelligent solutions for identifying and addressing cyber threats, institutions can enhance their security stance and decrease the likelihood of data breaches and other forms of cyber attacks.

Lessons Learned From Real-World Applications of AI and Machine Learning in Cybersecurity

The empirical evidence of AI and machine learning in cybersecurity has furnished valuable observations regarding the advantages and obstacles associated with these technologies. Here are some lessons learned from these case studies:

The implementation of AI and machine learning can enhance the detection and response to security threats: The capacity of AI and machine learning to identify and react to security threats promptly is one of their principal advantages in cybersecurity. The case studies demonstrated that a variety of cyber threats, including malware attacks and phishing attacks, can be identified and thwarted through the use of these technologies. By providing automated and intelligent tools for threat detection and response, organizations can improve their security posture and mitigate the likelihood of data breaches and other forms of cyber attacks (Dua & Du, 2019).

Machine learning models need to be trained on quality data: For machine learning models to be efficacious in cybersecurity, they necessitate being trained on high-quality data. This implies that the data utilized to train the models must be precise, comprehensive, and representative of the varieties of threats that the models will be employed to identify. The case studies showed that organizations that invested in quality data achieved better results in threat detection and response.

The establishment of transparency is crucial for engendering confidence in AI and machine learning: A predicament in utilizing AI and machine learning in cybersecurity is the absence of transparency in the decision-making process of these technologies. This can impede security teams from comprehending how the models are reaching decisions and can engender a distrust in the technology. The case studies showed that organizations that provided transparency into their machine learning models were better able to build trust in the technology and achieve better results in threat detection and response.

Human expertise is still needed to interpret and act on the results: While AI and machine learning can provide automated and intelligent tools for threat detection and response, human expertise is still needed to interpret and act on the results. The case studies showed that organizations that had a strong security team with expertise in both cybersecurity and data science were better able to make sense of the data and take action to prevent cyber threats.

Collaboration between different security tools is important for comprehensive threat protection: Numerous case studies demonstrated that AI and machine learning were employed along with other security tools like firewalls and antivirus software, to furnish inclusive protection against security threats. By merging these various tools, institutions can enhance their overall security stance and decrease the likelihood of data breaches and other types of cyber attacks.

The evolving nature of cyber threats requires continuous monitoring and adaptation: One of the primary takeaways from the case studies is that cybersecurity threats are constantly changing and advancing, and organizations need to continuously monitor and adapt their security strategies in response. This means that machine learning models need to be retrained on new data and new threat patterns, and thus, security teams must keep themselves abreast with the latest threats and methods of attack.

To conclude, the empirical case studies of AI and machine learning in cybersecurity have offered significant insights for institutions seeking to enhance their security stance. By investing in quality data, providing transparency into machine learning models, and integrating different security tools, organizations can improve their threat detection and response capabilities and mitigate the likelihood of data breaches and other forms of cyber attacks. However, human expertise is still needed to interpret and act on the results, and continuous monitoring and adaptation is required to stay ahead of evolving cyber threats (Fasbender & Siddiqui, 2019).

Future of AI and Machine Learning in Cybersecurity

There is a promising future for the application of AI and machine learning in the field of cybersecurity. As cyber threats continue to become more sophisticated and complex, organizations are turning to these technologies to improve their security posture and protect against data breaches and other cyber attacks. Below are a few examples of how cybersecurity is expected to be impacted by AI and machine learning in the future:

Improved threat detection and response: The use of AI and machine learning will remain crucial in enhancing the identification and handling of security threats. As these technologies advance, they will be capable of real-time detection and response to a broader spectrum of threats, thereby offering prompt and precise threat detection and response.

Enhanced automation: Automation will persist as a primary impetus behind the utilization of AI and machine learning in cybersecurity. This will enable organizations to automate security tasks that are repetitive, such as threat detection and patching, freeing up security teams to concentrate on more intricate and strategic undertakings.

Advanced threat hunting: Machine learning algorithms will enable security teams to identify patterns and behaviors associated with sophisticated attacks that may otherwise go unnoticed. This will enable security professionals to better identify and track advanced threats, thereby reducing the time to detection and minimizing damage caused by cyber attacks.

Predictive threat intelligence: Machine learning will enable the identification of potential vulnerabilities and attacks before they occur. This will be achieved by analyzing historical data and identifying trends in cyber attacks, allowing security professionals to proactively defend against emerging threats (Grosse et al., 2017).

Improved endpoint security: Machine learning and AI will play a critical role in endpoint security, including the detection and prevention of malware and other malicious code. The ability to quickly identify and isolate infected endpoints can significantly reduce the potential for a widespread infection.

Better risk management: Risk management can also benefit from the application of AI and machine learning, such as identifying potential vulnerabilities and providing recommendations for mitigating risks.

AI-driven security operations centers (SOCs): The emergence of AI and machine learning will propel the creation of security operations centers (SOCs) that are driven by AI. These SOCs will be equipped with AI-powered tools that will provide intelligent and automated analysis of large volumes of data, enabling security professionals to quickly identify and respond to threats.

To sum up, AI and machine learning are expected to lead to better threat detection and response, increased automation, more advanced threat hunting, predictive threat intelligence, enhanced endpoint security, improved risk management, and the creation of AI-driven security operations centers (SOCs) in the future of cybersecurity. As these technologies continue to develop, organizations will be better equipped to defend against increasingly sophisticated and complex cyber threats. However, it is important to recognize that these technologies are not a panacea for all cybersecurity challenges, and that human expertise and a holistic approach to cybersecurity are still critical for effective cyber defense.

Trends and Future Directions for AI and Machine Learning in Cybersecurity

The rapid evolution of AI and machine learning is transforming our approach to cybersecurity. Here are some of the current trends and future directions for these technologies in cybersecurity:

Increased use of unsupervised learning: Unsupervised learning refers to a type of machine learning where algorithms can recognize patterns and irregularities in data without any explicit training on a predefined set of examples. This approach is gaining popularity in cybersecurity, as it allows security professionals to detect new and emerging threats that may not fit into pre-existing threat categories.

Integration with security orchestration, automation, and response (SOAR) platforms: As AI and machine learning become more prevalent in cybersecurity, they are also being combined with SOAR platforms to enhance the overall efficiency and effectiveness of security operations. These platforms can automate threat detection and response, provide real-time incident management, and help reduce response times.

Use of generative adversarial networks (GANs) for deepfake detection: Deepfakes are becoming increasingly common in cybersecurity, with malicious actors using these synthetic media to spread disinformation and manipulate public opinion. GANs, a kind of machine learning algorithm, have the ability to identify deepfakes by contrasting them with the original content and detecting discrepancies.

Increased focus on explainability and interpretability: AI and machine learning algorithms can sometimes be difficult to interpret and explain, leading to concerns about their reliability and transparency. As a result, there is an increasing focus on developing models that are more transparent and interpretable, allowing security professionals to understand how the algorithm is making decisions and why.

Use of AI for threat hunting: Threat hunting involves proactively searching for security threats that may have evaded traditional security measures. The involvement of AI in this process can aid in the examination of substantial amounts of data, recognizing patterns and inconsistencies that could indicate the existence of a potential threat.

Integration with IoT security: With the escalating number of Internet of Things (IoT) devices, there is an augmented requirement for better security measures. AI and machine learning can be utilized to detect and obstruct assaults on IoT devices, presenting an added level of defense for organizations.

Increased use of natural language processing (NLP) for threat intelligence: NLP, which is a form of AI, enables machines to comprehend and interpret human language. In cybersecurity, this technology can be used to analyze threat intelligence reports and extract valuable information that can be used to improve security measures.

Emphasis on privacy and data protection: The growing utilization of AI and machine learning in cybersecurity has led to a greater emphasis on safeguarding the privacy and security of sensitive data. This includes developing techniques for anonymizing data and ensuring that algorithms are not biased or discriminatory.

In conclusion, It is expected that unsupervised learning will be more widely adopted in the future of AI and machine learning in cybersecurity, integration with SOAR platforms, use of GANs for deepfake detection, increased focus on explainability and interpretability, use of AI for threat hunting, integration with IoT security, increased use of NLP for threat intelligence, and emphasis on privacy and data protection. These trends and future directions are likely to lead to more effective and efficient cybersecurity measures, providing a better defense against an ever-evolving range of cyber threats. However, as with any technology, It is crucial to acknowledge the constraints and probable hazards linked with implementing AI and machine learning in cybersecurity, and to guarantee that their application is responsible and ethical.

Potential Impact of AI and Machine Learning on Cybersecurity

The probable influence of AI and machine learning on cybersecurity is considerable and extensive. AI and machine learning are transforming the way cybersecurity professionals detect, analyze, and respond to cyber threats. Here are some potential impacts of AI and machine learning on cybersecurity:

Improved threat detection: Artificial intelligence and machine learning have the capability to swiftly and precisely identify potential dangers from vast quantities of data, surpassing the speed and accuracy of human detection. They can also identify patterns and anomalies in data that might be difficult for humans to detect, enabling organizations to identify and respond to threats more effectively (Hodge & Austin, 2004).

Increased efficiency: Artificial intelligence and machine learning have the ability to mechanize several everyday cybersecurity assignments, liberating cybersecurity experts to concentrate on more intricate tasks that mandate human involvement. This can lead to improved efficiency and productivity for cybersecurity teams.

Better incident response: AI and machine learning can help cybersecurity teams respond to incidents more quickly and effectively. For example, they can mechanize the procedures of incident response, which in turn curtails the duration required to recognize and restrain potential hazards.

More effective vulnerability management: AI and machine learning can help organizations identify vulnerabilities more quickly and accurately, enabling them to patch vulnerabilities before they can be exploited. This can reduce the risk of cyber attacks and data breaches.

Enhanced threat intelligence: AI and machine learning can analyze threat data to provide more accurate and actionable threat intelligence. This can help organizations stay ahead of emerging threats and proactively respond to potential cyber attacks.

Improved user authentication and access control: Artificial intelligence and machine learning can be utilized to enhance user authentication and access control, thereby heightening the difficulty for cybercriminals to access sensitive data and systems. One use case is the detection and prevention of deceptive login efforts by leveraging AI and machine learning.

Better fraud detection: The application of artificial intelligence and machine learning can enable real-time identification and prevention of fraud. As an illustration, financial organizations can utilize AI and machine learning to recognize deceitful transactions and obstruct their processing.

Enhanced security for IoT devices: The proliferation of IoT devices has created new cybersecurity challenges, as many of these devices are not designed with security in mind. The utilization of AI and machine learning can aid in the identification and handling of potential hazards on IoT devices, allowing companies to enhance the safety of their IoT ecosystems.

Increased use of predictive analytics: Predictive analytics enables the examination of data to anticipate potential risks or hazards in advance. This can help organizations proactively respond to potential threats and prevent cyber attacks.

Greater use of unsupervised learning: Unsupervised learning refers to a category of machine learning in which data can be scrutinized and patterns can be recognized without any explicit training. This can be useful for detecting new and emerging threats that might not be identified using traditional supervised learning techniques.

Overall, AI and machine learning have the potential to significantly affect cybersecurity. By leveraging these technologies, organizations can improve their cybersecurity posture and better protect themselves from cyber threats. It is essential to acknowledge that AI and machine learning alone are not a complete solution, and to achieve effectiveness, they need to be combined with additional cybersecurity measures.

Final Thoughts on the Potential of AI and Machine Learning in Cybersecurity

To sum up, the potential for AI and machine learning in the field of cybersecurity is extensive and optimistic. With the constant advancement and complexity of cyber threats, it has become crucial to rely on advanced technologies for detecting and responding to these threats. AI and machine learning have the capability to revolutionize the manner in which corporations deal with cybersecurity by delivering improved precision, productivity, and swiftness in identifying and addressing cyber hazards.

However, it is important to recognize that AI and machine learning are not a panacea, and there are still many challenges that need to be addressed before their full potential can be realized. One of the biggest obstacles is the problem of biased data, which may arise if AI and machine learning models are trained using incomplete or biased data sets. This can result in the models making inaccurate or unfair decisions, which can have serious consequences for individuals and organizations. To address this issue, it is essential that organizations ensure that their data sets are diverse and representative of the populations they serve.

Another challenge is the issue of explainability. Numerous AI and machine learning models are opaque systems, making it challenging to comprehend their decision-making process. This can be problematic from a regulatory perspective, as it can be difficult to demonstrate compliance with regulations such as the GDPR. As AI and machine learning are increasingly used in cybersecurity, it will be essential to develop explainable models that can be audited and explained to regulators and other stakeholders.

Apart from these difficulties, there are ethical implications that must be dealt with. For instance, there are apprehensions regarding the implementation of AI and machine learning in domains like facial recognition, where the technology can be utilized for biased objectives. To ensure that AI and machine learning are used in an ethical and responsible way, it will be essential for organizations to develop clear policies and frameworks that address these concerns.

Notwithstanding these obstacles, it is evident that AI and machine learning possess immense potential in the realm of cybersecurity. As the volume and complexity of cyber threats continue to increase, the need for advanced technologies to detect and respond to them becomes increasingly urgent. Through the utilization of AI and machine learning capabilities, organizations can enhance their defense against cyber threats and reduce the vulnerabilities associated with cyberattacks.

Organizations must allocate resources, talent, and infrastructure to enable the full potential of AI and machine learning for cybersecurity. This includes developing robust data sets, ensuring compliance with regulations, and providing ongoing training and development for cybersecurity professionals. By taking these measures, organizations can utilize the strength of AI and machine learning to formulate cybersecurity strategies that are more efficient and effective. This can help safeguard both the organization and its customers against potential cyber threats.

In conclusion, the potential of AI and machine learning in cybersecurity is considerable; however, it is crucial that organizations confront the difficulties and ethical implications linked with these technologies. By doing so, they can leverage the power of AI and machine learning to create more effective and efficient cybersecurity strategies, and better protect themselves from the evolving and complex cyber threats of today and tomorrow.

REFERENCES

Adadi, A., & Berrada, M. (2018). Peeking inside the black-box: A survey on Explainable Artificial Intelligence (XAI). *IEEE Access : Practical Innovations, Open Solutions, 6*, 52138–52160. doi:10.1109/ACCESS.2018.2870052

Ahmadi, H., Zhang, H., Kulkarni, S., & Yang, G. (2019). Cybersecurity Threats: A Machine Learning Perspective. In Y. Li, X. Li, & Y. Zhang (Eds.), *Guide to Vulnerability Analysis for Computer Networks and Systems*. Springer. doi:10.1007/978-981-13-7263-82

Akintoye, S. A., & Alaba, F. A. (2020). Artificial Intelligence and Cybersecurity: A Review of Applications and Future Directions. *Journal of Cybersecurity and Information Management, 3*(2), 55–72.

Al-Fuqaha, A., Guizani, M., Mohammadi, M., Aledhari, M., & Ayyash, M. (2015). Internet of Things: A Survey on Enabling Technologies, Protocols, and Applications. *IEEE Communications Surveys and Tutorials, 17*(4), 2347–2376. doi:10.1109/COMST.2015.2444095

Almgren, M., Jiang, Y., & Ramzan, Z. (2018). Adversarial Machine Learning: Attacks and Defenses. *IEEE Security and Privacy, 16*(6), 32–44. doi:10.1109/MSP.2018.2701193

Almukaynizi, M. (2020). Cybersecurity and Artificial Intelligence: A Review. *Journal of Artificial Intelligence and Data Science, 2*(1), 1–15.

Alom, M. Z., Yakopcic, C., Taha, T. M., Westberg, K., Sidike, P., Nasrin, M. S., ... Hasan, M. (2019). A state-of-the-art survey on deep learning theory and architectures. *Electronics (Basel), 8*(3), 292. doi:10.3390/electronics8030292

Alqurashi, M., & Mahmoud, Q. H. (2019). A survey on machine learning for cybersecurity. *IEEE Access : Practical Innovations, Open Solutions, 7*, 46127–46141.

Alvarez, R., & Vaisman, A. (2020). Machine Learning in Cybersecurity: Applications and Challenges. *IEEE Security and Privacy, 18*(1), 69–76.

Amin, S., Liao, K., Wang, D., & Singhal, A. (2019). A survey of deep learning for cyber security. *IEEE Communications Surveys and Tutorials, 22*(1), 270–309.

Amiri, S., Pouryazdanpanah, M., Heydari, M., & Abdar, M. (2020). A Machine Learning Approach for Network Security Based on NSL-KDD Dataset. *Journal of Ambient Intelligence and Humanized Computing, 11*(6), 2497–2507. doi:10.100712652-019-01311-x

Appelbaum, J., Gibson, A., Goetz, J., Kucherena, A., & Shubin, S. (2014). Edward Snowden: The whistleblower behind the NSA surveillance revelations. *The Guardian*, p. 10.

Arashloo, R. S., & Rabiee, H. R. (2019). Machine learning in intrusion detection: A comprehensive survey. *Journal of Network and Computer Applications, 135*, 1–25.

Arias-Oliva, M., Mendoza-Gonzalez, R., & de la Hoz-Manotas, A. (2020). Cybersecurity in smart cities: Challenges and opportunities. *Journal of Network and Computer Applications, 168*, 102680.

Arora, S., & Kapoor, V. (2019). Artificial intelligence for cybersecurity: A comprehensive review. *Journal of Network and Computer Applications, 130*, 114–133.

Arpaci-Dusseau, A. C., & Arpaci-Dusseau, R. H. (2018). *Operating systems: Three easy pieces*. Arpaci-Dusseau Books.

Baker, B., & Wilson, D. (2020). Explainable AI: Beware of inmates running the asylum or: How I learned to stop worrying and love the social and behavioral sciences. *Journal of Applied Research in Memory and Cognition, 9*(2), 298–307.

Banerjee, A., & Gupta, A. (2020). Intelligent anomaly detection in cyber security: A survey. *Journal of Network and Computer Applications, 150*, 102506.

Bhattacharya, S., Gudlaugsson, T., & Poddar, R. (2019). A Comprehensive Survey on Deep Learning for Cybersecurity. *Journal of Big Data, 6*(1), 24. doi:10.118640537-019-0187-3

Bhattacharyya, S., Chakraborty, S., Nandi, S., & Dutta, S. (2020). Cybersecurity in the era of industry 4.0: Challenges and opportunities. *Journal of Network and Computer Applications, 150*, 102524.

Bhowmik, T. K., Islam, M. R., & Rahman, M. M. (2020). An Overview of Cybersecurity and Artificial Intelligence. *International Journal of Advanced Science and Technology, 29*(2), 1261–1271.

Bishop, M. (2019). Artificial intelligence and cybersecurity. *Computer Fraud & Security, 2019*(6), 13–16.

Bouzeghoub, A., & Zeghidour, N. (2021). AI and cybersecurity: A review of current trends and future directions. *Journal of Ambient Intelligence and Humanized Computing, 12*(4), 3355–3368.

Buczak, A. L., & Guven, E. (2016). A Survey of Data Mining and Machine Learning Methods for Cyber Security Intrusion Detection. *IEEE Communications Surveys and Tutorials, 18*(2), 1153–1176. doi:10.1109/COMST.2015.2494502

Buczak, A. L., & Guven, E. (2018a). Deep Learning-Based Anomaly Detection: A Survey. *ACM Computing Surveys, 51*(3), 46. Advance online publication. doi:10.1145/3186243

Buczak, A. L., & Guven, E. (2018b). A survey of data mining and machine learning methods for cyber security intrusion detection. *IEEE Communications Surveys and Tutorials, 18*(2), 1153–1176. doi:10.1109/COMST.2015.2494502

Bukhari, S. A., & Awad, A. I. (2019). A survey on machine learning techniques for anomaly detection in network traffic. *Journal of Network and Computer Applications, 133*, 114–137.

Buonocunto, P., de Oliveira, S. H., Gomes, J. P., dos Santos, J. A., da Silva, J. M., & de Castro, L. N. (2019). A Review on Machine Learning and Artificial Intelligence Approaches for Cybersecurity. *Journal of Information Security and Applications, 48*, 102387. doi:10.1016/j.jisa.2019.102387

Cai, W., & Vasconcelos, N. (2018). Cascade R-CNN: Delving into high quality object detection. In *Proceedings of the IEEE conference on computer vision and pattern recognition* (pp. 6154-6162). 10.1109/CVPR.2018.00644

Calderon, M., & Zeadally, S. (2020). The internet of things in the era of 5G: Opportunities and challenges. *Journal of Network and Computer Applications, 168*, 102691.

Cao, Y., Zhang, X., Kang, J., Wang, X., & Sun, H. (2019). An effective end-to-end deep learning architecture for benign and malicious network traffic classification. *IEEE Access : Practical Innovations, Open Solutions*, *7*, 57522–57530.

Carlin, D. J., Kuleshov, V., Lupu, E. C., & Longstaff, T. A. (2018). Machine Learning and Security: Protecting Systems with Data and Algorithms. *IEEE Security and Privacy*, *16*(5), 68–77. doi:10.1109/MSP.2018.2801080

Carlini, N., & Wagner, D. (2017). Towards evaluating the robustness of neural networks. In *2017 IEEE Symposium on Security and Privacy (SP)* (pp. 39-57). IEEE. 10.1109/SP.2017.49

Carrara, F., Böhme, R., & Caviglione, L. (2020). Cybersecurity of the internet of things: A review of the literature. *Computer Science Review*, *35*, 100212.

Cavoukian, A. (2015). *Privacy by design: The 7 foundational principles.* Information and Privacy Commissioner of Ontario.

Chandola, V., Banerjee, A., & Kumar, V. (2009). Anomaly Detection: A Survey. *ACM Computing Surveys*, *41*(3), 15. Advance online publication. doi:10.1145/1541880.1541882

Chen, L., He, K., & Sun, J. (2016). Deep residual learning for image recognition. In *Proceedings of the IEEE conference on computer vision and pattern recognition* (pp. 770-778). IEEE.

Chen, M., Mao, S., & Liu, Y. (2014). Big data: A survey. *Mobile Networks and Applications*, *19*(2), 171–209. doi:10.100711036-013-0489-0

Chen, X., Ma, H., Song, D., & Sun, X. (2020). Survey on Artificial Intelligence and Cybersecurity. *International Journal of Advanced Computer Science and Applications*, *11*(5), 88–98.

Chhetri, S. K., & Singh, B. (2020). Artificial Intelligence in Cybersecurity: A Review. *International Journal of Computer Science and Network Security*, *20*(1), 87–93.

Chollet, F. (2017). *Deep learning with Python.* Manning Publications.

Chu, C. H., & Chen, J. V. (2019). The application of artificial intelligence in cybersecurity. *International Journal of Innovative Computing, Information, & Control*, *15*(3), 1179–1193.

Cohen, R., & Toubiana, V. (2018). Explaining explanations: An overview of interpretability of machine learning. *IEEE 5th International Conference on Data Science and Advanced Analytics (DSAA).*

Cosgrave, J., O'Hara, K., & Blyth, A. (2021). Ethical considerations for the use of artificial intelligence in cybersecurity. *Journal of Cybersecurity*, *7*(1), 1–12.

Cui, Y., Yu, F. X., & Jain, A. K. (2019). Unsupervised learning of anatomy-aware embeddings for cross-modality liver segmentation. *IEEE Transactions on Medical Imaging*, *38*(6), 1436–1447.

Dal Pozzolo, A., Boracchi, G., Caelen, O., Alippi, C., & Bontempi, G. (2018). Learned lessons in credit card fraud detection from a practitioner perspective. *Expert Systems with Applications*, *104*, 72–84.

Dang, X. T., Li, J., Li, G., Li, Y., & Li, Z. (2019). A deep learning approach for malware classification using dynamic analysis. *Journal of Computer and System Sciences*, *105*, 143–157.

Debar, H., Dacier, M., & Wespi, A. (2020). AI and machine learning in cybersecurity: The good, the bad and the ugly. *Journal of Cybersecurity*, *6*(1), 1–16.

Demertzis, I., Tserpes, K., & Varvarigou, T. (2019). Anomaly detection in cybersecurity using machine learning algorithms. In *Proceedings of the 14th International Conference on Availability, Reliability and Security (ARES)* (pp. 1-10). Academic Press.

Dougan, J. (2019). Artificial intelligence in cybersecurity: A review. *Journal of Information Privacy and Security*, *15*(4), 191–210.

Dua, S., & Du, X. (2019). Building and explaining reliable anomaly detection models in a high-dimensional and imbalanced data space. *IEEE Access : Practical Innovations, Open Solutions*, *7*, 52466–52479.

Elgamal, T., & Rizk, M. (2020). Adversarial machine learning: A comprehensive survey. *Pattern Recognition Letters*, *131*, 138–145.

Farahmandi, R., Khodabandelou, G., & Aghakhani, H. (2019). A survey on machine learning methods for cybersecurity. *IEEE Communications Surveys and Tutorials*, *21*(3), 2753–2773.

Fasbender, D., & Siddiqui, S. (2019). Detection of phishing websites using machine learning. *Procedia Computer Science*, *151*, 574–579.

Grosse, K., Papernot, N., Manoharan, P., Backes, M., & McDaniel, P. (2017). Adversarial examples for malware detection. *Proceedings of the 10th ACM Workshop on Artificial Intelligence and Security*.

Hodge, V. J., & Austin, J. (2004). A survey of outlier detection methodologies. *Artificial Intelligence Review*, *22*(2), 85–126. doi:10.1023/B:AIRE.0000045502.10941.a9

Chapter 8
Assessing the Impact of GeoAI in the World of Spatial Data and Energy Revolution

Shradha Chavan
Symbiosis International University, India

Preeti Mulay
(iD) https://orcid.org/0000-0002-4779-6726
Symbiosis Institute of Technology, Symbiosis International University, India

ABSTRACT

Geospatial is going to be the absolute heart of making sense of trillions of bits of data that are going to be surveyed by big machines. The buzz word of the last 4-5 years has been artificial intelligence (AI) and is influencing every marketplace including GIS, healthcare, pollution, and the list is truly endless. It is the world of collaborative and multidisciplinary research where technology is applied in almost every domain and has proved extremely useful to end-users. The diversity of themes identified in this chapter can be grouped into the categories of renewable energy mapping: spatiotemporal analysis, and data mining. This chapter gives a comprehensive account of transformation from the classical ML clustering techniques with the potential of quantum clustering (QC) which can be applied or mapped to renewable energy solutions driven by use of GIS, or narrating the importance of GIS and quantum. This chapter highlights the relationship between GeoAI, cybersecurity, and quantum computing in the world of spatial data.

1. INTRODUCTION

History tells us that the value shift is triggered by a new perspective on the way of life. AI, the Internet of Things (IoT) and big data are changing economies, industries, societies and our lifestyles. The revolution is manifold and by far the most advanced with breakthroughs in sectors such as 3D printing, robotics, energy, blockchain, autonomous vehicles and more. Automation drastically upgrades the efficiency of organization and businesses empower people all over the world.

DOI: 10.4018/978-1-6684-9317-5.ch008

AI will become an absolute enabler in the utility of the future. The state-of-art technology is used to get insight from the volume of data to harvest from energy system. AI tools have the ability to identify patterns and trends within energy sets of data. From that energy data we can start making analytics and predictions. Generated insights and predictions can help to enact traders' decision support systems. The end-to-end story of an AI solutions, it could fit anywhere in the processes and operational chain of the energy provider companies. AI solutions helps in such a way that managing assets, trading, forecasts of the needs for the future. The good quality data i.e. weather data, geographical assets data, historical demand data, prices data, and supply data for the AI analytics to pickup patterns. The terminology ML further uses for decision making and optimization of energy system operations. The paper addresses uses of various ML techniques used to solve issues related to integration and generation of renewable energy (Adeniyi, 2016).

Expectations from AI:

A. Trends and patterns
B. Predictive analytics
C. Actionable insights
D. Automated actions based on predictions

Geospatial data and technologies aspire to be an integral part of the disruptive journey. Imagine a world where smart, connected and effective monitoring will make breathing easier for us and our surroundings more liveable. A map is a way of organizing all the information related to everybody's place. There is an entire information ecosystem that we have access to like never before. Anyone can broadcast their location and that is revolutionary. Geospatial technology approach can helpful to near-term opportunities to assessed regional and national energy targets for renewables. The design distribution and control of the energy system is highly complex and to address generation and storage of energy. The geospatial technology and AI combined model gives variety of options to improve smart distribution of energy surveillance the energy demand [49]. The tones of high resolution input data from the turbines via satellite to cloud can be stored every day. To handle such type of data, scientist move from classical techniques to quantum technology (Zhou,2021).

This chapter addresses how the renewable energy mapped with GeoAI and quantum technology. Section 2 covers basics of ML and approach of clustering with the help of classical clustering algorithm. And also discusses about strength of AI and ML for geospatial and renewable energy industry. Section 3 includes the concept of quantum computer, comparison between classical and quantum computer, and the glimpse of QML area for better understanding of quantum technology. Lastly the conclusion and discussion section 4 discuss about the use of and future scope of quantum technology in renewable energy sectors.

2. ARTIFICIAL INTELLIGENCE AND MACHINE LEARNING FOR THE GEOSPATIAL AND RENEWABLE ENERGY INDUSTRY

AI started back in the 1950s but it's becoming increasingly popular. ML is the science of getting the computer to act without being programmed. So it's a way of programming the computers to learn from the available data. ML continues to learn from data as new data is brought in. Therefore it can become increasingly more accurate as the ML algorithm moves on. It involves teaching a computer to recognize patterns, learn from the patterns and then be able to make predictions based on the data. Following Figure1 shows major categories of ML system based outputs. ML has simple steps, it makes data to be able to train itself, learn from patterns and then it can classify itself. The ability to repurpose the ML algorithm for different things such as identifying pervious vs impervious surfaces and using that same algorithm to be able to perform object identification makes ML extremely powerful. In ML the data and training the data is the most critical part as one needs to have enough unbiased data to be able to train the system effectively. Attributed which are features that are used to train the system and these are the properties of the objects. In ML, quality and quantity are directly related to accuracy and output. Building a geospatial data refinery, the first component of machinery is automated data ingestion pipelines which aggregate and collect raw data from multiple sources (Kotsiantis,2006). Then cleaning, processing, validating and storing of datasets can be done. Next, it proceeds to cloud-native AI and ML models where they are analyzed to give final actionable insights.

2.1 ML Workflow

- Gathering training data
- Selection of attributes
- Selection of the ML system/algorithm
- Train the ML system/algorithm
- Prediction

Figure 1. Categories of ML

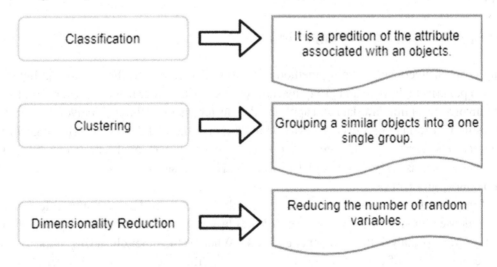

First of all, collecting training data is a major task. One then needs to select attributes that can later be used in training more data. Next, one needs to figure out an algorithm that is suitable for both the data as well as applications and then needs to train the system/algorithm. Finally, after the system/algorithm is trained we can use that training to predict in the dataset that the machine hasn't seen before. Let's jump into some of the ML algorithms, what they are all about and when they should be used for a variety of data.

- K-nearest Neighbours (Wei, 2016): This algorithm assumes that similar things exist near one another. It's an instance-based algorithm and this means that it does not generate a model based on the training data. K-nearest algorithm saves the training data info and when it's doing the prediction it compares the new data to training data to make predictions. K-nearest algorithm especially works for uniformly sampled data.

- Classification and Regression Tree (CART) (Loh,2014): CART a type of decision tree to represents alternatives of branches of predictions. CART is simple and easy to understand making it one of the most commonly used algorithms. CART is less influenced by outliers and anomalies so it's really good for classifying noisy data.

- Random Forest (Pal,2005): This algorithm grows multiple trees independent of one another, as opposed to a single tree in the CART model. Each tree gives a classification result. The forest chooses the class that has had most votes. The Random forest method is used across different disciplines and not just geospatial.

- Support Vector Machine (SVM) (Zheng,,2014): SVM is based on finding a hyperplane that separates classes and it works wonders when there are clear definitions and separations of classes. If the target classes are overlapping then this technique is not useful. For example, in vegetation when classes may be very similar. SVM also doesn't perform well on imbalanced or skewed training datasets.

- K-means (Agababov,2015): All previous classifiers were ML supervised classifiers. K-means is an unsupervised ML algorithm. It uses clusters of data to separate classes into a set number of classes that can be minimized by calculating the sum of the squares of the distances between the data points. The corresponding class centroids will then learn from this result to create such a cluster and identify a specific number of classes.

2.2 The Approach of Clustering in ML

Clustering is an unsupervised learning method used as a data analysis technique to highlight and discover hidden patterns in the data and grouping same characteristics of objects in clustering. The steps of clustering involve accepting raw data and applying the clustering algorithm to receive clusters of data as the final result. Clustering analyzes categorical, binary and numerical data. Clustering algorithms deal with large datasets, variety of attributes and handle low/high dimensional data (Loh, 2014). Figure2 illustrate the uses of clustering. In the social network analysis, clustering is used to recognize communities within a large group of people.

Most of the algorithms use distance measure or similarity between characteristics in feature space to discover the dense region of observation. Some of the clustering algorithms have to specify the random number of clusters to analyze the data (Zheng,, 2014). Whereas the other clustering algorithm requires the distance observation of data points to centroid whether they are close or connected. Such type of cluster analysis has the iterative process. Following are the different categories of clustering algorithms (Verma,,2012).

Figure 2. Various uses of clustering across a variety of industries

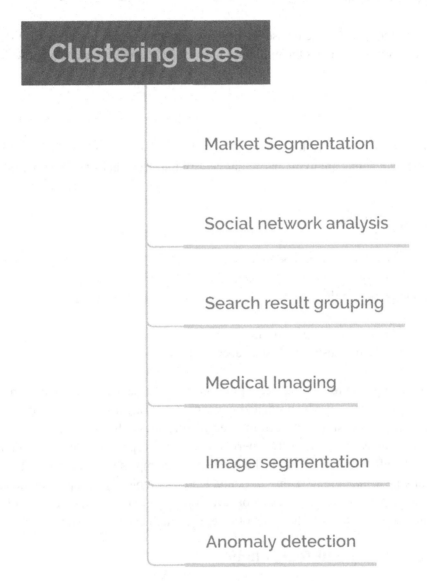

- Centroid based clustering:

In this methodology, choose the number of clusters that are required for a given situation. First, determine a centroid for each cluster and then see which data points belong to that cluster. It determines how far away the data points from the centroid. At the beginning of the algorithm choose the centroid randomly. The centroid based clustering algorithm works on pretty small datasets. Then normally iterate through many iterations to determine what the optimum groupings are.

- Density-based clustering:

Use density clustering when the datasets a little more offbeat and complicated. In density clustering, group the data points which has the minimum inter-cluster bond is present and how densely they're populated together.

- Hierarchical clustering:

Hierarchical clustering starts with individual clusters and creates cluster tree. Rather than determining how close the data points are to the particular centroid, it determines how the points are related to each other.

2.1.1 Clustering Workflow

To cluster data following steps should be followed:

1. Choosing and preparing the data.
2. Creating a similarity metric.
3. Running appropriate clustering algorithm.
4. Analyzing results and adjusts the clusters accordingly.

The data combining feature requires the data to have the same scale. One can transform data for multiple features to the same scale by normalizing the data. Making a similarity metric requires understanding the data and getting similar data from selected attributes (Zheng,,2014).

Improving the result requires iteratively experimenting with the previous steps of a running clustering algorithm to see the effect of clustering. If the dataset has examples with missing values for a certain feature the options are to either remove this particular feature completely or to predict the missing values from another example by using an ML model. For several years a great effort has been devoted to the study of geospatial data using clustering. The focus of recent research can be shown in the following Table1.

2.3 Brief About Geospatial Technology

The technology in itself extends human capabilities. Microscope extends our capabilities to seek things at a micro-level. The telescope does the opposite, like seeing things we can't see naturally so we can discern patterns and get an understanding. That's what geospatial technology does. It extends human interpretation beyond capabilities. Geospatial is the golden thread which links so many different datasets together while giving us the permission to connect, innovate and thread things together. Geospatial allows further levels of capabilities and provides more freedom for individuals to prioritise a profound impact on their country (DiBiase,,2010). The geospatial industry ecosystem is leveraging and enhancing its value to larger Information

Table 1. Literature review of geospatial data using clustering algorithms (data fetched from the Scopus database and Google scholar on 17 Feb, 2021)

Title	Year	Contributions	Datasets
"The spread of COVID-19 virus through population density and wind in Turkey cities" (Coşkun,2020)	2020	Findings presents that wind and population density were contributing in spreading the virus. The air pollution, sunny days, humidity & air temperature didn't affect the number of cases.	By TURKSTAT, population density and Population data was collected, "Ministry of Environment and Urbanization (2019) air pollution data"
"The effect of climate on the spread of the COVID-19 pandemic: A review of findings, and statistical and modelling techniques" (Briz-Redón,2020)	2020	Effects of climate on COVID-19's global expansion.	Carabayllo, Campo de Marte, San Juan de Lurigancho, Santa Anita, San Borja, Villa del Triunfo.
"Europe's war against covid-19: A map of countries' disease vulnerability using mortality indicators" (Horobet,2020)	2020	Author proposed how various patterns of disease contribute in growth and death rates.	"World Health Organization. European Mortality Database (MDB)"
"Assessing the spatial-temporal clustering and health implications of fine particulate matter (PM2.5)" (Liew,2020)	2020	Author analyzes the variations in mean annual exposure of PM 2.5. 1990 to 2000 air pollution data is considered and see the changes in deaths due to diseases using spatialtemporal clustering.	"World Bank Open Data and the World Health Organization's Global Health Observatory (GHO) Data Repository"
"Winter is coming: A socio-environmental monitoring and spatiotemporal modeling approach for better understanding a respiratory disease" (Marek, 2018)	2018	Explored combination of demographical, environmental and social conditions. Hospital admissions due to Chronic Obstructive Pulmonary Disease in an urban area of Christchurch (NZ).	"Demographic data used in the study came from the New Zealand census in 2013"
"Identification of Regions and Probable Health Risks Due to Air Pollution Using K-Mean Clustering Techniques" (Paulose, 2018)	2018	Identified the air pollutant in the specific areas of Delhi using the k-means clustering algorithm	"Central Pollution Control Board (CPCB) for five regions of Delhi namely, Dwarka, Rk Puram, Mandir Marg, Punjabi Bagh and Anand Vihar for the year 2015 and 2016"

Technology (IT) and engineering industries including automation and AI. Upcoming trends in geospatial technologies are expected to impact at multiple levels and diverse sectors. Thus, leading to accelerated growth rate and path-breaking innovations. With big data collecting a copious amount of data, this data needs to be churned to get meaningful information out of it. Handling such a huge amount of data demands advancements in analytics. Big Corporation relying on such data need to break this data in meaningful blocks promptly to implement it and to use it as a competitive edge in business. AI is one such technique that with advancement will be used in various sectors. In this age of Digitalization, bigger and wider networks are formed across boundaries leading to geospatial data getting more ubiquitous. Geospatial technology tells a story about a specific area, country or planet. Geospatial technology will continue to advance; especially aim to alter the way we live, work (DiBiase,,2010). The map of the earth changed forever, the volume of the iceberg is said to be twice as large as Lake Erie. The joint section of the ice shelf broke free in Antarctica in 2017. Satellites were used to keep an eye on Antarctica incident (Arthern, 2017) Geospatial technology can help observe the effects of climate change, prevent threats to biodiversity and improve natural resource management. Geospatial technologies can meet the needs of humanitarian access. Images are updated on daily basis, evolutions of natural disaster are observed along with their impacts on our populations in real-time. Geospatial technologies have a strong focus on data analytics and now more than ever to achieve developed outcomes. AI provides real-time resources allocation through satellite mapping and data analysis. Agriculture productivity is increased with the help of imaging with automated drones and satellites (Liew,,2020). Precision agriculture tools can go a long way in increasing agriculture produce and mitigating hunger. Billions of mobile devices such as smartphones and cameras are being used to diagnose heart, eye and blood disorders. Spatial data is information related to the shapes of geographic features and location, and the relationships between them stored as coordinates and topology. Following mindmap Figure6 shows the details of GeoAI for spatial analysis. This includes details of available platforms, algorithm and highlights the applications area. PostgreSQL support geometry and geography data types. PostGIS stores destinations as points and includes in the database using equalized [58]. Following Figure3 presents the top subject areas which use ML to analyze geospatial data.

Figure 3. Popular subject areas of GeoAI
(Fetched from Scopus on 10th Feb 2021)

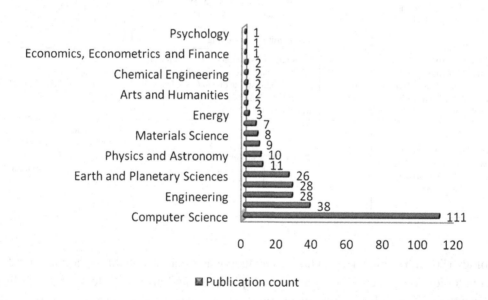

In Geographic Information System (GIS) when we target a problem it not only contains geographic data but also contains the exact time, temporal information and attributes information (DiBiase,,2010). GIS model is a conceptual framework which defines geographic data elements and their interrelationships. GIS data model has two types one is roster data model and other is vector data model. The geographic data represents in an array of grid or pixel forms in roster model. The roster model is also known as a gridded data model (Chaudhry,2019) .The pixel and grid contain information. The colour information contains precipitation value, temperature value or height in the GIS environment. The pair of (x,y) co-ordinates used to define the geographic data in conceptual framework of vector model (DiBiase,,2010). The relation of the points can create particular lines and closed rings can create polygons. In Figure6 the mind map shows a list of software, application areas and clustering algorithms for geospatial data.

2.4 Brief About Renewable Energy

Energy is the ability of an object to do some sort of work. Energy exists in different forms, depending upon the sources of generation which includes solar energy, geothermal energy, hydro-energy, wind energy, biomass energy, hybrid energy etc (Gulagi,,2021). The mind map shows the variety of renewable energy resources (See Figure6). Following points discuses the significant description of types of renewable energy sources:

- Solar Energy:

Earth receives huge amount of energy directly from the sun, using synthetic method and that energy is widely known as solar energy. AI driven solar forecasting could provide the better efficiency of solar power. Predicting the scale and timing of the variations in weather is crucial for demand and supply of energy. Solocast's technology employs a third generation satellite "Nowcasting" system. This can detect and predict cloud characteristics, track aerosols and utilise numerical weather model data (Nersesian,2014).

- Wind Energy:

Wind turbines are basically sleeker higher tech versions of the windmills of the past. Instead of using the wind to do farm work they are designed to use for wind energy into electricity. Smart AI and GIS technology can help to reduce the operating cost of wind energy plant. The previous study shows that wind speed forecasting and energy potential analysis (Infield,2020). The analysis maintains characteristics of the wind speed data assessment and presents original wind speed time series.

- Hydro Energy:

The hydro power provides 60% of total renewable electricity production. Hydro energy is leading in the energy market prices and plays an important role in green energy generation. The author apply ML methodology such as support vector machine, linear regression and neural networks to see the relationship between climate change variable, total water in reservoir and meteorological used in hydro energy generation (Casey, 2018). Some author presents production capacity of individual hydro energy plant using classical techniques (Russo, 2019).

Renewable energy presents some challenges it also offers environmental friendly alternative to the green house gas emissions and pollution of fossil fuels. As advance in technology make renewable energy more accessible affordable and efficient. AI generally refers to adaptive intelligence displayed independently by machine. The behaviour is not necessarily predator but sometimes adapts data inputs. ML is a subset of AI refers to the statistics to give computers to ability to learn from data. The most ML methods are suited to tackling some of the key problems i.e. predictions, clustering and classification problems. Some of the key uses of GeoAI and renewable energy are explained in Figure4.

Government and private companies across the world are taking step into the production and research of the renewable energy resources and facilities. Leading research on various control and power system data, the United States, Germany, Italy, United Kingdom and India are on the top. (See Figure5)

Figure 4. The rules of GeoAI and the transformation of the renewable energy sector
(Gielen, 2019, Infield, 2020, Olabi,2017)

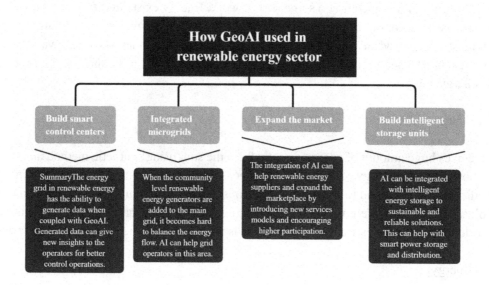

Figure 5. The leaders of the renewable energy research.
The data fetch from Scopus research database (On 27 Feb, 2021)

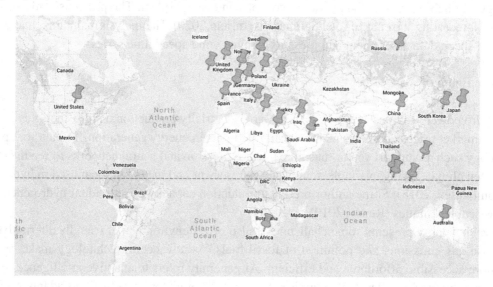

2.5 The Thematic Cluster of GeoAI Analysis and Renewable Energy

Geospatial is a key component of digital transformation. Geospatial technology is about the location and all about how the information revolution will be effective to humankind and the environment in its vicinity. Geospatial refers to everything on earth having relational aspects in space and time. Therefore, the distinction lies in the time scale of change concerning the human experience. The author (Seager,2009) reviews recent research assessment of bio-energy, wind and solar energy generation and distribution

Figure 6. Mind map shows the overview of the GeoAI and renewable energy for spatial analysis (Briz-Redón, Liew, Liu, Bhadane,2020, Marek, Bonetti, 2018)

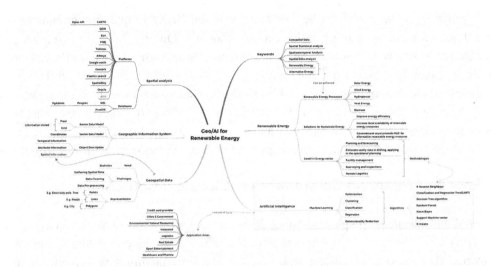

using geospatial aspects. The number of new studies contribution related to use of land and life cycle and its implications of energy technologies. Those studies have come from atmospheric science, geospatial technology, industrial ecology and economics.

To understand permeable reservoir rocks and its relevant sedimentary basins, expanded geothermal energy production is being used. Use of Geospatial technology shows promising signs for the search of geologically stored CO2. The paper's (Maldonado, 2020) search result shows and discusses the suitable position for power plant construction and power generation capacities. The paper (Maldonado, 2020) presents the case study analysis of temporal accounting and geospatial technical potentials suggest reshaping of city-energy relationship.

Data gathered from historic and current national and regional energy production can be analyzed using supply & demand trend combined with forecasting. To take decisions on energy demand and supply the author (Taminiau, 2021) presents the geospatial framework to see the power demand maps. The demand maps can be used for forecast power demand and power infrastructure planning. The author (Maclaurin, 2019) introduces renewable energy platform for examination of energy resources and respective geospatial intersections with land characteristics and grid infrastructure. The fetched results helps to analysis to generation from wind turbine on a particular location, to calculate maintain cost and capital expenditures to present future estimated cost from energy resources or emerging technology.

The author (Hay, 2011) presents Home Energy Assessment Technologies (HEAT) which provides real time energy usage movement. The HEAT specially designed to visualize the location and amount of waste energy of a particular home with the help of Google maps. The presented monitoring solution using GeoAI, achieve to reduce the green house gas emissions and save customers money.

As of now wind energy projects are limited to economic zones of coastal states. With advancement of technology it opens up new avenues of using it across high seas. The author (Elsner, 2019) describes the potential use of geospatial model in generating renewable energy from the high seas.

3. THE CONCEPT OF QUANTUM COMPUTER

In classical computing, a bit can either be 0 or 1 (M. Losada, 2018). In quantum computing [36] a bit can be both 0 and 1 simultaneously. Quantum bits are known as Qubits. Quantum computer (Flammia, 2020) uses Qubits to supply information and communicate through the system. Let's take an example where a user or person has saved word file on the server. This word file is placed on the server that is hosted on the cloud along with many servers. Classical computers sort through all the servers available on the cloud. A Qubit from a quantum computer using a concept of superposition on the other hand (Feig, 2020) can scan multiple servers simultaneously and provide lightning-fast outputs compared to classical computers. Companies providing quantum computers are D-wave, Google, IBM, Microsoft, and Intel.

3.1 The Speed of Quantum Computers vs. Classical Computer

For some problems, quantum computers (Adler, 2004) are faster than classical computers. It is not like a quantum computer is going to completely replace traditional classical computers. Quantum computers (Feynman, 2011) are great at solving problems that involve quantum data or anything involving a simulation just like the universe. Universe operates using both classical and quantum mechanics and that is in fact why Richard Feynman wrote in his paper combining both theories (Feynman, 2011). A couple of decades ago Feynman envisioned a computer that simulates reality perfectly, the only way to do that is via using quantum computers. A quantum computer can solve ML algorithms quickly and efficiently. QML (Fastovets, 2019) is part of the quantum world and objectives defined in QML have a major impact in defining problems.

In the quantum world, ML is used for defining an objective function. The objective function is going to learn from a function with the proper coefficients using some optimization scheme like gradient descent to solve defined objectives. Neural networks are the brain behind deep learning. A lot of experts suggest that neural networks and QML works on similar lines. What does Neural Network use? The Neural Network uses matrix operation. Graphics processing unit (GPUs) to speed up the matrix operations, GPU operations are executed in parallel. Marrying QML and Neural Networks will no doubt enhance its processing speed and capabilities (Altaisky, 2001).

3.2 Quantum Machine Learning Area

QML is one of interest area of researchers and data modellers'. Quantum tools are handy for classical ML and these have to do with linear algebra. Linear algebra is one of the crucial aspects and quantum machine using this feature provides a basis for exploration.

Swap test helps the researcher determine the distance between two Qubits. This present useful information is relevant to both ML (De Martini, 2003) and QML and it is termed as the estimated distances between Qubits. Figure7 represents the salient features of QML over ML. The reason why quantum (Biamonte, 2017) is an interesting field for ML, it already has to deal with a lot of noise. Because the data is very noisy many times even after training using Neural Networks. Due to the above-mentioned drawback, researchers need to come up with an algorithm that has to deal with this noise. Quantum computers are well equipped to deal with noisy data. As ML is known to have noisy data, a quantum computer is better suited to handle it. Additionally, the processing speed of a quantum computer is high. Algorithms executed via quantum computers provide various results. Their results need not be accurate but can be explained, by saying so it gets its property of explainability by considering various scenarios. This is crucial especially to people in healthcare where they wish to use ML to understand the pattern that can help them make informed decisions. There are still issues around how to upload classical data as a Qubit. As of now linear algebra tools will serve this purpose and might help us with future methods. The term quantum computing creates a machine that could go simulate the fundamental nature of physics. Quantum lays the solution to solving a lot of hard problems that we face today. Figure8 outlines the quantum technology advanced enhancement.

Table 2. Comprehensive look of research in spatiotemporal analysis and renewable energy

Authors	Title	Year	Take away	Author Keywords
Uribe-Hurtado A.-L., Ribeiro B.Lopes N., et al.	"GPU-based fast clustering via K-Centres and k-NN mode seeking for geospatial industry applications" (Elsner, 2019)	2020	Geospatial datasets used to demonstrate the performances using GPUs. Provides GPU implementation for clustering.	"Clustering algorithms, Geospatial data industry, Heterogeneous,architectures, K-Centres, k-NN mode seeking"
Fouedjio F.	"Clustering of multivariate geostatistical data" (Uribe-Hurtado,2020)	2020	The articles give systematic review of clustering algorithms which are designed for multivariate geo statistical data. Focus on spatially contiguous clusters by accounting for the spatial dependency of data locations.	"Spatial dependency geostatistics, Cluster analysis, Geospatial data, Multivariate spatial contiguity"
Raj A., Minz S.	"Spatial clustering using neighborhood for multispectral images" (Fouedjio,2016)	2020	Author proposed spatial clustering using neighbourhood (SCN), in which similar neighbouring pixels groups together to form a cluster.	"Calinski-Harabasz index, clustering; Davies Bouldin index, Silhouette coefficient; spatial data"
Bhadane C., Shah K.	"Clustering Algorithms for Spatial Data Mining" (Bhadane, 2020)	2020	clustering algorithms used to find important places of interest using large GPS based mobility datasets. Performance is tested using real-time data of 50 users collected over 2 - 5 years.	"GPS; Region of Interest; Spatial Clustering; Trajectory mining"
Saleh M., Bauke V.,Azarakhsh R.	"An exploratory study on the impact of physical and geospatial characteristics of the urban built environment on the buildings annual electricity usage" (Mohammadi, 2021)	2021	The paper focuses on usages of electricity in the urban built environment. It shows annual usages using building connections.	"Electricity demand modelling, Built environment physical And geospatial characteristics, Multiple linear regression, Ordinary least Squares technique"
Ashish G., Myron A., Amitrii B., Eugene E., Joey O., Christian B.	"Transition pathway towars 100% renewable energy across the sectors of power, heat, transport, and desalination for the Philippines" (Gulagi, 2021)	2021	The paper propose the study related of resource utilization using spatial resolution data and high temporal data from 2015 to 2050 in the Philippines	"Energy transition,100% renewable, Solar energy, Battery storage"
Evangelos T.,Demetrios N., Constantios N., Vagelis G.	"Planning and assessment of an off-grid power supply system for small settlements"(Tsiaras, 2020)	2020	Analyzes the environmental impact and improve design and integration of off-grid hybrid system.	"Wind turbine/PV system, Off-grid power production, Renewable, Energy policy"
Daneil R., Asami M.	"Benefits, challenges, and analytical approaches to scaling up renewable through regional planning and cooradination of power system in Africa" (Russo,2019)	2019	Paper explains challenges and benefits, planning recent studies related to regional and national power systems of Africa.	"Africa, Renewable energy, Regional integration, Power pools, Planning, Modelling, Capacity expansion"

Figure 7. Salient features of QML

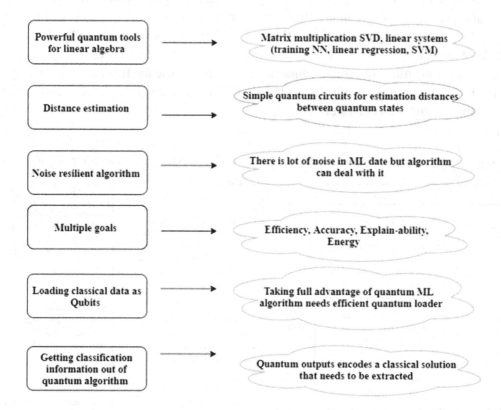

Figure 8. Quantum technology enhancement

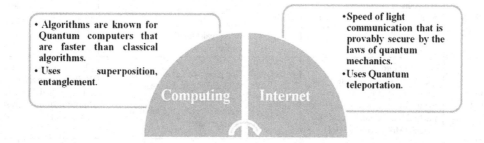

A machine that could help us understands how nature evolves and answers a lot of the problems. Quantum gives a new way to understand how we can find the hidden characteristics that we don't know about the data such as diseases. Quantum computing has various advantages in optimizing and for that reason the researchers put forward to combine the two different fields i.e. quantum technology and a learning algorithm hoping to acquaint or to introduce the benefits of quantum computing. A new type of clustering algorithm with quantum theory is QC algorithm. QC seeks the attention of the researchers and has achieved extensive success in various fields. In the following Table3, several theories have been proposed to explain QC.

3.3. Application of GeoAI and Quantum Computing in the World of Spatial Data and Energy Revolution

The application of GeoAI and quantum computing in the world of spatial data and the energy revolution can bring about transformative advancements and innovative solutions. Here are some specific applications where GeoAI and quantum computing can have a significant impact:

A. **Renewable Energy Site Selection** (Shao, Asadi,2023): GeoAI techniques can analyze spatial data such as terrain characteristics, solar radiation, wind patterns, and proximity to infrastructure to identify optimal locations for renewable energy projects. Quantum computing can enhance the computational power required for complex optimization algorithms, enabling more accurate site selection that maximizes energy generation and minimizes environmental impact.

B. **Grid Optimization and Load Balancing** (Parvin, Javadpour,2023) : Quantum computing can optimize energy grid management, considering factors such as power flow, demand patterns, and distribution constraints. By integrating GeoAI with quantum algorithms, it becomes possible to balance energy loads across the grid, minimize transmission losses, and ensure efficient energy distribution. This can lead to improved grid stability, reduced energy waste, and better utilization of renewable energy sources.

C. **Energy Demand Forecasting and Energy Trading** (Işık, Acquah, 2023): GeoAI techniques can integrate spatial data, weather patterns, historical energy consumption, and other relevant factors to forecast energy demand accurately. Quantum computing can enhance the accuracy and speed of demand forecasting algorithms, enabling real-time predictions and optimal energy trading strategies. This can facilitate efficient energy resource allocation, pricing, and supply-demand balancing.

D. **Energy Infrastructure Planning and Optimization** (Moudgil, Daneshvar, 2023): GeoAI, coupled with quantum computing, can optimize the planning and design of energy infrastructure. By considering spatial factors such as population density, land use, and environmental impacts, along with the computational power of quantum algorithms, it becomes possible to develop optimal infrastructure layouts that minimize costs, maximize energy efficiency, and ensure reliable energy supply.

E. **Climate Change Impact Analysis** (García-del-Amo, Coelho, 2023): GeoAI techniques can analyze spatial data to assess the impact of climate change on energy systems. Quantum computing can enhance the accuracy and speed of climate modeling simulations, enabling better predictions of climate change effects on energy demand, renewable energy potential, and infrastructure resilience. This information can guide decision-making for adapting and mitigating climate change impacts in the energy sector.

F. **Sensor Networks and Real-time Monitoring** (El-Fouly,,2023): Quantum computing can optimize the processing of real-time spatial data from sensor networks deployed in energy systems. By leveraging GeoAI techniques, quantum algorithms can analyze and interpret sensor data, enabling real-time monitoring of energy infrastructure, early detection of faults or anomalies, and proactive maintenance strategies.

G. **Energy Storage Optimization** (Mazzoncini, Das, 2023: Quantum computing can optimize the management and deployment of energy storage systems. By considering spatial factors such as energy demand patterns, renewable energy availability, and grid constraints, quantum algorithms can determine optimal storage locations, sizes, and charging/discharging strategies. This can enhance the integration of renewable energy sources into the grid, improve energy storage efficiency, and support grid stability.

These applications demonstrate how the combination of GeoAI and quantum computing can revolutionize spatial data analysis, energy planning, and optimization in the context of the energy revolution. While many of these applications are still in the research and development phase, they hold significant promise for shaping a more sustainable and efficient energy future.

3.4. Relationship Between GeoAI, Cyber Security, and Quantum Computing

The future scope of the relationship between GeoAI, cybersecurity, and quantum computing in the world of spatial data and the energy revolution is vast. Here are some potential advancements and opportunities in this field:

A. **Quantum-Safe Cryptography for GeoAI:** As quantum computing matures, the development and implementation of quantum-resistant encryption algorithms will become increasingly important. In the context of GeoAI and spatial data, ensuring the confidentiality, integrity, and authenticity of sensitive information will require quantum-safe cryptographic solutions. Future research and advancements will focus on developing robust and efficient quantum-resistant encryption methods specifically tailored for GeoAI applications in the energy sector.

B. **Secure Quantum Communications:** Quantum computing can also be leveraged to enhance secure communication protocols. Quantum key distribution (QKD) enables the secure exchange of encryption keys using the principles of quantum mechanics. Future advancements will explore the integration of QKD into GeoAI systems, ensuring secure transmission of spatial data and preventing unauthorized access or tampering during data transfer processes.

C. **Quantum-Safe Authentication and Access Control:** Quantum computing can also play a role in developing advanced authentication and access control mechanisms. Quantum-resistant authentication protocols can help protect GeoAI systems from unauthorized access and identity spoofing. Future research will focus on exploring quantum-safe authentication methods such as zero-knowledge proofs, quantum-resistant digital signatures, and post-quantum access control mechanisms for secure spatial data management in the energy sector.

D. **Quantum-Based Intrusion Detection Systems:** Intrusion detection systems (IDS) are crucial for identifying and responding to cyber attacks. Quantum computing can contribute to the development of advanced IDS algorithms that can analyze large-scale spatial data for detecting anomalies and potential security breaches. Quantum-based algorithms, combined with GeoAI techniques, can improve the accuracy and speed of intrusion detection in energy systems, ensuring the resilience and security of critical infrastructure.

E. **Quantum-Simulated Risk Assessment:** Quantum computing can enable more accurate and efficient risk assessment models for spatial data and energy systems. Quantum simulators can simulate complex scenarios and evaluate the potential impact of cyber threats on energy infrastructure. By combining GeoAI with quantum simulations, future advancements may allow for more comprehensive risk assessments that consider spatial data, cyber vulnerabilities, and potential consequences, facilitating better decision-making in energy planning and management.

F. **Quantum-Enhanced Incident Response:** Incident response is critical in cybersecurity, including the detection, containment, and recovery from cyber attacks. Quantum computing can enhance the speed and effectiveness of incident response processes by enabling real-time analysis of spatial data, detection of security incidents, and rapid decision-making. Future advancements may lead to the development of quantum-enhanced incident response frameworks that enable faster response times and better threat mitigation in energy system

Table 3. The contribution of QC

Paper Name	year	Methodologies	Contribution
"Quantum clustering in non-spherical data distributions: Finding a suitable number of clusters" (Fastovets, 2019)	2017	Hierarchical Clustering.	Extension of the Concordance and Separation framework already proposed K-means clustering.
"K-means Clustering on Noisy Intermediate Scale Quantum computers, Sumasam, Quantum" (Khan, 2019)	2018	Quantum K-means algorithms.	Solutions experimented using IMB Q computer and its simulator
"Analyzing Big Data with Dynamic Quantum Clustering (DQC)" (Weinstein, 2013)	2013	Quantum evolution algorithm to efficiently move	Demonstrated three examples of complex datasets
"Quantum Speed-up for unsupervised learning" (Sarma, 2019)	2016	Nearest neighbor & K-median algorithm	Quantized versions of clustering via minimum spanning tree

4. CONCLUSION AND DISCUSSION

Geospatial technology has made a significant impact on the renewable energy sector. It helps in identifying locations where specific awareness or emergency programs are required, contributes to searching the available resources within the community and also identifies the gaps and crafts out what actions need to be taken. By accessing demographics and energy-related data, GIS enables professionals to figure out energy consumption trends and more thoroughly target efforts. Using geography and other inputs GIS helps in finding where actual need of renewable energy is. The smart surveillance technology collects a very broad amount of information such as peak hours, seasonal demand etc. Such information helps in predicting risks and taking timely preventive measures. Satellite imagery enables decision-makers to monitor the infrastructure required for dealing with an emergency situation. United States has extensively used both these technologies along with GeoAI for location tracking of resources, automation in control center, and surveillance with the help of drones to contain records of all renewable energy resources. AI has its foundations in a machine that learns from experience for example an algorithm that gets better at chess every time it plays. Also, quantum computing is a new type of computer that replaces bits with qubits. This allows both 1 and 0 as choices to be considered at the same time producing vastly faster solutions to the same type of problems. Combining quantum AI and ML is not simply to make ML faster. It's a fundamentally different approach to problem-solving. QML replaces probabilities with amplitudes. Amplitudes are like arrows as they include a direction as well as magnitude. This is crucial because depending on their direction amplitudes can either cancel each other out or they can be added together which allows sophisticated decision making. There are many applications for this new way of thinking for example in medicine and health. Researchers have already made advances in pattern recognition, anomaly detection and other areas of ML. QML that are run exponentially faster than classical algorithm so the quantum algorithms are like poly-logarithmic time algorithm. QML algorithms are running in time logarithmic in a dimension where standard ML runs in time linear in the dimensions. So we can use quantum computing to make ML exponentially faster. Geospatial technology integrates and visualizes the enormous amount of data for better decision making. AI provides the backbone to the geospatial technology with classical and quantum ML. The exponential growth of data can be handled by the QC to give an accurate output in less time. Researchers are exploring the options with the help of QC to trace and locate data insights. When we go into more complex data structures and have non-linear datasets. Those data can have higher dimensions and these dimensions can go up to an infinite amount. That's where classical computers fail because the classical computer doesn't have enough computational power to be able to understand data structures at high complexity. Development in AI becomes important to better accurate forecasting and energy efficiency. Since its emergence, AI has produced a variety of tools use to solve complicated practical problems. Process large amount of atmospheric and oceanic data coupled with data from ocean and weather trackers. For current modelling, analytic computer codes use complex algorithms solving differential equations. This requires substantial computing power and time to develop accurate predictions. But AI systems can learn key information patterns removing the need for complex rules and mathematical routines. This offers the potential for better and more practical predictions than traditional methods.

Now technologies like GeoAI and QML are turning out to be an effective way to distribute and manage renewable energy supply. Following research directions can be achieved using the potential of both GeoAI and Quantum Clustering technologies to take precautions in a timely manner.

- Informed supply & demand management for suppliers
- Any congestion related issues can be addressed using GeoAI systems
- Identify energy consumption data points and in-turn derive meaningful information out of it
- Help in troubleshooting and maintenance activities like leakages and efficiency of units operating in system

The future scope of GeoAI and quantum computing in the world of spatial data and the energy revolution holds immense potential. The combination of these two fields can bring about significant advancements and transformative capabilities. Here are some areas where GeoAI and quantum computing can have a profound impact:

A. Spatial Data Analysis and Modeling: Quantum computing has the potential to greatly enhance the processing capabilities required for complex spatial data analysis. By leveraging quantum algorithms, it can handle large-scale spatial data sets and perform computations that are currently infeasible for classical computers. This can lead to more accurate modeling, simulation, and optimization of spatial systems, enabling better decision-making in energy planning, resource allocation, and infrastructure design.

B. Optimization of Energy Systems: Quantum computing can revolutionize optimization algorithms, enabling more efficient and faster solutions to complex energy system optimization problems. It can tackle optimization challenges related to energy generation, distribution, and storage, considering multiple variables and constraints simultaneously. By integrating quantum algorithms with GeoAI techniques, it becomes possible to optimize the placement of renewable energy sources, enhance energy grid efficiency, and facilitate demand-side management.

C. Advanced Geospatial Analysis: Quantum machine learning algorithms can enable more sophisticated geospatial analysis techniques. Quantum-based algorithms can process and analyze spatial data in novel ways, extracting patterns, correlations, and insights that are not easily discoverable with classical approaches. This can lead to more accurate land cover classification, geospatial feature recognition, and change detection, which are essential for monitoring and managing energy infrastructure and environmental factors.

D. Climate Modeling and Prediction: Climate modeling is a complex task that requires extensive computational power. Quantum computing has the potential to significantly speed up climate simulations and improve prediction accuracy. By combining quantum computing with GeoAI, it becomes possible to incorporate high-resolution spatial data, satellite observations, and climate models to better understand climate change impacts, assess renewable energy potential, and develop adaptive strategies for energy systems.

E. Quantum Sensors for Spatial Data Collection: Quantum sensors, such as quantum magnetometers and quantum gravimeters, can enhance the quality and precision of spatial data collection. These sensors can detect subtle variations in the Earth's magnetic and gravitational fields, providing highly accurate geospatial information. Integrating quantum sensors with GeoAI techniques enables more precise mapping of energy resources, underground infrastructure, and geological features, facilitating optimal planning and management of energy systems.

F. Energy Optimization Algorithms: Quantum computing can drive advancements in solving complex optimization problems related to energy systems. It can enhance algorithms for energy scheduling, load balancing, and grid management. By combining GeoAI with quantum optimization techniques, it becomes possible to develop sophisticated energy optimization models that consider real-time spatial data, energy demand patterns, renewable energy availability, and infrastructure constraints.

While the future scope of GeoAI and quantum computing in spatial data and the energy revolution is promising, it's important to note that quantum computing is still in its early stages of development, and practical applications are limited. Overcoming technical challenges, scaling quantum systems, and ensuring the availability of suitable quantum algorithms are key areas of ongoing research and development. Nonetheless, the synergy between GeoAI and quantum computing has the potential to revolutionize how we analyze, model, and optimize spatial data for energy systems and contribute to sustainable energy solutions.

REFERENCES

Acquah, M. A., Jin, Y., Oh, B. C., Son, Y. G., & Kim, S. Y. (2023). Spatiotemporal Sequence-to-Sequence Clustering for Electric Load Forecasting. *IEEE Access : Practical Innovations, Open Solutions, 11*, 5850–5863. doi:10.1109/ACCESS.2023.3235724

Adler. (2004). *Quantum Theory as an Emergent Phenomenon.* Cambridge: Cambridge University Press.

Agababov, V., Buettner, M., Chudnovsky, V., Cogan, M., Greenstein, B., McDaniel, S., & Yin, B. (2015). Flywheel: Google's data compression proxy for the mobile web. *In 12th {USENIX} Symposium on Networked Systems Design and Implementation* ({NSDI} 15) (pp. 367-380).

Arthern, R. J., & Williams, C. R. (2017). The sensitivity of West Antarctica to the submarine melting feedback. *Geophysical Research Letters, 44*(5), 2352–2359. doi:10.1002/2017GL072514

Asadi, M., Pourhossein, K., & Mohammadi-Ivatloo, B. (2023). GIS-assisted modeling of wind farm site selection based on support vector regression. *Journal of Cleaner Production, 390*, 135993. doi:10.1016/j.jclepro.2023.135993

Bhadane, C., & Shah, K. (2020, April). Clustering algorithms for spatial data mining. *In Proceedings of the 2020 3rd International Conference on Geoinformatics and Data Analysis* (pp. 5-9). ACM. 10.1145/3397056.3397068

Biamonte, J., Wittek, P., Pancotti, N., Rebentrost, P., Wiebe, N., & Lloyd, S. (2017). Quantum machine learning. *Nature, 549*(7671), 195–202. doi:10.1038/nature23474 PMID:28905917

Binkley, P. F., Frontera, W., Standaert, D. G., & Stein, J. (2003). Predicting the potential of wearable technology. *IEEE Engineering in Medicine and Biology Magazine, 22*(3), 23–27. doi:10.1109/MEMB.2003.1213623 PMID:12845813

Bonetti, F., Warnaby, G., & Quinn, L. (2018). Augmented reality and virtual reality in physical and online retailing: A review, synthesis and research agenda. In *Augmented reality and virtual reality* (pp. 119–132). Springer. doi:10.1007/978-3-319-64027-3_9

Briz-Redón, Á., & Serrano-Aroca, Á. (2020). The effect of climate on the spread of the COVID-19 pandemic: A review of findings, and statistical and modelling techniques. *Progress in Physical Geography, 44*(5), 0309133320946302. doi:10.1177/0309133320946302

Cameron, D., & Jones, I. G. (1983). John Snow, the Broad Street pump and modern epidemiology. *International Journal of Epidemiology, 12*(4), 393–396. doi:10.1093/ije/12.4.393 PMID:6360920

Casey, D., & Pearce, D. (Eds.). (2018). *More Than Management Development: Action Learning at General Electric Company*. Routledge. doi:10.4324/9780429452567

Chaudhry, N., & Yousaf, M. M. (2019, February). Spatial querying of mineral resources using PostGIS. *In 2019 2nd International Conference on Advancements in Computational Sciences* (ICACS) (pp. 1-6). 10.23919/ICACS.2019.8688999

Clematis, A., Mineter, M., & Marciano, R. (2003). High performance computing with geographical data. *Parallel Computing, 29*(10), 1275–1280. doi:10.1016/j.parco.2003.07.001

Coelho, S., Ferreira, J., Carvalho, D., Miranda, A. I., & Lopes, M. (2023). Climate Change Impact on Source Contributions to the Air Quality in Aveiro Region. In *Air Pollution Modeling and its Application XXVIII* (pp. 207–212). Springer International Publishing.

Coşkun, H., Yıldırım, N., & Gündüz, S. (2020). The spread of COVID-19 virus through population density and wind in Turkey cities. *The Science of the Total Environment, 751*, 141663. doi:10.1016/j.scitotenv.2020.141663 PMID:32866831

Daneshvar, M., Mohammadi-Ivatloo, B., Zare, K., & Anvari-Moghaddam, A. (2023). *IoT Enabled Multi-Energy Systems: From Isolated Energy Grids to Modern Interconnected Networks*.

Das, N. K., Mishra, D. K., Naik, P. K., Dehury, P., Bose, S., & Banerjee, T. (2023). Dihydrolevoglycosenone as a novel bio-based nanofluid for thermal energy storage: Physiochemical and quantum chemical insights. *Journal of Energy Storage*, *59*, 106365. doi:10.1016/j.est.2022.106365

De Martini, F., Mazzei, A., Ricci, M., & D'Ariano, G. M. (2003). Exploiting quantum parallelism of entanglement for a complete experimental quantum characterization of a single-qubit device. *Physical Review A*, *67*(6), 062307. doi:10.1103/PhysRevA.67.062307

DiBiase, D., Tripp Corbin, T. F., Francica, J., Green, K., Jackson, J., Jeffress, G., & Smith, C. (2010). The New Geospatial Technology Competency Model: Bringing Workforce Needs into Focus. *URISA Journal*, *22*(2).

El-Fouly, F. H., Kachout, M., Alharbi, Y., Alshudukhi, J. S., Alanazi, A., & Ramadan, R. A. (2023). Environment-Aware Energy Efficient and Reliable Routing in Real-Time Multi-Sink Wireless Sensor Networks for Smart Cities Applications. *Applied Sciences (Basel, Switzerland)*, *13*(1), 605. doi:10.3390/app13010605

Elsner, P., & Suarez, S. (2019). Renewable energy from the high seas: Geo-spatial modelling of resource potential and legal implications for developing offshore wind projects beyond the national jurisdiction of coastal States. *Energy Policy*, *128*, 919–929. doi:10.1016/j.enpol.2019.01.064

Esser, H. J., Liefting, Y., Ibáñez-Justicia, A., van der Jeugd, H., Van Turnhout, C. A., Stroo, A., & de Boer, W. F. (2020). Spatial risk analysis for the introduction and circulation of six arboviruses in the Netherlands. *Parasites & Vectors*, *13*(1), 1–20. doi:10.118613071-020-04339-0 PMID:32912330

Fastovets, D. V., & Yu, I. & Lukichev, V. (2019). Machine learning methods in quantum computing theory. *In International Conference on Micro-and Nano-Electronics*. International Society for Optics and Photonics. 10.1117/12.2522427

Feig, M., & Potter, A. (2020). Matrix product state simulations on a quantum computer. *Bulletin of the American Physical Society*.

Feynman, R. P., Leighton, R. B., & Sands, M. (2011). The Feynman lectures on physics: Vol. I. *The new millennium edition: mainly mechanics, radiation, and heat*. Basic books.

Flammia, S. (2020). Quantum Computer Crosscheck. *Physics (College Park, Md.)*, *13*, 3. doi:10.1103/Physics.13.3

Fouedjio, F. (2016). Clustering of multivariate geostatistical data. *Wiley Interdisciplinary Reviews: Computational Statistics*, 1510.

García-del-Amo, D., Mortyn, P. G., & Reyes-García, V. (2023). Local reports of climate change impacts in Sierra Nevada, Spain: Sociodemographic and geographical patterns. *Regional Environmental Change*, *23*(1), 1–16. doi:10.100710113-022-01981-5 PMID:36540304

Gielen, D., Boshell, F., Saygin, D., Bazilian, M. D., Wagner, N., & Gorini, R. (2019). The role of renewable energy in the global energy transformation. *Energy Strategy Reviews*, *24*, 38–50. doi:10.1016/j.esr.2019.01.006

Gulagi, A., Alcanzare, M., Bogdanov, D., Esparcia, E. Jr, Ocon, J., & Breyer, C. (2021). Transition pathway towards 100% renewable energy across the sectors of power, heat, transport, and desalination for the Philippines. *Renewable & Sustainable Energy Reviews, 144*, 110934. doi:10.1016/j.rser.2021.110934

Hay, G. J., Kyle, C., Hemachandran, B., Chen, G., Rahman, M. M., Fung, T. S., & Arvai, J. L. (2011). Geospatial technologies to improve urban energy efficiency. *Remote Sensing (Basel), 3*(7), 1380–1405. doi:10.3390/rs3071380

Heipke, C. (2010). Crowdsourcing geospatial data. *ISPRS Journal of Photogrammetry and Remote Sensing*, (65), 550-557.

Horobet, A., Simionescu, A. A., Dumitrescu, D. G., & Belascu, L. (2020). Europe's War against CO-VID-19: A Map of Countries' Disease Vulnerability Using Mortality Indicators. *International Journal of Environmental Research and Public Health, 17*(18), 6565. doi:10.3390/ijerph17186565 PMID:32916973

Infield, D., & Freris, L. (2020). *Renewable energy in power systems*. John Wiley & Sons.

Işık, G., Öğüt, H., & Mutlu, M. (2023). Deep learning based electricity demand forecasting to minimize the cost of energy imbalance: A real case application with some fortune 500 companies in Türkiye. *Engineering Applications of Artificial Intelligence, 118*, 105664. doi:10.1016/j.engappai.2022.105664

Javadpour, A., Sangaiah, A. K., Pinto, P., Ja'fari, F., Zhang, W., Abadi, A. M. H., & Ahmadi, H. (2023). An energy-optimized embedded load balancing using DVFS computing in cloud data centers. *Computer Communications, 197*, 255–266. doi:10.1016/j.comcom.2022.10.019

Khan, S. U., Awan, A. J., & Vall-Llosera, G. (2019). *K-Means Clustering on Noisy Intermediate Scale Quantum Computers*. arXiv preprint arXiv:1909.12183

Kotsiantis, S. B., Zaharakis, I. D., & Pintelas, P. E. (2006). Machine learning: A review of classification and combining techniques. *Artificial Intelligence Review, 26*(3), 159–190. doi:10.100710462-007-9052-3

Liew, H. P., & Eidem, N. (2020). Assessing the spatial-temporal clustering and health implications of fine particulate matter (PM2. 5). *Journal of Public Health*, 1–11.

Liu, C., Cao, Y., Yang, C., Zhou, Y., & Ai, M. (2020). Pattern identification and analysis for the traditional village using low altitude UAV-borne remote sensing: Multifeatured geospatial data to support rural landscape investigation, documentation and management. *Journal of Cultural Heritage, 44*, 185–195. doi:10.1016/j.culher.2019.12.013

Loh, W. Y. (2014). Classification and regression tree methods. *Wiley StatsRef: Statistics Reference. Online (Bergheim)*. doi:10.1002/9781118445112.stat03886

Losada, S. F., & Holik, F. (2018, February). Classical Limit and Quantum Logic. *International Journal of Theoretical Physics, 57*(2), 465–475. doi:10.100710773-017-3579-0

Maclaurin, G. J., Grue, N. W., Lopez, A. J., & Heimiller, D. M. (2019). *The Renewable Energy Potential (reV) Model: A Geospatial Platform for Technical Potential and Supply Curve Modeling (No. NREL/TP-6A20-73067)*. National Renewable Energy Lab. doi:10.2172/1563140

MaldonadoS. B.BielickiJ. M.MirandaM.Ogland-HandJ. D.HowardC.AdamsB.SaarM. O. (2020). Geospatial Estimation of the Electric Power Potential in Sedimentary Basin Geothermal Resources Using Geologically Stored Carbon Dioxide. In *World Geothermal Congress*. doi:10.3929/ethz-b-000449699

Marek, L., Campbell, M., Epton, M., Kingham, S., & Storer, M. (2018). Winter Is Coming: A Socio-Environmental Monitoring and Spatiotemporal Modelling Approach for Better Understanding a Respiratory Disease. *ISPRS International Journal of Geo-Information*, *7*(11), 432. doi:10.3390/ijgi7110432

Mazzoncini, F., Cavina, V., Andolina, G. M., Erdman, P. A., & Giovannetti, V. (2023). Optimal control methods for quantum batteries. *Physical Review. A*, *107*(3), 032218. doi:10.1103/PhysRevA.107.032218

Mohammadi, S., de Vries, B., Rafiee, A., Esfandiari, M., & Dias, E. (2021). An exploratory study on the impact of physical and geospatial characteristics of the urban built environment on the buildings annual electricity usage. *Journal of Building Engineering*, *102359*, 102359. Advance online publication. doi:10.1016/j.jobe.2021.102359

Moudgil, V., Hewage, K., Hussain, S. A., & Sadiq, R. (2023). Integration of IoT in building energy infrastructure: A critical review on challenges and solutions. *Renewable & Sustainable Energy Reviews*, *174*, 113121. doi:10.1016/j.rser.2022.113121

Nersesian, R. (2014). Energy for the 21st century: a comprehensive guide to conventional and alternative sources. Routledge

O'Grady, N. P., Alexander, M., Dellinger, E. P., Gerberding, J. L., Heard, S. O., Maki, D. G., & Raad, I. I. (2002). Guidelines for the prevention of intravascular catheter-related infections. Centers for Disease Control and Prevention. MMWR. Recommendations and reports: Morbidity and mortality weekly report. *Recommendations and reports*, *51*(RR-10), 1-29.

Olabi, A. G. (2017). Renewable energy and energy storage systems. *Energy*, *136*, 1–6. doi:10.1016/j.energy.2017.07.054

Pal, M. (2005). Random forest classifier for remote sensing classification. *International Journal of Remote Sensing*, *26*(1), 217–222. doi:10.1080/01431160412331269698

Parvin, M., Yousefi, H., & Noorollahi, Y. (2023). Techno-economic optimization of a renewable micro grid using multi-objective particle swarm optimization algorithm. *Energy Conversion and Management*, *277*, 116639. doi:10.1016/j.enconman.2022.116639

Paulose, B., Sabitha, S., Punhani, R., & Sahani, I. (2018). Identification of Regions and Probable Health Risks Due to Air Pollution Using K-Mean Clustering Techniques. *In 2018 4th International Conference on Computational Intelligence & Communication Technology (CICT)* (pp. 1-6). IEEE.

Resch, B., Sagl, G., Törnros, T., Bachmaier, A., Eggers, J. B., Herkel, S., Narmsara, S., & Gündra, H. (2014). GIS-based planning and modeling for renewable energy: Challenges and future research avenues. *ISPRS International Journal of Geo-Information*, *3*(2), 662–692. doi:10.3390/ijgi3020662

Russo, D., & Miketa, A. (2019). Benefits, challenges, and analytical approaches to scaling up renewables through regional planning and coordination of power systems in Africa. Current *Sustainable/Renewable. Energy Reports*, *6*(1), 5–12. doi:10.100740518-019-00125-4

Sarma, A., Chatterjee, R., Gili, K., & Yu, T. (2019). *Quantum Unsupervised and Supervised Learning on Superconducting Processors.* arXiv preprint arXiv:1909.04226.

Seager, T. P., Miller, S. A., & Kohn, J. (2009, May). Land use and geospatial aspects in life cycle assessment of renewable energy. *In 2009 Ieee International Symposium on Sustainable Systems and Technology* (pp. 1-6). IEEE. 10.1109/ISSST.2009.5156724

Shao, M., Zhao, Y., Sun, J., Han, Z., & Shao, Z. (2023). A decision framework for tidal current power plant site selection based on GIS-MCDM: A case study in China. *Energy, 262*, 125476. doi:10.1016/j.energy.2022.125476

Taminiau, J., Byrne, J., Kim, J., Kim, M. W., & Seo, J. (2021). Infrastructure-scale sustainable energy planning in the cityscape: Transforming urban energy metabolism in East Asia. *Wiley Interdisciplinary Reviews. Energy and Environment, 397*(5), e397. doi:10.1002/wene.397

Tomlinson, R. F. (2007). *Thinking about GIS: geographic information system planning for managers* (Vol. 1). ESRI, Inc.

Tsiaras, E., Papadopoulos, D. N., Antonopoulos, C. N., Papadakis, V. G., & Coutelieris, F. A. (2020). Planning and assessment of an off-grid power supply system for small settlements. *Renewable Energy, 149*, 1271–1281. doi:10.1016/j.renene.2019.10.118

Uribe-Hurtado, A. L., Orozco-Alzate, M., Lopes, N., & Ribeiro, B. (2020). GPU-based fast clustering via K-Centres and k-NN mode seeking for geospatial industry applications. *Computers in Industry, 122*, 103260. doi:10.1016/j.compind.2020.103260

Verma, M., Srivastava, M., Chack, N., Diswar, A. K., & Gupta, N. (2012). A comparative study of various clustering algorithms in data mining. [IJERA]. *International Journal of Engineering Research and Applications, 2*(3), 1379–1384.

Wei, Z., & Yongquan, Y. (2016). Automated web usage data mining and recommendation system using K-Nearest Neighbor (KNN) classification method. *Applied Computing and Informatics, 12*(1), 90–108. doi:10.1016/j.aci.2014.10.001

Weinstein, M., Meirer, F., Hume, A., Sciau, P., Shaked, G., Hofstetter, R., & Horn, D. (2013). Analyzing big data with dynamic quantum clustering. arXiv preprint arXiv:1310.2700.

Zheng, B., Yoon, S. W., & Lam, S. S. (2014). Breast cancer diagnosis based on feature extraction using a hybrid of K-means and support vector machine algorithms. *Expert Systems with Applications, 41*(4), 1476–1482. doi:10.1016/j.eswa.2013.08.044

Zhou, Y., & Zhang, P. (2021). Quantum Machine Learning for Power System Stability Assessment. arXiv preprint arXiv:2104.04855.

Chapter 9
Cloud–Based Malware Detection Using Machine Learning Methods

Pham Sy Nguyen
Government Office of Vietnam, Vietnam

Nguyen Ngoc Cuong
University of Technology-Logistics of Public Security, Vietnam

Hoang Viet Long
ⓘD https://orcid.org/0000-0001-6657-0653
University of Technology-Logistics of Public Security, Vietnam

ABSTRACT

Malware in the cloud can affect many users on multiple platforms, while traditional malware typically only affects a system or a small number of users. In addition, malware in the cloud can hide in cloud services or user accounts, making it more difficult to detect and remove than traditional malware. Information security solutions installed on servers (such as anti-malware solutions) are not considered very effective as malware (especially sophisticated solutions) can bypass the detection capabilities of these solutions. Moreover, these solutions often cannot detect new and unknown malware patterns. To address this issue, machine learning (ML) methods have been used and proven effective in detecting malware in many different cases. This chapter per the authors focuses on introducing malware detection techniques in the cloud and evaluating the effectiveness of machine learning methods used, as well as proposing an effective model to support malware detection in the cloud.

DOI: 10.4018/978-1-6684-9317-5.ch009

1. INTRODUCTION

In recent years, malware attacks have become increasingly prevalent, and their impact is not limited to individual users or companies. These attacks can have a significant impact on the global economy. One of the most notable examples of the economic impact of malware attacks is the WannaCry ransomware attack that occurred in May 2017. The WannaCry attack not only caused financial losses for individuals and companies but also disrupted critical infrastructure such as hospitals and transportation systems. In the UK, the attack disrupted the National Health Service, causing many hospitals to cancel surgeries and appointments, and in some cases, forcing them to revert to paper-based systems.

Another example of the economic impact of malware attacks is the SolarWinds attack that occurred in late 2020. The attack targeted the US government and many private companies, and the full extent of the damage is still being assessed. However, initial estimates suggest that the attack could cost billions of dollars in damages. This type of attack can have a significant impact on the global economy, as many companies rely on third-party vendors for critical services.

Overall, malware attacks pose a significant threat to the global economy. They can cause financial losses for individuals and companies, disrupt critical infrastructure, and undermine confidence in the security of digital systems. Malware can include various types of malicious software such as viruses, worms, rootkits, backdoors, and ransomware, and often performs dangerous actions on the victim's computer without their permission (Ömer Aslan, 2020).

Figure 1 shows the results of a study by the AV-TEST Institute describing the rapid increase of malware over the past decade. More than 450,000 samples of harmful software applications and Potentially Unwanted Applications (PUA) are recorded every day. In the past decade, the rate of increase of malware has raised significant concerns, and there is no method that can detect all types of practical malware. Modern malware can automate their activities and even automatically adjust to avoid antivirus software and other security tools. They may use techniques such as "packing", in which the malware is packed into different files, making detection more difficult. Therefore, detecting malware through traditional methods has become complex and almost impossible.

Figure 1. The increase in the number of malware over the past decade

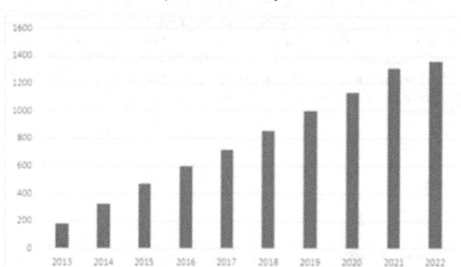

Traditional techniques for malware analysis and detection typically focus on detecting signs of malware on the system. These signs may be special character strings in files, abnormal code snippets written into memory, or abnormal behavior of the program compared to normal operations. Manual malware analysis techniques involve using specialized tools to analyze suspect files, monitor network transactions, and files downloaded from the internet. Malware analysts use special search techniques and tools to find malware on the system. They then analyze the structure of the suspect files to identify malware and determine their behavior. Other traditional malware detection techniques include using virus scanning tools to detect malicious programs, monitoring network traffic to detect abnormal behavior, and using heuristic rules to detect abnormal behavior of the program.

The methods for detecting malware are undergoing a shift from traditional methods to new ones. One of the methods that brings many advantages is detecting malware on the cloud. Detecting malware on the cloud offers easier scalability compared to detection on traditional environments. System administrators can easily increase or decrease centralized processing power without the need to change hardware. Using cloud services also allows organizations to reduce costs of investing in hardware, maintenance, and upgrading of malware detection systems. Cloud providers also offer flexible service packages for businesses at affordable prices. Additionally, the malware detection system on the cloud is built with high fault-tolerant architecture and provides strong security features to protect business data.

In this article, we will provide a detailed assessment of cloud-based malware detection methods and make the following contributions:

- Describe the role of cloud computing and the importance of protecting cloud infrastructure from malware.
- Explain malware generation trends and some cloaking techniques. Discuss current challenges and analyze malware detection techniques.
- Provides a summary of current academic research on cloud-based malware detection using machine learning.
- Propose a malware detection model in the cloud with the support of advanced techniques including machine learning/deep learning.

2. OVERVIEW OF CLOUD COMPUTING

Cloud computing, or simply "the cloud," is a revolutionary technology that allows users to access and store data over the internet rather than on their personal computers or local servers. This technology has been rapidly adopted by individuals, small and large businesses, and even governments. Cloud computing is often used for data storage, hosting websites and applications, and running software programs. The use of cloud computing has many benefits, including flexibility, scalability, and cost-effectiveness. With the cloud, users can quickly and easily increase or decrease the amount of computing resources they need, without having to purchase new hardware or software. One of the most common applications of cloud computing is in data backup and disaster recovery. Businesses and individuals can store their data on remote servers, which are typically spread across multiple geographic locations, ensuring that data is safe and available in the event of a disaster or outage. This approach also provides a higher level of security, as cloud providers often employ advanced security measures and protocols to protect data from hackers and other threats.

Cloud computing has also enabled new forms of collaboration and communication. Teams can work on the same project simultaneously, from different locations and devices, with real-time updates and feedback. This has been particularly useful during the COVID-19 pandemic, where remote work has become more common.

Overall, cloud computing has transformed the way we store, access, and process data. It has become an integral part of our daily lives and is expected to continue to evolve and expand in the coming years.

Figure 2. Cloud computing architecture process

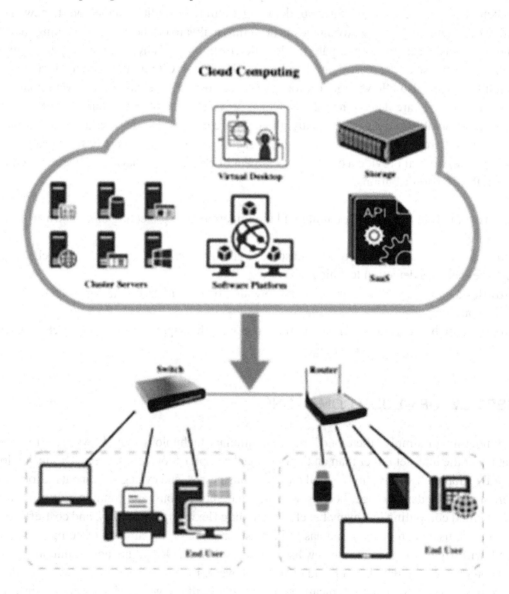

According to the definition of NIST (Peter Mell, 2011), cloud computing is a form of providing computing power, storage, networking, applications, and other IT resources through a cloud service platform. The cloud model allows customers to access these resources on demand and pay based on their usage. The cloud model provides several basic characteristics and three service models, as well as four deployment models. The management and interaction of the service provider with these resources are reduced to a minimum level.

Cloud computing services are diverse and flexible to meet different user needs, including the following service models:

- SaaS (Software as a Service): Users use applications hosted on the cloud and provided by the service provider, such as Microsoft 365's application.
- PaaS (Platform as a Service): Users deploy their own applications on the cloud platform provided by the service provider, using programming languages and development tools supported by the provider, such as VMware (Pivotal) Cloud Foundry.
- IaaS (Infrastructure as a Service): Users can be provided with resources such as storage, networking, processing, and can deploy and operate arbitrary software on the cloud infrastructure, from applications to operating systems, such as Microsoft Azure.

The emergence of cloud computing has changed the way organizations deploy and manage their IT services. With cloud computing, organizations can rent and utilize server resources, storage, networks, and software more flexibly and cost-effectively, instead of investing in complex and expensive infrastructure. Cloud computing has many economic, technological, and security benefits for individuals and businesses. Cloud computing provides convenience and cost savings through resource sharing, the ability to access anytime anywhere, flexible service expansion, and minimized technical details such as software upgrades and maintenance. The cloud also has a security advantage over individual servers due to the hired cloud provider's security experts and the readily available resources and recovery architecture after an attack. However, the cloud faces the threat of malware distribution, especially in cases where virtual machines are configured similarly, and an attack can spread to many different virtual machines. This can lead to data loss and affect the reliability of the cloud computing system. In most cases, administrators are unaware that their servers have been compromised, even though intrusion detection/malware prevention solutions have been deployed on the servers. In other cases, the breach is only discovered after a long time when significant damage has already occurred. Therefore, detecting a virtual server that has been infected with malware is critical to an organization's security efforts. An overview of commonly used malware detection methods as well as malware detection in the cloud is presented in the following section.

3. OVERVIEW OF CLOUD-BASED MALWARE DETECTION

Malware can be used to steal data, create a backdoor for unauthorized access to the system, distribute spam, launch DDoS attacks, encrypt data and demand ransom, or perform other malicious activities (Tech Term, n.d.). Malware can be distributed through email, malicious websites, fake software, file attachments, and other media. Malware attack can be carried out through various methods, including DDoS (Distributed Denial of Service) attacks, malware attacks through cloud applications and services, and unauthorized access to cloud systems. In DDoS attacks, the attacker uses thousands or millions of infected devices to attack cloud systems. This can cause disruptions in accessing cloud services, disrupt business operations, and create a sense of insecurity for users. Another method for spreading malware is through cloud applications and services. Attackers can upload malicious files to cloud storage services and then distribute them to other systems through sharing links or file attachments in emails. Unauthorized access to cloud systems is also a risk for spreading malware. Attackers can use methods such as exploiting security vulnerabilities or password guessing attacks to access cloud systems and spread malware from within. The next section discusses trends in malware creation and some commonly used hiding techniques.

3.1. Trends In Malware Creation and Hiding Technologies

Currently, creating malware is becoming one of the most common illegal activities on the internet. Attackers create malware to exploit the weaknesses of security systems or the lack of knowledge of users. Threats from malware can lead to information security breaches, security vulnerabilities, and even loss of property. Hackers and cybercriminals have used many new and sophisticated techniques to create various types of malware. In fact, creating malware has become a professional job that brings economic benefits. Hackers and cybercriminals can create and sell malware on the dark web or dangerous websites. At a reasonable price, these criminals can sell malware to various targets, from novice hackers to large criminal groups.

To create malware, attackers use various methods, from simple conventional techniques such as inserting a special code into a program file, to complex techniques using complex algorithms to create polymorphic and complex malware. The type of malware created by conventional techniques can be easily identified by extracting some unique characteristics to combine and match, known as signatures.

One of the most common trends is the creation of polymorphic malware. This type of malware is capable of automatically changing itself to avoid detection by traditional antivirus software. It can create millions of different versions of itself, each with a different code. This makes it extremely difficult to detect and remove the malware. Polymorphic malware is a type of malware in which the syntax of the code changes with each infection, but the semantics remain the same. Encryption techniques are the most common method used in polymorphic malware.

Another trend is the use of encryption techniques to hide malware. Hackers can use strong encryption algorithms to encrypt parts of the malware, making it harder to detect. This makes it more difficult to analyze and detect malware.

In addition, hackers are also using new techniques to attack IoT (Internet of Things) devices. IoT devices, such as security cameras, smart air conditioners, or smart light bulbs, are often poorly protected and can become a weak point in the network security system.

Obfuscated malware is a type of malware that is intentionally designed to be difficult for security researchers and antivirus programs to analyze and detect. This is typically achieved by using various techniques to conceal or obfuscate the true nature and behavior of the malware, such as encryption, code obfuscation, and anti-analysis measures. The goal of obfuscation is to make it more challenging for security professionals to understand how the malware operates, thereby prolonging the amount of time that the malware can remain undetected and active on a system.

Remote execution of malicious code is performed by hackers to achieve their intentions remotely using the infrastructure of the Internet and benefiting from existing remote execution methods.

Due to the fact that there are many ways to detect malware, there are also ways to prevent malware from being detected. Malware is usually created using concealment techniques to avoid detection by antivirus software, so understanding these techniques is essential for studying modern malware detection techniques. Some techniques commonly used by attackers to distribute malware include:

3.1.1. Encryption

Malware can use encryption techniques to hide itself on the system it has infiltrated. Malware often uses encryption to hide a part or all of its content, which helps it avoid detection by antivirus software and malware analysis tools (B. Rad, 2012).

Some encryption techniques commonly used include:

- Encrypting strings, files, or network packets to prevent the unwanted discovery of these entities.
- Using different encryption techniques for different parts of the program or file, making it difficult to find the entire malware.
- Using dynamic encryption algorithms, meaning algorithms executed at runtime instead of being pre-installed.

3.1.2. Obfuscation

Malware obfuscation techniques are methods used by attackers to obscure or conceal the true nature and behavior of malware. The goal of obfuscation is to make it more difficult for security researchers and antivirus programs to detect and analyze the malware.

Some obfuscation techniques commonly used include:

- Syntax transformation: Changing the syntax of the source code by adding or removing whitespace, changing variable, function or class names, changing the order of statements to make the source code look different from the original.
- Encryption: Using encryption algorithms to encrypt malware source code, making it harder to read and analyze.
- Dynamic decoding: Decoding the malware directly at runtime.
- Malware distribution: Distributing malware into multiple files to make detection more difficult.

3.1.3. Packing

Packing is a technique used by malware to hide itself and evade detection by antivirus programs. This technique works by using a packing program (Packer) to compress or encrypt the malicious file into a different form that antivirus programs cannot recognize. When executed, the packing program will decompress or decrypt the malware file and run it. This process helps the malware avoid antivirus software but also makes it more difficult to analyze the malware code.

Some common packing techniques for malware include UPX, ASPack, and Themida. However, dynamic analysis tools can detect packed files by decompressing them and analyzing their contents.

3.1.4. Code Injection

Code injection is a method of inserting malicious code into allocated memory regions of applications, systems, or other processes running on a computer without permission. When the malware is injected into the memory region, it can execute malicious functions, such as collecting personal information, stealing passwords, creating security vulnerabilities, or installing other malicious software.

Common methods of code injection techniques include:

- DLL Injection: injecting malware into a dynamic link library (DLL) to execute malicious functions when the application is running.
- Shellcode Injection: injecting malware into a buffer memory area used to store the executable commands of the program.
- Process Injection: injecting malware into a running process to perform malicious functions.
- Registry Injection: injecting malware into the registry to perform malicious functions.

3.1.5. Techniques for Attacking Anti-Virus Software (Anti-Virus Evasion)

Using techniques to avoid detection by anti-virus software such as using malware that is "safe" or inserting malware into unrelated files to prevent infection. These techniques may include:

- Resigning malware: The malware is resigned with a new signature to avoid detection by anti-virus software.
- Renaming file names: This technique is used to rename malware files to avoid detection by anti-virus software. The files can be renamed according to a random string or encrypted.
- Attacking anti-virus software: Malware will attack anti-virus software and disable or delete it to avoid detection.

3.1.6. Rootkit Technique

Rootkit technique is a technique used by malware to conceal its existence on a computer system. Rootkits often interfere with the operating system to hide infected files, processes, and drivers. It also often uses hooking techniques to hide abnormal activities and avoid detection by anti-virus software and system management tools.

Malware rootkits typically operate at the kernel level of the operating system, which gives them complete control over the system and the ability to intercept and manipulate system calls. This allows attackers to execute commands, steal data, and perform other malicious actions without being detected.

To install a rootkit as part of a malware campaign, attackers may use a variety of techniques, such as exploiting vulnerabilities in the system or tricking users into downloading and installing the malware. Once the rootkit is installed, it can be used to maintain persistent access to the system, even after the initial malware infection has been detected and removed.

3.1.7. Reverse Connection Technique

Reverse connection technique is a network attack technique in which malware creates a connection from the infected machine to another computer that the hacker controls, instead of the hacker's computer having to connect to the infected machine. This technique is often used to bypass network security mechanisms such as firewalls or Network Address Translation (NAT) and allows hackers to remotely access the infected system without being detected.

To carry out this technique, the malware will create a connection to a command and control server controlled by the hacker. The hacker will then use this server to send commands and requests to the infected computer and retrieve information from the system. The reverse connection technique is often used in network attacks targeting valuable organizations, businesses, or individuals.

To prevent the reverse connection technique, users need to maintain strong network security measures such as firewalls and regularly update their security patches to protect their systems. Additionally, anti-virus programs should also be updated regularly to detect and remove malware that uses the reverse connection technique.

3.1.8. User Attention Avoidance Technique

User attention avoidance technique help malware avoid detection from a user perspective through methods such as:

- Automatic startup: Malware can automatically start when the operating system is turned on or when the user logs into the system. This allows the malware to operate in the background without the need for user intervention.
- System process spoofing: Malware can spoof the name or information of other system processes to avoid detection.
- Slow attack: Some malware can attack slowly and control access traffic to avoid user attention or anti-malware systems.
- Hiding in other files: Malware can hide in other files, such as system files or files attached to emails or messages.
- Use of user deception techniques: Some malware can use user deception techniques, such as displaying fake notifications or changing the user interface to trick users into performing unintended actions.

3.2. Malware Analysis Techniques Using Machine Learning

Malware analysis using machine learning involves using algorithms and statistical models to analyze and detect malware. There are two main approaches to malware analysis using machine learning: static and dynamic analysis.

3.2.1. Machine Learning-Based Static Analysis Technique

In the static analysis method, the executable/binary file is not executed to check its code. Instead, the analysis process is performed by examining the source code of the executable/binary file. Typically, the process of static analysis of malware involves analyzing the structure of the program, searching for malware by scanning files with antivirus software, and reading and decoding the malware using malware analysis tools. Static analysis of malware is often used to identify the malicious features of malware, such as creating a backdoor or collecting information. It can also help detect the malicious behavior of malware, such as creating unauthorized network connections or creating unauthorized new processes.

Static analysis of malware is often used as a tool to identify the malicious features of a program, find ways to decode malware, and make recommendations on how to prevent its spread. It is an effective method to help security experts identify potential threats from malware and detect malicious programs on their systems. Static malware analysis using machine learning is a technique that involves analyzing the characteristics and behavior of malware without running it. Static analysis techniques used in machine learning include analyzing the file header, strings, imports, exports, and disassembly of the executable code. Other advanced techniques such as graph-based analysis, machine code analysis, and byte-level analysis can also be used. Nonetheless, it should be emphasized that machine learning models are not immune to errors and may still generate false positives or fail to detect new forms of malware that do not conform to their learned patterns. Studies have used different machine learning techniques including ANN and DT (Maloof, 2006) (Abou-Assaleh, 2004) (Shabtai, 2009). Similarly, the authors in (Stokes B. A., 2017) used DL models such as LSTM, GRU, and CNN to statically analyze malware files without executing them.

3.2.2. Machine Learning-Based Dynamic Analysis Technique

Although static analysis is effective in detecting malware, it is not effective in detecting polymorphic malware. Polymorphic malware often uses techniques to hide text and binary data to avoid detection by conventional static analysis methods. In addition, malware authors also use packing techniques, where the malware is compressed or encrypted during runtime to avoid detection by static analysis methods. Fileless malware always tries to avoid static analysis methods, but their goal remains the same: to harm the target system. For example, a malware may want to steal the system's secret key, and the malware will continue to do so even if it is obfuscated. Therefore, behavior-based detection methods are extremely important.

Dynamic analysis of malware using machine learning involves monitoring the behavior of a program during its execution in a controlled environment. This approach enables the analysis of the program's actions, interactions with other software and system resources, and network communications. Machine learning algorithms can then be applied to the data generated during the analysis process to identify malicious behavior. Dynamic analysis is often performed in a sandbox environment, which is an isolated virtual machine that allows the program to run in a controlled environment without affecting the host system. The program's execution is monitored and logged, and various metrics are collected such as API calls, system events, and network traffic. Machine learning algorithms can then be trained on these metrics to identify malicious behavior.

Overall, dynamic analysis of malware using machine learning provides an effective way to detect previously unseen malware that may evade traditional signature-based detection methods. This allows researchers to better understand how malware operates in the system and how it interacts with other components of the system. Dynamic analysis also allows researchers to detect unexpected behaviors of malware in a real-world running environment. It can detect various behaviors of malware, including data changes, creating new files or modifying the system, and help identify malicious agents or infected systems.

Static and dynamic analysis are preventive mechanisms that involve not running suspicious exe files on the target system until they have been analyzed and determined to be safe. However, the limitations of static and dynamic analysis, along with new threats to cloud systems, allow malware to successfully execute on the target virtual machine. Therefore, online malware detection is essential for cloud infrastructure.

Unlike static and dynamic analysis, online malware detection focuses on the entire system rather than just one suspicious executable file. This helps to overcome the issue of malware not displaying its malicious activity, as it will be detected and stopped as soon as it begins its harmful operations. At present, there have been some investigations into detecting malware online, especially for cloud systems. The majority of prior research has adapted conventional malware detection methods for virtual machines.

According to recent studies, cloud-based malware detection has been applied in many fields and has shown higher efficiency compared to other methods. The use of cloud-based methods helps to provide more detailed analysis results for each malware sample and improve the detection rate of known and unknown malware (Ömer Aslan, 2020), (Hao Sun, 2017). This method is based on main ideas and feature extraction techniques, using advanced algorithms/techniques.

With the ability to learn and automatically update, machine learning algorithms can analyze data from network activities, files, and software to search for indications of malicious behavior. Machine learning algorithms can learn from data samples and discover patterns and rules to detect new malicious behaviors. By using machine learning techniques such as classification, clustering, and reinforcement learning, malware detection systems can automatically analyze and assess risks to identify potential threats. Machine learning can learn from previous data to make predictions about potential malicious behavior and issue necessary warnings to prevent cyber attacks.

In summary, the role of using machine learning for malware detection is very important in protecting networks and systems from harmful cyber attacks. Machine learning-based malware detection systems can automatically detect and assess threats, enhancing the reliability and safety of networks and systems. Next, this article will delve into the study of detecting malware on the cloud using machine learning.

4. EVALUATING OF CLOUD-BASED MALWARE DETECTION USING MACHINE LEARNING APPROACH

4.1. Overview Of Machine Learning Methods

This section introduces the machine learning methods commonly used in recent research works related to detecting malware in cloud computing.

Figure 3. Classification of machine learning methods

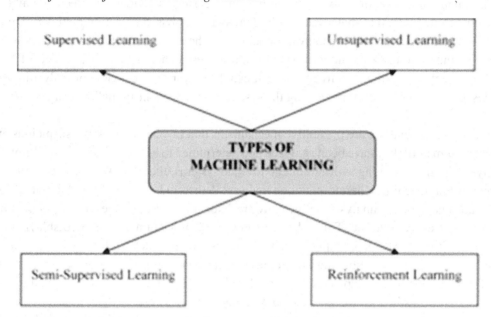

4.1.1. Supervised Learning

Supervised Learning is the process of acquiring knowledge by providing precise input and output samples to statistical models. This process is carried out during the training phase and uses labeled datasets to train algorithms, which can then predict outputs for new inputs. Supervised Learning can be classified into classification and regression. After machine learning is trained with input and output samples, it is tested with different datasets to evaluate its ability to predict outputs.

4.1.2. Unsupervised Learning

Unsupervised Learning is the process of training models on unclassified or unlabeled data, allowing the model to automatically discover the structure of the data without supervision. Unsupervised Learning is often used in data exploration tasks to discover features and classify data into groups. This process relies on computers finding potential patterns in the input data. Popular unsupervised learning methods include clustering, dimensionality reduction, and rule association.

4.1.3. Semi-Supervised Learning

Semi-supervised learning is a type of machine learning that involves training a model on a combination of labeled and unlabeled data. Semi-supervised learning combines the advantages of both approaches to achieve better performance with fewer labeled data. Semi-supervised Learning is used when data is insufficient to build supervised learning models, or when labeling data is costly and time-consuming. Popular semi-supervised learning algorithms include Self-training, Transfer Learning, and Multi-Task Learning.

4.1.4. Reinforcement Learning

Reinforcement Learning is a machine learning method where an agent interacts with the environment by performing a sequence of actions to achieve a predefined goal. In Reinforcement Learning, the agent receives feedback from the environment about the effectiveness of the actions performed, helping the agent improve its decisions and learn how to optimize the execution of actions to achieve the goal. Reinforcement Learning methods include using algorithms such as Q-learning, Policy Gradient, Actor-Critic, and Deep Reinforcement Learning. Reinforcement Learning has many applications in various fields, including robot learning, automatic control, electronic games, and even finance.

4.2. Cloud-Based Malware Detection Using Machine Learning

The technique of using ML to detect malware is a new approach applied to make malware detection more accurate and faster. ML enables systems to learn automatically from sample data to identify and classify new objects. In the case of detecting malware, the sample data are files containing malware that have been previously analyzed and marked as malicious or benign. After the system is trained with sample data, it will be able to automatically detect similar patterns in new files. From there, researchers can determine whether these files contain malware and, if so, what type of malware it is.

When using the technique of detecting malware using ML, researchers must provide the computer with a large amount of malware samples. The computer will use ML algorithms to analyze the characteristics of these samples, thereby identifying the common features of malware. Then, the computer will be trained to detect these features in different files. The technique of detecting malware using ML has many advantages. First, it allows for the quick and accurate detection of new malware patterns. Second, it helps to reduce false positives, such as mistakenly identifying a valid file as malware. Finally, this technique also helps researchers develop automated and more effective malware detection tools.

To detect malware using Machine Learning, researchers often use algorithms such as Random Forest, SVM, or Neural Networks. These algorithms have the ability to automatically classify files based on their features, such as size, structure, or lines of code. These features are called features, and researchers will select appropriate features to include in the system's training process.

In this section, we introduce machine learning-based malware detection methods, focusing on detecting malware in cloud infrastructure. However, cloud-based malware detection methods can be applied to both standalone and cloud systems. The overview diagram below describes the malware detection techniques based on machine learning and the extracted features.

File classification technique is the process of analyzing files or executable programs to determine if they contain malware or not. There are two commonly used file classification methods, static analysis and dynamic analysis. Static analysis is a method of analyzing files or programs without running them. This technique focuses on analyzing the structure of the file to find suspicious characteristics such as special character strings, incorrect file size, or malware hidden inside other files. Static analysis is often used to detect simple types of malware such as viruses or worms. Dynamic analysis is a method of analyzing files or programs by running them in a simulated environment or virtual machine. This technique allows the analysis of program behavior to determine if it has malicious actions. Dynamic analysis is often used to detect more complex types of malware such as Trojans or spyware. Static and dynamic analysis techniques are often used together to detect malware. Combining both methods provides malware analysts with a comprehensive understanding of the program or file being suspected of containing malware.

Figure 4. Classification of malware detection techniques using machine learning

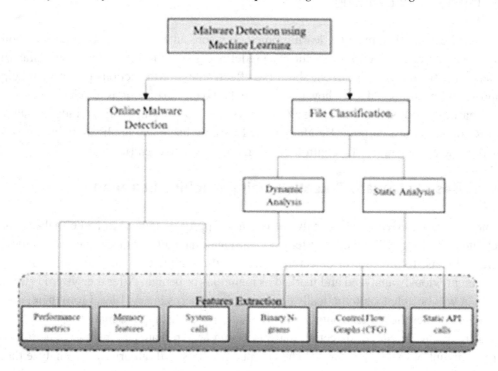

Meanwhile, online detection method continuously monitors the entire system to detect the presence of malware. The features monitored in this method are time-series and more dynamic, including performance indicators, memory features, and system call/API invocation. Figure 5 depicts the entire process of the machine learning-based malware detection approach, providing a more thorough comprehension of its methodology.

4.3. Studying Techniques for Cloud-Based Malware Detection Using Machine Learning

Detecting malware on the cloud is a crucial issue in information security. When applications and data are stored on the cloud, they can be attacked by various types of malware. To deal with these threats, the online detection technique can be used. Online detection is a method of detecting malware in real-time while data is being accessed and processed. This technique allows for the detection and prevention of malicious behavior before it causes damage to the system. Online detection is often used in cloud systems to detect malicious behavior, such as malware attacks, DDoS attacks, and exploiting security vulnerabilities. This technique uses data analysis algorithms to detect malicious patterns and abnormal activities in cloud data. To detect malware on the cloud using online detection technique, data analysis algorithms are deployed in network devices, application firewalls, or network monitoring devices. These algorithms analyze cloud data in real-time and issue alerts when malicious behavior is detected. Online detection data analysis algorithms can use machine learning techniques to analyze malware patterns and abnormal activities. These techniques allow for the detection of malicious behavior without knowing specific malware patterns beforehand.

Figure 5. Malware detection and training process

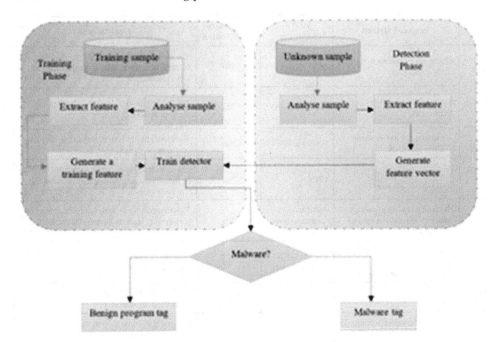

Table 1 summarizes the recent time machine learning-based malware detection methods on the cloud.

In (Michael R. Watson, 2015), Watson introduced a method for online anomaly detection in cloud computing by using specialized detection components in the fault-tolerant architecture of the cloud. This method uses features collected at the system and network level of cloud nodes and applies novelty detection using the Support Vector Machine (SVM) formula in virtualization level. The experimental results show high accuracy of over 90% and the ability to detect malware as well as DDoS attacks.

Bojan (Bojan Kolosnjaji, 2016) used a neural network with convolutional and regression layers to generate the best features for malware classification. The author used a combination of n-gram convolution and full sequence model to create a hierarchical feature extraction architecture. The author's evaluation results show that their method outperforms previous methods used in malware classification.

In her study, Xiaoyue Wan (Xiaoyue Wan, 2017) investigated the competition between wireless transmission bandwidth and sharing data of security servers to detect dynamic malware. Mobile devices were used to select the application trace load reduction speed for security servers. The author proposes to use deep Q-network with deep convolutional neural network to optimize load reduction strategy and improve speed and accuracy of malware detection. Simulation results show that load reduction strategy based on hotbooting-Q improves malware detection performance better than strategy based on Q-learning.

Together with other methods, Ye (Yanfang Ye, 2017) proposes a non-homogeneous deep framework for detecting unknown new malware. This model consists of a stacked AutoEncoder with multiple restricted Boltzmann machines and a combined memory layer. The training process of this model starts by unsupervised feature learning using greedy layer-wise training method, then fine-tuning the supervised parameters.

Table 1. Statistics of cloud-based malware detection approaches using machine learning methods

Paper	Proposed Method	ML/DL Algorithm	Malware classification	Goal/Success	Year
Watson (Michael R. Watson, 2015)	Online anomaly detection in cloud computing	SVM	No	The model provides the ability to flexibly detect new malware with a small amount of input information	2015
Mishra (Preeti Mishra E. S., 2016)	NvCloudIDS security architecture	C4.5 DT	No	The model has some better results than previous methods	2016
Bojan (Bojan Kolosnjaji, 2016)	A model using a combination of CNN and RNN	CNN and RNN	No	The model brings better results than simpler neural architectures	2016
Xiaoyue Wan (Xiaoyue Wan, 2017)	Using deep Q-network with deep CNN	CNN	No	The Q-learning based strategy is outperformed by the scheme, as confirmed by preliminary simulation results.	2017
Ye (Yanfang Ye, 2017)	Heterogeneous deep learning model consisting of a stacked AutoEncoder	Autoencoder (heterogeneous deep network)	No	This framework has better malware detection performance than traditional shallow learning methods	2017
Yuxin (Ding Yuxin, 2017)	Using a recursive neural network to extract n-gram features and predict malware	Deep Belief Network (DBN)	No	This model can provide a useful tool for malware analysis	2017
Kalash (Mahmoud Kalash, 2018)	A malware detection architecture using CNN	CNN	No	The model achieves very high accuracy on certain specific datasets.	2018
Cui (Zhihua Cui, 2018)	Propose a new deep learning method to enhance the ability to detect variations of malware	CNN	Yes	Compared to other malware detection models, the model demonstrates both high accuracy and speed according to the test results.	2018
Abdelselam (Mahmoud Abdelsalam, 2018)	A model using a combination of 2D CNN and 3D CNN.	CNN	No	The accuracy of the model is improved with 3D CNN.	2018
Patil (Rajendra Patil, 2019)	A malware detection model that combines signature-based and anomaly-based approaches.	Random Forest	No	The model can be improved and expanded to detect ransomware.	2019
Yadav (Yadav, 2018)	WFCM-AANN homogeneous malware detection technique	WFCM-AANN	No	Malware detection technique with high accuracy	2019
Huhua Li (Huhua Li, 2019)	Memory analysis model for malware detection, using deep learning	CNN	Yes	The model demonstrates security and accuracy during experimentation.	2019
Rahul Kumar (Rahul Kumar, 2020)	The TLSH framework	DT, RF, and LR	No	The model helps reduce training time while ensuring accuracy in detecting malware.	2020
Aldribi (Abdulaziz Aldribi, 2020)	A cloud anomaly detection model based on hypervisor to develop an intrusion detection system (IDS)	PCA	No	Model used machine learning algorithms with heterogeneous classifiers to detect malicious code inside virtual machines from the hypervisor	2020
Kimmell (Jeffrey C. Kimmell, 2021)	Malware detection in Cloud Virtual Machines (VMs) using RNN	LSTM RNN and BIDI	No	In certain instances, the performance of the trained RNN models can be affected by the input order, as demonstrated by the results.	2021
Tom (Tom Landman, 2021)	Linux-based cloud malware detection	CNN	No	The model achieves high effectiveness and accuracy in detecting and classifying unknown malware.	2021
Mishra (Preeti Mishra A. G., 2022)	vServiceInspector	CNN	No	Compared to previously proposed techniques, vServiceInspector exhibits higher accuracy and greater resistance to attacks.	2022

Yuxin (Ding Yuxin, 2017) uses a recursive neural network to extract n-gram features and predict malware. The model can classify files into two classes, benign and malicious, with an accuracy of 97.11%. The author also uses the recursive neural network to extract features for the t-SNE visualization algorithm, which can visualize the clustering of malware samples. This study shows that the recursive neural network can extract effective features for malware detection and provide a useful tool for malware analysis.

In Cui's (Zhihua Cui, 2018) study, a new deep learning method was proposed to enhance the ability to detect variations of malware. The author used CNN to automatically extract features of malware images after converting them into grayscale images. To address the data imbalance between different types of malware, the author used the bat algorithm. The author's approach demonstrated superior speed and accuracy compared to other malware detection models.

Abdelselam (Mahmoud Abdelsalam, 2018) used a standard 2D CNN structure to train with available meta-data for each process in the virtual machine (VM). Then, by using a new 3D CNN model, they improved the accuracy of the classifier to reduce the number of mislabeled samples. Experiments were performed on data containing different types of malware (mostly Trojan and Rootkit) executed on the virtual machine. They randomly selected malware samples in the experiments and achieved a good detection rate.

A malware detection system proposed by Patil (Rajendra Patil, 2019) for virtual machines in cloud computing uses two different techniques to detect malware. The anomaly system checks for unidentified executable files by analyzing their static features and using a random forest classification model, while the signature-based technique is implemented within the VM and uses signatures to detect known types of malware.

In Yadav's (Yadav, 2018) study, they proposed a WFCM-AANN homogeneous malware detection technique to identify the presence of malware in a system. The method is composed of two major components: a clustering component and a classification component. The authors believe that the proposed method has higher sensitivity for detecting malware than existing classifiers and may improve system performance in the future.

Huhua Li (Huhua Li, 2019) proposed a method using deep learning to detect malware through memory analysis during execution. The author extracts memory snapshots and uses a CNN to detect malware. However, to reduce runtime, the author only analyzes periodic snapshots.

Aldribi (Abdulaziz Aldribi, 2020) proposed a cloud anomaly detection model based on hypervisor to develop an intrusion detection system (IDS). The researchers utilized a combination of machine learning algorithms with diverse classifiers to detect malware on virtual machines within the hypervisor.

Deep-Hook (Tom Landman, 2021) connects to the volatile memory of a virtual machine in a reliable way and collects memory dumps to discover traces of malware while the virtual machine is running. The evaluation results of the experiment conducted by the author demonstrate the effectiveness, efficiency, and accuracy of the model in detecting and classifying unknown malware (even rootkits).

Recently, Mishra (Preeti Mishra A. G., 2022) proposed a method named vServiceInspector for monitoring the virtual machine process both internally and externally. The author utilized advanced memory introspection to extract system call strings at the Out-VM position (i.e., the virtualization layer), then used a Genetic Algorithm (GA) to identify the most discriminative system call strings and extract optimized feature sets. Then, the author employed CNN to learn and detect various types of malicious program execution. vServiceInspector is more accurate and better at preventing attacks compared to previous proposed techniques.

5. PROPOSED FRAMEWORK

This section presents a proposed framework aimed at enhancing malware detection in the cloud using machine learning/deep learning algorithms. The objective is to design a universal model. A working diagram of the framework and a comprehensive description of the process approach depicted in Figure 6 will be presented.

Figure 6. Proposed model for cloud-based malware detection using machine learning

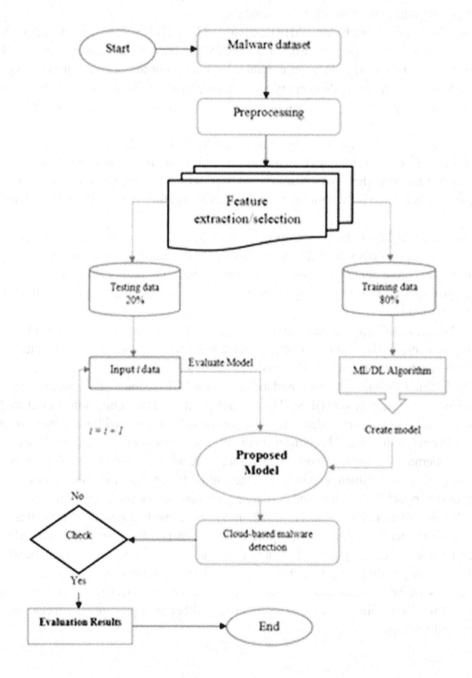

Accordingly, the malware dataset used as input for the model can be obtained from publicly available data sets such as VirusShare, UNSW-NB, UNM, Barecloud, etc. In addition, it is possible to build a dataset for training machine learning algorithms in malware detection. This dataset needs to contain all types of malware, including both known and unknown ones. These types of malware can include viruses, worms, trojans, rootkits, backdoors, spyware, adware, and other types of malware. To build the dataset, malware analysis tools can be used to search, classify, and extract malware files from various sources. These sources can include collections of malware samples on the internet, malware files collected from attacks, and official updates from security software providers. After identifying the malware files, data preprocessing steps need to be performed to prepare for the training process. These steps include dividing the malware files into smaller samples, removing unnecessary malicious code segments, and standardizing the data format. The data patterns in these datasets include malicious and benign code.

To improve the ability to detect malware in the cloud, it is necessary to design a general model supported by machine/deep learning algorithms. However, before feeding the data into the model, data preprocessing is needed to integrate and remove unsuitable samples. This helps to simplify the process of malware detection and improve the accuracy of detection as well as data processing time. The data preprocessing process includes removing null value samples and samples with different behavior from other samples. Data preprocessing techniques include handling missing data, encoding categorical variables, data normalization, data scaling, and some other techniques.

Next, the selected prominent features through the improvement presented in this study can be implemented through algorithms such as Random Forest, Decision Tree, SVM, etc. The use of semantic logic assists in the identification of salient features, resulting in more precise feature selection and increased accuracy in the detection process with minimal error rates. The goal of feature selection is to eliminate redundant and unimportant features from the feature set when it becomes too large. The three commonly used methods in the feature selection process are filter method (statistical scores of features are used. Features with high scores will be retained, while features with low scores will be removed), wrapper method (features are combined into different sets and tested on the prediction model. The feature set with the most accurate result will be selected), and embedding method (evaluating attributes used in building the model).

Next, the data is divided into two parts: training data and testing data. Training data and testing data are two important components in building a machine learning model. Training data is used to "train" the model by providing it with examples of inputs and their corresponding outputs. The model will use this data to learn and optimize its parameters so that it can make accurate predictions for new inputs. Testing data is used to evaluate the performance of the trained model. When the model is applied to new data, testing data will evaluate whether the model can make accurate predictions or not. If the evaluation result is not good, we can adjust the model or change the training method to increase the accuracy of the model. The division is done randomly and the sample data is split into two parts at a ratio of 80% for training and 20% for testing.

To apply ML/DL algorithms to data with special characteristics, the data samples are randomly classified to create training and testing sets. Appropriate ML/DL algorithms can be used, such as CNN, LSTM, RNN, DNN, VGG16, etc. In addition, to evaluate the model accurately, performance evaluation methods such as confusion matrix, accuracy, recall, precision, and F1-score should be used.

After training and building an effective malware detection model in the cloud, the model can be deployed on dedicated hardware devices with appropriate resources to achieve the highest malware detection efficiency. Figure 8 illustrates the process of detecting malware in the cloud when applying the proposed model in practice. Suspicious files/traffic from personal devices, mobile devices or IoT devices during exploitation, using cloud services, browsing the web, sending/receiving emails or transmitting files will be input for the cloud-based malware detection system. Depending on the trained model, appropriate input data will be analyzed and recorded for the existence of malware in one or more execution streams.

Figure 7. The proposed framework in practice

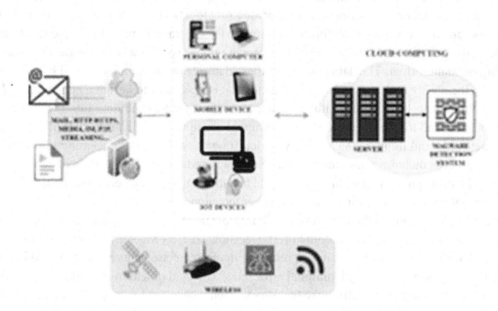

6. EXPERIMENTAL DESIGN

6.1. Datasets

The dataset from the UNSW Canberra Cyber Center's laboratory was collected, including 69.3 GB of pcap files with over 72 million records. The dataset simulate a realistic network environment with a mix of normal and botnet traffic. Considering the sample dataset is too large, the experiment uses only 5% of the extracted data from the sample dataset, including four files with a total size of ~1GB, with over 3,600,000 records in csv format.

The label ratio in the dataset shows that 99.987% - 3,668,045 samples are malware, with only 0.013% - 477 samples being benign. The sample dataset will be divided into two subsets: the training dataset (80%) and the testing dataset (20%), and will be randomly split.

6.2. Data Preprocessing

Data preprocessing steps will include: handling missing data, encoding categorical variables, and normalizing data.

Figure 8. Malware ratio in the sample dataset

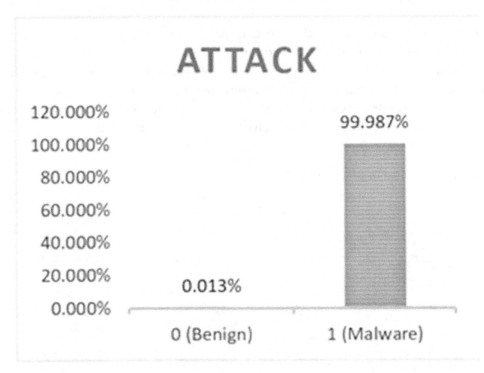

- Handling missing data: The dataset being used does not have any missing data points, so this step is skipped.
- Encoding categorical variables: There are 5 categorical features that need to be encoded into numerical values: "flgs", "proto", "sport", "dport", "state".
- Normalizing data: Using standardization helps transform the distribution of data so that each feature has a mean value of 0 and a standard deviation of 1.

6.3. Feature Selection

In this dataset, there are not too many features, and some of them are redundant and unimportant, including:

- 'state_number', 'proto_number', 'flgs_number': These fields only represent the number of different values in the existing columns.
- 'category', 'subcategory': Fields representing sub-labels.
- 'saddr', 'daddr': Fields containing information about source and destination addresses. From the original 45 features, after running the algorithm for feature selection, there are 38 remaining features.

6.4. Training and Testing the Malware Detection Model

Apply the Random Forest algorithm to the sample dataset. Then, the results of the machine learning algorithms will be compared and conclusions drawn.

Random Forest is an algorithm that leverages the power of randomness by constructing multiple decision trees (forest). The fundamental concept of the algorithm is to construct decision trees using separate subsets of the provided dataset. In each node, a few randomly selected feature values are assessed until the optimal split is discovered. In summary, the algorithm can be illustrated in Figure 9.

Figure 9. Description of the random forest algorithm

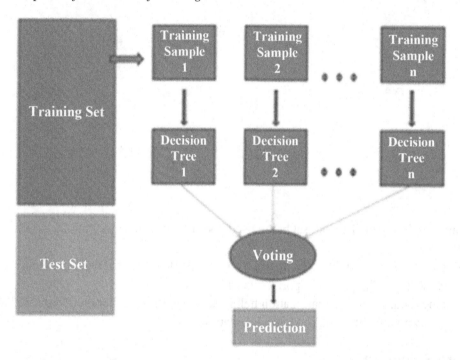

After feature extraction and selection, this dataset will be used to train machine learning techniques, including KNN, SVM, Decision Tree, Naive Bayes, and Random Forest. The library packages used for these algorithms are Scikit-Learn Classifiers.

The experimental environment is conducted on Google Colab.

6.5. Results and Evaluation

The algorithms produced different results. The best-performing algorithm is Random Forest with accuracy, recall, and precision all achieving 100%. Next is KNN with 99.99% accuracy, 98.94% recall, and Decision Tree with 99.99% accuracy and precision, and 86% recall. Naïve Bayes achieved 99.73% accuracy, 90% recall, and 52% precision. The algorithm with the lowest accuracy is SVM, which achieved 56.28% accuracy, 78% recall, and 50% precision. The effectiveness of the algorithms is shown in Table 2.

Table 2. The result of experiment

Model	Accuracy	Recall	Precision	F1 score	TPR	FPR	AUC-ROC	Training time
Random Forest	100%	100%	100%	100%	100%	0%	100%	10 minutes
Decision Tree	99.99%	86%	99,99%	92%	100%	26%	86%	1 minutes
Naïve Bayes	99,73%	90%	52%	53%	99,73%	19%	99%	40 second
SVM	56,28%	78%	50%	36%	56%	0%	82%	2 minutes
KNN	99,99%	98,94%	99,46%	99%	99,99%	2,1%	99%	2 hours 36 minutes

The most important feature is the Total number of packets per protocol (TnP_PerProto), which contributes approximately 50% to the predictive performance of the model.

Different machine learning algorithms often rely on a set of hyper-parameters or a hypothesis about the data distribution, so there is no single algorithm that is always good and performs best for all applications and datasets. It is worth noting that hyper-parameters are not automatically learned in machine learning classification models, but can be adjusted by users. Therefore, to find the best machine learning algorithms for a given dataset, experimentation may be needed to try out different algorithms. Among the five techniques mentioned above, the thesis recommends applying the Random Forest algorithm to the malware detection problem with the collected dataset, achieving 100% accuracy and coverage, the lowest false positive rate (FPR) - 0%, and being suitable for large datasets because it can be parallelized across multiple machines to train multiple trees simultaneously.

6.6. Experiment With a Recent Cloud-Based Dataset

The dataset was constructed by (A Alfred Raja Melvin, 2021) based on VMI (Virtual Machine Introspection) technology, consisting of a total of 273 samples of both malicious and benign files. It includes 175 Virus samples, 50 Trojan samples, 30 utility files, and 18 system files.

The dataset was evaluated using 10-fold cross-validation with different algorithms, specifically:

- LMT (Logistic Model Tree): LMT combines the decision tree model with logistic regression to build a decision tree with good classification capabilities. The LMT algorithm creates a decision tree by dividing the data based on features and uses logistic regression to make predictions for each branch of the tree. Applying the LMT algorithm to the dataset resulted in a runtime of 0.7s, with both ROC and PRC achieving absolute values.

- Random Tree: Random Tree generates multiple random decision trees and combines their results to make predictions. When applying the Random Tree algorithm, the True Positive rate reached 96% and the False Positive rate was 10.7%.
- OneR: OneR evaluates all possible features and selects the one with the best performance in classification. It then constructs a rule using the selected feature and threshold value to classify the samples. Applying the OneR algorithm to the dataset mentioned above, the runtime was reduced to 0.02s, but the TP, FP, and MCC scores remained at an average level.

Table 3. The result of experiment with a recent cloud-based dataset

Model	TP	FP	Precision	Recall	F-Measure	MCC	ROC	PRC	Training Time
LMT	0.989	0.052	0.989	0.989	0.989	0.962	1.0	1.0	0.7s
Random Tree	0.960	0.107	0.959	0.960	0.960	0.860	0.936	0.951	0.02s
OneR	0.868	0.618	0.886	0.868	0.833	0.464	0.625	0.778	0.02s
NaiveBayes	0.923	0.049	0.941	0.923	0.927	0.781	0.963	0.947	0.03s
SGD	0.985	0.020	0.986	0.985	0.985	0.951	0.983	0.981	0.18s
AdaBoostM1	1.0	0.0	1.0	1.0	1.0	1.0	1.0	1.0	0.16s

- NaiveBayes: The algorithm calculates the probability of each class based on the features and uses Bayes' theorem to make classification predictions. The classification results of the Naive Bayes algorithm for the dataset are 92.3% True Positive (TP) and 4.9% False Positive (FP).

- SGD (Stochastic Gradient Descent): SGD is an optimization algorithm used for training machine learning models. The SGD algorithm optimizes the loss function by updating the weights randomly for each data point (stochastic). Updating the weights based on each data point helps the algorithm converge faster compared to traditional optimization methods. When applying the SGD algorithm to the dataset, the results are relatively high, with 98.5% TP and 2.0% FP. With a Precision of 98.6% and F-measure of 98.5%, it can be seen that the model is capable of accurately predicting Positive samples with a rate of 98.6%. At the same time, the F-measure of 98.5% indicates a high level of accuracy and recall, demonstrating good performance in classifying Positive samples. Both of these metrics indicate that the model achieves good performance in classification and accurate predictions.

- AdaBoostM1. AdaBoost creates versions of weak models based on generating training samples with different weights. These weak models are then combined to make the final prediction. The algorithm yields optimal results when applied to the aforementioned dataset. With a runtime of 0.16s, the TP reaches 100%, indicating accurate classification of all Positive samples. FP reaches 0%, indicating no Negative samples misclassified as Positive. Precision, Recall, and F-measure all reach 100%, demonstrating perfect accuracy and recall in classification. MCC is a measure of the correlation between predictions and true labels, and a value of 100% indicates a perfect correlation between predictions and labels. ROC and PRC both reach 100%, indicating excellent classification performance across the entire range of decision thresholds. Overall, these metrics indicate that the model achieves perfect performance in data classification.

7. CONCLUSION

In today's era, malware attacks are becoming increasingly common in terms of quantity, complexity, and severity. However, there is no detection method that can detect all newly created types of malware. The future development direction of cloud-based malware detection techniques using machine learning in the cloud is expected to focus on several areas: incorporating more advanced deep learning models, such as CNN, RNN, and transformers; developing more sophisticated feature extraction techniques to identify and extract more informative features from malware samples; utilizing more diverse and comprehensive datasets for model training; investigating new methods for dealing with adversarial attacks, where attackers attempt to evade or deceive the detection models by crafting malicious samples that can bypass the detection mechanisms; exploring the possibility of integrating different detection techniques and models into a unified system that can leverage the strengths of each individual technique and provide a more comprehensive and effective solution for malware detection on the cloud. Overall, the development of cloud-based malware detection techniques using machine learning is expected to continue to advance rapidly in the coming years, driven by the increasing demand for more efficient and effective methods to detect and mitigate the growing threat of malware attacks on cloud environments.

ACKNOWLEDGMENT

Pham Sy Nguyen was funded by Vingroup Joint Stock Company and supported by the Domestic Master/ PhD Scholarship Programme of Vingroup Innovation Foundation (VINIF), Vingroup Big Data Institute (VINBIGDATA), code VINIF.2022.TS.086.

REFERENCES

Melvin, A. (2021). *The Practicality of using Virtual Machine Introspection Technique with Machine Learning Algorithms for the Detection of Intrusions in Cloud.* EUDL.

Abdulaziz Aldribi, I. T. (2020). *ypervisor-based cloud intrusion detection through online multivariate statistical change tracking.* Elsevier Computer and Security.

Abou-Assaleh, T. (2004). *N-gram-based detection of new malicious code.* COMPSAC. doi:10.1109/CMPSAC.2004.1342667

Ajeet Singh, A. J. (2018). Study of cyber-attacks on cyber-physical system. In *Proceedings of 3rd International Conference on Internet of Things and Connected Technologies (ICIoTCT).* SSRN.

Berlin, S. (2015). Deep neural network based malware detection using two dimensional binary program features. IEEE.

Bojan Kolosnjaji, A. Z. (2016). Deep learning for classification of malware system call sequences. [Springer.]. *Intelligence*, 137–149.

Chengwei, W. (2009). Ebat: online methods for detecting utility cloud anomalies. In *Proceedings of the 6th Middleware Doctoral Symposium.* ACM.

Cui, Z. F. X.-g. (2018). Detection of Malicious Code Variants Based on Deep Learning. IEEE.

Dahl, G. E. J. W. (2013). Large-scale malware classification using random projections and neural networks. ICASSP. IEEE.

Davis, R. S. (2019). *McAfee Mobile Threat Report Q1.* McAfee.

Ding, Y. Z. S. (2017). *Malware detection based on deep learning algorithm.* The Natural Computing Applications Forum.

Hao Sun, X. W. (2017). CloudEyes: Cloud-based malware detection with reversible sketch for resource-constrained internet of things (IoT) devices. *Software, Practice & Experience.*

Jeffrey, C., & Kimmell, A. D. (2021). *Recurrent Neural Networks Based Online Behavioural Malware Detection Techniques for Cloud Infrastructure.* IEEE.

Jensen, N. G. (2020). *Attack surfaces: A taxonomy for attacks.* IEEE CLOUD.

Joel, A., & Dawson, J. T. (2018). Space detection of virtual machine cyber events through hypervisorlevel system call analysis. *2018 1st International Conference in IEEE.* IEEE.

Kim, S. S. (2016). *Visualized malware classification based-on convolutional neural network.* Information Security and Cryptology.

Li, H. D. Z. (2019). Using Deep-Learning-based Memory Analysis for Malware Detection in Cloud. *IEEE 16th International Conference on Mobile Ad Hoc and Sensor Systems Workshops (MASSW).* IEEE.

Mahmoud Abdelsalam, R. K. (2018). Malware Detection in Cloud Infrastructures using Convolutional Neural Networks. *IEEE 11th International Conference on Cloud Computing.* IEEE. 10.1109/CLOUD.2018.00028

Mahmoud Kalash, M. R. (2018). *Malware Classification with Deep Convolutional Neural Networks.* IEEE.

Maloof, J. Z. (2006). Learning to detect and classify malicious executables in the wild. *Machine Learning.*

Michael, R. Watson, N.-u.-h. S. (2015). Malware Detection in Cloud Computing Infrastructures. *IEEE Transactions on Dependable and Secure Computing.*

Morgan, S. (2019). *Cybersecurity almanac: 100 facts, figures, predictions and statistics.* Cybercrime Magazine Cisco and Cybersecurity Ventures.

Ömer Aslan, R. S. (2020). Using a Subtractive Center Behavioral Model to Detect Malware. *Security and Communication Networks*, 2020.

Peter Mell, T. G. (2011). *The NIST Definition of cloud computing.*

Preeti Mishra, A. G. (2022). vServiceInspector: Introspection-assisted evolutionary bag-of-ngram approach to detect malware in cloud servers. *Ad Hoc Networks, 131.*

Preeti Mishra, E. S. (2016). NvCloudIDS: A Security Architecture to Detect Intrusions at Network and Virtualization Layer in Cloud Environment. *Intl. Conference on Advances in Computing, Communications and Informatics (ICACCI).*

B. Rad, M. M. (2012). *Camouflage in Malware: from Encryption to Metamorphism.* Journal of Computer and Science Network Securrity.

Rahul Kumar, K. S. (2020). *Machine Learning based Malware Detection in Cloud Environment using Clustering Approach.* IEEE.

Rajendra Patil, H. D. (2019). *Designing in-VM-assisted lightweight agent-based malware detection framework for securing virtual machines in cloud computing.* Springer.

Samet, Ö. A. (2020). A comprehensive review on malware detection approaches. *IEEE Access : Practical Innovations, Open Solutions*, 8.

Shabtai, A., Moskovitch, R., Elovici, Y., & Glezer, C. (2009). Detection of malicious code by applying machine learning classifiers on static features: A state-of-the-art. *Information Security Technical Report*, *14*(1), 16–29. doi:10.1016/j.istr.2009.03.003

Stokes, B. A. (2017). *Malware classification with LSTM and GRU language models and a character-level cnn.* IEEE.

Stokes, W. H. (2016). MtNet: a multi-task neural network for dynamic malware classification. Detection of Intrusions and Malware, and Vulnerability Assessment. Springer.

Tahan, G., L. R. (2012). Mal-ID: Automatic malware detection using common segment analysis and meta-features. *Journal of Machine Learning Research.*

Tobiyama, Y. Y. (2016). *Malware detection with deep neural network using process behavior.* COMPSAC.

Tom Landman, N. N. (2021). Deep-Hook: A trusted deep learning-based framework for unknown malware detection and classification in Linux cloud environments. *Neural Networks*, *144*, 648–685. doi:10.1016/j.neunet.2021.09.019 PMID:34656885

Wan, X. G. S. (2017). Reinforcement Learning Based Mobile Offloading for Cloud-based Malware Detection. IEEE.

Yadav, R. M. (2018). Effective Analysis Of Malware Detection In Cloud Computing. *Computers & Security.*

Yanfang Ye, L. C. (2017). *DeepAM: a heterogeneous deep learning framework or intelligent malware detection.* Springer-Verlag London 2017.

Yim, I. Y. (2010). *Malware obfuscation techniques: A brief survey.* Wirel. Comput. Commun. Appl. BWCCA.

Chapter 10
Cyber Security Risk Assessment and Management Using Artificial Intelligence and Machine Learning

Sangeetha Ganesan

R.M.K. College of Engineering and Technology, India

A. Indumathi

Sri Venkateswara College of Engineering, India

Kumaravel Subramani

Sri Venkateswara College of Engineering, India

N. Uma

Sri Venkateswara College of Engineering, India

M. Sugacini

Sri Venkateswara College of Engineering, India

S. Kavishree

Sri Venkateswara College of Engineering, India

ABSTRACT

The threat of cyber-attacks and wireless communication technologies are now affecting a number of private and public organizations around the world. It is a challenge to protect today's data from cyber-attacks since it is highly dependent on electronic technology. It is possible to mitigate or reduce these risks by identifying them. Risk assessments can help to develop a plan for responding to and recovering from a cyber attack. It is crucial to continuously monitor and assess the risk environment to identify any changes in the organization's context and to keep track of the entire risk management process. Researchers from all around the world have proposed a number of methods to thwart cyber-attacks or minimize the harm they do. The aim of this chapter is to present in-depth analysis of the typical improvements achieved in the field of cyber security risk assessment and management and examines the impact of artificial intelligence and machine learning in cyber security risk assessment, and management.

DOI: 10.4018/978-1-6684-9317-5.ch010

1. INTRODUCTION

Cyber attacks are attempts to compromise or damage computer systems, networks, or devices by unauthorized individuals or groups. These attacks can come in many different forms, including viruses, malware, phishing, and denial-of-service attacks. The motives behind cyber attacks can vary, but they often include theft of sensitive data, financial gain, or political activism. Protecting against cyber attacks involves implementing security measures such as firewalls, anti-virus software, and encryption protocols, as well as educating individuals and organizations on safe online practices. Cyber security risk assessment and management are processes that organizations use to identify, analyze, and evaluate the risks and vulnerabilities associated with their information systems, data, and networks. This allows them to implement appropriate security measures to minimize or mitigate those risks.

In a world where cyber threats are increasing, conducting a cyber security risk assessment is essential for any organization that handles sensitive or confidential data. A risk assessment can help an organization identify potential threats, evaluate the likelihood and potential impact of those threats, and determine the appropriate measures to reduce or eliminate the risks. The cyber security risk management process involves several steps, including identifying assets and threats, assessing the risks associated with those assets and threats, selecting and implementing appropriate controls to mitigate those risks, and continuously monitoring and reviewing the effectiveness of those controls.

A thorough cyber security risk assessment and management program should involve all stakeholders within an organization, including IT personnel, risk management professionals, and executive leadership. By involving all relevant parties, an organization can ensure that its cyber security program is comprehensive, effective, and aligned with its overall business objectives. Overall, cyber security risk assessment and management are critical components of any organization's overall security strategy. By identifying and addressing potential risks and vulnerabilities, organizations can protect themselves from cyber threats and maintain the confidentiality, integrity, and availability of their data and systems.

Cyber security risk assessment and management can be enhanced by the use of AI and machine learning technologies. These technologies enable organizations to identify potential security threats and vulnerabilities in their systems and data more quickly and accurately, as well as automate and improve the effectiveness of their risk management strategies. One way that AI and machine learning can be used for cyber security risk assessment is by analyzing large datasets of network traffic, system logs, and other security-related data to identify patterns and anomalies that may indicate a security threat. Machine learning algorithms can be trained on this data to recognize patterns and behaviors that are indicative of a cyber attack or other security breach, allowing organizations to respond quickly and proactively to potential threats.

Another way that AI and machine learning can be used for cyber security risk management is through the development of predictive analytics models. These models can analyze historical data to identify potential future threats and vulnerabilities, enabling organizations to implement proactive security measures to prevent attacks before they occur. In addition, AI and machine learning can be used to automate certain cyber security tasks, such as vulnerability scanning and patch management, which can help organizations identify and remediate vulnerabilities more quickly and efficiently. However, it's important to note that AI and machine learning are not a silver bullet for cyber security risk assessment and management. These technologies require careful development, monitoring, and evaluation to ensure that they are accurate and effective, and they should be used in conjunction with other cyber security strategies and best practices.

2. LITERATURE SURVEY

"Cyber security Risk Assessment for SCADA and DCS Networks: A Systematic Literature Review" by Othman Alshammari, Abdulrahman Almutairi, and Khalid Alghathbar. The paper aims to provide a systematic literature review of the current state of research on cyber security risk assessment for SCADA (Supervisory Control and Data Acquisition) and DCS (Distributed Control Systems) networks. The objective of the paper is to identify the existing research gaps and suggest future research directions in this area. The paper reviews a total of 69 research articles published between 2000 and 2020 that focus on cyber security risk assessment for SCADA and DCS networks. The review highlights the importance of addressing the unique cyber security challenges associated with these networks, which are often used in critical infrastructure systems such as power plants and water treatment facilities. The authors identify several key research gaps in the existing literature, including the need for more comprehensive risk assessment frameworks, improved threat modeling techniques, and more effective security controls. They also suggest that future research should focus on developing more advanced machine learning and AI-based techniques for cyber security risk assessment and mitigation. Overall, this paper provides a valuable overview of the current state of research on cyber security risk assessment for SCADA and DCS networks and highlights several important research gaps that need to be addressed. Future work in this area could help improve the security and resilience of critical infrastructure systems and protect them against cyber threats.

"A Comprehensive Literature Review on Cyber security Risk Management" by Arshad Ali, Mohammad Zakaria, and Abdulaziz Almehmadi. This paper provides a comprehensive literature review on cyber security risk management, covering various aspects such as risk assessment, risk mitigation, risk governance, and risk communication. The authors analyze the existing literature and provide insights into the challenges and opportunities of cyber security risk management.The objective of the paper is to identify the key themes and trends in the literature and to highlight the research gaps that need to be addressed. The paper reviews a total of 109 research articles published between 2000 and 2020 that focus on cyber security risk management. The review covers a wide range of topics, including risk assessment, threat modeling, security controls, incident response, and governance. One of the key strengths of this paper is its emphasis on identifying the research gaps in the existing literature. The authors highlight several important research areas that need to be addressed, including the need for more comprehensive risk assessment frameworks, improved threat modeling techniques, and more effective security controls. In terms of future work, the authors suggest that research in this area should focus on developing more advanced machine learning and AI-based techniques for cyber security risk management. They also emphasize the importance of developing more effective communication and collaboration mechanisms between stakeholders in the cyber security ecosystem. Overall, this paper provides a valuable overview of the current state of research on cyber security risk management and highlights several important research gaps that need to be addressed. Future work in this area could help improve the effectiveness of cyber security risk management strategies and help organizations better protect against cyber threats.

"Machine Learning for Cyber security Risk Management: A Survey" by Arvind S. Raju, S. Sathappan, and U. Srinivasan. This paper presents a survey of the literature on the use of machine learning in cyber security risk management. The authors discuss various machine learning techniques used in this field, such as anomaly detection, classification, and prediction, and provide insights into the challenges and opportunities of using machine learning for cyber security risk management. The objective of the paper is to identify the key trends and challenges in this area and to provide insights into future research directions. The paper reviews a total of 99 research articles published between 2000 and 2019 that focus on machine learning for cyber security risk management. The review covers a wide range of topics, including intrusion detection, malware analysis, vulnerability assessment, and threat intelligence. One of the key strengths of this paper is its emphasis on identifying the challenges and limitations of using machine learning for cyber security risk management. The authors highlight several important challenges, including the lack of high-quality training data, the difficulty of interpreting machine learning results, and the need for more effective feature engineering techniques. In terms of future work, the authors suggest that research in this area should focus on developing more advanced machine learning algorithms that can handle the complexity and variability of cyber threats. They also emphasize the importance of integrating machine learning with other cyber security technologies, such as threat intelligence and incident response systems. Overall, this paper provides a valuable survey of the current state of research on machine learning for cyber security risk management and highlights several important challenges and research directions. Future work in this area could help improve the effectiveness of cyber security risk management strategies and help organizations better protect against cyber threats.

"Cyber security Risk Assessment and Management: A Review of the Current State of the Art" by Mohammad J. Al-Muhtadi, Mahmoud A. Al-Qutayri, and Qassim Nasir. This paper presents a review of the current state of the art in cyber security risk assessment and management. The authors discuss various approaches and techniques used in this field, such as threat modeling, vulnerability assessment, and risk analysis, and provide insights into the challenges and opportunities of cyber security risk assessment and management. The objective of the paper is to identify the key challenges and opportunities in this area and to suggest future research directions. The paper reviews a total of 45 research articles published between 2000 and 2019 that focus on cyber security risk assessment and management. The review covers a wide range of topics, including risk assessment methodologies, threat modeling techniques, security controls, and incident response. One of the key strengths of this paper is its emphasis on identifying the challenges and limitations of current cyber security risk assessment and management approaches. The author highlights several important challenges, including the need for more comprehensive risk assessment frameworks, the difficulty of accurately measuring cyber security risk, and the lack of effective incident response strategies. In terms of future work, the author suggests that research in this area should focus on developing more advanced risk assessment and management approaches that can handle the complexity and variability of cyber threats. This may involve integrating machine learning and AI-based techniques into existing risk assessment and management frameworks, as well as developing more effective incident response strategies. Overall, this paper provides a valuable review of the current state of the art in cyber security risk assessment and management and highlights several important challenges and research directions. Future work in this area could help improve the effectiveness of cyber security risk assessment and management strategies and help organizations better protect against cyber threats.

"A Review of Cyber security Risk Assessment Frameworks for Industrial Control Systems" by Md Rashedul Islam and Asif Ullah Khan. This paper presents a review of the existing cyber security risk assessment frameworks for industrial control systems (ICS). The authors discuss various frameworks used in this field, such as NIST SP 800-82, ISA/IEC 62443, and ISO 27001, and provide insights into the challenges and opportunities of cyber security risk assessment in ICS. The objective of the paper is to identify the key features and limitations of existing frameworks and to suggest future research directions. The paper reviews a total of 19 research articles published between 2010 and 2020 that focus on cyber security risk assessment frameworks for ICSs. The review covers a wide range of topics, including risk assessment methodologies, threat modeling techniques, security controls, and incident response. One of the key strengths of this paper is its emphasis on identifying the features and limitations of existing cyber security risk assessment frameworks for ICSs. The authors highlight several important features, including the need for asset identification and classification, vulnerability assessment, and threat analysis. They also identify several limitations, such as the lack of standardization and the need for more effective metrics for measuring cyber security risk. In terms of future work, the authors suggest that research in this area should focus on developing more comprehensive and standardized cyber security risk assessment frameworks for ICSs. This may involve integrating machine learning and AI-based techniques into existing frameworks, as well as developing more effective incident response strategies. Overall, this paper provides a valuable review of the current state of research on cyber security risk assessment frameworks for ICSs and highlights several important features and limitations. Future work in this area could help improve the effectiveness of cyber security risk assessment frameworks for ICSs and help organizations better protect against cyber threats in critical infrastructure systems.

"The Cyber Risk Handbook: Creating and Measuring Effective Cyber security Capabilities" by Domenic Antonucci and Mieke Kooij. This comprehensive handbook provides a detailed overview of the cyber security risk assessment and management process, as well as practical guidance on how to implement effective cyber security strategies. The paper's objective is to provide a structured approach for managing cyber risks that is both practical and actionable. The handbook covers a wide range of topics, including understanding the cyber threat landscape, identifying and prioritizing cyber security risks, implementing cyber security controls, and managing incident response. It also provides guidance on how to measure the effectiveness of cyber security strategies using key performance indicators (KPIs) and other metrics. One of the key strengths of this handbook is its emphasis on practicality. The authors provide concrete examples and case studies throughout the book to illustrate how organizations can implement effective cyber security strategies in real-world scenarios. In terms of future work, the authors note that the cyber security threat landscape is constantly evolving, and organizations must remain vigilant and adapt their risk management strategies accordingly. They suggest that future research should focus on developing more advanced cyber security metrics and analytics tools to help organizations better understand and manage cyber risks. Overall, "The Cyber Risk Handbook" is a valuable resource for organizations looking to develop effective cyber security risk management strategies, and it provides a useful framework for ongoing cyber security risk management efforts.

"NIST Cyber security Framework" by the National Institute of Standards and Technology (NIST). This framework provides a set of best practices for managing cyber security risks, including how to identify and prioritize risks, implement cyber security controls, and manage incident response. The objective of this paper is to provide a detailed overview of the NIST Cyber security Framework, including its core components and implementation guidance. The paper provides a comprehensive overview of the five core components of the NIST Cyber security Framework, which include Identify, Protect, Detect, Respond, and Recover. It also discusses the implementation guidance provided by NIST, which includes a seven-step process for implementing the framework within an organization. One of the key strengths of this paper is its emphasis on practical guidance for implementing the NIST Cyber security Framework. The authors provide detailed explanations of each of the core components and offer practical examples of how organizations can implement them. In terms of future work, the paper suggests that organizations and researchers should continue to refine and improve the implementation guidance provided by NIST. This may involve developing more specific guidance for different industry sectors, as well as incorporating new technologies and cyber security threats into the framework. Overall, this paper provides a valuable overview of the NIST Cyber security Framework and its implementation guidance. The framework has become widely adopted by organizations across different sectors as a useful tool for managing and reducing cyber security risk, and future work in this area could help improve its effectiveness and applicability to different organizations and contexts.

"Cyber security Risk Management: A Review of Current Approaches" by Andrew Simpson and Marcus Sachs. This article provides an overview of different cyber security risk management approaches, including qualitative and quantitative risk assessment, as well as emerging technologies such as AI and machine learning. The objective of the paper is to provide a comprehensive overview of the various approaches to cyber security risk management, including their strengths and weaknesses, and to identify areas for future research. The paper reviews a range of approaches to cyber security risk management, including quantitative and qualitative approaches, as well as hybrid approaches that combine both quantitative and qualitative methods. The review covers a variety of topics, including risk assessment methodologies, threat modeling techniques, and risk management frameworks. One of the key strengths of this paper is its comprehensive review of different approaches to cyber security risk management, which provides readers with a broad understanding of the different options available for managing cyber security risk. The paper also highlights the strengths and weaknesses of each approach and provides practical examples of their use. In terms of future work, the paper suggests that research in this area should focus on developing more standardized and effective approaches to cyber security risk management. This may involve developing more comprehensive risk assessment methodologies, improving the accuracy of threat modeling techniques, and developing better metrics for measuring cyber security risk. Overall, this paper provides a valuable overview of the current state of research on cyber security risk management and highlights several important areas for future research. Improved cyber security risk management is becoming increasingly important in the face of growing cyber security threats, and future work in this area could help organizations better protect against cyber attacks and minimize the impact of security breaches.

"Cyber security Metrics: A Practical Guide for Effective Security and Risk Management" by Andrew Jaquith. This book provides practical guidance on how to develop effective cyber security metrics to measure the effectiveness of cyber security risk management strategies. The objective of the paper is to provide a comprehensive overview of the key concepts and best practices for developing and using cyber security metrics, as well as to provide practical examples of their use. The paper covers a range of topics related to cyber security metrics, including the benefits of using metrics, key performance indicators (KPIs) for cyber security, and how to measure the effectiveness of cyber security programs. The paper also provides guidance on how to develop and use metrics to support risk management practices, such as risk assessment and risk mitigation. One of the key strengths of this paper is its practical focus, which provides readers with practical guidance on how to develop and use cyber security metrics in their organizations. The paper provides a range of examples of cyber security metrics and offers guidance on how to measure their effectiveness. In terms of future work, the paper suggests that further research is needed to refine and improve the use of cyber security metrics. This may involve developing more standardized metrics and benchmarks for different industry sectors, as well as developing more sophisticated methods for measuring the effectiveness of cyber security programs. Overall, this paper provides a valuable guide for organizations looking to develop and use cyber security metrics to improve their security and risk management practices. Cyber security metrics are becoming increasingly important in the face of growing cyber security threats, and future work in this area could help organizations better protect against cyber attacks and minimize the impact of security breaches.

"The Art of Cyber Risk Oversight: CISOs and Boards" by Thomas J. Parenty and Jack J. Domet. This book focuses on the relationship between CISOs and corporate boards in managing cyber security risks, including how to communicate cyber security risks effectively to the board and how to develop effective risk management strategies. The objective of the paper is to highlight the challenges facing CISOs and boards in managing cyber risks, and to provide practical guidance on how to overcome these challenges. The paper covers a range of topics related to cyber risk oversight, including the roles and responsibilities of CISOs and boards, how to establish effective communication and reporting structures, and best practices for managing cyber risks. One of the key strengths of this paper is its focus on the importance of collaboration between CISOs and boards in managing cyber risks. The paper highlights the need for CISOs to engage with boards in a meaningful way, and provides practical guidance on how to establish effective communication channels. In terms of future work, the paper suggests that further research is needed to refine and improve the collaboration between CISOs and boards in managing cyber risks. This may involve developing more standardized approaches to reporting cyber risks to boards, as well as developing more effective methods for assessing the effectiveness of cyber risk management programs. Overall, this paper provides a valuable guide for CISOs and boards looking to establish effective collaboration in managing cyber risks. As cyber threats continue to evolve, effective cyber risk oversight is becoming increasingly important for organizations, and future work in this area could help organizations better protect against cyber attacks and minimize the impact of security breaches. There are many different types of cyber attacks, each with its own specific tactics, techniques, and objectives. Here are some of the most common types: Malware attacks: Malware refers to any type of malicious software that is designed to infiltrate a computer or network and cause harm. Examples include viruses, worms, trojan horses, and ransomware. Phishing attacks: Phishing is a type of social engineering attack that involves tricking users into divulging sensitive information, such as passwords or credit card numbers. This is usually done through fake emails or websites that appear to be legitimate. Denial-of-service (DoS) attacks: DoS attacks are designed to overwhelm a network or website with traffic, rendering it unusable. Distributed denial-of-service (DDoS) attacks are a more advanced version that use multiple sources to flood the network. Man-in-the-middle (MitM) attacks: MitM attacks involve intercepting communications between two parties, allowing the attacker to eavesdrop, steal information, or manipulate the data being transmitted. SQL injection attacks: SQL injection attacks target databases by injecting malicious code into SQL statements, allowing attackers to access sensitive data. Zero-day attacks: Zero-day attacks exploit previously unknown vulnerabilities in software or hardware, giving attackers the advantage of surprise and making them difficult to defend against. Advanced persistent threats (APTs): APTs are long-term attacks that are designed to remain undetected for extended periods of time. They involve sophisticated techniques such as social engineering, malware, and targeted attacks on specific individuals or organizations. These are just a few examples of the many types of cyber attacks that exist. As cyber threats continue to evolve, it is important for organizations to stay informed and take appropriate measures to protect themselves.

"A Survey of Cyber Attacks and Their Classification" by Zhiwei Wang and Tingting Zhang: This paper provides a comprehensive survey of cyber attacks, including malware attacks, phishing attacks, DoS attacks, MitM attacks, and many others. The paper also proposes a classification scheme for cyber attacks based on their characteristics. The authors begin by discussing the general concepts of cyber attacks and their impacts on organizations and individuals. They then provide an overview of the various categories of cyber attacks, including: Malware attacks, Phishing attacks, Denial-of-service (DoS) attacks, Man-in-the-middle (MitM) attacks, Password attacks, SQL injection attacks. The authors then propose a classification scheme based on three characteristics of cyber attacks: the attack vector, the attack target, and the attack objective. This classification scheme provides a useful framework for understanding the different types of cyber attacks and their implications for cyber security. Overall, this paper provides a useful survey of different types of cyber attacks and their classification. The authors' proposed classification scheme is a valuable tool for researchers and practitioners in the field of cyber security, as it provides a systematic way to analyze and understand cyber attacks.

"A Survey of Cyber security Threats and Defenses" by Rajarajan et al.: This paper provides an overview of various types of cyber threats, including malware, phishing, DoS, and social engineering attacks. The paper also discusses various defense mechanisms, including intrusion detection and prevention systems, firewalls, and encryption. The authors begin by discussing the current state of cyber threats and the impact they have on organizations and individuals. They then provide an overview of the various categories of cyber threats. The authors then discuss various defense mechanisms that can be used to protect against these threats, including firewalls, intrusion detection and prevention systems, and encryption. They also discuss the importance of user awareness and training in preventing cyber attacks. Overall, this paper provides a useful survey of cyber security threats and defenses. The authors' discussion of defense mechanisms is particularly valuable, as it provides a roadmap for organizations looking to improve their cyber security posture. The paper is a valuable resource for researchers and practitioners in the field of cyber security.

"A Taxonomy of Cyber Attacks and Defensive Techniques for Cyber Physical Systems" by Saurabh Kumar et al.: This paper provides a comprehensive taxonomy of cyber attacks and defensive techniques for Cyber Physical Systems (CPS). CPS refers to systems that are composed of physical and cyber components that interact with each other to achieve a common goal. The paper covers a range of attack types, including DoS attacks, code injection attacks, and insider attacks, and also discusses various defensive techniques. The authors begin by discussing the unique challenges associated with securing CPS, including the need to protect both physical and cyber components, the complexity of these systems, and the potential impact of a successful cyber attack. They then provide a taxonomy of cyber attacks that are specific to CPS, including: Denial-of-service (DoS) attacks, Physical attacks, Malware attacks, Man-in-the-middle (MitM) attacks, Spoofing attacks. The authors then discuss various defensive techniques that can be used to protect against these attacks, including network segmentation, intrusion detection and prevention systems, and cryptography. Overall, this paper provides a valuable taxonomy of cyber attacks and defensive techniques for CPS. The authors' focus on CPS is particularly valuable, as these systems have unique security challenges that are not present in traditional IT systems. The paper is a useful resource for researchers and practitioners in the field of CPS security.

"Cyber Attacks: A Literature Review" by Gerasimos Kambourakis et al.: This paper provides a literature review of cyber attacks, covering a range of attack types and their characteristics. The paper also discusses various defense mechanisms, including intrusion detection systems, firewalls, and encryption. The paper discusses the types of cyber attacks, their characteristics, and their potential impact on individuals and organizations. The paper begins by defining cyber attacks and highlighting their increasing frequency and severity in recent years. It then provides a classification of cyber attacks based on the type of attack, including: Denial of service (DoS) attacks, Malware attacks, Phishing attacks, Man-in-the-middle (MitM) attacks, Distributed denial of service (DDoS) attacks, Advanced persistent threats (APTs). The paper then discusses the characteristics of cyber attacks, such as their stealthiness, scalability, and the ability of attackers to launch attacks from anywhere in the world. It also highlights the potential impact of cyber attacks, including financial loss, reputational damage, and legal and regulatory consequences. The paper also discusses the various techniques that can be used to prevent and mitigate the impact of cyber attacks, such as firewalls, intrusion detection and prevention systems, and encryption. It also discusses the importance of incident response plans and the need for continuous monitoring and improvement of cyber security measures. Overall, the paper provides a valuable overview of the literature on cyber attacks. It highlights the types, characteristics, and potential impact of cyber attacks, as well as the techniques that can be used to prevent and mitigate their effects. The paper is a useful resource for researchers and practitioners in the field of cyber security.

"A Survey on Cyber Security Attacks and Countermeasures in Cloud Computing" by Jia et al.: This paper provides a survey of cyber attacks and countermeasures in cloud computing environments, covering a range of attack types, including DoS attacks, virtual machine attacks, and data breaches. The paper also discusses various defense mechanisms, including access control, encryption, and intrusion detection and prevention systems. However, the paper does highlight some potential areas for future work in the field. For example, the paper suggests that more research is needed to develop effective intrusion detection and prevention systems for cloud computing environments. The authors also note that there is a need for more research on the use of machine learning and other advanced analytics techniques for detecting and mitigating cyber security attacks in the cloud. Additionally, the paper notes that there is a need for more research on the impact of cyber security attacks on the availability, integrity, and confidentiality of data in cloud computing environments. The authors suggest that this research could help inform the development of more effective countermeasures for preventing and mitigating the effects of cyber security attacks.Overall, the paper provides a valuable overview of the state of the art in cyber security attacks and countermeasures in cloud computing, and highlights several potential areas for future research and development.

These papers provide a useful overview of the different types of cyber attacks that exist and the defense mechanisms that can be used to protect against them. As cyber threats continue to evolve, it is important for researchers and practitioners to stay informed about the latest trends and best practices in cyber security.

Figure 1. Types of cyber risks

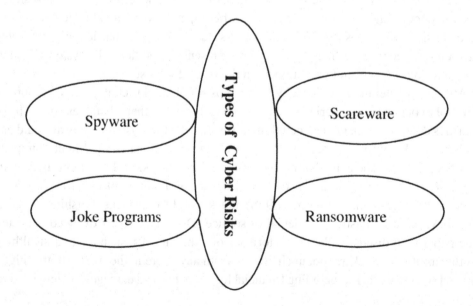

3. CYBERSECURITY RISKS AND SECURITY MONITORING

In addition to innovations, technological developments also bring some negative aspects. As a result of the globalization of technology, organizations, and institutions host their data in a distributed structure based on multiple data centers and cloud platforms. Various risks pose a threat to corporate and personal data as they become more valuable [16]. Cybercriminals are also developing new ways to attack computer-based systems to benefit from them. "Cyber Risks" describe the various activities that can occur from data theft to ransomware attacks. The most common cyber risks is shown in Figure 3.1.

3.1 Importance of Security Monitoring

It is typical for organizations to design and implement cybersecurity controls across the organization in order to ensure information assets are protected from unauthorised access, disclosure, and corruption. Security monitoring is crucial for protecting an organization's assets, reputation, and operations. It involves constantly monitoring the organization's network, systems, and data for any signs of suspicious activity or potential threats. It allows organizations to detect and respond to security incidents quickly, reduce the impact of attacks, and ensure compliance with regulatory requirements. Here are some reasons why security monitoring is important:

- Early Detection of Threats: Security monitoring can help identify threats early, before they have a chance to do serious damage. This allows organizations to take action to prevent or mitigate the impact of an attack.
- Reduced Response Time: By detecting and responding to security incidents quickly, organizations can reduce the amount of time that their systems and data are at risk.

Figure 2. Importance of security monitoring

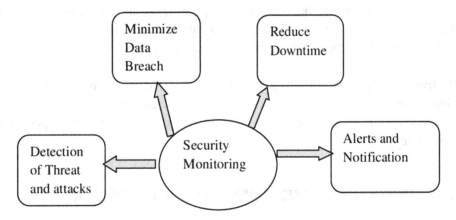

- Compliance Requirements: Many industries have compliance requirements that mandate security monitoring, such as the Payment Card Industry Data Security Standard (PCI DSS) and the Health Insurance Portability and Accountability Act (HIPAA).

- Protection of Sensitive Data: Security monitoring can help protect sensitive data from being accessed, stolen, or compromised by unauthorized individuals or malicious actors.
- Increased Awareness: Security monitoring can help increase awareness of security risks and potential vulnerabilities within an organization. This can lead to improved security practices and a more proactive approach to cybersecurity. There are different types of security monitoring that an organization can use to protect its assets and information. Here are some of the most common types of security monitoring:
- Network Security Monitoring (NSM): NSM involves monitoring network traffic for signs of suspicious activity, such as unusual data transfer patterns, malicious IP addresses, or known attack signatures.
- Endpoint Detection and Response (EDR): EDR involves monitoring endpoints such as laptops, desktops, and mobile devices for signs of malicious activity, such as unauthorized access, file changes, or unusual processes.
- Cloud Security Monitoring: Cloud security monitoring involves monitoring cloud environments for potential security threats, such as unauthorized access to cloud resources, misconfigured security settings, or data breaches.
- Application Security Monitoring: Application security monitoring involves monitoring applications and their underlying infrastructure for signs of potential security threats, such as unauthorized access attempts, SQL injection attacks, or buffer overflow exploits.
- Identity and Access Management (IAM) Monitoring: IAM monitoring involves monitoring user activity and access rights to detect potential unauthorized access or changes to user privileges.
- Physical Security Monitoring: Physical security monitoring involves monitoring physical access to an organization's facilities, such as surveillance cameras, access control systems, and security guards.
- Cybersecurity Threat Monitoring (CTM): CTM enables us to observe the network in real-time and aids in the detection of suspicious or malicious activity. This will make it easier for the cybersecurity professional to take precautions before an attack incidence occurs. By using security protocols, the unknown packet that enters the company's network is stored in the database so that experts can examine it, determine whether it is harmful, and take the necessary action. They will also send an alert to the cybersecurity professional team if necessary.

Thus, Effective security monitoring requires a comprehensive approach that covers all aspects of an organization's infrastructure, systems, and applications. By combining multiple types of security monitoring, organizations can gain a more complete understanding of their security posture and reduce the risk of security incidents.

4. CYBER SECURITY RISK ASSESSMENT AND MANAGEMENT

Cybersecurity risk assessment and management are crucial components of any organization's security strategy. With the increasing complexity and frequency of cyber attacks, traditional risk assessment methods may no longer be sufficient. Artificial intelligence (AI) and machine learning (ML) can be used to enhance cybersecurity risk assessment and management. AI and ML can help organizations identify potential threats and vulnerabilities, analyze data, and make predictions based on patterns and historical data. These technologies can also automate routine security tasks and free up security personnel to focus on more complex issues. Here are some ways AI and ML can be used in cybersecurity risk assessment and management:

- Threat Detection: AI and ML algorithms can be used to detect threats in real-time by analyzing patterns and anomalies in network traffic and user behavior. These algorithms can learn from past attacks and identify new threats, enabling organizations to take proactive measures to prevent them.
- Vulnerability Assessment: AI and ML can be used to conduct automated vulnerability assessments of networks, applications, and systems. This typically involves using tools to scan for known vulnerabilities, such as outdated software, misconfigured systems, or unpatched vulnerabilities. The goal of vulnerability assessment is to identify potential weaknesses in the system, so that they can be addressed before they are exploited by an attacker.
- Risk Assessment: AI and ML can help identify risks and their potential impact on an organization's operations, assets, and reputation. These algorithms can provide insights into potential vulnerabilities, identify areas where controls may be insufficient, and recommend appropriate mitigation strategies.
- Incident Response: AI and ML can assist in incident response by automating the identification and containment of cyber threats. These algorithms can detect and respond to security breaches in real-time, minimizing the impact of the attack.
- Compliance Monitoring: AI and ML can be used to monitor compliance with security policies and regulations. These algorithms can identify areas of non-compliance, assess the risk associated with non-compliance, and recommend corrective actions.

In conclusion, AI and ML can help organizations automate and streamline cybersecurity risk assessment and management processes, enabling them to identify and respond to potential threats more quickly and effectively. However, it's important to note that AI and ML are not a silver bullet for cybersecurity and should be used in conjunction with other security measures and practices.

4.1 Threat Detection and Categorization

Threat detection is the process of identifying potential security threats in an organization's network, systems, applications, or data. The goal of threat detection is to identify and respond to security incidents before they can cause damage or loss to the organization. Threat detection typically involves a combination of automated tools and human analysis. Automated tools such as intrusion detection systems (IDS), security information and event management (SIEM) systems, and endpoint detection and response (EDR) systems can monitor network traffic, system logs, and user behavior to detect potential threats. These tools use a range of techniques, including signature-based detection, behavior-based detection, and anomaly detection, to identify threats. Human analysis is also an important component of threat detection. Security analysts can investigate potential threats identified by automated tools to determine whether they are real threats or false positives. They can also conduct forensic investigations to identify the root cause of security incidents and prevent similar incidents from occurring in the future.

Effective threat detection requires a combination of technology, processes, and people. Organizations need to have a comprehensive security strategy that includes regular vulnerability assessments, threat intelligence, and incident response planning. They also need to invest in security tools and technologies that can help detect and respond to threats in real-time. Finally, organizations need to have trained security staff who can analyze security incidents, investigate threats, and respond to security incidents in a timely and effective manner. A robust approach is required to detect (automated and evolutionary) cyberattacks of the new generation and respond accordingly. Machine learning (ML) and artificial intelligence (AI) have become increasingly important in threat detection and categorization. These technologies can help organizations detect and respond to security threats faster and more accurately than traditional methods. Due to its ability to learn from experiences and respond to newer attacks on time, machine learning is a possible solution to combat such attacks quickly. There are many articles that describe the use of ML to predict cyber threats on the dark web or deep web. Here are some ways ML and AI are used in threat detection and categorization:

- Anomaly detection: ML algorithms can learn the normal patterns of behavior within an organization's network and alert security teams when there are deviations from the norm. This can help detect anomalies such as unauthorized access attempts or unusual data transfer activities that could be signs of a security breach. It's particularly effective for detecting unknown and emerging threats.
- Behavioral based detection: AI algorithms can be used to analyze user behavior to detect unusual patterns of activity that may indicate a potential security threat. This can include monitoring user logins, access to sensitive data, and network traffic to identify unusual or suspicious behavior. It's commonly used for detecting insider threats and advanced persistent threats (APTs).
- Signature-based detection - This technique uses a database of known attack signatures to identify and block attacks. It's a common technique used in antivirus software and intrusion detection systems.
- Threat intelligence - This technique involves collecting and analyzing data about current and potential threats to identify patterns and trends that may indicate an attack. Threat intelligence is often used in conjunction with other threat detection techniques.
- Network traffic analysis - This technique involves analyzing network traffic to identify and block malicious traffic. It can be used for detecting a range of threats, including malware infections, denial-of-service attacks, and data exfiltration.
- Sandboxing - This technique involves running potentially malicious software in a controlled environment to observe its behavior and determine whether it's a threat. Sandboxing is commonly used for detecting zero-day attacks and other unknown threats.Top of Form
- Predictive analytics: ML algorithms can be trained to predict potential security threats based on historical data and patterns. This can help organizations take proactive measures to prevent security breaches before they occur.
- Categorization and prioritization: AI algorithms can be used to categorize and prioritize security threats based on their severity and likelihood of occurrence. This can help security teams focus their resources on the most critical threats and respond more quickly to mitigate their impact. There are several threat detection techniques used in various fields such as cybersecurity, physical security, and healthcare[17-25].

Bottom Overall, ML and AI are becoming increasingly important in threat detection and categorization. By leveraging these technologies, organizations can improve their ability to detect and respond to security threats quickly and accurately, reducing the risk of data breaches and other security incidents.

4.2 Threat Prevention Technologies

Threat prevention techniques refer to measures taken to prevent or reduce the likelihood of cyber attacks or security breaches on computer networks, systems, and devices. These techniques are critical in ensuring the safety and security of sensitive data and information. These techniques may include various strategies, such as implementing security software, conducting staff training, and establishing strict security protocols. G. S. Grewal et. al., presented an overview of various threat prevention techniques in cybersecurity, including firewalls, intrusion detection systems, and access control mechanisms. D. P. Lohrmann emphasized the importance of threat intelligence in preventing cyber attacks. They discussed the role of threat intelligence in identifying potential threats and developing effective prevention strategies. N. B. P. D. Silva et. al., focused on threat prevention techniques specifically for cloud computing environments. They elaborated the challenges of securing cloud-based systems and provides recommendations for effective prevention strategies. S. S. Wijekoon et. al., discussed the unique challenges of securing Internet of Things (IoT) devices and presented an overview of effective prevention techniques, including secure boot, firmware updates, and network segmentation. S. R. Caine et. al., examined the role of human factors in threat prevention, including the importance of staff training and education and presented the recommendations for improving the effectiveness of prevention strategies through increased awareness and education. Understanding of different categories of threats is important for developing effective security strategies and implementing appropriate security controls to protect against potential threats. Threats can be categorized based on the risk they pose or their type. Some of the threats are given below:

- Malware - Malware is any software designed to harm a computer system or steal data. This can include viruses, worms, trojans, ransomware, and spyware.
- Social engineering attacks - Social engineering attacks are designed to trick people into revealing sensitive information or taking a specific action. Examples include phishing, spear phishing, and pretexting.
- Insider threats - Insider threats are threats that come from within an organization. This can include employees who intentionally or unintentionally cause harm to the organization's network, systems, or data.
- Advanced persistent threats (APTs) - APTs are targeted attacks that are designed to gain unauthorized access to an organization's network, systems, or data. APTs can be difficult to detect and often involve multiple stages of attack.
- Denial-of-service (DoS) attacks - DoS attacks are designed to overwhelm a network, server, or application with traffic, rendering it unavailable to legitimate users.
- Physical threats - Physical threats include theft, vandalism, and other physical attacks that can cause damage to an organization's assets, data centers, or facilities.
- Web-based attacks - Web-based attacks are designed to exploit vulnerabilities in web applications or web servers. Examples include SQL injection, cross-site scripting (XSS), and directory traversal attacks.

- Zero-day attacks - Zero-day attacks are attacks that exploit vulnerabilities that are unknown to the organization or security community. Zero-day attacks can be difficult to detect and defend against.

Here are some threat prevention techniques that can help:

- Use two-factor authentication: Two-factor authentication adds an extra layer of security by requiring users to provide two forms of authentication before granting access to a network or system.
- Access control: Limit access to sensitive information: Only grant access to sensitive information to those who need it, and limit access to only what is necessary. This can help minimize the risk of data breaches and insider threats. According to the paper "Access Control in Cloud Computing Environment: A Review" by A. Shah et al., published in the Journal of Information Security and Applications, access control is a crucial technique for ensuring the security of cloud computing environments.
- Use encryption: Encryption can help protect data from unauthorized access by encoding it, making it unreadable without a key or password. . It is an effective technique for preventing data breaches and theft. The paper "Encryption Techniques for Data Security: A Comparative Study" by M. P. Singh et al., published in the International Journal of Computer Science and Mobile Computing, discusses various encryption techniques and their effectiveness in ensuring data security.
- Firewalls: Firewalls are software or hardware-based security systems that protect a network by monitoring and controlling incoming and outgoing traffic based on predefined security rules. It is an effective technique for preventing unauthorized access to computer systems and networks. The paper "Firewall Technologies: A Comprehensive Survey" by N. Singh et al., published in the Journal of Network and Computer Applications, provides a detailed review of various firewall technologies and their effectiveness in preventing security threats.
- Intrusion detection/prevention systems (IDS/IPS): IDS/IPS are security systems that monitor network traffic and detect and prevent potential security threats. They are effective in preventing various types of cyber attacks such as viruses, malware, and denial of service (DoS) attacks. The paper "A Survey of Intrusion Detection and Prevention Systems in Cloud Computing" by S. S. Alzahrani et al., published in the Journal of Network and Computer Applications, provides a comprehensive review of IDS/IPS techniques in cloud computing environments.
- Be cautious of phishing attacks: Phishing attacks are attempts to trick users into giving away sensitive information, such as passwords or credit card numbers, by posing as a legitimate source. Be cautious of suspicious emails, links, and attachments, and never give away personal information unless you are certain of the source.
- Vulnerability assessments: Vulnerability assessments are used to identify and eliminate security vulnerabilities in a network or system.
- Security information and event management (SIEM): SIEM is a software solution that provides real-time analysis of security alerts generated by network hardware and software.
- Use strong and unique passwords: Strong passwords with a mix of upper and lowercase letters, numbers, and special characters can help prevent unauthorized access to your accounts. Also, using unique passwords for each account can minimize the risk of multiple accounts being compromised if one password is compromised.

- Keep software up to date: Make sure that your operating system, software programs, and antivirus/malware protection are up to date with the latest security patches and updates. This can help protect your system from known vulnerabilities and threats.

- Regularly back up data: Regularly backing up data to a secure location can help ensure that important information is not lost in the event of a security breach or system failure.

- Security awareness training: Security awareness training is a technique that educates users on the importance of security and how to prevent security threats. It is an effective technique for preventing human error and negligence, which are major causes of security breaches.

5. THE ROLE OF MACHINE LEARING IN THREAT DETECTION AND RESPONSE TECHNIQUES

Threat detection using machine learning (ML) algorithms is an increasingly popular approach to detecting and responding to potential security threats. ML algorithms can analyze large amounts of data to identify patterns and anomalies that may indicate malicious activity, and can do so in near-real time. Threat detection requires a deep understanding of the data sources and features that are most relevant to your environment, as well as a strong understanding of machine learning algorithms and techniques. It's important to continuously monitor and evaluate the performance of the model and adjust the feature extraction techniques and model parameters as needed to ensure optimal performance. Here are some common steps in using ML for threat detection:

- Data Collection - The first step is to collect data from various sources, such as log files, network traffic, or system activity. This data is then prepared for use in the ML model by cleaning, transforming, and normalizing it.

- Feature Extraction - Next, features are extracted from the data that can be used to train the ML algorithm. These features can include information about the behavior of users, devices, or networks, as well as contextual information about the environment in which the data was collected. By extracting relevant features from data, the machine learning algorithm can learn to distinguish between normal and anomalous behavior and identify potential threats. The steps involved for using feature extraction to detect threats:

- Determine relevant data sources - The first step is to identify the data sources that are most relevant for detecting threats in your environment. This could include log files, network traffic, system activity, or user behavior data.

- Define features – Next, define the features that will be used to train the machine learning algorithm. These features should be relevant to the types of threats that you are looking to detect. For example, if you are looking to detect insider threats, have to extract features related to user behavior, such as login times, file access patterns, and network activity.

- Extract features - Once the features have been defined, extract them from the raw data. This can involve a variety of techniques, such as statistical analysis, frequency analysis, or time series analysis, depending on the type of data and the features that you are looking to extract.

- Normalize features - Before using the extracted features to train the machine learning algorithm, normalize them to ensure that they are on a consistent scale. This can involve techniques such as standardization, normalization, or scaling.

- Train the machine learning model - Finally, use the extracted and normalized features to train the machine learning model. This typically involves a process of supervised or unsupervised learning, where the algorithm learns to recognize patterns in labeled or unlabeled data. Once the model is trained, it can be used to detect threats in real-time by analyzing incoming data and flagging potential threats based on deviations from the learned patterns.
- Model Evaluation - Once the model is trained, it is evaluated to ensure that it is effective in detecting threats while minimizing false positives and false negatives. This evaluation may involve testing the model against known threats or simulating attacks to see how the model performs in detecting them.
- Deployment and Monitoring - Finally, the ML model is deployed in the production environment and monitored for ongoing performance. As new threats emerge or the environment changes, the model may need to be updated or retrained to ensure continued effectiveness.

There are many different types of machine learning algorithms that can be used for threat detection, including supervised learning, unsupervised learning, and reinforcement learning. M. Di Mauro et. al., 2021 have discussed about Supervised feature selection techniques to detect network intrusion. John Oche Onah et. al., 2021 have used feature selection based on Genetic algorithm and Naïve Bsyes to detect anomalies in the Fog computing Environment. Sydney Mambwe Kasongo et. al., 2023 have discussed various Recurrent Neural Networks (RNN) such as simple RNN, Long-Short Term Memory (LSTM), and Gated Recurrent Unit (GRU) for intrusion detection. Jiaming Pei et. al., 2022 proposed LSTM – auto encoder for network traffic anomaly detection. Here are a few examples of machine learning algorithms used in threat detection.

- Support vector machines (SVMs) - SVMs are a type of supervised learning algorithm that can be used for classification and regression analysis. SVMs have been used in threat detection to classify different types of network traffic as either normal or anomalous based on features such as packet size, protocol type, and source/destination IP addresses. Hu et al. classify anomalies with the help of a variation of support vector machines. A one-class support vector machine classifier was used by Wagner et al. to detect anomalies and different types of attacks including NetBIOS scanning, DoS attacks, POP spams, and Secure Shell (SSH) scanning. Moskovitch, R et. al. detected unknown computer worms' activity by using SVM Classifier.
- Convolutional neural networks (CNNs) - CNNs are a type of deep learning algorithm commonly used in image and video analysis. In threat detection, CNNs can be used to analyze network traffic in a similar way to image analysis, identifying patterns and anomalies in data. Ullah, S et. al. 2022 presented an Intrusion detection system based on deep CNN. Cao B et. al., 2022 have used CNN for spatial feature extraction.
- Random forests - Random forests are a type of ensemble learning algorithm that combines multiple decision trees to improve accuracy. Random forests have been used in threat detection to classify malware samples based on features such as file size, file type, and code structure. Wu, T., et. al., 2022 have used advanced Random Forest algorithm in addition to synthetic minority oversampling technique (SMOTE)

- K-means clustering - K-means clustering is an unsupervised learning algorithm that can be used to group data points into clusters based on similarity. In threat detection, K-means clustering has been used to identify groups of IP addresses or network traffic that may be associated with malicious activity.
- Reinforcement learning - Reinforcement learning is a type of machine learning that involves an agent learning through trial and error to maximize a reward signal. In threat detection, reinforcement learning has been used to develop dynamic security policies that can adapt to changing threat landscapes.
- These are just a few examples of the many machine learning algorithms that can be used in threat detection. As the field continues to evolve, it is likely that new and more sophisticated algorithms will be developed to address increasingly complex security threats.
- ML algorithms can be a powerful tool for threat detection, allowing organizations to proactively identify and respond to potential security threats. However, it is important to note that ML algorithms are not a silver bullet, and must be used in conjunction with other security measures, such as access controls, encryption, and employee training, to create a comprehensive security strategy.

6. CONCLUSION

In the process of technological evolution, cyber-attacks are continually growing and changing, improving their malicious performance. This study examines the types of cyber-attacks, defence countermeasures, and applications of machine learning, deep learning for cyber-security, and advantages of using AI and ML for security. This article discusses the various technologies used for cyber-attack detection, prevention, and mitigation. Taking the current study as a reference, future studies will be able to address the issues associated with cyber-security. We provide insights into cyber-security for the research community, enabling them to better structure defences against potential attacks through this study. With the development of cybernetic technologies applied both to defense and attack in the context of Industry 4.0, there is a constant need for updating future requirements to implement cyber-security actions.

REFERENCES

Al-Muhtadi, M. J., Al-Qutayri, M. A., & Nasir, Q. (2019). Cybersecurity Risk Assessment and Management: A Review of the Current State of the Art. *IEEE Access : Practical Innovations, Open Solutions*, 7, 112103–112122. doi:10.1109/access.2019.2932952

Alaa, A. & van der Schaar, M. (2018). *A Review of Machine Learning Techniques for Healthcare Risk Prediction.*

Ali, A., Zakaria, M., & Almehmadi, A. (2021). A Comprehensive Literature Review on Cybersecurity Risk Management. *Computers & Security*, *108*, 102242. doi:10.1016/j.cose.2021.102242

Alshammari, O., Almutairi, A., & Alghathbar, K. (2019). Cyber security Risk Assessment for SCADA and DCS Networks: A Systematic Literature Review. *Journal of Computer Networks and Communications*, *2019*. doi:10.1155/2019/8190167

Antonucci, D., & Kooij, M. (2017). *The Cyber Risk Handbook: Creating and Measuring Effective Cybersecurity Capabilities*. John Wiley & Sons. doi:10.1002/9781119309741

Cao, B., Li, C., Song, Y., & Fan, X. (2022, April 12). Network Intrusion Detection Technology Based on Convolutional Neural Network and BiGRU. *Computational Intelligence and Neuroscience, 1942847*, 1–20. doi:10.1155/2022/1942847 PMID:35463242

Dahbur, K., Mohammad, B., & Tarakji, A. B. (2011). A survey of risks, threats, and vulnerabilities in cloud computing. In *Proceedings of the 2011 International conference on intelligent semantic Web-services and applications*, Amman, Jordan. 10.1145/1980822.1980834

Di Mauro, M., Galatro, G., Fortino, G., & Liotta, A. (2021). Supervised feature selection techniques in network intrusion detection: A critical review. *Engineering Applications of Artificial Intelligence, 101*. doi:10.1016/j.engappai.2021.104216

Ghazaleh, R. A. (2019). A Survey of Machine Learning Techniques for Cybersecurity.

Hossain, M. (2020). *Anomaly Detection in ECG Signals Using Machine Learning Techniques: A Survey*.

Hu, W., Liao, Y., & Vemuri, V. R. (2003). *Robust Support Vector Machines for Anomaly Detection in Computer Security*. In Proceedings of the International Conference on Machine Learning and Applications, Los Angeles, CA, USA.

Islam, M. R., & Khan, A. U. (2020). A Review of Cybersecurity Risk Assessment Frameworks for Industrial Control Systems. *Computers & Security, 94*, 101812. doi:10.1016/j.cose.2020.101812

Jaquith, A. (2011). *Cyber security Metrics: A Practical Guide for Effective Security and Risk Management*. Pearson Education.

Jia, Y., Zhang, X., Xiang, Y., & Zhou, W. (2019). A Survey on Cyber Security Attacks and Countermeasures in Cloud Computing. *Journal of Network and Computer Applications, 135*, 1–11. doi:10.1016/j.jnca.2019.02.012

Kambourakis, G., Damopoulos, D., Panaousis, E., & Katos, V. (2019). Cyber Attacks: A Literature Review. *Journal of Information Security and Applications, 50*, 1–12. doi:10.1016/j.jisa.2019.02.008

Kasongo, S. (2023). A deep learning technique for intrusion detection system using a Recurrent Neural Networks based framework. *Computer Communications, 199*.

Korhonen, P. (2018). *Automated Threat Detection in Airport Security: A Survey*.

Kumar, S., Gupta, B. B., & Misra, S. (2019). A Taxonomy of Cyber Attacks and Defensive Techniques for Cyber Physical Systems. *Journal of Ambient Intelligence and Humanized Computing, 10*(10), 3821–3842. doi:10.100712652-019-01361-4

Kumar, S. (2018). Anomaly Detection in Network Traffic Using Deep Learning.

Makris, D. (2018). Review of Video-Based Threat Detection Approaches for Public Safety.

Moskovitch, R., Nissim, N., Stopel, D., Feher, C., Englert, R., & Elovici, Y. (2007). *Improving the detection of unknown computer worms activity using active learning.* In *Proceedings of the Annual Conference on Artificial Intelligence*, Osnabrück, Germany. 10.1007/978-3-540-74565-5_47

National Institute of Standards and Technology (NIST). (2018). *NIST Cybersecurity Framework.* NIST. https://www.nist.gov/cyberframework

Onah, J. O., Shafi'i, M. A., Abdullahi, M., Hassan, I. H., & Al-Ghusham, A. (2021). Genetic Algorithm based feature selection and Naïve Bayes for anomaly detection in fog computing environment. *Machine Learning with Applications, 6.*

Parenty, T. J., & Domet, J. J. (2014). The Art of Cyber Risk Oversight: CISOs and Boards. *MIS Quarterly Executive, 13*(4), 197–213. doi:10.17705/2msqe.00012

Pei, J., & Zhong, K. (2022). Personalized federated learning framework for network traffic anomaly detection. *Computer Networks, 209.*

Rajarajan, M., Zisman, A., & Dimitrakos, T. (2013). A Survey of Cyber security Threats and Defenses. *Journal of Network and Computer Applications, 36*(1), 1–11. doi:10.1016/j.jnca.2012.08.005

Raju, A. S., Sathappan, S., & Srinivasan, U. (2021). Machine Learning for Cybersecurity Risk Management: A Survey. *Journal of Ambient Intelligence and Humanized Computing, 12*(8), 7941–7962. doi:10.100712652-021-03517-6

Simpson, A., & Sachs, M. (2018). Cyber security Risk Management: A Review of Current Approaches. *Computers & Security, 78*, 398–416. doi:10.1016/j.cose.2018.07.006

Stone, E. (2016). Detecting Clinical Deterioration in Hospital Patients: A Survey of Methods.

Troester, G. (2017). Threat Detection Using Millimeter Wave Radar: A Review.

Ullah, S., Ahmad, J., Khan, M. A., Alkhammash, E. H., Hadjouni, M., Ghadi, Y. Y., Saeed, F., & Pitropakis, N. (2022). A New Intrusion Detection System for the Internet of Things via Deep Convolutional Neural Network and Feature Engineering. *Sensors (Basel), 22*(10), 3607. doi:10.339022103607 PMID:35632016

Wagner, C., François, J., & Engel, T. (2011). Machine learning approach for ip-flow record anomaly detection. In *Proceedings of the International Conference on Research in Networking*, Valencia, Spain. 10.1007/978-3-642-20757-0_3

Wang, Z., & Zhang, T. (2019). A Survey of Cyber Attacks and Their Classification. *Journal of Network and Computer Applications, 126*, 46–69. doi:10.1016/j.jnca.2018.11.013

Wang, X. (2020). Deep Learning for Network Intrusion Detection: A Survey.

Wu, T., Fan, H., & Zhu, H. (2022). Intrusion detection system combined enhanced random forest with SMOTE algorithm. *J. Adv. Signal Process, 39.* doi:10.1186/s13634-022-00871-6

Chapter 11
Fake News Detection With the Help of Computation Time to Increase Accuracy

P. Umamaheswari

iD https://orcid.org/0000-0003-2007-697X

SASTRA University, India

N. Umasankari

iD https://orcid.org/0000-0002-6952-6794

Sathyabama Institute of Science and Technology, India

Selvakumar Samuel

Asia Pacific University of Technology and Innovation, Malaysia

ABSTRACT

Newspapers were the primary source of receiving news. Though they were slow in getting us the news, they were reliable since almost every piece of an article printed in newspapers is proofread. But things are changing rapidly and we are reliant on other sources for news (such as Facebook, Twitter, YouTube, WhatsApp). This paved the way for information, whether it is fake or real, that has never been witnessed in human history before. However, ever since social media boomed and the spread of information became easy, it has been difficult to find and stop the spread of fake and fabricated news. Existing solutions identify fake news usage either or some of the machine learning algorithms. In this work, an ensemble machine learning model is developed using ensemble method and evaluate their performance for the computation time to increase the accuracy of fake news detection using datasets. The experimental evaluation confirms the superior performance of our proposed ensemble learner approach in comparison to individual learners.

DOI: 10.4018/978-1-6684-9317-5.ch011

1. INTRODUCTION

Since the advent of social media, the rapid dissemination of information has been paralleled by the spread of misinformation. This rise in misleading content or "fake news" often results from people sharing unverified information or due to their misconceptions. To combat this, many have explored automated systems for detecting fake news using machine learning techniques. Various classifiers, such as Logistic Regression, Multilayer Perceptron, Passive Aggressive Classifier, Decision Tree, Random Forest, and various Naive Bayes classifiers, have been tested for this purpose. Recently, deep learning methods, especially those tailored for natural language processing tasks, have shown promise in offering improved solutions. The study evaluates the efficiency and accuracy of different models in distinguishing between genuine and fake news.

In present days, the hybrid deep learning model built by the authors by combining a Convolutional neural network (CNN) and recurrent neural network (RNN) (Nasir et al., 2021). The primary aim of combining these two models was that they needed good results. Since these are bio-inspired algorithms, they have very good computational power. Since this is a classification problem, the major problem overcome and was bridging the gap created due to a lack of thorough investigation and a lack of combinations of deep learning models built to detect fake news. Then they evaluated the model using two publicly available datasets namely, FA-KES (FakevsSatire) (Brewer et al., 2013) and ISO.

In the logistic regression model, a logistic function for modelling the occurrence of a particular class in the target column is present in the dataset and it is generally of Boolean type. Concerning the proposed solution, it is either true or fake. Even if a problem does not have a Boolean column as an output, LR can be used. This is done by mapping the output to a numerical value, which is between 0 and 1. The basic structure of the Multilayer Perceptron is that it has three layers of perceptron. The first layer is the input layer, the second layer is the hidden layer and the third layer is the output layer. Using a non-linear activation function, each node performs its job except the input nodes. For training, it uses back propagation.

The Passive Aggressive Classifier is one of the models used for applications using large-scale data is a passive aggressive classifier. There are a set of online learning algorithms out of which this is one. The online learning algorithms work with data that is sequential. Decision Tree Classifier belongs to the family of machine learning (Aldwairi, Hasan, & Balbahaith, 2017) models which works by questioning and being answered. The questions are based on the dataset that is used for training the model. The model works this way- firstly it asks for an answer, if it gets the answer, then that path is chosen and further questions of that path are asked. This process continues unless and until a value from the target column is reached. Random forest classifier, one of the algorithms present in the family of machine learning algorithms (Aldwairi, Hasan, & Balbahaith, 2017), itself, is an ensemble of many decision trees that are built as part of its algorithm. The ensemble algorithm is the maximum voting classifier. A theorem proposed by Bayes was based on independent events and this resulted in yet another model called Naïve Bayesian Classifier. Each result produced by the classifiers under this family of machine learning models (Aldwairi, Hasan, & Balbahaith, 2017) is independent of all the results produced by every other model present in the world. Bernoulli Naive Bayes, BernoulliNB implements the naive Bayes training and classification algorithms for data that is distributed according to multivariate Bernoulli distributions; i.e., there may be multiple features but each one is assumed to be a binary-valued (Bernoulli, Boolean) variable. The kaggle dataset is used to implement the proposed system. This paper is organized as follows: Section 2 describes the related work, while Section 3 presents the Proposed Framework of the system. Section 4 depicts the Implementation Results and Evaluation of the proposed system. The conclusion and suggestions for future work are presented in Section 5.

2. RELATED WORK

Fake news, the dissemination of false or misleading information disguised as legitimate news, has become a significant concern in today's digital age. Detecting and combatting fake news is crucial to maintain the integrity of information in the era of social media and online communication. Researchers and practitioners have made significant progress in developing techniques and algorithms to identify fake news. This literature survey provides an overview of key studies and approaches in the field of fake news detection.

2.1 Traditional Approaches

Content-Based Analysis: Early fake news detection methods primarily relied on content analysis, examining linguistic and structural features of news articles. Researchers used natural language processing (NLP) techniques to identify patterns of deception, bias, or misinformation within the text.

   Source Reputation: Another traditional approach involved assessing the reputation and credibility of news sources. This method relied on predefined trustworthiness scores for various media outlets, flagging content from dubious sources as potentially fake.

Machine Learning and Statistical Techniques

Supervised Learning: Machine learning models, such as Logistic Regression, Random Forest, and Support Vector Machines (SVMs), have been applied to classify news articles as real or fake based on labeled training data. Feature engineering, often involving TF-IDF or word embeddings, plays a critical role in this approach.

   Deep Learning: More recently, deep learning models like Convolutional Neural Networks (CNNs) and Recurrent Neural Networks (RNNs) have shown promise in capturing complex linguistic patterns, making them suitable for fake news detection. Long Short-Term Memory (LSTM) networks, in particular, have been effective in modeling sequential data.

Network Analysis

Social Network Analysis: Researchers have also explored the spread of fake news through social networks. Network analysis techniques aim to identify influential nodes and detect patterns of information propagation, helping pinpoint the sources and dynamics of fake news dissemination.

Fact-Checking and External Resources

Fact-Checking and External Databases: Fact-checking organizations and databases like Snopes and PolitiFact have been integrated into fake news detection pipelines. Automated systems cross-reference news articles with known fact-checks to verify claims and assess the credibility of information

2.2 Hybrid Approaches

Ensemble Methods: Combining multiple models and approaches into ensemble systems has become a common practice. Ensemble methods leverage the strengths of various techniques, enhancing overall detection accuracy.Despite significant progress, fake news detection remains a challenging task due to evolving tactics used by misinformation spreaders. Future research directions include:

- Multimodal Analysis: Integrating text, images, and videos for more comprehensive fake news detection.
- Explainable AI: Developing models that provide interpretable explanations for their decisions.
- Real-Time Detection: Creating systems that can identify fake news as it emerges.
- Adversarial Attacks: Studying methods to defend against adversarial attempts to deceive fake news detectors.

In conclusion, the field of fake news detection is continuously evolving, with researchers exploring a wide range of techniques and strategies to combat misinformation. Effective solutions require a combination of content analysis, machine learning, network analysis, and fact-checking, all integrated into robust and adaptable systems.

3. PROPOSED FRAMEWORK

This Section describes the process flow of the proposed system. The proposed system has been implemented in the following steps. First, the datasets- true and fake are read. Now, to each of these datasets (Aldwairi & Al-Salman, 2011), are added to a target column and fill it with "True" and "Fake" (Aldwairi & Alwahedi, 2018; Conroy et al., 2016; Marchi, 2012) in their respective datasets. And then both of these datasets are concatenated. After that datasets are shuffled for the better accuracy. In the Second step the input data are pre-processed. Here, the "Date" column is dropped followed by the drop of the "Title" column. Then, convert all the data to lowercase followed by the removal of all punctuation marks, a step performed as a part of natural language processing techniques. Then, exclude stopping words from the dataset, again a part of natural language processing techniques. After that tokenize all the words from the dataset. Now, the pre-processed dataset is ready for being used in the models.

CNNs have been traditionally used for image processing, but researchers have also used them for text-based tasks including fake news detection. Embedding Layer: Textual data, such as news articles, is first converted into numerical format through embeddings (like word2vec or GloVe). This helps in converting words into vectors that capture semantic meaning. Convolutional Layer: Once the text is in a numerical format, it can be passed through convolutional layers. The convolution operation helps to identify patterns or features in the text, similar to how it identifies features in images. Pooling Layer: After convolution, pooling layers help to reduce the dimensionality, capturing only the most essential information.Fully Connected Layers: After several convolutional and pooling layers, the data might be passed through one or more dense layers for final classification - to determine whether a news article is fake or real. The idea behind using CNNs for text is that they can recognize patterns (like certain phrases or word combinations) that might be indicative of fake news. When trained on a large dataset of genuine and fake articles, a CNN can, in theory, learn the textual nuances that differentiate legitimate news from fake ones.

While CNNs have shown promise in some fake news detection tasks, they are often used in combination with other models (like RNNs or LSTMs) or as part of more complex architectures to handle the sequential nature of textual data. Third step of this system is split the training and test data from the dataset for further processing. The proposed system used the different learning models for evaluating, whether the given news is true or false. Now, the data is subject to four machine learning models and two deep learning models. The models are Logistic Regression, Multilayer Perceptron (MLP), Passive Aggressive Classifier (PAC), Decision Tree Classifier (DTC), Random Forest Classifier (RFC), Naive Bayesian Classifier (NBC). The final result is then summarised from the voting classifier.

In each of the models, the data split into the following way. That is 80 percent of training data and 20 percent of testing data. Since this is full of words, before any model, vectorize it and assign IDs to each word followed by the model itself. In Fourth step, the different machine learning models are evaluated. Performed Logistic Regression (LR) with a random state of 42 for the best accuracy. In each model, after the model is applied, we convert all the true values to 1 and all the false values to 0 followed by their evaluation with the testing data. Next, the training data is subjected to DTC with a random state of 42 and with the entropy criterion as that is the parameter with which run DTC and also set the maximum depth to 17. This is the optimal value obtained for the depth in DTC. Next, perform the RFC with several forests or estimators as 50, the optimal value obtained and the criteria used is entropy. Next, the dataset is subject to NBC. Next, PAC is performed with several iterations as 50 which is the optimal value obtained for PAC. Then, perform the Multilayer Perceptron (MLP) (Aldwairi, Abu-Dalo, & Jarrah, 2017) with 'adam' as the solver and alpha as 0.0001. Run it with three hidden layers each having 20 perceptron. With a random state of 1 and an initial learning rate of 0.001, it performs best at a maximum number of iterations of 200. At last, the result is obtained from the maximum voting ensemble algorithm. Based on the prediction of all machine learning models, the result of the news displayed whether the news is true or fake. Figure 1 shows the Block diagram of the Proposed system.

The basic logic behind the proposed work is combine a certain number of models, we can expect better results than the results we get using one model. This also ensures that, take the input data and process it in all possible ways possible to get better results. The proposed hybrid model works with six models out of which four are from the family of machine learning models and two are from the family of deep learning models (Aldwairi, Hasan, & Balbahaith, 2017). The ensemble algorithm then takes into account the results of all these models and gives the combined output which will be reliable.

3.1 Logistic Regression

It has a logistic equation to model a binary dependent variable. The dependent variables or features present in a logistic function may be of two types- continuous or Boolean. The dataset used in the proposed solution has non-Boolean features. It's one of the simple and yet powerful algorithms used in binary classification problems.In the context of fake news detection:

- Feature Extraction:

Before employing Logistic Regression, the text data (news articles or headlines) needs to be transformed into a format that's understandable by the model. This is often achieved through techniques like:
Bag of Words (BoW),Term Frequency-Inverse Document Frequency (TF-IDF),Word embeddings (though rarer with logistic regression)

Figure 1. The block diagram of the proposed system

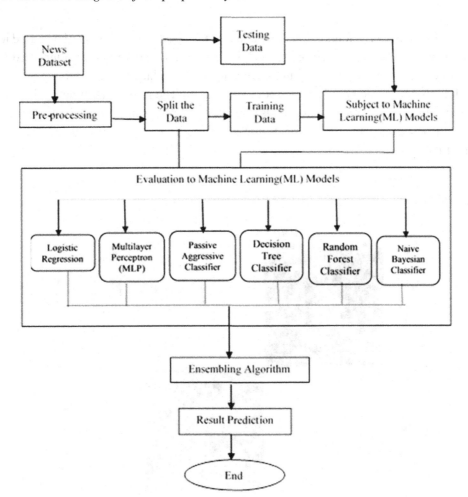

- Model Training:

Once features are extracted from the textual data, they can be fed into the Logistic Regression algorithm. The model will then adjust its weights based on the input features to predict whether an article is real or fake.

- Prediction:

For any new piece of news, the model will output a probability score between 0 and 1. Based on a predetermined threshold (commonly 0.5), this score will be categorized as 'fake' or 'real'. If the score is greater than the threshold, the news might be classified as real; otherwise, it's considered fake.

- Usage:

While Logistic Regression is a foundational method for text classification and has been used in initial studies on fake news detection, more complex models (like neural networks) are often used in more recent approaches due to their ability to capture nuanced patterns in large textual data.

This algorithm got this name based on the following reason. The role of the function is to map the log of the odds to the result variable. The log-odds scale is measured using a unit called logit and hence it got the name logistic regression. Figure 2&3. Represents the confusion matrix and Evaluation metrics of a Logistic Regression.

Figure 2. Confusion matrix obtained for logistic regression

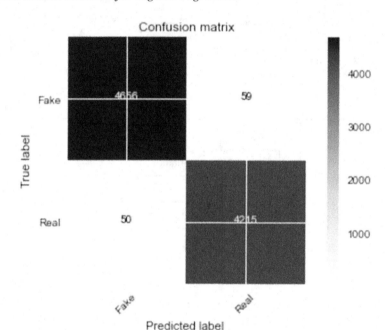

A point to note that it can also use analogous functions. The logistic regression model itself models outcome likelihood in terms of input and does not perform statistical classification (it is not a classifier). But it can be used to create a classifier, e.g., by selecting a cut-off value and by classifying inputs with a probability greater than the cut-off as one class, below the cut-off as the other; this is a typical way to make a binary class. Here logistic regression is used to classify the given news is fake or not (Wang, 2017; Conroy et al., 2016; Marchi, 2012). It is performed by using the Kaggle dataset. With a random state of 66, LR was performed on the dataset which gave an accuracy of over 95 percent as seen in Figure 3.

Figure 3. Evaluation metrics for logistic regression

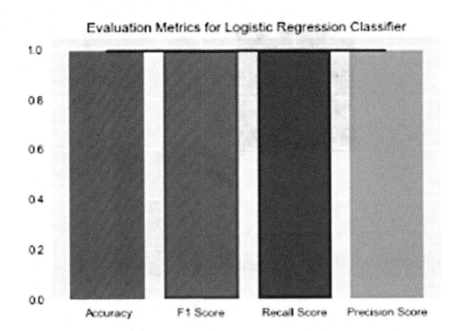

3.2 Multilayer Perceptron

This is the only deep learning model the application has in its back end. This model comes under the family of feed forward artificial neural networks. Figure 4 represents the Confusion matrix of Multilayer Perceptron and 5 shows the Evaluation metrics for Multilayer Perceptron.

Generally, this term is also used to mean any model present in the family of feed forward neural networks and this term might also refer to networks that have one or more layers of perceptrons, each having activation concerning threshold values. Whenever the number of layers is one, it is called a vanilla network (Nasir et al., 2021; Shanmuganathan & Raviraj, 2012). The difference between an MLP and a linear perceptron (Aldwairi, Hasan, & Balbahaith, 2017) is that the former uses a non-linear activation function and has multiple layers. With a random state of 99, the algorithm was executed. Ranging from 1 till 99 it was run to find the optimal value of 'k'. It was observed that at k=11, the best accuracy was obtained for both pieces of training as well as testing data. Hence k was fixed to be 11. As seen in Figure 5, it got an accuracy of 95 percent. We set the solver as 'adam' and alpha to 0.0001. The number of hidden layers is three and the number of perceptrons in each layer is 20. The random state was set to 1 to get the best accuracy. At a maximum of 200 iterations, we get the best output for the initial learning rate as 0.001.

Figure 4. Confusion matrix obtained for multilayer perceptron

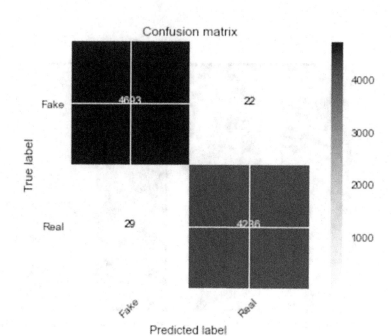

Figure 5. Evaluation metrics for multilayer perceptron

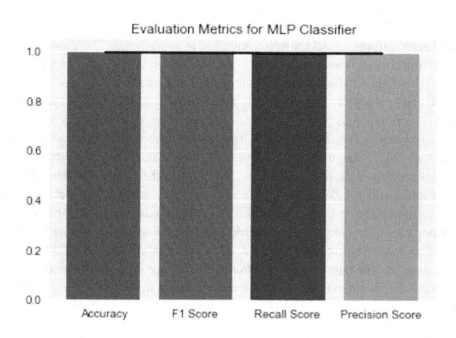

3.3 Passive Aggressive Classifier

Generally, machine learning models use batch learning as their basis where they use the entire dataset at the beginning and at once. But, this model uses a step-by-step updating process, meaning, it changes itself once a particular data comes in. This comes in handy when the data is big (for example, big data). The random-access memory cannot hold such data for processing in them at once (Aldwairi & Al-Salman, 2011). So, the way the online learning algorithm Figure 4(a) work is that they get a sample of data with which they can update themselves and then discard the sample for the next one to come. Because of this reason, this method has been selected to detect the fake news (Wang, 2017; Marchi, 2012). The data on social media (Chakraborty et al., 2016) is dynamic and we can't process it statically. Though it is not implemented for the same, this would be better if done because the data is sequential, dynamic, and huge. Figure 6 and 7 represents the Confusion Matrix obtained for Passive Aggressive Classifier and Evaluation Metrics for Passive Aggressive Classifier respectively.

The model works in the following way. If the prediction or the result is correct, the model need not change itself and it has not got enough data to change itself because the prediction is right. If the prediction is incorrect, it means that the model still has to make changes to itself so that it can reduce the number of incorrect predictions. The former case makes the model passive Figure 7 and the latter makes the model aggressive. This is the reason why it got its name as "Passive-Aggressive Classifier". Set the number of iterations to 50 as it was the most optimal value got for this model. It has been denoted in the Figure 4b. This model got an accuracy of over 99 percent which is quite good.

Figure 6. Confusion matrix obtained for passive aggressive classifier

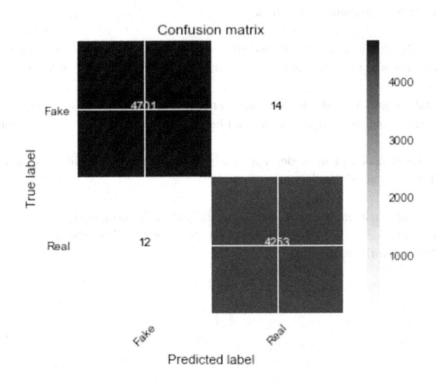

Figure 7. Evaluation metrics for passive aggressive classifier

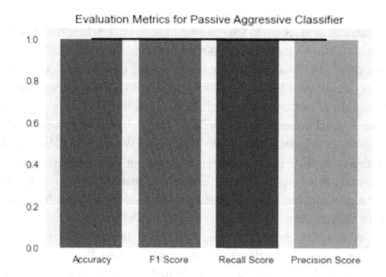

3.4 Decision Tree Classifier

The collection of all paths leads to a tree which is how this model got its name. A decision tree is a hierarchical data structure. A tree in a data structures is defined to be tuple that consists of a set of vertices and a set of edges. A point to note is that each edge present in the set of edges is depicted in Figure 8.

Now, these are basic measures that form a tree:

1. The root node is defined as the start node of the tree out of which every other subtree has come. Since this is the start node, it doesn't have any incoming edges and it may have one or more outgoing edges.
2. The second category of nodes are the internal nodes which are the ones having exactly one edge and at least one outgoing edge. If they don't have any outgoing edges, they come under the last category.
3. Leaf or terminal nodes are the nodes that have one incoming node, just like any internal node, but strictly don't have an edge going out from them.

It can be seen that each leaf node is assigned a class label in the decision tree.

Figure 8 and 9 represents the Confusion Matrix for Decision Tree Classifier and Evaluation Metrics for Decision Tree Classifier respectively.

Figure 8. Confusion matrix obtained for decision tree classifier

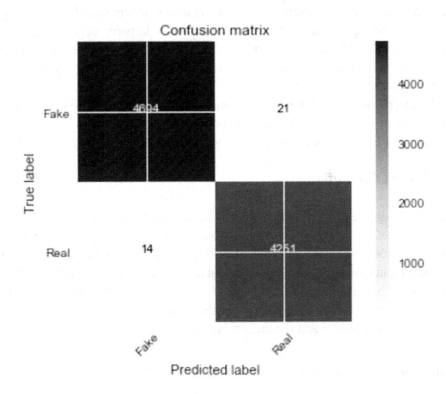

Figure 9. Evaluation matrix for decision tree classifier

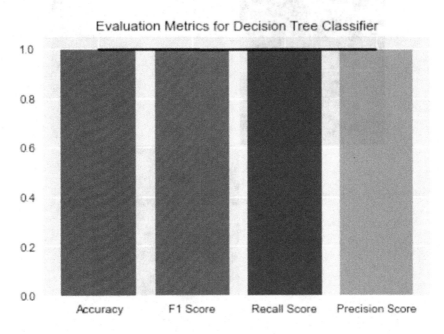

Decision-making Figure 9 is done by all the internal nodes and the root node. The job of the root node and the internal nodes is to act as conditional determiners to decide which child node does the current data belong to. For best fitting the data that have, the child nodes' impurity degrees are considered. The distribution of the class will be skewed if the impurity chosen is less. To check if a test is correct or not, the model compares the impurity degrees of the parent and the child nodes. The impurity degree of the parent is taken before the split and that of the child node is taken after a split. This says that a test condition is good based on the difference observed. If it is high, it means that the test condition or the split is good else it is poor. Another factor to be determined is the depth of the tree and in our project for the best accuracy, we limited the depth to 17. As seen in Figure 9, DTC with a depth of 17 got an accuracy of 99 percent.

3.5 Random Forest Classifier

The is an ensemble of many decision trees that are built as part of its algorithm. The ensemble algorithm is the maximum voting classifier. This is because it gives the output as the majority of the output produced by the decision trees built as a part of the algorithm Figure 10. The basis of this model is that it is better to give the output based on several independent trees rather than a single tree. The following is the reason: why it is one of the best models available: "A large number of relatively uncorrelated models (trees) operating as a committee will outperform any of the individual constituent models." Figure 10 and 11 represents the Confusion Matrix and Evaluation Metrics for Random Forest Classifier respectively.

Figure 10. Confusion matrix obtained for random forest classifier

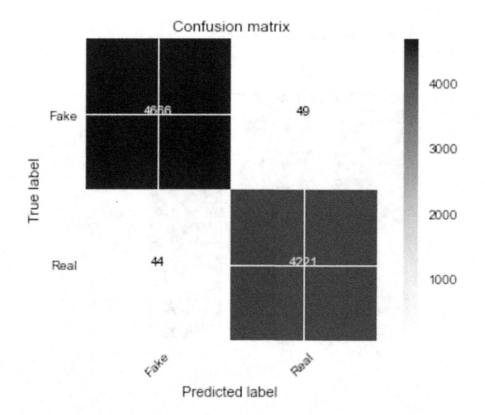

Figure 11. Evaluation metrics for random forest classifier

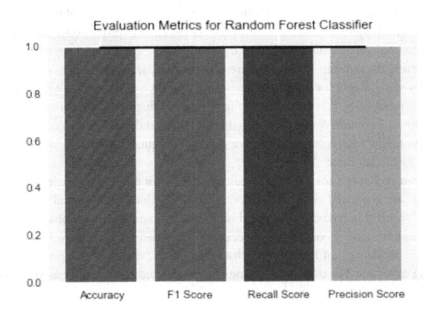

The logic behind the entire working of this model is that since the co-relation between the individual trees is so less, it means that each tree is independent of all the other trees. Another point to note is that the prediction made by a single tree may not be reliable. Hence the output is the combined result of all the trees. The errors made by all of the trees would not be in a single direction.

This is the core reason why this is such a good model. Assume the number of trees giving the correct output is "I" and that the other "n-I" trees give the wrong output. It is a prerequisite to this model that the value of "I" remains less than "n/2". This is also one of the reasons why this is a good machine learning model.The correlation between the individual trees needs to be low so that each tree performs work as an independent unit. To get the maximum accuracy the number of estimators was fixed to 50 and the criterion used was entropy and it achieved an accuracy of 98 percent as seen in Figure 11.

3.6 Naive Bayesian Classifier

Figure. 12 and 13 shows the Confusion Matrix and Evaluation Metrics for Naive Bayesian Classifier respectively. This model constitutes a set of Naive Bayesian Classifiers. The dataset presented to our application does not contain so many features. It initially contained three and after pre-processing, it has only one. Now, let us consider the dataset that was present before pre-processing.

The date has nothing to do with the news or the title. Similarly, for every other column present in the dataset, it can get such pairs. Now, consider that it need an answer for particular news which is shown in Figure 12. The model presents all the input data, which is called the input feature vector, and the output is called the response vector. This set of classifiers divide the data into two major components. They are the response vector and the feature matrix. The matrix contains all the parameters values or the rows of the data set and hence it is treated as a matrix as far as Naive Bayesian Classifiers are concerned. In the dataset for this application, the feature is news itself. The response vector is the collection of all values present in the target column or feature of the dataset which in our case, is the truth of the news. In our dataset, the class variable name is 'Result. Figure 13 shows the prerequisites of this set of classifiers are that each parameter makes an independent contribution and an equal contribution to the result of the model.

A point that can be noted is that it had several input features, each would have been given the same weightage for getting the output. Also, no feature is completely irrelevant to the outcome and each parameter is equally accountable for the outcome. Even if one such column which is irrelevant is present in the dataset, conventionally, it is removed during pre-processing. Now, this gives rise to Naive Bayes classifiers as follows: *Bernoulli Naive Bayes:* In this classifier, the features are either a '1' or a '0'. This can be used in problems where, for example, we need the frequencies of each word in a document or the runs scores in a cricket match.

Multinomial Naive Bayes Classifier: In a multinomial distribution, if we represent the frequencies with which events are generated as feature vectors, it comes under a multinomial Naive Bayesian Classifier. Figure 12. shows this type classifier used in document classification problems. In this proposed system, with a random state of 66, we got an accuracy of 97 percent as seen in Figure 13. At last, the results of all these models as an input to the ensemble model, which in this proposed system, is the maximum voting classifier. The maximum voting classifier decides the result based on the majority of the results that came from all these models.

Figure 12. Confusion matrix obtained for Naïve Bayesian classifier

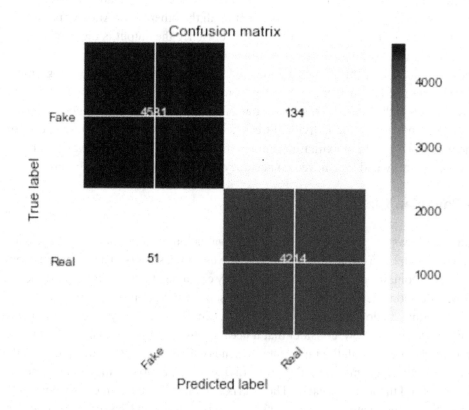

Figure 13. Evaluation metrics for Naïve Bayesian classifier

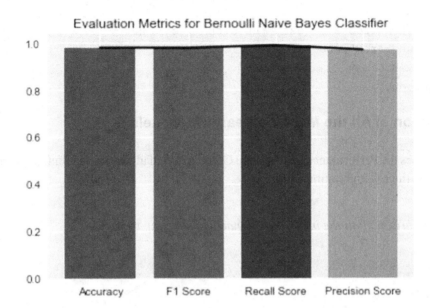

4. RESULTS AND EVALUATION

The proposed system implemented by using the open source software Python GUI programming with Tkinter module. Even if there are much researchers conducted in the files of fake news detection, the model generalization issue is still present. To promote this type of work, the model that was built was extensively trained with ISO dataset and tested with FA-KES dataset.

Accuracy: To view the accuracies of all models implemented, Fake News Detector: To go to the interface for probing into a news, Computation Time: To view the computation times of all the models, Choose the model: To select a model from the list of models displayed, Predict: To check if the entered news is Real news or True News.

4.1 Python Implementation Using Machine Learning Models

```
# Calculate accuracy time and computation time for all Machine Learning Model
# This applies the new style 'combostyle' to all ttk.Combobox
combostyle.theme_use('combostyle')
n14=tk.StringVar()
v14=ttk.Combobox(root21, width=28, height=7, textvariable="", font= ("serif",
13,'bold'), state='readonly')
v14['values'] = ['          <--Choose the Model-->        ','Logistic Regression
Classifier ','Decision Tree Classifier          ','Random Forest Classi-
fier        ','Bernoulli Naive Bayes Classifier','Passive Aggressive Clas-
sifier    ','MLP Classifier                        ','Voting Classifier
']
```

```
v14.place(x=196, y=310)
v14.current(0)
btn1 = Button (root21, text ="Predict ", command = Take_
input,foreground='red', bg="green yellow", font=("serif", 9, 'bold')).
place(x=522, y=310)
 root21.mainloop()
```

4.2 Comparison of All the Machine Learning Models

Figure 14 describes the Performance analysis and Comparison of all the Implemented Machine Learning Models based on their Computation Time.

Figure 14. Comparison of all the implemented machine learning models

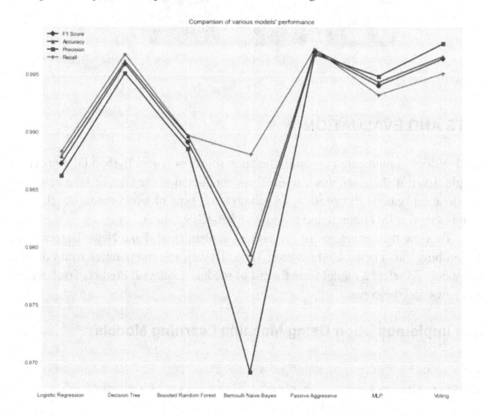

The proposed system evaluated, in terms of accuracy and precision are the best evaluation metrics that should be used to judge the models. This is because, unlike the other two evaluation metrics, accuracy and precision, are at the middle of the two extremes. Hence, this proposed models evaluated by using measure accuracy. It can also see that almost all the models tend to have the evaluation metrics high for the ensemble model. The voting classifier, thus, it is very effective as expected. Results are obtained using the proposed system and that too short period of time. The corresponding precision, recall and F1 scores can be calculated by using the following Equations (1), (2) and (3)

$$Precision = \frac{True\ Positive}{True\ Positive + False\ Positive} \tag{1}$$

$$Recall = \frac{True\ Positive}{True\ Positive + False\ Negative} \tag{2}$$

$$F1Score = 2 \times \frac{Precision \times Recall}{Precision + Recall} \tag{3}$$

$$Accuracy = \frac{True\ Positive + True\ Positive}{True\ Positive + True\ Negative + False\ Positive + False\ Negative} \tag{4}$$

It is robust to various sets of news. The proposed application needs good dataset for better results and an aim of integrating it with the internet for real time data would be fruitful. Latest and real time data would be the best for this kind of applications. It is obvious because news and events change day by day. Figure 10 shows the user input screen.

Figure 16 & 17 displays the Accuracy and the Computation Time of the Implemented Machine Learning Models respectively.

Figure 18 shows the Sample snap shot of User Input News and Machine Learning Model.

Figure 19 displays the Entered input value and selected Machine Learning Model from the User.

Figure 15. User input screen

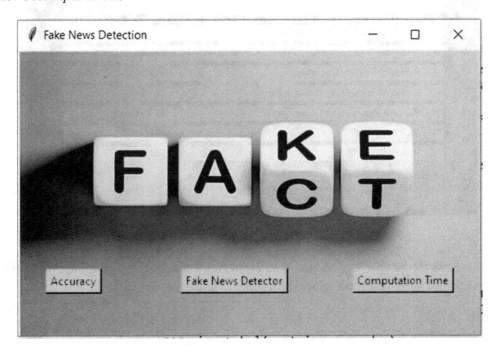

Figure 16. Window that displays the accuracy of all the implemented machine learning models

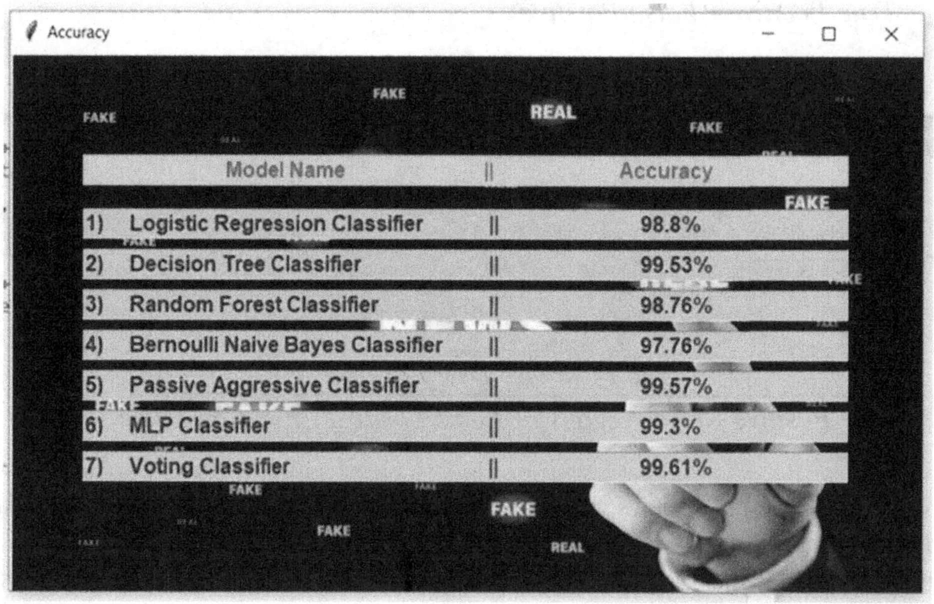

Figure 17. Window that displays the computation time of all the implemented machine learning models

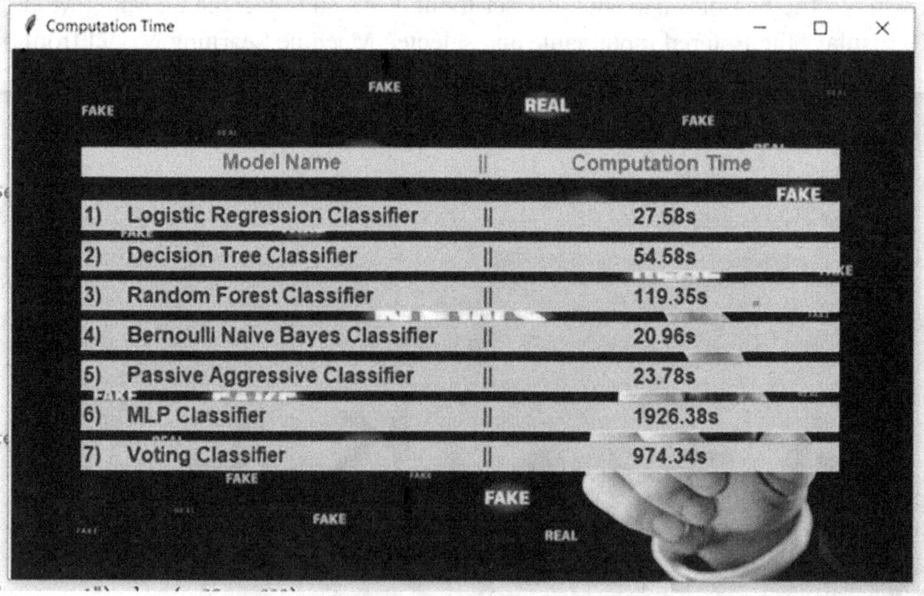

Figure 20 shows the Sample snap shot of User Input News and Machine Learning Model. Figure 21 displays the Entered input value and selected Machine Learning Model from the User.

Figure 18. Window that gets the input of the news and the machine learning model from the user

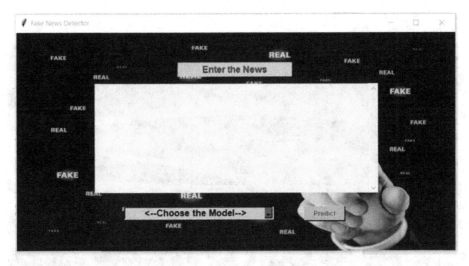

Figure 19. Window after entering the input of the news and the machine learning model from the user

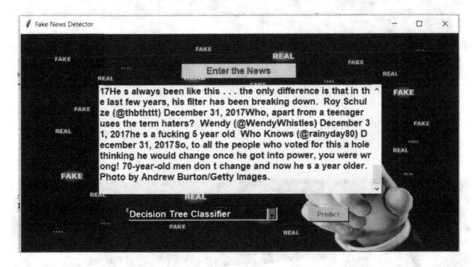

5. CONCLUSION AND FUTURE ENHANCEMENT

Despite significant advancements in fake news detection, the ever-changing landscape of misinformation requires continuous research dedication. As progress in NLP, machine learning, and deep learning continues, researchers are constantly pushing the boundaries to develop more dependable and efficient systems for identifying fake news.For the application to function correctly, it must be installed on the user's device, ensuring all required packages and environments are present. The datasets utilized by the application should also be available on the system. When these prerequisites are satisfied, the application should operate as designed. The proposed solution's performance metrics, especially accuracy, are commendable, outshining many existing systems. Furthermore, this solution is available at no charge. We aspire for this tool to excel in its primary objective: detecting fake news.

Figure 20. Output if the news is fake

Figure 21. Output if the news is real

Future research directions could involve exploring different machine learning and deep learning models, or even combinations thereof. Finding the right hybrid model might further optimize the application's performance. It's advisable to run deep learning tasks on systems with superior configurations, including enhanced RAM and processors. Parallel processing during model training and prediction can also expedite the application's run-time, particularly when implementing various machine-learning algorithms in Python. The system could be enhanced to assess multimedia elements such as images, videos, and audio alongside text, given that misinformation frequently manifests in various formats.

REFERENCES

Al Messabi, K., Aldwairi, M., Al Yousif, A., Thoban, A., & Belqasmi, F. (2018). Malware Detection using DNS Records and Domain Name Features. *International Conference on Future Networks and Distributed Systems (ICFNDS)*. ACM. .3231082.10.1145/3231053.3231082

Aldwairi, M., & Alwahedi, A. (2018). Detecting Fake News in Social Media Networks. *Science Direct, Procedia Computer Science, 141*, 215-222. . doi:10.1016/j.procs.2018.10.171

Aldwairi, M., Abu-Dalo, A. M., & Jarrah, M. (2017). Pattern Matching of Signature-based IDS using Myers algorithm under MapReduce framework. *EURASIP Journal of Information Security*. doi:10.1186/s13635-017-0062-7

Aldwairi, M., & Al-Salman, R. (2011). Malurls: Malicious URLs Classification System. *Annual International Conference on Information Theory and Applications, GSTF Digital Library (GSTF-DL)*, Singapore.

Aldwairi, M., & Alsaadi, H. H. (2017). Flukes: Autonomous Log Forensics, Intelligence and Visualization Tool. *ICFNDS'17: Proceedings of the International Conference on Future Networks and Distributed Systems*. ACM. 10.1145/3102304.3102337

Aldwairi, M., Hasan, M., Balbahaith, Z. (2017). *Detection of Drive-by Download Attacks using Machine Learning Approach*. ACM. . doi:10.4018/IJISP.2017100102

Avery, E. (2011). Journalists, Social media, and the use of Humor on Twitter. *The Electronic Journal of Communication, Texas, 21*, 1–2.

Baym, G., & Jones, J.P., (2012). News Parody in Global Perspective: Politics, Power, and Resistance. *Popular Communication*. Taylor and Francis. doi:10.1080/15405702.2012.638566

Brewer, P.R., Young, D.G., & Morreale, M. (2013). The Impact of Real News about Fake News: Intertextual Processes and Political Satire. *International Journal of Public Opinion Research, 25*(3), 323–343. doi:10.1093/ijpor/edt015

Chakraborty, A., Paranjape, B., Kakarla, S., & Ganguly, N. (2016). Stop Clickbait: Detecting and Preventing Clickbaits in Online News Media. *IEEE/ACM International Conference on Advances in Social Networks Analysis and Mining (ASONAM), Computer Science and Information Networks*, (pp. 9–16). IEEE. https://arxiv.org/abs/1610.09786 10.1109/ASONAM.2016.7752207

Chen, Y., Conroy, N. J., & Rubin, V. L. (2015). News in an Online World: The Need for an Automatic Crap Detector. *Proceedings of the 78th ASIS&T Annual Meeting, Research in and for the Community.* American Society for Information Science, Silver Springs. 10.1002/pra2.2015.145052010081

Conroy, N. J., Rubin, V. L., & Chen, Y. (2016). *Automatic Deception Detection: Methods for Finding Fake News.* Proceedings of the ASIS&T Annual Meeting, Information Science and Technology, Silver Springs, MD, USA. 10.1002/pra2.2015.145052010082

Marchi, R. (2012). With Facebook, Blogs, and Fake News, Teens Reject Journalistic "objectivity". *Journal of Communication Inquiry.* doi:10.1177/0196859912458700

Masri, R., & Aldwairi, M. (2017). Automated Malicious Advertisement Detection using virustotal, urlvoid, and trendmicro. *8th International Conference on Information and Communication Systems (ICICS).* IEEE. .10.1109/IACS.2017.7921994

Nasir, J., Khan, O., & Varlamis, K. (2021). Fake News Detection: A Hybrid CNN-RNN based Deep Learning Approach. International Journal of Management Data Insights. *International Journal of Information Management Data Insights.* Elsevier.

Shanmuganathan, C., & Raviraj, P. (2012, April). Performance Measures of Wireless Protocols for ATM Networks. *International Journal of Mobile Network Communications & Telematics*, 2(2), 31–44. doi:10.5121/ijmnct.2012.2203

Wang, W. (2017). *"liar, liar pants on fire": A New Benchmark Dataset for Fake News Detection.:* arXiv:1705.00648.

Zahedi, F., Abbasi, A., & Chen, Y. (2015). Fake-Website Detection Tools: Identifying Elements that Promote Individuals use and Enhance their Performance. *Journal of the Association for Information Systems, 16,*(6). doi:10.17705/1jais.00399

Chapter 12
Hybrid Feature Selection Model for Detection of Android Malware and Family Classification

Sandeep Sharma
The NorthCap University, India

Prachi
https://orcid.org/0000-0002-6241-7659
The NorthCap University, India

Rita Chhikara
The NorthCap University, India

Kavita Khanna
Delhi Skill and Entrepreneurship University, India

ABSTRACT

Android OS based applications offer services in various aspects of our daily lives such as banking, personal, professional, social, etc. Increased usage of Android applications makes them extremely vulnerable to various malware threats. A resilient and attack resistant machine learning based Android malware detector is desired to achieve a safe working environment. This work employs feature selection on static and dynamic features and proposes a hybrid feature selection method that can identify most informative features while eliminating the irrelevant ones. Information gain from filter and recursive feature elimination from wrapper feature selection methods outperform other evaluated feature selection techniques. Thereafter, different classification algorithms are trained on the features selected through hybrid feature selection technique and experimental results showed that XGBoost obtained maximum accuracy i.e., 98% and 89% for binary and multiclass classification respectively using only 50 features.

DOI: 10.4018/978-1-6684-9317-5.ch012

1. INTRODUCTION

Android Operating System (OS) is one of the prominent mobile platforms that is dominating the smartphone industry worldwide for more than a decade. According to the report of Statista, Android operating system has captured nearly 71.8% market as compared to iOS which has captured around 27.6% in the last quarter of 2022 (Laricchia, 2023). The popularity of Android platform and its open-source nature encourages developers to design applications that can fulfil users day-to-day needs such as online shopping, instant messaging, banking, official meetings, and so on. These applications store vast amount of personal data for users including their password, credit/debit card information, images and messages, etc.

With the proliferation of Android applications, malicious Android applications are also increasing at an alarming rate. Cybercriminals use the open nature of Android to exploit the vulnerabilities present in the OS. They design malicious applications or inject malicious code into existing applications for stealing sensitive information, send premium SMS or remotely control/damage a machine (Faruki et al., 2015; Felt et al., 2011; Surendran et al., 2018). Nowadays, adversaries use advanced technological solutions such as automatic code generators, code obfuscators, etc to create more and more sophisticated Android malware. These malware evade signature-based or manual analysis based malware detection methods and often suffer from low detection accuracy, late detection, etc. Consequently, it is important to design an automated method of Android malware detection that can protect smartphone users and their information from these malicious attacks.

A number of industry experts and security researchers are conducting research to propose proficient malware detection techniques. The techniques for detecting malware are largely classified as static, dynamic, and hybrid analysis. Static analysis based detection methods reverse engineer the applications and analyze their source code to identify malicious components (Wagner & Dean, 2001). They offer high code coverage by exploring all execution paths within an application (Fraser & Arcuri, 2014) but fail to analyze encrypted, obfuscated and dynamically loaded code within applications. Dynamic analysis-based techniques execute the applications in an isolated environment to observe their runtime behavior (Kang & Srivastava, 2011). They can effectively deal with obfuscated as dynamically loaded code of applications (Fraser & Arcuri, 2014) but fail to cover complete code of an application. Consequently, hybrid analysis-based techniques have been proven more useful in malware detection (Zhang et al., 2011; Zhang et al., 2012). However, most of these existing methods use a dataset of applications that are collected over a short timeframe.

Therefore, it is extremely important to devise a new detection technique known as hybrid Android malware detection and classification technique which can perform on a wide range of Android applications evolved over a larger period of time. Further, malware writers frequently reuse the code of existing applications to write new but similar applications. Classification of malware into families helps malware analysts to segregate the already known malware with minimal effort. Furthermore, Android applications are composed of a large number of static and dynamic features. Some of the features are redundant in nature and don't provide any significant information about detection and classification of malware into its respective family.

As a result, the proposed work presents an effective method that can detect as well as classify Android malware with high performance using a small number of informative features extracted from an extensive set of applications developed over 2008-2020 years.

The following contributions are made to the work presented:

- Android malware detection and classification technique has been presented that uses hybrid features extracted from Android applications.
- Proposes a hybrid (wrapper + filter) feature selection technique that selects the most effective features for identifying Android malware and classifying them into different families efficiently.
- Selects the most significant 50 features to detect Android malware i.e, 22 static and 28 dynamic features.

The organization of the remaining paper is as follows:

Section 2 highlights the related work of techniques for detecting Android malware. In section 3, detailed information about the suggested methodology is provided. Section 4 specifics the outcomes and discussion of experimental work. Section 5 accomplishes the research.

2. RELATED WORK

Researchers are constantly evolving the methods of predicting and detecting Android malwares through various classification techniques. Modern malware detection methods evolve from traditional machine learning algorithms to deep learning algorithms. These techniques have their own strengths and weaknesses. This section describes the identification of benign and malicious Android applications aided by various machine-learning approaches.

2.1 Static Analysis Based Android Malware Detection

Static analysis techniques analyse the source code of applications to expose their malicious behaviour. This subsection discusses the work focused on static analysis of Android applications:

Li et al. (Li et al., 2018) suggested SIGPID to find out the most substantial permissions that can discriminate between benign and malware samples. Authors employed classification algorithms for classifying the malware into its respective family. Experimentation was conducted on over 2,000 malware samples and results showed that they were able to detect 93.62% malware in the dataset with only 22 permissions. Zhu et al. (Zhu et al., 2018) offered an effective and robust Android malware detection technique that uses complex APIs, permissions, and monitoring system events as features. Authors designed a Rotation Forest model and evaluated it with 2,130 samples to achieve 88.26% accuracy. Yerima and Sezer (Yerima & Sezer, 2018) employed a multi-level classifier fusion approach that combines multiple classification algorithms to improve accuracy in Android malware detection. Authors further applied four ranking algorithms on predictive accuracies to generate the final classifier. Empirical results calculated using DREBIN, Malgenome, and McAfee datasets showed that it surpassed the predictive accuracy of Stacked generalization.

To reflect a wide range of features of apps in Android, Kim et al. (Kim et al., 2018) examined a multimodal deep neural network approach and explored whether it could be exploited for maximizing use of several types of features. The authors were 98% accurate with the dataset which included 41,260 samples. Feizollah and colleagues investigated the usefulness of Android intents for distinguishing benign samples of malware from malicious samples (Feizollah et al., 2017). Authors claimed that intents are semantic rich in nature and they can be used in conjunction with other known features for further improving the performance. Experiments were done on 7,406 applications and a detection rate of 91% was reported with Intents and 95.5% when Intents were used in combination with permissions.

Turker and Kan (Türker & Can, 2019) proposed a ML based framework that uses statically extracted features such as permissions and API calls to classify respective families of Android malwares. Authors used AMD and DREBIN dataset and attained accuracy ranging from 91% to 97%. Cai et al. (Cai et al., 2021) extracted static features from eight different categories and selected the most contributing features. Authors assigned initial weights to the selected features using ML classifiers and used weight mapping functions to convert them into final weights. Experimentation used 3000 benign and 3000 malware samples and attained 98.1% accuracy in Android malware detection.

Bayazit et al. (Bayazit et al., 2022) evaluated the performance of BiLSTM, RNN based LSTM and GRU algorithms on CICInvesAndMal2019 dataset consisting of 8115 static features extracted from Android samples. Experimental results showed that BiLSTM performed best with 98.85% accuracy for the detection of malware. Sahin et al. (Şahın et al., 2022) used multiple Linear Regression method based classifiers to find the Android malware using permissions. These classifiers were evaluated on 4 different datasets and compared with various conventional ML algorithms. Experimental results showed that authors achieved f-measure ranging from 83% to 97%.

Khari et al. presented a tool (Khari et al., 2020) that automatically extracts features from APK files and creates the dataset of several static features like permissions, intent, etc in a CSV file format. The tool has been implemented in Python and it can be executed on any set of APK files and it will create a dataset by using AndoroidManifest.xml and Classes.dex files of APKs.

Despite the numerous approaches to detect malware suggested by machine learning methods, there is a wide variety of models that are not sufficiently transparent and interpretable which could lead to difficulties in understanding Android's decision-making process and limit its application in practice. In order to gain insight into model behaviour and improve confidence in the results, techniques such as feature importance analyses, rule extraction or visualizations can be used. With manipulated or encrypted malware, the static analysis methods are unable to work. In such cases, the static analysis approach is outshone by dynamic analysis techniques.

2.2 Dynamic Analysis Based Android Malware Detection

Hou et al. presented a method that automatically executes code routines and extracts system calls to design weighted directed graphs that can detect unknown malware (Hou et al., 2016). In experimentation, authors achieved 93.68% accuracy with 5% false positives with 1500 benign and 1500 malware samples. A new method (Lashkari et al., 2017) to protect organizations and companies from malicious Android applications based on the monitoring of changes in network traffic has been planned by Lashkari et al. The experimental outcomes showed that, with 1500 benign and 400 malicious samples, the proposed method has an average accuracy of 91.41%.

Alzaylaee et al. (Alzaylaee et al., 2017) introduced a technique to elevate the limitations of limited code coverage and enhance the dynamic analysis of Android applications. Experimentation is conducted on 1200 benign and 1200 malware samples and results showed that they are able to extract more dynamic features and uncover malicious behaviour from the applications. Yang et al. introduced DroidWard (Yang et al., 2018), a dynamic analysis method that extracts the most effective features to characterize the malware behaviour. This method also identified some novel features through dynamic analysis of applications. Empirical evidence shows that 98.54% of malicious applications can be correctly classified by the proposed method. Alzaylaee et al. (Alzaylaee et al., 2020) used stateful input generation to enhance code coverage and increase accuracy for Android malware detection. Authors claimed that accuracy with 97.8% detection rate can be achieved with dynamic features.

A slightly supervised method to classify Android malware into categories has been introduced by Mahdavifar et al. (Mahdavifar et al., 2020). The authors have also introduced a new database of 17,341 android applications with static and dynamic features divided into different categories. DeLADY, a dynamic analysis technique for the detection of Android malware using Deep Learning was presented by Sihag et al (Sihag et al., 2021). De-LADY was evaluated on 13533 applications in different categories and attained 98.08% detection rate. Khalid and Hussain (Khalid & Hussain, 2022) performed a broad analysis on different classes of dynamic features to classify the most significant categories and relevant features in those categories. Dynamic analysis based methods can detect obfuscated or encrypted malware with good accuracy but fail to cover the entire code of applications. On the contrary, static analysis based methods can cover all execution paths within an application. The advantages of both static and dynamic can be combined by using a hybrid feature based technique.

While some of the papers do use both approaches, there may be room for further research on how to effectively integrate them in a more robust and efficient manner. Additionally, while deep learning methods are gaining popularity for Android malware detection, there may be a need for more explainable models that can provide insights into why certain apps are classified as malicious. In addition, it might be useful to assess whether existing methods for managing the increasing number of variants of Android malware are feasible in terms of scalability and if there is a realistic possibility of Real Time detection on Mobile Devices.

2.3 Hybrid Analysis Based Android Malware Detection

Surendran et al. (Surendran et al., 2020) suggested a hybrid Android malware detection and analysis system that involves the interdependency of both static and dynamic features into consideration. They trained 3 Logistic Regression classifiers on features and determined whether an app is malicious or not with 97% accuracy by employing a special Bayesian network termed as Tree Augment Naïve Bayes that combines the output of these classifiers. Ding et al. (Ding et al., 2021) applied several feature selection techniques and machine learning algorithms on permissions and intents extracted from Android applications to identify the most critical static features and most proficient classification algorithm. Thereafter, authors performed dynamic analysis using network traffic to detect and classify malware and low-trust benign applications identified during static analysis.

Wang et al. presented FGL_Droid to alter dynamic API call sequences into function call graphs so that length of the sequence can be reduced significantly while preserving the order of execution (Wang et al., 2022). Additionally, authors used information extracted from permissions to compensate for loss of information. Accuracy of 97.5% was obtained when experimentation was conducted on 3950 malware and 4219 benign applications.

Tong and Yan (Tong & Yan, 2017) executed applications and gathered their runtime system calls. Subsequently, they performed a static procedure for extracting patterns from system calls of malicious and harmless applications in isolation. In order to ascertain the behaviour of unknown apps for Google's Android operating system, authors applied these patterns.

Lu et al. (Lu et al., 2020) applied Deep Belief network on static features and Gate Recurrent Unit on dynamic features to design a hybrid malware detection model. Experimentation was conducted on 7000 benign and 6298 malware applications and attained 96.82% accuracy.

Martinelli (Martinelli et al., 2017) presented BRIDEMAID to combine analysis of Android applications i.e, both static and dynamic analysis through n-gram matching and monitoring of user and application behaviour at multiple levels. It reported 99.7% detection accuracy with 2794 malicious applications.

In order to find the best Android malware detection methods, Dhalaria and Gandotra were able to obtain a variety of static and interactive features using Information Gain technique (Dhalaria & Gandotra, 2021). Hybrid features Machine learning classifiers trained on only static or dynamic features achieved a 98.53% accuracy for Dataset 1 and 90.1% accuracy for Dataset 2, more accurately than those trained solely on dynamic features.

Hadiprakoso et al. (Hadiprakoso et al., 2020) combined DREBIN and CICMalDroid datasets to extract 261 hybrid features for Android malware detection. Authors reported their best accuracy i.e. around 99% accuracy with extreme gradient boosting model.

Arshad et al. (Arshad et al., 2018) combined local and remote host, static and dynamic analysis and machine learning for Android applications to extant a three-layer hybrid malware detection model. Authors operated in both local as well as remote hosts to achieve computation efficiency.

On the basis of these references for malware detection and classification, there is a research gap that can be explored in developing more effective and efficient multimodal analysis approaches. In terms of correctness, speed and scalability, there are still potential improvements even though a number of new studies have been carried out with regard to various combination methods.

Machine learning based malware detection has become more crucial after the evolution of IOT and Industry 4.0. Few research work has been presented in the literature to deal with such kind of issues. Le et al. discuss about the concepts like the increase in cybercrime, hidden image detection, malware, the market for malware, data mining, security challenges, cyberattacks, steganography, and more (Le et al., 2019). The need for security arrangements of user data in mobiles is also included along-with ransomware, crypto mining and crypto-jacking malware. It also includes various case studies that include the development of strategies to defend against such data threats.

Khari et al. proposed Elliptic Galois cryptography (EGC) method to defend the IoT network against possible data breaches (Khari et al., 2019). It enciphers the sensitive data received from various medical sources using CNN and embeds it inside an image using XOR based encoding scheme. It further optimizes the proposed technique with the Adaptive Firefly algorithm. The proposed method reported 86% steganography embedding efficiency when implemented on MATLAB simulator.

Chaudhary et al. proposed a semi-supervised threat detection method for IoT-powered grid systems (Chaudhary et al., 2023). It uses a bi-directional generative convolutional network to find patterns of threat data from partially labeled grid systems. Federated learning is introduced so that several remote servers can work on the training without their private local data being compromised. Blockchain technology is used to allow the communication between cloud layers and the edge layers. The results clearly show the superiority of FSEI-Net over other latest detection techniques.

The growing complexity and variety of cyber crime needs to be taken into account by the proposed techniques. This work examines the impact of a variety of features, models and algorithms on the effectiveness of hybrid analysis based Android malware detection approaches.

3. PROPOSED METHODOLOGY

This section depicts the overall working of the proposed methodology, with 4 major phases (as shown in Figure 1): Dataset collection and feature extraction, Data pre-processing, Feature selection, and Classification algorithms.

Figure 1. Architecture of the proposed methodology

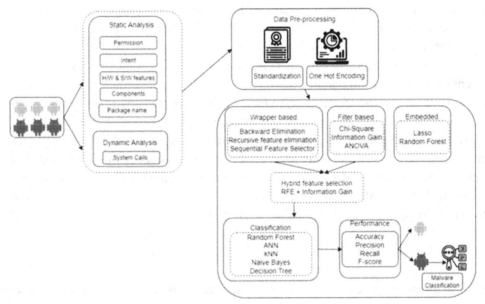

The pseudocode of the proposed work is given in Algorithm 1:

Algorithm 1: Hybrid feature selection technique

```
Input: Set of features (F={f1,f2,….fn})
Initialize: FSTs ← Feature Selection Techniques, W ← Wrapper Techniques, S ←
Filter techniques, E ← Embedded techniques
Output: Performance and Set of features (F') providing the best performance,
F' ⊆ F
Convert numeric features ← non-numeric features
for each t in W, S, E
         Identify maximum performance and best-performing features
End
Integrate two best-performing techniques from W, S and E
Find best-performing features (F') using integrated technique
Give F' as an input to the best-performing classification algorithm
Calculate results
```

3.1 Dataset Collection and Feature Extraction

This paper uses Kronodroid dataset, a dataset encompassing hybrid features of benign and malicious Android applications from different sources over a time frame from 2008 to 2020. The dataset includes 200 static and 289 dynamic features that are collected on emulators as well as on real devices because dynamic behaviour of applications might change (may show variation) on the basis of data source. Emulator dataset is composed of 35,246 benign and 28,745 malicious applications whereas the real device dataset is composed of 36,755 benign and 41,382 malicious applications. Static features were collected in two different phases: The first phase extracts APK package name, components of app, hardware and software requirements, permissions, and intent from AndroidManifest.xml file of Android applications using AndroGuard (Desnos et al., 2018), Android Asset Packaging Tool (aapt) (Android, 2021) and Exif tool (Harvey, 2021). The second phase further enrich the static features by analyzing applications on the Anti-virus engine of Virus Total portal.

The most common behavioral features of Android applications are kernel calls or system calls. They're used as interfaces between applications and the Operating System kernel. Therefore, they illustrate the actual behavior of applications. To capture these system calls, applications were installed and executed for a duration of 60 seconds without any interruption and the frequency of each system call issued by an application is taken into consideration. These calls are captured with Android Debug Bridge (ADB), strace (Levin, 2021) and monkey (Android, 2021) tools. Kronodroid has extracted a total of 489 properties to classify the applications on both emulators and real device datasets after performing those steps.

3.2 Data Pre-Processing

This section performs pre-processing of features retrieved in the aforementioned step to enhance the efficiency of machine learning algorithms while minimizing the chances of overfitting:

- **Transformation:** The features comprise numeric as well as non-numeric values. To achieve better performance with classification algorithms, non-numeric attributes are converted to numeric values through one-hot encoding method.
- **Standardization:** In machine learning, the datasets need to be standardized as there is a possibility that values in larger ranges tend to be given more importance, and also features in different ranges can have a negative impact on the classification algorithm.

This is avoided in our study by subtracting each input value from the mean of respective feature and dividing by the corresponding standard deviation. This standardization method shifts the distribution to zero mean value and one standard deviation.

$$Standardized\ value = \frac{X_i - \mu}{\sigma} \tag{1}$$

Where X_i is the value of the respective feature, μ is the mean of the respective feature and σ is the standard deviation.

3.3 Feature Selection

This phase inspects the feature space to get rid of irrelevant and redundant features. This phase has paramount importance because it analyses the features, inspects the performance gain by the presence or absence of these features, and optimizes the evaluation capability of learning algorithms. The feature selection techniques are categorized into three categories: Filter Selection Technique, Wrapper Selection Technique, and Embedded Selection Technique.

Filter based feature selection techniques rank features using various statistical or information-theory based techniques. Thereafter, the best subset of features is passed as input to the learning model. They are independent of classifier performance.

The value of the features shall be measured based on classification accuracy using Wrapper Feature Selection techniques. The featured subsets are used to assess the efficiency and capability of learning algorithms and choose the addition or removal of features in the feature subset based on the inferences drawn from the earlier model. Filter methods are more effective than the wrapper method when it comes to computation, but often they do not find the best subsets of features in a feature vector.

An embedded method is also used for selecting features, in addition to these two types of methods. These methods integrate the characteristics of filter and wrapper processes, in contrast with filters and wrappers. The identification of the features along with classification is a key part of these embedded methods. Embedded algorithms (Deng et al., 2019) take advantage of their in-built feature selection and perform feature selection and classification simultaneously. They are quite similar to wrapper method in the sense that they try to optimize the performance of the learning model but they are computationally efficient like filter methods. They are less prone to over-fitting, obtain the most relevant set of features, and their computational cost lies between wrapper and filter method.

3.3.1 Filter Methods

For the purpose of selecting subsets of important features and calculating their importance scores, advanced filter methods such as Information Gain, ANOVA, and Chi-Square have been applied. The feature vector deletes features with 0 and low scores.

- **Information Gain**

In machine learning, Information Gain (MacKay & Mac Kay, 2003) is a common selection method for filtering features in which important elements are selected from the collected data. The objective of selecting filter features is to discover the maximum useful features which have strong relationship with the dependent(target) variable while removing features that are irrelevant or redundant.

In this method, the information gain value is used to assess each feature of a dataset and measures how much it contributes to its model's predictive power. The characteristics with high information gains are considered more important, and those that have low Information Gains are discarded.

The first step to evaluate Information Gain of a feature is to calculate entropy of the dependent(target) variable for the complete dataset. Entropy measures the level of uncertainty or randomness in the data and is evaluated as given in equation below.

$$E(S) = \sum_{i=1}^{c} - p_i log_2 p_i \qquad (2)$$

where 'p_i' is the frequentist probability of element 'i' in data

The dataset with low entropy provides high degree of confidence when it comes to forecasting the target. Secondly, for each subset that has been divided into features according to their values, we have calculated the entropy of the target variable.

Information gain is then measured by comparing the entropy of a target variable across all datasets with the weighted average for entropies between subsets. A feature with a high information gain is that it divides the data into subsets with low entropy and high purity, which means that it has a high predictive capacity for the target variable. In contrast, features with low Information Gain do not provide much additional information beyond what is already captured by other features in the dataset and are therefore less useful for prediction.

Information gain may assist to decrease the dimensionality of the data, and increase accuracy and performance of machine learning models by selecting filter features with a little bit of efficiency. For the purpose of classification, features that achieve information exceeding a certain threshold are selected because they provide maximum information about the target variable.

- **Chi-square:** It evaluates the independence between two features/events. Chi-square (Kenney & Keeping, 1951) of each independent feature is calculated w.r.t dependent feature to determine the independence between these two features.

$$x_c^2 = \frac{\Sigma(O_i - E_i)^2}{E_i} \qquad (3)$$

Here O and E are observed and expected values and C is the degree of freedom (number of variables that can vary in the calculation)

A low Chi-Square value represents that two features are independent whereas a high Chi-Square score represents dependence between the independent feature and target feature. Features having high Chi-square scores are selected in the feature set for training the model.

- **ANOVA**

ANOVA (Analysis of Variance) – This method is applied in statistics to compare the mean of different groups (in our case we used this method for malware and benign samples) and evaluate the significance based on differences (Fisher, 1992). It's generally helpful in identifying the most relevant variables of the dataset that are related to a target variable or outcome of interest.

Depending on the value of a particular variable (feature) the data is grouped to allow ANOVA to be used for selecting features. The mean and variance of the target variable are then calculated for each group, and the F-statistic is used to measure the difference between the group means relative to the variation within the groups.

$$f = \frac{Between\ group\ variance}{Within\ group\ variance} \tag{4}$$

Taking the degree of freedom into consideration the F-statistic is compared to a critical value. If the F-statistic is higher than the critical value then the null hypothesis is rejected. This helps in deciding whether the groups are significantly different in terms of their resources, indicating that this feature could be an excellent predictor of the target variable.

Features with a high F-statistic and a low p-value (indicating a high degree of statistical significance) are considered to be the most significant and informative features for predicting the target variable. They can be retained in the final dataset for further analysis or used as input variables in machine learning models.

Although ANOVA is a powerful and widely used method for filter feature selection, it has certain limitations, such as the assumption of equal variances across the groups and the sensitivity to outliers and non-normal distributions. The assumption and limitation of ANOVA should therefore be considered in a careful way so that it is possible to select suitable alternatives if required.

3.3.2 Wrapper Methods

This subsection deliberates upon a few of the most prominent wrapper based methods for feature selection. Details of the same are given below:

- **Sequential Forward Selection**

SFS is generally used wrapper feature selection technique in machine learning (Ferri et al., 1994). It works with a greedy search approach to detect the most pertinent subset of features that correspond to the target variable. The method adds features to the subset iteratively and assesses the model with the newly added feature.

The process begins with an empty set and then one feature is selected based on a performance measure, such as accuracy or AUC, when the model is trained with that feature alone. This selected feature becomes the first feature in the subset. A subset is further created by adding all remaining features one by one and the performance of these features is gauged through a selected classifier. This process is repeated until a certain number of features are selected or the output of the model is not improving, the feature that boosts the performance the most is added to the subset, and the process is repeated.

SFS has several advantages. It can find a subset of features that works well with a particular machine learning model and can handle interactions between features. Also, it is computationally efficient compared to exhaustive search methods.

However, SFS has some limitations. The search space can be large and there may be many local optima, meaning that the algorithm may get stuck in a suboptimal subset of features. Furthermore, if the number of characteristics chosen is too large compared to sample volumes, it can be prone to over proportion.

SFS method improves the accuracy and effectiveness of learning models by selecting the most relevant features. However, selecting appropriate performance measures and termination criteria for algorithms must be taken into account with great care in relation to the performance of a given algorithm and its computation efficiency.

- **Recursive Feature Elimination (RFE)**

RFE is one of the most prevalent techniques of feature selection. It reduces the number of input variables and selects only the relevant ones by evaluating the performance of the subset through a learning model. working in a predictive model.

The functionality of RFE involves removing variables from the dataset in a recursive manner and creating a model using the remaining variables. The variables are evaluated based on their significance, and the ones that are considered less important are eliminated. This process should be repeated till the preferred number of variables is achieved.

To execute RFE, a model shall be trained on the complete dataset, and the significance of each feature is assessed. The feature that is considered least significant is subsequently eliminated, and the model is retrained on the new reduced dataset.

RFE is a powerful technique because it not only selects the most important features, but it also considers the interactions between features. For example, if two features are highly correlated, RFE may select one of them and discard the other.

RFE is an effective approach to simplify a model and enhance its performance. Nevertheless, it is crucial to cautiously choose the number of features to preserve since retaining too few features could lead to an underfit model, while retaining too many features could result in an overfit model.

- **Backward Elimination**

Machine learning works with Backward Elimination to diminish the size of input variables utilized in a model to boost its accuracy and efficiency. The algorithm of Backward Elimination works by first training the model with the entire feature set. The significance for each feature is determined using a significance test, such as p-value or F-statistic. The model eliminates features with the highest p-value or the lowest F-statistic, and the model is subsequently retrained on the reduced dataset.

The process of eliminating features is repeated until a stoppage criterion is fulfilled, like accomplishing a specific level of accuracy or achieving a predetermined number of features. The choice of stopping criterion is based on the individualities in the dataset.

It may be noted that Backward Elimination shall not produce the top feature subset for a given problem. It can be sensitive to the choice of significance test and stopping criterion, and may not be effective for datasets with highly correlated features.

3.3.3 Embedded Method

Further, this paper explored embedded feature selection techniques, Random Forest and Lasso.

- **Random Forest (RF)**

RF is also known as a collection of Decision Trees (DTs). Each DT calculates the importance of features on the basis of impurity decreased by the feature. It is repeated for every tree within Random Forest and the average is taken across all trees to calculate the final feature importance. This method is less prone to over-fitting.

- **Lasso**

Lasso means Least Absolute Shrinkage and Selection Operation. It focuses on the optimization of the cost function and shrinks the regression coefficients. It selects features with non-zero coefficient values and discards features with zero coefficient values. A cost function is the sum of the difference between the projected and true value, the formula is given below:

$$Cost\ Function = \sum_{i=1}^{n}\left(y_i - \beta_o - \sum_{j=1}^{p}\beta_i x_{ij} \right)^2 = \sum_{i=1}^{n}\left(y_i - \hat{y}_l \right) \tag{5}$$

where β_j are the regression coefficients, also known as the Weights, associated with each feature $y_i =$ predicted value and $\hat{y}_i$ = actual value

In this phase, the features vector size is substantially reduced, training time decreased and the performance of classification models improved in order to be able to use them for the early detection of malware.

3.4 Application of Classification Algorithms

In this phase, classification algorithms are used to automatically discriminate between benign and malicious applications with the features selected using feature selection techniques. Further, malware writers often use the source code of already-known malware to design a new malware with minimal effort. These types of malware belong to a single malware family. Consequently, this paper further attempts to classify malware into its respective families. This process is popular as multi-class classification problem. This work identified 42 families in Kronodroid dataset that have at least 100 samples. The Figure 2 below gives the list of all Android Malware families which are included during the experimentation.

Figure 2. Families with more than one hundred samples in Kronodroid dataset

The process uses Artificial Neural Network (ANN), XGBoost, Decision Tree, Support Vector Machine (SVM) and k Nearest Neighbour (kNN) algorithms to construct classification models that can process the selected features to detect as well as classify malware. To avoid overfitting, classification algorithms used 10-fold cross validation and the feature set is segregated into 80:20 ratios as training and test set.

- **Artificial Neural Network**

ANN is one of the categories of learning algorithms that demonstrate the structure and functioning of the human brain. ANN contains multiple layers of nodes which are connected with each other and are referred as neurons, which work collectively to learn and make forecasts from data.

Every neuron in an ANN takes input signals from other neurons or directly from the input data. It then applies an activation function to the input signals and generates an output signal then sent to other neurons in the next layer. This process is repeated through multiple layers till the final output.

The connections between neurons in an ANN have weights that are adjusted during training to reduce the error between the outputs; predicted and actual. The process of backpropagation in ANN adjusts the weights, and it permits the ANN to learn from the input and enhance its predictions. They have demonstrated high accuracy and flexibility in many applications and a significant tool in machine learning and artificial intelligence. They give good results with large amounts of data.

- **XGBoost**

XGBoost can be applied iteratively by accumulating decision trees to the model, and each tree fixes an error from a previous tree. An algorithm optimizes the cost function to take into account the difference between expected and actual outputs during training. Optimisation is a process in which an algorithm learns faster and improves model accuracy through the calculation of the gradient and second derivative of the cost function.

The ability to resolve null information and outliers in input data was one of the main features of XGBoost. Regularisation techniques such as L1 and L2 regularisation, which are used to prevent overloads and improvements in generalization will also be included.

XGboost is renowned for its speed and scalability, which makes it a favorite choice in big datasets as well as real-time applications. Without the need for pre-processing, it will also be able to deal with a variety of types of data such as numerical and categorical.

- **Decision Tree (DT)**

This algorithm splits the data into chunks on the values of one of the input features selected by evaluating the statistical value of all features. It then recursively applies the splitting process to every subset and creates a tree-like structure of nodes as well as branches.

During training, the algorithm determines the features which are most informative for making decisions by calculating the Gini impurity or Information Gain. The algorithm continuously split the data till a stopping benchmark is encountered. Decision Trees are a common choice for exploratory data analysis and decision-making tasks.

- **Support Vector Machine (SVM)**

SVM is an algorithm that generates a decision boundary to separate n-dimensional space into different classes and consequently, through this model new data samples are correctly classified in the future. There can be multiple decision boundaries but the purpose of SVM is to clearly find the best decision boundary (hyperplane) that will maximize the margins between different classes. The distance of the hyperplane from the closest points is called margin which are also referred as support vectors. There are two types of SVM algorithm: Linear and Non-Linear SVM. To handle Non-Linear SVM, various kernel methods like Radial Basis Function, Polynomial etc. are designed.

- **K Nearest Neighbour (kNN)**

kNN is a simple yet popular algorithm that works on the methodology of proximity to predict the class of a new sample. It identifies k nearest neighbors of a given dataset and then counts the number of neighbors in each class. Thereafter, it assigns the new sample to a class that possesses maximum number of neighbors. It can use different distance metrics, to name a few; Hamming, Euclidean, Manhattan, and Minkowski distance to identify the k nearest neighbours of a given sample. One of the most used distance metrics is Euclidean distance. It is crucial to select an optimal value of 'k' to handle the situation of overfitting or underfitting of the classification model.

3.4.1 Performance Metrics

This work uses the following performance metrics: accuracy, AUC (Area Under Curve) and F1-score to measure the performance of classification algorithms.

- **Accuracy** evaluates the percentage of correct predictions by a classification model. Mathematically it is written as:

$$Accuracy = \frac{TP + TN}{TP + TN + FP + FN} \tag{6}$$

where TP is True Positive, TN is True Negative, FP is False Positive and FN is False Negative)

- **AUC score** promotes high True Positives and low False Positives. Mathematically, TPR- True Positive Rate and FPR- False Positive Rate are expressed as:

$$TPR = \frac{TP}{TP + FN} \tag{7}$$

$$FPR = \frac{FP}{FP + TN} \tag{8}$$

- **F1-score**

F1 score is based on the precision and recall metrics, which measure how accurately a model classifies positive and negative instances. Precision is the ratio of TP predictions to all positive predictions, while recall is the ratio of TP predictions to all actual positive instances.

The formula for F1 score is:

$$F1 = 2* (precision*recall)/(precision+recall) \tag{9}$$

A classification model with high F1-score indicates that both precision and recall are high.

4. EXPERIMENTAL RESULTS AND ANALYSIS

This section presents the overall performance of the proposed method using various feature selection techniques with machine learning algorithms. Experiments are conducted on Intel(R) Core i7-1165G7 @ 2.80 GHz with 16 GB RAM and 64-bit Windows 10 operating system.

4.1 Performance of Machine Learning Algorithms for Malware Detection

This subsection evaluates the performance of KNN, ANN, SVM, decision tree and XGBoost algorithms for detecting malware using the entire feature set. Results of experiments are given in Table 1.

Table 1. Results of Android malware detection with entire dataset

Classifier	Overall Accuracy (in %)	Classwise Accuracy (in %)	F1 score (in %)	AUC score
KNN	73	0->69 1->76.9	69 78	0.73
SVM	60	0->52 1->68	57 62	0.59
Decision Tree	96	0->96 1->97	96 97	0.92
ANN	**98.8**	**0->97** **1->99**	**98** **98**	0.97
Xgboost	98	0->98 1->99	98 99	0.98

It is clear from Table 1 that ANN algorithm is giving the best accuracy while XGBoost is giving the best AUC score. Figure 3 presents the AUC score of the XGBoost algorithm. In binary classification, accuracy is given more preference than AUC score if the dataset is balanced. Therefore, this work uses ANN for feature selection with Adam optimizer and 100 epochs to classify the dataset.

4.2 Performance of the Feature Selection Methods for Malware Detection

This section reduces the dimension of the feature set by getting rid of redundant and obsolete features while enhancing the performance of classification models through feature selection methods. It also helps in minimizing the computational and time complexity of classification models.

Figure 3. ROC (AUC) of XGBoost

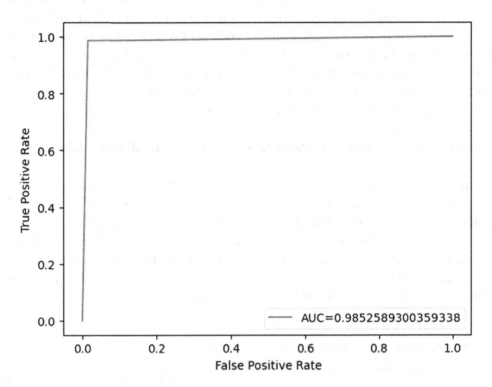

As discussed in section 3.3, three methods are used for the selection of features i.e, Filter, Wrapper and Embedded method. The experimental results are performed with three filter methods (IG, Chi-square and ANOVA), three wrapper methods (SFS, RFE and BE) and two embedded methods (Random Forest and LASSO). The outcomes are shown in Table 2.

Table 2. Outcome of malware detection with selected features

Method	Number of Features	Accuracy (in %)	AUC	F1 (in %)
Wrapper FS				
Sequential Feature Selector	178	95.4	0.94	94.6
Recursive Feature Elimination	**151**	**98.5**	**0.98**	**99**
Backward Elimination	183	96.4	0.95	95.1
Filter FS				
Information Gain	**111**	**96.9**	**0.96**	**99.8**
Chi-square	192	93.2	0.92	93
Embedded				
Random Forest	92	97	0.97	98
Lasso	112	62	0.63	61

The performance of each feature selection method was tested using an ANN classifier. The results exhibited that the Information Gain filter method and RFE wrapper method had the best performance from their respective pools. It is also interesting to note that LASSO embedded method showed poor performance. Based on this analysis, IG and RFE have been ensembled iteratively to design a hybrid model that combined the strengths of both filter and wrapper techniques. It identifies the optimal subset of features to detect malicious Android applications. As shown in subsequent sections, the same hybrid model is also tested for the multiclass classification of Android malware.

4.3 Performance of Machine Learning Methods for Multiclass Classification

This subsection assesses the performance of classification algorithms in classifying Android malware into their respective families. The Kronodroid dataset employed for experimentation in this study consists of 209 families. However, this work considers 42 families of Kronodroid dataset as discussed in section 3.4. The binary classification techniques of some of the classification methods like KNN, ANN, Decision Tree, Naïve Bayes etc. can be easily expanded to multiclassification problems. However, in some cases the multiclass classification problem is solved by decomposing into many two-class problems and then solved with efficient binary classifiers. SVM falls under this category of classifiers.

Table 3. Results of malware classification with entire feature set

Classifier	Overall Accuracy (in %)	F1 score (in %)
KNN	63	59
SVM	54	55
Decision Tree	81	78
XGBoost	**90**	**90**
ANN	88	87

As observed from Table 3, XGBoost outperformed all other classification algorithms in terms of multiclass classification by attaining 90% F1 score and Accuracy. F1 score is also taken into account, as the multiclassification dataset has an unbalanced dataset and accuracy alone does not provide sufficient criteria for testing model performance in the case of unbalanced dataset. It is closely followed by ANN by achieving 88% accuracy and 87% F1 score.

4.4 Proposed Hybrid Model for Binary and Multiclass Classification

This section uses the hybrid feature selection model (Information Gain + RFE) proposed in section 4.2 to overcome the weaknesses of Filter and Wrapper approaches.

Thereafter, a novel model is designed that combines IG and RFE using XGboost as the classifier, referred as IGRFM and IGRFB for Multiclass and Binary classification respectively. To the best of our knowledge, this combination of filter, wrapper, and machine learning algorithm has not been explored in the domain of Android malware detection.

Table 4. Results of malware detection and classification with hybrid model

Hybrid Model	Number of Features	Accuracy	F1-score	AUC
IGRFM	50	89%	89%	88.4%
IGRFB	50	98%	98%	97.9%

Table 4 shows that the proposed model achieved 89%, 89% and 88.4% accuracy, F1-score and AUC for multiclass classification. Further, it reported 98%, 98% and 97.9% accuracy, F1-score and AUC for binary classification with 90% reduction in features. Similar values in accuracy, F1-score and AUC highlight the robustness of the proposed methodology for balanced as well as unbalanced datasets because accuracy alone is not sufficient to determine the performance of a classification model.

Table 5 represents 50 topmost features i.e, 28 dynamic features (system calls) and 22 static features (permissions, metadata etc.) for the detection and classification of Android malware.

4.5 Comparison With Other State-of-Art Methods

This section compares the performance of proposed work with other similar works evaluated on Kronodroid dataset. Chaudhari et al. (Chaudhuri et al., 2022) proposed a novel deep learning based Android malware detection method. Authors used 4-layer feed forward network with ReLU and sigmoid as activation function for hidden and output layer respectively. Renjith and Aji (Renjith & Aji, 2022) utilized dynamic features of applications from Kronodroid dataset and presented a Liblinear incremental learning-based algorithm for detection of Android malware. Authors reported that their proposed model attained the highest incremental accuracy of 97.94%.

It is clear from Table 6 that the proposed approach is able to outperform state-of-art methods evaluated on the same dataset. This proves the potency of our work over earlier presented approaches.

CONCLUSION

The paper presents a novel method of binary and multiclass classification of Android malware using both static as well dynamic features of applications. The proposed study explored several feature selection techniques to discard inappropriate or redundant features and select features that can contribute towards detection and classification of malware into its respective family. Experimentation results showed that Information Gain from filter and Recursive Feature Elimination from wrapper outperformed all other filter, wrapper and embedded feature selection techniques evaluated in this paper. Extensive experimentation was conducted using various classification algorithms and results revealed that XGBoost and ANN achieved higher accuracy and F1-score as compared to other classification algorithms. In the end, a hybrid model of Information Gain and Recursive Feature Elimination feature selection method is designed to select features that can obtain 98% and 89% accuracy for binary and multiclass classification respectively using XGBoost algorithm.

Table 5. Top fifty features selection for Android malware detection

S.No.	Features	S.No.	Features
1	'getuid32'	26	'SYS_329'
2	'getpriority'	27	'SYS_339'
3	'prctl'	28	'nr_syscalls'
4	'read'	29	'ACCESS_NETWORK_STATE'
5	'write'	30	'GET_TASKS'
6	'munmap'	31	'MOUNT_UNMOUNT_FILESYSTEMS'
7	'mprotect'	32	'READ_PHONE_STATE'
8	'madvise'	33	'RECEIVE_BOOT_COMPLETED'
9	'ioctl'	34	'SEND_SMS'
10	'writev'	35	'nr_permissions'
11	'fcntl64'	36	'normal'
12	'dup'	37	'dangerous'
13	'fsync'	38	'signature'
14	'fstat64'	39	'nr_custom'
15	'rt_sigprocmask'	40	'total_perm'
16	'recvfrom'	41	'CFileSize'
17	'getsockopt'	42	'UFileSize'
18	'wait4'	43	'FilesInsideAPK'
19	'clock_gettime'	44	'TimesSubmitted'
20	'gettimeofday'	45	'Activities'
21	'futex'	46	'NrIntServices'
22	'pread'	47	'NrIntActivities'
23	'SYS_310'	48	'NrIntReceiversActions'
24	'SYS_312'	49	'TotalIntentFilters'
25	'SYS_317'	50	'NrServices'

Table 6. Comparison of the proposed work with other state-of-art methods

	Accuracy	F1-Score
DW FedAvg (2022) (Chaudhuri et al., 2022)	96.32% 95.96%	96.51% 96.18%
Linear Incremental Algorithm (2022) (Renjith & Aji, 2022)	97.94%	-
Proposed Approach	98.8%	98%

REFERENCES

Alzaylaee, M. K., Yerima, S. Y., & Sezer, S. (2017, June). Improving dynamic analysis of android apps using hybrid test input generation. In *2017 International Conference on Cyber Security And Protection Of Digital Services (Cyber Security)* (pp. 1-8). IEEE. 10.1109/CyberSecPODS.2017.8074845

Alzaylaee, M. K., Yerima, S. Y., & Sezer, S. (2020). DL-Droid: Deep learning based android malware detection using real devices. *Computers & Security*, *89*, 101663. doi:10.1016/j.cose.2019.101663

Android. (2021). Aapt2. Android. https://developer.android.com/studio/command-line/aapt2.

Android. (2021). *Ui/application exerciser monkey*. Android. https://developer.android.com/studio/test/monkey,.

Arshad, S., Shah, M. A., Wahid, A., Mehmood, A., Song, H., & Yu, H. (2018). SAMADroid: A novel 3-level hybrid malware detection model for android operating system. *IEEE Access : Practical Innovations, Open Solutions*, *6*, 4321–4339. doi:10.1109/ACCESS.2018.2792941

Bayazit, E. C., Sahingoz, O. K., & Dogan, B. (2022, June). A Deep Learning Based Android Malware Detection System with Static Analysis. In *2022 International Congress on Human-Computer Interaction, Optimization and Robotic Applications (HORA)* (pp. 1-6). IEEE. 10.1109/HORA55278.2022.9800057

Cai, L., Li, Y., & Xiong, Z. (2021). JOWMDroid: Android malware detection based on feature weighting with joint optimization of weight-mapping and classifier parameters. *Computers & Security*, *100*, 102086. doi:10.1016/j.cose.2020.102086

Chaudhary, G., Srivastava, S., & Khari, M. (2023). Generative Edge Intelligence for Securing IoT-assisted Smart Grid against Cyber-Threats. *International Journal of Wireless & Ad Hoc Communication*, *6*(1), 38–49. doi:10.54216/IJWAC.060104

Chaudhuri, A., Nandi, A., & Pradhan, B. (2022). *A Dynamic Weighted Federated Learning for Android Malware Classification*. arXiv preprint arXiv:2211.12874.

Deng, X., Li, Y., Weng, J., & Zhang, J. (2019). Feature selection for text classification: A review. *Multimedia Tools and Applications*, *78*(3), 3797–3816. doi:10.100711042-018-6083-5

Desnos, A., Gueguen, G., & Bachmann, S. Androguard, https://androguard.readthedocs.io/en/latest, 2018.

Dhalaria, M., & Gandotra, E. (2021). *A hybrid approach for android malware detection and family classification*. Research Gate.

Ding, C., Luktarhan, N., Lu, B., & Zhang, W. (2021). A hybrid analysis-based approach to android malware family classification. *Entropy (Basel, Switzerland)*, *23*(8), 1009. doi:10.3390/e23081009 PMID:34441149

Faruki, P., Bharmal, A., Laxmi, V., Ganmoor, V., Gaur, M. S., Conti, M., & Rajarajan, M. (2015). Android security: A survey of issues, malware penetration, and defenses. *IEEE Communications Surveys and Tutorials*, *17*(2), 998–1022. doi:10.1109/COMST.2014.2386139

Feizollah, A., Anuar, N. B., Salleh, R., Tangil, G. S., & Furnell, S. (2017). Androdialysis: Analysis of android intent effectiveness in malware detection. *Computers & Security*, *65*, 121–134. doi:10.1016/j.cose.2016.11.007

Felt, A. P., Finifter, M., Chin, E., Hanna, S., & Wagner, D. (2011). A survey of mobilemalware in the wild. In: *Proc. 1st ACM Work. Secur. Priv. smartphones Mob. devices.* ACM.

Ferri, F. J., Pudil, P., Hatef, M., & Kittler, J. (1994). Comparative study of techniques for large-scale feature selection. *Pattern Recognition in Practice*, *IV*, 403–413.

Fisher, R. A. (1992). *Statistical methods for research workers.* Springer New York. doi:10.1007/978-1-4612-4380-9_6

Fraser, G., & Arcuri, A. (2014). Automated test generation for java generics. In: *Int. Conf. Softw. Qual.* Springer.

Hadiprakoso, R. B., Kabetta, H., & Buana, I. K. S. (2020, November). Hybrid-based malware analysis for effective and efficiency android malware detection. In *2020 International Conference on Informatics, Multimedia, Cyber and Information System (ICIMCIS)* (pp. 8-12). IEEE. 10.1109/ICIMCIS51567.2020.9354315

Harvey, P. (2021). *Exiftool.* Exiftool. https://exiftool.org/.

Hou, S., Saas, A., Chen, L., & Ye, Y. (2016, October). Deep4maldroid: A deep learning framework for android malware detection based on linux kernel system call graphs. In *2016 IEEE/WIC/ACM International Conference on Web Intelligence Workshops (WIW)* (pp. 104-111). IEEE. 10.1109/WIW.2016.040

Kang, B. B. H., & Srivastava, A. (2011). Dynamic malware analysis. In *Encycl. Cryptogr. Secur* (pp. 367–368). Springer. doi:10.1007/978-1-4419-5906-5_846

Kenney, J. F., & Keeping, E. S. (1951). *Mathematics of Statistics, Pt. 2* (2nd ed.). Van Nostrand.

Khalid, S., & Hussain, F. B. (2022, May). Evaluating Dynamic Analysis Features for Android Malware Categorization. In *2022 International Wireless Communications and Mobile Computing (IWCMC)* (pp. 401-406). IEEE.

Khari, M., Dalal, R., Misra, U., & Kumar, A. (2020). AndroSet: An automated tool to create datasets for Android malware detection and functioning with WoT. *Smart Innovation of Web of Things, 187*.

Khari, M., Garg, A. K., Gandomi, A. H., Gupta, R., Patan, R., & Balusamy, B. (2019). Securing data in Internet of Things (IoT) using cryptography and steganography techniques. *IEEE Transactions on Systems, Man, and Cybernetics. Systems*, *50*(1), 73–80. doi:10.1109/TSMC.2019.2903785

Kim, T., Kang, B., Rho, M., Sezer, S., & Im, E. G. (2018). A multimodal deep learning method for Android malware detection using various features. *IEEE Transactions on Information Forensics and Security*, *14*(3), 773–788. doi:10.1109/TIFS.2018.2866319

Laricchia, F. (2023). *Mobile operating systems' market share worldwide from 1st quarter 2009 to 4th quarter 2022.* Statista. https://www.statista.com/statistics/272698/global-market-share-held-by-mobile-operating-systems-since-009/#:~:text=Android%20maintained%20its%20position%20as,the%20mobile%20operating%20system%20market

Lashkari, A. H., Kadir, A. F. A., Gonzalez, H., Mbah, K. F., & Ghorbani, A. A. (2017, August). Towards a network-based framework for android malware detection and characterization. In *2017 15th Annual conference on privacy, security and trust (PST)* (pp. 233-23309). IEEE. 10.1109/PST.2017.00035

Le, D., Kumar, R., Mishra, B. K., & Chatterjee, J. (2019). Cyber security in parallel and distributed computing: Concepts, techniques, applications and case studies. John Wiley & Sons.

Levin, D. (2021). *Strace - linux syscall tracer*. Strace. https://strace.io.

Li, J., Sun, L., Yan, Q., Li, Z., Srisaan, W., & Heng, Y. (2018). Significant permission identification for machine-learning-based android malware detection. *IEEE Transactions on Industrial Informatics*, *14*(7), 3216–3225. doi:10.1109/TII.2017.2789219

Lu, T., Du, Y., Ouyang, L., Chen, Q., & Wang, X. (2020). Android malware detection based on a hybrid deep learning model. *Security and Communication Networks*, *2020*, 2020. doi:10.1155/2020/8863617

MacKay, D. J., & Mac Kay, D. J. (2003). *Information theory, inference and learning algorithms*. Cambridge university press.

Mahdavifar, S., Kadir, A. F. A., Fatemi, R., Alhadidi, D., & Ghorbani, A. A. (2020). Dynamic android malware category classification using semi-supervised deep learning. In *2020 IEEE Intl Conf on Dependable, Autonomic and Secure Computing,* (DASC/PiCom/CBDCom/CyberSciTech). (pp. 515-522). IEEE.

Martinelli, F., Mercaldo, F., & Saracino, A. (2017, April). Bridemaid: An hybrid tool for accurate detection of android malware. In *Proceedings of the 2017 ACM on Asia conference on computer and communications security* (pp. 899-901). ACM. 10.1145/3052973.3055156

Renjith, G., & Aji, S. (2022). On-device Resilient Android Malware Detection using Incremental Learning. *Procedia Computer Science*, *215*, 929–936. doi:10.1016/j.procs.2022.12.095

Şahın, D. Ö., Akleylek, S., & Kiliç, E. (2022). LinRegDroid: Detection of Android malware using multiple linear regression models-based classifiers. *IEEE Access : Practical Innovations, Open Solutions*, *10*, 14246–14259. doi:10.1109/ACCESS.2022.3146363

Sihag, V., Vardhan, M., Singh, P., Choudhary, G., & Son, S. (2021). De-LADY: Deep learning based Android malware detection using Dynamic features. *J. Internet Serv. Inf. Secur.*, *11*(2), 34–45.

Surendran, R., Thomas, T., & Emmanuel, S. (2018). *Detection of malware applications in an- droid smartphones*. World Sci Book Chapter.

Surendran, R., Thomas, T., & Emmanuel, S. (2020). A TAN based hybrid model for android malware detection. *Journal of Information Security and Applications*, *54*, 102483. doi:10.1016/j.jisa.2020.102483

Tong, F., & Yan, Z. (2017). A hybrid approach of mobile malware detection in Android. *Journal of Parallel and Distributed Computing*, *103*, 22–31. doi:10.1016/j.jpdc.2016.10.012

Türker, S., & Can, A. B. (2019). Andmfc: Android malware family classification framework. In *2019 IEEE 30th International Symposium on Personal, Indoor and Mobile Radio Communications (PIMRC Workshops)* (pp. 1-6). IEEE.

Wagner, D., & Dean, R. (2001). Intrusion detection via static analysis. In: *Secur. Privacy,. S&P 2001. Proceedings.* IEEE. 10.1109/SECPRI.2001.924296

Wang, W., Ren, C., Song, H., Zhang, S., & Liu, P. (2022). FGL_Droid: An Efficient Android Malware Detection Method Based on Hybrid Analysis. *Security and Communication Networks, 2022*, 2022. doi:10.1155/2022/8398591

Yang, Y., Wei, Z., Xu, Y., He, H., & Wang, W. (2018). Droidward: An effective dynamic analysis method for vetting android applications. *Cluster Computing, 21*(1), 265–275. doi:10.100710586-016-0703-5

Yerima, S. Y., & Sezer, S. (2018). Droidfusion: A novel multilevel classifier fusion approach for android malware detection. IEEE transactions on cybernetic. IEEE.

Zhang, R., Huang, S., Qi, Z., & Guan, H. (2011). Combining static and dynamic analysis to dis- cover software vulnerabilities. In: *Innov. Mob. Internet Serv. Ubiquitous Com- put. (IMIS), Fifth Int. Conf.* IEEE.

Zhang, R., Huang, S., Qi, Z., & Guan, H. (2012). Static program analysis assisted dynamic taint tracking for software vulnerability discovery. *Computers & Mathematics with Applications (Oxford, England), 63*(2), 469–480. doi:10.1016/j.camwa.2011.08.001

Zhu, H. J., You, Z. H., Zhu, Z. X., Shi, W. L., Chen, X., & Cheng, L. (2018). DroidDet: Effective and robust detection of android malware using static analysis along with rotation forest model. *Neurocomputing, 272*, 638–646. doi:10.1016/j.neucom.2017.07.030

Chapter 13

Identifying and Assessing Risk Factors to Lower Hazards in Cyber Security Penetration Testing

Mayukha Selvaraj

https://orcid.org/0000-0002-3463-2722

Bharathiar University, India

R. Vadivel

https://orcid.org/0000-0001-9684-909X

Bharathiar University, India

ABSTRACT

Penetration testing is a rapidly growing field. In today's technological exposure to cyber-attacks, there is a need for easily understandable metrics of cyber-attacks and the impact that it causes on enterprises. The measurement metrics are significant challenges in assessing a cyber-crime incident or a penetration testing audit. There are so many factors in the cyber security field that a penetration tester must consider determining the risk of a particular event or attack. Without any measurement or metrics, there is a chance that the pentesters or penetration testing can get stuck in a bottomless pit without arriving at a defined result. A tool called CVSS attempts to calculate risk based on specific parameters. There are complex technicalities involved in arriving at a risk index to be understood by the board members of an enterprise to make an informed decision about the enterprise's cyber security plan.

INTRODUCTION

Cyber security is the need of the hour in today's technological world. Everything and everyone are connected. Therefore, the exposure of everyone right from a newborn baby whose details are entered into a hospital management system that is connected to the internet to a death of a person which is recorded

DOI: 10.4018/978-1-6684-9317-5.ch013

by a government administrative software is inevitable. To make cyberspace more secure, cyber security experts and Chief Information Security Officers (CISOs) everywhere are contributing and fighting unknown and undiscovered threats and threat actors all the time. The information security team everywhere has faced a challenge in conveying the processes and threats behind the systems and inside the wires to the decision-makers or management board. Since it is almost impossible for anyone outside of the cyber security field to fathom the seriousness and the impact of any cyber threat, it is the responsibility of the information security officers that are employed in an enterprise to clarify and make the management board or decision-makers understand the risks involved and take the necessary mitigation steps to minimalize or prevent the risks of the cyber threats. The security field of IT(Klaus 2013) is a vast area that requires skill, dedication and resources, which are lacking currently. People have a general misconception that the cybersecurity field comes will have high risk and impact. But if the learning and the implementation are all done adhering to standards with understanding then it is a piece of cake which can be secured for years to come. In an increasingly interconnected digital landscape, the significance of cybersecurity cannot be overstated. Cyberattacks are a constant threat to organizations, and the consequences of a security breach can be catastrophic, ranging from financial losses to reputational damage. To fortify their defenses and safeguard their digital assets, organizations employ various security measures, one of which is cybersecurity penetration testing.

This chapter explores the critical domain of "Identifying and Assessing Risk Factors to Lower Hazards in Cyber Security Penetration Testing." Penetration testing, often referred to as ethical hacking, is a proactive approach to identifying vulnerabilities within an organization's systems, networks, and applications. However, the effectiveness of penetration testing hinges on a systematic understanding and assessment of risk factors.

In the following sections, we will delve into the fundamental concepts, methodologies, and best practices associated with identifying and assessing risk factors in cybersecurity penetration testing. We will explore how organizations can systematically pinpoint vulnerabilities, evaluate their potential impact, prioritize remediation efforts, and ultimately lower the hazards posed by cyber threats. As the cyber landscape evolves, it is imperative for organizations to adapt their risk assessment practices continually, ensuring that they remain ahead of emerging threats and vulnerabilities.

CYBER SECURITY

Cyberspace is the technology space in the digital world where everything is stored and connected. Securing this cyberspace is called cyber security. Cyber security also means protecting the data via data security (Rossouw and Johan 2013) governed by three main factors: Confidentiality, Integrity and Accessibility (CIA) as illustrated in Figure 1.1

Cyber security is a field where resources like the Chief Information Security Officer(CISOs) of an enterprise plan the defensive strategy to take care of the risks involved in business transactions of data. An enterprise that conducts business will have to share resources and data between the vendors, suppliers and customers. Once the sharing begins, the exposure starts from there. Once the exposure is initiated there come risks that the enterprise is now open to any kind of cyber-attack.

Figure 1. Cybersecurity foundation

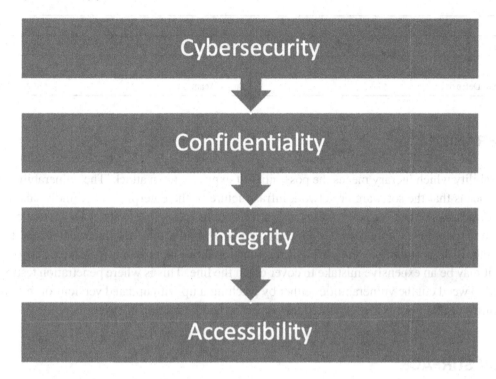

PENETRATION TESTING

Penetration Testing (Mayukha & Vadivel 2022) or often referred to as pentesting is a part of the cyber security field. Pentesting is where the enterprise or an individual who is using any kind of software or network infrastructure hires a penetration tester or pentester to penetrate the enterprise's system thereby exposing any kind of vulnerabilities that may have been in the software or network infrastructure.

PENTESTERS

Pentesters or penetration testers can be an individual or cyber security company which offers a range of services to audit and fix any vulnerabilities in the software or network infrastructure. There are various types of Pentesters as well as pentesting methods. Pentesters are the good guys. Pentesters carry out a series of processes to identify and patch vulnerabilities if any. The main factor to be included in the penetration testing is the risk factor. The risk factor plays a vital role in the field of cyber security. Any business small, medium or large is prone to cyber-attack. The businesses that do not take these kinds of attacks seriously end up losing more than just money. The Pentester's job is to minimize the risk or prevent the risk altogether if possible

There are various types of penetration testing and with it, there are various types of pentesters involved as described in Table 1. The approach with which penetration testing is carried out makes all the difference.

Table 1. Types of penetration testing and pentesters

Penetration Testing Type	Pentester Type
Defensive	Blue Team
Offensive	Red Team
Offensive & Defensive	Purple Team

VULNERABILITY

A vulnerability which literary means the possibility of exposure to an attack. The vulnerability in cyber security means that the software or network infrastructure of the enterprise or an individual has some kinds of drawbacks or bugs or errors which makes the system vulnerable to attacks from malicious hackers. When a system is designed and developed in an enterprise it must be rigorously tested for access controls etc. If the testing does not cover all the functionalities or possibilities which may or may not happen, it may be an expensive mistake to cover down the line. This is where penetration testing comes in needed to weed out the vulnerabilities either by patching it up with updated versions or mitigating the vulnerability so that even if it is exploited the impact would be minimal or zero.

ATTACK SURFACE

Attack surface in cyber security refers to the expanse of user interaction of the software or network infrastructure that is open to the public, employees or the management. Attack surface doesn't mean only the larger audience portal gets attacked because of the number of users. Though that may be true at some point, it would be only the initial access that will be done on that level. Another concept called privilege escalation comes into play when the hacker tries to escalate the access controls of the employees or the management. The hacker always goes for the root privilege so that the hacker can make the maximum impact carrying out an attack.

The attack surface today has risen exponentially because a person is always connected to the internet. The more devices that an enterprise or an individual uses, the more possibility of the attack surface. Attack surface doesn't necessarily mean that it pertains only to the software or network infrastructure of the enterprise or an individual. There are other factors such as third-party API integration for Vendors, Customers etc. If the third-party plugins or libraries are vulnerable then integrating those plugins or libraries with the enterprise's system poses more attack surface and increased vulnerability level.

EXPOSURES

Exposure happens when the system is taken online. When software or network infrastructure is deployed on the servers that are connected to the internet, it is exposed to the world. Exposure is the point where it all starts. Exposures give the malicious hackers the time and opportunity to reconnaissance and prepare for their attack. Since this all happens virtually there is no way to know about these kinds of stalking until after the attack has been initialized. There are offline exposures as well which happen due to physical reconnaissance such as eavesdropping, tailgating etc.

HACKERS

Hackers can be anyone in this world with a vengeance or a malicious intent of attacking the enterprise or an individual for monetary benefits or even for the fun of it. There are two types of hackers in general.

(a) Ethical Hackers
(b) Malicious Hackers

ETHICAL HACKERS

Ethical hackers are freelancers that work on a project basis to audit and secure an enterprise or an individual. Ethical hackers tend to stay inside the legal system thereby ethical hackers do not break the law by hacking. Before the audit, scope and contracts between the ethical hacker and the enterprise are put in place. So, anything that the ethical hacker tries to adhere to the contract is legal. The golden rule for ethical hackers is the consent of the enterprise or individual for whom the audit is being carried out. Ethical hacker often mimics the behaviours of the malicious hacker and try to enter the system by any means. Once it is successful then the ethical hacker submits the audit report along with suggestions of how that attack can be prevented in future if some malicious hacker tends to exploit it.

MALICIOUS HACKERS

Malicious hackers are any individual or group that performs cyber-attacks on an enterprise or individual for personal gain or monetary gain. Malicious hackers can target certain people and attack or let loose some trojan or malware like ransomware and get benefitted when the victims transfer bitcoins to their wallets. In the case of ransomware, there is no specific group of targets. Almost all the countries in the world fell prey to ransomware attacks. Following this, there has been an increased malware deployment like ransomware. Malicious hackers are like any other criminals, except instead of physically breaking the law by committing some physical crime, these malicious hackers get into the systems and wires virtually and do anything because as of the present situation there aren't enough cyber security engineers that can thwart the plans of the malicious hackers.

EXPLOITS

When hackers meet vulnerabilities, exploits happen. Hackers are persistent beings. There is a reason why any hacker is willing to break the law to gain something monetary or to boost one's ego. It is because the hackers stop at nothing. If not this way, another way will be exploited. Cyber security requires equally bull-headed persons to secure the systems and would stop at nothing to take down or find the person responsible for the attack. The hackers exploit without worry because at a click of starting the VPN the hackers become almost impossible to identify. Exploits are vulnerabilities that are not patched up. Coincidentally, some malicious hackers find those vulnerabilities and launch a stream of attacks to penetrate the system and gain access to the data as described in the flow of the hack of an enterprise in Figure 2.

Figure 2. Flow of hack of an enterprise

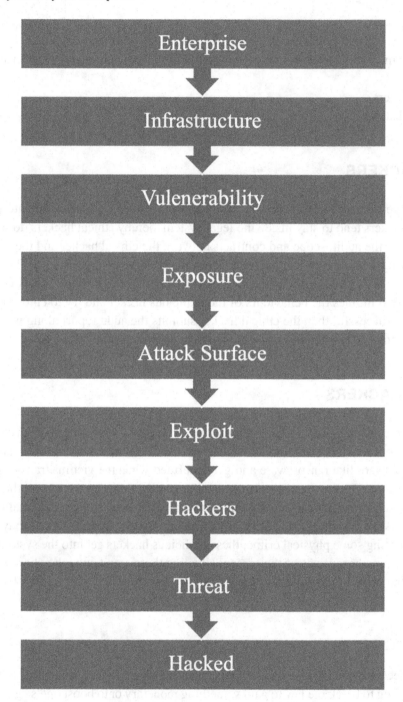

Unless and until some monitoring system is in place for the system that sweeps for exploits there is no way for the enterprise or an individual to know that such an exploit has taken place. This gives the hackers even more time to penetrate the system deeper and laterally get into all the sub-systems that are present in the system. This is far more dangerous because the hacker's presence inside the system is unknown to the enterprise, which complicates things. One fine day after gathering enough data and intel on everything and backing up everything as a personal copy, the malicious hacker launches a series of attacks against the enterprise. This would be the end of the enterprise either financially or in reputation. This exact scenario happened to the global enterprise of sony pictures in 2014.

Here's a brief description of key aspects related to exploits:

Vulnerabilities Exploits target vulnerabilities, which are security flaws or weaknesses in software, hardware, or configurations. These vulnerabilities can result from programming errors, misconfigurations, or unpatched software.

Malicious Intent Exploits are used with malicious intent. Hackers and cybercriminals employ exploits to breach systems, often for financial gain, data theft, espionage, or causing disruption.

Delivery Mechanisms Exploits can be delivered through various means, including malicious emails, websites, or network attacks. These delivery methods aim to trick or force users or systems to execute the exploit code.

Payloads Exploits typically include a payload, which is the malicious code or script that runs once the vulnerability is successfully exploited. Payloads can perform actions such as installing malware, stealing data, or taking control of the compromised system.

Zero-Day Exploits Zero-day exploits target vulnerabilities that are not yet known to the software vendor or the public. These are especially dangerous because there are no available patches or fixes, making them highly effective for attackers.

Exploit Kits Some attackers use pre-packaged exploit kits that contain multiple exploits for various vulnerabilities. These kits streamline the process of launching attacks, making them more accessible to a wider range of threat actors.

Patch Management One of the primary defenses against exploits is keeping systems and software up to date with security patches and updates. Timely patch management can mitigate the risk of known vulnerabilities being exploited.

Ethical Use In ethical hacking and cybersecurity, professionals may also use exploits in a controlled and authorized manner as part of penetration testing or vulnerability assessment to identify weaknesses and help organizations strengthen their security defenses.

Overall, exploits are a significant cybersecurity concern, and organizations must employ robust security measures, such as regular patching, intrusion detection systems, and security awareness training, to defend against these threats and protect their digital assets from unauthorized access and compromise.

THREATS

Threats (Thakur, Qiu, Gai and Ali 2015) are defined as exploiting vulnerabilities. Before the hackers get a chance to exploit the vulnerability in the attack surface, the pentesters have to identify the threat and neutralize it. Any threat if identified by the pentesters, can launch a series of defensive strategies to minimalize the impact of the threat should it ever be exploited. Any possible way of exploiting is a threat to the system. Identifying and resolving these threats is the responsibility of the enterprise with the help of a pentester. This opens up a new and upcoming stream inside cyber security called threat modelling.

THREAT MODELLING

Threat modelling is the process of refining a software or network infrastructure by identifying exposure and vulnerabilities which are considered threats and taking the necessary steps to mitigate those threats. Threat modelling also covers the process of countermeasures that has to be taken in the event of any threat. Threat modelling is one way to identify the weaknesses in the enterprise's system and convey it in quantifiable measures to the management. Thus, with these threat modelling techniques, necessary actions can be taken to mitigate those threats. In the scope of this chapter, threat modeling serves as an invaluable framework for understanding and addressing potential hazards associated with the penetration testing process itself, as well as the broader implications for an organization's security posture.

Threat modeling involves a structured analysis of various elements, including:

Assets Identifying and categorizing the digital assets that require protection. This can encompass data, applications, networks, and critical infrastructure elements relevant to penetration testing.

Attack Vectors Examining potential attack vectors and entry points that threat actors could exploit to compromise the integrity, confidentiality, or availability of assets. In the context of penetration testing, understanding these attack vectors is vital for simulating real-world scenarios.

Vulnerabilities Identifying known and potential vulnerabilities within the systems and applications under scrutiny. This includes both technical vulnerabilities (e.g., software flaws) and human-related vulnerabilities (e.g., social engineering).

Threat Actors Evaluating potential threat actors, their motivations, capabilities, and tactics. In penetration testing, this may involve simulating the actions of malicious actors to uncover vulnerabilities from an attacker's perspective.

Risk Assessment Assessing the risks associated with identified threats and vulnerabilities. This includes evaluating the likelihood of an exploit and the potential impact on the organization.

Countermeasures Developing countermeasures and mitigation strategies to reduce the risks associated with identified threats. These countermeasures can include technical controls, policy changes, and security awareness training.

Documentation Thoroughly documenting the threat modeling process, findings, and recommended mitigation steps. Documentation ensures transparency, facilitates communication with stakeholders, and provides a basis for tracking progress and compliance.

Iterative Process Recognizing that threat modeling is not a one-time activity but an iterative process that evolves as the organization's technology stack, threat landscape, and regulatory environment change.

In this chapter, we will explore how organizations can effectively apply threat modeling techniques to penetration testing scenarios. By doing so, organizations can gain a deeper understanding of the potential risks associated with their security testing efforts and develop targeted strategies to lower those hazards. Threat modeling serves as a proactive framework that complements the penetration testing process, helping organizations stay one step ahead of cyber threats and maintain a resilient security posture.

THREAT ACTORS

In the world of threat modelling, any person or group that threatens an enterprise or an individual is known as a threat actor (Giri 2019). Identifying a threat actor is very important. Once the threat actor is identified then a pentester can identify the associated risks with that threat actor. Once this mapping is done, then the pentester can proceed with necessary actions that can be taken to mitigate the risks that can be potentially caused by the threat actor. There are various kinds of threat actors, even employees or employees with the admin privilege can also be taken as a threat actor in case there is a scenario when some malicious hacker gains access to that employee's account and spoof their control access.

THREAT ASSESSMENT

Threat assessment is the evaluation of the possible event of attacks from any person or vulnerability in the system. So, to measure any risk in an enterprise, a threat assessment has to be done by the pentester. Threats play a vital role in assessing the risk thereby impacting the actions that have to be taken to mitigate the risk. The threats are analysed and indexed according to the following major categories

- Actual Threat
- Inherent Threat
- Potential Threat

Classification of the threats can lead to actual quantification of the risk that is involved with each threat. With this, the management board of an enterprise can take an informed decision about the possibility of a threat and the associated mitigation strategy (Mayukha & Vadivel 2021) of that threat. This goes a long way in helping secure an enterprise from possible attacks which could save face and millions of rupees for the enterprise.

EXISTING RISK INDEXING IN CYBER SECURITY

Risk indexing in cyber security has always been a qualitative analysis rather than a quantitative one. Many experts believe that in the field of cyber security one doesn't have enough data or the data is too volatile to analyse objectively and predict what is going to be the future of any enterprise in the terms of cyber security. Though there are many organisations such as MITRE, NIST and OWASP that have been fighting against the attacks by spreading awareness of the possible attacks and the necessary mitigations that can be done to reduce the risk, Cyber security officers and enthusiasts still face a conundrum in explaining all these threats, vulnerabilities and the potential losses that the enterprise can face in the event of an attack to the management board. It is not that non-IT people cannot understand the issues and scenarios of cyber security settings. It is that security officials are not able to label a measure on these attacks that may or may not happen to the enterprise thereby rendering this useless and an unwanted expense on the enterprise's budget. But due to the recent rise in cyber-attacks that have been terrorising people all over the world, even non-IT people could understand the consequences of unsecured or exposed software or network infrastructure.

Risk indexing in cyber security has always been classifying the severity of risk in the event of a cyber-attack into four categories. Those four categories are as below:

- Low
- Medium
- High
- Extreme

The main aim of the pentesters is to index risks according to the threats. Then the mitigation strategy aims to reduce the severity of risks that are faced by the enterprise to the category low from the other two categories. That is all that past risk indexing was all about. There was no quantifying metric in which the pentester could convey this would be the cost of the attack if the mitigation is not in place or this would be the cost of implementing the mitigation and when comparing the two the management can make the right decision rather than crossing the expensive cyber security budget immediately due to non-availability of clear data statistics.

RISK RATING MATRIX

The traditional model of rating the risks into one of the three categories against the likelihood of the attack was not working. No matter whether this model was adopted by the majority of the industry, it wasn't the correct way of rating the risk of cyber threats which could make a reasonable impact in securing an enterprise. Table 2. represents the risk matrix that is adopted widely by security experts all over the world.

Table 2. Existing risk rating matrix in cyber security

Risk Rating		Severity			
		Acceptable	Tolerable	Undesirable	Intolerable
Likelihood	Improbable	Low	Medium	Medium	High
	Possible	Low	Medium	High	Extreme
	Probable	Medium	High	High	Extreme

CVSS

CVSS is the acronym for Common Vulnerability Scoring System. This was developed by the research team National Infrastructure Advisory Council (NIAC) and launched the CVSS 1.0 in the year Feb 2005. After that NIAC in April 2005 delegated the Forum of Incident Response and Security Teams (FIRST) to head the CVSS tool for future development. The CVSS tool is for measuring the severity index of any given to assess the vulnerabilities in any system. This was accepted as a quantifiable metric for the vulnerability.

Over the years the CVSS tool has undergone so many changes to adapt to the challenging issues of the cyber security field. The CVSS is an industry-accepted standard for assessing vulnerability. The CVSS tool is the third version now. The acceptable parameters for the CVSS tools are as follows

- Base Score Metrics
- Temporal Score Metrics
- Environmental Score Metrics

The base score metrics deal with the basic parameters such as

- Attack Vector - AV
- Attack Complexity - AC
- Privileges Required - PR
- User Interaction - UI
- Scope - S
- Confidentiality Impact - C
- Integrity Impact - I
- Availability Impact – A

These parameters are subjective based. So any severity of the vulnerability can be calculated. The main important thing is that the penetration tester who is auditing the system should be aware of what is in place and what is not. In the case of black box penetration testing, these details would not be available for the pentester. So in some rare cases, this might be rendered unusable until all the factors and variables are known by the pentester. This is one of the main drawbacks of the CVSS tool.

In the case of white box penetration testing. These parameters are applicable for measuring the vulnerability of the system. The explanation of the parameters are as below.

Attack Vector has 4 options - Network, Adjacent, Local, and Physical. If the vulnerability exploitation requires a network connection. Even if the attack is not launched via the network. Once the exploit happens, the malicious application sends the data over to the hacker server through the network connection then the attack vector should be selected as the network. So Attack Vector here describes how the data is transferred from a victim to the host after the successful exploit.

Attack Complexity is scored as low or high. In a scenario where the vulnerability can be exploited by the hacker anytime and anywhere then the attack complexity score is low. When any vulnerability requires an attack that is dependent on other factors out of the reach of the hacker then the attack complexity is high.

Privileges Required is scored with three options – None, Low, High. When the privileges to successfully exploit a vulnerability are not required then it is none. If a user-level privilege is required to execute the attack at the host system then the privileges required score is low. If the exploit requires administrator-level or root-level access to successfully exploit the vulnerability then the privileges required score is high.

User Interaction is scored none or required. The user interaction score is none if the attack launched by the hacker does not require any user interaction. The user interaction score is required if the attack requires user interaction to be successful. For e.g. if the user has to click on a link for the successful deployment of payload on the system then user interaction is required in this scenario.

Scope has two states that are changed and unchanged.When the exploited vulnerability affects another system logically or physically that is controlled by another application then the scope is scored as changed. If the exploit cannot alter any other programs or data then the scope remains unchanged.

Confidentiality Impact score depicts the access of data by the hacker which has three options – None, Low and High. When the exploitation of the vulnerability does not affect any data then the confidentiality option can be set to none. If the exploit can access any publicly available data of the user then the confidentiality is scored as low. If the exploit can access sensitive data then the confidentiality score is high. If the sensitive data is encrypted and stored then confidentiality can be scored as a medium in another parameter that comes under the environmental score.

Integrity Impact score describes the accuracy of the data that is stored or used. This score is validated depending on whether the data is sensitive or not. For example, any data that deals with any monetary transaction or identifying a person should have an integrity score as high. If the data is trivial to anyone such as common information from the web etc. then the integrity score can be selected as low. If the vulnerability assessment does not cover the data then the integrity score would be none.

Availability Impact describes whether the uptime of the server is crucial for the execution of the application. If cluster devices or multiple servers are run then this impact would be none. But if the application cannot run if the server is unavailable and the recovery should be done within 24 hours then the availability impact is high. If the applications can be executed without immediate availability of the server and can run for 1-5 days then the availability impact for this is medium. Even if a server is down for more than 5 days then the score is low. It all depends on the availability of the application to the users.

This covers the base score metrics of the CVSS tool. Next are the temporal metrics. The temporal metrics are described in terms of the following parameters

- Exploit code maturity - E
- Remediation level - RL
- Report Confidence – RC

The exploit code maturity has the values Not defined – if the exploit code isn't required or known, unproven that exploit exists – for zero-day payloads, proof of concept code – for working exploit codes, functional exploit exists – exists in the CVE or CWE and high. If the exploitation code (payload) is easy to acquire and the resulting impact of this code is devastating then the score for this parameter is high.

Remediation level is the recovery method that can be done for the vulnerability. This has the values described below. Not applicable – unknown status of the recovery method. official fix – when the vendor has to deploy the patch for the vulnerability, Temporary fix – when something can be done for the time being to restore the services until the official fix can come. Workaround – when the vulnerability can be overcome with an alternative process, this is mostly discouraged because vulnerability can be exploited at any time. Unavailable is the option where no recovery tasks can be done.

Report Confidence is the confidence level in the existence of the vulnerability. This level may vary depending on the existence of the vulnerability in the databases such as CVE or CWE. This parameter has the values Not defined – when it is not applicable. Unknown when the existence of the vulnerability is not known. Reasonable – might exist in the database of vulnerabilities. Confirmed – exists in the vulnerability databases.

Next are the environmental score metrics. Since any cyber vulnerability would have so many different facets to its characteristics CVSS tool has done a good job in trying to quantify the severity of the vulnerability. All these metrics are subjective. What may apply to one company's scope and objectives might not be the same for another company. The environmental score metrics are a repetition of the other metrics which are tailored for the environment of the company. For example, if the server is in the cloud it would have a different set of options rather than the generic options that are to be selected for the base and temporal metrics. The metrics involved in environmental score metrics are as below

- Attack Vector - MAV
- Attack Complexity - MAC
- Privileges Required - MPR
- User Interaction - MUI
- Scope - MS
- Confidentiality Impact - MC
- Integrity Impact - MI
- Availability Impact - MA
- Confidentiality Requirement - CR
- Integrity Requirement - IR
- Availability Requirement – AR

Except for the last three parameters, the other parameters are all the same but optional. If the severity of the vulnerability is to be quantified, using the formula given in the CVSS tool and the inputs of the user, the tool generates a percentage for the severity of the vulnerability.

DISCUSSION OF THE EXISTING METHODS

There are a lot of methods that claim that risk measurement in terms of low, medium and high is only possible. But this does not change the fact that quantification of the cyber security risk is an issue. The measurement is not accurate and cannot be explained to the decision-makers of a company. The decision-makers could not understand the risk factors due to which the decision-makers are hesitant to decide about the security implementation of the organization. The decision-makers think of cyber security as an optional commodity rather than a necessity. This causes breaches and exposure of the data to hackers. The data out there can cause more harm to the people of the world and the company also.

The decision-makers do not take the time to understand the technicality of the cyber security measures and actions to be taken for an organization. This becomes a huge problem for the CISOs in the event of any breach. Risk-measuring methods should be quantifiable so that with these metrics the decision makers can take an informed decision in the aspects of securing the organization.

So far the risk-measuring terms in cyber security are qualitative. The need for quantifiable risk detection measurements is required for understanding and betterment of security in case of any cyber-attack. The metrics should be able to convey a quantifiable measure for the following directions.

- The frequency of threat.
- The preventive measures that should be incorporated to reduce the threat percentage
- The effect of vulnerability open the organization to an exploit?

There are so many questions that can be posed for which quantifiable answers are expected by the decision-makers.

RISK MEASURING METHODS

After lots of conundrums and research, it was finally clarified by Douglas W. Hubbard, a generalist in measurement methods, and Richard Seirsen(2016), a Cyber security expert came up with "quantifiable methods to assess risk". Both authors have done a commendable job in making the readers understand how to measure anything in cybersecurity risk. Following the steps mentioned in the book, the two most important points stand out and pave the way for how to quantify cyber risk.

- Since most cyber security assessment has to be done on a hypothesis of whether the identified threat might or might not happen, the analysis of a probability should be measured subjectively rather than objectively
- Prior Data is relevant no matter how small which can be helpful in the Pentester's assumptions using the Bayesian Monte Carlo measurement (Jial, Neil and Fenton 2020;Wu,Knag and Li 2015; Ganin et al. 2020; Zhang et al. 2018; Sommestad, Ekstedt and. Johnson 200; Fielder et al. 2018; Zhang et al. 2016; Goel, Kumar and Haddow 2020)
- Quantification of risk is very much possible provided the assumptions of event and probability are relevant and on point to the threat of the subjected enterprise.

Following this quantification method, this paper suggests what kind of parameters a pentester should consider when presenting the assessment of the software or network infrastructure. This could help the pentester to quantify every threat (Kolokotronis and Shiaeles 2021) and also quantify the before and after the impact of the mitigation strategy rather than simply stating the risk category has been reduced to a low level. This opens up so many possibilities in letting the decision-makers understand the quantifiable threats and mitigation strategy and the return of mitigation as well i.e., quantifiable loss which has been reduced due to the implementation of mitigation strategy. As per Hubbard's Decision Research, the probability distribution for any risk parameter can be calculated with the formula 1 where P(r) is the Probability distribution of any given risk. The assumption of any threat event happening is based on probability given by rand(). UB is the Upper Bound Value and LB is the Lower Bound value.

$$P(r) = if\left(rand() < 0.5, lognorm.inv\left(rand(), \frac{\ln(UB) + lb(LB)}{2}, \frac{\ln(UB) - lb(LB)}{3.29} \right), 0 \right)$$

With the help of this formula one can calculate the risk in terms of percentage. This is done with the setting of lower bound value and a upper bound value. The authors have 90% confidence in the assumption of the percentage for the lower bound and upper bound values. For e.g. If an attack affects the system of a downtime for a minimum

where P(r) is the Probability distribution of any given risk. The assumption of any threat event happening is based on probability given by rand(). UB is the Upper Bound Value and LB is the Lower Bound value.

IDENTIFYING SECURITY PARAMETERS

Once the risk indexing method is sorted out next comes the conundrum of what to index for the risk. Should the pentester take into account the downtime of a threat or the denial of accessibility following an attack or some other aftermath of the attack? As described earlier, the pentesting should be subjective rather than objective. Even subjectively a pentester can face the dilemma as to which to focus on and which is irrelevant. Securing an enterprise is not an easy feat. But the Pentester's ability to what should be indexed matters here. The three pillars on which the cyber security foundation is built would be the optimal choice in assessing any threat subjectively. The foundation of cyber security is as follows

- Confidentiality
- Integrity
- Accessibility

For any threat, the pentester should be able to assess the quantity of disruption that can be caused to any of these three qualities in an enterprise. This would give a benchmark on the threats. E.g., a Denial of System (DoS) attack would disrupt the confidentiality of the enterprise by 5%, the Integrity of the enterprise by 30% and the accessibility of the enterprise by 99%. The pentester doesn't need to index all three. But whichever parameter is taken the quantification of the same parameter after the mitigation strategy should also be done. E.g., implementing one of the mitigations of DoS attacks such as detecting illegitimate traffic and blocking it at the routing level might bring down the disruption of confidentiality to 1%, integrity by 1% and accessibility also to 1% which is a huge step in almost nullifying the impact of the DoS attack. This can exponentially increase the quantifiability for assessing any threat. The GDPR policies that are enforced by the European Union cover that all enterprises should adhere to these three cores to be followed with the explicit consent of the user and the necessary logs and documentation as the data processor and data controller if called for auditing.

CONFIDENTIALITY

Confidentiality is one of the cores of cyber security. Confidentiality conveys that the system of the enterprise protects the data it holds from unauthorized disclosure or access by third parties. By this an enterprise should take steps in any event of any threat, the data from the enterprise's software or network infrastructure should never be exposed to anybody outside the intended users of the enterprise. Any threat that disrupts this can be quantified by how deep can it be affected or for how long can it be disrupted.

Confidentiality Risk is quantified by the possibility of untrusted access to the infrastructure of the enterprise. It should be as low as possible in the range of 0% - 100%.

INTEGRITY

Integrity conveys that the enterprise's software or network infrastructure is protected from unauthorized alteration of data or access. The pentester has to assess from the standpoint of whether a given threat at any given point of time compromises the integrity of the system. If yes, then for how deep or for how long till the integrity of the enterprise can be restored. All these parameters can be easily quantified.

Integrity Risk is quantified by the possibility of incorrect data offered by the infrastructure of the enterprise. It should be as low as possible in the range of 0% - 100%.

ACCESSIBILITY

Accessibility is the availability of the enterprise's software or network infrastructure for all the intended users all across the world. At no point in time should any threat deny the intended users access to the enterprise's system. If so, then the necessary mitigation should be immediately deployed to restore accessibility to the system. A threat's probability to disrupt the accessibility is also quantifiable for the period and the impact.

Accessibility Risk is quantified by the possibility of inaccessibility to the infrastructure of the enterprise. It should be as low as possible in the range of 0% - 100%.

Given that the cyber security foundation cores CIA can be used as the risk parameters for any given threat. There are a few other parameters that can guide the pentesters and management board to the right decision for threat assessment. From a cyber security POV, the three cores may be important in assessing the threat. But from a management POV, another three parameters should be taken into consideration as well so that a pentester has covered the whole nine yards from both perspectives. The three other parameters are as follows:

- Frequency
- Value
- Time

These parameters help the pentesters in convincing the decision-makers which threat can be expensive to mitigate or threat can disrupt great value etc. Understanding what exactly is conveyed in these terms of assessment is very important for a pentester.

FREQUENCY

The frequency of a threat is the likelihood of the threat happening to an enterprise. For example, a simple Nmap Scan can happen to an enterprise daily by various threat actors. This means the frequency of a Nmap scan by any threat actor scanning our system for vulnerabilities would be around 90% - 100%. So, any threat can be quantified with the help of prior data by organisations like MITRE (Mayukha & Vadivel 2023; Georgiadou, Mouzakitis and Askounis 2021) etc.

VALUE

Value conveys the cost of the enterprise in terms of monetary or reputation which would take a hit in the event of a threat. Monetary value alone is enough for value but some enterprises might consider reputation a value. Though the selection of the parameters can be done by the pentesters subjectively. The parameters specified here convey a quantifiable measure of the impact of a threat.

TIME

Time is another factor that many enterprises calculate when assessing threats. In this present age where time equals money, a pentester should be able to quantify that in case of a threat then what's the downtime or the time for recovery from the attack etc. Similar to the value parameter, the pentester can choose to factor in either the downtime or the recovery time for this parameter. This purely depends on the enterprise's choice since the assessment should be done subjectively.

MEASURING RISK

Measurement of risk is an assumption that in the event of any threat, what are the possible disruptions that can happen to an enterprise's software or network infrastructure. For categorization of the stage of an attack and to better measure and manage the risk, the process of threat can be categorized accordingly. A pentester should be well versed in the impacts of the threats. Risk measurement can be taken in three stages as well.

- Pre threat
- During threat
- Post Threat

PRE THREAT

Pre-threat is where reconnaissance of the targeted victim happens. If the enterprise had audited the software or network system for vulnerabilities and constantly monitor the access logs and activity in the system, then there is a chance that the enterprise can thwart an attack at this stage itself. If Pentester's suggestion to safeguard the enterprise involves the right set of processes then the malicious hacker wouldn't be able to gather info about the enterprise to proceed with an attack.

DURING THREAT

The threat isn't an instant process. A threat can be executed in 10 seconds or an hour or even a day. It is similar to hijacking any building and taking control of it before doing any kind of damage. It might take a while for a threat to destroy or damage an enterprise. If the enterprise is smart enough to bring in a pentester or ethical hacker to combat the situation then the impact of the threat drastically gets reduced. This can apply to almost all threats. For a few threats, there are only pre-threat and post-threats because of how fast the threats are executed and traversed inside the system of the enterprise.

POST THREAT

Even after the damage is done, there might be some possibilities to mitigate the attack if the pentester could recover any of the evidence of the attack. Post threat measures should be taken with due diligence as building the infrastructure up from infiltration is a tedious job. It would be a progressive act to investigate how and what happened so that, this kind of same threat can be avoided by others in future. The pentesters could also come up with an action plan to mitigate these kinds of threats even before happening.

If the pentester can quantify the risk parameters in these three stages as summarized in Table 3. and suggest the necessary mitigation steps, an enterprise can save face and a lot of money despite any attack. For this to become a reality, the pentester should be able to follow the prior data and events about the threat and approach it realistically based on probability followed up by the decision-makers making the right mitigation process as well.

Table 3. Summary of risk indexing factor

Phases	Parameters
Pre Threat	Confidentiality
During Threat	Integrity Accessibility
Post Threat	Frequency Value – Monetary or Reputation Time – Taken for Attack or Taken to Recover

MANAGING RISK

Managing risk in cyber security in and itself is a vast major field. In this context, managing risk covers the quantifiability of the parameters in the three stages. Risk management is an art. Some steps can be involved in managing risk in the pre-threat stage. E.g., the regular sweep of logs can alert the pentester of any suspicious login or activity before the threat actor got a chance to launch an attack on the enterprise. In the field of cyber security identifying that the enterprise is under attack is the first step in managing risk. Once the attack is discovered or identified, the impact of the attack should be assessed followed by the mitigation process.

MITIGATING RISK

Mitigation (Nicholas and Shiaeles 2021) is the process of either reducing the attack's impact or rendering the impact null by a series of incident responses to the threat. Mitigating risk happens either during the threat or post threat. Because no matter how much precaution an enterprise takes to neutralize the risk, a realistic approach would be to assume there are always unidentified risks that are even more dangerous than the identified risk. So, the enterprise should always be prepared to counteract any threat which opens up the door of threat intelligence.

GRAPHS AND DISCUSSION: ALL VALUES SHOULD BE LOW

For a case study, a risk assessment for a social engineering attack which is a common threat to an enterprise has to be performed based on assumptions and prior data from MITRE, NIST, OWASP etc., Table 4. Describes the social engineering threat risk Indexing parameters.

Table 4. Risk Index Parameters

Risk Index Parameters			
Parameters		**Description**	**Units**
Confidentiality		No. of Untrusted Access	Nos.
Integrity		Possibility of incorrect data	%
Accessibility		No. of Inaccessibility	Nos.
Frequency		No. of Probable Attacks	Days
Value	Money	Potential loss	Rs.
	Reputation	(C + I + A)/3	%
Time	For Attack	Time taken to recover from threats	Hours
	For Recovery	Time taken for the attack	Hours

Table 5. Random event generation

Random Event Probability (x)	0.00529059

The random event generation is generated by the RAND() function as described in Table 5. Table 6 furnishes the pre-threat associated risk percentage with X. Figure 3. Plots the risk parameters in the pre-threat stage.

Table 7 furnishes the during threat associated risk percentage with X. There is a difference between the LB and the UB in this stage compared to the previous stage. Figure 4. Plots the risk parameters during threat stage.

Table 8 furnishes the post threat associated risk percentage with X. Figure 5. Plots the risk parameters in the post threat stage. Comparing the three stages, the risk is lower in the pre-threat then gradually has increased to the post threat stage.

Table 6. Pre-threat risk indexing for social engineering attack

Pre Threat					
Social Engineering	**LB**	**UB**	**Probability**	**Percentage**	**Percentage Round off**
Confidentiality	5	250	1.692017259	0.676806904	1
Integrity	40	60	35.75097089	59.58495149	60
Accessibility	8	150	3.552267853	2.368178568	2
Frequency	12	100	6.670237018	6.670237018	7
Value Money	10000	100000	5284.80687	5.28480687	5
Value Reputation	-	-	-	-	21
Time Recovery	48	76	42.26350458	55.60987444	56
Time Attack	24	48	19.80772962	41.26610338	41

Figure 3. Pre-threat risk index graph

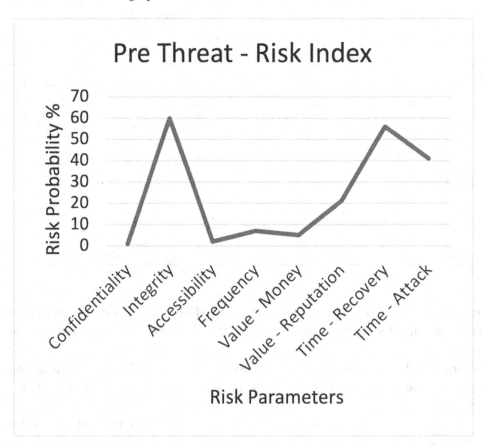

284

Table 7. During threat- risk indexing for social engineering attack

During Threat					
Social Engineering	**LB**	**UB**	**Probability**	**Percentage**	**Percentage Round off**
Confidentiality	250	500	206.3305169	41.26610338	41
Integrity	60	80	55.40473202	69.25591503	69
Accessibility	150	300	123.7983101	41.26610338	41
Frequency	100	200	82.53220675	41.26610338	41
Value Money	100000	200000	82532.20675	41.26610338	41
Value Reputation					50
Time Recovery	76	90	72.52302666	80.58114073	81
Time Attack	10	20	8.253220675	41.26610338	41

Figure 4. During threat risk index graph

Table 8. Post-threat risk indexing for social engineering attack

Post Threat					
Social Engineering	**LB**	**UB**	**Probability**	**Percentage**	**Percentage Round off**
Confidentiality	500	750	446.8871362	59.58495149	60
Integrity	80	100	75.20534978	75.20534978	75
Accessibility	300	450	268.1322817	59.58495149	60
Frequency	200	300	178.7548545	59.58495149	60
Value Money	200000	500000	155171.5869	31.03431738	31
Value Reputation					65
Time Recovery	90	120	83.10709804	69.25591503	69
Time Attack	1	10	0.528480687	5.28480687	5

Figure 5. Post-threat risk index graph

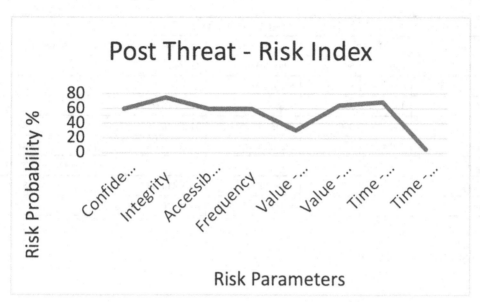

It is clear as day that if the mitigations are not initiated during the pre-threat stage itself there would be a huge loss and gap in recovering from any attack. Using this any CISO or management of an enterprise can take an informed decision about the mitigation process and implement suitable controls in place to minimalize the risk probability percentage of the parameters which the enterprise considers the most important. As mentioned earlier all the assessments of the risk should be subjective rather than objective to clearly assess the need of the enterprise.

CONCLUSION

In conclusion, identifying and assessing risk factors is an indispensable component of effective cybersecurity penetration testing. This chapter has delved into the critical aspects of this process, emphasizing the importance of a systematic and comprehensive approach to risk evaluation in the context of penetration testing. By meticulously examining potential vulnerabilities, understanding the threat landscape, and prioritizing risks, organizations can substantially lower hazards and enhance the overall security posture of their digital assets.

Risk Identification Properly identifying risks involves analyzing the organization's infrastructure, applications, and systems, as well as recognizing the potential attack vectors that threat actors might exploit. It's essential to document all identified risks systematically.

Risk Assessment Once risks are identified, a rigorous assessment is necessary. This involves evaluating the likelihood and impact of each risk, considering both the technical and business aspects. Assigning risk scores can aid in prioritizing remediation efforts.

Prioritization Not all risks are created equal, and resources are finite. Prioritizing risks based on their potential impact on the organization and the likelihood of exploitation is crucial. High-priority risks should be addressed promptly and effectively.

Holistic Approach A successful risk mitigation strategy should encompass both technical and non-technical aspects of cybersecurity. This includes addressing human factors, such as employee training and awareness, alongside technical vulnerabilities.

Continuous Improvement Cyber threats evolve continuously, making it imperative for organizations to conduct regular risk assessments and penetration testing. A static approach to risk assessment is ineffective in the ever-changing landscape of cybersecurity.

Documentation and Communication Transparent and clear documentation of the risk assessment process, findings, and recommended mitigations is vital. Effective communication with stakeholders, including executive leadership, is essential for garnering support for security initiatives.

Regulatory Compliance In many industries, compliance with regulatory standards is mandatory. A robust risk assessment process can assist in meeting these compliance requirements.

By implementing a robust risk assessment methodology and integrating it into the penetration testing process, organizations can better understand their vulnerabilities, prioritize mitigation efforts, and ultimately lower the hazards associated with cybersecurity threats. It is crucial to view risk assessment as an ongoing and adaptive process, reflective of the dynamic nature of cyber threats. In doing so, organizations can proactively safeguard their digital assets and maintain a strong defence against evolving cyber threats. Cyber threats and cyber actors have become more resilient. Cyber-attacks have reached a new level. Almost all the operations across the world are dependent on one or the other electronic device. This means that the malicious hackers have great exposure to the attack surface of any enterprise. Whether the enterprise is small, medium or big is irrelevant. If there are vulnerabilities in the system, the malicious hackers would stop at nothing to exploit it. It is up to the cyber security officers and enthusiasts to balance the scales or to secure the enterprises even more than before.

Due to the lack of understanding of measurement in cyber security, there are a lot of conundrums. The management board of the enterprises must be convinced of the threat risk and the impact of the cyber security strategy to increase the security around the enterprise's software and network infrastructure. This could help prevent cyber-attacks that cost time, money and even lives in many cases. Identifying the risk parameters and quantifying the parameters would be the right direction in understanding the impact of a threat and its mitigation.

FUTURE SCOPE

Cyber security is an ever-growing field. It has taken years to understand the impact of cyberspace attacks and even more so to fill the gap between attack and mitigation. Cyber security is not a field where assumptions and faith could save the day. It relies on hard data and statistics to prove whether a threat should be taken seriously and whether the cost of implementing the mitigation is less than the threat value itself. There are so many factors dependable on identifying, managing and mitigating the risks. A tool where for any given threat, data calculation of the parameters is automatically generated based on prior data and events would be a good way to proceed in the future direction. Another would be to assess the phases of risk before and after penetration testing to calculate the return on controls implemented by the enterprise. These parameters can be refined even more subjectively or objectively to yield even more scrutinized and secured enterprises. The future scope for the chapter on "Identifying and Assessing Risk Factors to Lower Hazards in Cyber Security Penetration Testing" encompasses several key areas that will continue to evolve and shape the field of cybersecurity:

Advanced Threat Intelligence Integration As cyber threats become more sophisticated and dynamic, the integration of advanced threat intelligence tools and platforms will be critical. Future penetration testing methodologies should leverage real-time threat data to enhance risk assessments and provide timely insights into emerging threats.

AI and Machine Learning in Risk Assessment Artificial intelligence (AI) and machine learning (ML) technologies are poised to play a significant role in risk assessment. These technologies can automate the analysis of vast datasets to identify patterns and anomalies, improving the accuracy and efficiency of risk assessments.

IoT and Cloud Security The proliferation of Internet of Things (IoT) devices and cloud computing environments introduces new attack vectors. Future penetration testing must adapt to assess the security of IoT devices, cloud services, and their interactions within complex ecosystems.

DevSecOps Integration The DevSecOps approach emphasizes integrating security into the software development lifecycle. Future penetration testing methodologies should align more closely with DevSecOps practices, ensuring that security is built in from the outset rather than bolted on afterward.

Quantitative Risk Assessment While qualitative risk assessments are valuable, the industry is moving toward more quantitative risk assessments. These assessments use metrics and data-driven approaches to provide a clearer picture of potential financial and operational impacts of security vulnerabilities.

Regulatory Changes The landscape of cybersecurity regulations and compliance standards is constantly evolving. Future penetration testing efforts will need to adapt to these changes and ensure that organizations remain compliant with relevant laws and industry-specific regulations.

Human-Centric Security As social engineering and insider threats continue to pose significant risks, future penetration testing should place greater emphasis on assessing and mitigating human-related vulnerabilities through targeted training and awareness programs.

Red and Blue Teaming Red teaming (offensive security) and blue teaming (defensive security) will continue to evolve, with more organizations adopting a collaborative approach. Future scope should explore methodologies for combining red and blue team efforts to simulate realistic attacks and defence scenarios.

Blockchain Security As blockchain technology becomes more prevalent in various industries, there will be a need to assess the security of blockchain-based systems and smart contracts. Future penetration testing methodologies should address the unique challenges posed by blockchain technology.

Ethical Considerations As penetration testing involves simulating real attacks, ethical considerations will remain paramount. Future scope should include discussions on the ethical boundaries of penetration testing and guidelines for responsible testing practices.

Global Threat Landscape Analysis The global threat landscape is interconnected, with threats originating from various regions. Future scope should involve a broader analysis of the global threat landscape and its implications for risk assessment and penetration testing.

In summary, the future scope for this chapter should encompass the continuous evolution of technology, threat landscapes, and regulatory environments. It should also emphasize the need for adaptability, automation, and collaboration to address emerging challenges in the field of cybersecurity penetration testing. Keeping pace with these developments will be essential for organizations to maintain robust security postures in an ever-changing digital landscape.

REFERENCES

Fielder, A., König, S., Panaousis, E., Schauer, S., & Rass, S. (2018). Risk Assessment Uncertainties in Cybersecurity Investments. *Games*, *9*(2), 34. doi:10.3390/g9020034

Ganin, A. A., Quach, P., Panwar, M., Collier, Z., Keisler, A., Marchese, D., & Linkov, I. (2020). Multi-criteria Decision Framework for Cybersecurity Risk Assessment and Management. *Risk Analysis*, *40*(1), 183–199. doi:10.1111/risa.12891 PMID:28873246

Georgiadou, A., Mouzakitis, S., & Askounis, D. (2021). Assessing MITRE ATT&CK Risk Using a Cyber-Security Culture Framework. *Sensors (Basel)*, *21*(9), 3267. Advance online publication. doi:10.339021093267 PMID:34065086

Giri, S. (2019). Cyber crime, cyber threat, cyber security strategies and cyber law in Nepal. *Pramana Research Journal*, *9*(3), 662–672.

Goel, R., Kumar, A., & Haddow, J. (2020). PRISM: A strategic decision framework for cybersecurity risk assessment. *Information and Computer Security*, *28*(4), 591–625. doi:10.1108/ICS-11-2018-0131

Hubbard, D. W., & Seiersen, R. (2016). *How to Measure Anything in Cybersecurity Risk*. Wiley. doi:10.1002/9781119162315

Jial, W., Neil, M., & Fenton, N. (2020). A Bayesian network approach for cybersecurity risk assessment implementing and extending the FAIR model. *Computers & Security*, *89*, 101659. Advance online publication. doi:10.1016/j.cose.2019.101659

Klaus, J. (2013). Understanding and overcoming cyber security anti-patterns. *Computer Networks*, *57*(10), 2206–2211. doi:10.1016/j.comnet.2012.11.023

Kolokotronis, N., & Shiaeles, S. (2021). *Cyber-Security Threats*. Actors, and Dynamic Mitigation.

Mayukha, S., & Vadivel, R. (2023). Reconnaissance for Penetration Testing Using Active Scanning of MITRE ATT&CK. In M. S. Kaiser, J. Xie, & V. S. Rathore (Eds.), *Information and Communication Technology for Competitive Strategies (ICTCS 2021). Lecture Notes in Networks and Systems*. Springer., doi:10.1007/978-981-19-0098-3_66

Mayukha S, Vadivel R. 2021. *Various Possible Attacks and Mitigations of the OSI Model Layers Through Pentesting – An Overview*. New Frontiers in Communication and Intelligent Systems, 799–809. Computing & Intelligent Systems, SCRS, India. doi:10.52458/978-81-95502-00-4-78

Nicholas, K., & Shiaeles, S. (Eds.). (2021). *Cyber-Security Threats, Actors, and Dynamic Mitigation*. CRC Press.

Rossouw, S., & Johan, N. (2013). From information security to cyber security. *Computers & Security*, *38*, 97–102. doi:10.1016/j.cose.2013.04.004

Sommestad, T., Ekstedt, M., & Johnson, P. (2009). Cyber Security Risks Assessment with Bayesian Defense Graphs and Architectural Models. *42nd Hawaii International Conference on System Sciences*. IEEE. 10.1109/HICSS.2009.141

Thakur, L., Qiu, M., Gai, K., & Ali, M. L. (2015). An Investigation on Cyber Security Threats and Security Models. *IEEE 2nd International Conference on Cyber Security and Cloud Computing*. IEEE. 10.1109/CSCloud.2015.71

Vadivel, R., & Mayukha, S. (2022). Port Scanning Mitigation Strategies for Penetration Testing: Blue Team Perspective, *2022 International Conference on Engineering and Emerging Technologies (ICEET)*, Kuala Lumpur, Malaysia. 10.1109/ICEET56468.2022.10007258

Wu, W., Kang, R., & Li, Z. (2015). Risk assessment method for cyber security of cyber physical systems. *First International Conference on Reliability Systems Engineering (ICRSE)*. IEEE. 10.1109/ICRSE.2015.7366430

Zhang, Q., Zhou, C., Tian, Y.-C., Xiong, N., Qin, Y., & Hu, B. (2018). A Fuzzy Probability Bayesian Network Approach for Dynamic Cybersecurity Risk Assessment in Industrial Control Systems. *IEEE Transactions on Industrial Informatics, 14*(6), 2497–2506. doi:10.1109/TII.2017.2768998

Zhang, Q., Zhou, C., Xiong, N., Qin, Y., Li, X., & Huang, S. (2016). Multimodel-Based Incident Prediction and Risk Assessment in Dynamic Cybersecurity Protection for Industrial Control Systems. *IEEE Transactions on Systems, Man, and Cybernetics. Systems, 46*(10), 1429–1444. doi:10.1109/TSMC.2015.2503399

Chapter 14
Implementation of Image Steganography and Combination of Cryptography and Steganography

S. Rashmi

Independent Researcher, India

ABSTRACT

Information transmission over the net is a very common process and securing the information plays an important role. Cryptography and Steganography are the two important techniques that provides secure transmission of data over the internet medium. Cryptography converts the data into an unreadable format, steganography is used to hide the encrypted text into any file like an audio, video, image, etc. In this paper we have explained Cryptography and Steganography as well as combined cryptography and steganography.

INTRODUCTION

Over the decade, a lot of applications based on network are discovered such as online shopping, stock trading business, net-banking and bill payment etc. These transactions take place over the connection-oriented(wired) orconnection-less/virtual connection(wireless) networks which asks for the need of secure connections, secrecy and integrity of the data.Encryption is one of the method to ensure the guaranteed way of securing the sensitive information. There are many ciphering algorithms that perform substitution and transformation of plaintext into unreadable form. This method is Cryptography. There is also way to hide the information in digital files, this process is Steganography.Steganography fails when the presence of the cipher text in the multimedia file is found out by the intruder (Shelke et al., 2014). Cryptography fails when the cipher-text is cracked by the intruder. Overall cryptography and steganography provides confidentiality of information but they have some drawbacks. Combination of both these technique results in a very powerful technique to secure data and helps in keeping it confidential (Rohmani et al., 2015).

DOI: 10.4018/978-1-6684-9317-5.ch014

LITERATURE SURVEY

Cryptography

Cryptography is the study of mathematical methods regarding information or data security such as secrecy, entity authentication, integrity of data and message's original authentication(Vishnu & Babu, 2015). The main objective is to make information impossible to read by an eavesdropper. Cryptographic algorithms are divided into symmetric and asymmetric network cryptographies (Vishnu & Babu, 2015). Symmetric algorithms are used to convert the plaintext to cipher text and cipher text to original messages (plaintext) by using the same secret key. While Asymmetric algorithms uses public-key to exchange key and then uses the secret key algorithms to ensure secrecy of stream of data (Vishnu & Babu, 2015). In asymmetric cryptography, there is are two kinds of keys, one key is public-key which is known to public, and is used to encrypt data to be sent by the sender to a receiver who owns the respective secret-key. In order for transmission to occur, secret and public keys are both different and they need to be exchanged between the sender and the receiver.

Figure 1. Encryption and decryption

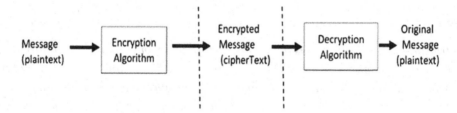

Steganography

Steganography is derived from Greek language which means "secrecy writing" (Khosravi et al., 2011). The main objective of steganography is to send sensitive information under the cover of a carrier signal. It is generally known that any

steganographic method must havethese two properties: good imperceptibility and enough data capacity (Thomas, 2014). The property ensures that the secret messages that are embedded are difficult to discover, and the second implies effective secret communication. Even though Steganography and cryptography both aim at security, but they are different. The goal of cryptography is to communicate securely by changing the data into an unreadable form that an intruder cannot understand.

METHODOLOGY

In the implementation we have made use of blowfish algorithm and AES for encrypting the plain text, and LSB algorithm and the random padding algorithm for image steganography.Initially text documents of four different sizes are encrypted using the blowfish and AES algorithm each. Then, these eight encrypted text documents were embedded into an image file with a .jpg extension. The results of the embedded image files were stored and PSNR value was calculated for the same. The LSB algorithm as well as random padding was used to implement image steganography. The main requirements include transparency, hiding capacity and robustness.

Figure 2. Steganography system model

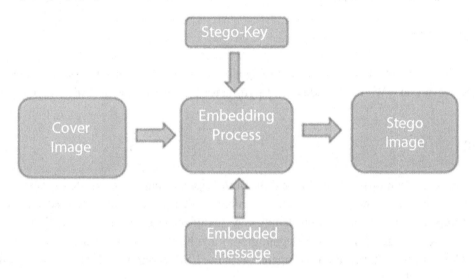

Blowfish

It is a symmetric block cipher (Singh & Malik, 2013). Since it is symmetric the same secret key is used for both encryption and decryption; the key has to be kept secret from public except for the sender and receiver. A block cipher is crypto-technique that takes any amount of plain text and converts it into cipher-text (Singh & Malik, 2013). It performs this routine on lump of text called blocks. And in order for the text to be decrypted on the receiver side, the function also generates a key to unlock the cipher-text. Variable length key is used to encrypt the text. Blowfish is used since it is fast, simple to implement and very effective.

AES

AES or Advanced Encryption Standard is one more way of encrypting the information. AES is also a symmetric block cipher; that can process data blocks of 128 bits, using the key size of 2^7 bits, 192 bits, and 2^8 bits. The AES algorithm defines different types of transformations that are performed on information. This info is stored in an array. The first step of putting the info in an array is done; then transformation is performed for a number of times. The number of rounds is determined by the length of the key. Say,14 rounds for 256-bit keys, 12 rounds for 192-bit keys and 10 rounds for 128-bit keys (Singh et al., 2011).

LSB Algorithm

LSB or Least Significant Bit Steganographic method in which the information is hidden inside an image. Here the least significant bit is replaced with the secret message. Images are made of pixels each have their own RGB values, this technique makes use of these pixels by replacing every least significant bit of every byte with the encrypted/cipher text which may or may not result in minor distortion. These distortions are not visible to naked eyes.

Random Padding

Random padding is a technique in which the image is converted in to flat array of pixels and the text is hidden in between them. We have made use of python for the implementation of steganography.

OUTPUT

Figure 3 shows the result of proposed algorithm. Both original image and the stego image after inserting the text are shown below. Table I shows the analysis of PSNR values obtained for the proposed method. Encrypted text files of different lengths are obtained by Blowfish and AES encryption. And the same files are analyzed for the two steganography methods- LSB and Random Padding. It shows Random Padding gives better result as compared with the LSB steganography algorithm for both types of encryption methods.

Figure 3. The result of cryptography and image steganography

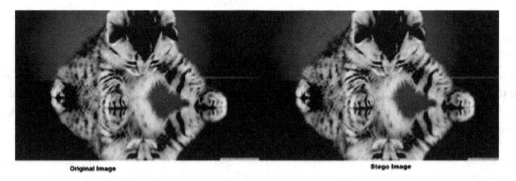

Original Image   Stego Image

CONCLUSION

In this paper we have studied about Cryptography and Steganography as well as their combination. Both Steganography and Cryptography provides security but their combination provides us with a higher security. First, we encrypt the message and then that message is embedded into an image. In this way, if an attacker tries to crack the hidden messages from the image, the combined security due to cryptography and steganography will not make it possible as it will only showcase the encrypted message; which in turn enhances the security capacity.

Table 1. PSNR values for different algorithms

Cryptographic Algorithm	Blowfish		AES	
Hiding Algorithm	LSB	Random Padding	LSB	Random Padding
File Size				
20kb	43.38	54.36	38.51	49.39
40kb	43.37	54.35	38.51	49.39
60kb	43.36	54.34	38.50	49.38
80kb	43.36	54.33	38.50	49.38

REFERENCES

Khosravi, S., Dezfoli, M. A., & Yektaie, M. H. (2011). A new steganography method based HIOP (Higher Intensity Of Pixel)algorithm and Strassen's matrix multiplication. *Journal of Global Research in Computer Science, 2*(1).

Rohmani, K., & Goyal, A. K., & Mudgal, M. (2015). Study of Cryptography and Steganography System. *International Journal of Engineering and Computer Science, 4*(8), 2319-7342

Shelke, F., Dongre, A., Soni, P. (2014). Comparison of Different techniques for steganography in images. *International Journal of Application or Innovation in Engineering And Management, 3*(2).

Singh, A. & Malik, S. (2013). Securing Data by Cryptography with Steganography", *International Journal of Advanced Research in Computer Science and Software Engineering, 3*(5).

Singh, G., Singla, ASandha, K. (2011). Cryptography Algorithm Comparison forSecurity Enhancement in Wireless Intrusion DetectionSystem. *International Journal of MultidisciplinaryResearch, 1*(4), 143-151, August.

Thomas, P. (2014). Literature Survey on Modern Image Steganographic Techniques. *International Journal of Engineering Research and Technology, Vol 2,* Issue 5, May, ISSN 2278-0181

Vishnu, S. & Babu, H. (2015). A Study on combined Cryptography and Steganography. *International Journal of Research Studies in Computer Science and Engineering, 2*(5).

Chapter 15
Managing Cyber Threats in the Age of Technology:
The Role of Risk Detection and Cyber Security

R. Shobarani

ⓘ https://orcid.org/0000-0003-0183-3867

Dr. M.G.R. Educational and Research Institute, India

Chitrakala Muthuveerappan

Victoria University of Wellington, New Zealand

I. Sujiban

Dr. M.G.R. Educational and Research Institute, India

K. SuryaPrakhash

SRM University, India

S. Pratheepa

J.H.A. Agarsen College, India

M. J. Bharathi

St. Thomas College of Arts and Science, India

ABSTRACT

This chapter highlights the importance of risk detection and cybersecurity in modern computing systems. As technology continues to advance, these components become increasingly critical for ensuring the successful operation of these systems. The chapter suggests that failure to properly address these issues can result in serious consequences, including the compromise of sensitive information and the disruption of critical systems. Therefore, it is essential for organizations to prioritize risk detection and cybersecurity as a foundational element of their computing infrastructure.

DOI: 10.4018/978-1-6684-9317-5.ch015

1. INTRODUCTION

In today's era of technology, computing has become an integral part of our lives. From online banking to social media, we use computing for a variety of tasks on a daily basis. However, with the increasing use of technology, there has also been an increase in cyber threats and risks. In order to ensure the success of contemporary computing, it is essential to have robust risk detection and cyber security measures in place.

With the rapid advancement of technology, cybersecurity has become an increasingly important concern for individuals and organizations. Cyber threats such as hacking, phishing, and malware attacks are becoming more sophisticated and frequent, and organizations must implement effective risk detection and cybersecurity measures to protect themselves from these threats. In this article, we will explore the role of risk detection and cybersecurity in managing cyber threats in the age of technology.

Cyber security is the practice of protecting electronic devices, systems, and networks from unauthorized access, theft, and damage to information. It encompasses a wide range of technologies, processes, and practices that are designed to prevent and mitigate cyber threats. Risk detection, on the other hand, involves the identification of potential threats and vulnerabilities in a system, which can then be addressed through appropriate security measures.

There are several reasons why risk detection and cyber security are critical for the success of contemporary computing. First and foremost, cyber threats can result in significant financial losses and reputational damage. For example, a data breach can result in the theft of sensitive information, which can then be used for malicious purposes such as identity theft or financial fraud. Such incidents can have a significant impact on the affected individuals, as well as the organizations that are responsible for protecting their data.

Secondly, cyber threats can also disrupt business operations, leading to significant downtime and loss of productivity. For example, a ransomware attack can encrypt critical files, rendering them inaccessible and disrupting business operations until the ransom is paid. In some cases, even after paying the ransom, the data may still be lost, resulting in further downtime and costs.

In order to address these risks and ensure the success of contemporary computing, it is essential to have robust risk detection and cyber security measures in place. These measures can include a range of technologies, processes, and practices, such as firewalls, antivirus software, intrusion detection systems, vulnerability assessments, and incident response plans.

One of the most critical components of risk detection and cyber security is education and awareness. Employees and users must be educated about the risks and best practices for using electronic devices, systems, and networks. This can include training on topics such as password management, phishing awareness, and data protection.

Another essential component is the adoption of best practices and standards in cyber security. For example, the National Institute of Standards and Technology (NIST) has developed a Cybersecurity Framework, which provides a set of guidelines and best practices for organizations to follow. Adhering to such frameworks and standards can help organizations to identify and mitigate risks more effectively.

In the age of technology, managing cyber threats has become a critical aspect of any organization's operations. The increasing reliance on digital systems and the interconnectedness of networks have created new vulnerabilities and opportunities for malicious actors to exploit. In this context, risk detection and cyber security play crucial roles in safeguarding sensitive information, protecting infrastructure, and mitigating the impact of cyber attacks.

Risk detection involves identifying potential vulnerabilities and threats to an organization's digital assets. This can be achieved through various methods such as risk assessments, vulnerability scans, penetration testing, and threat intelligence gathering. By understanding the potential risks, organizations can prioritize their security efforts and allocate resources effectively to mitigate those risks. For example, a financial institution might conduct regular vulnerability scans on its network to identify weak points that hackers could exploit to gain unauthorized access to customer data.

Cyber security encompasses the measures and practices employed to protect systems, networks, and data from unauthorized access, disruption, or damage. It involves a range of technical, administrative, and physical controls designed to secure information and maintain the integrity of digital assets. Examples of cyber security measures include firewalls, intrusion detection systems, encryption, multi-factor authentication, security awareness training for employees, and incident response plans. For instance, an e-commerce platform may implement encryption protocols to protect customers' credit card information during online transactions.

Phishing and Social Engineering: These attacks involve tricking individuals into revealing sensitive information or performing actions that could compromise their security. Phishing emails, fake websites, and social media scams are common examples.

Credential Stuffing and Brute Force Attacks: Cybercriminals use automated tools to attempt login credentials obtained from data breaches on various websites and services, hoping that users reuse passwords across multiple accounts.

Business Email Compromise (BEC): BEC attacks involve impersonating executives or high-level employees to deceive employees into performing fraudulent actions, such as making unauthorized wire transfers.

Cloud Security Risks: With the increasing adoption of cloud services, security risks associated with misconfigurations, weak authentication, and insecure APIs have become more prominent. Unauthorized access to cloud resources and data breaches are common consequences of cloud security vulnerabilities.

One example of the role of risk detection and cyber security is seen in the defense sector. Governments and military organizations face sophisticated cyber threats from state-sponsored actors and hackers seeking to gain access to classified information or disrupt critical infrastructure. Risk detection techniques, such as continuous monitoring and threat intelligence analysis, are used to identify potential vulnerabilities and proactively respond to emerging threats. Cyber security measures are implemented to secure classified networks, safeguard sensitive data, and ensure the reliability of communication systems.

Another example is the financial industry, where risk detection and cyber security are of paramount importance. Banks and financial institutions handle vast amounts of sensitive customer data, making them attractive targets for cyber criminals. Risk detection methods, including penetration testing and security audits, help identify vulnerabilities in banking systems and prevent potential breaches. Cyber security measures, such as secure authentication protocols and real-time transaction monitoring, are employed to protect customer accounts, prevent fraud, and ensure the integrity of financial transactions.

In summary, risk detection and cyber security play vital roles in managing cyber threats in the age of technology. They help organizations identify vulnerabilities, proactively respond to emerging threats, and protect digital assets from unauthorized access, disruption, or damage. By implementing robust risk detection practices and comprehensive cyber security measures, organizations can enhance their resilience against cyber attacks and safeguard the trust of their stakeholders.

2. RELATED WORKS

K. Zarrineh and S. Raza (2016) provides an overview of the challenges and risks associated with modern computing, including the rise of cyber threats and the need for effective risk detection and cyber security measures.

M. Abdel-Aziz, M. Al-Eroud, and F. Alsulaiman (2019) provides a comprehensive review of various cybersecurity frameworks, standards, and guidelines, including the NIST Cybersecurity Framework, ISO/IEC 27001, and PCI DSS.

F. Gao, Y. Liao, and Y. Tao (2020) provides a review of the cybersecurity risks and best practices in the context of smart manufacturing, including the need for risk detection and cyber security measures to protect critical infrastructure.

S. Kaur and P. Bansal (2020) provides a survey of machine learning techniques for cybersecurity applications, including the use of machine learning for risk detection and intrusion detection.

Alqahtani, S., & Khan, M. K. (2020) Provides a systematic review that summarizes the use of machine learning techniques in intrusion detection systems. The authors reviewed a number of studies and highlighted the strengths and weaknesses of different machine learning approaches in this area.

Y. Albalawi, M. Aldossary, and A. Alghamdi (2020) highlights the unique cybersecurity challenges faced by healthcare systems and discusses research and development trends in addressing these challenges. It emphasizes the importance of secure data sharing, secure communication, and employee training.

S. Gupta, S. Kapoor, and D. Sharma (2020) provides a systematic literature review of blockchain technology's applications in cybersecurity and privacy. It covers topics such as secure data sharing, identity management, and secure communication.

S. S. Sood, S. Kaur, and A. J. Singh (2021) highlights the threat posed by social engineering attacks and discusses best practices for preventing these attacks. It emphasizes the importance of employee training, phishing awareness, and incident response planning.

A. R. Awan, R. N. Akhtar, and Z. A. Khan (2021) discusses the potential applications of quantum computing in cybersecurity and highlights the challenges associated with quantum computing's implementation. It emphasizes the need for research and development in quantum-resistant cryptography and the importance of post-quantum security protocols.

S. S. Kaur, G. S. Brar, and S. S. Jha (2022) discusses the unique cybersecurity challenges posed by cloud computing and highlights the need for a comprehensive security strategy that includes data security, network security, and cloud service provider security. It emphasizes the importance of threat intelligence, risk assessment, and incident response planning.

Christopher T. Johnson, Aaron M. French, William R. Rose (2017) proposes a framework for assessing cybersecurity risks in supply chains, considering factors such as vulnerabilities, threats, and impacts. It provides insights into managing cyber risks within complex supply chain networks.

Ugochukwu Chinonso Okoroafor, Hongmei Chi, Andrew N. Smith (2018) discusses the limitations of vulnerability scanning as the sole approach to cybersecurity risk assessment and highlights the need for a more comprehensive approach. It presents a methodology that integrates threat intelligence, vulnerability assessment, and attack simulation to improve risk assessment accuracy.

Aaron F. Brantly, Karen Renaud, Marianthi Theoharidou (2016) discusses the importance of incident response planning in managing cyber threats effectively. It presents insights from a large-scale cybersecurity exercise and provides recommendations for developing and testing incident response plans.

Steve C. Oney, Frank S. Lineberry, David A. Dampier (2018) focuses on insider cyber attacks and proposes effective measures for preventing and responding to such threats. It discusses the role of access controls, monitoring systems, training programs, and incident response plans in mitigating insider threats.

Timothy C. Tobin, Robert S. Zapata, Neil C. (2017) explores the role of cyber threat intelligence in enhancing cybersecurity capabilities. It discusses the collection, analysis, and utilization of threat intelligence and provides recommendations for organizations to establish mature cybersecurity programs

These papers provide a good starting point for further research on the topic of risk detection and cyber security for the success of contemporary computing. They highlight the importance of effective risk detection and cyber security measures in protecting electronic devices, systems, and networks from cyber threats, and provide insights into various technologies, processes, and best practices that can be used to mitigate these risks.

3. RISK DETECTION IMPLEMENTATION

Risk detection is the process of identifying potential risks and vulnerabilities in an organization's systems, infrastructure, and processes. This is an essential step in managing cyber threats, as it enables organizations to identify and mitigate potential risks before they can be exploited by cybercriminals. There are several ways that organizations can implement risk detection:

Vulnerability Assessments: Vulnerability assessments involve testing an organization's systems, infrastructure, and processes to identify potential vulnerabilities that can be exploited by cybercriminals. These assessments can be conducted by internal teams or external consultants and can help organizations prioritize their cybersecurity efforts. An organization might hire an external cybersecurity consultant to conduct a vulnerability assessment of their network infrastructure. The consultant would use specialized tools and techniques to identify potential weaknesses in the organization's systems and processes, such as outdated software versions or misconfigured settings. Based on the results of the assessment, the organization could prioritize their cybersecurity efforts and take steps to address the identified vulnerabilities.

Penetration Testing: Penetration testing involves simulating a cyber attack on an organization's systems to identify potential weaknesses and vulnerabilities. This can help organizations identify weaknesses in their cybersecurity defenses and improve their overall security posture. A company might hire a team of ethical hackers to conduct a penetration test of their website. The hackers would simulate a cyber attack on the website to identify potential weaknesses in its security defenses, such as a lack of encryption or weak password policies. The company could then use the results of the penetration test to improve their website security and prevent future attacks.

Threat Intelligence: Threat intelligence involves monitoring and analyzing the latest cyber threats and trends to identify potential risks to an organization's systems. An organization might subscribe to a threat intelligence service that monitors the latest cyber threats and trends. The service would provide regular reports and updates on potential risks and vulnerabilities to the organization's systems. For example, if the service detected a new type of malware that was targeting a specific software application, the organization could proactively take steps to mitigate the risk, such as updating their antivirus software or implementing additional security control.

Real-time examples of risk detection methods in action:

Vulnerability Assessments: In 2017, Equifax suffered a massive data breach that exposed the personal information of over 140 million individuals. The breach was caused by a vulnerability in the company's website software that could have been easily identified and patched with a vulnerability assessment. Equifax later faced significant backlash and financial penalties for its failure to adequately prioritize its cybersecurity efforts.

Penetration Testing: In 2020, Microsoft conducted a penetration test of its Azure cloud computing platform. The test simulated a cyber attack on the platform and identified several vulnerabilities in its security defences. Microsoft used the results of the test to improve its security controls and prevent future attacks. Penetration testing, also known as ethical hacking, involves simulating real-world cyber attacks to identify vulnerabilities in an organization's systems and networks. This proactive approach helps organizations understand their security weaknesses and take appropriate measures to mitigate the identified risks.

Threat Intelligence: In 2021, the SolarWinds supply chain attack exposed several US government agencies and private companies to significant cyber risks. In late 2020, it was discovered that sophisticated hackers compromised SolarWinds, a leading IT management software provider, to distribute a trojanized software update. This update, when installed by SolarWinds customers, allowed the attackers to gain unauthorized access to the networks of numerous organizations, including government agencies and major technology companies. The attack highlighted the risks associated with supply chain vulnerabilities and the potential for wide-reaching impact.

In the wake of the attack, threat intelligence services were used to monitor the spread of the malware and identify potential risks to other organizations. This allowed organizations to proactively take steps to prevent the spread of the malware and protect their systems from future attacks.

Target Data Breach (2013): In one of the most high-profile data breaches, hackers gained unauthorized access to Target's network through a third-party vendor's compromised credentials. Target had an Intrusion Detection System (IDS) in place, which generated alerts when the attackers started moving laterally within the network. Unfortunately, these alerts were not adequately investigated, and the breach continued, resulting in the theft of millions of customer payment card details. This incident highlights the importance of not only having risk detection measures but also ensuring that proper response procedures are in place to address detected threats.

WannaCry Ransomware Attack (2017): The WannaCry ransomware attack spread rapidly worldwide, targeting vulnerable systems with unpatched Windows operating systems. Organizations utilizing effective vulnerability management and threat intelligence platforms were able to detect and respond to the attack promptly. By actively monitoring the threat landscape and promptly applying security patches, organizations minimized the impact of the attack and prevented the encryption of their systems.

Kaseya Ransomware Attack (2021)

The Kaseya cyber attack that occurred in July 2021, targeted a software company called Kaseya, which provides remote management and monitoring services to managed service providers (MSPs). The attackers exploited a vulnerability in the company's software called VSA (Virtual System Administrator) to deploy ransomware on the networks of numerous MSPs and their clients.

The attack affected an estimated 1,500 organizations worldwide, leading to service disruptions and, in some cases, data breaches. The attackers demanded a ransom in exchange for a decryptor tool to restore the encrypted files. This incident highlighted the potential impact of supply chain attacks and the wide-reaching consequences they can have on organizations and their customers.

Insider Trading Detection: Financial institutions employ sophisticated User Behavior Analytics (UBA) tools to detect and prevent insider trading activities. These tools analyze various factors, such as abnormal trading patterns, access to sensitive data, and unauthorized data transfers. By utilizing UBA, financial institutions can detect suspicious behavior and promptly investigate and take appropriate actions to mitigate the risks associated with insider trading.

Advanced Persistent Threats (APTs) Detection: APTs are sophisticated, targeted attacks that aim to gain prolonged unauthorized access to systems. Organizations often employ Security Information and Event Management (SIEM) systems to detect APTs by correlating various security events and indicators. For example, if a SIEM system identifies multiple failed login attempts from different locations followed by unauthorized access to critical systems, it can trigger an alert for a potential APT and initiate an incident response process.

These examples highlight the importance of implementing risk detection methods and the potential impact they can have on mitigating cyber threats. However, it is crucial to continuously evaluate and enhance these methods to keep pace with evolving threats and ensure effective risk management.

4. CYBERSECURITY

Machine learning is a type of artificial intelligence (AI) that enables computers to learn from data without being explicitly programmed. Machine learning algorithms are designed to identify patterns in data and to make predictions or decisions based on those patterns. Machine learning algorithms can be trained on large datasets to improve their accuracy and to make better predictions over time.

Cybersecurity refers to the technologies, processes, and practices used to protect an organization's systems, infrastructure, and data from cyber threats. Here are some key cybersecurity measures that organizations can implement:

Access Controls: Access controls involve implementing authentication and authorization mechanisms to control who can access an organization's systems and data. This can help prevent unauthorized access and data breaches.

Firewalls: Firewalls are a key cybersecurity technology that can help prevent unauthorized access to an organization's systems and data. Firewalls monitor incoming and outgoing network traffic and can block unauthorized access attempts.

Antivirus and Anti-malware Software: Antivirus and anti-malware software can help detect and remove malicious software such as viruses, worms, and Trojan horses. These technologies can help prevent malware infections and data breaches.

Encryption: Encryption involves encoding data so that it can only be read by authorized parties with the appropriate decryption keys. Encryption can help protect sensitive data from unauthorized access and data breaches.

Leveraging Machine Learning in Cybersecurity

Machine learning has emerged as a powerful tool for cybersecurity, and it has the potential to improve our ability to detect and respond to cyber threats. Machine learning has several advantages over traditional cybersecurity approaches. First, machine learning can analyze vast amounts of data in real-time, which is essential in the rapidly evolving cybersecurity landscape. Second, machine learning algorithms can identify patterns and anomalies that may be missed by traditional cybersecurity measures. Finally, machine learning can automate many cybersecurity tasks, allowing organizations to respond more quickly to cyber threats.

Here are some ways that organizations can leverage machine learning in cybersecurity:

Threat detection: Machine learning algorithms can be trained to detect and classify various types of cyber threats, such as malware, phishing attacks, and insider threats. They can analyze large volumes of data to identify patterns and anomalies that may indicate a cyber attack.

Network security: Machine learning can be used to detect and respond to network attacks, such as Distributed Denial of Service (DDoS) attacks. Machine learning algorithms can be trained to detect abnormal network traffic patterns and to take appropriate actions to mitigate the attack.

Predictive analytics: Machine learning can be used to analyze historical data to predict future cyber attacks. This can help organizations to proactively identify vulnerabilities and take appropriate actions to prevent cyber attacks.

Fraud detection: Machine learning can be used to detect fraudulent activity, such as credit card fraud or identity theft. Machine learning algorithms can be trained to detect unusual patterns of behavior that may indicate fraudulent activity.

Vulnerability management: Machine learning can be used to identify and prioritize vulnerabilities in software and systems. This can help organizations to prioritize their patching and remediation efforts and reduce their exposure to cyber attacks.

With the increasing frequency and complexity of cyber attacks, cybersecurity has become a major concern for organizations across all industries. Traditional security measures, such as firewalls and antivirus software, are no longer sufficient to protect against sophisticated cyber threats.

5. AUTHENTICATION TECHNIQUES

Organizations should evaluate their specific security requirements, user needs, and the sensitivity of the systems or data being protected to determine the appropriate authentication techniques to implement. Implementing a layered approach with multiple authentication factors can significantly enhance security and protect against various attacks.

Password-Based Authentication: Password-based authentication is the most widely used method. Users provide a unique password or passphrase that is compared against a stored password in a database. However, password-based authentication is susceptible to various attacks, such as brute force, dictionary attacks, and password reuse. To enhance security, organizations should enforce strong password policies, encourage the use of password managers, and implement mechanisms like password hashing and salting.

Two-Factor Authentication (2FA): 2FA requires users to provide two different types of authentication factors to access a system. It adds an extra layer of security beyond passwords. Common 2FA methods include:

One-Time Passwords (OTP): Users receive a unique OTP via SMS, email, or generated by an authentication app. The OTP is valid for a limited time and provides an additional authentication factor.

Hardware Tokens: Physical devices generate time-based or event-based OTPs that users input during authentication. These tokens can be separate devices or integrated into smart cards or USB tokens.

Software Tokens: Mobile applications or software generate OTPs on a user's device, eliminating the need for a separate hardware token.

Biometric Verification: In some cases, biometrics like fingerprints or facial recognition are used as the second factor in 2FA.

Multi-Factor Authentication (MFA): MFA expands on the concept of 2FA by requiring users to provide multiple authentication factors, typically combining something the user knows (password), something the user has (token), and something the user is (biometric data). MFA significantly enhances security by adding multiple layers of authentication.

Biometric Authentication: Biometric authentication uses unique physical or behavioral characteristics of an individual for identification. Examples include fingerprint recognition, iris or retina scanning, voice recognition, or facial recognition. Biometrics are difficult to replicate, providing a high level of security. However, biometric authentication requires specialized hardware and software, and privacy concerns must be addressed.

Certificate-Based Authentication: Certificate-based authentication utilizes digital certificates issued by a trusted authority. Certificates are used to verify the identity of users or devices. Public Key Infrastructure (PKI) is commonly employed in certificate-based authentication. The authentication process involves verifying the digital certificate, validating the issuer's trust, and ensuring the certificate is not expired or revoked.

Risk-based Authentication: Risk-based authentication assesses the risk level of an authentication attempt based on various factors such as device information, location, IP address, and user behavior. A risk score is calculated, and authentication requirements are adjusted accordingly. For example, if a user attempts to log in from an unfamiliar location or device, additional authentication steps may be required to mitigate potential risks.

Single Sign-On (SSO): SSO enables users to authenticate once and gain access to multiple applications or systems without re-entering credentials. It simplifies user access management and reduces the burden of remembering multiple passwords. SSO can be achieved through protocols like Security Assertion Markup Language (SAML) or OpenID Connect.

Adaptive Authentication: Adaptive authentication dynamically adjusts the authentication requirements based on risk factors and user behavior. It uses contextual information such as device type, location, time of access, and previous user behavior to determine the level of authentication required. Adaptive authentication helps balance security and usability by adjusting the authentication process based on the risk level associated with the access attempt.

6. ADVANCED SECURITY TECHNIQUES

It's important to note that these advanced security techniques are not standalone solutions but are often implemented as part of a comprehensive cybersecurity strategy. Organizations should assess their specific needs, risk profile, and industry best practices to determine which techniques are most relevant and effective for their environment.

Threat Intelligence: Shabtai, A., et al. (2012) discussed the threat intelligence involves gathering and analyzing information about potential threats, adversaries, and vulnerabilities. It helps organizations stay informed about emerging threats, attack techniques, and indicators of compromise (IOCs). Threat intelligence can be obtained from various sources, such as security research firms, threat feeds, open-source intelligence (OSINT), and information sharing platforms. It provides valuable insights to enhance threat detection, incident response, and proactive defense measures. The use of threat intelligence platforms that leverage machine learning and AI to analyze vast amounts of data and provide real-time threat intelligence feeds. These platforms collect information from various sources, such as dark web monitoring, malware analysis, and security research, to identify emerging threats and indicators of compromise.

Behavioral Analytics: Ahmad, I., et al. (2017), focuses on monitoring user and entity behavior to detect anomalies and potential security incidents. This technique leverages machine learning algorithms and statistical models to establish a baseline of normal behavior and identify deviations that may indicate malicious activity. By continuously monitoring user behavior, network traffic, and system activities, behavioral analytics can detect advanced threats that may bypass traditional signature-based security controls. User and entity behavior analytics (UEBA) solutions that apply machine learning algorithms to analyze user behavior and detect anomalies. These solutions can identify unusual patterns of activity, such as privileged user abuse or insider threats, by establishing a baseline of normal behavior and flagging deviations.

Machine Learning and Artificial Intelligence (AI): Biggio, B., et al. (2018), explained on Machine learning and AI technologies are increasingly being used in cybersecurity to enhance threat detection, automate security operations, and enable intelligent decision-making. These techniques can analyze large volumes of data, identify patterns, and detect anomalies in real-time. AI-powered solutions can automate routine security tasks, such as log analysis, malware detection, and incident response, freeing up security teams to focus on more complex issues. The application of machine learning algorithms for network intrusion detection. Intrusion detection systems (IDS) can use machine learning techniques to identify patterns in network traffic and detect anomalies or known attack signatures, enabling proactive threat detection and response.

Deception Technologies: Kharraz, A., et al. (2015) discussed deception technologies involve the deployment of decoy systems, applications, and data to mislead attackers and divert their attention. Deception techniques can be used to detect and identify attackers early in the cyber kill chain by luring them into interacting with decoy assets. Deception technologies can include decoy servers, honey pots, deceptive files or documents, and deceptive network segments. By engaging attackers in deceptive interactions, organizations can gain valuable insights into their tactics, techniques, and intentions, helping to strengthen defenses and improve incident response. Deploying decoy systems and honeypots to deceive and lure attackers. Deception technologies create virtual assets that mimic real systems, applications, or data, tricking attackers into interacting with them. The interactions can provide valuable insights into attacker tactics, techniques, and motivations.

Zero Trust Security: Wang, Y., et al. (2020), Zero Trust is an approach to security that assumes no inherent trust for any user, device, or network within an organization's environment. It requires continuous verification and authentication of users and devices, strict access controls, and granular security policies. Zero Trust architectures aim to minimize the potential attack surface and prevent lateral movement within a network. Key components of Zero Trust include identity and access management (IAM), multifactor authentication (MFA), network segmentation, micro-segmentation, and continuous monitoring. Implementing zero trust network access (ZTNA) solutions that enforce strict access controls and continuously verify user and device trust worthiness. ZTNA solutions authenticate and authorize users and devices before granting access to resources, regardless of their location or network context.

Endpoint Detection and Response (EDR): Garcia, S., et al. (2018) provides EDR solutions are real-time monitoring, detection, and response capabilities at the endpoint level. They collect and analyze data from endpoints, such as workstations, laptops, and servers, to identify suspicious activities and respond to threats. They provide organizations with visibility into endpoint activities, facilitate incident investigation, and enable rapid response to security incidents. Advanced EDR solutions can identify and block malicious activities, provide real-time visibility into endpoint events, and support incident response.

Cloud Security: Rizvi, S. T., et al. (2018) discussed as organizations increasingly adopt cloud computing and services, advanced security techniques specific to the cloud have emerged. Cloud security focuses on protecting data, applications, and infrastructure in cloud environments. Techniques include cloud-native security tools, data encryption, secure configuration management, identity and access management (IAM) controls, and continuous monitoring. Cloud-specific security controls help organizations address the unique challenges and risks associated with cloud-based systems and ensure the confidentiality, integrity, and availability of cloud resources.

These advanced security techniques go beyond traditional security measures to provide enhanced protection against sophisticated threats. Organizations should assess their specific needs, risk profile, and industry best practices to determine which techniques are most relevant and effective for their environment. A holistic and layered approach to security, incorporating multiple advanced techniques, can provide robust defenses against evolving cyber threats. Cloud workload protection platforms (CWPP) that provide security controls and visibility into cloud-based workloads. These platforms offer features such as data encryption, access controls, threat detection, and continuous monitoring to protect sensitive data and applications in the cloud.

7. CYBER-PHYSICAL SYSTEMS (CPS)

As CPS technology continues to evolve, the integration of physical and cyber components opens up new opportunities for optimization, automation, and efficiency in various domains. However, it also brings forth the need for careful consideration of security, safety, and privacy aspects to ensure the reliable and resilient operation of these complex systems.

Integration of Physical and Cyber Components: In CPS, physical components and computational devices are tightly integrated, forming a unified system. Physical components include sensors that collect data about the environment, actuators that control physical processes, and machines or devices that perform physical tasks. The cyber components consist of computational devices such as computers, embedded systems, and networks that process data, perform analysis, and make decisions.

Real-Time Monitoring and Control: CPS systems often require real-time monitoring and control of physical processes. For example, in a smart grid CPS, sensors continuously monitor electricity consumption, generation, and distribution. The collected data is analyzed in real-time to optimize power flow, manage demand, and ensure reliability. Control actions are then implemented through actuators to adjust power generation or distribution.

Interconnectedness and Communication: CPS heavily relies on interconnectedness and communication between physical and cyber components. This is facilitated through communication networks, such as wired or wireless connections and the Internet of Things (IoT). Physical sensors gather data and transmit it to computational devices for analysis and decision-making. Conversely, cyber components send control signals to physical actuators to effect changes in the physical world.

Wide Range of Applications: CPS has diverse applications across various domains. In transportation systems, CPS can optimize traffic flow, monitor vehicle conditions, and enable intelligent transportation management. In manufacturing, CPS enables smart factories with connected machines, real-time monitoring of production lines, and adaptive manufacturing processes. In healthcare, CPS can support remote patient monitoring, personalized medicine, and smart medical devices. CPS also finds applications in agriculture (precision farming), energy management (smart grids), infrastructure management (smart cities), and more.

Security Challenges: CPS introduces unique security challenges due to its integration of physical and cyber components. Cyber attacks on CPS can have real-world consequences, including physical damage, disruption of critical services, or compromise of public safety. Ensuring the security of CPS systems requires robust authentication and access control mechanisms, encryption of communication channels, anomaly detection algorithms, and regular security updates to protect against evolving threats.

Safety Considerations: CPS must address safety concerns, as failures or malfunctions in the cyber components can have direct implications for physical processes. Safety measures include redundancy and fault-tolerant designs, rigorous testing and verification of system behavior, and compliance with industry safety standards.

Data Analytics and AI: CPS leverages data analytics and artificial intelligence (AI) techniques to extract insights, detect anomalies, and optimize system performance. Machine learning algorithms can analyze large volumes of data generated by CPS components to identify patterns, predict system behavior, and enable proactive decision-making.

Here are some recent examples of CPS:

Smart Grids: CPS technology is being used in modern power grids to enable efficient energy management, real-time monitoring, and control. Smart grids integrate power generation, distribution, and consumption with advanced communication and control systems to optimize energy usage, detect faults, and improve grid resilience.

Autonomous Vehicles: The development of autonomous vehicles involves the integration of sensors, actuators, computing systems, and connectivity to create vehicles capable of navigating and interacting with the physical environment. CPS techniques are employed to ensure safe and reliable operation, collision avoidance, and real-time decision-making.

Industrial Internet of Things (IIoT): CPS is at the core of IIoT, where physical devices and machines are connected to the internet to enable data exchange and intelligent decision-making. In manufacturing, CPS allows for the integration of production systems with data analytics and control algorithms, leading to improved efficiency, predictive maintenance, and flexible production processes.

Smart Healthcare Systems: CPS is transforming healthcare by integrating medical devices, electronic health records, wearables, and communication systems. This integration enables real-time monitoring of patients, remote healthcare services, and data-driven decision support systems for diagnosis and treatment.

Smart Cities: CPS technologies are used to create smart cities, where various infrastructure systems such as transportation, energy, water, and waste management are interconnected and optimized. CPS enables intelligent traffic management, efficient resource allocation, environmental monitoring, and enhanced public safety.

These examples demonstrate how CPS technology is being deployed in real-world applications to improve efficiency, productivity, and safety. As CPS continues to evolve, it brings new opportunities and challenges for ensuring the security, privacy, and resilience of these interconnected systems.

8. TOOLS AND TECHNIQUES USED FOR RISK DETECTION

There are various tools that can be used to detect risks in a computing system. Some of the commonly used tools are:

Vulnerability Scanners: These are tools that scan a system for vulnerabilities such as outdated software, missing patches, and other security flaws that can be exploited by attackers.

Intrusion Detection and Prevention Systems (IDPS): These tools monitor network traffic for signs of malicious activity and can help to prevent unauthorized access or attacks.

Security Information and Event Management (SIEM) Systems: These tools collect and analyze data from various sources to identify potential security threats and suspicious activity.

Penetration Testing Tools: These are tools used to simulate attacks on a system to identify vulnerabilities and weaknesses that can be exploited by attackers.

Web Application Firewalls: These are tools designed to protect web applications from attacks such as SQL injection and cross-site scripting (XSS).

Anti-malware Software: This software is designed to detect and remove malware such as viruses, trojans, and spyware.

The field of cybersecurity is constantly evolving, and new tools and technologies are continually being developed to address emerging threats. Here are some recent tools used in cybersecurity:

Endpoint Detection and Response (EDR) Tools: EDR tools are designed to detect and respond to threats on endpoints, such as desktops, laptops, and mobile devices. These tools can monitor and analyze endpoint activity in real-time, allowing organizations to quickly detect and respond to potential threats.

Identity and Access Management (IAM) Solutions: IAM solutions are designed to manage user identities and access to systems and applications. These solutions can help organizations to ensure that only authorized users have access to sensitive data and systems, reducing the risk of data breaches and insider threats.

Network Traffic Analysis (NTA) Tools: NTA tools can help organizations to monitor and analyze network traffic to detect potential threats, such as malware, phishing attempts, and insider threats. These tools can help organizations to quickly identify and respond to potential threats before they can cause significant damage.

User and Entity Behavior Analytics (UEBA): UEBA solutions analyze user and entity behavior to detect anomalies and potential security threats. By establishing baseline behavior patterns, UEBA tools can identify deviations that may indicate insider threats, compromised accounts, or other suspicious activities.

Security Orchestration, Automation, and Response (SOAR): SOAR platforms integrate security tools and automate incident response processes. They can automatically detect and respond to security incidents, streamline investigation workflows, and orchestrate remediation actions, helping organizations detect and mitigate risks more efficiently.

Data Loss Prevention (DLP) Solutions: DLP solutions help organizations detect and prevent the unauthorized transmission or leakage of sensitive data. They use techniques such as content analysis, data classification, and user activity monitoring to identify and mitigate risks associated with data breaches or data loss.

Threat Hunting: Threat hunting involves proactively searching for signs of compromise or hidden threats within an organization's network. It often involves using advanced analytics, threat intelligence feeds, and specialized tools to identify indicators of compromise that may have been missed by traditional security controls.

Cloud Security Monitoring and Configuration Management: As organizations increasingly adopt cloud services, tools and techniques specific to cloud security monitoring and configuration management are becoming more important. These tools help detect misconfigurations, vulnerabilities, and unauthorized access in cloud environments, ensuring the security and compliance of cloud-based systems and data.

These are a few examples of the latest tools and techniques used for risk detection. It's important to stay updated with the rapidly evolving landscape of cybersecurity and explore emerging technologies and practices that can help organizations detect and mitigate risks effectively.

9. RISK DETECTION ALGORITHMS

A comparative study of risk detection algorithms is important to understand the strengths and weaknesses of different approaches, and to determine the most suitable algorithm for a given situation. Here are some examples of a comparative study of risk detection algorithms:

In a study comparing decision trees, neural networks, and SVM for credit risk assessment, it was found that decision trees performed the best, while SVM had the lowest accuracy. However, the study also noted that the choice of algorithm would depend on the specific goals.

9.1 Decision Trees, Neural Networks, and SVM for Credit Risk Assessment

In this study, the three algorithms were compared for their ability to accurately predict credit risk. The dataset used in the study contained information on customer credit history, financial information, and other relevant factors.

The results showed that decision trees performed the best with an accuracy of 77%, while neural networks and SVM had lower accuracies of 74% and 70% respectively. The study noted that decision trees were better at identifying the most important factors for predicting credit risk, while SVM had a tendency to overfit the data.

However, the study also noted that the choice of algorithm would depend on the specific goals and requirements. For example, if the goal was to identify the most important factors for credit risk assessment, decision trees would be the most suitable algorithm. However, if the goal was to prioritize accuracy over interpretability, neural networks might be a better choice.

9.2 Bayesian Networks, Decision Trees, and SVM for Network Intrusion Detection

In another study, Bayesian networks, decision trees, and SVM were compared for their ability to detect network intrusions. The dataset used in the study contained network traffic data from a real-world network.

The results showed that decision trees and Bayesian networks had higher detection rates than SVM, with decision trees achieving the highest detection rate of 98.6%. However, SVM had the lowest false positive rate, which could be an important consideration in situations where false alarms could have serious consequences.

9.3 Neural Networks, SVM, and Decision Trees for Malware Detection

A study compared the performance of neural networks, SVM, and decision trees in detecting malware. The study used a dataset containing samples of known malware and benign files.

The results showed that neural networks outperformed SVM and decision trees in terms of detection accuracy. However, decision trees had the advantage of being more interpretable, which could be useful in understanding the characteristics of malware.

9.4 Clustering and SVM for Anomaly Detection in Network Traffic

Another study compared clustering and SVM for detecting anomalies in network traffic. The study used a dataset containing network traffic data from a real-world network.

The results showed that clustering had a higher false positive rate than SVM, but was more effective at detecting previously unseen anomalies. SVM had a lower false positive rate but was less effective at detecting unknown anomalies.

The study concluded that a combination of clustering and SVM could be effective for detecting anomalies in network traffic, with clustering used to identify previously unseen anomalies and SVM used to reduce false positives.

9.5 Bayesian Networks and SVM for Predicting Insider Threats

A study compared the performance of Bayesian networks and SVM for predicting insider threats. The study used a dataset containing information on employee behavior and other relevant factors.

The results showed that both Bayesian networks and SVM were effective at predicting insider threats, with Bayesian networks achieving slightly higher accuracy. However, the study noted that Bayesian networks were more complex and difficult to interpret, while SVM was simpler and easier to use.

Overall, these studies highlight the importance of selecting the appropriate algorithm for a given situation, considering factors such as accuracy, interpretability, and false positives. It's also important to consider the nature of the data and the specific risks being targeted when selecting a risk detection and cyber security algorithm.

9.6 Latest Risk Detection Algorithms

The field of risk detection is continuously evolving, and researchers are developing new algorithms to improve the accuracy and efficiency of risk detection systems. Here are some of the latest risk detection algorithms used:

Deep Learning Algorithms: Deep learning algorithms, such as Convolutional Neural Networks (CNNs) and Recurrent Neural Networks (RNNs), are being applied to risk detection tasks. These algorithms can automatically learn complex patterns and features from large-scale data, making them effective in detecting risks and anomalies in various domains, including cybersecurity and fraud detection.

Graph-based Algorithms: Graph-based algorithms, such as Graph Neural Networks (GNNs) and community detection algorithms, are increasingly used for risk detection in networks and interconnected systems. These algorithms can model relationships and dependencies between entities, allowing for the identification of anomalous behaviors, malicious actors, or vulnerabilities in complex networks.

Ensemble Learning: Ensemble learning techniques combine multiple classifiers or models to improve the accuracy and robustness of risk detection systems. Algorithms such as Random Forests, Gradient Boosting, and Stacking are commonly used in ensemble learning to leverage the collective intelligence of diverse models for more effective risk detection.

One-Class Classification: One-class classification algorithms aim to detect anomalies or risks by modeling the normal behavior of a system or dataset. Algorithms such as Support Vector Machines (SVM), Isolation Forest, and Autoencoders are used to create models that capture the characteristics of normal instances, enabling the identification of outliers or anomalies.

Reinforcement Learning: Reinforcement learning algorithms are increasingly explored for risk detection in dynamic and evolving environments. These algorithms learn optimal decision-making policies by interacting with the environment, allowing for adaptive risk detection and response in real-time.

Evolutionary Algorithms: Evolutionary algorithms, such as Genetic Algorithms and Particle Swarm Optimization, are used to optimize risk detection models and feature selection processes. These algorithms mimic natural evolution to search for the best combination of features or parameters, improving the effectiveness of risk detection systems.

It's important to note that the choice of algorithm depends on the specific risk detection task, the available data, and the context in which the risk occurs. Researchers and practitioners continue to explore and develop new algorithms to address the evolving challenges of risk detection in various domains.

10. COMPARATIVE PERFORMANCE FOR RISK DETECTION AND CYBER SECURITY ALGORITHMS

These studies illustrate that there is no one-size-fits-all solution for risk detection and cyber security. The best approach depends on the specific goals and requirements, the nature of the data, and the specific risks being targeted.

Comparative Study of Decision Trees, Neural Networks, and SVM for Credit Risk Assessment

Decision Trees: Accuracy of 77%
Neural Networks: Accuracy of 74%
SVM: Accuracy of 70%

Comparative Study of Bayesian Networks, Decision Trees, and SVM for Network Intrusion Detection

Decision Trees: Detection rate of 98.6%
Bayesian Networks: Detection rate of 97.7%
SVM: Detection rate of 90.3%

Comparative Study of Neural Networks, SVM, and Decision Trees for Malware Detection

Neural Networks: Highest accuracy
Decision Trees: More interpretable

Comparative Study of Clustering and SVM for Anomaly Detection in Network Traffic

Clustering: More effective at detecting previously unseen anomalies
SVM: Lower false positive rate

Comparative Study of Bayesian Networks and SVM for Predicting Insider Threats

Bayesian Networks: Slightly higher accuracy
SVM: Simpler and easier to use

Here are some of the values that can be used to compare different risk detection and cyber security approaches:

Accuracy: This is a common metric used to evaluate the effectiveness of a risk detection algorithm. Accuracy is typically defined as the proportion of correctly classified instances over the total number of instances. Higher accuracy generally indicates a more effective approach.

False Positive Rate: False positives occur when a system generates an alarm or alert for a threat that is not actually present. The false positive rate is the proportion of false positives over the total number of negative instances. A lower false positive rate generally indicates a more reliable system.

Detection Rate: The detection rate is the proportion of actual positive instances that are correctly identified by the system. A higher detection rate indicates a more effective system.

Interpretability: Interpretability refers to the ability to understand how the system makes its decisions. In some cases, it may be important to have an interpretable system in order to understand the characteristics of the threats being detected.

Complexity: Complexity refers to the computational resources required to implement the system. A simpler system may be easier to implement and use, but may sacrifice accuracy or other metrics.

Time to Detect: This refers to the amount of time it takes for the system to detect a threat. Faster detection times may be more desirable in situations where quick action is needed to prevent a security breach.

Robustness: Robustness refers to the ability of the system to perform well in different situations or against different types of threats. A more robust system may be better able to handle new or unknown threats.

Cyber threats are increasingly becoming a significant concern for organizations of all sizes and types. Cybersecurity breaches and attacks can have significant financial and reputational impacts, as well as disrupting business operations. Here are some detailed explanations of how cyber threats can impact an organization:

Financial Impacts: Cyber threats can result in significant financial losses for organizations. These losses can come from a variety of sources, such as stolen funds, lost revenue due to downtime or service disruptions, legal and regulatory fines, and costs associated with repairing or replacing damaged systems. For example, in the case of the 2017 Equifax data breach mentioned earlier, the company faced over $1 billion in costs related to the breach, including legal settlements, regulatory fines, and cybersecurity improvements.

Reputational Impacts: Cyber threats can also damage an organization's reputation and erode customer trust. Data breaches and other cybersecurity incidents can result in the theft or exposure of sensitive information, such as personal data or financial information. This can lead to negative media coverage, public backlash, and a loss of customer confidence. In some cases, organizations may also face lawsuits from affected individuals or groups. For example, in the aftermath of the 2013 Target data breach, the company faced significant reputational damage and a loss of customer trust.

Operational Impacts: Cyber threats can disrupt an organization's operations, resulting in downtime, service disruptions, or even the complete shutdown of business activities. This can result in lost revenue, missed deadlines, and damage to customer relationships. In some cases, organizations may also face legal or regulatory consequences for failing to maintain adequate cybersecurity defenses. For example, in 2020, the Australian logistics company Toll Group was forced to shut down several of its systems due to a ransomware attack, resulting in significant operational disruptions and delays.

Resolving cyber attacks requires a multi-faceted approach that involves both immediate response and long-term remediation. Here are some general steps that organizations can take to resolve and mitigate the impact of cyber attacks:

Incident Response Plan: Have a well-defined incident response plan in place that outlines the steps to be taken when an attack is detected. This plan should include procedures for isolating affected systems, preserving evidence, notifying relevant parties, and restoring operations.

Contain and Isolate: Immediately isolate affected systems to prevent further spread of the attack. Disconnect compromised devices from the network and take them offline. This step aims to limit the attacker's ability to move laterally and cause additional damage.

Assess the Scope and Impact: Conduct a thorough assessment to understand the extent of the attack and the potential damage caused. Determine what systems or data have been compromised and evaluate the impact on critical operations.

Engage Security Experts: Involve cybersecurity experts, either from your internal team or through external incident response services, to provide specialized knowledge and assistance in analyzing the attack, identifying vulnerabilities, and recommending mitigation strategies.

Restore Systems and Data: Restore affected systems and data from secure backups or clean copies. Ensure that backups are regularly performed and verified to avoid any data loss. Verify the integrity of restored systems and validate their security posture before reconnecting to the network.

Implement Security Enhancements: Strengthen security measures to prevent similar attacks in the future. This may involve patching software vulnerabilities, implementing stronger access controls, deploying intrusion detection and prevention systems, and regularly updating security software.

Conduct Forensic Analysis: Perform a detailed forensic analysis to determine the root cause of the attack and identify any indicators of compromise. This analysis can provide valuable insights into the attacker's tactics, techniques, and motives.

Improve Security Awareness and Training: Enhance security awareness and training programs for employees to prevent future attacks. Educate staff about the importance of strong passwords, recognizing phishing emails, and following security protocols.

Learn from the Incident: Conduct a post-incident review to identify lessons learned and areas for improvement. Update policies, procedures, and security controls based on the insights gained from the incident response process.

Share Information: If appropriate, share relevant information about the attack with law enforcement, industry organizations, or cybersecurity vendors to help prevent similar attacks and contribute to collective defense efforts.

It's important to note that the specific steps to resolve cyber attacks may vary depending on the nature and severity of the incident. It is recommended to consult with cybersecurity professionals and incident response experts for tailored guidance based on your organization's specific circumstances.

Implementing a range of technologies, processes, and practices is essential for organizations to effectively identify and mitigate risks and protect their electronic devices, systems, and networks from cyber threats. Here's a detailed study of some of the key measures that organizations can take:

Technology Measures: Organizations can implement a range of technological measures to enhance their cybersecurity. This can include firewalls, antivirus software, intrusion detection systems, encryption, and multi-factor authentication. These technologies can help to detect and prevent unauthorized access, identify potential threats, and protect data from theft or exposure.

Process Measures: Process measures refer to the policies and procedures that organizations put in place to manage cybersecurity risks. This can include incident response plans, disaster recovery plans, and regular backups of critical data. By having these plans and procedures in place, organizations can quickly respond to security incidents and minimize the impact of any disruptions.

Best Practices and Standards: Adopting best practices and standards is another crucial step for organizations to enhance their cybersecurity posture. This can include implementing the National Institute of Standards and Technology (NIST) Cybersecurity Framework or complying with the Payment Card Industry Data Security Standard (PCI DSS). These standards provide a framework for managing cybersecurity risks and can help organizations to identify and prioritize their cybersecurity efforts.

Education and Awareness: Education and awareness initiatives can also help to strengthen an organization's cybersecurity posture. This can include providing regular cybersecurity training to employees, promoting good security practices, and raising awareness of potential threats. By educating employees and users, organizations can help to ensure that everyone is equipped to recognize and respond to potential threats.

Governments play a crucial role in preventing and mitigating cyber attacks. Here are some steps that governments often take to address cyber threats:

Legislation and Regulation: Governments enact laws and regulations to establish legal frameworks for cybersecurity. These laws may include requirements for organizations to protect sensitive data, disclose breaches, and adhere to specific security standards. Governments also regulate critical infrastructure sectors to ensure robust cybersecurity measures are in place.

National Cybersecurity Strategies: Governments develop comprehensive national cybersecurity strategies that outline their approach to cybersecurity, including prevention, detection, response, and recovery. These strategies often involve collaboration with various stakeholders, such as industry, academia, and international partners.

Establishing National Cybersecurity Agencies: Governments create specialized agencies responsible for cybersecurity at the national level. These agencies coordinate efforts, develop policies, provide guidance, and conduct cybersecurity awareness and education programs.

Cybersecurity Standards and Best Practices: Governments establish cybersecurity standards and promote best practices to help organizations improve their security posture. These standards can cover areas such as secure coding practices, incident response planning, encryption, authentication, and network security.

Information Sharing and Collaboration: Governments facilitate information sharing and collaboration between public and private sectors. They establish platforms and mechanisms for sharing threat intelligence, vulnerability information, and best practices to enhance situational awareness and enable proactive defense.

Public-Private Partnerships: Governments foster partnerships with the private sector to leverage their expertise and resources in addressing cyber threats. These partnerships may involve joint initiatives, information sharing, research and development collaborations, and capacity-building programs.

International Cooperation: Governments engage in international cooperation to combat cyber threats. This involves sharing information, collaborating on investigations, establishing norms of behavior in cyberspace, and participating in international cybersecurity initiatives and agreements.

Education and Workforce Development: Governments invest in cybersecurity education and workforce development programs to build a skilled cybersecurity workforce. This includes promoting cybersecurity education at all levels, offering training programs, and supporting research and development in the field.

Incident Response and Forensics: Governments establish capabilities for incident response and digital forensics to investigate cyber incidents, identify perpetrators, and support law enforcement efforts. These capabilities often involve specialized cybersecurity teams and forensic labs.

Continuous Monitoring and Threat Intelligence: Governments implement systems for continuous monitoring of networks and critical infrastructure to detect and respond to cyber threats promptly. They leverage threat intelligence sources to identify emerging threats and share this information with relevant stakeholders.

It's worth noting that the specific steps taken by governments may vary depending on their jurisdiction, resources, and the evolving threat landscape. Additionally, governments collaborate with international organizations, participate in cyber exercises and simulations, and support research and development in emerging technologies to strengthen their cybersecurity posture.

In summary, implementing a range of technologies, processes, and practices, as well as education and awareness initiatives, is crucial for organizations to effectively manage cybersecurity risks and protect against cyber threats. By taking these measures, organizations can enhance their security posture, minimize the impact of security incidents, and safeguard their operations and reputation.

11. CONCLUSION

In conclusion, the success of contemporary computing depends on robust risk detection and cyber security measures. Cyber threats can have significant financial and reputational impacts, as well as disrupting business operations. By implementing a range of technologies, processes, and practices, organizations can help to identify and mitigate risks more effectively, and protect their electronic devices, systems, and networks from cyber threats. Furthermore, education and awareness, as well as the adoption of best practices and standards, can help to ensure that all users and employees are equipped to recognize and respond to potential threats.

Managing cyber threats in the age of technology requires effective risk detection and cybersecurity measures. Organizations must implement vulnerability assessments, penetration testing, and threat intelligence to identify potential risks and vulnerabilities. In addition, organizations must implement access controls, firewalls, antivirus and anti-malware software, encryption, and incident response plans to prevent, detect, and respond to cyber attacks. By implementing these measures, organizations can improve their overall security posture and protect themselves from cyber threats.

REFERENCES

Abdel-Aziz, M., Al-Eroud, M., & Alsulaiman, F. (2019). A Comprehensive Review of Cybersecurity Frameworks, Standards, and Guidelines. *IEEE Access, 7*.

Ahmad, I. (2017). A survey on behavior-based malware analysis techniques: Static, dynamic, and hybrid analysis. *ACM Computing Surveys, 50*(6), 1–36.

Albalawi, Y., Aldossary, M., & Alghamdi, A. (2020). Cybersecurity in Healthcare: A Systematic Review of Trends in Research and Development. *Journal of Medical Systems, 83*.

Alqahtani, S., & Khan, M. K. (2020). A systematic review of intrusion detection using machine learning techniques. *Journal of King Saud University - Computer and Information Sciences, 32*(8), 944-956.

Awan, A. R., Akhtar, R. N., & Khan, Z. A. (2021). Quantum Computing for Cybersecurity: Challenges and Opportunities. *Journal of Ambient Intelligence and Humanized Computing, 12*(8).

Biggio, B., & Roli, F. (2018). Wild patterns: Ten years after the rise of adversarial machine learning. *Pattern Recognition, 84*, 317–331. doi:10.1016/j.patcog.2018.07.023

Brantly, Renaud, & Theoharidou. (2016). Cybersecurity Incident Response Planning: Lessons from a Large-Scale Exercise. *Computers & Security, 56.* doi:10.1016/j.cose.2015.11.001

Gao, F., Liao, Y., & Tao, Y. (2020). A Review of Cybersecurity Risks and Best Practices in Smart Manufacturing. *IEEE Access, 8.*

Garcia, S. (2018). A survey on intrusion detection and prevention systems. *IEEE Communications Surveys and Tutorials, 20*(4), 3193–3235.

Gupta, S., Kapoor, S., & Sharma, D. (2020). Blockchain Technology for Cybersecurity and Privacy: A Systematic Literature Review. *Journal of Information Security and Applications, 88.*

Johnson, French, & Rose. (2017). A Framework for Cybersecurity Risk Assessment in the Supply Chain. *International Journal of Business and Systems Research, 11*(3).

Kaur, S., & Bansal, P. (2020). Machine Learning Techniques for Cyber security Applications: A Survey. *Journal of Computer Science and Technology, 35*(6).

Kaur, S., Brar, G. S., & Jha, S. S. (2022). Cybersecurity Challenges in Cloud Computing: A Systematic Review. *Journal of Ambient Intelligence and Humanized Computing, 92.*

Kharraz, A. (2015). Cutting the Gordian knot: A look under the hood of ransomware attacks. *Proceedings of the Network and Distributed System Security Symposium (NDSS).*

Okoroafor, U. C., Chi, H., Smith, A. N., & Assessment, C. R. (2018). Moving Beyond Vulnerability Scanning. *IEEE Security & Privacy, 16*(3). DOI: .2701204 doi:10.1109/MSP.2018

Oney, Lineberry, & Dampier. (2018). Effective Measures for Preventing and Responding to Insider Cyber Attacks. *International Journal of Critical Infrastructure Protection, 21.* DOI: . 2018.08.002 doi:10.1016/j.ijcip

Rizvi, S. T. (2018). A comprehensive survey on cloud security attacks and defense mechanisms. *Journal of Network and Computer Applications, 107,* 57–82.

Shabtai, A. (2012). A survey of machine learning methods for detecting malicious executables. *Information Security Technical Report, 16*(1), 2–14.

Sood, S. S., Kaur, S., & Singh, A. J. (2021). The Role of Social Engineering in Cybersecurity: A Systematic Literature Review. *Journal of Cybersecurity, 103.*

Tobin, Zapata, & Rowe. (2017). Cyber Threat Intelligence: Analysis and Recommendations for a Mature Cybersecurity Program. *Computers & Security, 68.* doi:10.1016/j.cose.2016.10.008

Wang, Y. (2020). Survey on zero trust networks: Towards the next generation of secure network architectures. *IEEE Access : Practical Innovations, Open Solutions, 8,* 100736–100752.

Zarrineh, K., & Raza, S. (2016). Cybersecurity Challenges for Modern Computing. *Journal of Cyber Security and Mobility, 4*(2).

Chapter 16
Proactive DDoS Attacks Detection on the Cloud Computing Environment Using Machine Learning Techniques

Kishore Babu Dasari

iD https://orcid.org/0000-0001-6920-0674

Keshav Memorial Institute of Technology, India

Srinivas Mekala

Keshav Memorial Institute of Technology, India

ABSTRACT

Distributed Denial of Service (DDoS) is a cyber-attack targeted on availability principle of information security by disrupts the services to the users. Cloud computing is very demand service in internet to provide computing resources. DDoS attack is one of the severe cyber-attack to disrupt the resource unavailable to the legitimate users. So DDoS attack detection is more essential in cloud computing environment to reduce the effect of circumstances of the attack. This Chapter proposed DDoS attack detection with network flow features instead of conventional researchers use network type features in cloud computing environment. This study evaluate the DDoS attack detection in cloud computing environment using uncorrelated network type features selected by Pearson, Spearman and Kendall correlation methods. CIC-DDoS2019 dataset used for experiments this study which is collected from Canadian Institute for Cyber Security. Finally, Pearson uncorrelated feature subset produces .better results with KNN and MLP classification algorithms.

DOI: 10.4018/978-1-6684-9317-5.ch016

1. CLOUD COMPUTING

Cloud computing is on-demand access, via the internet, to computing resources-applications, servers (physical servers and virtual servers), data storage, development tools, networking capabilities, and more hosted at a remote data center managed by a cloud services provider (CSP). The CSP makes these resources available for a monthly subscription fee or bills them according to usage.

Cloud computing is the delivery of computing services—including servers, storage, databases, networking, software, analytics, and intelligence—over the Internet ("the cloud") to offer faster innovation, flexible resources, and economies of scale. You typically pay only for cloud services you use, helping you lower your operating costs, run your infrastructure more efficiently, and scale as your business needs change.

Cloud computing is the on-demand delivery of IT resources over the Internet with pay-as-you-go pricing. Instead of buying, owning, and maintaining physical data centers and servers, you can access technology services, such as computing power, storage, and databases, on an as-needed basis from a cloud provider like Amazon Web Services (AWS).

Cloud computing is the on-demand availability of computing resources as services over the internet. It eliminates the need for enterprises to procure, configure, or manage resources themselves, and they only pay for what they use.

The term cloud refers to a network or the internet. It is a technology that uses remote servers on the internet to store, manage, and access data online rather than local drives. The data can be anything such as files, images, documents, audio, video, and more.

1.1 Cloud Security

Cloud security is an important area of research. Many consultants and security agencies have issued warnings on the security threats in the cloud computing model. Besides, potential users still wonder whether the cloud is secure. There are at least two concerns when using the cloud. One concern is that the users do not want to reveal their data to the cloud service provider. For example, the data could be sensitive information like medical records. Another concern is that the users are unsure about the integrity of the data they receive from the cloud. Therefore, within the cloud, more than conventional security mechanisms will be required for data security.

The following technical challenges need to be addressed in order to make cloud computing acceptable for common consumers:

1. Open security profiling of services that is available to end users and verifiable automatically. Service providers need to disclose in detail the levels of specific security properties rather than providing blanket assurances of "secure" services.
2. The cloud service/infrastructure providers are required to enable end users to remotely control their virtual working platforms in the cloud and monitor others' access to their data. This includes the capability of fine grained accessing controls on their own data, no matter where the data files are stored and processed. In addition, it is ideal to possess the capability of restricting any unauthorized third parties from manipulating users' data, including the cloud service provider, as well as cloud infrastructure providers.

3. Security compliance with existing standards could be useful to enhance cloud security. There must be consistency between the security requirements and/or policies of service consumers and the security assurances of cloud providers.

4. It is mandatory for the providers to ensure that software is as secure as they claim. These assurances may include certification of the security of the systems in question. A certificate—issued after rigorous testing according to agreed criteria (e.g., ISO/IEC 15408)—can ensure the degree of reliability of software in different configurations and environments as claimed by the cloud providers.

2. DISTRIBUTED DENIAL OF SERVICE (DDOS) ATTACKS

A Distributed Denial of Service (DDoS) attack is a type of cyber attack in which multiple compromised computers or devices are used to flood a target system, network, or website with a high volume of traffic or requests. The aim of a DDoS attack is to overwhelm the target's resources and make it unavailable to legitimate users.

Here's a general overview of how a DDoS attack works:

Botnet Formation: The attacker first creates or gains control over a large number of computers or devices, known as a botnet. These compromised devices are often part of a network of computers infected with malware or controlled through other means, such as a botnet-for-hire service.

Command and Control: The attacker manages the botnet through a command and control (C&C) infrastructure, which allows them to coordinate and control the attack. The C&C infrastructure communicates with the compromised devices, instructing them to send traffic or requests to the target.

Traffic Generation: The attacker initiates the attack by sending instructions to the compromised devices within the botnet. These devices then generate a massive amount of traffic or requests towards the target system. The traffic can be in the form of data packets, HTTP requests, or other network protocols.

Target Overload: The target system becomes overwhelmed by the flood of traffic, exhausting its resources such as network bandwidth, processing power, memory, or disk space. As a result, the target system or network becomes slow, unresponsive, or completely unavailable to legitimate users.

Impact: The consequences of a successful DDoS attack can vary depending on the target. For businesses and organizations, it can lead to financial losses due to disrupted services, decreased customer trust, and potential damage to their reputation. For individuals, it can cause inconvenience or disruption of access to online services.

Duration: DDoS attacks can last for a few hours to several days, depending on the attacker's intentions and the countermeasures in place to mitigate the attack. During an attack, the attacker may also change attack vectors or switch between different compromised devices to evade detection or mitigation efforts.

Mitigating DDoS attacks typically involves a combination of strategies such as traffic filtering, rate limiting, and deploying specialized hardware or software solutions to detect and block malicious traffic. Internet service providers (ISPs) and content delivery networks (CDNs) may also have measures in place to absorb or redirect attack traffic before it reaches the target.

It's important for organizations and individuals to maintain robust security measures, such as keeping software up to date, using strong passwords, and implementing firewalls and intrusion detection systems, to reduce the risk of their devices becoming part of a botnet used for DDoS attacks.

3. DDOS ATTACKS ON CLOUD COMPUTING ENVIRONMENT

DDoS attacks on cloud computing environments can have severe consequences due to their potential to disrupt services for multiple customers sharing the same infrastructure. Here are some key aspects to consider regarding DDoS attacks on cloud computing environments:

Shared Infrastructure: Cloud computing environments are built on shared infrastructure, where multiple customers or tenants utilize the same pool of resources. This shared nature means that an attack on one tenant can impact the availability and performance of other tenants' services, leading to collateral damage.

Elasticity and Scalability: Cloud environments are designed to be elastic and scalable, allowing resources to be dynamically allocated and scaled up or down based on demand. While this flexibility is advantageous for normal operations, it can also make cloud environments more susceptible to DDoS attacks that exploit the scaling capabilities to amplify their impact.

Multi-vector Attacks: DDoS attacks on cloud environments often involve multiple attack vectors, combining various techniques to overwhelm different layers of the infrastructure. These attacks can target network bandwidth, application-layer resources, or even the control and management layers of the cloud environment.

Reflection and Amplification Attacks: Attackers may leverage reflection and amplification techniques to magnify the scale of their DDoS attacks. By spoofing the source IP address and sending requests to vulnerable services, they can elicit large responses that are directed towards the victim's infrastructure, causing a significant impact with relatively minimal effort.

Resource Starvation: DDoS attacks can also aim to exhaust specific resources within the cloud environment, such as compute instances, storage systems, or network components. By overwhelming these resources, attackers can disrupt the services of targeted tenants and potentially impact the overall performance of the cloud infrastructure.

4. EFFECTS OF THE DDOS ATTACKS ON CLOUD COMPUTING

The rise of DDoS attacks has presented a new challenge to cloud computing environments. The primary goal of DDoS attacks is to significantly impair customer experience, and without effective DDoS protection in place, it is not uncommon for DDoS attacks to go unnoticed and instead blight customer experience in cloud environments. Organizations need to take preventative measures to avoid unnecessary reoccurring spend and leverage an understanding of utilization to drive a better understanding of customer experience and predicting forward demand for their products. Additionally, it is crucial to have a plan in place to deal with pulse attacks and ensure that the auto-scaling triggers are firing correctly to prevent mass over-provisioning. With these measures in place, organizations can mitigate the impact of DDoS attacks on cloud computing environments and ensure a seamless customer experience.

5. CLOUD DDOS ATTACKS DETECTION

DDoS attacks are a significant threat to cloud computing infrastructure, as they can disrupt cloud services and prevent users from accessing them. These attacks are becoming increasingly sophisticated, with attackers using multiple sources to generate traffic, making it difficult to distinguish between legitimate traffic and attack traffic. Traditional approaches to DDoS detection, such as appliance-based detection, are no longer sufficient to track the massive amount of traffic and identify individual IP addresses.

Cloud DDoS detection and protection have evolved to address these challenges by utilizing cloud computing scale to detect and mitigate DDoS attacks. By using cloud-scale compute and storage resources, cloud DDoS protection solutions can collect and examine network flow data in highly granular fashion, with superior baselining intelligence. This approach ensures greater accuracy in stopping DDoS attacks than is possible with legacy DDoS detection appliances.

Detecting a DDoS attack is the first critical step in avoiding or stopping it. To detect an attack in progress, it is necessary to collect enough network traffic information to perform an analysis to determine if the traffic is legitimate or not. DDoS detection can be performed manually by a network engineer or automatically through mechanisms built into the DDoS detection mechanism.

The effectiveness of a DDoS defense depends on two critical success criteria: speed of detection and accuracy of detection. Fast and effective detection mechanisms are essential for implementing a consistently effective DDoS defense.

5.1 Cloud-Based DDoS Protection

Cloud-based DDoS protection solutions provide a more intelligent approach to identifying and mitigating DDoS attacks. These solutions use big data to continuously scan network-wide data on a multi-dimensional basis without constraints. Big data detection systems provide deep, forensic analytics, as well as the ability to incorporate network performance, planning, and other capabilities.

Kentik Protect is an example of a cloud-based DDoS protection solution that offers the industry's most accurate DDoS detection. It can automatically trigger mitigation via RTBH, Cloudflare, Radware DefensePro, or A10 Thunder TPS mitigation.

5.2 Machine Learning Approaches

Machine learning algorithms are also being used to detect and mitigate DDoS attacks. Naive Bayes classifiers, random forest techniques, and artificial neural networks are some of the machine learning methods that have been proposed to solve cloud security challenges.

Perplexed-based classifiers with and without feature selection are being compared with existing machine learning algorithms to prove the effectiveness of the perplexed-based classification algorithm. The proposed algorithm has an accuracy of 99%, which is higher than the existing algorithms, proving that the proposed algorithm is highly efficient in detecting DDoS attacks in cloud computing systems.

5.3 Nature-Inspired Computing

Nature-inspired computing is also being explored to handle the issues related to cloud vulnerabilities. Particle swarm optimization (PSO) is being used to optimize delivery and increase the network lifetime. However, due to its nonsupervised machine learning approach, the model needs to be enhanced for all possible DDoS attacks.

6. MACHINE LEARNING CLASSIFICATION ALGORITHMS

Machine learning is a part of artificial intelligence (AI) that gives machines the ability to learn automatically from training data to classify target classes and predict the values. Machine learning algorithms are classified into supervised learning algorithms and unsupervised learning algorithms. Supervised learning algorithms trained with target classes while unsupervised learning algorithms trained without target classes. Supervised learning algorithms (Kotsiantis et al., 2007;Mishra et al., 2019) used for classification and regression. Classification is the task of predicting discrete class labels while regression is the task of predicting continuous value. DDoS attack detection is the task of predicting attack and benign class labels. So machine learning classification algorithms (Dasari & Devarakonda, 2022) are used to detect DDoS attacks.

In order to implement the classification models to classify the network traffic into attack and benign class labels implemented using the following machine learning classification algorithms with selected uncorrelated features subsets.

- Logistic regression
- Decision tree
- Random forest
- Ada boost
- Gradient boost
- K-Nearest Neighbor
- Naive bayes
- Multilayer perceptron

6.1 Logistic Regression

Logistic regression (Yan et al., 2019; Yadav & Selvakumar, 2015) is a classification algorithm for classifying binary class labels. It classifies the binary classes using a logistic function. Logistic function calculated by

$$\varnothing(z) = \frac{1}{1 + e^{-z}} \tag{4.1}$$

z is the linear combination of weights and features.

$$z = w^T x = w_1 x + w_2 x^2 + w_3 x^3 + \cdots + w_n x^n \tag{4.2}$$

6.2 Decision Tree

Decision Tree (Lakshminarasimman et al., 2017; Wu et al., 2011) is a non-parametric tree structured classification algorithm. Its internal nodes contain dataset features, while leaf nodes contain class labels and edges contain decision rules. Based on the feature set, the decision tree makes a series of decisions to produce the outcome.

6.3 Random Forest

Random forest (Pinto & Sebastian, 2021; Chen, 2020) is an ensemble classification learning algorithm. In order to solve the complex problems and improve performance, ensemble learning algorithms combine multiple classification algorithms. Random forest contains multiple decision trees with controlled variance and uses randomly picked features as their input. Classification results decided by voting weights.

6.4 K-Nearest Neighbors

K-Nearest Neighbor (Dong & Sarem, 2019; Fouladi et al., 2016) is a non-parametric similarity based classification algorithm. It assumes every data point close to one another in the same class. The distance between the features calculated by standard Euclidean distance.

$$(x, y) = \sqrt{\sum_{i=1}^{n} (x_i - y_i)^2} \tag{4.3}$$

n is the total number of features and x_i, y_i are the ith instance values of x, y

6.5 Naive Bayes

Naive bayes (Rachmadi et al., 2021; Mazini et al., 2019) is a probabilistic based classification algorithm using Bayes theorem.

Naive Bayes theorem is calculated as

$$P(C_k / X) = \frac{P(X / C_k) P(C_k)}{P(X)} \tag{4.4}$$

Here $X = (X_1, X_2, X_3, \ldots, X_n)$ represents a independent feature vector and C_k represents each target class.

6.6 AdaBoost

Adaptive boosting (AdaBoost) (Islam, 2020; Chen et al., 2018) is a boosting based ensemble classification algorithm. AdaBoost classifiers construct strong classifiers from a collection of weak decision tree classifiers identified by high weight data points then after training the weak models again and again until lower error is output.

6.7 Gradient Boost

Gradient boosting (Wang et al., 2020) is a boosting based ensemble classification algorithm. Gradient classifiers construct strong classifiers from weak decision tree learners identified by gradient value then training the weak models again and again until lower error is output.

6.8 Multilayer Perceptron

Multilayer perceptron (MLP) () is an artificial neural network based classification algorithm. It has one input layer, one output layer and one or more hidden layers. It is fully connected with dense layers. MLP is classified as a classification algorithm based on linear predictor function based on weights and feature vectors.

7. EVALUATION OF MACHINE LEARNING CLASSIFICATION ALGORITHMS FOR PROACTIVE CLOUD DDOS ATTACKS DETECTION WITH EXPERIMENTS RESULTS

The DrDoS attack dataset collected from CIC-DDoS2019 (Mishra et al., 2019) datasets and operations performed performed on it. Because the quality of data and the significant information that may be extracted from dataset has a direct impact on our model's capacity to train, so data preprocessing (Kotsiantis et al., 2007) is a pivot point in machine learning. Preprocessing process, remove constant socket features and remove missing and infinite value records. Use 0 and 1 to encode the Benign and DrDoS attacks, respectively. To improve the performance of the classification algorithms, standardize the feature values.

Feature selection (Chen, 2020) is a method of removing redundant, irrelevant, or noisy features from total features in order to pick a subset of the most relevant features. Filter, Wrapper, Embedded, and Hybrid approaches are the types of feature selection methods. Using multiple metrics, the filter technique removes undesired features of the model. The feature selection in wrapper techniques is based on a machine learning algorithm that tries to fit a certain dataset. Wrapper and filter methods are used in embedded methods, which enhance feature interactions while maintaining the computational expenses low. In this study, feature selection is done utilizing filter-based feature selection methods such variance threshold and correlation methods (Chen, 2020). All features whose variance fall below a certain threshold are removed b variance threshold. By default, it removes all zero-variance features that have the same value across all samples. It removes all 0.01-variance features, those features are called quasi-constant features. Correlation (Chen, 2020) is a statistical word that describes how closely two features are related in a linear manner. High correlation features have a similar influence on the dependent variable since they are more linearly dependent. When there is a strong association between two features, one of them may be dropped. The correlation coefficients' values range from -1 to +1, indicating how strong the relationship between the features is. When the coefficient value is ±1 it represents high correlation among features. When the coefficient value is zero, the traits are highly unrelated. The Pearson, Spearman, and Kendall (Dasari & Devarakonda, 2022) correlation approaches are used in this study to identify uncorrelation properties. A linear relationship between two continuous variables is measured using Pearson's. Spearman's is a non-parametric test that uses ranked data to measure a monotonic connection. Spearman's has the advantage of being simpler to calculate. Kendall's method is non-parametric, which means it doesn't require the two variables to be on a bell curve. Kendall's does not require continuous data as well. It will work with continuous data because it is based on the ranked values of each variable, but it can also be used with ordinal data. Although ordinal data have a ranking, the intervals between rankings are not always consistent.

The correlation coefficient calculated by Pearson is

$$r = \frac{\Sigma\left(X_i - \bar{X}\right)\left(Y_i - \bar{Y}\right)}{\sqrt{\Sigma\left(X_i - \bar{X}\right)^2 \Sigma\left(Y_i - \bar{Y}\right)^2}} \tag{1}$$

Here r is the correlation coefficient

X_i - is the X-feature values in a sample
$\bar{X}$ – is the X-features mean value.
Y_i - is the Y-feature values in a sample
$\bar{Y}$ – is the Y-features mean value.

The Spearman correlation coefficient calculated by

$$\rho = 1 - \frac{6\Sigma d_i^2}{n\left(n^2 - 1\right)} \tag{2}$$

Here ρ is the Spearman's rank correlation coefficient

d_i is the difference among the two ranks of each observation
n is the total observations

The correlation coefficient calculated by Kendall is

$$\tau = \frac{N_c - N_d}{\dfrac{n\left(n-1\right)}{2}} \tag{3}$$

Here τ is the Kendall rank correlation coefficient

N_c is the total of concordant

N_d is the total of discordant

Machine learning classification algorithms applied for DDoS attacks detection with following feature sets.

- Without feature selection feature subset mean all features after preprocessing
- Variace threshold feature set mean features after remove constant and quasi-constant features
- Pearson uncorrelated features subset
- Spearman uncorrelated features subset
- Kendall uncorrelated features subset

Table 1 depicts the accuracy values of the different classification algorithms on the DrDDoS dataset for DDoS attack detection. KNN and MLP produce the best accuracy values with all feature subsets. Pearson uncorrelated features subset produces the best accuracy values with all classification algorithms compared to remaining uncorrelated feature subsets. It produces the equal or more accuracy results compared to the results without feature selection and variance threshold features sets.

Table 1. Accuracy values of the different classification algorithms for DDoS attack detection on DrDoS dataset

Feature sets	Without Feature Selection	Variance Threshold	Uncorrelated feature subsets		
Classification Algorithms			Pearson	Spearman	Kendall
Logistic Regression	99.28	99.24	99.37	99.30	99.32
Decision Tree	99.43	99.65	99.50	98.22	98.19
Random Forest	99.63	99.45	99.56	99.38	99.32
Ada Boost	99.21	99.10	99.35	98.86	99.19
Gradient Boost	99.56	99.57	99.59	99.54	99.54
KNN	99.93	99.92	99.91	99.76	99.76
Naive Bayes	98.54	98.38	97.85	97.64	97.58
MLP	99.90	99.90	99.89	99.77	99.77

Table 2 depicts the K-Fold Cross (KFC) validation accuracy values of the different classification algorithms on the DrDoS dataset for DDoS attack detection. Decision tree and Random forest classification algorithms produce the best K-fold cross validation accuracy values with all feature subsets. Gradient descent and MLP classification algorithms also produce better accuracy values with all feature subsets. Pearson uncorrelated feature subset produces the best K-Fold cross validation accuracy values with all classification algorithms compared to remaining uncorrelated feature subsets. It produces the equal or more K-Fold cross validation accuracy results compared to the results without feature selection and variance threshold features sets.

Table 2. K-Fold cross validation accuracy values of the different classification algorithms for DDoS attack detection on DrDoS dataset

Feature sets	Without Feature Selection	Variance Threshold	Uncorrelated feature subsets		
Classification Algorithms			Pearson	Spearman	Kendall
Logistic Regression	99.3668% (0.0239%)	99.3626% (0.0264%)	99.3872% (0.0110%)	99.3336% (0.0103%)	99.3547% (0.0369%)
Decision Tree	99.9802% (0.0028%)	99.9800% (0.0019%)	99.9808% (0.0051%)	99.8869% (0.0115%)	99.8847% (0.0124%)
Random Forest	99.9840% (0.0041%)	99.9832% (0.0032%)	99.9864% (0.0037%)	99.8966% (0.0136%)	99.8968% (0.0136%)
Ada Boost	99.8711% (0.0112%)	99.8711% (0.0112%)	99.8800% (0.0100%)	99.1899% (0.0337%)	99.1576% (0.0284%)
Gradient Boost	99.9721% (0.0022%)	99.9707% (0.0018%)	99.9690% (0.0060%)	99.8413% (0.0062%)	99.8525% (0.0161%)
KNN	99.8788% (0.0041%)	99.8758% (0.0036%)	99.9425% (0.0071%)	99.8788% (0.0141%)	99.8573% (0.0130%)
Naive Bayes	98.6391% (0.0697%)	98.5703% (0.0818%)	97.9895% (0.1208%)	97.6374% (0.1272%)	97.5609% (0.1071%)
MLP	99.9120% (0.0157%)	99.9114% (0.0089%)	99.9014% (0.0092%)	99.7614% (0.0126%)	99.7725% (0.0124%)

Table 3. Specificity values of the different classification algorithms for DDoS attack detection on DrDoS dataset

Feature sets	Without Feature Selection	Variance Threshold	Uncorrelated feature subsets		
Classification Algorithms			Pearson	Spearman	Kendall
Logistic Regression	1.00	1.00	1.00	0.99	0.99
Decision Tree	0.92	0.98	0.97	0.77	0.73
Random Forest	0.94	0.90	0.91	0.87	0.83
Ada Boost	0.97	1.00	0.87	0.99	0.99
Gradient Boost	0.99	0.99	0.99	1.00	1.00
KNN	0.99	0.99	0.98	0.97	0.98
Naive Bayes	1.00	1.00	1.00	0.99	0.99
MLP	0.98	0.98	0.97	0.96	0.96

Table 4 depicts the ROC-AUC scores of the different classification algorithms on the DrDoS dataset for DDoS attack detection. MLP classification algorithm produces the best ROC_AUC score values with all features subsets. All uncorrelated features subsets produce the better ROC-AUC values with all classification algorithms. Figure 4.1 to Figure 4.5 depicts the ROC-AUC curves of the different classification algorithms using, without feature selection, features selected by variance threshold, Pearson, Spearman and Kendall uncorrelated features subsets for DDoS attack detection on DrDoS dataset respectively.

Table 4. ROC-AUC values of the different classification algorithms for DDoS attack detection on DrDoS dataset

Feature sets Classification Algorithms	Without Feature Selection	Variance Threshold	Uncorrelated feature subsets		
			Pearson	Spearman	Kendall
Logistic Regression	0.998327	0.998238	0.996582	0.996565	0.996576
Decision Tree	0.958071	0.989299	0.985105	0.881367	0.862427
Random Forest	0.999675	0.999562	0.999682	0.999409	0.999270
Ada Boost	0.999084	0.998571	0.998907	0.997183	0.997278
Gradient Boost	0.998773	0.998289	0.998533	0.089070	0.089407
KNN	0.998563	0.998431	0.997552	0.991193	0.991445
Naive Bayes	0.930140	0.905593	0.605798	0.992774	0.993059
MLP	0.999724	0.999952	0.999680	0.999786	0.999758

Figure 1. ROC-AUC curve of the different classification algorithms for DDoS attack detection on DrDoS dataset without feature selection

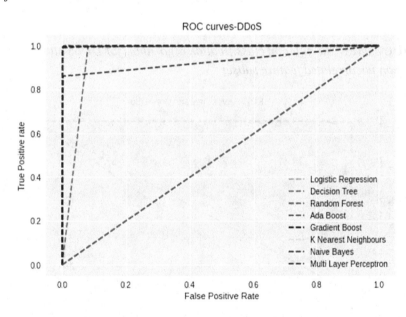

Table 5 depicts the Log-loss values of the different classification algorithms on the DrDoS dataset for DDoS attack detection. MLP classification algorithm produces the best log-loss values with all features subsets. Pearson uncorrelation features subset produces the best log-loss value than other uncorrelated features subsets.

Figure 2. ROC-AUC curve of the different classification algorithms for DDoS attack detection on DrDoS dataset with features selected by Variance Threshold

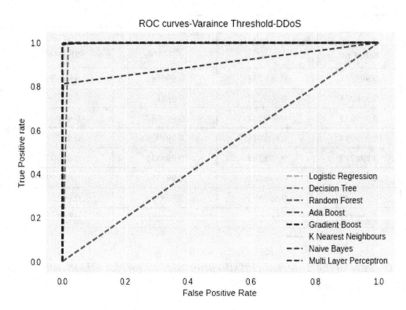

Figure 3. ROC-AUC curve of the different classification algorithms for DDoS attack detection on DrDoS dataset with Pearson uncorrelated feature subset

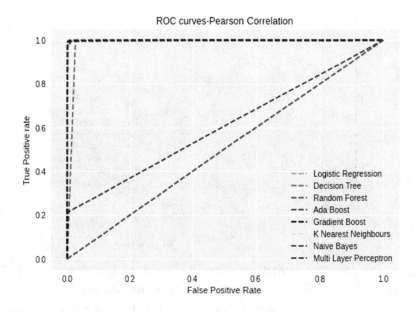

Figure 4. ROC-AUC curve of the different classification algorithms for DDoS attack detection on DrDoS dataset with Spearman uncorrelated feature subset

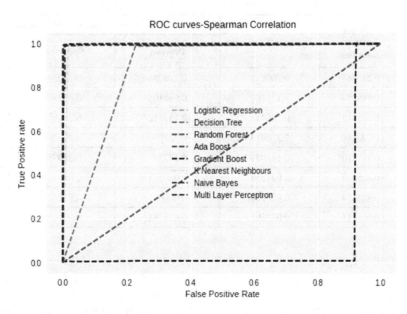

Figure 5. ROC-AUC curve of the different classification algorithms for DDoS attack detection on DrDoS dataset with Kendall uncorrelated feature subset

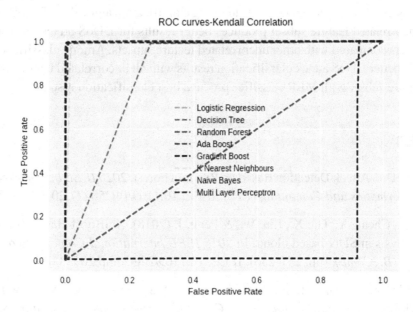

Table 5. Log-loss values of the different classification algorithms for DDoS attack detection on DrDoS dataset

Feature sets	Without Feature Selection	Variance Threshold	Uncorrelated feature subsets		
Classification Algorithms			Pearson	Spearman	Kendall
Logistic Regression	0.249088	0.260832	0.216040	0.240348	0.235978
Decision Tree	0.198289	0.121267	0.985105	0.613165	0.625730
Random Forest	0.128915	0.188457	0.151312	0.214951	0.235162
Ada Boost	0.274489	0.310813	0.223690	0.392204	0.278039
Gradient Boost	0.151310	0.148033	0.142297	0.330756	0.328571
KNN	0.025674	0.027859	0.030317	0.083849	0.083303
Naive Bayes	0.855374	0.880228	0.000651	0.813632	0.836574
MLP	0.034141	0.033595	0.038784	0.078660	0.078660

8. SUMMARY

This study describes Cloud computing, DDoS attacks and impact of DDoS attacks on Cloud computing environment. It used network flow features for detecting DDoS attacks instead of using network type features. And this study used uncorrelated independent features to classify dependent target class feature. In this study, Pearson, Spearman and Kendall correlation methods used for finding uncorrelated features. The study evaluates different machine learning classification algorithms for DDoS attack detection. Pearson uncorrelated feature subset produces better results for DDoS attack detection with KNN and MLP classifiers compared with other uncorrelated feature subsets. Among classification algorithms MLP produce the better DDoS attack classification results with all uncorrelated feature subsets. Pearson uncorrelated feature subset with MLP classifier produce best classification results.

REFERENCES

Chen, Y. (2020). DDoS Attack Detection Based on Random Forest. *2020 IEEE International Conference on Progress in Informatics and Computing (PIC)*. IEEE. 10.1109/PIC50277.2020.9350788

Chen, Z., Jiang, F., Cheng, Y., Gu, X., Liu, W., & Peng, J. (2018). XGBoost classifier for DDoS attack detection and analysis in SDN-based cloud. In *2018 IEEE International Conference on Big Data and Smart Computing (BigComp)*, (pp. 251-256). IEEE. 10.1109/BigComp.2018.00044

Dasari, K. B., & Devarakonda, N. (2022). Detection of DDoS Attacks Using Machine Learning Classification Algorithms. *International Journal of Computer Network and Information Security*, *14*(6), 89–97. doi:10.5815/ijcnis.2022.06.07

Dasari, K. B., & Devarakonda, N. (2022). TCP/UDP-based exploitation DDoS attacks detection using AI classification algorithms with common uncorrelated feature subset selected by Pearson, Spearman and Kendall correlation methods. *Revue d'Intelligence Artificielle*, *36*(1), 61–71. doi:10.18280/ria.360107

Dong, S., & Sarem, M. (2019). DDoS attack detection method based on improved KNN with the degree of DDoS attack in software-defined networks. *IEEE Access : Practical Innovations, Open Solutions*, *8*, 5039–5048. doi:10.1109/ACCESS.2019.2963077

Fouladi, R. F., Kayatas, C. E., & Anarim, E. (2016). Frequency based DDoS attack detection approach using naive Bayes classification. *2016 39th International Conference on Telecommunications and Signal Processing (TSP)*. IEEE. 10.1109/TSP.2016.7760838

Islam, M. K. (2020). Network anomaly detection using lightgbm: A gradient boosting classifier. *2020 30th International Telecommunication Networks and Applications Conference (ITNAC)*. IEEE. 10.1109/ITNAC50341.2020.9315049

Kotsiantis, S. B., Zaharakis, I., & Pintelas, P. (2007). Supervised machine learning: A review of classification techniques. *Emerging artificial intelligence applications in computer engineering*, *160*(1): 3-24.

Lakshminarasimman, S., Ruswin, S., & Sundarakandam, K. (2017). Detecting DDoS attacks using decision tree algorithm. *Fourth International Conference on Signal Processing, Communication and Networking (ICSCN)*, (pp. 1-6). IEEE. 10.1109/ICSCN.2017.8085703

Mazini, M., Shirazi, B., & Mahdavi, I. (2019). Anomaly network-based intrusion detection system using a reliable hybrid artificial bee colony and AdaBoost algorithms. *Journal of King Saud University-Computer and Information Sciences*, *31*(4), 541–553. doi:10.1016/j.jksuci.2018.03.011

Mishra, P., Varadharajan, V., Tupakula, U., & Pilli, E. S. (2019). A detailed investigation and analysis of using machine learning techniques for intrusion detection. *IEEE Communications Surveys and Tutorials*, *21*(1), 686–728. doi:10.1109/COMST.2018.2847722

Pinto, T., & Sebastian, Y. (2021). Detecting DDoS attacks using a cascade of machine learning classifiers based on Random Forest and MLP-ANN. *2021 IEEE Madras Section Conference (MASCON)*, (pp. 1-6). IEEE. 10.1109/MASCON51689.2021.9563266

Rachmadi, S., Mandala, S., & Oktaria, D. (2021). Detection of DoS attack using AdaBoost algorithm on IoT system. *2021 International Conference on Data Science and Its Applications (ICoDSA)*, (pp. 28-33). 10.1109/ICoDSA53588.2021.9617545

Wang, M., Lu, Y., & Qin, J. (2020). A dynamic MLP-based DDoS attack detection method using feature selection and feedback. *Computers & Security*, *88*, 101645. doi:10.1016/j.cose.2019.101645

Wu, Y.-C., Tseng, H. R., Yang, W., & Jan, R. H. (2011). DDoS detection and traceback with decision tree and grey relational analysis. *International Journal of Ad Hoc and Ubiquitous Computing*, *7*(2), 121–136. doi:10.1504/IJAHUC.2011.038998

Yadav, S., & Selvakumar, S. (2015). Detection of application layer DDoS attack by modeling user behavior using logistic regression. *2015 4th International Conference on Reliability, Infocom Technologies and Optimization (ICRITO)(Trends and Future Directions)*. IEEE. 10.1109/ICRITO.2015.7359289

Yan, Y. D., Tang, D., Zhan, S. J., Dai, R., Chen, J. W., & Zhu, N. B. (2019). Low-rate DoS attack detection based on improved logistic regression. *IEEE 21st International Conference on High-Performance Computing and Communications*, (pp. 468-476). IEEE. 10.1109/HPCC/SmartCity/DSS.2019.00076

Chapter 17
Profile Clone Detection on Online Social Network Platforms

Anthony Doe Eklah
University of Ghana, Ghana

Winfred Yaokumah
iD https://orcid.org/0000-0001-7756-1832
University of Ghana, Ghana

Justice Kwame Appati
iD https://orcid.org/0000-0003-2798-4524
University of Ghana, Ghana

ABSTRACT

Successful profile cloning attacks have far-reaching consequences for the victims. People whose profiles are cloned suffer defamation, mistrust, loss of job, interdiction, public disgrace, dent of reputation, and defrauding. This chapter aims to identify and propose a model that detects profile cloning attacks on online social network platforms. The proposed model is based on unsupervised machine learning clustering and statistical similarity verification methods for the filtration of profiles. The model computes statistical values for attribute similarity measure (ASM) and friends network similarity measure (FNSM). The model has a precision score of 100%. The attribute weight and friends network similarity measures show percentile figures ranging from 0.45 to 1.00. Profile accounts that fall within this range for both ASM and FNSM measures are likely to turn out to be cloned. The higher the figures, the more the suspicion of being a fake account to the supposed original one. The strength of the model is that it exposes the actual clone using the outcome of the computation.

DOI: 10.4018/978-1-6684-9317-5.ch017

INTRODUCTION

Advancements in technology and web development have given rise to social networking among people using the internet. The Internet provides web services such as e-mails, e-commerce website services, and online social network site services. The increasing use of the internet has been remarkable. A recent report shows that the global human resource of almost 2.6 million, representing 7.9 percent permanently work from home using the internet, even before the COVID-19 pandemic. After the outbreak of the pandemic, about 18 percent of workers work from home (Venkatesha et al., 2021). One of the fast-growing internet services is the online social network (OSN) sites. Online social network platforms enable people to register and share messages, share career interests, ideas, audio, and images. It allows enhancing social skills, building, and networking among businesses and partners (Jain et al., 2021b; Rao et al., 2020b; Roy & Chahar, 2021).

Several people connect on OSNs including presidents, business leaders, and prominent personalities to share information. The information shared on these platforms may include names, careers and professions, birth dates, photos, and videos. People also read what others have to share. A large number of users patronize OSN services. Currently, even governmental and non-governmental agencies, businesses, and organizations have operational accounts on at least one of these OSN sites to reach out and receive information from the populace (Jain et al., 2021b; Kharaji et al., 2014). Recent statistics show that in the first quarter of 2020, Facebook had more than 2.5 million monthly active users and Twitter chalks up to 330 million active users in a day (Hu et al., 2021; Jain et al., 2021b; Kumar, Kumar Gupta, et al., 2013). The OSN users share large amounts of data with friends in their network by the very nature of OSNs.

Although OSN services provide several benefits, there also exist inherent vulnerabilities. Users especially those who are new to these platforms, oftentimes, are less selective and security conscious, thereby inviting and accepting friends of varied backgrounds. People turn to accept all manner of friends including wrongdoers – malicious intruders, who prey on innocent users by misconducting themselves in cyber-bullying, spamming, phishing, and above all, engaging in profile cloning (Liyanage & Premarathne, 2021a; Rao et al., 2020b). While the core principles that underpin social networking are openness, connecting, and sharing with others, these give rise to unscrupulous OSN users preying on the profile accounts of unsuspecting persons, invading their privacy, and cloning their profiles. There has been exposure to extremely volatile information by OSN platform users (Rao et al., 2020a). What is more alarming is the lack of privacy and its related crime (Liyanage & Premarathne, 2019; Venkatesha et al., 2021). Personal and corporate information which must be protected from public consumption are rather exposed, out of naivety and ignorance of privacy security settings. At large, online social sites are susceptible to risks such as phishing attacks, malware attacks, cyberbullying, and identity theft (Mustafa et al., 2019).

Profile cloning or fake profiles, which is a type of identity theft, is becoming a great concern on OSN platforms. Profile cloning is an act of stealing other OSN platform users' profile details. A profile is a collection of a user's biodata used on the same or other platforms as an identity (Zabielski, Kasprzyk, et al., 2016). Profile cloning attacks can be classified into two. The first type involves cloning an existing social media account and sending multiple requests to the friends of the original account user. As a result, this intruder shares the friends of his/her victim by impersonating him or her and creating an identical account in the same OSN platform. Same-site profile cloning is the term used for this form of profile cloning (Chatterjee, 2019). The second type of profile cloning is a more advanced attack in which the victim's contacts are re-established in another social network where the victim has not yet registered (Kharaji et al., 2014). In profile cloning, an attacker uses the fake profile account to send requests to the friends of the victim whose account has been cloned. Unsuspecting friends may accept the request. In some instances, the attacker may use a prominent businessman's account to advertise fake job opportunities for those interested and ask them to pay an amount of money for the job. Since the original account holder is known in public life as a business leader, unsuspecting job seekers do little or no cross-checking of the facts before involving themselves.

The harm caused by profile cloning to victims and neighbors or friends is enormous and have far-reaching consequence. When an individual falls victim to fake profile attack, the attacker could publish or post information that dents the reputation of the victim or even defraud friends of the victim thereby causing misunderstanding and mistrust for the victim. Individuals such as corporate executives, celebrities, and government business leaders suffer abuse of names and credentials resulting in loss of job or contract, interdiction, and disgrace as a result of profile attacks (He et al., 2014; Mohammadrezaei et al., 2018). Therefore, if social media security issues are not taken seriously enough, many people will be vulnerable to a wide variety of threats and have their confidential data at risk (Jain et al., 2021a). In light of these, this chapter aims to identify and propose a model, referred to as the EAD Model, that detects profile cloning on OSN platforms.

BACKGROUND

Social Media Platforms and Privacy Concerns

Social networking is a means of expanding one's contact circles with others, mostly through social media platforms like Facebook, Twitter, Instagram, and LinkedIn (Jain et al., 2021a). The public exposure of user account details or biodata of those who create accounts on social network sites has their privacy opened to attack by intruders. Zabielski et al. (2016) opined that the breakthrough in technology for the storage of user personal information led to the violation of user privacy but the rate of popularity and patronage of OSN services has continuously seen tremendous increases over the years due to its effectiveness in communication for all online social media (Rao et al., 2020a).

Today, online businesses enjoy a larger customer base due to social media and internet facilities. Businesses and marketers transact business through online social media. This has increased the number of people present on these platforms, as well as increased the amount of time spent online by existing customers (Venkatesha et al., 2021). However, the online customer might fall into the hands of a fraudster. Fraudsters create replica company or product accounts of the original thereby misleading the unsuspecting customer dealing with the wrong person. This eventually causes a loss of money on the part of the customer and raises trust issues on the part of businesses hence OSN patrons prefer dealing in face-to-face transactions to the virtual. The attackers also turn to publish false comments on products causing fear and panic among patrons of such sites and platforms. The result is that a good number of customers shy away from transacting business with the victims (Liyanage & Premarathne, 2021a; Mohammadrezaei et al., 2018). Moreover, the government and its agencies suffer profile attacks in many ways. And duplication of OSN accounts of government officials and agencies is on the rise. Distinguishing the real accounts from the overwhelming fake ones has become difficult for those who have an interest in such accounts. This causes vital information from government agencies to get lost, treated with doubt, or even misleading. The effect is that government opinion polls are no longer effective on OSN platforms (Mohammadrezaei et al., 2018).

Privacy protection has become a contentious subject among both suppliers and users of online social networks. Facebook and other social media platforms have been chastised for making users' profiles public to as large an audience as possible by default. If users do not modify their privacy settings, their information becomes accessible not only to their friends but in the worst-case scenario, to everyone on the same social networking service. Kumar et al. (2016) suggested that the service provider's user interface might be a factor in why users make so few changes to their settings. In any case, privacy features are useless if the user does not use them. Kumar et al. (2016) noted that just a small percentage of Facebook users alter the default privacy settings, which are designed to increase the exposure of users' profiles. Most users seldom modify the default settings on many of the software packages they use, despite attempts to build user interfaces and functionality. Users may not alter their settings for a variety of reasons, including time constraints, misunderstanding, or fear of "messing up" their settings (Kumar et al., 2016).

Users' faith in their social network providers depends on their ability to control privacy choices. Because Internet users come from a diverse variety of cultures and ages, privacy settings should be straightforward, and simple to use. Users must be able to manage their privacy settings at any moment. As a result, the link between data protection legislation and privacy policies is critical (Aldhafferi, Watson, & Sajeev, 2013). These privacy options allow users to accept or reject the dissemination of their information to others. For example, some users do not want to publish sensitive information such as health or medical information (Samavi & Consens 2010). To promote safe participation, a site should respect privacy standards and provide user-friendly profile control and setup.

Profile Cloning Attacks

He et al. (2014) established that OSN attacks occur in two forms.

- The first is when an attacker copies and replicates the same attributes of an original account that has been set up such that there is no difference between the original and the fake accounts on that same social network site. The attacker tries to send friend request links to some friends of the original account. The victim's friend may see this request to be genuine and accept the request. By linking up with the fake account user, the tendency to make your account public to those in your circle of friends is high. A naïve user often sets the account to default which is public or opens to all to view their information or biodata. This fake friend now has unauthorized access and use of the biodata and gradually defrauds the unsuspecting friends of the original account owner. This form of attack is termed Profile Cloning Attack in the same social network.
- The second form of this attack is described as Cross-site Cloning. This kind of profile attack works when a user registers or opens an account on one OSN site but not on other OSN sites. The attacker accesses the victim's profile details or biodata and steals it to register or open similar profiles on different OSN sites other than where the biodata is stolen from. The attacker then sends friend requests to the same unsuspecting friends of his/her victim on this new site and eventually defrauds them. This usually brings about mistrust and acrimony between the original account owner and the unsuspecting friends.

Best Practices on Online Social Networks

Online social networking and the usage of social platforms are now more important than ever. As more individuals use these platforms, their reputation grows, as do the hazards associated with utilizing them. As the number of users grows year after year, it becomes increasingly important to safeguard themselves against malicious and unscrupulous users. Here are a few reasonably safe practices that users can engage in when using OSNs.

- Users of any OSN platform thoroughly learn and understand the privacy and security issues relating to the individual platforms.
- Users should learn to apply the privacy and security settings of the various platforms. Each platform has its peculiar privacy and security settings and configurations to limit other users as to what degree of exposure the user profile is accessible to the public or even friends in their circles. Let us consider the following processes employed by the under-listed platforms to reinforce privacy on their sites: Take, for example, how individuals can limit the display of their profiles to others on various social networking sites:
  - Facebook: For new users, Facebook's privacy setting is Friends Only. Go to Settings > Privacy > Who can see your future posts to change this.
  - Twitter: Protect my Tweets may be found under Settings > Security and Privacy> Privacy > Tweet Privacy > Protect my Tweets. LinkedIn: To make a change, edit your public profile by going to Settings > Account > Helpful Links > Edit your public profile. Google+: Before you publish your article, write the name of a Circle in the "To" section underneath it to modify this setting (Jain et al., 2021b; Senthil Kumar et al., 2016).
- It is unreasonably prudent for a user to accept to use of the default privacy setting of OSN sites. It is oftentimes, loosely set. One must always bear in mind that the internet is public but there exist precautionary measures that can be afforded to hide in public places (A. Kumar, Kumar Gupta, et al., 2013).
- It is advisable to be very economical with the kind of information one puts on OSN platforms. Sensitive and detailed information is better kept away from the eyes of the public. It attracts malicious or unscrupulous users to steal or reproduce a fake profile account of yours to defraud your close allies or tarnish your reputation hence the need to limit the information you share on such platforms. Examples of such information include social security numbers, bank account details, sensitive photographs, and videos. Once it is posted, "it could not be retrieved". Public eyes would have seen it at all costs hence the need to protect one's social reputation. For example, recruiters reject about 70% of job seekers due to information found on their online social media platforms about company ethics (Jain et al., 2021b; A. Kumar, Kumar Gupta, et al., 2013).
- The internet makes it highly practicable for people to misrepresent their true identity and motives. Make sure you check the profile or background of would-be-friends of yours on the OSN platforms or that the one requesting your friendship is known to you. One can create different groups for sharing different messages or information. For example group for family members and another for coworkers and colleagues (Jain et al., 2021a).
- Before sharing information relating to your workplace or company as an employee be sure of the policy regarding sharing content online by the company.

- More often than not suspicious links are shared by friends. Be sure to pay attention while you attempt to click such links, it may be a Bot attempting to copy your credentials once you click such links.

- One must be vigilant about the domain address shared with you. Obnoxious sites' URLs may look compelling and very similar to genuine ones but careful checks would inform you about slight inconsistencies in the spelling of domain names (Jain et al., 2021b).

- One should be vigilant and suspicious of messages that request you to act promptly or offer you something that looks like a bonanza or windfall and even request personal information about you. They are often baits to entangle you.

- Advertisements or links concerning employment should be treated with great caution, often it ends up being a hoax as a result of you not cross-checking facts before engaging in it. Such advertisements or publications could be verified by public relations officers and human resource officers before engaging oneself in them (Jain et al., 2021b).

Related Works

Previous works on profile cloning presented various models to deal with the risk. Alharbi et al. (2021) built on social sensing, a paradigm that permits crowd-sourcing. A unique unsupervised Social Sensor (SocSen) Service Provider Identity Cloning Detection Approach was developed in the study. A multi-view account representation, an embedding learning model, and a prediction model were the three primary components of the proposed approach. The proposed method was tested using a real-world dataset. NPS-AntiClone considerably surpasses existing state-of-the-art identity cloning detection algorithms. The machine learning methodologies achieved a precision score of 88.70%, recall of 82.83%, F1-Score of 85.66%, and F2-Score of 83.94%. According to the study, future work should focus on developing a mechanism that can identify which account of a pair of accounts is the cloned identity.

In a related study, Liyanage and Premarathne (2021) used a clustering algorithm on profile attributes and network linkages to provide a novel approach to detecting clone profiles on Facebook. Filter by name, clustering using weighted categorical features, and estimating the strength of friend links between profiles were the three primary stages of the detection procedure. The study offered a strategy with three primary phases for detecting clone profiles on Facebook; the amount of computation done at each level was decreased by filtering the profiles in each stage. The method was straightforward, yet it was more effective and precise. When non-anonymized features are given, the goal of this study was to include cross-platform detections where the clone on multiple platforms may be recognized, utilizing string-matching algorithms to match the real text of a name. This model precision measure obtained the highest score of 88.75% above the state-of-the-art. Also, Shree et al. (2021) employed machine learning and natural language processing (NLP) technologies in the proposed work to increase the percentage of fake profile prediction. The Support Vector Machine (SVM) and the Naive Bayes algorithms are the two algorithms used in the classification that provide better results. In evaluating the dataset, NLP preprocessing techniques were used; and the detection accuracy rate was improved using ML algorithms.

Moreover, Nagariya et al. (2021) tested eight different classification algorithms and calculated their accuracy on an Online Social Network dataset. Random Forest, Support Vector Machine, Logistic Regression, KNN, and Decision Trees were employed in the study. The study examined the results of each hybrid technique, concluding that the best accuracy was obtained by combining SVM, Logistic Regression, and Neural Networks. By testing and training the dataset on multiple hybrid approaches of classification algorithms, the study claimed to have achieved higher accuracy in detecting cloned profiles with the score best score of 99.33%. Likewise, Spoorthy and Sinha (2021) proposed a two-phase approach to detesting clones. Phase one deals with the probability of some features of a chosen profile and phase two deals with affinity measure. If there exists a cluster of profiles with high similarity accounts, then they are regarded as false profiles. The study has identified that future work should improve on precision by engaging more user events and also improve on the approaches to the detection of fake nodes.

Purba et al. (2020) targeted user behavior to prune out fake nodes by using machine learning approaches in classifying profile accounts into real or fake ones. The classification comes in three ways. These include classification into 2 classes and 4 classes and the last stage is the Metadata. The dataset contains authentic users and fake users, which were filtered using human annotators. Analysis of user comments and other messages posted, analyzing graphical representations of social relations including photographs. The study achieved a classification accuracy of 91.76%. Joshi et al. (2020) also suggested a model that relies on account attributes (user-based, graph-based, content-based, and time-based) and several classification algorithms to recognize accounts on social networking sites (as false or authentic). The study obtained with its two datasets (D1 and D2) experiments, the classification accuracies of 97.3% and 99.56% respectively in the hybrid technique of RF+LR+NN. The study concluded that a system with an approach that can understand user information in a faster, more reliable, and more efficient manner is required.

PROPOSED MODEL AND IMPLEMENTATION

System Platform and Tools

This research seeks to introduce a new algorithm that reacts more effectively to catching clones on the Facebook social platform and then proceeds to educate OSN platform users on possible ways to stay safe on such platforms. This way the online community becomes aware and alert of a possible clone. The research depended on the Stanford University SNAP-trained dataset to test the new algorithm for effectiveness and efficiency using a unified modeling language. Finally, In the implementation of the proposed solution, some tools and applications will be utilized to find effective and competent solutions to the problem. The proposed software would be written in PHP, a web application hosted on a MySQL server. It would be readily accessible to most platforms using Android, windows, and others. MySQL server in XAMPP with Apache server was used to host and accommodate the system locally throughout development. MySQL server also will provide a database for temporal storage of details in the system. Web technologies and frameworks like Java Script will be employed to deploy the system. There will be computer software developed to solve the problem in the real world.

The Characteristics of the Dataset

The SNAP of Stanford University, an online data repository was the source of data for this study. For this project, the dataset was obtained through the University's online repository. The dataset according to Stanford has a total user of 4039 and 88234 connections to the nodes with a total of 26 attributes. The network users were uniquely represented with integer IDs. The related attributes of all nodes were also substituted by integer values https://snap.stanford.edu/data/ego-Facebook.html. This dataset does not contain clones or duplicate profiles. Otherwise, it would be difficult to find similar profiles from the original dataset, therefore 81 of the profiles were altered as clones to have resemblance or similarity with their victims. Also altered were some of those profiles with null values. This number represents about 2% of the total dataset. A similar alteration was carried out on some friend circles of the artificial clones to appear similar to the original users. A user may have about one to four clones (Kharaji et al., 2014; Liyanage & Premarathne, 2019). A clone will attempt to imitate comparable network information in addition to replicating a victim's qualities. This can be due to a desire to befriend the same people as their victims. Thus, the clone's friend network would be modified to be similar, if not exact, to the victim's network. Besides, the dataset was designed in such a way that an original user account might have one to three related users. clones.

Table 1. Profile attributes

Profile Attributes	
No.	**Attributes Selected**
1	First Name
2	Last Name
3	Birthday
4	Gender
5	Location
6	Hometown
7	Education (School)
8	Work (Employer)
9	Work Position
10	Work Location

The Proposed Model

Figure 1 shows the design flowchart of the proposed system. The proposed system model has three main stages namely, the Information Distiller, Profile Hunter, and Profile Verifier for finding fake profiles. Profiles through the three stages would be screened and sorted or pruned down to be suitable as input for the next stages. The figure demonstrates the flow of detection of a clone. From the start, the name attributes of the supposed original account owner are fed into the Distiller. This enables the Distiller to extract all accounts with similar attributes (Similarity List) for further cross-examinations. The Profile Hunter accepts the Similarity List and uses the Similarity Weight Measure Mechanism to further classify the Similarity List to a Candidate List. Then the Profile Verifier checks network similarities of the Candidates List to ascertain the candidate(s) with the highest similarities as a clone. The detailed processes are explained in the following:

1) **Information Distiller**: The credentials of the Facebook user who wants to check for clones of his profile information are required as input for this component. The output of the component is a user record that contains a set of keywords that match pieces of information from the user's profile and that, singly or in combination, identify that profile. This component parses the HTML elements contained in the user's profile to identify the different types of information present once the user logs in with the service. The first stage accepts the named attributes of the supposed original account owner or the victim's name credential. With this attribute fed into the Information Distiller (ID), all accounts bearing similar names (attribute), are sorted to form the Similarity List – the output of stage one and an input for the next stage. In profile cloning, attempt to make the features of the clone similar to that of the original account or profile such that, friends could hardly notice any difference and concede to the "oneness" of the two accounts or profiles.

2) **Profile Hunter.** This component examines user records and locates social network accounts that may or may not belong to the user using user-identifying keywords. Profiles are gathered via social-network-specific inquiries that include these phrases and the user's true name, utilizing each network's search function. A profile record is built by combining all of the returned results. A link to the user's authentic profile is included in the profile records, as well as links to all of the profiles retrieved in the results. The second stage accepts the Similarity List input for detection processing by the profile similarity weight measure mechanism to cluster or classify the list to produce the Candidates List – the input for the next stage, Profile Verifier. The Candidate's List is expected to have somehow, much resemblance with the original profile or account.

3) **Profile Verifier.** This component parses profile records and pulls the data from the social profiles that have been gathered. The resemblance of each profile to the user's original profile is then assessed. The common values of information fields are used to create a similarity score. Also compared are profile images, since cloned profiles will use the victim's photo to appear more real. After all of the extracted profiles have been compared to the real ones, the user is given a list of all of them, along with a similarity score. The Information Distiller begins by extracting user-identifying information from a verified social media page. This is used to build a user record that the Profile Hunter may utilize. Profile Hunter then uses the information from the user record to search online social networks for profiles. The Profile Verifier receives all of the Hunter's returning profiles, which are subsequently put into a profile record. After that, the Profile Verifier compares all of the profiles from the profile record to the original legitimate profile, calculating a similarity score based on the common values of certain fields. The user is supplied with the profiles, as well as similarity ratings and a prediction of which profiles are most likely to be cloned, and the procedure is completed. The third stage verifies the similarity between friends' networks and recommended friends, and computes the profile similarity value between the victim and each profile on the candidate's list. If any of the computations go beyond the stipulated threshold, and the same user with a higher score of attribute match and with even a lesser score of Friends' network relationship (minimum RS) with the same friends' circles of the victim is selected as the possible clone of the original account.

Figure 1. Design algorithm for fake profile detection

DESIGN ALGORITHM FOR FAKE PROFILE DETECTION

```
Information                    start  ──►  Extract the
Distiller                                 contents of node
                                          (A) to set criteria
                                                │
                                                ▼
Receive as input of next   Output "Similarity" ◄── Yes ── Is A = B(i)?  ── No ──  Profile
condition                  List" of nodes              next B                     Hunter
                                 │
                                 ▼
              No ──  Is unique attribute of ── Yes ──  Output "Candidates
                     A = B(i....n)?                    List"
                                                          │
                                                          ▼
                     Display Clone  ◄── Yes ──  compare
                     List                       node A to node B for
                                                network similarity         Profile
                        │                              │                   Verifier
                        │                              No
                        ▼                              │
                       End  ◄──────────────────────────┘
```

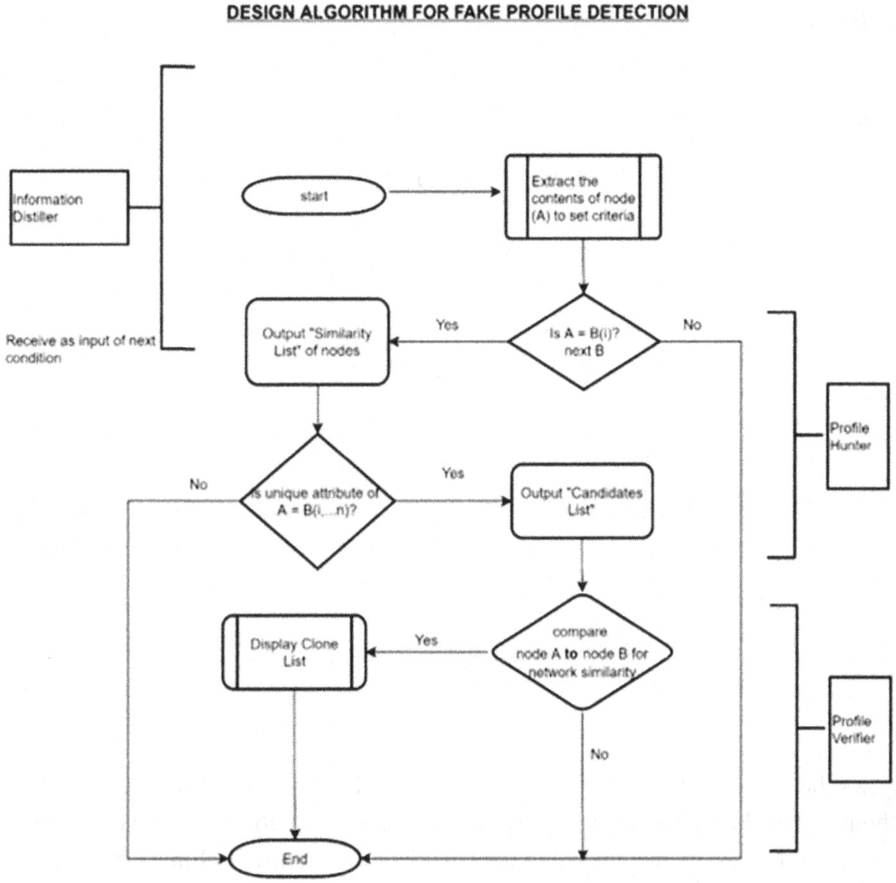

Building the Model

The model is built to filter by name and by user clustering

Filter by Name: To minimize the scope of the search, the account user's name (first name) is a key attribute that is usually considered to remain the same on a clone profile or with minimal altering. Therefore, the first step to 'phishing out' clones is using the user's name as a criterion for filtering other profiles before forwarding the list to the next stage of detection. Figure 2 shows the filtering process.

User Clustering: Attribute Weight Computation: Weights are representations of the impact of each characteristic on the detection and decision-making process. The second detection stage includes clustering where weight is put on the various considered attributes for computations including names. During the detection and decision-making processes, weight can reveal the value or relevance of a characteristic. Formulas such as rank order centroid and rank exponent have been discovered in various investigations. The formula employed in this study is equally used in Liyanage & Premarathne (2021a), this method considers the values of attributes distributed in a dataset. The values of each clone and the victim pair were compared for resemblance. Finally, the average of the estimated similarities is used to determine the attribute's weight. Because the clone and victim pairings are predetermined by any given dataset, this approach of attribute weight computation is more adaptable to practically every case (Liyanage & Premarathne, 2021b).

Figure 2. Model filtering process

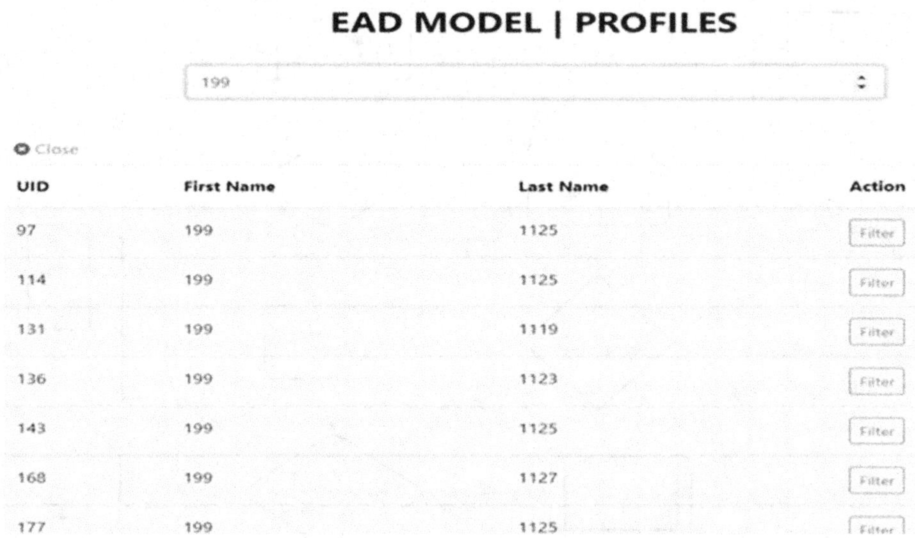

EAD MODEL | PROFILES

| 199 | | | ⇕ |

O Close

UID	First Name	Last Name	Action
97	199	1125	Filter
114	199	1125	Filter
131	199	1119	Filter
136	199	1123	Filter
143	199	1125	Filter
168	199	1127	Filter
177	199	1125	Filter

Table 2 shows the process of weight estimation. It could be observed that victim 1 and clone 1 have different Birthdays, thus 2 and 209 respectively. Therefore, the Attribute Similarity Measure for Birthday produces 0 (zero) hence the weight value for Birthday for victim 1, clone 1 is 0. Another attribute checked for victim 1 and clone 1 is the Last_Name. The Last_Names for victim 1 and clone 1 correspond producing a similarity weight of 1. The same applies to victim 2 and clone 2, they have Birthdays 6 and 0 respectively hence ASM is 0, on the contrary, they have the same Last_Names which results in a weight of 1. Victim 3 and clone 3 have the same Birthday, 2 and 2 which produces an ASM of 1; the weight value of 1 but dissimilar Last_Names produce a weight of 0.

Similarity Computations

The similarity computations are in two folds. The Attribute Similarity Measure and Friends Network Similarity Measure.

Attribute Similarity Measure (ASM). Equation 1 shows Lei Jin et al approach for computing Attribute Similarity called Attribute Similarity Measure:

$$Satt\left(Pc, Pv\right) = \frac{SAcv}{\sqrt{Ac \cdot Av}} \tag{1}$$

Table 2. Weight estimation process

ATTRIBUTE WEIGHT CALCULATION					
User	Row_No.	Birthday	Similarity	LastName	Similarity
Victim 1	97	2	0	1125	1
Clone 1	143	209		1125	
Victim 2	63	6	0	277	1
Clone 2	104	0		277	
Victim 3	97	2	1	1125	0
Clone 3	136	2		1123	
Weight/Avg		1/3 = 0.33		2/3 = 0.66	

Where:

S_{att} - Attribute Similarity

Pc – Profile of potential clone

Pv - Profile of the potential victim

SAcv – Total of Similar Attributes between Pc and Pv

Ac – Total Attributes of the Clone (Pc)

Av – Total Attributes of the Victim (Pv)

Table 3 displays the results of aggregate attributes similarity weight calculation for victims and their respective clones for 10 selected attributes. Each of the 10 attributes is weighted 0.1. victim 1 and clone 1 had all 10 attribute items to be the same including First_Name. therefore, the Aggregate Similarity Value for clone 1, victim 1 equals 1.0. This is similar to Victim 3 and Clone 3. On the other hand, victim 2 and clone 2 have more attributes in common including First_Name but not all 10 of the selected attribute items hence the aggregate attribute similarity value is 0.8.

Table 3. Weights of Aggregate Similar Attributes

AGGREGATE ATTRIBUTE SIMILARITY MEASURE				
(Total Attributes Items = 10)				
	Row_No.	First_Name	Aggr_Sim_Value (Sim_Weight=0.1)	ASM
CLONE 1	107	200	1.0	1.0000
VICTIM 1	95	200		
CLONE 2	104	900	0.8	0.0894
VICTIM 2	63	900		
CLONE 3	130	73	1.0	1.0000
VICTIM 3	1	73		

Figure 3 shows the results obtained from the model. Figure 4 above is additional information on Table 3 above. In this figure, the details of selected attributes considered for the calculation of the ASM were all displayed. In the exception of the Account ID (UID) which shows the difference in accounts under consideration, the attribute items were First Name, Last Name, Gender, Birthday, Home Town, Location, Education, Work Employment, Work Location, and Work Position were extracted from the victim's account and matched against those on the list for similarity rating – (how many attribute items are common to the potential victim (Pv) and the potential clone (Pc) taking in to account the weight/ value of each item to be 0.1. Therefore, ID 95 and 107 have a similarity rating of 1.0 (having all 10 attribute items in common) and ASM calculation – Satt (Pc, Pv) also shows 1.00 for the two accounts. This means Satt (Pc, Pv) = 1.00 is a 100% score in imitation of attributes of the original account. The higher the score, the higher the rate of suspicion of being a potential clone.

Friends Network Similarity Measure (FNSM). Network similarity calculation is shown in Equation 2. It is called the Friend Network Similarity Measure.

$$Sff\left(Pc, Pv\right) = \frac{MFFcv}{\sqrt{Fc \cdot Fv}}$$ (2)

Where:

    Pc – Profile of potential clone
    Pv - Profile of the potential victim
    S_{ff} – Total of Friend Similarity

Fc – Friend list of clone profiles.

Fv – Friend list of victim profile.

MFFcv – Set of Mutual Friends of Pc and Pv

Figure 3. Model results for Clone1 and Victim1

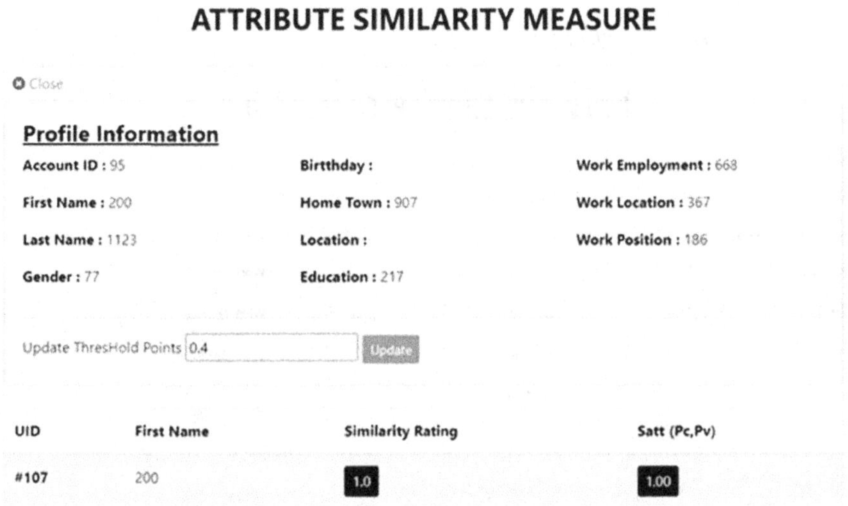

ATTRIBUTE SIMILARITY MEASURE

⊘ Close

Profile Information

Account ID : 95	**Birtthday :**	**Work Employment :** 668
First Name : 200	**Home Town :** 907	**Work Location :** 367
Last Name : 1123	**Location :**	**Work Position :** 186
Gender : 77	**Education :** 217	

Update ThresHold Points `0.4`   Update

UID	First Name	Similarity Rating	Satt (Pc,Pv)
#107	200	1.0	1.00

Table 4 below shows the Friends Network Measure of some Fc and Fv. From Table 4 above, it can be observed that Friends of Clone (Fc) 1 and Friends Victim (Fv) 1 are 92 and 133 respectively. Mutual friends (MFFcv) of both clone 1 and victim1 stood at 78 with friends' network similarity measure (FNSM) rating at 0.7052 out of 1.0 and in percentage, it stood at 70.51%. The foregoing scores reveal the intention of the clone. Having successfully passed the ASM stage with a high rating and also scoring a high rate at the FNSM means that the clone intends to make friends in the victim's circle his/her friends. Most often a clone attempts to send friend invitations to the victim's friends, win their confidence, and eventually defraud them.

Table 4. FNSM of clones and their respective victims

FRIENDS NETWORK SIMILARITY MEASURE					
	ROW_NO.	**FIRST NAME**	**MFFcv**	**Fc / Fv**	**FNSM**	**PERCENTAGE**
CLONE 1	107	200	78	92	0.7052	70.51%
VICTIM 1	95	200		133		
CLONE 2	125	900	80	223	0.4360	43.60%
VICTIM 2	63	900		151		
CLONE 3	130	73	153	271	0.4790	47.90%
VICTIM 3	1	73		371		

Figure 4 lends credence to Table 4. From the figure, Account ID 95 with First Name 200 has a suspected account ID of UID 107 with the same First Name 200. The Friends Network Similarity Measure (FNSM) shows the victim and the clone have common friends as part of their respective friends' networks. The victim has 133 friends and the clone has 92. Out of these numbers, 78 friends representing 70.51% of the victim's total friends are equally friends to the clone. This, therefore, means that the clone is gradually wooing the friends of the victim.

Figure 4. FNSM computation of a clone pair

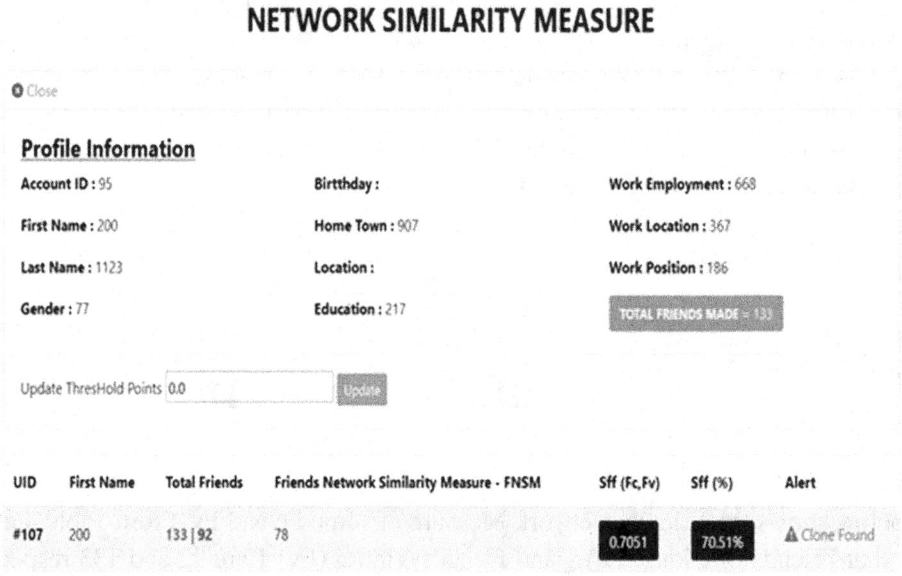

NETWORK SIMILARITY MEASURE

⊗ Close

Profile Information

Account ID : 95	Birtthday :	Work Employment : 668
First Name : 200	Home Town : 907	Work Location : 367
Last Name : 1123	Location :	Work Position : 186
Gender : 77	Education : 217	TOTAL FRIENDS MADE = 133

Update ThresHold Points 0.0 [Update]

UID	First Name	Total Friends	Friends Network Similarity Measure - FNSM	Sff (Fc,Fv)	Sff (%)	Alert
#107	200	133 | 92	78	0.7051	70.51%	⚠ Clone Found

Generating the Similarity Threshold

The estimated similarity threshold value is based on the combined network weight values of the known clone and victim pair. To avoid the loss of some of the genuine clone profiles without being identified by the threshold, the minimum among all known pairings is used as the threshold instead of the average aggregate network similarity (Liyanage & Premarathne, 2019). In Table 5, the clones had aggregate network similarity of 0.89, 0.78, and 0.9 against the victim. In order not to leave out any genuine clones, the minimum figure among the pairs is selected and set as the threshold. In the table above, 0.78 is the best fit to be set as the threshold. Table 5 below demonstrates the generation of a Threshold value

Figure 5 illustrates the concept of determining the threshold. The account with ID 1 has a suspicious list of UIDs 91, 130, 141, 176, and 181 as suspected clones. For any of the suspected accounts not to be let loose through the system, the least of the similarity rating of suspected clones to the victim's attributes must be used to set the threshold. In the case of Figure 5, the lowest attribute rating was obtained by account with ID 91 and a similarity rating of 0.2. Therefore, the threshold must be updated to 0.2, then click the corresponding button to update.

Table 5. The generation of a threshold value for the ASM check

Similarity Threshold Calculation		
User	Aggregate Network Similarity	Similarity Threshold
Victim 1	0.89	0.78
Clone 1		
Victim 2	0.78	
Clone 2		
Victim 3	0.9	
Clone 3		

For a known pair, the lowest threshold was 0.93. A percentage was assigned to all suspect profiles with a similarity weight value, showing how similar they are to the true victim. A real-time validation mechanism should be included in the application to ensure that the actual clone profiles are correct (Liyanage & Premarathne, 2019).

Figure 5. Sets threshold to zero to determine the least threshold value

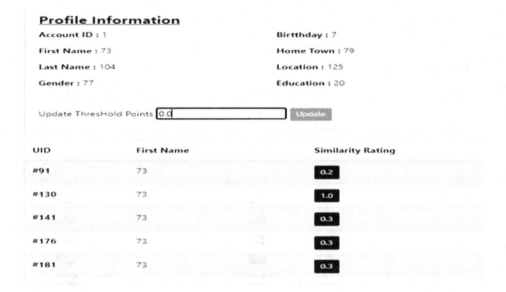

EVALUATION AND RECOMMENDATIONS

The study developed a model based on clustering and statistical similarity verification methods for the filtration of profiles. The clustering technique was an unsupervised learning method which is the evaluation process used to observe how the model measures up to the Gold Standard (Liyanage & Premarathne, 2021b; Xu et al., 2018). Gold Standard calculates statistical values like Attribute Weight, Similarity Threshold, and Network Similarity Weight, among others (Xu et al., 2018). The use of this technique increases the model's performance and efficiency. Table 6 shows the summary of the cluster based on First Name. Figure 6 shows the display on the application interface of a cluster, based on the First Name of record number 97.

Table 6. Cluster data based on first name

Row_No.	Cluster_1	F_Name	L_Name	Gender	Birthday	Hometown	Location	Educ_Sch	Work_Empl.	Work_Loc	Work_Position
97	1	199	1125	77	2	88	134		536	176	184
114	1	199	1125	77	2	88	134		536	176	184
131	1	199	1119	77	4	174	286	221	515	933	184
136	1	199	1123	77	2	84	126	54	533	174	184
143	1	199	1125	78	209	905	1142	411	656	176	184
168	1	199	1127	77	5	89	88	59	532	173	182
177	1	199	1125	77	2	88	617	41	142	175	182
178	1	199	1621	77	739	87	616	41	142	175	185

Figure 6. Display cluster based on first name

Model Performance

The Model shows how close or distinguishable the similarity of the authentic clone is to other suspected profiles. In most of the victim–clone pairs below, the precision is [TP / (TP + FP)], where TP is the victim and FP is the clone (True Positive). The number of clone nodes detected as fake nodes, as well as the number of actual nodes classified as false nodes (FP). The model has a precision score of 100%. The performance of the system depends on the clustering algorithm and similarity measurements. This study was modeled alongside the most current model using clustering and similarity measure approach, Liyanage & Premarathne (2021) and the precision score of their work stood at 88.75% and was considered as good work. Again, Liyanage and Premarathne compared their model performance to that of Kontaxis and Lei Jin for which it was accepted to have performed creditably well with 88.75% score.

The Stanford Library Facebook dataset was used to test the Cloned Profile Detection Model. Two hundred (200) profiles, were created artificially to test run the model. The following figures show the output from the Model of a known victim of ID = 97 with an authentic clone of ID = 114. From the dataset of 200 profiles, 8 were filtered based on the First Name cluster including the victim. From the 7 profiles, one was identified and proven to be a clone. Based on the illustration of Table 6, Figure 7 displays the clone. A clone of a profile turns to make friends from the friends' circle of the victim purposely for malicious reasons. Therefore, for a true clone to be identified, there is a need to investigate friends' network similarity. If this could be proven like in Figure 8 then it is a clone.

Figure 7. Clone based on first name

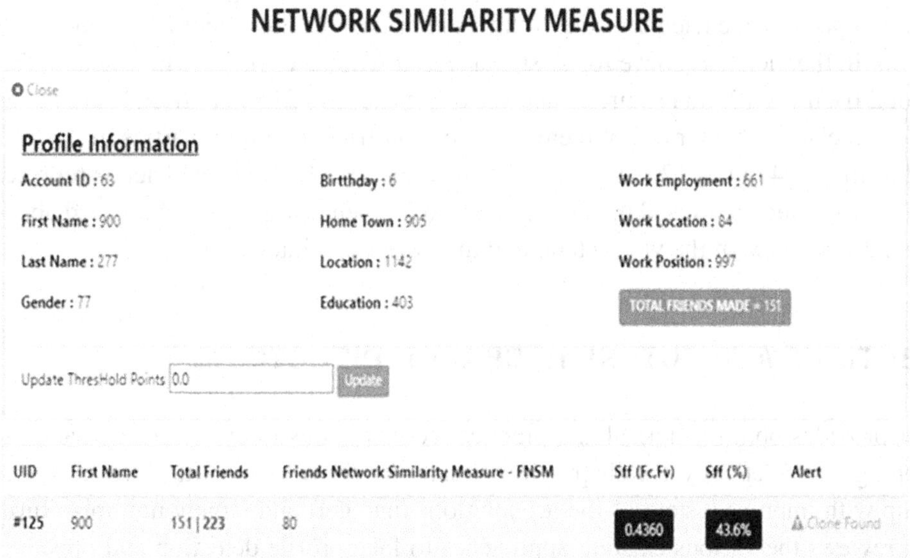

NETWORK SIMILARITY MEASURE

O Close

Profile Information

Account ID : 63	Birtthday : 6	Work Employment : 661
First Name : 900	Home Town : 905	Work Location : 84
Last Name : 277	Location : 1142	Work Position : 997
Gender : 77	Education : 403	TOTAL FRIENDS MADE = 151

Update ThresHold Points 0.0   Update

UID	First Name	Total Friends	Friends Network Similarity Measure - FNSM	Sff (Fc,Fv)	Sff (%)	Alert
#125	900	151	223	80	0.4360	43.6%	Clone Found

In Figure 8, a victim with ID 63 had 151 friends' network while the clone with ID 125 had 223 friends and 80 of the friends of the victim are also friends of the clone. No other profile accounts with high attribute ratings attempted to woo the friends from the victim's circle.

The closeness of biodata attributes alone does not determine a clone. A true clone has intention. It, therefore, goes further than just profile similarity. Friends network similarity is vital to conclude whether or not a profile is a clone of the other.

Figure 8. Displays the closeness of attributes of suspected profiles of victim 199

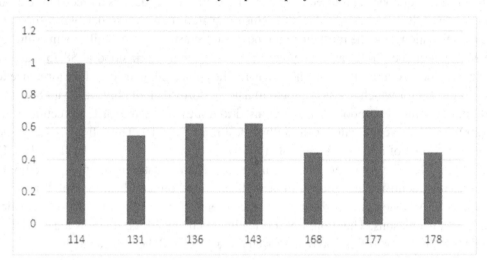

Figure 9, the pie chart represents stage 2 of ASM with a threshold of 0.0, seven (7) profiles were potentially clone candidates with varied similarity check weights. Stage 3 seeks to verify whether or not a clone attempts to make friends of the victim his/her friends, the outcome concludes the processes of verification. In the pie chart above for First Name 199 with User ID 97 who wants to find his clone (Pv) has a total friend of 125 in his circles and the clone (Pc) has 215 total friends in his/her circles. In the evaluation to check whether or not there are common friends to both parties, it has been revealed that the Pc has made 94 out of 125 of the Pv's friends his. This figure of 94 friends represents 75.20% of the total friends of the victim and put victim–clone pair friends together as displayed above, common friends form 22%, less 7% of the victim total and this reveals an intention.

CONTRIBUTIONS AND FUTURE RESEARCH DIRECTIONS

This chapter provides both theoretical and practical contributions to cyber security and identity theft (Profile Cloning). Theoretically, the chapter investigates Profile Cloning Attack Detection Approaches and comes up with improved, state-of-the-art solutions that alert and largely minimize further attacks. The chapter reviews the various existing approaches to fake profile detection and prevention through categorization and comparison to adopt and improve on the limitations of some of those existing approaches for better and more robust fake profile detection and prevention approaches. The literature review will bring to the fore, the types of user activities and experiences that made the individual susceptible to such attacks to fine-tune such knowledge through user education.

Figure 9. Network similarity of Victim: Clone pair in percentages

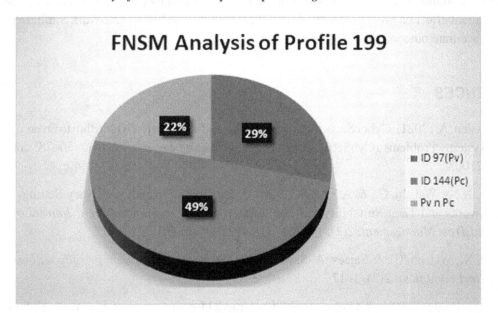

Practically, the chapter seeks to improve on data filtering of the existing approaches for the detection of suspicious profiles. It also aims to be robust and user-friendly for OSN patrons seeking to understand how profile cloning works. The study developed an application that accepts user (original profile details) input and uses this input as criteria to search and process the dataset to find suspiciously fake profiles, then any OSN user or a victim could use knowledge and experiences gained from the Detector Model to fortify his or her security on the platform.

For future work, there could be a testing of this model with more attributes than the ten used. It would expand the relationship between attributes and suspected fake profiles or clones. Secondly, work on the model could further be implemented on cross-platforms to detect clones through the matching of attributes and finally move this work from the mock stage to the real-life stage to detect live clones on OSN platforms to unmask the true culprits behind these unscrupulous acts will be a dream come true.

CONCLUSION

This chapter focuses mainly on developing an algorithm that uses clustering and similarity measures to design a model to detect clones on the OSN dataset as a mock-up to solving the real-life challenge. The techniques of clustering, similarity measures, and precision measures all lend credence to the effectiveness and robust nature of the EAD Model. The chapter also came up with some privacy and security strategies to adopt by OSN users whilst on these platforms as a user intervention realizing the gravity of the real situation. This is so because real-life occurrences like pandemics are causing a paradigm shift in human activities mainly from live or reality to virtual modes including using OSN platforms for business transactions, education, and job-seeking avenues. Therefore, if OSN platform users are educated and become aware of possible dangers including profile cloning, it would go a long way to minimize the effects of profile cloning attacks. The performance of the model was measured with Precision to meet the Gold Standard taking into consideration TF and FT parameters. The efficiency of the model and its resultant effect on profiles stemmed from the Attribute and Friends Network Similarity Measure indicating accurate outcomes in every instance.

REFERENCES

Abdou Hussien, A. (2021). Cyber Security Crimes, Ethics and a Suggested Algorithm to Overcome Cyber-Physical Systems Problems (CybSec1). *Journal of Information Security, 12*(01), 56–78. doi:10.4236/jis.2021.121003

Aldhafferi, N., & Watson, C., & A.S.M, S. (. (2013). Personal Information Privacy Settings of Online Social Networks and Their Suitability for Mobile Internet Devices. *International Journal of Security. Privacy and Trust Management, 2*(2), 1–17. doi:10.5121/ijsptm.2013.2201

Aldhafferi, N., Watson, C., & Sajeev, A. S. M. (2013). *Personal information privacy settings of online social networks and their. 2*(2), 1–17.

Alflen, N. C., Prado, E. P. V., & Grotta, A. (2020). A model for evaluating requirements elicitation techniques in software development projects. *ICEIS 2020 - Proceedings of the 22nd International Conference on Enterprise Information Systems, 2*(Iceis), 242–249. 10.5220/0009397502420249

Ali, M. K., Ali, M. K., & Hassan, K. A. (2020). *Factors Affecting Information Privacy and Protection Behavior on Social Network Sites. VII*(Ix), 406–418.

Ali, S., Islam, N., Rauf, A., Din, I. U., Guizani, M., & Rodrigues, J. J. P. C. (2018). Privacy and security issues in online social networks. *Future Internet, 12*(12), 1–12. doi:10.3390/fi10120114

Bilge, L., Strufe, T., Balzarotti, D., & Kirda, E. (2009). All your contacts belong to us: Automated identity theft attacks on social networks. *WWW'09 - Proceedings of the 18th International World Wide Web Conference*, 551–560. 10.1145/1526709.1526784

Bin Othman Mustafa, M. S., Nomani Kabir, M., Ernawan, F., & Jing, W. (2019). An Enhanced Model for Increasing Awareness of Vocational Students Against Phishing Attacks. *2019 IEEE International Conference on Automatic Control and Intelligent Systems, I2CACIS 2019 - Proceedings, June*, (pp. 10–14). IEEE. 10.1109/I2CACIS.2019.8825070

Bródka, P., Sobas, M., & Johnson, H. (2014). Profile cloning detection in social networks. *Proceedings - 2014 European Network Intelligence Conference, ENIC 2014*, (pp. 63–68). IEEE. 10.1109/ENIC.2014.21

Diebold, P., & Scherr, S. A. (2017a). Software process models vs descriptions: What do practitioners use and need? *Journal of Software (Malden, MA), 29*(11), e1879. doi:10.1002mr.1879

Diebold, P., & Scherr, S. A. (2017b). Software process models vs descriptions: What do practitioners use and need? *Journal of Software (Malden, MA), 29*(11), e1879. doi:10.1002mr.1879

Edwards, C. (2017). Waterfall Model. The Bloomsbury Encyclopedia of Design, 1–4. doi:10.5040/9781472596154-BED-W004b

Ganney, P. S., Pisharody, S., & Claridge, E. (2013). Software Engineering. In Clinical Engineering: A Handbook for Clinical and Biomedical Engineers. Academic Press. doi:10.1016/B978-0-12-396961-3.00009-3

He, B. Z., Chen, C. M., Su, Y. P., & Sun, H. M. (2014). A defence scheme against Identity Theft Attack based on multiple social networks. *Expert Systems with Applications, 41*(5), 2345–2352. doi:10.1016/j.eswa.2013.09.032

Hiatt, D., & B, Y. (2016). Role of Security in Social Networking. *International Journal of Advanced Computer Science and Applications, 7*(2), 12–15. doi:10.14569/IJACSA.2016.070202

Hoda, R., & Murugesan, L. K. (2016). Multi-level agile project management challenges: A self-organizing team perspective. *Journal of Systems and Software, 117*, 245–257. doi:10.1016/j.jss.2016.02.049

Hu, X., Zhang, X., & Lovrich, N. P. (2021). Forecasting Identity Theft Victims: Analyzing Characteristics and Preventive Actions through Machine Learning Approaches. *Victims & Offenders, 16*(4), 465–494. doi:10.1080/15564886.2020.1806161

Jain, A. K., Sahoo, S. R., & Kaubiyal, J. (2021a). Online social networks security and privacy: Comprehensive review and analysis. *Complex & Intelligent Systems, 0123456789*(5), 2157–2177. Advance online publication. doi:10.100740747-021-00409-7

Jain, A. K., Sahoo, S. R., & Kaubiyal, J. (2021b). Online social networks security and privacy: Comprehensive review and analysis. *Complex & Intelligent Systems, 7*(5), 2157–2177. doi:10.100740747-021-00409-7

Joshi, S., Nagariya, H. G., Dhanotiya, N., & Jain, S. (2020). Identifying Fake Profile in Online Social Network: An Overview and Survey. *Communications in Computer and Information Science, 1240 CCIS*. doi:10.1007/978-981-15-6315-7_2

Kamhoua, G. A., Pissinou, N., Iyengar, S. S., Beltran, J., Kamhoua, C., Hernandez, B. L., Njilla, L., & Makki, A. P. (2017). Preventing Colluding Identity Clone Attacks in Online Social Networks. *Proceedings - IEEE 37th International Conference on Distributed Computing Systems Workshops, ICDCSW 2017*, (pp. 187–192). IEEE. 10.1109/ICDCSW.2017.64

Kaur, C., & Kumar, V. (2016). Comparative Analysis of Iterative Waterfall Model and Scrum. *International Journal of Computer Science Research, 3*(1), 11–14.

Khairuddin, S. N., Sarlan, A., & Ahmad, R. (2021). Challenges in Requirement Management Process: An Overview. *Proceedings of International Conference on Computer and Information Sciences: Sustaining Tomorrow with Digital Innovation.* (pp. 120–124). IEEE. 10.1109/ICCOINS49721.2021.9497213

KharajiM. Y.RiziF. S.KhayyambashiM. R. (2014). *A New Approach for Finding Cloned Profiles in Online Social Networks. 6*(April), 25–37. https://arxiv.org/abs/1406.7377

Khayyambashi, M. R., & Rizi, F. S. (2013). An approach for detecting profile cloning in online social networks. *2013 7th Intenational Conference on E-Commerce in Developing Countries: With Focus on e-Security.* IEEE. 10.1109/ECDC.2013.6556739

Kontaxis, G., Polakis, I., Ioannidis, S., & Markatos, E. P. (2011). Detecting social network profile cloning. *2011 IEEE International Conference on Pervasive Computing and Communications Workshops, PERCOM Workshops 2011, November 2014*, (pp. 295–300). IEEE. 10.1109/PERCOMW.2011.5766886

Kumar, A., Gupta, S. K., Rai, A. K., & Sinha, S. (2013).. . *Social Networking Sites and Their Security Issues.*, *3*(4), 1–5.

Kumar, A., Kumar Gupta, S., Rai, A. K., & Sinha, S. (2013). Social Networking Sites and Their Security Issues. *International Journal of Scientific and Research Publications*, *3*(4). www.ijsrp.org

Kumar, N. (n.d.). *Automatic Detection of Fake Profiles in Online Social Networks R . Nithin Reddy (108CS043) & Automatic Detection of Fake Profiles in Online Social Networks*. NIT Rourkela.

Liyanage, C. R., & Premarathne, S. C. (2019). *A Walkthrough on Clone Profile Resolution in Social Networks*. *10*(9), 1334–1337.

Liyanage, C. R., & Premarathne, S. C. (2019). A Walkthrough on Clone Profile Resolution in Social Networks. *International Journal of Scientific and Engineering Research*, *10*(9). http://www.ijser.org

Liyanage, C. R., & Premarathne, S. C. (2021a). *Clustered Approach for Clone Detection in Social Media*. *11*(1).

Liyanage, C. R., & Premarathne, S. C. (2021b). Clustered Approach for Clone Detection in Social Media. *International Journal on Advanced Science, Engineering and Information Technology*, *11*(1), 99–104. doi:10.18517/ijaseit.11.1.9272

Meligy, A. M., Ibrahim, H. M., & Torky, M. F. (2015). A Framework for Detecting Cloning Attacks in OSN Based on a Novel Social Graph Topology. *International Journal of Intelligent Systems and Applications*, *7*(3), 13–20. doi:10.5815/ijisa.2015.03.02

Mohammadrezaei, M., Shiri, M. E., & Rahmani, A. M. (2018). Identifying Fake Accounts on Social Networks Based on Graph Analysis and Classification Algorithms. *Security and Communication Networks*, *2018*, 1–8. doi:10.1155/2018/5923156

Mushtaq, J. (2016). Different Requirements Gathering Techniques and Issues. *International Journal of Scientific and Engineering Research*, *7*(9), 835–840.

Navarro, J. C., & Higgins, G. E. (2017). Familial Identity Theft. *American Journal of Criminal Justice*, *42*(1), 218–230. doi:10.100712103-016-9357-3

Nyandongo, K. M., & Khoza, L. (2018). Assessing the performance of agile methodology: A customer perspective. *Towards Sustainable Technologies and Innovation - Proceedings of the 27th Annual Conference of the International Association for Management of Technology, IAMOT 2018*, (pp. 1–17). IEEE.

Okesola, O. J., Okokpujie, K., Goddy-Worlu, R., Ogunbanwo, A., & Iheanetu, O. (2019). Qualitative comparisons of elicitation techniques in requirement engineering. *Journal of Engineering and Applied Sciences (Asian Research Publishing Network)*, *14*(2), 565–570.

P, S., & Chatterjee, M. (2019). Detection of Fake and Cloned Profiles in Online Social Networks. *SSRN Electronic Journal*, 1–5. doi:10.2139/ssrn.3349673

Policy, P. (2020). *Got It ! Got It !* 1–6.

Purba, K. R., Asirvatham, D., & Murugesan, R. K. (2020). Classification of instagram fake users using supervised machine learning algorithms. *Iranian Journal of Electrical and Computer Engineering, 10*(3), 2763–2772. doi:10.11591/ijece.v10i3.pp2763-2772

Rao, S., Verma, A. K., & Bhatia, T. (2020a). *Evolving Cyber Threats, Combating Techniques, and Open Issues in Online Social Networks*, 219–235. IGI Global. doi:10.4018/978-1-7998-5728-0.ch012

Rao, S., Verma, A. K., & Bhatia, T. (2020b). *Evolving Cyber Threats*. Combating Techniques, and Open Issues in Online Social Networks. doi:10.4018/978-1-7998-5728-0.ch012

Revathi, S., & Suriakala, M. (2018). Profile Similarity Communication Matching Approaches for Detection of Duplicate Profiles in Online Social Network. *Proceedings 2018 3rd International Conference on Computational Systems and Information Technology for Sustainable Solutions, CSITSS 2018*, (pp. 174–182). IEEE. 10.1109/CSITSS.2018.8768751

Riswanto, & Sensuse, D. I. (2021). Knowledge management systems development and implementation: A systematic literature review. *IOP Conference Series: Earth and Environmental Science, 704*(1). doi:10.1088/1755-1315/704/1/012015

Rizi, F. S., Khayyambashi, M. R., & Kharaji, M. Y. (2014). A New Approach for Finding Cloned Profiles in Online Social Networks. In *Int* (Vol. 6). J. of Network Security.

Romanov, A., Semenov, A., Mazhelis, O., & Veijalainen, J. (2017). Detection of fake profiles in social media: Literature review. *WEBIST 2017 - Proceedings of the 13th International Conference on Web Information Systems and Technologies, Webist*, (pp. 363–369). 10.5220/0006362103630369

Roy, P. K., & Chahar, S. (2021). Fake Profile Detection on Social Networking Websites: A Comprehensive Review. *IEEE Transactions on Artificial Intelligence, 1*(3), 271–285. doi:10.1109/TAI.2021.3064901

Royce, W. W. (2021). Managing the Development of Large Software Systems (1970). *Ideas That Created the Future*, (August), 321–332. doi:10.7551/mitpress/12274.003.0035

Saranya Shree, S., Subhiksha, C., & Subhashini, R. (2021). Prediction of Fake Instagram Profiles Using Machine Learning. SSRN *Electronic Journal, 25*(5), 4490–4497. doi:10.2139/ssrn.3802584

Sarode, A. J., & Mishra, A. (2015). Audit and analysis of impostors: An experimental approach to detect fake profile in online social network. *ACM International Conference Proceeding Series, 25-27-Sept*, 1–8. 10.1145/2818567.2818568

Senthil Kumar, N., Saravanakumar, K., & Deepa, K. (2016). On Privacy and Security in Social Media - A Comprehensive Study. *Physics Procedia, 78*(December 2015), 114–119. doi:10.1016/j.procs.2016.02.019

ShaydulinR.SybrandtJ. (2017). *To Agile, or not to Agile: A Comparison of Software Development Methodologies*. 1–11. https://arxiv.org/abs/1704.07469

Spoorthy, A. S., & sinha, S. (2021). Trust Based Fake Node Identification in Social Networking Sites. *IOP Conference Series. Materials Science and Engineering, 1123*(1), 012036. doi:10.1088/1757-899X/1123/1/012036

Szabo, B., & Hercegfi, K. (2017). Research questions on integrating user experience approaches into software development processes. *8th IEEE International Conference on Cognitive Infocommunications, CogInfoCom 2017 - Proceedings, 2018-Janua*(CogInfoCom), (pp. 243–246). IEEE. 10.1109/CogInfoCom.2017.8268250

Van Casteren, W. (2017). The Waterfall Model And The Agile Methodologies : A Comparison By Project Characteristics-Short The Waterfall Model and Agile Methodologies. *Academic Competences in the Bachelor.* (pp. 10–13). Research Gate. https://www.researchgate.net/publication/313768860

Venkatesha, S., Reddy, K. R., & Chandavarkar, B. R. (2021). Social Engineering Attacks During the COVID-19 Pandemic. *SN Computer Science, 2*(2), 1–9. doi:10.100742979-020-00443-1 PMID:33585823

Wang, Y., & Nepali, R. K. (2015). Privacy threat modeling framework for online social networks. *2015 International Conference on Collaboration Technologies and Systems, CTS 2015*, (pp. 358–363). IEEE. 10.1109/CTS.2015.7210449

Wani, M. A., Agarwal, N., Jabin, S., & Hussain, S. Z. (2019). Analyzing Real and Fake users in Facebook Network based on Emotions. *2019 11th International Conference on Communication Systems and Networks, COMSNETS 2019, 2061*, (pp. 110–117). IEEE. 10.1109/COMSNETS.2019.8711124

Xu, Z., Harzallah, M., & Guillet, F. (2018). Comparing of term clustering frameworks for modular ontology learning. *IC3K 2018 - Proceedings of the 10th International Joint Conference on Knowledge Discovery, Knowledge Engineering and Knowledge Management.* IEEE. 10.5220/0006960401280135

Zabielski, M., Kasprzyk, R., Tarapata, Z., & Szkółka, K. (2016). Methods of Profile Cloning Detection in Online Social Networks. *MATEC Web of Conferences, 76.* IEEE. 10.1051/matecconf/20167604013

Zabielski, M., Tarapata, Z., Kasprzyk, R., & Szkółka, K. (2016). Profile Cloning Detection in Online Social Networks. *Computer Science and Mathematical Modelling, 0*(0), 39–46. doi:10.5604/01.3001.0009.4502

Zorzetti, M., Signoretti, I., Salerno, L., Marczak, S., & Bastos, R. (2022). Improving Agile Software Development using User-Centered Design and Lean Startup. *Information and Software Technology, 141*(October 2020), 106718.

KEY TERMS AND DEFINITIONS

Active Friend: An active friend in social networking is said to be two or more users who frequently share posts, otherwise, communicate very often. It represents the interaction frequency of a user with his/her friend(s) in the network.

Attribute Similarity: Attribute similarity is the comparison between the same fields of two or more profiles to measure the degree of likeness or similarity in contents. The attribute similarity metric determines how comparable a couple of profile accounts are concerning the weight of similar attributes in their fields. Users' profiles frequently contain categorical data in each field, according to the Similarity Measure. The fundamental measures to compare two attributes are if two profiles have the same value in the same field. Return 1 if the condition is true; else, return 0.

Cross-Site Profiles: Cross-site profiles are user accounts on two or more social networking sites that bear a resemblance in nature (appearance and content). Often social networking enthusiasts have multiple accounts across various sites available to them and keep them active or otherwise. In contrast, a user account or profile on one social site is secretly replicated by an intruder on another social site and lures friends of the original account user's friends on the new social site to accept his friend request the blind side of the original account user's. When an account is stolen from one site and replicated by another person on a different site it is known as cross-site profile cloning.

Internet: The Internet is a facility used to provide web services such as e-mails, e-commerce website services, and online social network site services.

OSN website: Online Social Networking (OSN) sites provide a common pattern for the required profile information and the fields allow entries of all kinds including hobbies, relationships, and career interests. There are also options for introducing additional fields.

Profile Cloning (Fake Profile): According to Bródka & Sobas (2014), a fake profile is an attempt to duplicate or reproduce illegally the credentials or biodata of an existing account by creating an identical one without the original account holder's knowledge or permission to eavesdrop or tap exchanges between the original profile owner and friends.

Profile Evaluation: It is a method of gathering suspected profiles for investigation based on attribute similarity and relationship strength measurements in comparison to the original profile. A clone profile is identified when the quantity of profile similarity exceeds a predetermined threshold of relationship and is less than others.

Same-Site Profiles: Same-site profiles are profiles that exist on one particular social networking site. When two or more profiles on the same site appear similar or share likeness, it is believed that one is a clone of the other.

Social Network: An online platform networking is a collection of social structures among a group of people that are linked in some way. People may share their interests, activities, and circle of contacts with their families, loves, and friends thanks to social networks' offer of social presence via the web and virtual environment. An OSN platform networking is a collection or a community of people that are linked in some way. People may share their interests, activities, and circle of contacts with their families, loves, and friends thanks to social networks' offer of social presence via the web and virtual environment.

Suspicious Profiles: A suspicious profile is a profile having common or similar attributes with the real or original profile such that there is highly no distinction between the two. Profile attributes such as first name, last name, and user name, are taken from a profile that the owner is willing to duplicate profile of his/hers. The data gathered is used to create test queries in search engines available on OSNs. The outcome of the search is used to create a suspected list of profiles-accounts which is further screened.

APPENDIX

List of Abbreviations

ID Information Distiller / Identification
URL Uniform Resource Locator
ASM Attribute Similarity Measure
FNSM Friends Network Similarity Measure
OSN Online Social Network
NSCM Network Similarity Computation Measure
COVID-19 Coronavirus of 2019
HTTP Hypertext Transfer Protocol
HTTPS Hypertext Transfer Protocol Secure
XAMPP Apache HTTP Server Mysql Database Php and Perl
SQL structured Query Language
HTML Hypertext Markup Language
EAD Model Eklah Anthony Doe Model
NSPCD Network Similarity Profile Clone Detection
ASPCD Attribute Similarity Profile Clone Detection
TPR True Positive Rate
FPR False Positive Rate
NLP Natural Language Processing
SVM Support Vector Network
KNN K-Nearest Neighbor

Chapter 18
Risk Detection and Assessment in Digital Signature

R. Hemalatha
PSG College of Arts and Science, India

R. Amutha
PSG College of Arts and Science, India

ABSTRACT

Nowadays people are living in a digital era in which all aspects of our lives depend on computers, networks, software applications and other electronic devices. Due to the technological development the security tasks and threat intelligence is a challenging task. Information theft is one of the most expensive segments of cybercrime. It is essential to protect information from cyber threats. In business, the digital signature plays an important role in authorizing the digital data. The receiver or some third party can verify this binding. In larger business, the signing process supports regulating the business. It uses asymmetric cryptography, which provides a layer of validation and security to the message communication through a non-secure channel. There are some risks in digital signature like forgery, fraud, and exclusions. This chapter discusses how to identify the risks and methods practices to mitigate the risks in adopting digital signature. Reasonable risk analysis can enhance the chance of successful electronic business.

1. INTRODUCTION TO DIGITAL SIGNATURES

The world of business changing rapidly and no company can keep up. It is witnessed several technological advances that have revolutionized business around the world such as customer relationship management systems, integrated communications and social media marketing.

Gone are the days of printing documents, physically signing them, scanning them and sending them back. Wet signatures had become standard in offices around the world. Today, however, this practice, like everything else, has moved to a digital format. The digital transformation of business faces growing concerns about the authentication, verification, trust, recognition, security and trustworthiness of digital transactions.

DOI: 10.4018/978-1-6684-9317-5.ch018

In today's highly connected world, the traditional approaches like signing and authenticating documents increasingly take over by electronic signatures, sometimes called digital signatures. Digital signatures are becoming a standard practice in the modern world and new developments can make a big difference for businesses and save a lot of time for individuals and entire businesses.

1.1 Digital Signature

Public key cryptography used in digital signature to verify identity, ensure data and transaction integrity. This signature means that the data written by the signatory and unaltered, certifying the legitimacy of the developed company digital signature. Any modification of the signed data invalidates the entire signature.

Traditional pen and ink signatures are less secure and less protective than digital signatures. With handwritten signatures, it is not always possible to identify who signed and when. In addition, it is not possible to check if the document has changed after adding a handwritten signature.

Digital signature technology has around for quite some time and is largely standardized and recognized by businesses, organizations and governments around the world. Digital signatures are more widely accepted internationally than the simpler (and less secure) type of electronic signature. Once a document has signed with a digital signature, it becomes legally binding and remains so for years.

Digital signatures used in:

- Mortgage application
- Real estate contracts and closing documents
- Purchase agreement
- Supplier Agreement
- Virtual recruitment and on-boarding documents

Figure 1. Digital signature

1.2 Example for Digital Signature

Let's look at a step-by-step example of digital signatures to better understand the process.
Suppose a person needs to send a message to someone at particular office.

- The first step is to type the message or prepare a file to send. The private key acts as a stamp for this file as a code or password. Then press Send and the mail will reach the particular office over the Internet.
- In the second step, the office receives the file and the signature verified with its public key. Then the user can access the encrypted files.
- In the final step, the office Bureau needs to unlock the file using the private key that shared. If the recipient does not have the private key, the information in the document is not accessible.

Figure 2. Example for digital signature

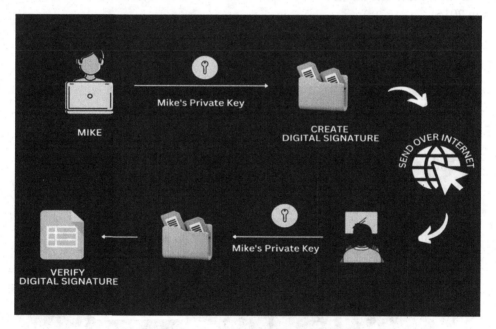

1.3 Digital Signature Secure

It is a special type of signature backed by a digital certificate proves the identity. It considered a more secure type of electronic signature because it cryptographically bound and verified to the signed document. The document obtains a digital signature using a digital certificate obtained from a trusted third party, it is virtually impossible to forge the resulting digital signature. In addition, it provides proof of the identity of the signer. That is, the signed document is not amended and the signature is valid.

1.4 Evolution of Digital Signature

Whitfield Diffie and Martin Hellman introduced the digital signature concept and there were no practical implementation of the concept in 1976.

Ronald Rivest, Adi Shamir, and Len Adleman developed the RSA algorithm that used to develop the first digital signatures in 1977.

Lotus Notes 1.0 uses RSA algorithms that became the first widely marketed software that could offer digital signatures in 1988.

Embedding the digital signatures on documents added to the format like PDF in 1999.

Digital signatures become a legally binding through ESIGN law in 2000.

The International Organization for Standardization known as ISO 32000, the PDF format becomes an open standard in 2008.

GetAccept founded with the goal of becoming a global leader in eSigning and assisting businesses in implementing in 2015. In business transactions, it is a standard for all of their business activities.

eIDAS (electronic Identification, Authentication, and trust Services) is an EU regulation on electronic signatures in 2016.

Figure 3. Evolution of Digital Signature

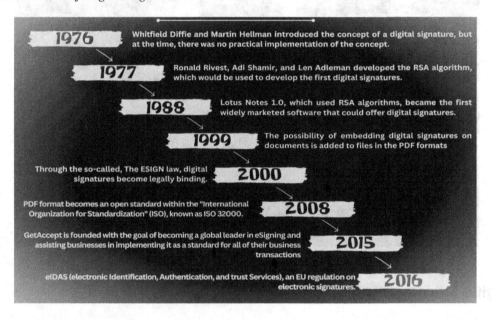

1.5 Application of Digital Signature in Real Life

Digital signatures are becoming more widely used by businesses in the private and public sectors to modernize workflows and increase the security of document processing processes. There are many applications for digital signatures in the 21st century, which play a vital role for restructuring and modernizing any enterprises, market place, corporation, agencies, etc.,

- **Human Resources**

HR professionals deal with legal agreements and agreements where digital signatures have a significant impact on their ability to process digital documents efficiently. From non-disclosure agreements to employee agreements to initiations, digital signatures provide the security and transparency needed to ensure all forms and documents are secure and trustworthy.

- **Financial Services**

The financial sector has entered a new banking era with digital signatures. Banking transaction, customer loan servicing, Contracts, mortgages, insurance documents and more made possible by the secure and efficient technology behind digital signatures.

- **HealthCare**

The advent of digital signatures has improved the efficiency of administrative and treatment processes and enhanced data security in health care industry. Both doctors and patients use digital signatures to distribute prescriptions, patient information, and process other documents. Most healthcare companies must comply with specific laws and regulations that require them to prove their authenticity to government agencies using digital signatures.

- **Banking Industry**

It used in the banking industry for contracts, loan processes, mortgages and many other documents. The user should follow the guidelines of the E-Signature Act, the Federal Examination Council for Financial Institutions, and the Uniform Electronic Business Transactions Act.

- **Government Agency**

Governments use it to release sensitive documents such as budgets, tax returns, invoices and contracts. They follow very strict protocols and use digital signatures such as smart cards to identify employees. Only these cardholders have access to the digital signatures that secure the institution's systems.

- **Government**

Governments use digital signatures for variety of reasons, including ratifying laws and administering contracts, processing tax returns, and validating transactions between businesses and governments. The digitization of these processes has reduced costs and increased security when handling sensitive documents. Government agencies follow strict laws, standards and regulations while using digital signatures. Public officials use smart cards to identify employees and citizen. These physical cards contain a digital signature that grants the cardholder access to buildings and internal systems.

- **Crypto currencies**

Digital signatures play a central role in crypto currency security like Bitcoin. Cryptocurrencies use digital signatures to authenticate the blockchain upon which they are constructed. To use Bitcoin from a particular Bitcoin address, the user has to prove their "ownership" (or knowledge) of the private key and private key associated with the public key.

- **Legal Offices**

Law firms handle some of the most confidential documents in the country. Implementing digital signatures has significantly reduced paper and labour costs. Storage of confidential documents also plays a role.

- **Military**

The military is one of the largest and most sensitive sectors in any country that has seen many improvements with the advent of digital signatures. Above all, information sharing and security have improved him tenfold.

- **Manufacturing**

Manufacturing, like other industries, relies heavily on paperwork for process approvals, contract management, invoice signing, and document management. Digital signature software helps manufacturing companies digitally manage all documents related to every point in the manufacturing process. This prompted manufacturers to speed up the process. This enables better product design, increased production and sales.

1.6 Benefits of Digital Signatures

Data authentication, Data integrity and non-repudiation support can offered by digital signatures. Documents signed electronically, and verified by the signers. This mathematical code verifies the sender of the document and makes sure that the recipient did not alter it. The advantages of digital signatures are as follows:

- **Enhanced Security**: Digital signatures have security measures built in to make sure that official documents haven't been tampered with and that the signature is valid. Asymmetric encryption, personal identification numbers (PINs), cyclic redundancy checks (CRC),checksums and verification by CAs and trust service providers (TSPs) are among the security features.
- **Save time:** Besides signing documents and contracts with the click of a button, digital signature certificates allow businesses to save both time and money. Particularly when people need to sign from different locations, it saves a lot of money and time.

Figure 4. Benefits of digital signature

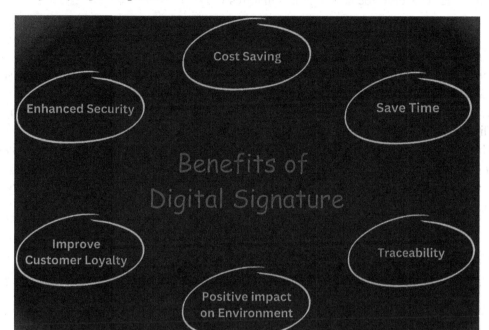

- **Improve customer loyalty:**
  Digital signatures are advantageous to stakeholders, partners, and customers as well. Instead of physically visiting a branch, office, or store, you can sign whenever you want, from any location, using any device. E-signatures enhance external business processes more than internal ones. By enhancing the shopping experience, it also raises customer satisfaction and loyalty. Electronic signatures provide customers with a number of advantages in addition to accelerating the signing process and getting rid of office printers. This superior experience results in quicker turnaround times as well as greater customer retention and satisfaction.
- **Positive impact on the environment:** Cutting back on paper use also lessens the physical waste it produces and the harmful effects that transporting paper documents has on the environment.
- **Traceability:** Digital signatures produce an audit trail that marks managing internal records in an organization easier. There are fewer opportunities for the handwritten signer or note-maker to make a mistake or forget something because everything is recorded and stored digitally.

1.7 How Does Digital Signature Work?

A digital signature works by proving that a digital document or message not modified either intentional or unintentional. It generates unique hash for the document. Send a document or message and encrypt the message with the sender's private key. Digital signature is a framework for generating private keys, signature algorithms, and verification algorithms for comparison with public keys and verifies the authenticity of private keys and digital signatures.

The following steps describe how digital signatures work.

Step 1: A sender has to select a file to digitally signing.
Step 2: Once a file selected, the sender computes a unique hash value of the file contents.
Step 3: The hash of the selected file encrypted with the private key of sender's to create a digital signature.
Step 4: The original file will be sent to the recipient along with a digital signature.
Step 5: Recipients use the relevant document application. This marks the file as digitally signed.
Step 6: The receiver uses the sender's public key to decrypt the digital signature.
Step 7: The recipient's computer calculates the original file's hash value and compares the calculated hash with the decrypted hash of the sender's file.
Step 8: If any differences found, the received message is more likely to be considered tampered with than the original message.

Figure 5. The figure shows how the digital signature works

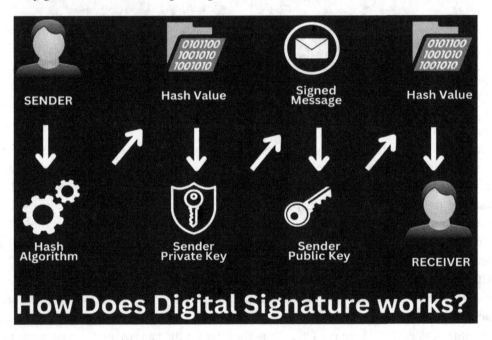

1.8 Types of Digital Signature

Different document processing platforms support various types of digital signatures. They are described below.

1.8.1 Certified Signatures

Authenticated and digitally signed documents have a unique blue band across the top of the document. A notarized signature contains the names of the person who signed the document and the issuer of the certificate, indicating the authenticity and authorship of the document.

Figure 6. Types of digital signature

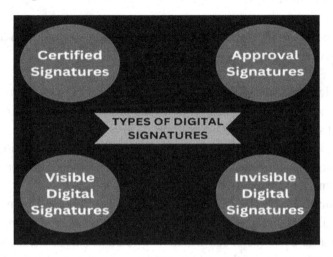

1.8.2 Approval Signatures

In an organization's business processes, documents can be approved using digital signatures. It makes the organization's approval procedure more efficient. In order to complete this process, permissions granted by both us and other parties must be obtained and embedded in PDF files. The signature approval contains information like a picture of the area, a real signature, a date, and an official seal.

1.8.3 Visible Digital Signature

It allows a user to digitally sign the documents. This signature will appear on the document in the same way the signature appears on the physical document.

1.8.4 Invisible Digital Signature

Invisible digital signatures have a blue band visual cue within the document on the taskbar. Invisible digital signatures can be used when you don't have a signature or don't want to see it, but need to demonstrate the authenticity, integrity, and provenance of a document.

1.9 Understanding the Importance of Rules and Standards

1.9.1 Digital Signature Standard (DSS)

DSS presented within the year of 1994 by US National Established of Benchmarks and Innovation (NIST). It is the standard for electronic archive confirmation in US government. Government Data Preparing Standard (FIPS) 186 indicates DSS. It proposed in 1991 and changed in 1993 due to open concerns approximately framework security.

1.9.2 Types of Digital Signatures

All electronic signatures must comply with DSS rules, but not all are created equal. There are three types of digital signatures that can be used to sign documents:

1. **Simple Electronic Signature (SES)** – It is the most basic form of electronic signature. SES is quick and easy to add to your documents, but it's not protected by encryption. In other words, they are unsure. Email signatures are a good example of SES.
2. **Advanced Electronic Signatures (AES)** – Although not yet legally binding, AES tracks changes made to documents after they are signed. This provides better security, but he still may not want to use AES for important contracts and documents.
3. **Qualified Advanced Electronic Signature (QES)** - The foremost secure electronic signature strategy. Qualified electronic marks, too known as advanced marks, utilize open key foundation, deviated encryption, and two-factor confirmation to guarantee the most noteworthy level of security. It can confirm the personality of the endorser and is as secure and lawful as a physical signature.

2. ALGORITHMS IN DIGITAL SIGNATURE

The Digital Signature Algorithm (DSA) is one of the Federal Information Processing Standards for creating digital signatures. It uses the discrete logarithm problem and the modular exponentiation formulas to cryptograph the signature digitally.

It uses the public-key primitives of message confirmation in cryptography are advanced marks. In truth, at this minute, written by hand marks on written or transcribed writings are broadly utilized within the physical world. They utilized to tie signatories to the message in arrange to secure it.

Therefore, a digital signature is a method that binds an individual or organization to the digital information in the signature. Now the recipient of the information and any other party with access to the information can independently verify that it is binding. Here, a digital signature is a cryptographic value that created by the signer or the person whose signature it is, with a secret key known only to them.

In reality, the recipient of a communication must be certain that it originates from the sender and should not be able to hack the message's origin to use it inappropriately or for any other reason. This requirement is particularly crucial in commercial applications and other domains since there is a very high likelihood of a disagreement concerning transmitted data.

2.1 Digital Signature: Block Diagram

The digital signature scheme works based on public-key cryptography algorithm.

- To begin with, each user using this technique possesses a cryptographic public-private key pair.
- Each signature uses a unique set of key pairs for encryption, decryption, signing, and verification. In this approach, the public key serves as the verification key while the private key is utilised to sign documents.
- The data from the signer fed into hash function and hash value of the message generated.

Figure 7. Block diagram of digital signature

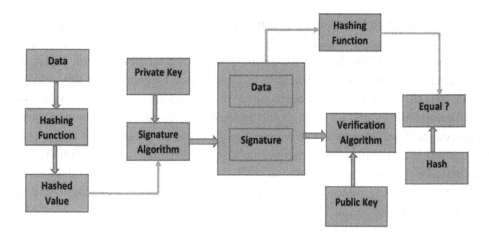

- The signing key and hash value are input to the signing algorithm. Algorithm generates a digital signature for a given hash value of this message. Then add your signature data and both sent to the verifier.
- After that, the verifier runs the DSA's verification algorithm with the verification key and digital signature and. As a result, the verification algorithm outputs a cipher text with some value. In order to obtain hash value for this algorithm, the verifier also applies the same hash function on the data it receives.
- The signature and its hash value and the results of the verification process compared with each other for verification. The verifier decides whether the digital signature is valid for this based on the comparison result.
- Because the signer's private key used to create the digital signature and no one else can use it to shelter the data, the signer is unable to change their mind about signing the data in the future.

2.2 Significance of Digital Signature Algorithm

Digital signatures are very important tool in cryptography. Let's find out the reasons.

To achieve data security in cryptography and cryptanalysis, the cryptographic analysis of all digital signatures using public key cryptography is therefore considered a very important or important and valuable tool. As a result, digital signature in crypto also ensures message authentication and data integrity in addition to ensuring message non-repudiation. The following are accomplishes by using a digital signature.

Message Authentication

Message authentication helps to handle identity protection. The merchant uses the handwritten signature as an authentication mechanism when comparing the signature on the back of the credit card with the signature on the receipt to verify that the person presenting the credit card is the person presenting the card. As a result, by utilising this procedure, the verifier can be sure that the digital signature were created by the sender alone and by no one else when he examines it using the sender's public key.

Data Integrity

A ensure that the information has not been adjusted since it was marked. Transcribed marks themselves do not give information astuteness administrations, but the security hones customarily encompassing manually written marks, such as the utilize of permanent ink and tamper-resistant paper, do give a few degree of information astuteness. Confirmation of the advanced signature for this calculation on the getting conclusion falls flat in case an assailant gets to and adjusts the information. As a result, the yield of the confirmation strategy and the hash of the updated information do not coordinate the signature created by this calculation. It is sensible to accept that the information judgment of this calculation has been compromised since the beneficiary has securely rejected the message. Computerized marks give fabulous information keenness administrations since the value of a computerized signature may be a work of the message process. Indeed minor changes to carefully marked messages will continuously cause signature confirmation to fall flat.

Non-Repudiation

This incorporates giving prove to a third party (such as a judge or jury) that one party taken part within the exchange. This avoids other parties to the exchange from being accidentally denied to take an interest. The buyer's signature on the credit card deals slip proves the buyer's interest within the exchange and avoids dealers and card-issuing banks from incorrectly denying the buyer's cooperation within the exchange.

Since the signer knows the signing key, he creates a unique signature only for specific data in this message. The recipient can present the data and digital signature as evidence to a third party in the event of a future dispute regarding the backup of the data. Recipients have the opportunity to prove the authenticity of their data to third parties in the event of a dispute while at the same time protecting it. Only the known signer's signature key is used. so a unique signature can be created over the data of a given message only when using encryption. To protect data, recipients can now provide third parties with digital signatures and evidence in the event of data discrepancies.

2.3 Encryption With Digital Signature

To guarantee privacy in cryptography, it is better to trade scrambled messages instead of plaintext. In open key encryption plot, the sender's open or encryption key uncovered within the open space, making it conceivable for anyone to accept his character and utilize this calculation to send scrambled message to the beneficiary.

2.4 DSA Algorithm Steps

- In the key generation process like public key and private key generation processtakes place during the first phase of the DSA algorithm, can be described as follows:
- First, select a prime number q, also referred to as the prime divisor in this.
- Choose another prime modulus in this case is p, which should choose so that p-1 mod q = 0.
- After that, select an integer g such that 1<g<p, g**q mod p = 1 and g = h**((p-1)/q) mod p. The multiplicative order modulo p of g was also referred to as q in this approach.

Figure 8. Encryption using Hash function

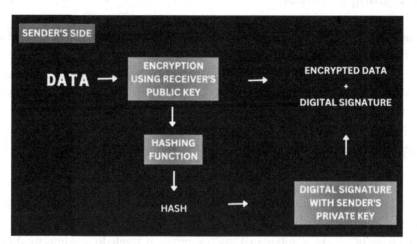

- Select an integer so that 0< x <q is true for this.
- Then, calculate y as g**x mod p.
- As a result, this is how to package the public key: p, q, g, y.
- Furthermore, the private key should be packaged as p, q, g, x.

Then, the sender can take the following actions to create a message signature:

- Create the message digest h first by employing a hashing method like SHA1.
- The next step is to create a random number k such that 0 < k< q.
- Compute (g**k mod p) mod q. Use a different k if r = 0.
- Moreover, calculate i so that k*i mod q = 1. In this, i is referred to as the modular multiplicative inverse of k modulo q.
- Calculate s = i*(h+r*x) mod q after that. Use a different k if s = 0.
- Pack the digital signature as {r,s} as a result.

The recipient of the communication and the digital signature can then take the following additional steps to confirm the message's signature:

- Create the message digest h first, employing the same hashing technique.
- Next, determine w such that s*w mod q = 1. In this context, w denoted as the modular multiplicative inverse of s modulo q.
- Next, determine u1 = h*w mod q.
- Furthermore, determine u2 = r*w mod q.
- Next, determine v = (((g**u1)*(y**u2)) mod p) mod q.
- The digital signature is valid wherever v == r.

2.5 ElGamal Signing Protocol

The ElGamal signature is a digital signature system based on the challenge of discrete logarithm computation. Taher ElGamal first described it in 1984.

The Digital Signature Algorithm, a variation created at the NSA, is far more popular. There are numerous further variations [2]. Taher ElGamal also created the ElGamal encryption, which should not be confuse with the ElGamal signature technique.

The ElGamal signature system enables a verifier to validate the validity of a message given to him through an insecure channel by the signer.

2.5.1 System Settings

- Assume H is a hash function that resists collisions.
- Assume that p is a big prime number, making computing discrete logarithms modulo p challenging.
- Assume that g is a generator selected at random from the multiplicative group of integers modulo p.

Users might exchange these system settings.

2.5.2 Key Generation

- Using $1 < x < p - 1$ select a secret key x at random.
- Determine $y = gx \bmod p$.
- The public key is (p, g, y).
- X is the secret key.

The signer just needs to complete these steps once.

2.5.3 Creation of Signatures

The signer follows these steps in order to certify a communication.

- Choose k at random such that $\gcd(k, p\ 1) = 1$ and $0 < k < p-1$.
- Calculate $r \equiv g^k (\bmod p)$.
- Calculate $s \equiv (H(m)-xr)k^{-1} (\bmod p-1)$.
- Restart if s=0.

The pair (r,s) is afterwards m's digital signature. For each signature, the signer goes through these processes again.

Verification

A signature (r,s) of a message m is verified as follows.

- $0 < r < p$ and $0 < s < p-1$.
- $gH(m) \equiv y^r r^s (\bmod p)$

If it met, all requirements the verifier accepts a signature; if not rejected.

2.5.4 Correctness

Insofar as the verifier will always accept a signature produced using the signing procedure, the algorithm is accurate.

The production of the signature suggests

$H(m) \equiv xr + sk \pmod{p-1}$

Hence, Fermat's Little Theorem suggests

$$g^{H(m)} \equiv g^{xr}g^{ks}$$

$$\equiv (g^x)^r (g^k)^s$$

$$\equiv (y)^r(r)^s \pmod{p}$$

2.5.5 Security

In order to counterfeit a signature, a third party must either discover the signer's secret key, x, or look for collisions in the hash function $H(m) \equiv H(M) \pmod{p-1}$. It is thought that both issues are challenging. To ensure that k, or even some information about k is not disclosed, the signer must be careful to select various k uniformly at random for each signature. If not, an attacker might be able to figure out the secret key x with less difficulty, which might be sufficient to allow a viable attack. A particular scenario where an attacker could directly calculate x is when two messages are delivered using the same key and k value.

2.6 Elliptic Curve Digital Signature Algorithm (ECDSA)

ECDSA is the method employed by Bitcoin to ensure that their rightful owners may only spend funds. Depending on the hash function and selected curve order. For bitcoin, these are Secp256k1 and SHA256 (SHA256 ()), respectively.

2.6.1 Concepts regarding ECDSA

- **Secret key:** a personal number that accessed by the creator. A private key is essentially a number that selected at random. Only those who own the private key linked to the funds can spend them in Bitcoin. In Bitcoin, a private key is a single unsigned 256-bit integer that takes up 32 bytes.
- **Public Key:** A numerical value functions similarly to a private key but does not need to be kept secret. It is possible to calculate a public key using a private key, but not the other way around. A public key can be used to verify if a signature is genuine (i.e., created with the correct key) without revealing the private key. Public keys may or not compressed in Bitcoin. The 33 bytes that make up compressed public keys consist of a 256-bit integer called x with a prefix of either 0x02 or 0x03. The previous uncompressed keys are 65 bytes long, contain a constant prefix (0x04), and two 256-bit integers called x and y (2 * 32 bytes). The prefix of a compressed key makes it possible to determine the y value from the x value.

- **Signature:** A code proving the signing process truly took place. A signature is produced mathematically by fusing a private key and the object to be hashed. The two integer's r and s make up the signature. A mathematical approach employing the public key on the signature can be used to prove that it was originally made from the hash and the private key without having access to the private key. With probabilities of about 25%, 50%, or 25%, respectively, the resulting signatures are 73, 72, or 71 bytes long. However, with exponentially decreasing chances, sizes far smaller than that are possible.

2.6.2 Primitives

The ECDSA verification and signing algorithms use a few fundamental variables to generate signatures and reverse the process of generating messages from signatures.

- r and s: The signature is identified by these letters and numerals.
- z: The hash of the message has to sign. There is no need for truncation because the length of the employed hash function, SHA256, is equal to the number of bits in the secp256k1 curve (256). Typically, user only permitted to use the message hash's left-most N bits, where N is the size of the employed hash function.
- K: A cryptographically secure nonce that used to calculate the values of r and s.
- dA and QA: These stand for the private key and public key of the message, respectively.

2.6.3 Algorithm for Signing

- The signing algorithm takes an input message msg****+ private key**** and generates an output signature. It consists of pair of integers{r,s}. It consists of following steps.
- Compute the hash value of the message using cryptographic hash function like SHA256. h=hash(msg)
- Generate random number k from the range of 1 to n-1.
- Calculate the random point R=k*G (G is the secp256k1 curve's generating point)
- Calculate the Signature proof s= k^{1} *(h+r*privatekey) (mod n)
- Return the signature{r, s}

2.6.4 Verification Method

The r and s, QA, and z signature pair consistency examined by the verification procedure.

- Ensure that both r and s fall between the range of 1 and n-1.
- The values of u1 = z*s-1 mod n and u2 = r*s-1 mod n should be determined.
- Check to make sure the point at infinity is not the outcome of (x, y) = u1*G + u2*QA. The strange point known as the point at infinity is produced when two points joined that would not ordinarily produce a point on the curve, such as two points with the same X value but inverted Y values.
- If r=x mod n, the signature is valid. If any of the checks fail or something else goes wrong, the signature is void.

3. ISSUES IN DIGITAL SIGNATURE

3.1 Universal Signature Forgery (USF)

Modify the signature entity by adding inappropriate content to it or removing references to it. Signature object, Universal Signature Forgery (USF) attack aims to defeat digital signature verification procedure. This object holds all the data required for signature verification.

The USF attack messed up the signature verification mechanism and prevented the correct one from being applied the cryptographic operations required to verify the signature, despite the presence of the signature object, and still included in the electronic signature. Online Verification Once Hacker Successfully Hits His USF Attack The logic or view program shows on the display panel that the electronic signature is valid. Belonging to a particular person or organization.

3.2 Incremental Saving Attack (ISA)

An incremental save to a document by altering its structure is the aim of an incremental saving attack (ISA). Therefore, the incremental saving or incremental updating capability of a PDF document, which when utilised properly enables a user to add annotations to their PDF, is the focus of this attack. After the PDF's original content, these annotations saved progressively as a new PDF body. The PDF signed using the incremental saving capability, which enables the signature object to be added to the file's original content.

Any changes made to a document after it has been signed typically result in a notice that the document has been tampered with. However, if an ISA attack is being carried out, the attacker might add new pages or annotations to a PDF that has already been signed. This violation is technically not an attack. Instead, this is an abuse of PDF's incremental save feature. However, vulnerabilities occur when the signature verification logic is unaware that the contents of the PDF file have changed. The person or organization that originally created the electronic signature for the document only sees the unsigned text. Added after the document was signed as an update. A successful ISA attack looks like this: Although the new content/text changes are indicated, the signature verification process will cause the PDF to documentation changed or updated.

3.3 Signature Wrapping (SWA)

An attack known as Signature Wrapping (SWA) employs a novel strategy to get around a PDF's signature protection without using its incremental saving function. It works by adding the second byte of the signed /Byte Range to the end of the document that violated. The attacker then references his altered xref using the xref pointer that was previously present in the signed trailer of the document. The attacker also wrap the relocated second half in a stream object or dictionary. Online signature protection function used to avoid this attack.

An attacker can insert malicious unsigned objects into the document with a successful SWA attack. These items positioned either before or after the modified xref if he has opted to wrap the relocated second section. The harmful objects would be positioned after the modified xref if no wrapping was added. To open the PDF file and avoid signature verification without the alterations noticed, the attacker may duplicate the file's last trailer and place it after his modified xref, depending on the PDF viewer.

3.4 Man-in-the-Middle (MITM) attack

When an outsider intercepts a communication between two systems, it is known as an MITM attack. Any type of online communication, social media, including email, site browsing, etc., might experience this. They can target all the data stored on the devices in addition to listening in on the private talks. When all the intricacies removed, a straightforward example used to explain the idea of an MITM attack.

Imagine returning to the past, when snail mail was widely used. After years of keeping his affections for Jackie hidden, Jerry writes a letter to her declaring his love for her. He drops the letter off at the post office, where an inquisitive mail man picks it up. Before delivering the mail to Jackie, he opened it and, for laughs only, decided to modify the letter. Because of "Jerry" calling Jackie a fat cow, Jackie develops a lifelong hatred for him. The lesson of the story is that hackers are jerks, just like the mail man.

A more contemporary illustration would be a hacker who sits in between browser and the website, which is viewing, capturing and intercepting any data provide to the site, including login credentials or sensitive information.

4. DIGITAL SIGNATURE TOOLS AND VENDORS

There are many e-signature technologies and tools on the market includes the following:

4.1 Adobe Sign

Adobe's services offer numerous features and functionality. Available on both web and mobile apps, it's easy to use e-signatures on the go. We offer authentication services to ensure that those applied to important documents are aware of basic legal compliance, and ofcourse user can personalize your electronic signature. This eSign software meets various regulated industries and EUsigning requirements. Recent improvements include life sciences and pharmaceutical compliance and integration with SAP Success factors.

Use this tool to track the status of the documents and know when documents has opened, signed and returned. Ofcourse, Adobe Sign works with all Microsoft Office products.

4.2 Xodo Sign

Xodo Sign (formerly ever sign) helps both small businesses and large enterprises. We support your digital leap. Many companies are reluctant to manage and manage processing sensitive data in the cloud, such as contracts and business agreements, stands for eversign. Build a highly secure and monitored e-signature platform. The product offers user-friendliness Affordable for all businesses, yet packed with features.

4.3 SignNow

The main purpose of SignNow is to sign documents from any device. This can be a PC, tablet or mobile phone. This app allows you to import documents and digitally sign them. Many features help to achieve this easily such as document import functionality, team collaboration, reusable templates, two-factor authentication, management tools, and more. A convenient software enables individuals and businesses to create legally binding products without stress.

4.4 PandaDoc

PandaDoc is an all-in-one tool for creating, editing, and tracking and e-signing business documents quickly and easily. Find a better way to create professional looking documents. Win more deals with unlimited e-signatures, reusable templates, in-app editing, CRM integration, APIs, and 24/7 human support.

4.5 Secured Signing

Secured Signing is a more affordable piece of software than the e-signature solutions above. Being cloud-based, user can easily access and use e-signatures from the laptop, desktop or mobile. It also supports PDF files with multiple signature fields for the similar witness and multi-page signatures.

4.6 OneSpan Sign

OneSpan Sign still says it works for both small and large businesses with its streamlined and user-friendly workflows for devices and staff. Deploy in public or private clouds, within your computing infrastructure, or any combination of the three. However, inaddition to flexibility, the software also focuses on protecting enterprise security.

4.7 Dotloop

For realtors, brokers, and teams, Dotloop is an all-in-one digital signature and transaction management platform. Dotloop gives you more support than just document sharing, editing, and e-signing. Additionally, it offers transactional insights, allows text-based document transmission and reception, and supports document compliance and storage.

4.8 Signeasy

Signeasy obviously be used from your office or home computer, and a lot of effort seems to have gone into making it mobile friendly. It's cloud-based, so you can access it on the go, and the mobile experience on your phone or tablet is so intelligently designed. Otherwise, it has many of the same features as the e-signature service above, but with a focus on simplicity (as the name suggests). Signature fields can be annotated to make it clear who should sign and how. In addition, if you need to e-sign the same type of document repeatedly, template scan be easily set up and reused. Signeasy is an e-signature solution for all businesses, SMBs and enterprises in industries such as transportation, realestate, financial and legal services.

4.9 Soda PDF

The first fully functional PDF solution that is both a desktop and a web-based app is Soda PDF Anywhere. Users have unrestricted access to the features of any web-enabled device, including desktops, laptops, smartphones, and tablets. A wealth of cutting-edge features, including PDF conversion, editing, verification, security tools, award-winning e-signature solutions, Bates numbering, cloud integration, and more all of which intended to increase productivity.

4.10 FoxiteSign

FoxiteSign's goal is to provide versatile, intuitive and adaptable solutions for customers' e-signature needs. Send, sign, and reply to documents in seconds, helping users across all industries work more efficiently and streamline their workflows.

5. RISKS OF DIGITAL SIGNATURES

Forgery – As with traditional paper and ink signatures, forgery or identity theft are real risks with electronic signatures. To reduce this risk, electronic signatures should be protected with password protection and 2FA (two-factor authentication) whenever possible.

Fraud –A digitally signed document can be tampered with even after signing. Of course, such fraud risk is not limited to electronic signatures. Like traditional paper and ink contracts, both parties should keep a copy of the contract just in case.

Exclusions – Certain types of documents (such as deeds, wills and transfers of property) cannot be signed with an electronic signature because the signature must be verified by an independent third party. If these types of documents are signed with an electronic signature, they may expire.

6. BEST PRACTICES TO MITIGATE THE ISSUES IN ADOPTING E-SIGNING

For a multitude of reasons, esignatures are safer and less secure than paper based or wet signatures. It's less likely that they're going to be manipulated, forged, copied or misused. For future reference, digital signatures have multiple layers of authentication and security, as well as court admissible proof of transactions. As far as electronic signatures are concerned, here are the best practices can apply for business processes:

In order to ensure a further layer of protection against potential Hacking and Other Cyber Security attacks, recommend to use cloud based eSignature Platform for the authentication of contract process as well as signer authorisation platform. In order to guarantee safety in the use of digital signatures, it is necessary to establish an internal eSignature Procedure or develop a formal policy. In the interests of protecting sensitive information, it may also considered to incorporate antifraud controls with certain compliance measures.

Protect Sensitive information follow the following.

If necessary, approve additional signers.

Update the list of signers on a regular basis.

If electronic signatures used for some sensitive transactions, consult with lawyer.

It is useful to know what to do with digital signatures. It is time saver and more environments friendly compared with wet signature. However, there is a risk that your business processes are at risk of being adversely affected by the lack of use of digital signatures that may lead to fraud, identity abuse and forgery if we do not properly manage them.

6.1 Digital Signature Security

Security is the major benefit of using digital signatures. Security features and methods used in digital signature include the following:

- **PINs, passwords and codes.** They utilized to confirm and authenticate the identity of the signatory and confirm their signatures. Email, username and password are the most common methods used.
- **Asymmetric cryptography.** This strategy employment open key calculation that includes private and open key encryption and verification.
- **Checksum.** This long string of letters and numbers utilized to decide the genuineness of the transmitted information. The checksum is the result of performing a cryptographic hash work on the information. The initial record esteem compared with the computed record esteem to distinguish blunders or changes. The checksum acts as a information unique finger impression.
- **CRC.** A sort of checksum, this mistake discovery code and confirmation work is utilized in advanced systems and capacity gadgets to distinguish changes in crude information.
- **CA validation.** Certificate specialists issue computerized marks and act as trusted third parties by tolerating, confirming, issuing and putting away advanced certificates. Utilizing CAs makes a difference avoid the creation of fake computerized certificates.
- **TSP validation.** This individual or legitimate substance confirms the advanced signature on sake of the company and gives signature confirmation reports.

6.2 Digital Signature Attacks

Possible attacks on digital signatures include the following:

- **Chosen-message attack.** The assailant either gets the victim's open key or traps the casualty into carefully marking archive they do not proposed to sign.
- **Known-message attack.** The aggressor gets the messages sent by the casualty and a key that permits the aggressor to manufacture the victim's signature on archives.
- **Key-only attack.** An aggressor as it were has get to the victim's open key and can reproduce the victim's signature to carefully sign archives or messages that the casualty does not proposed to sign.

REFERENCES

Atreya, M. & Paine, S. (2002). *Digital Signatures*. McGraw-Hill.

Bishop, M. (2004). *Introduction to Computer Security*. Addison-Wesley Professional.

Dunbar, F. E. S. (2002). *Digital Signature Scheme Variation*. University of Waterloo.

Menezes, A., Van Oorschot, P., & Vanstone, S. (1996). Handbook of Applied Cryptography. CRC Press.

Meyer, C., & Matyas, S. M. (1982). *Cryptography-A New Dimension in Computer Data Security*. John Wiley & Sons.

Mollin, R. (2002RSA and Public-Key Cryptography. CRC Press.

Smid, M. E. & Branstad, D. K. (1992). Response to comments on the NIST proposed Digital Signature Standard. *Crypto '92*.

Stallings, W. (2020). *Cryptography and Network Security Principles and practices*. Pearson Education.

Chapter 19
Securing the Future:
The Vital Role of Risk Detection and Cyber Security in Modern Computing Systems

R. Shobarani
https://orcid.org/0000-0003-0183-3867
Dr. M.G.R. Educational and Research Institute,
India

Chitrakala Muthuveerappan
Victoria University of Wellington, New Zealand

G. Aarthy Priscilla
St. Anne's Arts and Science College, India

T. Suganthi
https://orcid.org/0009-0000-0502-2565
D.B. Jain College, India

S. SriVidhya Santhi
Dr. M.G.R. Educational and Research Institute,
India

R. Surekha
St. Anne's Arts and Science College, India

ABSTRACT

Risk detection and cybersecurity are critical components for the success of contemporary computing systems. With the increasing reliance on technology and the Internet, cyber threats have become more complex and sophisticated, posing a significant challenge to the security of computer systems. In this chapter, the authors examine the importance of risk detection and cybersecurity measures in contemporary computing, highlighting the potential risks and threats that can impact system performance and integrity. They explore various techniques and tools used in risk detection and cybersecurity, including intrusion detection systems, firewalls, and encryption methods. Additionally, the authors discuss the role of risk management in identifying and mitigating potential threats to computing systems. They conclude that risk detection and cybersecurity measures are essential for the successful operation of contemporary computing systems and highlight the need for continued investment and innovation in this critical area.

DOI: 10.4018/978-1-6684-9317-5.ch019

1. INTRODUCTION

The increasing reliance on technology and the internet in today's world has made cybersecurity and risk detection essential for the success of contemporary computing. Cybersecurity threats are becoming more advanced, and cybercriminals are continuously evolving to find new ways to exploit vulnerabilities in computer systems. Ransomware attacks have been on the rise in recent years, and they remain a significant threat to organizations and individuals alike. In a ransomware attack, hackers typically encrypt an organization's data and demand payment in exchange for the decryption key. In some cases, hackers may also threaten to publish stolen data if their demands are not met. Phishing attacks are a type of social engineering attack that targets individuals by tricking them into providing sensitive information, such as login credentials or financial information. Phishing attacks often use emails or messages that appear to be from a legitimate source, such as a bank or a company that the target is familiar with. As more organizations move their data and applications to the cloud, cloud security has become an increasingly important issue. Cloud providers offer a range of security features, but organizations still need to ensure that they are using the cloud securely and that their data is protected.

This paper aims to explore the importance of risk detection and cybersecurity measures for the success of contemporary computing systems. We will examine various techniques and tools used for risk detection and cybersecurity, including intrusion detection systems, firewalls, and encryption methods. Additionally, we will discuss the role of risk management in identifying and mitigating potential threats to computing systems.

Latest cyber threats and trends: In recent years, there has been an increase in the number and sophistication of cyber threats. These include ransomware attacks, phishing attacks, and data breaches. Some of the latest trends in cyber threats include supply chain attacks, where attackers target third-party vendors to gain access to their customers' networks, and attacks on critical infrastructure, such as power grids and water treatment plants.

Effectiveness of Security Information and Event Management (SIEM) systems: SIEM systems are designed to detect and respond to security events in real-time. However, there is ongoing debate about their effectiveness in preventing and mitigating cyber attacks. Some studies have found that SIEM systems can be effective when used correctly, while others have found that they can generate too many false positives, leading to alert fatigue and a decrease in their effectiveness.

The human factor in cybersecurity: Human error is a significant contributor to cybersecurity incidents. This includes mistakes such as weak passwords, falling for phishing scams, and misconfiguring systems. To address this, organizations need to provide regular cybersecurity training to employees and establish policies and procedures to promote good security hygiene. Additionally, some studies have explored the use of behavioral analytics to identify and address risky behavior among employees.

2. LITERATURE SURVEY

Jajodia and Subrahmanian (2011) discuss the importance of a proactive cybersecurity approach to address emerging threats. They emphasize the need for collaboration between researchers, practitioners, and policymakers to ensure effective cybersecurity.

Tan and Ewe (2014) provide an overview of intrusion detection and prevention systems, describing the two main types of IDS (signature-based and anomaly-based) and their respective strengths and weaknesses. They emphasize the importance of IDS in detecting and preventing cyber attacks.

Cheswick and Bellovin (1994) discuss the role of firewalls in network security. They describe the different types of firewalls and their respective benefits, and provide guidance on how to implement a firewall policy that balances security needs with business requirements.

Bhatia (2019) highlights the importance of encryption in protecting sensitive information from unauthorized access. They describe the different types of encryption algorithms and their respective strengths and weaknesses, and provide guidance on how to implement an encryption strategy.

NIST (2018) provides a comprehensive framework for managing risks to information systems and organizations. The framework includes five core functions: identify, protect, detect, respond, and recover. It provides guidance on how to implement a risk management strategy that is tailored to an organization's specific needs.

Tsai and Hsieh (2018) review the current state of risk management in cybersecurity. They discuss the importance of a proactive, risk-based approach to cybersecurity and provide guidance on how to identify, assess, and mitigate risks to a computer system.

Check Point Research (2022) provides a comprehensive overview of the cyber threat landscape in 2021, including emerging threats and trends in various industries. The report highlights the importance of proactive threat intelligence and the need for continuous monitoring and incident response.

The National Cyber Security Centre (2021) provides an overview of the cyber threats faced by UK businesses, including phishing attacks, ransomware, and supply chain attacks. The report provides guidance on how to mitigate these risks and improve cybersecurity posture.

Felske et al. (2020) evaluate the effectiveness of security information and event management (SIEM) systems in detecting and responding to cyber threats. They highlight the importance of SIEM in providing a centralized view of an organization's security posture and enabling rapid response to incidents.

Kim and Trivedi (2020) provide a comprehensive review of cybersecurity risk management, including the key components of a risk management framework and the challenges associated with implementing such a framework. They emphasize the importance of a proactive, risk-based approach to cybersecurity and the need for continuous improvement.

Ransbotham and Kiron (2017) discuss the human factor in cybersecurity, including the importance of employee training and awareness programs, and the need for a culture of cybersecurity within organizations. They highlight the lessons learned from the US Department of Defense's approach to cybersecurity.

Chen, T., Wang, X., & Yang, Y. (2017) describes a malware detection approach that uses deep learning techniques based on auto encoders. The authors applied this approach to raw executable files and achieved good detection accuracy.

Duda, R. O., & Hart, P. E. (1973). This is a classic book on pattern classification and scene analysis. It covers the mathematical foundations of pattern recognition, including decision trees and other classification techniques.

Grosse, K., Papernot, N., Manoharan, P., Backes, M., & McDaniel, P. (2017). This paper explores the concept of adversarial examples for malware detection. The authors demonstrate that it is possible to create malicious software that can evade detection by machine learning algorithms, and propose potential solutions to this problem.

Kaur, H., & Verma, A. K. (2019). This paper provides a review of user behavior analysis using deep learning techniques. The authors summarize recent studies in this area and highlight the different approaches.

Liao, H., & Chen, M. (2021). This paper is a systematic literature review of fraud detection using clustering algorithms. The authors review a number of studies and summarize the different clustering techniques that have been used for this purpose.

Verma, A. K., & Dheeraj, R. (2019). This paper describes a decision tree-based password security system. The authors applied this approach to a dataset of passwords and achieved good performance in identifying weak passwords.

Alomari, M. H., & Mahdi, M. N. (2019). This paper presents a comparative study of different machine learning algorithms for intrusion detection systems (IDSs). The authors analyzed the performance of five different algorithms (K-NN, SVM, Naive Bayes, Decision Trees, and Random Forests) on the KDD Cup 1999 dataset. The study found that Random Forests outperformed the other algorithms with an accuracy of 99.88%.

Basu, M., Bhattacharyya, D., & Kundu, M. (2018). This survey paper provides an overview of different machine learning techniques that can be used for malware detection. The authors analyzed 66 research papers on the topic and found that Decision Trees and Random Forests are the most commonly used algorithms for malware detection.

Farooq, M., Mahmood, T., &Basalamah, S. (2020). This paper provides a systematic literature review of different user authentication methods using keystroke dynamics. The authors analyzed 111 research papers on the topic and found that the most commonly used machine learning algorithms for keystroke dynamics-based user authentication are SVM and Neural Networks.

Ghahremanlou, R. S., &Soltani, S. (2021). This review paper provides a comprehensive analysis of different user authentication systems that use keystroke dynamics. The authors analyzed 105 research papers on the topic and found that SVM is the most commonly used machine learning algorithm for keystroke dynamics-based user authentication.

Jin, X., Liu, F., Zhang, Y., & Jiang, X. (2019). This survey paper provides an overview of different machine learning techniques that can be used for Android malware detection. The authors analyzed 70 research papers on the topic and found that SVM and Random Forests are the most commonly used algorithms for Android malware detection.

Wang, X., &Xie, Y. (2019). This survey paper provides an overview of different user authentication schemes that use mouse dynamics. The authors analyzed 74 research papers on the topic and found that the most commonly used machine learning algorithms for mouse dynamics-based user authentication are SVM and Neural Networks.

Overall, these references emphasize the importance of a proactive, risk-based approach to cybersecurity, including the need for continuous monitoring, incident response, and employee training and awareness programs. They also highlight the importance of threat intelligence and the challenges associated with implementing a risk management framework and provide guidance on how to implement various security measures, including intrusion detection systems, firewalls, encryption, and risk management strategies. These study cover a range of topics related to cybersecurity, including the latest cyber threats and trends, the effectiveness of security information and eventmanagement (SIEM) systems, risk management strategies, and the human factor in cybersecurity.

3. CYBERSECURITY RISKS IN CONTEMPORARY COMPUTING

With the ever-growing use of the internet, the risks to cybersecurity have increased. Malware, phishing, hacking, and ransomware are some of the significant cybersecurity risks that computing systems face today. Malware refers to malicious software that can be installed on a computer without the user's knowledge or consent. Phishing is a type of social engineering attack that tricks users into revealing sensitive information like passwords or credit card details. Hacking is the unauthorized access to a computer system, while ransomware is a type of malware that encrypts a user's files and demands payment in exchange for the decryption key.

These threats can cause significant damage to a computer system, leading to the loss of data, financial loss, and reputational damage. Cybercriminals can use stolen data for financial gain or to cause harm to individuals or organizations. Therefore, it is essential to implement risk detection and cyber security measures to protect computer systems from these threats.

3.1 Techniques and Tools for Risk Detection and Cybersecurity

There are various techniques and tools used for risk detection and cybersecurity in contemporary computing systems. Techniques and tools for risk detection and cybersecurity are essential in today's digital age, where cyber threats and attacks are becoming more prevalent and sophisticated. These techniques and tools help organizations identify and mitigate potential risks to their systems, data, and networks. These techniques and tools are used to detect and prevent cybersecurity threats from causing damage to computer systems.

Here are some of the most commonly used techniques and tools:

3.1.1 Vulnerability Scanning

Vulnerability scanning is the process of identifying vulnerabilities in a system or network. This technique involves using automated tools to scan for weaknesses in software, hardware, and network configurations. The results of the scan can be used to prioritize the remediation of vulnerabilities.

However, I can provide some information on vulnerability scanning and recent trends in the field.

Vulnerability scanning is a critical component of an organization's cybersecurity strategy. It is an automated process that checks for known vulnerabilities in software, hardware, and network configurations. Vulnerability scanning tools can identify potential weaknesses in an organization's IT infrastructure before they are exploited by cybercriminals.

In recent years, there has been an increase in the number and sophistication of cyber attacks, making vulnerability scanning more critical than ever. One recent trend in vulnerability scanning is the use of machine learning algorithms to improve the accuracy of vulnerability detection. These algorithms can help identify and prioritize vulnerabilities based on their severity and the likelihood of exploitation.

Another trend in vulnerability scanning is the integration of scanning tools with other cybersecurity tools, such as intrusion detection and prevention systems (IDPS) and security information and event management (SIEM) tools. This integration can help organizations to detect and respond to potential threats more quickly and effectively.

Overall, vulnerability scanning remains a critical component of an organization's cybersecurity strategy, and recent trends in the field are focused on improving the accuracy and efficiency of vulnerability detection and response.

3.1.2 Penetration Testing

Penetration testing is a technique used to identify vulnerabilities in a system by simulating an attack. This technique involves hiring ethical hackers to try and penetrate the system's defenses, identify any weaknesses, and provide recommendations for remediation.

Intrusion detection and prevention systems: Intrusion detection and prevention systems (IDPS) are tools that monitor a system or network for suspicious activity. These tools can detect and prevent attacks by monitoring network traffic, looking for known attack patterns, and alerting security teams of potential threats.

Penetration testing, also known as pen testing, is a technique used to identify vulnerabilities in a system by simulating an attack. The goal of penetration testing is to identify weaknesses in an organization's IT infrastructure before they are exploited by cybercriminals.

During a penetration test, ethical hackers simulate real-world attacks on an organization's systems and networks to identify vulnerabilities that could be exploited by cybercriminals. The penetration testing process typically involves several stages, including:

Planning and reconnaissance: In this stage, the ethical hackers gather information about the organization's systems and network architecture.

Scanning: The ethical hackers use automated tools to scan for vulnerabilities in the organization's systems and networks.

Exploitation: The ethical hackers attempt to exploit any vulnerabilities they have identified to gain access to the organization's systems and networks.

Post-exploitation: Once access has been gained, the ethical hackers assess the extent of the access they have and attempt to escalate their privileges.

Reporting: The ethical hackers document their findings and provide recommendations for remediation.

Penetration testing is an essential component of an organization's cybersecurity strategy, as it can identify vulnerabilities that may not be identified through other security measures, such as vulnerability scanning. Penetration testing can also provide insight into an organization's overall security posture and help identify areas where additional security measures may be needed.

It is essential to note that penetration testing should only be performed by trained and ethical professionals to ensure that the testing is conducted safely and without causing damage to the organization's systems or data.

3.1.3 Security Information and Event Management (SIEM)

SIEM tools are used to monitor and analyze security-related events across an organization's systems and networks. These tools collect and analyze data from multiple sources, including logs, network traffic, and security devices, to identify potential threats and provide real-time alerts to security teams.

Security Information and Event Management (SIEM) is a cybersecurity technology that helps organizations collect, analyze, and interpret data from various sources to identify security threats and incidents. The primary function of a SIEM system is to centralize and correlate security events and alerts from multiple sources, such as firewalls, intrusion detection and prevention systems, and endpoint protection platforms.

SIEM systems work by collecting log data from various devices and applications in the organization's network and analyzing that data to detect potential security threats. The system uses rules and algorithms to identify patterns and anomalies in the data, which can be an indication of a security incident.

SIEM systems can also automate the process of alerting security teams when potential threats are detected. Alerts can be sent to security teams in real-time, enabling them to respond quickly to potential security incidents.

One of the key benefits of a SIEM system is its ability to provide a unified view of an organization's security posture. This enables security teams to identify potential threats that may be missed by individual security tools and take appropriate action to mitigate those threats.

Another benefit of SIEM is its ability to provide valuable insights into an organization's security environment. By analyzing data from various sources, SIEM systems can identify trends and patterns in security incidents, which can help organizations make more informed decisions about their security strategies and policies.

Overall, SIEM is an essential component of an organization's cybersecurity strategy. It provides a centralized platform for collecting and analyzing security data, enabling security teams to detect and respond to potential threats quickly and effectively.

3.1.4 Multi-Factor Authentication (MFA)

MFA is a security technique that requires users to provide multiple forms of authentication to access a system or network. This technique can include something the user knows (like a password), something the user has (like a token), or something the user is (like biometric data).

Multi-factor authentication (MFA) is a security technique that requires users to provide multiple forms of authentication to access a system or network. MFA is becoming increasingly popular as a security measure because it adds an additional layer of protection beyond traditional usernames and passwords, which can be easily compromised by cybercriminals.

MFA typically involves three types of authentication factors:

Something the user knows: This could be a password or PIN.

Something the user has: This could be a smart card, token, or mobile device.

Something the user is: This could be a biometric factor, such as a fingerprint, facial recognition, or iris scan.

By requiring users to provide multiple forms of authentication, MFA makes it much more difficult for cybercriminals to gain unauthorized access to a system or network. Even if a cybercriminal manages to steal a user's password, they would still need to provide the additional authentication factors to gain access.

MFA can be implemented in a variety of ways, including through hardware devices like tokens or smart cards, software-based solutions such as mobile apps, or biometric factors like fingerprint scanners. Some organizations may also use location-based authentication, where the user's location is verified in addition to the other authentication factors.

MFA is an essential component of an organization's cybersecurity strategy and can significantly improve security by reducing the risk of unauthorized access. However, it is important to ensure that the MFA solution is implemented correctly and that users are educated on how to use it effectively to avoid potential security risks.

In conclusion, these techniques and tools are essential for identifying and mitigating potential risks to a system or network. Organizations should implement a combination of these tools and techniques to ensure that they have a comprehensive cybersecurity strategy in place

4. REASONS FOR USING MACHINE LEARNING IN CYBER SECURITY

Machine learning, a subfield of artificial intelligence, has shown great potential in enhancing Cyber Security. Machine learning algorithms can analyze large amounts of data, identify patterns and anomalies, and detect potential security threats.

Here are a few examples of how machine learning can be used in Cyber security:

Intrusion detection: Machine learning algorithms can be used to analyze network traffic and detect anomalies that may indicate a potential security breach. For example, machine learning algorithms can be trained to recognize patterns in network traffic that are indicative of a distributed denial-of-service (DDoS) attack or other types of cyber attacks.

Malware detection: Machine learning algorithms can be trained to recognize patterns in the code of malicious software, such as viruses and trojans. By analyzing these patterns, machine learning algorithms can detect new strains of malware that may not be detected by traditional antivirus software.

User behavior analysis: Machine learning algorithms can analyze user behavior patterns to detect anomalies that may indicate a potential security threat. For example, machine learning algorithms can be trained to recognize patterns in user login behavior that are indicative of a brute force attack.

Fraud detection: Machine learning algorithms can be used to detect fraudulent activity in financial transactions. By analyzing patterns in transaction data, machine learning algorithms can detect anomalies that may indicate fraud.

Password security: Machine learning algorithms can be used to analyze password data to identify weak passwords and password reuse. By analyzing these patterns, machine learning algorithms can provide recommendations for improving password security.

4.1 Machine Learning Algorithms in Cyber Security

Here are a few examples of **Machine learning algorithms** that can be used in Cyber security:

Support Vector Machines (SVM): SVM is a type of machine learning algorithm that can be used for intrusion detection. It works by finding the optimal boundary between two classes of data (normal traffic and malicious traffic) and classifying new data points based on their position relative to the boundary.

Random Forest: Random Forest is a type of machine learning algorithm that can be used for malware detection. It works by combining multiple decision trees to form a forest, where each tree predicts the class of a data point. The final prediction is based on the majority vote of the individual trees in the forest.

Deep Learning: Deep Learning is a subset of machine learning that is based on neural networks. Deep learning algorithms can be used for user behavior analysis, where they can analyze patterns in user behavior data to detect anomalies that may indicate a potential security threat.

Clustering: Clustering is a machine learning technique that can be used for fraud detection. It works by grouping similar data points together based on their features. Data points that are significantly different from their respective clusters may be indicative of fraudulent activity.

Decision Trees: Decision Trees are machine learning algorithms that can be used for password security. They work by analyzing password data and identifying common patterns in weak passwords. Based on this analysis, decision trees can provide recommendations for improving password security.

These are just a few examples of machine learning algorithms that can be used in cyber security. By leveraging these algorithms, organizations can better protect their data and systems from potential security threats. However, it's important to note that machine learning algorithms are not a silver bullet for cyber security. They should be used in conjunction with other security measures, such as firewalls, antivirus software, and access controls. Additionally, machine learning algorithms should be continuously updated and retrained to ensure they remain effective against evolving security threats.

4.1.1 Support Vector Machines (SVM) Can Be Used for Intrusion Detection

The goal of intrusion detection is to identify any unauthorized access or activities within a computer system or network. SVM is one of the machine learning algorithms that can be used for this purpose. The basic idea behind SVM is to find the optimal boundary (or hyperplane) that separates the two classes of data: normal traffic and malicious traffic. The boundary is chosen such that it maximizes the margin, or the distance between the boundary and the closest data points of each class.

In practice, SVM works by taking a set of labeled training data, which consists of input features and their corresponding class labels (normal or malicious traffic). The algorithm then constructs a hyperplane that separates the two classes with maximum margin. The hyperplane is defined by a set of coefficients that are learned during the training process.

Once the hyperplane has been trained, SVM can classify new data points based on their position relative to the hyperplane. If a new data point falls on one side of the hyperplane, it is classified as normal traffic; if it falls on the other side, it is classified as malicious traffic.

There are several techniques that can be used to improve the performance of SVM for intrusion detection. One such technique is feature selection, which involves selecting the most relevant features (such as packet size, source and destination IP addresses, and protocol type) that are most indicative of a security threat. Another technique is kernel selection, which involves choosing the appropriate kernel function that can map the input features into a higher-dimensional space where the classes are better separable.

SVM can also be used in combination with other machine learning algorithms to improve its performance. For example, an ensemble of SVM classifiers can be used, where each SVM classifier is trained on a different subset of the training data. The final classification decision is then made by combining the outputs of the individual SVM classifiers.

In conclusion, SVM is a powerful machine learning algorithm that can be used for intrusion detection. By finding the optimal boundary between normal and malicious traffic, SVM can accurately identify potential security threats in real-time. However, to achieve the best performance, SVM must be carefully tuned and trained on high-quality data.

4.1.2 Random Forest Can Be Used for Malware Detection

Malware detection is the process of identifying malicious software that can harm a computer system or network. Random Forest is one of the machine learning algorithms that can be used for this purpose. The basic idea behind Random Forest is to create an ensemble of decision trees, where each tree is trained on a random subset of the input features and data points. The final prediction is based on the majority vote of the individual trees in the forest.

In practice, Random Forest works by taking a set of labeled training data, which consists of input features (such as file size, file type, and system calls) and their corresponding class labels (malware or benign). The algorithm then constructs a forest of decision trees, where each tree is trained on a random subset of the input features and data points.

During the training process, each decision tree is constructed by recursively splitting the input space into smaller regions based on the values of the input features. The splits are chosen such that they maximize the information gain or reduce the impurity of the data in each region. The decision rules learned by each tree are then combined to form the final decision boundary between malware and benign samples.

Once the forest has been trained, Random Forest can classify new data points by passing them through each tree in the forest and aggregating the results. The final prediction is based on the majority vote of the individual trees in the forest.

There are several techniques that can be used to improve the performance of Random Forest for malware detection. One such technique is feature selection, which involves selecting the most relevant features that are most indicative of a malware threat. Another technique is ensemble pruning, which involves removing the trees that contribute the least to the accuracy of the forest.

Random Forest can also be used in combination with other machine learning algorithms to improve its performance. For example, a hybrid model of Random Forest and Support Vector Machines (SVM) can be used, where Random Forest is used to pre-select a subset of relevant features, and SVM is used to classify the data points based on the selected features.

In conclusion, Random Forest is a powerful machine learning algorithm that can be used for malware detection. By combining multiple decision trees to form a forest, Random Forest can accurately identify potential security threats in real-time. However, to achieve the best performance, Random Forest must be carefully tuned and trained on high-quality data.

4.1.3 Deep Learning Can Be Used for user Behavior Analysis in Cyber Security

Deep Learning is a subset of machine learning that is based on neural networks. Deep Learning algorithms can be used for user behavior analysis, where they can analyze patterns in user behavior data to detect anomalies that may indicate a potential security threat. The algorithm works by learning patterns in the data through multiple layers of nonlinear transformations.

The basic idea behind Deep Learning for user behavior analysis is to train a neural network on a large dataset of user behavior data, where each data point is represented by a set of features such as login time, IP address, and access location. The neural network then learns to recognize patterns in the data that are indicative of normal behavior, and can flag any anomalous behavior as a potential security threat.

There are several techniques that can be used to improve the performance of Deep Learning for user behavior analysis. One such technique is data preprocessing, which involves normalizing and scaling the input data to improve the convergence of the neural network. Another technique is regularization, which involves adding constraints to the neural network to prevent overfitting.

In addition to these techniques, there are several types of neural networks that can be used for user behavior analysis. One common type is the recurrent neural network (RNN), which is well-suited for modeling sequences of data such as user login times. Another type is the convolutional neural network (CNN), which is well-suited for modeling image data such as screenshots of user activity.

Once the neural network has been trained on the user behavior data, it can be used to analyze new data in real-time. For example, if a user logs in from an unusual location or at an unusual time, the neural network can flag this behavior as a potential security threat and alert the system administrator.

In conclusion, Deep Learning is a powerful machine learning algorithm that can be used for user behavior analysis in information security. By analyzing patterns in user behavior data, Deep Learning algorithms can detect anomalies that may indicate a potential security threat. However, to achieve the best performance, Deep Learning must be carefully tuned and trained on high-quality data.

4.1.4 Clustering Can Be Used for Fraud Detection in Cyber Security

Clustering is a machine learning technique that can be used for fraud detection. It works by grouping similar data points together based on their features. Data points that are significantly different from their respective clusters may be indicative of fraudulent activity. The algorithm works by first identifying the relevant features of the data, and then grouping similar data points together based on those features.

One common technique used in clustering is k-means clustering. K-means clustering works by first randomly selecting k initial cluster centers, and then iteratively assigning each data point to the nearest cluster center based on a distance metric. The cluster centers are then updated to the mean of the data points assigned to each cluster, and the process is repeated until convergence.

To improve the performance of k-means clustering for fraud detection, several techniques can be used. One such technique is feature engineering, which involves selecting and transforming the most relevant features of the data to better capture the underlying patterns. Another technique is outlier detection, which involves identifying and removing data points that are significantly different from their respective clusters.

In addition to k-means clustering, there are several other clustering algorithms that can be used for fraud detection. One such algorithm is hierarchical clustering, which works by building a tree-like structure of nested clusters based on the distance between data points. Another algorithm is DBSCAN, which works by grouping together data points that are close together in density-based clusters.

Once the clustering algorithm has been applied to the data, the system administrator can examine the clusters and identify any data points that are significantly different from their respective clusters. These data points may be indicative of fraudulent activity, and can be further investigated to determine if a security breach has occurred.

In conclusion, clustering is a powerful machine learning technique that can be used for fraud detection in information security. By grouping similar data points together based on their features, clustering algorithms can detect data points that are significantly different from their respective clusters, which may be indicative of fraudulent activity. However, to achieve the best performance, clustering algorithms must be carefully tuned and trained on high-quality data.

4.1.5 Decision Trees Can Be Used for Password Security

Decision trees are machine learning algorithms that can be used for password security. They work by analyzing password data and identifying common patterns in weak passwords. Based on this analysis, decision trees can provide recommendations for improving password security.

The algorithm works by first collecting and preprocessing a dataset of password data. This dataset should include a large number of passwords along with their associated characteristics, such as length, complexity, and use of common patterns or words. The data should also be labeled as either "strong" or "weak" passwords based on a predefined criteria.

Once the dataset has been prepared, the decision tree algorithm can be applied to the data. The algorithm works by recursively partitioning the data into subsets based on the most informative features. At each step, the algorithm selects the feature that best separates the data into strong and weak password groups, and creates a decision node based on that feature. The algorithm then continues to partition the data based on the remaining features until all nodes are either decision nodes or leaf nodes.

To improve the performance of the decision tree algorithm for password security, several techniques can be used. One such technique is feature selection, which involves selecting the most informative features from the dataset. This can be done using methods such as information gain or chi-square tests. Another technique is pruning, which involves removing decision nodes that do not significantly improve the performance of the decision tree.

Once the decision tree has been trained on the dataset, it can be used to analyze new password data and provide recommendations for improving password security. This can be done by traversing the decision tree based on the characteristics of the new password and following the recommended path to the leaf node. The leaf node will then provide a recommendation for improving the security of the password.

In conclusion, decision trees are a powerful machine learning algorithm that can be used for password security. By analyzing password data and identifying common patterns in weak passwords, decision trees can provide recommendations for improving password security. However, to achieve the best performance, decision trees must be carefully trained and tuned on high-quality data.

5. INTRUSION DETECTION SYSTEMS

Intrusion detection systems (IDS) are an essential component of any cybersecurity strategy. This is a type of security software that monitors network traffic for signs of malicious activity. IDS can be classified into two categories: signature-based and anomaly-based IDS. Signature-based IDS identify known threats based on their signatures, while anomaly-based IDS detect deviations from normal network behavior.

IDS can be implemented at various points in the network, such as at the network perimeter, on individual hosts, or on critical network segments. IDS can be configured to generate alerts or take automated actions when an attack is detected, such as blocking traffic or disconnecting a device from the network. IDS is an effective way to detect and prevent cyberattacks, but it requires regular monitoring and maintenance to ensure its effectiveness.

5.1 Firewalls

A firewall is a network security device that monitors and filters incoming and outgoing network traffic based on a set of predetermined security rules. Firewalls can be hardware or software-based, and they act as a barrier between a trusted internal network and an untrusted external network like the internet.

Firewalls are a critical component of any cybersecurity strategy and they can be configured to allow or deny traffic based on various criteria, such as source IP address, destination IP address, port number, and protocol.

Firewalls can be configured to block traffic from known malicious IP addresses or to prevent traffic from known malware domains. Firewalls can also be used to prevent unauthorized access to sensitive information or to limit access to specific applications or services. Firewalls require regular maintenance to ensure that they are up to date with the latest threats and to modify their rules to meet changing business needs.

Here are some more recent details about firewalls:

Next-Generation Firewalls (NGFW): These are an advanced type of firewall that not only monitor traffic, but also perform deep packet inspection, application-level filtering, and can even detect and prevent certain types of attacks. NGFWs often include features such as VPN connectivity, intrusion prevention, and antivirus capabilities.

Cloud-based Firewalls: As more and more businesses move their operations to the cloud, traditional firewalls are no longer sufficient. Cloud-based firewalls offer the same level of security as traditional firewalls, but with the added benefit of being able to protect cloud-based resources, such as SaaS applications, cloud storage, and virtual machines.

Zero Trust Architecture: This is a security model that assumes all traffic is potentially malicious, and requires strict authentication and authorization measures before granting access. Firewalls are a critical component of zero trust architectures, as they help to enforce access policies and limit lateral movement within a network.

Firewall-as-a-Service (FWaaS): This is a cloud-based firewall solution that is managed by a third-party provider. FWaaS offers the same level of security as traditional firewalls, but with the added benefit of being scalable, easily deployed, and managed through a web-based interface.

Application Programming Interface (API) Integration: Many modern firewalls offer API integration, which allows them to work seamlessly with other security solutions, such as SIEMs, threat intelligence platforms, and security orchestration tools. This integration can help to automate security processes, improve visibility, and reduce response times to security incidents.

5.2 Encryption

Encryption is the process of converting data into a form that is unintelligible to unauthorized users. Encryption is used to protect sensitive information like passwords, credit card numbers, and personal information from unauthorized access. There are two types of encryption: symmetric and asymmetric encryption. Symmetric encryption uses a single key for both encryption and decryption, while asymmetric encryption uses two keys, one for encryption and one for decryption. Asymmetric encryption is more secure than symmetric encryption, but it is also more computationally expensive. Encryption is an effective way to protect data from unauthorized access, but it requires careful key management and regular maintenance to ensure its effectiveness.

Encryption can be used to secure data at rest, in transit, or in use. Encryption uses various cryptographic algorithms to convert data into a form that is unintelligible to unauthorized users. Encryption requires the use of a key to encrypt and decrypt data.

Here are some recent details about encryption:

Quantum Encryption: Quantum computing is expected to revolutionize the field of encryption. Quantum encryption uses the principles of quantum mechanics to generate and distribute encryption keys. This approach is considered to be unbreakable, as any attempt to intercept the key would result in its destruction. However, quantum encryption is still in the early stages of development and is not yet widely used.

Homomorphic Encryption: This is a form of encryption that allows computations to be performed on encrypted data without the need to decrypt it first. This approach is useful for situations where data needs to be analyzed without compromising its privacy, such as medical or financial data. Homomorphic encryption is still in the research stage, but it has the potential to become a valuable tool for data privacy.

Post-Quantum Cryptography: As quantum computing becomes more powerful, it will be able to break many of the encryption algorithms that are currently in use. Post-quantum cryptography is a field of research that is focused on developing encryption algorithms that are resistant to quantum computing attacks. This approach is still in its early stages, but it is expected to become more important as quantum computing advances.

End-to-End Encryption: This is a form of encryption that ensures that only the sender and recipient of a message can read its contents. End-to-end encryption is becoming more popular in messaging apps and email services. It ensures that messages cannot be intercepted or read by third parties, including service providers.

Hybrid Encryption: This is an approach that combines symmetric and asymmetric encryption to provide both speed and security. In this approach, data is encrypted using a symmetric key, which is then encrypted using an asymmetric key. This approach is useful for situations where both speed and security are important, such as in online transactions.

5.3 Risk Management Strategies

Effective risk management is essential for protecting against cyber threats. This includes identifying and assessing risks, developing risk mitigation strategies, and regularly monitoring and updating security measures. Some common risk management strategies include conducting regular vulnerability assessments, implementing multi-factor authentication, and establishing incident response plans.

The risk management process involves the following steps: risk identification, risk assessment, risk mitigation, and risk monitoring. Risk management is a critical component of any cybersecurity strategy.

Risk identification involves identifying potential threats to a computer system, such as malware, phishing, hacking, and ransomware. Risk assessment involves analyzing the likelihood and potential impact of each identified risk. This analysis can be used to prioritize risks and allocate resources to address them. This can be done through various methods, such as analyzing past security incidents, conducting vulnerability scans, and performing risk assessments. Once potential threats are identified, they are documented and categorized.

Risk assessment: Once potential threats have been identified, the next step is to assess the likelihood and potential impact of each risk. This involves analyzing the probability of the risk occurring and the potential impact it could have on the organization. The analysis should consider factors such as the likelihood of the risk occurring, the impact it could have on business operations, and the cost of mitigating the risk.

Risk mitigation: Based on the risk assessment, the next step is to develop risk mitigation strategies to reduce the likelihood and potential impact of the identified risks. Risk mitigation strategies may include implementing technical controls, such as firewalls, intrusion detection systems, and anti-virus software, or implementing administrative controls, such as security policies, procedures, and training programs. The effectiveness of risk mitigation strategies should be regularly monitored and evaluated.

Risk monitoring: The final step of the risk management process involves monitoring risks to ensure that risk mitigation strategies are effective and that new risks are identified and addressed in a timely manner. This includes regularly reviewing security policies and procedures, conducting regular vulnerability assessments and penetration testing, and maintaining incident response plans.

involves regularly monitoring and evaluating the effectiveness of implemented risk management measures.

Effective risk management is an ongoing process that requires constant monitoring and updating as new threats emerge and business operations change. By following the risk management process and implementing appropriate risk mitigation strategies, organizations can better protect themselves against cyber threats and minimize the impact of security incidents.

6. SOME RECENT TRENDS IN RISK DETECTION AND CYBERSECURITY USED TO DETECT THE ALGORITHMS

Artificial Intelligence (AI) and Machine Learning (ML): AI and ML are increasingly being used to detect and mitigate cyber threats. AI and ML can analyze large amounts of data and identify patterns that are difficult for humans to detect. AI and ML can also automate threat detection and response, improving the speed and efficiency of cybersecurity operations.

Cloud Security: With the increasing use of cloud services, there is a growing need for cloud security. Organizations need to ensure that their cloud environments are secure and that they are implementing appropriate security measures to protect their data.

Zero Trust: Zero trust is a security model that assumes that all users, devices, and applications are untrusted and requires continuous authentication and verification for access. With the growing number of remote workers and the increasing use of mobile devices, zero trust is becoming an increasingly popular approach to cybersecurity. Zero Trust Architecture aims to reduce the attack surface by segmenting the network and limiting access to sensitive data and applications.

Internet of Things (IoT) Security: With the proliferation of IoT devices, there is a growing need for IoT security. IoT devices are often vulnerable to cyber attacks, and organizations need to implement appropriate security measures to protect these devices and the data they generate.

Threat Intelligence: Threat intelligence involves analyzing data to identify potential threats and risks. Threat intelligence can help organizations stay ahead of cyber threats by identifying emerging threats and vulnerabilities.

Cyber Insurance: This is a type of insurance that provides coverage for losses incurred as a result of cyber attacks or data breaches. Cyber insurance can help organizations recover from a cyber attack more quickly, by providing financial resources for incident response, remediation, and legal expenses.

Security Automation: Security automation involves automating security processes and tasks, such as threat detection and incident response. Security automation can improve the speed and efficiency of security operations and help organizations respond to threats more quickly.

Supply Chain Attacks: Supply chain attacks involve targeting third-party vendors and suppliers to gain access to an organization's network. These attacks have become more common in recent years, with attackers using a variety of tactics, such as malware injection, to compromise the supply chain.

Ransomware Attacks: Ransomware attacks continue to be a significant threat to organizations of all sizes. These attacks involve encrypting an organization's data and demanding a ransom for its release. Attackers are now using more sophisticated tactics, such as double extortion, where they not only encrypt the data but also threaten to publish it unless the ransom is paid.

Overall, these trends reflect the increasing sophistication of cyber threats and the growing need for effective risk detection and cybersecurity measures to protect against them.

As technology evolves, so do the techniques used by cyber attackers. As a result, risk detection and cybersecurity measures must also evolve to keep pace with new threats.

7. IMPACTS FOR GLOBALIZATION, INTERNATIONALIZATION, AND INDUSTRIALIZATION

Globalization, internationalization, and industrialization have had significant impacts on risk detection and cybersecurity in contemporary computing.

Globalization: Globalization refers to the increasing interconnectedness of the world's economies, cultures, and societies. It has led to increased trade, investment, and migration across borders. The benefits of globalization include increased economic growth, job creation, and access to a wider variety of goods and services. However, it has also led to economic inequality, job displacement, and environmental degradation.

Internationalization: Internationalization refers to the process of a company or organization expanding its operations to other countries. It has led to increased competition, access to new markets, and the transfer of technology and knowledge across borders. However, it has also led to cultural clashes, language barriers, and challenges in navigating foreign legal and regulatory systems.

Industrialization: Industrialization refers to the transition from an agrarian-based economy to a manufacturing-based economy. It has led to increased productivity, job creation, and higher standards of living. However, it has also led to environmental degradation, the exploitation of workers, and the displacement of traditional ways of life.

Overall, these three processes have had significant impacts on the global economy and society. While they have brought many benefits, they have also created new challenges that must be addressed to ensure a sustainable and equitable future for all.

Here are some of the key ways in which these factors have influenced cybersecurity.

Increased connectivity and data sharing: Globalization and internationalization have led to increased connectivity and data sharing between organizations, which has increased the risk of cyber attacks. With more data being shared, the potential for data breaches and other security incidents increases. The emergence of global markets and the increased availability of online communication technologies have led to a greater degree of interconnectivity between businesses, governments, and individuals. As a result, there is a higher level of data sharing between organizations, which can create additional security risks. Hackers and cyber criminals may target these channels to gain unauthorized access to sensitive data and information, which can lead to data breaches, financial losses, and reputational damage.

Greater complexity of IT environments: Industrialization and technological advancements have led to more complex IT environments, with a larger number of devices and systems connected to the network. This increased complexity creates more opportunities for cyber attackers to exploit vulnerabilities in the system. Industrialization and technological advancements have led to more complex IT environments. As organizations have become more reliant on technology, the number of devices, systems, and applications that need to be secured has increased. This complexity makes it more challenging for organizations to maintain the necessary level of security across all of their systems and applications. This can leave gaps in security that can be exploited by cyber criminals.

The complexity of IT environments has increased significantly over the past few years, which has resulted in several challenges for organizations. Here are some details on the greater complexity of IT environments:

Cloud computing: Cloud computing has become increasingly popular in recent years, with many organizations using multiple cloud providers and services. This has led to a more complex IT environment with distributed systems and data.

Mobility: With the rise of remote work and mobile devices, organizations must manage and secure a wide variety of devices and networks, including smartphones, tablets, laptops, and IoT devices.

Integration: Organizations are increasingly integrating different systems and platforms to streamline processes and improve efficiency. This has led to a more complex IT environment with multiple systems and applications that need to work seamlessly together.

Data volume: The volume of data that organizations generate and manage has increased significantly, which has resulted in the need for more powerful and sophisticated data management systems.

Cyber threats: Cyber threats have become more sophisticated and frequent, which has resulted in the need for more advanced cybersecurity measures. Organizations must protect against a wide variety of threats, including malware, phishing, ransomware, and insider threats.

Compliance: Organizations must comply with a wide variety of data protection and privacy regulations, which can vary by country and industry. Compliance requires more sophisticated IT systems and processes to ensure that data is protected and managed in accordance with regulations.

In summary, the greater complexity of IT environments has resulted from several factors, including cloud computing, mobility, integration, data volume, cyber threats, and compliance. Organizations must adapt to these challenges by implementing more sophisticated IT systems and processes to ensure that data is protected, managed, and used effectively.

More sophisticated cyber attacks: As technology advances, cyber attackers have become more sophisticated in their methods. This includes the use of advanced malware, social engineering, and other techniques to bypass security measures. The scale and complexity of these attacks can be overwhelming for many organizations, and it can be difficult to stay ahead of these threats.

Need for cross-border cooperation: With the global nature of cyber threats, international cooperation is increasingly important for effective risk detection and cybersecurity. This includes sharing information and resources across borders to better detect and respond to cyber attacks.

8. GREATER IMPORTANCE OF DATA PROTECTION REGULATIONS

With the increase in data sharing and cyber threats, data protection regulations have become increasingly important. Organizations must comply with these regulations, such as the EU's General Data Protection Regulation (GDPR), to protect the privacy and security of personal data. Cybersecurity threats often originate from one country and target organizations in another. As a result, cross-border cooperation is essential for detecting and responding to these threats effectively.

In order to be successful in contemporary computing, organizations must prioritize risk detection and cybersecurity. This includes implementing advanced security measures, staying up to date on the latest threats and trends, and complying with data protection regulations. It also requires ongoing monitoring and evaluation of security measures to ensure they remain effective in the face of evolving cyber threats.

As a result of the increased risks associated with global data sharing and cyber attacks, data protection regulations have become increasingly important. Regulations like GDPR and the California Consumer Privacy Act (CCPA) have been implemented to protect personal data and ensure that organizations are held accountable for any breaches that occur.

Overall, to succeed in contemporary computing, organizations must prioritize risk detection and cybersecurity. This requires a holistic approach that includes implementing advanced security measures, staying up to date on the latest threats and trends, complying with data protection regulations, and ongoing monitoring and evaluation of security measures.

The importance of data protection regulations has been highlighted by numerous studies and incidents related to cyber threats and data breaches. Here are some examples:

Cost of data breaches: According to the 2021 Cost of a Data Breach Report by IBM, the average cost of a data breach is $4.24 million. This includes expenses related to detection, response, notification, and lost business.

Public concern about data privacy: A survey conducted by Pew Research Center in 2019 found that 79% of US adults are concerned about the way their personal data is being used by companies. This concern has led to increased demand for stricter data protection regulations.

Increase in cyber attacks: The number of cyber attacks has been on the rise in recent years. According to a report by the Cybersecurity and Infrastructure Security Agency (CISA), there were over 2,400 reported incidents in 2020, a 25% increase from the previous year.

Regulatory fines: Non-compliance with data protection regulations can result in significant fines. For example, under GDPR, organizations can be fined up to €20 million or 4% of their global annual revenue, whichever is higher.

Cross-border cooperation: Cyber threats often originate from one country and target organizations in another. Therefore, cross-border cooperation is essential for detecting and responding to these threats effectively. This requires adherence to common data protection regulations and information sharing among nations.

Overall, data protection regulations are crucial for protecting personal data and ensuring the security of digital systems. Adherence to these regulations can help prevent data breaches, reduce the financial impact of cyber attacks, and promote cross-border cooperation in the fight against cyber threats.

Importance of data protection regulations:

Consumer trust: Data protection regulations help to build consumer trust by assuring individuals that their personal data is being collected and processed in a responsible and secure manner. This trust is essential for fostering long-term relationships between organizations and their customers.

Data breaches and reputational damage: Data breaches can result in significant reputational damage for organizations. The loss of customer trust can have a lasting impact on an organization's brand and bottom line. Compliance with data protection regulations can help minimize the risk of data breaches and the associated reputational damage.

Employee awareness: Data protection regulations require organizations to provide employee training on data privacy and security. This awareness helps to foster a culture of data security within the organization and can prevent insider threats.

International data transfers: Cross-border data transfers are a common occurrence in today's global economy. Data protection regulations provide a framework for ensuring that personal data is protected when it is transferred across borders.

Compliance with industry-specific regulations: Many industries have their own specific data protection regulations. Compliance with these regulations is necessary for organizations to operate within those industries.

Innovation: Data protection regulations can stimulate innovation by encouraging the development of new technologies and approaches to data privacy and security. For example, GDPR's "privacy by design" principle encourages organizations to consider data privacy and security from the outset of the development of new products and services.

In summary, data protection regulations are essential for ensuring the privacy and security of personal data in today's digital world. Compliance with these regulations can help organizations build consumer trust, prevent data breaches, minimize reputational damage, and foster a culture of data security and innovation.

9. CONCLUSION

In conclusion, risk detection and cybersecurity measures are essential for the success of contemporary computing systems. Cybersecurity threats like malware, phishing, hacking, and ransomware can cause significant damage to a computer system, leading to the loss of data, financial loss, and reputational damage. Cybersecurity threats are becoming more advanced, and cybercriminals are continuously evolving to find new ways to exploit vulnerabilities in computer systems. Intrusion detection systems, firewalls, and encryption are essential tools used for risk detection and cybersecurity. Therefore, it is essential to implement risk detection and cybersecurity measuresrequires ongoing monitoring and maintenance to ensure their effectiveness. Risk management is a crucial process used to identify, assess, and mitigate risks to a computer system.

REFERENCES

Alomari, M. H., & Mahdi, M. N. (2019). Intrusion detection systems using machine learning algorithms: A comparative study. *IEEE Access : Practical Innovations, Open Solutions, 7*, 74458–74477.

Basu, M., Bhattacharyya, D., & Kundu, M. (2018). Malware detection using machine learning techniques: A survey. *ACM Computing Surveys, 51*(4), 1–36. doi:10.1145/2501654.2501660

Bhatia, A. (2019). Encryption: A Critical Component of Cyber Security. *International Journal of Computer Science and Network Security, 19*(1), 11–16.

Check Point Research. (2022). *2022 Cyber Security Report*. Check Point Software Technologies.

Chen, T., Wang, X., & Yang, Y. (2017). Malware detection using deep learning based on autoencoder with raw executable files. *Journal of Information Security and Applications, 36*, 1–9.

Cheswick, W. R., & Bellovin, S. M. (1994). *Firewalls and Internet security: repelling the wily hacker*. Addison-Wesley Professional.

Duda, R. O., & Hart, P. E. (1973). *Pattern classification and scene analysis*. Wiley.

Farooq, M., Mahmood, T., & Basalamah, S. (2020). A systematic literature review of the state-of-the-art in user authentication using keystroke dynamics. *Information Sciences, 527*, 317–347.

Felske, S., Lai, D., & Yamaguchi, F. (2020). Evaluating the Effectiveness of Security Information and Event Management (SIEM) Systems in Cybersecurity. *Journal of Information Security, 11*(1), 24–33.

Ghahremanlou, R. S., & Soltani, S. (2021). A comprehensive review of user authentication systems using keystroke dynamics. *Journal of Ambient Intelligence and Humanized Computing, 12*(1), 157–189.

Grosse, K., Papernot, N., Manoharan, P., Backes, M., & McDaniel, P. (2017). Adversarial examples for malware detection. In *Proceedings of the 10th ACM Workshop on Artificial Intelligence and Security* (pp. 3-14). ACM.

Jajodia, S., & Subrahmanian, V. S. (2011). Cybersecurity: The Next Decade. *IEEE Security and Privacy, 9*(1), 70–73. doi:10.1109/MSP.2011.3

Jin, X., Liu, F., Zhang, Y., & Jiang, X. (2019). A survey of Android malware detection using machine learning. *IEEE Access : Practical Innovations, Open Solutions, 7*, 105855–105870.

Kaur, H., & Verma, A. K. (2019). User behavior analysis using deep learning techniques: A review. *Journal of Ambient Intelligence and Humanized Computing, 10*(11), 4417–4446.

Kim, J., & Trivedi, K. S. (2020). Cybersecurity Risk Management: A Review. *ACM Computing Surveys, 53*(3), 1–37.

Liao, H., & Chen, M. (2021). Fraud detection using clustering algorithms: A systematic literature review. *Journal of King Saud University - Computer and Information Sciences, 33*(2), 209-220.

National Cyber Security Centre. (2021). *The Cyber Threat to UK Business.* National Cyber Security Centre.

NIST. (2018). *Risk Management Framework for Information Systems and Organizations.* National Institute of Standards and Technology.

Ransbotham, S., & Kiron, D. (2017). Cybersecurity's Human Factor: Lessons from the Pentagon. *MIT Sloan Management Review, 58*(4), 41–48.

Tan, S. M., & Ewe, H. T. (2014). Network security: Intrusion detection and prevention systems. *Journal of Information Assurance and Security, 9*(2), 95–102.

Tsai, C. F., & Hsieh, H. Y. (2018). A Review of Risk Management in Cyber Security. *Journal of Information Security, 9*(2), 115–125. doi:10.4236/jis.2018.92007

Verma, A. K., & Dheeraj, R. (2019). Decision tree based password security system. In *Proceedings of the 3rd International Conference on Inventive Systems and Control* (pp. 1746-1749). IEEE.

Wang, X., & Xie, Y. (2019). A survey of user authentication schemes based on mouse dynamics. *Journal of Network and Computer Applications, 126*, 130–152.

Chapter 20
Vulnerability Assessment in Contemporary Computing

Umamageswari

SRM Institute of Science and Technology, Ramapuram, India

S. Deepa

ⓘD https://orcid.org/0000-0001-7690-0839

SRM Institute of Science and Technology, Ramapuram, India

ABSTRACT

Vulnerability assessments are an important aspect of contemporary computing and cyber security. It is a process of distinguishing and assessing potential security weaknesses and vulnerabilities in a computing system or network. It involves using various tools and techniques to denote vulnerabilities and supply recommendations for mitigating them. The primary goal of a vulnerability assessment is to identify weaknesses that attackers could exploit to gain unauthorized access or cause damage to the system or network. By identifying vulnerabilities early, organizations can take proactive steps to address them and prevent attacks. Some of the key steps involved in vulnerability assessments include: It is important to note that vulnerability assessments should be conducted on a regular basis, as new vulnerabilities are constantly being discovered. Additionally, organizations should consider conducting penetration testing in addition to vulnerability assessments, which involves simulating real-world attacks to identify potential weaknesses.

DOI: 10.4018/978-1-6684-9317-5.ch020

1. INTRODUCTION

1.1 Chapters

Here are some potential chapter topics related to vulnerability assessments in contemporary computing:

1. **Introduction to vulnerability assessments:** This chapter could provide an overview of vulnerability assessments, including their purpose, benefits, and the key steps involved in conducting them.
2. **Types of vulnerability assessments:** This chapter could explore different types of vulnerability assessments, such as network vulnerability assessments, application vulnerability assessments, and cloud vulnerability assessments.
3. **Vulnerability scanning techniques:** This chapter could delve into the various techniques used in vulnerability scanning, such as port scanning, vulnerability scanning, and web application scanning.
4. **Vulnerability assessment tools:** This chapter could provide an overview of the different vulnerability assessment tools available on the market, including open-source and commercial tools.
5. **Vulnerability assessment reporting:** This chapter could cover how to create vulnerability assessment reports, including what information to include, how to interpret the results, and how to provide actionable recommendations.
6. **Integrating vulnerability assessments into the software development life-cycle:** This chapter could explore how vulnerability assessments can be integrated into the software development life-cycle, including the benefits of conducting assessments during different stages of the development process.
7. **Case studies:** This chapter could provide real-world examples of how vulnerability assessments have helped organizations identify and mitigate vulnerabilities, as well as the lessons learned from these experiences.

1.2 Vulnerability Assessments

Vulnerability assessment is the process of identifying, quantifying, and prioritizing vulnerabilities in computer systems, networks, and applications. In contemporary computing, vulnerability assessment is a critical component of maintaining the security and integrity of computer systems and protecting them from potential cyberattacks.

The first step in vulnerability assessment is to identify all possible points of vulnerability, such as outdated software, unpatched systems, mis-configured systems, weak passwords, or lack of encryption (Mell, P., & Scarfone, K. 2011).

Once vulnerabilities are identified, they are typically prioritized based on their severity and potential impact. This allows organizations to focus their resources on the most critical vulnerabilities first. Figure 1.1 shows the various vulnerability assessment in contemporary computing.

After prioritization, organizations must then take steps to remediate vulnerabilities, which can include software patches, configuration changes, or other security measures. Finally, regular vulnerability assessments should be conducted to ensure that new vulnerabilities are not introduced over time.

Figure 1. Vulnerability assessment in contemporary computing

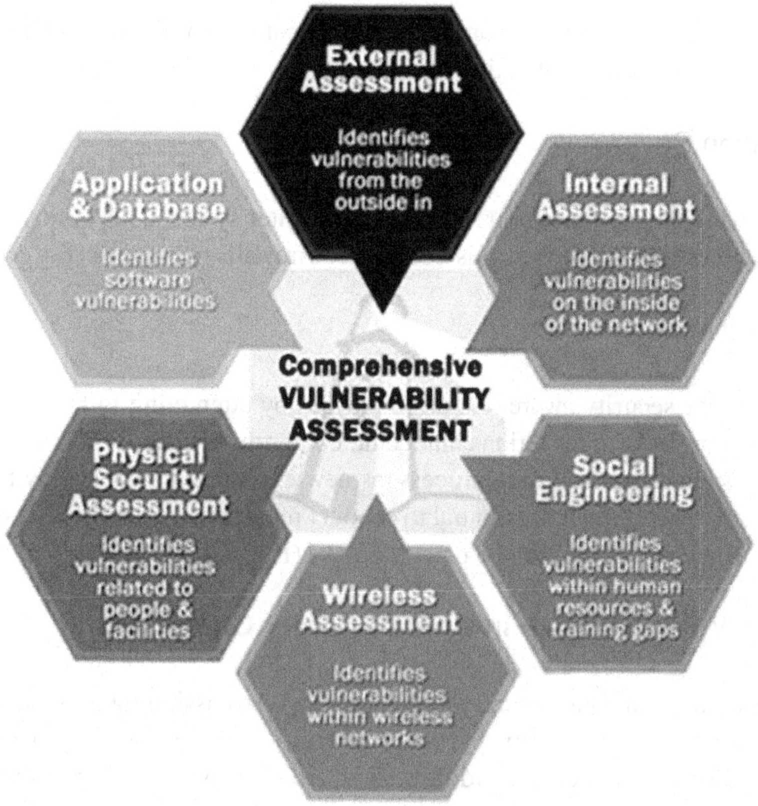

1.3 Identifying Vulnerabilities in Contemporary Computing

There are several methods to identify vulnerabilities in contemporary computing:

1.3.1 Vulnerability Scanning

This involves using software tools to scan computer systems, networks, and applications to identify known vulnerabilities. The tools will typically generate a report of identified vulnerabilities, along with recommended remediation steps.

1.3.2 Penetration Testing

This involves hiring ethical hackers to simulate attacks on computer systems, networks, and applications to identify vulnerabilities. Penetration testing can provide a more comprehensive view of potential vulnerabilities that may not be identified through vulnerability scanning.

1.3.3 Code Review

This involves reviewing the source code of software applications to identify potential vulnerabilities, such as coding errors or weak authentication mechanisms.

1.3.4 Configuration Review

This involves reviewing the configuration settings of computer systems, networks, and applications to identify potential vulnerabilities, such as mis-configured firewalls or weak access control policies.

1.3.5 Social Engineering

This involves testing the security awareness of employees by attempting to trick them into divulging sensitive information or performing actions that could compromise security.It is important to note that vulnerability identification is an ongoing process, as new exposure are constantly being revealed and employed by attackers. Therefore, it is essential to conduct regular vulnerability assessments and implement effective security controls to mitigate potential risks (Kizza, J. M. 2017).

1.3 Quantifying Vulnerabilities in Contemporary Computing

Quantifying vulnerabilities in contemporary computing involves assigning a numerical value or score to vulnerabilities based on their severity and potential impact. This allows organizations to prioritize vulnerabilities and allocate resources accordingly. Here are some ways to quantify vulnerabilities.

1.3.1 Common Vulnerability Scoring System (CVSS)

This is a widely used system for quantifying vulnerabilities. It assigns a score between 0 and 10 to vulnerabilities based on factors such as their impact on confidentiality, integrity, and availability, as well as the complexity of the attack required to exploit them.

1.3.2 Risk Assessment

This involves identifying and quantifying the potential impact of a vulnerability on the organization, such as financial loss, reputational damage, or legal liabilities. The severity of the vulnerability is then evaluated based on its likelihood of occurrence and the potential impact.

1.3.3 Exploitability Index

This involves assigning a numerical value to a vulnerability based on its ease of exploitation, such as the availability of exploit code or the level of technical knowledge required to exploit it.

1.3.4 Time-to-Fix (TTF)

This involves quantifying the time required to remediate a vulnerability. The severity of the vulnerability is then evaluated based on its potential impact during the time required to remediate it.

1.3.5 Business Impact Analysis (BIA)

This involves evaluating the impact of a vulnerability on critical business processes and operations. The severity of the vulnerability is then evaluated based on its potential impact on these processes and operations.It is important to note that different organizations may use different methods for quantifying vulnerabilities based on their unique needs and risk profiles. However, the ultimate goal is to prioritize.

1.4 Prioritization in Contemporary Computing

Prioritization is a critical aspect of contemporary computing. In computing, prioritization refers to the process of determining the relative importance of tasks or processes and allocating resources accordingly. Prioritization is essential in ensuring that critical processes are given the necessary resources to run efficiently, while less critical processes are given fewer resources.

One common example of prioritization in contemporary computing is in the context of multitasking operating systems. In such systems, the operating system is responsible for allocating system resources, such as CPU time, memory, and I/O bandwidth, to different processes or threads. The operating system must prioritize these processes to ensure that critical processes are given the necessary resources to function correctly. For example, in a web server, incoming requests must be prioritized based on their importance or urgency (Buczak, A. L.2016).

Another example of prioritization in contemporary computing is in the context of cloud computing. Cloud service providers often use prioritization algorithms to ensure that their customers' most critical workloads receive the necessary resources. These algorithms take into account factors such as workload importance, customer preferences, and available resources to ensure that the most critical workloads are given priority.

Finally, prioritization is also crucial in the context of real-time systems, where tasks must be completed within a specified time frame. In such systems, prioritization algorithms ensure that critical tasks are given the necessary resources to meet their deadlines, while less critical tasks are given lower priority (D'AmicoA.et.al., 2015).

In summary, prioritization plays a crucial role in contemporary computing by ensuring that critical processes and tasks are given the necessary resources to run efficiently. As computing continues to evolve, prioritization algorithms will continue to play a vital role in ensuring that the ever-increasing number of tasks and processes can be managed effectively.

2. TYPES OF VULNERABILITY ASSESSMENTS

There are several types of vulnerability assessments used in contemporary computing, including:

2.1 Network Vulnerability Assessment

The assessment typically involves scanning the network for known vulnerabilities and assessing the risk level of each identified vulnerability.Network vulnerability assessments are essential in contemporary computing to secure network infrastructure and prevent cyber-attacks.

The following are the steps involved in network vulnerability assessment:

- Network discovery: This step involves identifying all the devices and systems on the network, including servers, routers, switches, and firewalls.
- Vulnerability scanning: This step involves using vulnerability scanning tools to identify vulnerabilities in the network infrastructure. The scanning tools search for known vulnerabilities in operating systems, applications, and other network components.
- Vulnerability assessment: This step involves assessing the risk level of each identified vulnerability. The assessment takes into account factors such as the severity of the vulnerability, the likelihood of exploitation, and the potential impact on the network.
- Reporting: This step involves creating a report that summarizes the results of the vulnerability assessment. The report typically includes a list of identified vulnerabilities, their risk level, and recommended remediation steps.
- Remediation: This step involves addressing the identified vulnerabilities. Remediation may involve installing security patches, upgrading software, reconfiguring network devices, or implementing additional security controls.
- Follow-up testing: This step involves performing additional vulnerability assessments to ensure that the identified vulnerabilities have been remediated.

In summary, network vulnerability assessment is a critical component of contemporary computing. It involves identifying and evaluating security vulnerabilities in a network infrastructure, assessing the risk level of each identified vulnerability, and taking steps to address the vulnerabilities. By performing regular network vulnerability assessments, organizations can ensure that their network infrastructure remains secure and protected from cyber-attacks.

2.2 Web Application Vulnerability Assessment

Web applications are often targeted by attackers, making it essential to assess their security regularly. The assessment typically involves testing the web application for common vulnerabilities such as SQL injection, cross-site scripting (XSS), and cross-site request forgery (CSRF).Web application vulnerability assessment is an important aspect of contemporary computing, as the internet and web applications have become an integral part of our lives. With the rise of e-commerce, online banking, and social media, web applications have become a target for cyber attacks, making vulnerability assessment essential to ensure the security of users and their data (Zhang, Y. 2015).

Some popular automated scanning tools include Burp Suite, OWASP ZAP, and Nessus. These tools can detect vulnerabilities such as SQL injection, cross-site scripting, and insecure session management. However, they may not detect all vulnerabilities, and manual testing is still necessary to identify complex vulnerabilitiesDebar, H, et.al. (1999). Vulnerability management involves prioritizing and fixing vulnerabilities based on their severity and impact on the application and its users.Overall, web application vulnerability assessment is a critical aspect of contemporary computing, and it is essential for organizations to regularly assess and manage the security of their web applications to ensure the safety and privacy of their users. Figure 2.1 shows the Vulnerability Assessment and Penetration Testing of Web Application.

Figure 2. Vulnerability assessment and penetration testing of web application

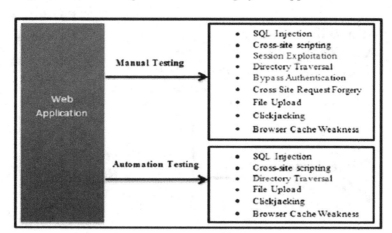

2.3 Wireless Network Vulnerability Assessment

The assessment typically involves scanning the network for wireless access points and assessing their security configurations. Wireless network vulnerability assessment is an important aspect of contemporary computing, as wireless networks have become an integral part of our daily lives. With the increasing use of wireless devices such as smartphones, tablets, laptops, and IoT devices, wireless networks have become a target for cyber attacks, making vulnerability assessment essential to ensure the security of users and their data. Figure 2.2 shows the Wireless vulnerability assessment in contemporary computing.

Wireless network vulnerability assessment is the process of identifying and assessing vulnerabilities in wireless networks that can be exploited by attackers. It involves the use of various tools and techniques to scan wireless networks for vulnerabilities such as weak passwords, unsecured access points, rogue access points, and man-in-the-middle attacks.

There are various methods and tools available for wireless network vulnerability assessment, ranging from manual testing to automated scanning tools. Manual testing involves the use of human expertise and skills to identify vulnerabilities in wireless networks, while automated scanning tools use algorithms and scripts to scan wireless networks for vulnerabilities.

Some popular automated scanning tools include Aircrack-ng, Wireshark, and Nmap. These tools can detect vulnerabilities such as weak encryption, open ports, and unauthorized access points. However, they may not detect all vulnerabilities, and manual testing is still necessary to identify complex vulnerabilities.In addition to vulnerability scanning, wireless network security can be improved through secure configuration, regular security testing, and vulnerability management. Secure configuration involves configuring wireless networks with security in mind, such as using strong encryption, disabling unused services and protocols, and implementing access controls.

Figure 3. Wireless vulnerability assessment in contemporary computing

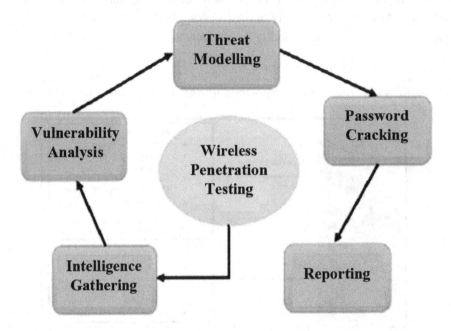

Regular security testing involves conducting regular vulnerability assessments and penetration testing to identify and fix vulnerabilities in wireless networks. Vulnerability management involves prioritizing and fixing vulnerabilities based on their severity and impact on the network and its users.

2.4 Physical Vulnerability Assessment

This type of assessment focuses on identifying physical security vulnerabilities, such as unlocked doors, unsecured equipment, and unsecured network ports. The assessment typically involves inspecting the physical infrastructure and identifying potential security weaknesses.Physical vulnerability assessment is an important aspect of contemporary computing, as the security of physical infrastructure is critical to the security of digital infrastructure. Physical vulnerabilities can provide attackers with access to critical infrastructure, such as servers, routers, and switches, which can lead to data breaches, service disruptions, and other security incidents.

Physical vulnerability assessment is the process of identifying and assessing physical vulnerabilities that can be exploited by attackers. It involves the use of various tools and techniques to evaluate physical security controls such as access controls, surveillance systems, and physical barriers.Some common physical vulnerabilities that can be assessed include unauthorized physical access, theft, vandalism, and natural disasters. Physical vulnerability assessment can also include assessing the security of data centers, server rooms, and other critical infrastructure.

Physical vulnerability assessment can be performed manually, by conducting physical inspections and audits, or through the use of automated tools such as surveillance cameras, motion sensors, and access control systems. Automated tools can provide real-time monitoring and alerts, which can improve the detection of physical security incidents.In addition to physical vulnerability assessment, physical security can be improved through security training and awareness, access control management, and security incident management. Security training and awareness can help employees recognize and respond to physical security incidents, while access control management can limit access to critical infrastructure.

Overall, physical vulnerability assessment is a critical aspect of contemporary computing, and it is essential for organizations to regularly assess and manage the physical security of their infrastructure to ensure the safety and privacy of their users and data.

2.5 Cloud Vulnerability Assessment

This type of assessment focuses on identifying vulnerabilities in cloud-based infrastructure, such as virtual machines, containers, and cloud-based applications. The assessment typically involves scanning the cloud infrastructure for known vulnerabilities and assessing the risk level of each identified vulnerability.

Cloud vulnerability assessment is the process of identifying and evaluating vulnerabilities in a cloud environment. With the increasing popularity of cloud computing, it has become essential to assess the security of cloud infrastructure and services to prevent cyber-attacks.

Contemporary cloud computing has brought many challenges for vulnerability assessment, such as the use of shared infrastructure and the dynamic nature of cloud environments. Cloud providers are responsible for securing the underlying infrastructure, but customers are responsible for securing their applications, data, and access to the cloud.

To assess cloud vulnerabilities, organizations can use a combination of automated tools and manual techniques. Automated tools can scan the cloud infrastructure and identify vulnerabilities such as unpatched software or misconfigured security settings. Manual techniques involve conducting penetration testing, code reviews, and vulnerability assessments to identify potential vulnerabilities (Conti, M. 2018).

Some common vulnerabilities in cloud computing include weak access controls, insecure interfaces, data leakage, and insufficient network security. These vulnerabilities can be exploited by attackers to gain unauthorized access, steal sensitive data, or disrupt cloud services.

To mitigate cloud vulnerabilities, organizations should adopt a comprehensive security strategy that includes regular vulnerability assessments, proper access controls, encryption, and monitoring of network traffic. Additionally, it's crucial to stay up-to-date with the latest cloud security best practices and to work closely with cloud service providers to ensure the security of cloud environments (Kaur, R., & Singh, A. 2017).

3. VULNERABILITY SCANNING TECHNIQUES

Vulnerability scanning is an essential part of contemporary computing security that helps organizations identify and address security weaknesses in their IT infrastructure. Here are some common vulnerability scanning techniques used in contemporary computing: Figure 3.1 shows the various phases of vulnerability scanning process.

3.1 Network Scanning

Network scanning is the process of identifying active devices on a network, including computers, servers, routers, and switches. Vulnerability scanners can detect open ports, services, and vulnerabilities in these devices, enabling organizations to take necessary action.

Figure 4. Vulnerability scanning process

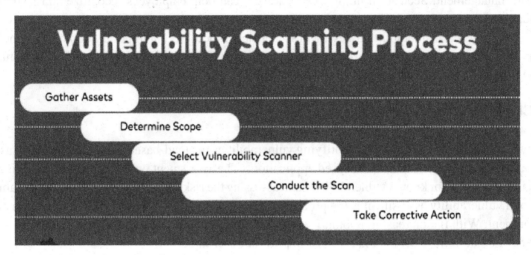

3.1.1 Ping Sweep

Ping sweep is a basic network scanning technique that sends ICMP echo requests to a range of IP addresses to identify active hosts. This technique is useful for identifying hosts that respond to ICMP packets and is quick to perform.

3.1.2 Port Scanning

Port scanning is a technique used to identify open ports on a network. Port scanners can detect open ports, services, and vulnerabilities in devices, enabling organizations to take necessary action. Port scanning can be performed using tools such as Nmap, Angry IP Scanner, and OpenVAS.

3.1.3 Protocol Scanning

Protocol scanning involves identifying the protocols running on a network. This technique can help identify vulnerabilities related to the protocols used on the network, such as outdated or unsecured protocols.

3.1.4 Vulnerability Scanning

Vulnerability scanning involves scanning for vulnerabilities in network devices, such as routers, switches, and firewalls. Vulnerability scanners can detect known vulnerabilities and misconfigurations in devices, enabling organizations to take necessary action.

3.1.5 Wireless Network Scanning

Wireless network scanning involves scanning wireless networks to identify potential vulnerabilities related to wireless security, such as weak encryption, default passwords, and unauthorized access.

3.2 Port Scanning

Port scanning is a technique that involves sending packets to a range of ports on a target device to identify which ports are open and what services are running on them. This technique can help identify potential vulnerabilities related to open ports and services.Port scanning is a vital vulnerability assessment technique used in contemporary computing to identify open ports and services on a target system. By scanning a system's ports, security professionals can identify potential vulnerabilities related to open ports, services, and applications.Here are some techniques used in port scanning vulnerability assessment for contemporary computing:

3.2.1 TCP Port Scanning

TCP port scanning is a technique used to identify open TCP ports on a target system. TCP port scanning tools send TCP packets to a range of port numbers to identify open ports and services running on them.

3.2.2 UDP Port Scanning

UDP port scanning is a technique used to identify open UDP ports on a target system. UDP port scanning tools send UDP packets to a range of port numbers to identify open ports and services running on them.

3.2.3 Service Scanning

Service scanning involves identifying the services running on open ports. Service scanning tools can identify the type of service running on a port and the version of the service, enabling security professionals to identify potential vulnerabilities related to the service.

3.2.4 Banner Grabbing

Banner grabbing is a technique used to identify the operating system and software running on a target system by examining the information contained in the banner message returned by the system.

3.2.5 Vulnerability Scanning

Vulnerability scanning involves scanning for vulnerabilities in services and applications running on open ports. Vulnerability scanners can detect known vulnerabilities and misconfigurations in services and applications, enabling organizations to take necessary action.Port scanning vulnerability assessment can be performed manually or using automated vulnerability scanning tools such as Nmap, Nessus, and OpenVAS. Organizations should conduct regular port scans to identify and address vulnerabilities in a timely manner and reduce the risk of cyber-attacks.

3.3 Credential Scanning

Credential scanning involves checking the strength of user passwords on devices and applications. The scanner tests for weak or default passwords, easily guessable passwords, and compromised credentials.

Credential scanning is a crucial vulnerability scanning technique used in contemporary computing to identify weak or compromised user credentials that could be exploited by attackers to gain unauthorized access to networks, systems, and applications.Here are some techniques used in credential scanning for contemporary computing:

3.3.1 Password Cracking

Password cracking is a technique used to crack or guess passwords using automated tools that test a large number of password combinations. Password cracking is useful in identifying weak passwords and enforcing stronger password policies.

3.3.2 Brute Force Attacks

Brute force attacks are a type of password cracking attack that involves testing all possible combinations of characters until the correct password is found. This technique can be used to identify weak passwords or default credentials that could be easily guessed.

3.3.3 Password Hashes

Password hashes are encrypted versions of user passwords that are stored in a database or system. Password scanning tools can extract password hashes from these databases and attempt to crack them to reveal the actual passwords.

3.3.4 Credential Stuffing

Credential stuffing is a type of attack that involves using lists of stolen or leaked credentials to gain access to systems and applications. Credential scanning tools can identify compromised credentials and help organizations prevent these types of attacks.

3.3.5 Multi-Factor Authentication

Multi-factor authentication (MFA) is a security technique that requires users to provide multiple forms of identification to access a system or application. Credential scanning tools can help identify systems and applications that do not use MFA, enabling organizations to implement additional security measures.

3.4 Web Application Scanning

Web application scanning involves scanning web applications to identify vulnerabilities, such as SQL injection, cross-site scripting (XSS), and other application-level vulnerabilities.

Web application scanning is an important component of vulnerability assessment in contemporary computing. With the increasing dependence on web-based applications and the rise of cyber threats, it is crucial to regularly scan web applications for vulnerabilities and potential security loopholes.

Web application scanning involves the use of automated tools to test web applications for security weaknesses, including injection flaws, cross-site scripting (XSS) vulnerabilities, insecure storage of sensitive data, and others. The tools scan the web application's source code, network traffic, and other relevant data to identify potential security risks.

3.5 Operating System Scanning

Operating system scanning involves scanning the operating system of a device or server to identify vulnerabilities related to software vulnerabilities, mi-sconfigurations, and other issues.

Operating system scanning is another important component of vulnerability assessment in contemporary computing. Operating systems are the backbone of any computing environment, and vulnerabilities in the operating system can lead to significant security risks, including unauthorized access, data theft, and system compromise.

Operating system scanning involves the use of automated tools to scan the operating system for vulnerabilities and potential security loopholes. These tools scan the operating system's configuration files, registry settings, network traffic, and other relevant data to identify potential security risks.

Some of the common vulnerabilities that can be identified through operating system scanning include missing security patches, weak passwords, outdated software, and mis-configured network settings. Once these vulnerabilities are identified, appropriate remediation actions can be taken to address them and reduce the risk of a security breach.

In addition to automated scanning, vulnerability assessment of operating systems may also involve manual testing by security professionals. Manual testing allows for a deeper analysis of the operating system's security posture and can help identify vulnerabilities that may be missed by automated scanning tools.

Overall, operating system scanning is an essential component of vulnerability assessment in contemporary computing, as it helps organizations identify and address potential security risks at the operating system level, which is critical for maintaining a secure computing environment.

3.6 Cloud Scanning

Cloud scanning involves scanning cloud infrastructure and services, such as virtual machines, storage, and databases, to identify vulnerabilities.Cloud scanning is an important component of vulnerability assessment in contemporary computing, as more and more organizations are adopting cloud-based infrastructure and services. With the increasing dependence on cloud computing, it is crucial to regularly scan cloud environments for vulnerabilities and potential security loopholes.

Some of the common vulnerabilities that can be identified through cloud scanning include mis-configured security settings, weak passwords, outdated software, and insecure data storage. Once these vulnerabilities are identified, appropriate remediation actions can be taken to address them and reduce the risk of a security breach.

Overall, cloud scanning is a critical component of vulnerability assessment in contemporary computing, as it helps organizations identify and address potential security risks in their cloud infrastructure and services. By conducting regular cloud scanning, organizations can ensure that their cloud environments remain secure and protected from cyber threats. These scanning techniques can be performed manually or through the use of automated vulnerability scanning tools. Organizations should conduct regular vulnerability scans to identify and address vulnerabilities in a timely manner and reduce the risk of cyber-attacks.

4. VULNERABILITY ASSESSMENT TOOLS

There are many vulnerability assessment tools available for contemporary computing, both open-source and commercial, that can help organizations identify and address potential security risks in their computing environment (Ali, S., &Alazab, M. 2019). Figure 4.1 shows the Here are some examples of popular vulnerability assessment tools:

Figure 5. Vulnerability assessment tools

4.1 Nessus

Nessus is a widely used vulnerability assessment tool that can help organizations identify and address potential security risks in their computing environment. Here are some key features and benefits of Nessus:

- Scanning Capabilities: Nessus can scan networks, operating systems, and applications for vulnerabilities and potential security risks. It can perform both internal and external scans, as well as authenticated scans to identify vulnerabilities that require user credentials to access.
- Vulnerability Detection: Nessus has a vast vulnerability database that is constantly updated with the latest threats and vulnerabilities. It uses advanced scanning techniques to identify and prioritize vulnerabilities, including critical vulnerabilities that could lead to system compromise.
- Reporting and Remediation: Nessus generates detailed reports that can help organizations understand their security posture and prioritize remediation efforts. It also provides recommendations for remediation and
- can integrate with other security tools to facilitate the remediation process.

- Integration: Nessus can integrate with a wide range of security tools, including security information and event management (SIEM) systems, endpoint protection solutions, and threat intelligence platforms.
- Flexibility: Nessus is highly customizable and can be tailored to meet the specific needs and requirements of different organizations. It can be deployed as a standalone tool or as part of a larger security framework.

4.2 OpenVAS

OpenVAS is a popular open-source vulnerability assessment tool that can help organizations identify and address potential security risks in their computing environment. Here are some key features and benefits of OpenVAS:

- Scanning Capabilities: OpenVAS can scan networks, operating systems, and applications for vulnerabilities and potential security risks. It can perform both internal and external scans, as well as authenticated scans to identify vulnerabilities that require user credentials to access.
- Vulnerability Detection: OpenVAS has a comprehensive vulnerability database that is constantly updated with the latest threats and vulnerabilities. It uses advanced scanning techniques to identify and prioritize vulnerabilities, including critical vulnerabilities that could lead to system compromise.
- Reporting and Remediation: OpenVAS generates detailed reports that can help organizations understand their security posture and prioritize remediation efforts. It also provides recommendations for remediation and can integrate with other security tools to facilitate the remediation process.
- Integration: OpenVAS can integrate with a wide range of security tools, including security information and event management (SIEM) systems, endpoint protection solutions, and threat intelligence platforms.
- Open-Source: OpenVAS is an open-source tool that can be customized to meet the specific needs and requirements of different organizations. It is also free to use, making it a cost-effective option for organizations with limited budgets.

4.3 Qualys

Qualys is a cloud-based vulnerability assessment tool that scans networks, operating systems, and applications for vulnerabilities and potential security risks.Here are some key features and benefits of Qualys:

- **Scalability:**Qualys can scan large and complex networks, making it ideal for organizations with a large number of assets to manage. It can also be used to scan cloud environments, including public and private clouds.
- **Vulnerability Detection:**Qualys has a comprehensive vulnerability database that is constantly updated with the latest threats and vulnerabilities. It uses advanced scanning techniques to identify and prioritize vulnerabilities, including critical vulnerabilities that could lead to system compromise.

- **Reporting and Remediation:**Qualys generates detailed reports that can help organizations understand their security posture and prioritize remediation efforts. It also provides recommendations for remediation and can integrate with other security tools to facilitate the remediation process.
- **Integration**: Qualys can integrate with a wide range of security tools, including security information and event management (SIEM) systems, endpoint protection solutions, and threat intelligence platforms.
- **Cloud-Based**: Qualys is a cloud-based tool that is accessible from anywhere with an internet connection. This makes it easy to manage and deploy across multiple locations and devices.

4.4 Nmap

Nmap is a powerful and widely used network exploration and security auditing tool that can be used for vulnerability assessment. It is capable of performing a variety of tasks such as scanning for open ports, identifying the operating system running on a target system, detecting services and their versions, and more.

- In terms of contemporary computing, Nmap is still a relevant tool for vulnerability assessment. As technology continues to evolve, new vulnerabilities and threats emerge, and Nmap is regularly updated with new features and capabilities to keep up with these changes.
- Some of the features and capabilities of Nmap that make it useful for contemporary vulnerability assessment include:
- Detection of new vulnerabilities: Nmap can be used to scan for known vulnerabilities in operating systems and applications, as well as to identify new vulnerabilities that have not yet been publicly disclosed.
- Integration with other tools: Nmap can be integrated with other vulnerability assessment tools, such as Metasploit, to provide a more comprehensive assessment of a target system's security posture.
- Scriptable automation: Nmap has a scripting engine that allows users to create custom scripts for automating vulnerability assessment tasks. This can be useful for scanning large numbers of systems or performing complex assessments.
- Support for IPv6: As the world moves towards IPv6, Nmap has added support for this protocol, allowing users to scan both IPv4 and IPv6 networks.
- Improved performance: Nmap has been optimized for modern computing environments, allowing it to scan networks faster and more efficiently than ever before.
- In summary, Nmap is still a relevant and useful tool for vulnerability assessment in contemporary computing environments. Its features and capabilities continue to evolve to keep up with changes in technology and the emergence of new threats.

4.5 Metasploit

Metasploit is a popular vulnerability assessment and penetration testing tool used by security professionals to identify and exploit vulnerabilities in computer systems. It provides a comprehensive framework for testing the security of networked systems and applications, and is regularly updated to keep up with changes in technology and the emergence of new threats.In contemporary computing, Metasploit remains a valuable tool for vulnerability assessment and penetration testing (Doupé, A.et.al., 2016). Some of the key features and capabilities of Metasploit that make it useful for contemporary security assessments include:

- **Comprehensive vulnerability scanning**: Metasploit can scan for vulnerabilities across a range of different systems, applications, and protocols, including web applications, databases, and mobile devices.
- **Automated exploitation:**Metasploit includes a range of automated exploit modules that can be used to test the security of vulnerable systems and applications. This can help to identify potential attack vectors and provide a more comprehensive assessment of a target's security posture.
- **Advanced payloads and encodings**: Metasploit includes a range of advanced payloads and en-codings that can be used to bypass common security controls and evade detection. This can help to test the resilience of systems against more sophisticated attacks.
- **Integration with other tools**: Metasploit can be integrated with other vulnerability assessment and penetration testing tools, allowing users to combine the strengths of multiple tools to create a more comprehensive assessment.
- **Community-driven development:**Metasploit is an open-source tool with a large and active com-munity of developers and users. This community-driven development model helps to ensure that the tool remains up-to-date and relevant in the face of emerging threats and changing technologies.

4.6 Burp Suite

Burp Suite is a widely used vulnerability assessment tool that can help identify security vulnerabilities in contemporary computing systems. It is a powerful platform that provides a range of tools to assess and test web applications and network infrastructures for security vulnerabilities.Some of the features that make Burp Suite an excellent tool for contemporary computing include:

- **Web Application Security Testing**: Burp Suite is designed to identify security vulnerabilities in web applications. It can scan for common vulnerabilities such as SQL injection, cross-site script-ing, and buffer overflow attacks.
- **Automation and Integration:** Burp Suite can be integrated with other tools to automate the test-ing process. It supports scripting languages such as Python, which can be used to automate the testing process.
- **Advanced Proxy Server:** Burp Suite has a built-in proxy server that can be used to intercept and modify web traffic. This makes it easier to identify vulnerabilities in web applications.
- **Collaborative Testing:** Burp Suite can be used to facilitate collaborative testing. It allows mul-tiple users to work together to identify vulnerabilities in a web application.
- **Reporting and Analysis:** Burp Suite provides detailed reports on vulnerabilities found during the testing process. It also offers analysis tools that help users identify the root cause of the vulner-ability and suggest remediation steps.

4.7 Nikto

Nikto is a popular open-source web server vulnerability scanner that can be used for contemporary computing systems. It is designed to scan web servers and identify security vulnerabilities that could be exploited by attackers.Here are some features of Nikto that make it an excellent tool for contemporary computing:

- **Comprehensive scanning**: Nikto can scan a wide range of web servers and web applications for vulnerabilities. It can detect outdated software versions, misconfigurations, and known security vulnerabilities.
- **Easy to use**: Nikto is easy to use and does not require any complex configuration. It can be run from the command line, and users can easily customize the scan parameters.
- **Integration**: Nikto can be integrated with other tools such as Metasploit and Nmap. This integration can provide a more comprehensive vulnerability assessment of web applications and web servers.
- **Regular updates**: Nikto is updated regularly to keep up with the latest security threats and vulnerabilities. This ensures that it remains a useful tool for contemporary computing systems.
- **Reporting and Analysis**: Nikto provides detailed reports on the vulnerabilities detected during the scan. It also offers analysis tools that help users identify the root cause of the vulnerability and suggest remediation steps.

These are just a few examples of the many vulnerability assessment tools available for contemporary computing. Each tool has its own strengths and weaknesses, and organizations should choose the tool that best fits their specific needs and requirements.

5. VULNERABILITY ASSESSMENT REPORTING

Vulnerability assessment reporting is a critical aspect of contemporary computing security. It provides insights into the security posture of an organization's IT infrastructure and highlights areas that need improvement (Saleh, M.et.al., 2017). Here are some essential elements that a vulnerability assessment report should include:

5.1 Executive Summary

The executive summary of a vulnerability assessment report provides a high-level overview of the assessment, highlighting the key findings, risks, and recommendations. It should be concise, easy to understand, and provide decision-makers with the information they need to make informed decisions about improving the organization's security posture (Al-Hamdani, Y., &Muttik, I.2017).The executive summary should include the following elements:

- **Scope**: A brief description of the scope of the assessment, including the systems, applications, and networks that were assessed.

- **Methodology:** A summary of the methodology used during the assessment, including the tools and techniques used to identify vulnerabilities.
- **Key Findings:** A summary of the critical vulnerabilities discovered during the assessment, including the severity of each vulnerability, the risk they pose to the organization, and the potential impact of each vulnerability.
- **Risk Analysis:** A summary of the risks posed by the vulnerabilities discovered during the assessment, including the potential impact and likelihood of exploitation.
- **Remediation Recommendations**: A summary of the remediation recommendations, including the steps that need to be taken to address each vulnerability and improve the organization's security posture.
- **Compliance Considerations**: A summary of any compliance considerations that the organization needs to adhere to, and how the vulnerabilities discovered during the assessment may impact compliance.
- **Conclusion:** A final summary of the key points and recommendations, highlighting the importance of addressing the vulnerabilities and improving the organization's security posture.

5.2 Vulnerability Summary

The vulnerability summary in a vulnerability assessment report provides a detailed breakdown of the vulnerabilities discovered during the assessment. It should include information about the severity of each vulnerability, the risk they pose to the organization, and the potential impact of each vulnerability. Here are some essential elements that should be included in a vulnerability summary:

- **Vulnerability Description:** A brief description of each vulnerability, including how it can be exploited and the potential impact on the organization.
- **Severity:** The severity of each vulnerability, based on the Common Vulnerability Scoring System (CVSS) or another similar rating system. This rating should provide an indication of the potential impact of the vulnerability on the organization.
- **Risk Assessment:** A risk assessment for each vulnerability, including the likelihood of exploitation and the potential impact on the organization. This assessment should provide decision-makers with an understanding of the risks posed by each vulnerability.
- **Proof of Concept:** If possible, provide proof-of-concept examples for each vulnerability to demonstrate how it can be exploited.
- **Recommendation:** A summary of the recommended steps to address each vulnerability, including patches, configuration changes, and other security measures that should be taken.
- **References:** References to external sources that provide additional information about each vulnerability, including vendor advisories, Common Vulnerabilities and Exposures (CVE) identifiers, and other resources.

5.3 Risk Analysis

The risk analysis section in a vulnerability assessment report provides an analysis of the risks posed by the vulnerabilities discovered during the assessment. It should outline the potential impact of each vulnerability and the likelihood of it being exploited. Here are some essential elements that should be included in a risk analysis section:

- **Potential Impact:** A description of the potential impact of each vulnerability on the organization, including financial loss, data breaches, system downtime, and reputational damage.
- **Likelihood of Exploitation:** An assessment of the likelihood of each vulnerability being exploited, based on the organization's threat landscape and the potential motivation of attackers.
- **Risk Assessment:** A risk assessment for each vulnerability, including a calculation of the risk score based on the severity, potential impact, and likelihood of exploitation. This assessment should provide decision-makers with an understanding of the risks posed by each vulnerability.
- **Mitigation Strategies:** A discussion of the mitigation strategies that can be implemented to reduce the risks posed by each vulnerability. This discussion should include the cost and effort required to implement each mitigation strategy.
- **Compliance Considerations:** A discussion of any compliance considerations that the organization needs to adhere to and how the vulnerabilities discovered during the assessment may impact compliance.
- **Prioritization:** A recommendation on the prioritization of vulnerabilities based on the risk assessment and potential impact on the organization. This recommendation should provide decision-makers with an understanding of which vulnerabilities need to be addressed first.

5.4 Remediation Recommendations

The remediation recommendations section in a vulnerability assessment report provides detailed recommendations on how to address the vulnerabilities discovered during the assessment. It should include specific steps that need to be taken to remediate each vulnerability, as well as best practices for improving the organization's security posture (Deshpande, A., & Jain, P.2018). Here are some essential elements that should be included in a remediation recommendations section:

- **Specific Steps:** Detailed steps that need to be taken to remediate each vulnerability, including patches, configuration changes, and other security measures that should be implemented.
- **Best Practices:** Best practices for improving the organization's security posture, including recommendations for password policies, network segmentation, and security training for employees.
- **Timeline:** A timeline for implementing the recommended remediation measures, including priority levels and estimated completion times.
- **Cost:** An estimate of the cost associated with implementing the recommended remediation measures, including hardware, software, and labor costs.
- **Impact:** An assessment of the impact that implementing the recommended remediation measures will have on the organization's operations and systems.
- **Verification:** A plan for verifying that the recommended remediation measures have been successfully implemented and that the vulnerabilities have been addressed.
- **Documentation:** A recommendation for documenting the remediation measures taken and maintaining an up-to-date inventory of systems and applications.

5.5 Technical Details

The technical details section in a vulnerability assessment report provides a detailed technical analysis of the vulnerabilities discovered during the assessment. It should include information on how the vulnerabilities were discovered, the tools and techniques used, and any technical details that may be relevant to understanding the vulnerabilities. Here are some essential elements that should be included in a technical details section:

- **Vulnerability Identification:** A description of the methodology used to identify the vulnerabilities, including the tools and techniques used and any manual testing performed.
- **Vulnerability Analysis:** A detailed analysis of each vulnerability, including information on the root cause, potential impact, and exploitability.
- **Proof of Concept:** A proof-of-concept demonstration of each vulnerability, demonstrating how the vulnerability can be exploited and the potential impact on the organization.
- **Recommendations:** Technical recommendations for remediation, including specific patches or configuration changes that need to be implemented.
- **False Positive Analysis:** An analysis of any false positives discovered during the assessment, including how they were identified and why they were determined to be false positives.
- **Risk Assessment:** A risk assessment of each vulnerability, including a calculation of the risk score based on the severity, potential impact, and likelihood of exploitation.
- **Relevant Standards:** A discussion of any relevant security standards, such as the OWASP Top Ten or the CIS Controls, and how the vulnerabilities discovered during the assessment may impact compliance.

5.6 Compliance Considerations

Compliance considerations are an important aspect of vulnerability assessment in contemporary computing. Compliance requirements are set by industry or regulatory bodies, and organizations need to meet these requirements to demonstrate that they are operating securely and responsibly. Here are some essential elements that should be included in a compliance considerations section:

- Relevant Regulations: A list of relevant regulations that the organization needs to comply with, such as HIPAA, PCI DSS, GDPR, or SOX.
- Applicable Standards: A discussion of any applicable security standards, such as the NIST Cybersecurity Framework or ISO 27001, and how the organization can use these standards to improve its security posture.
- Vulnerability Management: A discussion of how vulnerability management fits into the compliance framework and what specific compliance requirements need to be considered during the vulnerability assessment process.
- Reporting: A description of the specific reporting requirements for the organization, including how the organization needs to report on vulnerabilities and what information needs to be included in the reports.

- Risk Assessment: A discussion of how compliance requirements impact risk assessment, including how the organization needs to evaluate the risk associated with vulnerabilities and how risk should be prioritized.
- Remediation: A discussion of how compliance requirements impact remediation efforts, including what specific remediation measures need to be taken to address the vulnerabilities and how the organization needs to document the remediation process.
- Audit and Compliance Monitoring: A discussion of how the organization needs to monitor compliance with relevant regulations, including what specific metrics need to be tracked and how the organization needs to prepare for audits.

5.7 Appendices

Appendices are additional materials that are included in a vulnerability assessment report to provide supporting information, technical details, or additional context. Here are some essential elements that can be included in the appendices of a vulnerability assessment report:

- Tools and Techniques Used: A list of the tools and techniques used during the vulnerability assessment process, including their purpose, configuration, and any relevant technical details.
- Scan Results: A copy of the scan results obtained during the vulnerability assessment process, including any logs, reports, or other output generated by the tools used.
- Vulnerability Details: A detailed technical analysis of each vulnerability, including its impact, potential risk, and any recommended remediation steps.
- Risk Assessment Details: A description of the risk assessment methodology used during the vulnerability assessment process, including any relevant risk scoring models and criteria used.
- Compliance Frameworks: A description of the compliance frameworks used during the vulnerability assessment process, including their purpose, criteria, and any relevant technical details.
- Remediation Plan: A detailed remediation plan that outlines the specific steps to be taken to address each vulnerability discovered during the assessment, including prioritization, timelines, and any relevant technical details.
- Technical Diagrams: Technical diagrams that illustrate the organization's network architecture, system configurations, and other relevant technical details that provide context for the vulnerabilities discovered. Additionally technical details, supporting information, or context to help the reader understand the vulnerabilities discovered during the assessment process. In summary, a vulnerability assessment report should provide a comprehensive overview of the security posture of an organization's IT infrastructure. It should include an executive summary, vulnerability summary, risk analysis, remediation recommendations, technical details, compliance considerations, and appendices. The report should be clear, concise, and actionable, providing organizations with the information they need to improve their security posture.

6. INTEGRATING VULNERABILITY ASSESSMENTS INTO THE SOFTWARE DEVELOPMENT LIFECYCLE:

Integrating vulnerability assessments into the software development lifecycle (SDLC) is an important practice in contemporary computing to ensure that software is secure and free from vulnerabilities that could be exploited by attackers (Krol, K., &Misra, S.2019). This is especially important given the increasing prevalence and sophistication of cybe- attacks.

There are several ways in which vulnerability assessments can be integrated into the SDLC, including:

6.1 Threat Modeling

Threat modeling is a process used to identify and prioritize potential threats and vulnerabilities in a software system. It is a critical component of the software development lifecycle (SDLC) and vulnerability assessment process in contemporary computing.

There are several approaches to threat modeling in the SDLC of vulnerability assessment. One approach is to use a structured methodology, such as Microsoft's STRIDE (Spoofing, Tampering, Repudiation, Information disclosure, Denial of service, Elevation of privilege) or the more recent DREAD (Damage potential, Reproducibility, Exploitability, Affected users, Discoverability) frameworks. These frameworks provide a structured approach to threat modeling and help identify the most significant risks to a software system.

Another approach to threat modeling in the SDLC is to use threat modeling tools. These tools automate the process of identifying potential threats and vulnerabilities, allowing developers to quickly and efficiently prioritize their efforts to address the most significant risks.

Regardless of the approach used, threat modeling should be an iterative process that is conducted throughout the SDLC. As the software system evolves, so do the potential threats and vulnerabilities. Therefore, it is essential to review and update the threat model regularly to ensure that it accurately reflects the current state of the system.

6.2 Code Analysis

Code analysis is a process used to review the source code of a software system to identify potential security vulnerabilities, coding errors, and other issues that could compromise the system's security or stability. It is a crucial component of the vulnerability assessment process in the software development lifecycle (SDLC) in contemporary computing.

Code analysis can be performed manually, using a structured code review process, or using automated tools that scan the source code for potential vulnerabilities and issues. The use of automated code analysis tools is becoming increasingly popular, as they can identify potential vulnerabilities more quickly and efficiently than manual code reviews.

In the SDLC of vulnerability assessment in contemporary computing, code analysis should be integrated into the development process to ensure that potential vulnerabilities and issues are identified early and addressed promptly. This can be done by using automated code analysis tools as part of the continuous integration and continuous deployment (CI/CD) process or by conducting regular manual code reviews.

By integrating code analysis into the SDLC, developers and security professionals can identify potential vulnerabilities and issues before they are deployed into production, reducing the risk of security breaches and other issues that could compromise the system's security or stability. Overall, code analysis is an essential component of the vulnerability assessment process in contemporary computing and should be integrated into the SDLC to ensure that software systems are secure and protected against potential threats.

6.3 Penetration Testing

Penetration testing is a process used to simulate a real-world cyber attack on a software system, network, or application. It is an essential component of the vulnerability assessment process in the software development lifecycle (SDLC) in contemporary computing.

Penetration testing can be conducted manually or using automated tools. Manual penetration testing involves skilled cybersecurity professionals using their knowledge and experience to attempt to exploit potential vulnerabilities in the system. Automated penetration testing tools use pre-defined scripts to simulate cyber attacks and identify potential vulnerabilities.

Regardless of the approach used, penetration testing should be conducted regularly to ensure that the system remains secure over time. As new vulnerabilities and attack techniques are discovered, the system's security must be updated and tested to ensure that it remains protected against potential threats.

6.4 Security Training

Security training is a critical component of the vulnerability assessment process in the software development lifecycle (SDLC) in contemporary computing. It ensures that developers and other stakeholders in the development process have the knowledge and skills necessary to develop secure software systems.

Security training should be integrated into the SDLC as early as possible to ensure that security is considered throughout the development process. It should cover a range of topics, including secure coding practices, threat modeling, risk assessment, penetration testing, and incident response.

In addition to these technical approaches, it is essential to establish a culture of security throughout the development organization. This includes providing security training to developers, creating clear security policies and procedures, and ensuring that security is a top priority throughout the software development lifecycle(Raza, S., &Kavitha, C. (2020).

7. CASE STUDIES

Here are some examples of vulnerability assessment in contemporary computing that have been reported as case studies:

7.1 Equifax Data Breach

The Equifax data breach occurred in 2017 and was one of the largest data breaches in history, with the personal information of over 143 million individuals exposed. The breach was caused by a vulnerability in a web application framework that Equifax used.

The vulnerability in question was a flaw in the Apache Struts web application framework that Equifax used to power its online dispute portal. The vulnerability had been identified and a patch had been released, but Equifax failed to apply the patch in a timely manner, leaving the system vulnerable to attack (Kwak, D, et.al., 2019).

The attackers exploited the vulnerability to gain access to Equifax's systems and steal sensitive information, including names, addresses, birth dates, Social Security numbers, and other personal data. The breach had significant consequences for Equifax, including numerous lawsuits, congressional hearings, and regulatory fines.

The Equifax data breach highlighted the importance of conducting regular vulnerability assessments and patching known vulnerabilities in a timely manner. It also underscored the need for strong access controls, data encryption, and incident response plans to protect against potential cyber attacks.

7.2 WannaCryransomware Attack

The WannaCryransomware attack was a global cyberattack that occurred in May 2017. The attack affected over 200,000 computers in 150 countries, and is considered one of the most significant ransomwareattacks in history.

The WannaCry attack exploited a vulnerability in Microsoft Windows operating systems, using a worm-like feature to rapidly spread across networks. The vulnerability had been identified and a patch had been released by Microsoft, but many organizations had not applied the patch, leaving their systems vulnerable to attack.

Once the ransomware infected a computer, it encrypted the files and demanded a ransom payment in Bitcoin in exchange for the decryption key. The attack affected a wide range of organizations, including healthcare facilities, government agencies, and major corporations.

The WannaCry attack highlighted the importance of conducting regular vulnerability assessments and applying software updates and patches in a timely manner. It also underscored the need for effective incident response plans to quickly detect and respond to cyberattacks.

7.3 Capital One Data Breach

The Capital One data breach occurred in July 2019 and exposed the personal information of over 100 million people in the United States and Canada. The breach was caused by a vulnerability in a web application firewall that Capital One used to protect its data.

The vulnerability in question was caused by a misconfigured firewall that allowed an attacker to gain access to sensitive information stored in Capital One's cloud-based storage system. The attacker was able to obtain personal information such as names, addresses, phone numbers, and Social Security numbers.

Capital One discovered the breach in July 2019 and promptly reported it to law enforcement. The company also took immediate steps to contain the breach and notify affected individuals.

The Capital One data breach highlighted the importance of conducting regular vulnerability assessments, implementing strong access controls, and securing sensitive data. It also underscored the need for effective incident response plans to quickly detect and respond to cyberattacks.

7.4 SolarWinds Supply Chain Attack

The SolarWinds supply chain attack was a major cyberattack discovered in December 2020. The attack affected several US government agencies, including the Department of Defense, as well as private companies.

The attack was carried out by exploiting a vulnerability in SolarWinds' Orion platform, which is used for network management. The attackers inserted malicious code into a software update for the platform, allowing them to gain access to the networks of SolarWinds' customers who had installed the update.

Once the attackers gained access to a network, they were able to exfiltrate sensitive data and move laterally throughout the network. The attack was sophisticated and difficult to detect, with the attackers using multiple layers of obfuscation to evade detection (Alqahtani, S.et.al., 2021).

The SolarWinds supply chain attack highlighted the risk of supply chain attacks, where attackers target the software or hardware supply chain to gain access to networks and systems. It also underscored the importance of conducting regular vulnerability assessments, implementing strong access controls, and monitoring network traffic for suspicious activity.

These case studies demonstrate the importance of conducting regular vulnerability assessments, implementing effective security controls, and having strong incident response plans in place to protect against potential threats in contemporary computing.

REFERENCES

Al-Hamdani, Y., & Muttik, I. (2017). A review of vulnerability assessment and penetration testing tools. *International Journal of Advanced Computer Science and Applications*, 8(8), 190–198.

Ali, S., & Alazab, M. (2019). A review of vulnerability assessment tools for cloud computing. *Future Generation Computer Systems*, 92, 721–735.

Alqahtani, S., Alqahtani, F., Alqahtani, A., & Alshehri, M. (2021). Vulnerability assessment for industrial control systems using machine learning: A review. *IEEE Access : Practical Innovations, Open Solutions*, 9, 103149–103166.

Buczak, A. L., & Guven, E. (2016). A survey of data mining and machine learning methods for cyber security intrusion detection. *IEEE Communications Surveys and Tutorials*, 18(2), 1153–1176. doi:10.1109/COMST.2015.2494502

Conti, M., & Dehghantanha, A. (Eds.). (2018). *Security and privacy in cyber-physical systems: foundations, principles and applications*. CRC Press.

D'Amico, A., & Yang, B. (2015). Vulnerability assessment in the cloud computing environment. In *Proceedings of the 2015 International Conference on Computing, Networking and Communications (ICNC)* (pp. 117-121). IEEE.

Debar, H., Dacier, M., & Wespi, A. (1999). Towards a taxonomy of intrusion-detection systems. *Computer Networks*, 31(8), 805–822. doi:10.1016/S1389-1286(98)00017-6

Deshpande, A., & Jain, P. (2018). Vulnerability assessment of cloud-based systems. In *2018 International Conference on Advances in Computing, Communications and Informatics (ICACCI)* (pp. 1204-1209). IEEE.

Doupé, A., Celi, M., Chen, Y., & Lanzi, A. (2016). Evaluating automated vulnerability discovery using DARPA's cyber grand challenge. *IEEE Security and Privacy, 14*(5), 30–37.

Kaur, R., & Singh, A. (2017). A review of vulnerability assessment techniques in cloud computing. In *Proceedings of the 2017 2nd International Conference on Computing and Communications Technologies (ICCCT)* (pp. 35-38). IEEE.

Kizza, J. M. (2017). *Ethical and social issues in the information age.* Springer. doi:10.1007/978-3-319-70712-9

Krol, K., & Misra, S. (2019). Automated Vulnerability Assessment: A Survey. *IEEE Access : Practical Innovations, Open Solutions, 7*, 154760–154781.

Kwak, D., Kim, D., & Kim, H. (2019). Vulnerability assessment of web applications based on attack scenarios using a hybrid model of machine learning and logic reasoning. *Future Generation Computer Systems, 95*, 858–870.

Mell, P., & Scarfone, K. (2011). Vulnerability assessment: The state of the art. *IEEE Security and Privacy, 9*(4), 80–83.

Raza, S., & Kavitha, C. (2020). Vulnerability assessment techniques for internet of things (IoT) devices: A review. *Journal of Ambient Intelligence and Humanized Computing, 11*(5), 1895–1910.

Saleh, M., Ismail, R., & Al-Maashri, A. (2017). Vulnerability assessment in the internet of things: A review. In *Proceedings of the 2017 3rd International Conference on Cloud Computing Technologies and Applications (CloudTech)* (pp. 1-6). IEEE

Shrivastava, A., Tiwari, V., Kumar, R., & Khanna, A. (2018). A comprehensive survey on vulnerability assessment techniques for cloud computing. *Future Generation Computer Systems, 89*, 79–109.

Zhang, Y., Ye, Q., & Xu, Z. (2015). Cloud computing security: From single to multi-clouds. *Future Generation Computer Systems, 51*, 1–3.

APPENDIX

Abbreviations

CVSS - Common Vulnerability Scoring System
TTF - Time-to-Fix
BIA - Business Impact Analysis
XSS - Cross-Site Scripting
CSRF - Cross-Site Request Forgery
TCP - Transmission Control Protocol
UDP - User Datagram Protocol
MFA - Multi-factor authentication
SIEM - Security Information and Event Management
CVSS - Common Vulnerability Scoring System
CVE - Common Vulnerabilities and Exposures
HIPAA - Health Insurance Portability and Accountability Act
PCI DSS - Payment Card Industry Data Security Standard
GDPR - General Data Protection Regulation
SOX - Sarbanes-Oxley Act
NIST - National Institute of Standards and Technology
SDLC - Software Development Life cycle
STRIDE - Spoofing, Tampering, Repudiation, Information disclosure, Denial of service, Elevation of privilege
DREAD - Damage potential, Reproducibility, Exploitability, Affected users, Discoverability

Compilation of References

Abdel-Aziz, M., Al-Eroud, M., & Alsulaiman, F. (2019). A Comprehensive Review of Cybersecurity Frameworks, Standards, and Guidelines. *IEEE Access, 7.*

Abdou Hussien, A. (2021). Cyber Security Crimes, Ethics and a Suggested Algorithm to Overcome Cyber-Physical Systems Problems (CybSec1). *Journal of Information Security, 12*(01), 56–78. doi:10.4236/jis.2021.121003

Abdulaziz Aldribi, I. T. (2020). *ypervisor-based cloud intrusion detection through online multivariate statistical change tracking.* Elsevier Computer and Security.

Abhishek, B., Ranjit, S., Shankar, T., Eappen, G., Sivasankar, P., & Rajesh, A. (2020). Hybrid PSO-HSA and PSO-GA algorithm for 3D path planning in autonomous UAVs. *SN Applied Sciences, 2*(11), 1805. doi:10.100742452-020-03498-0

Abid, M., Abbas, H., Hassan, S. A., & Afzal, M. K. (2022). Internet of things security challenges and solutions: A review. *Journal of Ambient Intelligence and Humanized Computing.* doi:10.100712652-022-03655-6

Ablon, L., Libicki, M. C., & Golay, A. A. (2014). Markets for Cybercnme Tools and Stolen Data. Hackers' Bazaar, 1-85.

Abomhara, M., & Køien, G. (2015). Cyber security and the internet of things: vulnerabilities, threats, intruders and attacks. *Journal of Cyber Security and Mobility,* 65-88.

Abou-Assaleh, T. (2004). *N-gram-based detection of new malicious code.* COMPSAC. doi:10.1109/CMPSAC.2004.1342667

Abubakar, A. I., Sadiq, A. S., Dauda, M. D., & Garba, A. H. (2020). An overview of cyber security in digital banking and the role of machine learning and AI. *Procedia Computer Science, 172,* 78–85. doi:10.1016/j.procs.2020.07.347

Acquah, M. A., Jin, Y., Oh, B. C., Son, Y. G., & Kim, S. Y. (2023). Spatiotemporal Sequence-to-Sequence Clustering for Electric Load Forecasting. *IEEE Access : Practical Innovations, Open Solutions, 11,* 5850–5863. doi:10.1109/ACCESS.2023.3235724

Adadi, A., & Berrada, M. (2018). Peeking inside the black-box: A survey on Explainable Artificial Intelligence (XAI). *IEEE Access : Practical Innovations, Open Solutions, 6,* 52138–52160. doi:10.1109/ACCESS.2018.2870052

Adek, R. T., & Nasution, S. (2018). Tweet Clustering in Indonesian Language Twitter Social Media using Naive Bayes Classifier Method. *Eurasian Journal of Analytical Chemistry, 13*(6), 277–284.

Aditya Gautam, S. (2014). Path planning for unmanned aerial vehicle based on genetic algorithm & artificial neural network in 3D. *2014 International Conference on Data Mining and Intelligent Computing (ICDMIC).* IEEE.

Adler. (2004). *Quantum Theory as an Emergent Phenomenon.* Cambridge: Cambridge University Press.

Agababov, V., Buettner, M., Chudnovsky, V., Cogan, M., Greenstein, B., McDaniel, S., & Yin, B. (2015). Flywheel: Google's data compression proxy for the mobile web. *In 12th {USENIX} Symposium on Networked Systems Design and Implementation* ({NSDI} 15) (pp. 367-380).

Agrawal, R., & Srikant, R. (1994). *Fast algorithms for mining association rules*. In *Proceedings of the 20th International Conference on Very Large Data Bases*, Santiago, Chile.

Ahmad, I. (2017). A survey on behavior-based malware analysis techniques: Static, dynamic, and hybrid analysis. *ACM Computing Surveys, 50*(6), 1–36.

Ahmadi, H., Zhang, H., Kulkarni, S., & Yang, G. (2019). Cybersecurity Threats: A Machine Learning Perspective. In Y. Li, X. Li, & Y. Zhang (Eds.), *Guide to Vulnerability Analysis for Computer Networks and Systems*. Springer. doi:10.1007/978-981-13-7263-82

Ahmed. (2019). Modeling and Simulation of Office Desk Illumination Using ZEMAX. 2019 International Conference on Electrical, Communication, and Computer Engineering (ICECCE). IEEE. 10.1109/ICECCE47252.2019.8940756

Ajeet Singh, A. J. (2018). Study of cyber-attacks on cyber-physical system. In *Proceedings of 3rd International Conference on Internet of Things and Connected Technologies (ICIoTCT)*. SSRN.

Akhtar, N., Parwej, F., & Perwej, Y. (2017). A Perusal of Big Data Classification and Hadoop Technology. International Transaction of Electrical and Computer Engineers System (ITECES), USA. Doi:10.12691/iteces-4-1-4

Akintoye, S. A., & Alaba, F. A. (2020). Artificial Intelligence and Cybersecurity: A Review of Applications and Future Directions. *Journal of Cybersecurity and Information Management, 3*(2), 55–72.

Al Messabi, K., Aldwairi, M., Al Yousif, A., Thoban, A., & Belqasmi, F. (2018). Malware Detection using DNS Records and Domain Name Features. *International Conference on Future Networks and Distributed Systems (ICFNDS)*. ACM. .3231082.10.1145/3231053.3231082

Alaa, A. & van der Schaar, M. (2018). *A Review of Machine Learning Techniques for Healthcare Risk Prediction*.

Alazab, A., Hobbs, M., Abawajy, J., & Alazab, M. (2012). Using feature selection for intrusion detection system. In *Proceedings of the 2012 International Symposium on Communications and Information Technologies (ISCIT)*, Gold Coast, Australia. 10.1109/ISCIT.2012.6380910

Albalawi, Y., Aldossary, M., & Alghamdi, A. (2020). Cybersecurity in Healthcare: A Systematic Review of Trends in Research and Development. *Journal of Medical Systems, 83*.

Albert, A., Leira, F. S., & Imsland, L. (2017). UAV Path Planning using MILP with Experiments. *Modeling, Identification and Control, 38*(1), 21–32. doi:10.4173/mic.2017.1.3

Aldhafferi, N., Watson, C., & Sajeev, A. S. M. (2013). *Personal information privacy settings of online social networks and their. 2*(2), 1–17.

Aldhafferi, N., & Watson, C., & A.S.M, S. (. (2013). Personal Information Privacy Settings of Online Social Networks and Their Suitability for Mobile Internet Devices. *International Journal of Security. Privacy and Trust Management, 2*(2), 1–17. doi:10.5121/ijsptm.2013.2201

Aldmour, R., Burnap, P., & Lakoju, M. (2019). Risk assessment methods for converged IoT and SCADA systems: Review and recommendations. In *Proceedings of the Living in the Internet of Things (IoT 2019)*, London, UK. 10.1049/cp.2019.0130

Aldwairi, M., & Alwahedi, A. (2018). Detecting Fake News in Social Media Networks. *Science Direct, Procedia Computer Science, 141*, 215-222. . doi:10.1016/j.procs.2018.10.171

Aldwairi, M., Abu-Dalo, A. M., & Jarrah, M. (2017). Pattern Matching of Signature-based IDS using Myers algorithm under MapReduce framework. *EURASIP Journal of Information Security*. doi:10.1186/s13635-017-0062-7

Aldwairi, M., Hasan, M., Balbahaith, Z. (2017). *Detection of Drive-by Download Attacks using Machine Learning Approach*. ACM. . doi:10.4018/IJISP.2017100102

Aldwairi, M., & Alsaadi, H. H. (2017). Flukes: Autonomous Log Forensics, Intelligence and Visualization Tool. *ICFNDS'17: Proceedings of the International Conference on Future Networks and Distributed Systems*. ACM. 10.1145/3102304.3102337

Aldwairi, M., & Al-Salman, R. (2011). Malurls: Malicious URLs Classification System. *Annual International Conference on Information Theory and Applications, GSTF Digital Library (GSTF-DL)*, Singapore.

Alflen, N. C., Prado, E. P. V., & Grotta, A. (2020). A model for evaluating requirements elicitation techniques in software development projects. *ICEIS 2020 - Proceedings of the 22nd International Conference on Enterprise Information Systems, 2*(Iceis), 242–249. 10.5220/0009397502420249

Al-Fuhaidi, B. (2021). Literature Review on Cyber Attacks Detection and Prevention Schemes. *2021 International Conference on Intelligent Technology, System and Service for Internet of Everything (ITSS-IoE)*. IEEE. 10.1109/ITSS-IoE53029.2021.9615288

Al-Fuqaha, A., Alharbi, A., & Alsharif, M. (2020). A comprehensive review of blockchain technology: Applications, challenges, and opportunities in cyber security. *IEEE Internet of Things Journal, 8*(1), 528–545. doi:10.1109/JIOT.2020.2971403

Al-Fuqaha, A., Guizani, M., Mohammadi, M., Aledhari, M., & Ayyash, M. (2015). Internet of Things: A Survey on Enabling Technologies, Protocols, and Applications. *IEEE Communications Surveys and Tutorials, 17*(4), 2347–2376. doi:10.1109/COMST.2015.2444095

Al-Hamdani, Y., & Muttik, I. (2017). A review of vulnerability assessment and penetration testing tools. *International Journal of Advanced Computer Science and Applications, 8*(8), 190–198.

Alharbi, S., Qasim, S. M., & Alharbi, H. (2020). A Comprehensive Study on Blockchain-Based Cyber security: Applications, Opportunities, and Future Challenges. *IEEE Access : Practical Innovations, Open Solutions, 8*, 82598–82615. doi:10.1109/ACCESS.2020.2992273

Ali, M. K., Ali, M. K., & Hassan, K. A. (2020). *Factors Affecting Information Privacy and Protection Behavior on Social Network Sites. VII*(Ix), 406–418.

Ali, A., Zakaria, M., & Almehmadi, A. (2021). A Comprehensive Literature Review on Cybersecurity Risk Management. *Computers & Security, 108*, 102242. doi:10.1016/j.cose.2021.102242

Ali, S., & Alazab, M. (2019). A review of vulnerability assessment tools for cloud computing. *Future Generation Computer Systems, 92*, 721–735.

Ali, S., Islam, N., Rauf, A., Din, I. U., Guizani, M., & Rodrigues, J. J. P. C. (2018). Privacy and security issues in online social networks. *Future Internet, 12*(12), 1–12. doi:10.3390/fi10120114

Almgren, M., Jiang, Y., & Ramzan, Z. (2018). Adversarial Machine Learning: Attacks and Defenses. *IEEE Security and Privacy, 16*(6), 32–44. doi:10.1109/MSP.2018.2701193

Al-Muhtadi, M. J., Al-Qutayri, M. A., & Nasir, Q. (2019). Cybersecurity Risk Assessment and Management: A Review of the Current State of the Art. *IEEE Access : Practical Innovations, Open Solutions, 7*, 112103–112122. doi:10.1109/access.2019.2932952

Almukaynizi, M. (2020). Cybersecurity and Artificial Intelligence: A Review. *Journal of Artificial Intelligence and Data Science, 2*(1), 1–15.

Alomari, M. H., & Mahdi, M. N. (2019). Intrusion detection systems using machine learning algorithms: A comparative study. *IEEE Access : Practical Innovations, Open Solutions, 7,* 74458–74477.

Alom, M. Z., Yakopcic, C., Taha, T. M., Westberg, K., Sidike, P., Nasrin, M. S., ... Hasan, M. (2019). A state-of-the-art survey on deep learning theory and architectures. *Electronics (Basel), 8*(3), 292. doi:10.3390/electronics8030292

Alom, Z., Carminati, B., & Ferrari, E. (2018). Detecting spam accounts on Twitter. *IEEE/ACM International Conference on Advances in Social Networks Analysis and Mining.* IEEE.

Alqahtani, S., & Khan, M. K. (2020). A systematic review of intrusion detection using machine learning techniques. *Journal of King Saud University - Computer and Information Sciences, 32*(8), 944-956.

Alqahtani, S., Alqahtani, F., Alqahtani, A., & Alshehri, M. (2021). Vulnerability assessment for industrial control systems using machine learning: A review. *IEEE Access : Practical Innovations, Open Solutions, 9,* 103149–103166.

Alqurashi, M., & Mahmoud, Q. H. (2019). A survey on machine learning for cybersecurity. *IEEE Access : Practical Innovations, Open Solutions, 7,* 46127–46141.

ALRassan, I. (2020). XML Encryption and Signature for Securing Web Services. *International Journal of Computer Science & Information Technology (IJCSIT), 12*(4). https://ssrn.com/abstract=3688789

Alshahrani, A., & Zhang, X. (2020). Internet of things security: A survey. *Journal of Network and Computer Applications, 150,* 102506. doi:10.1016/j.jnca.2019.102506

Alshammari, O., Almutairi, A., & Alghathbar, K. (2019). Cyber security Risk Assessment for SCADA and DCS Networks: A Systematic Literature Review. *Journal of Computer Networks and Communications, 2019.* doi:10.1155/2019/8190167

Alvarez, R., & Vaisman, A. (2020). Machine Learning in Cybersecurity: Applications and Challenges. *IEEE Security and Privacy, 18*(1), 69–76.

Alzaylaee, M. K., Yerima, S. Y., & Sezer, S. (2017, June). Improving dynamic analysis of android apps using hybrid test input generation. In *2017 International Conference on Cyber Security And Protection Of Digital Services (Cyber Security)* (pp. 1-8). IEEE. 10.1109/CyberSecPODS.2017.8074845

Alzaylaee, M. K., Yerima, S. Y., & Sezer, S. (2020). DL-Droid: Deep learning based android malware detection using real devices. *Computers & Security, 89,* 101663. doi:10.1016/j.cose.2019.101663

Amin, S., Liao, K., Wang, D., & Singhal, A. (2019). A survey of deep learning for cyber security. *IEEE Communications Surveys and Tutorials, 22*(1), 270–309.

Amiri, F., Yousefi, M. R., Lucas, C., Shakery, A., & Yazdani, N. (2011). Mutual information-based feature selection for intrusion detection systems. *Journal of Network and Computer Applications, 34*(4), 1184–1199. doi:10.1016/j.jnca.2011.01.002

Amiri, S., Pouryazdanpanah, M., Heydari, M., & Abdar, M. (2020). A Machine Learning Approach for Network Security Based on NSL-KDD Dataset. *Journal of Ambient Intelligence and Humanized Computing, 11*(6), 2497–2507. doi:10.100712652-019-01311-x

Amor, N. B., Benferhat, S., & Elouedi, Z. (2004). Naive bayesvs decision trees in intrusion detection systems. *Proceedings of the 2004 ACM symposium on Applied computing,* ACM. 10.1145/967900.967989

Anderson, D., Lunt, T. F., Javitz, H., Tamaru, A., & Valdes, A. (1995). *Detecting unusual program behavior using the statistical component of the next-generation intrusion detection expert system (NIDES).* Computer Science Laboratory, SRI International.

Android. (2021). Aapt2. Android. https://developer.android.com/studio/command-line/aapt2.

Android. (2021). *Ui/application exerciser monkey*. Android. https://developer.android.com/studio/test/monkey,.

Antonucci, D., & Kooij, M. (2017). *The Cyber Risk Handbook: Creating and Measuring Effective Cybersecurity Capabilities*. John Wiley & Sons. doi:10.1002/9781119309741

Apiletti, E., Baralis, E., Cerquitelli, T., & D'Elia, V. (2009). Baralis, T. Cerquitelli, V. DElia, Characterizing network traffic by means of the netmine framework. *Computer Networks*, *53*(6), 774–789. doi:10.1016/j.comnet.2008.12.011

Appelbaum, J., Gibson, A., Goetz, J., Kucherena, A., & Shubin, S. (2014). Edward Snowden: The whistleblower behind the NSA surveillance revelations. *The Guardian*, p. 10.

Arashloo, R. S., & Rabiee, H. R. (2019). Machine learning in intrusion detection: A comprehensive survey. *Journal of Network and Computer Applications*, *135*, 1–25.

Arias-Oliva, M., Mendoza-Gonzalez, R., & de la Hoz-Manotas, A. (2020). Cybersecurity in smart cities: Challenges and opportunities. *Journal of Network and Computer Applications*, *168*, 102680.

Arora, S., & Kapoor, V. (2019). Artificial intelligence for cybersecurity: A comprehensive review. *Journal of Network and Computer Applications*, *130*, 114–133.

Arpaci-Dusseau, A. C., & Arpaci-Dusseau, R. H. (2018). *Operating systems: Three easy pieces*. Arpaci-Dusseau Books.

Arshad, M., Qaisar, S. B., & Choo, K. K. R. (2020). A review on blockchain security for cyber-physical systems. *IEEE Access : Practical Innovations, Open Solutions*, *8*, 167340–167362. doi:10.1109/ACCESS.2020.3024662

Arshad, S., Shah, M. A., Wahid, A., Mehmood, A., Song, H., & Yu, H. (2018). SAMADroid: A novel 3-level hybrid malware detection model for android operating system. *IEEE Access : Practical Innovations, Open Solutions*, *6*, 4321–4339. doi:10.1109/ACCESS.2018.2792941

Arthern, R. J., & Williams, C. R. (2017). The sensitivity of West Antarctica to the submarine melting feedback. *Geophysical Research Letters*, *44*(5), 2352–2359. doi:10.1002/2017GL072514

Arulkumaran, K., Deisenroth, M. P., Brundage, M., & Bharath, A. A. (2017). A Brief Survey of Deep Reinforcement Learning. *IEEE Signal Processing Magazine,* (Sept), 1–13. doi:10.1109/MSP.2017.2743240

Asadi, M., Pourhossein, K., & Mohammadi-Ivatloo, B. (2023). GIS-assisted modeling of wind farm site selection based on support vector regression. *Journal of Cleaner Production*, *390*, 135993. doi:10.1016/j.jclepro.2023.135993

Atreya, M. & Paine, S. (2002). *Digital Signatures*. McGraw-Hill.

Atzori, L., Iera, A., & Morabito, G. (2010). The internet of things: A survey. *Computer Networks*, *54*(15), 2787–2805. doi:10.1016/j.comnet.2010.05.010

Avery, E. (2011). Journalists, Social media, and the use of Humor on Twitter. *The Electronic Journal of Communication, Texas, 21,* 1–2.

Awan, A. R., Akhtar, R. N., & Khan, Z. A. (2021). Quantum Computing for Cybersecurity: Challenges and Opportunities. *Journal of Ambient Intelligence and Humanized Computing*, *12*(8).

B. Rad, M. M. (2012). *Camouflage in Malware: from Encryption to Metamorphism*. Journal of Computer and Science Network Securrity.

Bahrami, F., & Vahedian, Z. (2021). Developing an artificial intelligence-based approach for predicting cyber-attacks in cloud computing. *Journal of Cloud Computing (Heidelberg, Germany)*, *10*(1), 16. doi:10.118613677-021-00241-x

Baker, B., & Wilson, D. (2020). Explainable AI: Beware of inmates running the asylum or: How I learned to stop worrying and love the social and behavioral sciences. *Journal of Applied Research in Memory and Cognition, 9*(2), 298–307.

Balogun, A.O. & Jimoh, R.G. (2015). Anomaly intrusion detection using an hybrid of decision tree and K-nearest neighbor. J. *Adv. Sci. Res. Appl.*

Banerjee, A., & Gupta, A. (2020). Intelligent anomaly detection in cyber security: A survey. *Journal of Network and Computer Applications, 150*, 102506.

Ban, X., Chen, C., Liu, S., Wang, Y., & Zhang, J. (2015). A performance evaluation of machine learning-based streaming spam tweets detection. *IEEE Transactions on Computational Social Systems, 2*(3), 65–76. doi:10.1109/TCSS.2016.2516039

Bapat, R., Mandya, A., Liu, X., Abraham, B., Brown, D. E., Kang, H., & Veeraraghavan, M. (2018). *Identifying malicious botnet traffic using logistic regression*. In *Proceedings of the 2018 Systems and Information Engineering Design Symposium (SIEDS)*, Charlottesville, VA, USA. 10.1109/SIEDS.2018.8374749

Barry, M. (2009, October). Leiner at. al., "A Brief History of the Internet,". *Computer Communication Review, 39*(5).

Basu, M., Bhattacharyya, D., & Kundu, M. (2018). Malware detection using machine learning techniques: A survey. *ACM Computing Surveys, 51*(4), 1–36. doi:10.1145/2501654.2501660

Bayazit, E. C., Sahingoz, O. K., & Dogan, B. (2022, June). A Deep Learning Based Android Malware Detection System with Static Analysis. In *2022 International Congress on Human-Computer Interaction, Optimization and Robotic Applications (HORA)* (pp. 1-6). IEEE. 10.1109/HORA55278.2022.9800057

Baym, G., & Jones, J.P., (2012). News Parody in Global Perspective: Politics, Power, and Resistance. Popular Communication. Taylor and Francis. doi:10.1080/15405702.2012.638566

Bendavid, Y., Bagheri, N., Safkhani, M., & Rostampour, S. (2018). IoT Device Security: Challenging "A Lightweight RFID Mutual Authentication Protocol Based on Physical Unclonable Function". *Sensors (Basel), 18*(12), 4444. doi:10.339018124444 PMID:30558323

Benevenuto, F., Magno, G., Rodrigues, T., & Almeida, V. (2015). Detecting spammers on Twitter. *ACM International Conference on Collaboration, Electronic messaging. Anti-Abuse and Spam. ACM.*

Benferhat, S., Kenaza, T., & Mokhtari, A. (2008). A naive bayes approach for detecting coordinated attacks. In *Proceedings of the 2008 32nd Annual IEEE International Computer Software and Applications*. IEEE. 10.1109/COMPSAC.2008.213

Benisha, R., & Ratna, S. R. (2020). Detection of Interruption Attack in the Wireless networked closed loop industrial control systems. *Telecommunication Systems, 73*(3), 359–370. doi:10.100711235-019-00614-3

Berlin, S. (2015). Deep neural network based malware detection using two dimensional binary program features. IEEE.

Beskow, D. M., & Carley, K. M. (2019). *Social cybersecurity: an emerging national security requirement*. Carnegie Mellon University Pittsburgh United States.

Beyt, S. A. S., Rafie, M., & Mojtaba, G. S. (2021). Spam detection on Twitter using a support vector machine and users features by identifying their interactions. *Multimedia Tools and Applications, 8*(4), 11583–11605.

Beznosov, K., Flinn, S., Kawamoto, S., & Hartman, B. (2005). Introduction to Web services and their security. *Published in: Journal Information Security Tech., 10*(1).

Bhadane, C., & Shah, K. (2020, April). Clustering algorithms for spatial data mining. *In Proceedings of the 2020 3rd International Conference on Geoinformatics and Data Analysis* (pp. 5-9). ACM. 10.1145/3397056.3397068

Bhatia, A. (2019). Encryption: A Critical Component of Cyber Security. *International Journal of Computer Science and Network Security, 19*(1), 11–16.

Bhattacharya, S., Gudlaugsson, T., & Poddar, R. (2019). A Comprehensive Survey on Deep Learning for Cybersecurity. *Journal of Big Data, 6*(1), 24. doi:10.118640537-019-0187-3

Bhattacharyya, S., Chakraborty, S., Nandi, S., & Dutta, S. (2020). Cybersecurity in the era of industry 4.0: Challenges and opportunities. *Journal of Network and Computer Applications, 150*, 102524.

Bhatti, R., Bertino, E., Ghafoor, A., & Joshi, J. B. D. (2004, April). XML- Based Specification for Web Services Document Security. *Journal of Computers, 37*(4).

Bhowmik, T. K., Islam, M. R., & Rahman, M. M. (2020). An Overview of Cybersecurity and Artificial Intelligence. *International Journal of Advanced Science and Technology, 29*(2), 1261–1271.

Biamonte, J., Wittek, P., Pancotti, N., Rebentrost, P., Wiebe, N., & Lloyd, S. (2017). Quantum machine learning. *Nature, 549*(7671), 195–202. doi:10.1038/nature23474 PMID:28905917

Biggio, B., & Roli, F. (2018). Wild patterns: Ten years after the rise of adversarial machine learning. *Pattern Recognition, 84*, 317–331. doi:10.1016/j.patcog.2018.07.023

Bilge, L., Balzarotti, D., Robertson, W., Kirda, E., & Kruegel, C. (2012). Disclosure: detecting botnet command and control servers through large-scale netflow analysis. In: *Proceedings of the 28thAnnual Computer Security Applications Conference.* ACM. 10.1145/2420950.2420969

Bilge, L., Kirda, E., Kruegel, C., & Balduzzi, M. (2011). Exposure: Finding malicious domains using passive dnsanalysis. NDSS.

Bilge, L., Strufe, T., Balzarotti, D., & Kirda, E. (2009). All your contacts belong to us: Automated identity theft attacks on social networks. *WWW'09 - Proceedings of the 18th International World Wide Web Conference*, 551–560. 10.1145/1526709.1526784

Bin Othman Mustafa, M. S., Nomani Kabir, M., Ernawan, F., & Jing, W. (2019). An Enhanced Model for Increasing Awareness of Vocational Students Against Phishing Attacks. *2019 IEEE International Conference on Automatic Control and Intelligent Systems, I2CACIS 2019 - Proceedings, June*, (pp. 10–14). IEEE. 10.1109/I2CACIS.2019.8825070

Binkley, P. F., Frontera, W., Standaert, D. G., & Stein, J. (2003). Predicting the potential of wearable technology. *IEEE Engineering in Medicine and Biology Magazine, 22*(3), 23–27. doi:10.1109/MEMB.2003.1213623 PMID:12845813

Bishop, M. (2004). *Introduction to Computer Security.* Addison-Wesley Professional.

Bishop, M. (2019). Artificial intelligence and cybersecurity. *Computer Fraud & Security, 2019*(6), 13–16.

Bojan Kolosnjaji, A. Z. (2016). Deep learning for classification of malware system call sequences. [Springer.]. *Intelligence*, 137–149.

Bonetti, F., Warnaby, G., & Quinn, L. (2018). Augmented reality and virtual reality in physical and online retailing: A review, synthesis and research agenda. In *Augmented reality and virtual reality* (pp. 119–132). Springer. doi:10.1007/978-3-319-64027-3_9

Bouzeghoub, A., & Zeghidour, N. (2021). AI and cybersecurity: A review of current trends and future directions. *Journal of Ambient Intelligence and Humanized Computing, 12*(4), 3355–3368.

Braith, B., Hankison, W., Hiotis, A., Galbraith, B., Janakiraman, M., Prasad, D., & Trivedi, R. (2002). *Professional Web Service Security.* Wrox Publication.

Brantly, Renaud, & Theoharidou. (2016). Cybersecurity Incident Response Planning: Lessons from a Large-Scale Exercise. *Computers & Security, 56.* doi:10.1016/j.cose.2015.11.001

Brewer, P.R., Young, D.G., & Morreale, M. (2013). The Impact of Real News about Fake News: Intertextual Processes and Political Satire. *International Journal of Public Opinion Research, 25*(3), 323–343. doi:10.1093/ijpor/edt015

Bridges, V. (2000). Fuzzy Data mining and genetic algorithms applied to intrusion detection. In: *Proceedings of the National Information Systems Security Conference.* IEEE.

Briz-Redón, Á., & Serrano-Aroca, Á. (2020). The effect of climate on the spread of the COVID-19 pandemic: A review of findings, and statistical and modelling techniques. *Progress in Physical Geography, 44*(5), 0309133320946302. doi:10.1177/0309133320946302

Bródka, P., Sobas, M., & Johnson, H. (2014). Profile cloning detection in social networks. *Proceedings - 2014 European Network Intelligence Conference, ENIC 2014,* (pp. 63–68). IEEE. 10.1109/ENIC.2014.21

Buczak, A. L., & Guven, E. (2015). A survey of data mining and machine learning methods for cyber security intrusion detection. *IEEE Communications Surveys and Tutorials, 18*(2), 1153–1176. doi:10.1109/COMST.2015.2494502

Buczak, A. L., & Guven, E. (2018a). Deep Learning-Based Anomaly Detection: A Survey. *ACM Computing Surveys, 51*(3), 46. Advance online publication. doi:10.1145/3186243

Bukhari, S. A., & Awad, A. I. (2019). A survey on machine learning techniques for anomaly detection in network traffic. *Journal of Network and Computer Applications, 133,* 114–137.

Buonocunto, P., de Oliveira, S. H., Gomes, J. P., dos Santos, J. A., da Silva, J. M., & de Castro, L. N. (2019). A Review on Machine Learning and Artificial Intelligence Approaches for Cybersecurity. *Journal of Information Security and Applications, 48,* 102387. doi:10.1016/j.jisa.2019.102387

Cai, L., Li, Y., & Xiong, Z. (2021). JOWMDroid: Android malware detection based on feature weighting with joint optimization of weight-mapping and classifier parameters. *Computers & Security, 100,* 102086. doi:10.1016/j.cose.2020.102086

Cai, W., & Vasconcelos, N. (2018). Cascade R-CNN: Delving into high quality object detection. In *Proceedings of the IEEE conference on computer vision and pattern recognition* (pp. 6154-6162). 10.1109/CVPR.2018.00644

Calderon, M., & Zeadally, S. (2020). The internet of things in the era of 5G: Opportunities and challenges. *Journal of Network and Computer Applications, 168,* 102691.

Cameron, D., & Jones, I. G. (1983). John Snow, the Broad Street pump and modern epidemiology. *International Journal of Epidemiology, 12*(4), 393–396. doi:10.1093/ije/12.4.393 PMID:6360920

Cao, B., Li, C., Song, Y., & Fan, X. (2022, April 12). Network Intrusion Detection Technology Based on Convolutional Neural Network and BiGRU. *Computational Intelligence and Neuroscience, 1942847,* 1–20. doi:10.1155/2022/1942847 PMID:35463242

Cao, Y., Zhang, X., Kang, J., Wang, X., & Sun, H. (2019). An effective end-to-end deep learning architecture for benign and malicious network traffic classification. *IEEE Access : Practical Innovations, Open Solutions, 7,* 57522–57530.

Carlin, D. J., Kuleshov, V., Lupu, E. C., & Longstaff, T. A. (2018). Machine Learning and Security: Protecting Systems with Data and Algorithms. *IEEE Security and Privacy, 16*(5), 68–77. doi:10.1109/MSP.2018.2801080

Carlini, N., & Wagner, D. (2017). Towards evaluating the robustness of neural networks. In *2017 IEEE Symposium on Security and Privacy (SP)* (pp. 39-57). IEEE. 10.1109/SP.2017.49

Carrara, F., Böhme, R., & Caviglione, L. (2020). Cybersecurity of the internet of things: A review of the literature. *Computer Science Review*, *35*, 100212.

Casey, D., & Pearce, D. (Eds.). (2018). *More Than Management Development: Action Learning at General Electric Company*. Routledge. doi:10.4324/9780429452567

Cavoukian, A. (2015). *Privacy by design: The 7 foundational principles*. Information and Privacy Commissioner of Ontario.

Chakraborty, A., Paranjape, B., Kakarla, S., & Ganguly, N. (2016). Stop Clickbait: Detecting and Preventing Clickbaits in Online News Media. *IEEE/ACM International Conference on Advances in Social Networks Analysis and Mining (ASONAM), Computer Science and Information Networks*, (pp. 9–16). IEEE. https://arxiv.org/abs/1610.09786 10.1109/ASONAM.2016.7752207

Chandola, V., Banerjee, A., & Kumar, V. (2009). Anomaly Detection: A Survey. *ACM Computing Surveys*, *41*(3), 15. Advance online publication. doi:10.1145/1541880.1541882

Chang, L. Y., & Coppel, N. (2020). Building cyber security awareness in a developing country: Lessons from Myanmar. *Computers & Security*, *97*, 101959. doi:10.1016/j.cose.2020.101959

Chaudhary, G., Srivastava, S., & Khari, M. (2023). Generative Edge Intelligence for Securing IoT-assisted Smart Grid against Cyber-Threats. *International Journal of Wireless & Ad Hoc Communication*, *6*(1), 38–49. doi:10.54216/IJWAC.060104

Chaudhry, N., & Yousaf, M. M. (2019, February). Spatial querying of mineral resources using PostGIS. *In 2019 2nd International Conference on Advancements in Computational Sciences (ICACS)* (pp. 1-6). 10.23919/ICACS.2019.8688999

Chaudhuri, A., Nandi, A., & Pradhan, B. (2022). *A Dynamic Weighted Federated Learning for Android Malware Classification*. arXiv preprint arXiv:2211.12874.

Chebrolu, S., Abraham, A., & Thomas, J. P. (2005, June). Feature deduction and ensemble design of intrusion detection systems. *Computers & Security*, *24*(4), 295–307. doi:10.1016/j.cose.2004.09.008

Check Point Research. (2022). *2022 Cyber Security Report*. Check Point Software Technologies.

Chen, Y., Conroy, N. J., & Rubin, V. L. (2015). News in an Online World: The Need for an Automatic Crap Detector. *Proceedings of the 78th ASIS&T Annual Meeting, Research in and for the Community*. American Society for Information Science, Silver Springs. 10.1002/pra2.2015.145052010081

Chen, C., Wang, Y., Zhang, J., Xiang, Y., Zhou, W., & Min, G. (2016). Statistical Features Based Real-time Detection of Drifted Twitter Spam. *IEEE Transactions on Information Forensics and Security*, *12*(4), 914–925. doi:10.1109/TIFS.2016.2621888

Chengwei, W. (2009). Ebat: online methods for detecting utility cloud anomalies. In *Proceedings of the 6th Middleware Doctoral Symposium*. ACM.

Chen, L., He, K., & Sun, J. (2016). Deep residual learning for image recognition. In *Proceedings of the IEEE conference on computer vision and pattern recognition* (pp. 770-778). IEEE.

Chen, L., Zhou, H., & Shang, X. (2021). A survey on privacy-preserving machine learning for cyber security. *Journal of Cybersecurity*, *7*(1), tyaa006. doi:10.1093/cybsec/tyaa006

Chen, M., Mao, S., & Liu, Y. (2014). Big data: A survey. *Mobile Networks and Applications*, *19*(2), 171–209. doi:10.100711036-013-0489-0

Chen, T., Wang, X., & Yang, Y. (2017). Malware detection using deep learning based on autoencoder with raw executable files. *Journal of Information Security and Applications*, *36*, 1–9.

Chen, X., Ma, H., Song, D., & Sun, X. (2020). Survey on Artificial Intelligence and Cybersecurity. *International Journal of Advanced Computer Science and Applications, 11*(5), 88–98.

Chen, Y. (2020). DDoS Attack Detection Based on Random Forest. *2020 IEEE International Conference on Progress in Informatics and Computing (PIC)*. IEEE. 10.1109/PIC50277.2020.9350788

Chen, Y., Han, J., & Zhao, X. (2012). Three-dimensional path planning for unmanned aerial vehicle based on linear programming. *Robotica, 30*(Sept), 773–781. doi:10.1017/S0263574711000993

Chen, Z., Jiang, F., Cheng, Y., Gu, X., Liu, W., & Peng, J. (2018). XGBoost classifier for DDoS attack detection and analysis in SDN-based cloud. In *2018 IEEE International Conference on Big Data and Smart Computing (BigComp)*, (pp. 251-256). IEEE. 10.1109/BigComp.2018.00044

Cheswick, W. R., & Bellovin, S. M. (1994). *Firewalls and Internet security: repelling the wily hacker*. Addison-Wesley Professional.

Chhabra, S., Aggarwal, A., Benevenuto, F., & Kumaraguru, P. (2011). Phishing social: The phishing landscape through short URLs. *ACM International Conference on Collaboration Electronic messaging Anti-Abuse and Spam,* (pp. 92–101). ACM. 10.1145/2030376.2030387

Chhetri, S. K., & Singh, B. (2020). Artificial Intelligence in Cybersecurity: A Review. *International Journal of Computer Science and Network Security, 20*(1), 87–93.

Chollet, F. (2017). *Deep learning with Python*. Manning Publications.

Chowdhury, R., Das, K. G., Saha, B., & Bandyopadhyay, S. K. (2020). A Method Based on NLP for Twitter Spam Detection. Preprints, 283-291

Chu, C. H., & Chen, J. V. (2019). The application of artificial intelligence in cybersecurity. *International Journal of Innovative Computing, Information, & Control, 15*(3), 1179–1193.

Clematis, A., Mineter, M., & Marciano, R. (2003). High performance computing with geographical data. *Parallel Computing, 29*(10), 1275–1280. doi:10.1016/j.parco.2003.07.001

Coelho, S., Ferreira, J., Carvalho, D., Miranda, A. I., & Lopes, M. (2023). Climate Change Impact on Source Contributions to the Air Quality in Aveiro Region. In *Air Pollution Modeling and its Application XXVIII* (pp. 207–212). Springer International Publishing.

Cohen, R., & Toubiana, V. (2018). Explaining explanations: An overview of interpretability of machine learning. *IEEE 5th International Conference on Data Science and Advanced Analytics (DSAA)*.

Conference, T. Finland, 28 July–1 August 2008; pp. 704–709.

Conroy, N. J., Rubin, V. L., & Chen, Y. (2016). *Automatic Deception Detection: Methods for Finding Fake News*. Proceedings of the ASIS&T Annual Meeting, Information Science and Technology, Silver Springs, MD, USA. 10.1002/pra2.2015.145052010082

Conti, M., & Dehghantanha, A. (Eds.). (2018). *Security and privacy in cyber-physical systems: foundations, principles and applications*. CRC Press.

Cosgrave, J., O'Hara, K., & Blyth, A. (2021). Ethical considerations for the use of artificial intelligence in cybersecurity. *Journal of Cybersecurity, 7*(1), 1–12.

Coşkun, H., Yıldırım, N., & Gündüz, S. (2020). The spread of COVID-19 virus through population density and wind in Turkey cities. *The Science of the Total Environment, 751*, 141663. doi:10.1016/j.scitotenv.2020.141663 PMID:32866831

Craigen, D., Diakun-Thibault, N., & Purse, R. (2014). Defining cybersecurity. *Technology Innovation Management Review, 4*(10), 10. doi:10.22215/timreview/835

Cui, Z. F. X.-g. (2018). Detection of Malicious Code Variants Based on Deep Learning. IEEE.

Cui, Y., Yu, F. X., & Jain, A. K. (2019). Unsupervised learning of anatomy-aware embeddings for cross-modality liver segmentation. *IEEE Transactions on Medical Imaging, 38*(6), 1436–1447.

D'Amico, A., & Yang, B. (2015). Vulnerability assessment in the cloud computing environment. In *Proceedings of the 2015 International Conference on Computing, Networking and Communications (ICNC)* (pp. 117-121). IEEE.

Dahbur, K., Mohammad, B., & Tarakji, A. B. (2011). A survey of risks, threats, and vulnerabilities in cloud computing. In *Proceedings of the 2011 International conference on intelligent semantic Web-services and applications*, Amman, Jordan. 10.1145/1980822.1980834

Dahl, G. E. J. W. (2013). Large-scale malware classification using random projections and neural networks. ICASSP. IEEE.

Dainotti, A., Pescapé, A., & Ventre, G. (2007). *Worm traffic analysis and characterization.* In *Proceedings of the 2007 IEEE International Conference on Communications*, Glasgow, UK. 10.1109/ICC.2007.241

Dainotti, A., Pescapé, A., & Ventre, G. (2009). A cascade architecture for DoS attacks detection based on the wavelet transform. *Journal of Computer Security, 17*(6), 945–968. doi:10.3233/JCS-2009-0350

Dai, Y., Yang, Y., & Zou, C. (2021). A survey on privacy-preserving technologies for cloud-based cyber security. *Journal of Network and Computer Applications, 187*, 103027. doi:10.1016/j.jnca.2021.103027

Dal Pozzolo, A., Boracchi, G., Caelen, O., Alippi, C., & Bontempi, G. (2018). Learned lessons in credit card fraud detection from a practitioner perspective. *Expert Systems with Applications, 104*, 72–84.

Daneshvar, M., Mohammadi-Ivatloo, B., Zare, K., & Anvari-Moghaddam, A. (2023). *IoT Enabled Multi-Energy Systems: From Isolated Energy Grids to Modern Interconnected Networks.*

Dang, X. T., Li, J., Li, G., Li, Y., & Li, Z. (2019). A deep learning approach for malware classification using dynamic analysis. *Journal of Computer and System Sciences, 105*, 143–157.

Dasari, K. B., & Devarakonda, N. (2022). Detection of DDoS Attacks Using Machine Learning Classification Algorithms. *International Journal of Computer Network and Information Security, 14*(6), 89–97. doi:10.5815/ijcnis.2022.06.07

Dasari, K. B., & Devarakonda, N. (2022). TCP/UDP-based exploitation DDoS attacks detection using AI classification algorithms with common uncorrelated feature subset selected by Pearson, Spearman and Kendall correlation methods. *Revue d'Intelligence Artificielle, 36*(1), 61–71. doi:10.18280/ria.360107

Das, N. K., Mishra, D. K., Naik, P. K., Dehury, P., Bose, S., & Banerjee, T. (2023). Dihydrolevoglycosenone as a novel bio-based nanofluid for thermal energy storage: Physiochemical and quantum chemical insights. *Journal of Energy Storage, 59*, 106365. doi:10.1016/j.est.2022.106365

Davis, R. S. (2019). *McAfee Mobile Threat Report Q1.* McAfee.

Dawson, J., & Thomson, R. (2018). The future cybersecurity workforce: Going beyond technical skills for successful cyber performance. *Frontiers in Psychology, 9*(JUN), 1–12. doi:10.3389/fpsyg.2018.00744 PMID:29946276

De Martini, F., Mazzei, A., Ricci, M., & D'Ariano, G. M. (2003). Exploiting quantum parallelism of entanglement for a complete experimental quantum characterization of a single-qubit device. *Physical Review A, 67*(6), 062307. doi:10.1103/PhysRevA.67.062307

De Santis, R., Montanari, R., Vignali, G., & Bottani, E. (2018, May 16). Roberto Montanari. Giuseppe Vignali, 'An adapted ant colony optimization algorithm for the minimization of the travel distance of pickers in manual warehouses'. *European Journal of Operational Research*, *267*(1), 120–137. doi:10.1016/j.ejor.2017.11.017

Debar, H., Dacier, M., & Wespi, A. (1999). Towards a taxonomy of intrusion-detection systems. *Computer Networks*, *31*(8), 805–822. doi:10.1016/S1389-1286(98)00017-6

Debar, H., Dacier, M., & Wespi, A. (2020). AI and machine learning in cybersecurity: The good, the bad and the ugly. *Journal of Cybersecurity*, *6*(1), 1–16.

Deloitte. (2018). *Secure IoT by Design*. DeLoitte. https://www2.deloitte.com/us/en/pages/operations/articles/iot-platform-security.html

Demertzis, I., Tserpes, K., & Varvarigou, T. (2019). Anomaly detection in cybersecurity using machine learning algorithms. In *Proceedings of the 14th International Conference on Availability, Reliability and Security (ARES)* (pp. 1-10). Academic Press.

Deng, X., Li, Y., Weng, J., & Zhang, J. (2019). Feature selection for text classification: A review. *Multimedia Tools and Applications*, *78*(3), 3797–3816. doi:10.100711042-018-6083-5

Denning, D. E., & Neumann, P. G. (1985). Requirements and model for IDES – a real-time intrusion detection system. *SRI International Technical Report #83F83- 01-00*. Computer Science Laboratory.

Denning, D. (1987, February). An Intrusion-Detection Model. *IEEE Transactions on Software Engineering*, *SE-13*(2), 222–232. doi:10.1109/TSE.1987.232894

Deshpande, A., & Jain, P. (2018). Vulnerability assessment of cloud-based systems. In *2018 International Conference on Advances in Computing, Communications and Informatics (ICACCI)* (pp. 1204-1209). IEEE.

Desnos, A., Gueguen, G., & Bachmann, S. Androguard, https://androguard.readthedocs.io/en/latest, 2018.

Dhalaria, M., & Gandotra, E. (2021). *A hybrid approach for android malware detection and family classification*. Research Gate.

Di Mauro, M., Galatro, G., Fortino, G., & Liotta, A. (2021). Supervised feature selection techniques in network intrusion detection: A critical review. *Engineering Applications of Artificial Intelligence*, *101*. doi:10.1016/j.engappai.2021.104216

DiBiase, D., Tripp Corbin, T. F., Francica, J., Green, K., Jackson, J., Jeffress, G., & Smith, C. (2010). The New Geospatial Technology Competency Model: Bringing Workforce Needs into Focus. *URISA Journal*, *22*(2).

Diebold, P., & Scherr, S. A. (2017a). Software process models vs descriptions: What do practitioners use and need? *Journal of Software (Malden, MA)*, *29*(11), e1879. doi:10.1002mr.1879

Ding, Y. Z. S. (2017). *Malware detection based on deep learning algorithm*. The Natural Computing Applications Forum.

Ding, C., Luktarhan, N., Lu, B., & Zhang, W. (2021). A hybrid analysis-based approach to android malware family classification. *Entropy (Basel, Switzerland)*, *23*(8), 1009. doi:10.3390/e23081009 PMID:34441149

Dong, S., & Sarem, M. (2019). DDoS attack detection method based on improved KNN with the degree of DDoS attack in software-defined networks. *IEEE Access : Practical Innovations, Open Solutions*, *8*, 5039–5048. doi:10.1109/ACCESS.2019.2963077

Dougan, J. (2019). Artificial intelligence in cybersecurity: A review. *Journal of Information Privacy and Security*, *15*(4), 191–210.

Doupé, A., Celi, M., Chen, Y., & Lanzi, A. (2016). Evaluating automated vulnerability discovery using DARPA's cyber grand challenge. *IEEE Security and Privacy, 14*(5), 30–37.

Dua, S., & Du, X. (2019). Building and explaining reliable anomaly detection models in a high-dimensional and imbalanced data space. *IEEE Access : Practical Innovations, Open Solutions, 7,* 52466–52479.

Duda, R. O., & Hart, P. E. (1973). *Pattern classification and scene analysis.* Wiley.

Dunbar, F. E. S. (2002). *Digital Signature Scheme Variation.* University of Waterloo.

Dutse, I. I., Liptrott, M., & Korkontzelos, I. (2018). Detection of spam-posting accounts on Twitter. *Neurocomputing, 315*(13), 496–511. doi:10.1016/j.neucom.2018.07.044

Edwards, C. (2017). Waterfall Model. The Bloomsbury Encyclopedia of Design, 1–4. doi:10.5040/9781472596154-BED-W004b

El-Aziz, A. & Arputharaj, K.A. (2013). Comprehensive presentation to XML signature and encryption. *2013 International Conference on Recent Trends in Information Technology.* IEEE. doi:10.1109/ICRTIT.2013.6844276

El-Fouly, F. H., Kachout, M., Alharbi, Y., Alshudukhi, J. S., Alanazi, A., & Ramadan, R. A. (2023). Environment-Aware Energy Efficient and Reliable Routing in Real-Time Multi-Sink Wireless Sensor Networks for Smart Cities Applications. *Applied Sciences (Basel, Switzerland), 13*(1), 605. doi:10.3390/app13010605

Elgamal, T., & Rizk, M. (2020). Adversarial machine learning: A comprehensive survey. *Pattern Recognition Letters, 131,* 138–145.

Elsner, P., & Suarez, S. (2019). Renewable energy from the high seas: Geo-spatial modelling of resource potential and legal implications for developing offshore wind projects beyond the national jurisdiction of coastal States. *Energy Policy, 128,* 919–929. doi:10.1016/j.enpol.2019.01.064

Esser, H. J., Liefting, Y., Ibáñez-Justicia, A., van der Jeugd, H., Van Turnhout, C. A., Stroo, A., & de Boer, W. F. (2020). Spatial risk analysis for the introduction and circulation of six arboviruses in the Netherlands. *Parasites & Vectors, 13*(1), 1–20. doi:10.118613071-020-04339-0 PMID:32912330

Falak, A., Ghous, H., & Malik, M. (2021). Twitter Spam Detection Using Machine Learning. *International Journal of Scientific and Engineering Research, 12*(2), 792–815.

Fan, W., Miller, M., Stolfo, S., Lee, W., & Chan, P. (2004). Using artificial anomalies to detect unknown and known network intrusions. *Knowledge and Information Systems, 6*(5), 507–527. doi:10.100710115-003-0132-7

Farahmandi, R., Khodabandelou, G., & Aghakhani, H. (2019). A survey on machine learning methods for cybersecurity. *IEEE Communications Surveys and Tutorials, 21*(3), 2753–2773.

Farooq, M., Mahmood, T., & Basalamah, S. (2020). A systematic literature review of the state-of-the-art in user authentication using keystroke dynamics. *Information Sciences, 527,* 317–347.

Faruki, P., Bharmal, A., Laxmi, V., Ganmoor, V., Gaur, M. S., Conti, M., & Rajarajan, M. (2015). Android security: A survey of issues, malware penetration, and defenses. *IEEE Communications Surveys and Tutorials, 17*(2), 998–1022. doi:10.1109/COMST.2014.2386139

Fasbender, D., & Siddiqui, S. (2019). Detection of phishing websites using machine learning. *Procedia Computer Science, 151,* 574–579.

Fastovets, D. V., & Yu, I. & Lukichev, V. (2019). Machine learning methods in quantum computing theory. *In International Conference on Micro-and Nano-Electronics.* International Society for Optics and Photonics. 10.1117/12.2522427

Fayyad, U., Piatetsky-Shapiro, G., & Smyth, P. (1996). The KDD process for extracting useful knowledge from volumes of data. *Communications of the ACM*, *39*(11), 27–34. doi:10.1145/240455.240464

Fazil, M., & Abulaish, M. (2018). A Hybrid Approach for Detecting Automated Spammers in Twitter. *IEEE Transactions on Information Forensics and Security*, *13*(11), 2707–2719. doi:10.1109/TIFS.2018.2825958

Feig, M., & Potter, A. (2020). Matrix product state simulations on a quantum computer. *Bulletin of the American Physical Society*.

Feizollah, A., Anuar, N. B., Salleh, R., Tangil, G. S., & Furnell, S. (2017). Androdialysis: Analysis of android intent effectiveness in malware detection. *Computers & Security*, *65*, 121–134. doi:10.1016/j.cose.2016.11.007

Felske, S., Lai, D., & Yamaguchi, F. (2020). Evaluating the Effectiveness of Security Information and Event Management (SIEM) Systems in Cybersecurity. *Journal of Information Security*, *11*(1), 24–33.

Felt, A. P., Finifter, M., Chin, E., Hanna, S., & Wagner, D. (2011). A survey of mobilemalware in the wild. In: *Proc. 1st ACM Work. Secur. Priv. smartphones Mob. devices*. ACM.

Feron, E. (2008). *Aerial Robotics*. Springer Handbook of Robotics.

Ferrara, E., Varol, O., Davis, C., Menczer, F., & Flammini, A. (2016). The rise of social bots. *Communications of the ACM*, *59*(7), 96–104. doi:10.1145/2818717

Ferri, F. J., Pudil, P., Hatef, M., & Kittler, J. (1994). Comparative study of techniques for large-scale feature selection. *Pattern Recognition in Practice*, *IV*, 403–413.

Feynman, R. P., Leighton, R. B., & Sands, M. (2011). The Feynman lectures on physics: Vol. I. *The new millennium edition: mainly mechanics, radiation, and heat*. Basic books.

Fielder, A., König, S., Panaousis, E., Schauer, S., & Rass, S. (2018). Risk Assessment Uncertainties in Cybersecurity Investments. *Games*, *9*(2), 34. doi:10.3390/g9020034

Fisher, R. A. (1992). *Statistical methods for research workers*. Springer New York. doi:10.1007/978-1-4612-4380-9_6

Flammia, S. (2020). Quantum Computer Crosscheck. *Physics (College Park, Md.)*, *13*, 3. doi:10.1103/Physics.13.3

Fouedjio, F. (2016). Clustering of multivariate geostatistical data. *Wiley Interdisciplinary Reviews: Computational Statistics*, 1510.

Fouladi, R. F., Kayatas, C. E., & Anarim, E. (2016). Frequency based DDoS attack detection approach using naive Bayes classification. *2016 39th International Conference on Telecommunications and Signal Processing (TSP)*. IEEE. 10.1109/TSP.2016.7760838

Fraser, G., & Arcuri, A. (2014). Automated test generation for java generics. In: *Int. Conf. Softw. Qual.* Springer.

Fu, Z., Yu, J., Xie, G., Chen, Y., & Mao, Y. (2018). A Heuristic Evolutionary Algorithm of UAV Path Planning. *Wireless Communications and Mobile Computing*, *2018*(Sept), 11. doi:10.1155/2018/2851964

Gai, K., Tan, S., & Wang, L. (2021). A survey of machine learning in cyber security. *Journal of Information Security and Applications*, *62*, 102893. doi:10.1016/j.jisa.2021.102893

Galbraith, B., Hiotis, A., & Janakiraman, M. (2001). *Professional web services security*. Shroff Publishers & Distributors.

Gallaher, M., Link, A., & Rowe, B. (2008). *Cyber Security: Economic Strategies and Public Policy Alternatives*. Edward Elgar Publishing. doi:10.4337/9781781008140

Ganin, A. A., Quach, P., Panwar, M., Collier, Z., Keisler, A., Marchese, D., & Linkov, I. (2020). Multicriteria Decision Framework for Cybersecurity Risk Assessment and Management. *Risk Analysis*, *40*(1), 183–199. doi:10.1111/risa.12891 PMID:28873246

Ganney, P. S., Pisharody, S., & Claridge, E. (2013). Software Engineering. In Clinical Engineering: A Handbook for Clinical and Biomedical Engineers. Academic Press. doi:10.1016/B978-0-12-396961-3.00009-3

Gao, F., Liao, Y., & Tao, Y. (2020). A Review of Cybersecurity Risks and Best Practices in Smart Manufacturing. *IEEE Access, 8.*

Gao, H., Chen, Y., Lee, K., Palsetia, D., & Choudhary, A. N. (2012). Towards online spam filtering in social networks. *Network Distributed System Security*, *15*, 1–16.

Gao, Y., Chen, S. F., & Lu, X. (2004, January). Research on Reinforcement Learning Technology: A Review. *Acta Automatica Sinica, 30.* doi:10.16383/j.aas.2004.01.011

García-del-Amo, D., Mortyn, P. G., & Reyes-García, V. (2023). Local reports of climate change impacts in Sierra Nevada, Spain: Sociodemographic and geographical patterns. *Regional Environmental Change*, *23*(1), 1–16. doi:10.100710113-022-01981-5 PMID:36540304

Garcia, S. (2018). A survey on intrusion detection and prevention systems. *IEEE Communications Surveys and Tutorials*, *20*(4), 3193–3235.

Georgiadou, A., Mouzakitis, S., & Askounis, D. (2021). Assessing MITRE ATT&CK Risk Using a Cyber-Security Culture Framework. *Sensors (Basel)*, *21*(9), 3267. Advance online publication. doi:10.339021093267 PMID:34065086

Ghahremanlou, R. S., & Soltani, S. (2021). A comprehensive review of user authentication systems using keystroke dynamics. *Journal of Ambient Intelligence and Humanized Computing*, *12*(1), 157–189.

Ghate, S., & Agrawal, P. K. (2017). A literature review on cyber security in indian context. *J. Comput. Inf. Technol*, *8*(5), 30–36. doi:10.22147/jucit/080501

Ghazaleh, R. A. (2019). A Survey of Machine Learning Techniques for Cybersecurity.

Gielen, D., Boshell, F., Saygin, D., Bazilian, M. D., Wagner, N., & Gorini, R. (2019). The role of renewable energy in the global energy transformation. *Energy Strategy Reviews*, *24*, 38–50. doi:10.1016/j.esr.2019.01.006

Giri, S. (2019). Cyber crime, cyber threat, cyber security strategies and cyber law in Nepal. *Pramana Research Journal*, *9*(3), 662–672.

Goel, R., Kumar, A., & Haddow, J. (2020). PRISM: A strategic decision framework for cybersecurity risk assessment. *Information and Computer Security*, *28*(4), 591–625. doi:10.1108/ICS-11-2018-0131

Goyal, M., Ahuja, P., & Kaur, H. (2021). A novel approach for detecting malicious Android applications using machine learning. *Journal of Ambient Intelligence and Humanized Computing*, *12*(8), 8969–8980. doi:10.100712652-021-03548-0

Grosse, K., Papernot, N., Manoharan, P., Backes, M., & McDaniel, P. (2017). Adversarial examples for malware detection. *Proceedings of the 10th ACM Workshop on Artificial Intelligence and Security.*

Gulagi, A., Alcanzare, M., Bogdanov, D., Esparcia, E. Jr, Ocon, J., & Breyer, C. (2021). Transition pathway towards 100% renewable energy across the sectors of power, heat, transport, and desalination for the Philippines. *Renewable & Sustainable Energy Reviews*, *144*, 110934. doi:10.1016/j.rser.2021.110934

Gupta, S., Kapoor, S., & Sharma, D. (2020). Blockchain Technology for Cybersecurity and Privacy: A Systematic Literature Review. *Journal of Information Security and Applications, 88.*

Gupta, H., Jamal, M. S., & Madisetty, S. (2018). A Framework for Real-Time Spam Detection in Twitter. *International Conference on Communication Systems & Networks*. IEEE. 10.1109/COMSNETS.2018.8328222

Hadiprakoso, R. B., Kabetta, H., & Buana, I. K. S. (2020, November). Hybrid-based malware analysis for effective and efficiency android malware detection. In *2020 International Conference on Informatics, Multimedia, Cyber and Information System (ICIMCIS)* (pp. 8-12). IEEE. 10.1109/ICIMCIS51567.2020.9354315

Han, J., Pei, J., & Kamber, M. (2011). *Data mining: Concepts and Techniques*. Elsevier.

Hao Sun, X. W. (2017). CloudEyes: Cloud-based malware detection with reversible sketch for resource-constrained internet of things (IoT) devices. *Software, Practice & Experience*.

Harvey, P. (2021). *Exiftool*. Exiftool. https://exiftool.org/.

Hay, G. J., Kyle, C., Hemachandran, B., Chen, G., Rahman, M. M., Fung, T. S., & Arvai, J. L. (2011). Geospatial technologies to improve urban energy efficiency. *Remote Sensing (Basel)*, *3*(7), 1380–1405. doi:10.3390/rs3071380

He, B. Z., Chen, C. M., Su, Y. P., & Sun, H. M. (2014). A defence scheme against Identity Theft Attack based on multiple social networks. *Expert Systems with Applications*, *41*(5), 2345–2352. doi:10.1016/j.eswa.2013.09.032

Heckerman, D. (1995). *A tutorial on learning with Bayesian networks*. Microsoft Research.

Heipke, C. (2010). Crowdsourcing geospatial data. *ISPRS Journal of Photogrammetry and Remote Sensing*, (65), 550-557.

Hejazi, D., Liu, S., Farnoosh, A., Ostadabbas, S., & Kar, S. (2020). Development of use-specific high-performance cyber-nanomaterial optical detectors by effective choice of machine learning algorithms. *Machine Learning: Science and Technology*, *1*(2), 025007. doi:10.1088/2632-2153/ab8967

Herzallah, H., Faris, S., & Adwan, O. (2017). Feature engineering for detecting spammers on Twitter: Modelling and analysis. *Journal of Information Science*, *44*(2), 1–19.

Hiatt, D., & B, Y. (2016). Role of Security in Social Networking. *International Journal of Advanced Computer Science and Applications*, *7*(2), 12–15. doi:10.14569/IJACSA.2016.070202

Hoang, X. D., Hu, J., & Bertok, P. (2009). A program-based anomaly intrusion detection scheme using multiple detection engines and fuzzy inference. *Journal of Network and Computer Applications*, *32*(6), 1219–1228. doi:10.1016/j.jnca.2009.05.004

Hoda, R., & Murugesan, L. K. (2016). Multi-level agile project management challenges: A self-organizing team perspective. *Journal of Systems and Software*, *117*, 245–257. doi:10.1016/j.jss.2016.02.049

Hodge, V. J., & Austin, J. (2004). A survey of outlier detection methodologies. *Artificial Intelligence Review*, *22*(2), 85–126. doi:10.1023/B:AIRE.0000045502.10941.a9

Horobet, A., Simionescu, A. A., Dumitrescu, D. G., & Belascu, L. (2020). Europe's War against COVID-19: A Map of Countries' Disease Vulnerability Using Mortality Indicators. *International Journal of Environmental Research and Public Health*, *17*(18), 6565. doi:10.3390/ijerph17186565 PMID:32916973

Horovic, Sabrina, Marija Boban, and Ivana Stipanovic. "Cybersecurity and criminal justice in digital society." *Economic and Social Development: Book of Proceedings* (2021): 52-60.

Hosmer, H. H. (1993). *Security is fuzzy!: applying the fuzzy logic paradigm to the multipolicy paradigm*. Proceedings of the 1992-1993 workshop on New security paradigms, ACM.

Hossain, M. (2020). *Anomaly Detection in ECG Signals Using Machine Learning Techniques: A Survey*.

Hou, S., Saas, A., Chen, L., & Ye, Y. (2016, October). Deep4maldroid: A deep learning framework for android malware detection based on linux kernel system call graphs. In *2016 IEEE/WIC/ACM International Conference on Web Intelligence Workshops (WIW)* (pp. 104-111). IEEE. 10.1109/WIW.2016.040

Hu, J., Yu, X., Qiu, D., & Chen, H. (2009). A simple and efficient hidden Markov model scheme for host-based anomaly intrusion detection. *IEEE Transaction on Network*. IEEE. doi:10.1109/MNET.2009.4804323

Hu, W., Liao, Y., & Vemuri, V. R. (2003). *Robust Support Vector Machines for Anomaly Detection in Computer Security*. In Proceedings of the International Conference on Machine Learning and Applications, Los Angeles, CA, USA.

Hu, W., Liao, Y., & Vemuri, V. R. (2003). Robust Support Vector Machines for Anomaly Detection in Computer Security. In *Proceedings of the International Conference on Machine Learning and Applications—ICMLA*. IEEE.

Huang, C., & Fei, J. (2018). UAV Path Planning Based on Particle Swarm Optimization with Global Best Path Competition. *International Journal of Pattern Recognition and Artificial Intelligence, 32*.

Huang, Y.-W. Tsai, C.H-., Lin, T.-P., Huang, S., Lee, D., & Kuo, S.-Y. (2005). A testing framework for Web application security assessment. *Journal Computer Networks: The International Journal of Computer and Telecommunications Networking - Web security, 48*(5).

Hubbard, D. W., & Seiersen, R. (2016). *How to Measure Anything in Cybersecurity Risk*. Wiley. doi:10.1002/9781119162315

Humayun, M., Niazi, M., Jhanjhi, N. Z., Alshayeb, M., & Mahmood, S. (2020). Cyber security threats and vulnerabilities: A systematic mapping study. *Arabian Journal for Science and Engineering, 45*(4), 3171–3189. doi:10.100713369-019-04319-2

Hu, W., Liao, Y., & Vemuri, V. R. (2003). *Robust support vector machines for anomaly detection in computer security*. ICMLA.

Hu, X., Zhang, X., & Lovrich, N. P. (2021). Forecasting Identity Theft Victims: Analyzing Characteristics and Preventive Actions through Machine Learning Approaches. *Victims & Offenders, 16*(4), 465–494. doi:10.1080/15564886.2020.1806161

Igor, S. (2018). Large-scale cyber-attacks monitoring using Evolving Cauchy Possibilistic Clustering. Applied Soft Computing (Vol. 62). Elsevier.

Infield, D., & Freris, L. (2020). *Renewable energy in power systems*. John Wiley & Sons.

Ingre, B., Yadav, A., & Soni, A. K. (2017). Decision tree based intrusion detection system for NSL-KDD dataset. In *Proceedings of the International Conference on Information and Communication Technology for Intelligent Systems*, Ahmedabad, India.

Irdeto. (2019). *New 2019 Global Survey: IoT-Focused Cyberattacks Are the New Normal*. IRDETO. https://resources.irdeto.com/global-connected-industries-cybersecurity-survey/new-2019-globalsurvey-iot-focused-cyberattacks-are-the-new-normal.

Işık, G., Öğüt, H., & Mutlu, M. (2023). Deep learning based electricity demand forecasting to minimize the cost of energy imbalance: A real case application with some fortune 500 companies in Türkiye. *Engineering Applications of Artificial Intelligence, 118*, 105664. doi:10.1016/j.engappai.2022.105664

Islam, M. K. (2020). Network anomaly detection using lightgbm: A gradient boosting classifier. *2020 30th International Telecommunication Networks and Applications Conference (ITNAC)*. IEEE. 10.1109/ITNAC50341.2020.9315049

Islam, M. H., Karmakar, G. C., Kamruzzaman, J., Al Mamun, S. A., & Shahjalal, M. (2020). A review of current trends and challenges in cyber security for industrial control systems. *IEEE Access : Practical Innovations, Open Solutions, 8,* 49762–49785. doi:10.1109/ACCESS.2020.2982924

Islam, M. R., & Khan, A. U. (2020). A Review of Cybersecurity Risk Assessment Frameworks for Industrial Control Systems. *Computers & Security, 94,* 101812. doi:10.1016/j.cose.2020.101812

Jain, A. K., Sahoo, S. R., & Kaubiyal, J. (2021a). Online social networks security and privacy: Comprehensive review and analysis. *Complex & Intelligent Systems, 0123456789*(5), 2157–2177. Advance online publication. doi:10.100740747-021-00409-7

Jain, G., Sharma, G., Agarwal, M., & Basant, P. (2021). Spam Detection on Social Media Using Semantic Convolutional Neural Network. *International Journal of Knowledge Discovery in Bioinformatics, 8*(1), 12–26. doi:10.4018/IJKDB.2018010102

Jain, G., Sharma, M., & Agarwal, B. (2019). Spam detection in social media using convolutional and long short term memory neural network. *Annals of Mathematics and Artificial Intelligence, 85*(1), 21–44. doi:10.100710472-018-9612-z

Jajodia, S., & Subrahmanian, V. S. (2011). Cybersecurity: The Next Decade. *IEEE Security and Privacy, 9*(1), 70–73. doi:10.1109/MSP.2011.3

Jaquith, A. (2011). *Cyber security Metrics: A Practical Guide for Effective Security and Risk Management.* Pearson Education.

Javadpour, A., Sangaiah, A. K., Pinto, P., Ja'fari, F., Zhang, W., Abadi, A. M. H., & Ahmadi, H. (2023). An energy-optimized embedded load balancing using DVFS computing in cloud data centers. *Computer Communications, 197,* 255–266. doi:10.1016/j.comcom.2022.10.019

Jeffrey, C., & Kimmell, A. D. (2021). *Recurrent Neural Networks Based Online Behavioural Malware Detection Techniques for Cloud Infrastructure.* IEEE.

Jensen, N. G. (2020). *Attack surfaces: A taxonomy for attacks.* IEEE CLOUD.

Jial, W., Neil, M., & Fenton, N. (2020). A Bayesian network approach for cybersecurity risk assessment implementing and extending the FAIR model. *Computers & Security, 89,* 101659. Advance online publication. doi:10.1016/j.cose.2019.101659

Jia, Y., Zhang, X., Xiang, Y., & Zhou, W. (2019). A Survey on Cyber Security Attacks and Countermeasures in Cloud Computing. *Journal of Network and Computer Applications, 135,* 1–11. doi:10.1016/j.jnca.2019.02.012

Jilani, F. A., Nazir, S., Khan, S. A., & Shah, S. A. (2021). Anomaly detection in online banking: A review of machine learning techniques. *Journal of King Saud University - Computer and Information Sciences, 33*(1), 60-68. doi:10.1016/j.jksuci.2020.02.003

Jin, X., Liu, F., Zhang, Y., & Jiang, X. (2019). A survey of Android malware detection using machine learning. *IEEE Access : Practical Innovations, Open Solutions, 7,* 105855–105870.

Joel, A., & Dawson, J. T. (2018). Space detection of virtual machine cyber events through hypervisorlevel system call analysis. *2018 1st International Conference in IEEE.* IEEE.

John, E. (2017). Dickerson and Julie A. Dickerson, Fuzzy network profiling for intrusion detection. *Proceedings of NAFIPS 19th International Conference of the North American Fuzzy Infor mation Processing Society,* Atlanta, USA).

Johnson, French, & Rose. (2017). A Framework for Cybersecurity Risk Assessment in the Supply Chain. *International Journal of Business and Systems Research, 11*(3).

Joshi, S., Nagariya, H. G., Dhanotiya, N., & Jain, S. (2020). Identifying Fake Profile in Online Social Network: An Overview and Survey. *Communications in Computer and Information Science, 1240 CCIS.* doi:10.1007/978-981-15-6315-7_2

Joshi, S. S., & Phoha, V. V. (2005). Investigating hidden markov models capabilities in anomaly detection. *Proceedings of the 43rd annual Southeast regional conference-.* ACM. 10.1145/1167350.1167387

Jun, S., & Wei, F. (2012). Quantum behaved particle swarm optimization; analysis of individual particle behavior and parameter selection. *Evolutionary Computation.*

Junaid, A., & Ping, L. (2020). How to build a vulnerability benchmark to overcome cyber security attacks. *IET Information Security, 14*(1), 60–71. doi:10.1049/iet-ifs.2018.5647

Kamal, W. A., Gu, D.-W., & Postlethwaite, I. (2005). Real Time Trajectory Planning for UAVs Using MILP. *Proceedings of the 44th IEEE Conference on Decision and Control,* (pp. 3381-3386). IEEE. 10.1109/CDC.2005.1582684

Kamara, S., & Lauter, K. (2010). Cryptographic cloud storage. Proceedings of the 14th international conference on Financial crypto graphy and data security, (pp. 136-149). ACM.

Kambourakis, G., Damopoulos, D., Panaousis, E., & Katos, V. (2019). Cyber Attacks: A Literature Review. *Journal of Information Security and Applications, 50,* 1–12. doi:10.1016/j.jisa.2019.02.008

Kamhoua, G. A., Pissinou, N., Iyengar, S. S., Beltran, J., Kamhoua, C., Hernandez, B. L., Njilla, L., & Makki, A. P. (2017). Preventing Colluding Identity Clone Attacks in Online Social Networks. *Proceedings - IEEE 37th International Conference on Distributed Computing Systems Workshops, ICDCSW 2017,* (pp. 187–192). IEEE. 10.1109/ICDCSW.2017.64

Kamra, B., & Bertino, E. (2011). Design and Implementation of an Intrusion Response System for Relational Databases. *IEEE Transactions on Knowledge and Data Engineering, 23*(6), 875–888. doi:10.1109/TKDE.2010.151

Kang, B. B. H., & Srivastava, A. (2011). Dynamic malware analysis. In *Encycl. Cryptogr. Secur* (pp. 367–368). Springer. doi:10.1007/978-1-4419-5906-5_846

Kasongo, S. (2023). A deep learning technique for intrusion detection system using a Recurrent Neural Networks based fframework. *Computer Communications, 199.*

Kaur, S., & Bansal, P. (2020). Machine Learning Techniques for Cyber security Applications: A Survey. *Journal of Computer Science and Technology, 35*(6).

Kaur, S., Brar, G. S., & Jha, S. S. (2022). Cybersecurity Challenges in Cloud Computing: A Systematic Review. *Journal of Ambient Intelligence and Humanized Computing, 92.*

Kaur, A., & Rana, S. (2022). A review of machine learning-based techniques for malware detection. *Journal of Network and Computer Applications, 193,* 103131. doi:10.1016/j.jnca.2021.103131

Kaur, C., & Kumar, V. (2016). Comparative Analysis of Iterative Waterfall Model and Scrum. *International Journal of Computer Science Research, 3*(1), 11–14.

Kaur, H., & Verma, A. K. (2019). User behavior analysis using deep learning techniques: A review. *Journal of Ambient Intelligence and Humanized Computing, 10*(11), 4417–4446.

Kaur, R., & Singh, A. (2017). A review of vulnerability assessment techniques in cloud computing. In *Proceedings of the 2017 2nd International Conference on Computing and Communications Technologies (ICCCT)* (pp. 35-38). IEEE.

Kenney, J. F., & Keeping, E. S. (1951). *Mathematics of Statistics, Pt. 2* (2nd ed.). Van Nostrand.

Khairuddin, S. N., Sarlan, A., & Ahmad, R. (2021). Challenges in Requirement Management Process: An Overview. *Proceedings of International Conference on Computer and Information Sciences: Sustaining Tomorrow with Digital Innovation.* (pp. 120–124). IEEE. 10.1109/ICCOINS49721.2021.9497213

Khaleel, A. A., & Kaya, B. (2019). *Spam detection in online social networks by deep learning.* IEEE Xplore.

Khalid, S., & Hussain, F. B. (2022, May). Evaluating Dynamic Analysis Features for Android Malware Categorization. In *2022 International Wireless Communications and Mobile Computing (IWCMC)* (pp. 401-406). IEEE.

Khan, S. U., Awan, A. J., & Vall-Llosera, G. (2019). *K-Means Clustering on Noisy Intermediate Scale Quantum Computers.* arXiv preprint arXiv:1909.12183

Khan, M. S. A. (2011). Rule based network intrusion detection using genetic algorithm. *International Journal of Computer Applications, 18*(8), 26–29. doi:10.5120/2303-2914

KharajiM. Y.RiziF. S.KhayyambashiM. R. (2014). *A New Approach for Finding Cloned Profiles in Online Social Networks. 6*(April), 25–37. https://arxiv.org/abs/1406.7377

Khari, M., Dalal, R., Misra, U., & Kumar, A. (2020). AndroSet: An automated tool to create datasets for Android malware detection and functioning with WoT. *Smart Innovation of Web of Things, 187.*

Khari, M., Garg, A. K., Gandomi, A. H., Gupta, R., Patan, R., & Balusamy, B. (2019). Securing data in Internet of Things (IoT) using cryptography and steganography techniques. *IEEE Transactions on Systems, Man, and Cybernetics. Systems, 50*(1), 73–80. doi:10.1109/TSMC.2019.2903785

Kharraz, A. (2015). Cutting the Gordian knot: A look under the hood of ransomware attacks. *Proceedings of the Network and Distributed System Security Symposium (NDSS).*

Khayyambashi, M. R., & Rizi, F. S. (2013). An approach for detecting profile cloning in online social networks. *2013 7th Intenational Conference on E-Commerce in Developing Countries: With Focus on e-Security.* IEEE. 10.1109/ECDC.2013.6556739

Khosravi, S., Dezfoli, M. A., & Yektaie, M. H. (2011). A new steganography method based HIOP (Higher Intensity Of Pixel)algorithm and Strassen's matrix multiplication. *Journal of Global Research in Computer Science, 2*(1).

Khraisat, A., Gondal, I., Vamplew, P., & Kamruzzaman, J. (2019). Survey of intrusion detection systems: Techniques, datasets and challenges. *Cybersecurity, 2*(1), 1–22. doi:10.118642400-019-0038-7

Kim, J., & Trivedi, K. S. (2020). Cybersecurity Risk Management: A Review. *ACM Computing Surveys, 53*(3), 1–37.

Kim, S. S. (2016). *Visualized malware classification based-on convolutional neural network.* Information Security and Cryptology.

Kim, T., Kang, B., Rho, M., Sezer, S., & Im, E. G. (2018). A multimodal deep learning method for Android malware detection using various features. *IEEE Transactions on Information Forensics and Security, 14*(3), 773–788. doi:10.1109/TIFS.2018.2866319

Kizza, J. M. (2017). *Ethical and social issues in the information age.* Springer. doi:10.1007/978-3-319-70712-9

Klaus, J. (2013). Understanding and overcoming cyber security anti-patterns. *Computer Networks, 57*(10), 2206–2211. doi:10.1016/j.comnet.2012.11.023

Koc, L., Mazzuchi, T. A., & Sarkani, S. (2012). A network intrusion detection system based on a Hidden Naïve Bayes multiclass classifier. *Expert Systems with Applications, 39*(18), 13492–13500. doi:10.1016/j.eswa.2012.07.009

Kokila, R., Selvi, S. T., & Govindarajan, K. (2014). DDoS detection and analysis in SDN-based environment using support vector machine classifier. In *Proceedings of the 2014 Sixth International Conference on Advanced Computing (ICoAC)*, Chennai, India. 10.1109/ICoAC.2014.7229711

Kolokotronis, N., & Shiaeles, S. (2021). *Cyber-Security Threats*. Actors, and Dynamic Mitigation.

Konatowski, S., & Pawlowski, P. (2019). PSO algorithm for UAV autonomous path planning with threat and energy cost optimization. *XII Conference on Reconnaissance and Electronic Warfare Systems*, (pp. 1-6). IEEE. 10.1117/12.2524886

Kontaxis, G., Polakis, I., Ioannidis, S., & Markatos, E. P. (2011). Detecting social network profile cloning. *2011 IEEE International Conference on Pervasive Computing and Communications Workshops, PERCOM Workshops 2011, November 2014*, (pp. 295–300). IEEE. 10.1109/PERCOMW.2011.5766886

Korhonen, P. (2018). *Automated Threat Detection in Airport Security: A Survey.*

Kotpalliwar, M. V., & Wajgi, R. (2015). *Classification of Attacks Using Support Vector Machine (SVM) on KDDCUP'99 IDS Database*. In *Proceedings of the 2015 Fifth International Conference on Communication Systems and Network Technologies*, Gwalior, India. 10.1109/CSNT.2015.185

Kotsiantis, S. B., Zaharakis, I., & Pintelas, P. (2007). Supervised machine learning: A review of classification techniques. *Emerging artificial intelligence applications in computer engineering, 160*(1): 3-24.

Kotsiantis, S. B., Zaharakis, I. D., & Pintelas, P. E. (2006). Machine learning: A review of classification and combining techniques. *Artificial Intelligence Review, 26*(3), 159–190. doi:10.100710462-007-9052-3

Krol, K., & Misra, S. (2019). Automated Vulnerability Assessment: A Survey. *IEEE Access : Practical Innovations, Open Solutions, 7*, 154760–154781.

Kruegel, C., Mutz, D., Robertson, W., & Valeur, F. (2003). Bayesian event classification for intrusion detection. In: Computer Security Applications Conference. IEEE. doi:10.1109/CSAC.2003.1254306

Kruegel, C., Mutz, D., Robertson, W., & Valeur, F. (2003). Bayesian event classification for intrusion detection. In *Proceedings of the 19th Annual Computer Security Applications Conference*, Las Vegas, NV, USA.

Kruse, C. S., Frederick, B., Jacobson, T., & Monticone, D. K. (2017). Cybersecurity in healthcare: A systematic review of modern threats and trends. *Technology and Health Care, 25*(1), 1–10. doi:10.3233/THC-161263 PMID:27689562

Kumar, N. (n.d.). *Automatic Detection of Fake Profiles in Online Social Networks R . Nithin Reddy (108CS043) & Automatic Detection of Fake Profiles in Online Social Networks*. NIT Rourkela.

Kumar, S. (2018). Anomaly Detection in Network Traffic Using Deep Learning.

Kumar, A., Gupta, S. K., Rai, A. K., & Sinha, S. (2013).. . *Social Networking Sites and Their Security Issues., 3*(4), 1–5.

Kumar, A., Kumar Gupta, S., Rai, A. K., & Sinha, S. (2013). Social Networking Sites and Their Security Issues. *International Journal of Scientific and Research Publications, 3*(4). www.ijsrp.org

Kumar, J., Rajendran, B., Bindhumadhava, B. S., & Chandra Babu, N. S. (2017). XML wrapping attack mitigation using positional token. *International Conference on Public Key Infrastructure and its Applications (PKIA)*, Bangalore, India. 10.1109/PKIA.2017.8278958

Kumar, P. A. R., & Selvakumar, S. (2011). Distributed denial of service attack detection using an ensemble of neural classifier. *Computer Communications*, *34*(11), 1328–1341. doi:10.1016/j.comcom.2011.01.012

Kumar, S., Gupta, B. B., & Misra, S. (2019). A Taxonomy of Cyber Attacks and Defensive Techniques for Cyber Physical Systems. *Journal of Ambient Intelligence and Humanized Computing*, *10*(10), 3821–3842. doi:10.100712652-019-01361-4

Kwak, D., Kim, D., & Kim, H. (2019). Vulnerability assessment of web applications based on attack scenarios using a hybrid model of machine learning and logic reasoning. *Future Generation Computer Systems*, *95*, 858–870.

Lakshminarasimman, S., Ruswin, S., & Sundarakandam, K. (2017). Detecting DDoS attacks using decision tree algorithm. *Fourth International Conference on Signal Processing, Communication and Networking (ICSCN)*, (pp. 1-6). IEEE. 10.1109/ICSCN.2017.8085703

Laricchia, F. (2023). *Mobile operating systems' market share worldwide from 1st quarter 2009 to 4th quarter 2022.* Statista. https://www.statista.com/statistics/272698/global-market-share-held-by-mobile-operating-systems-since-009/#:~:text=Android%20maintained%20its%20position%20as,the%20mobile%20operating%20system%20market

Lashkari, A. H., Kadir, A. F. A., Gonzalez, H., Mbah, K. F., & Ghorbani, A. A. (2017, August). Towards a network-based framework for android malware detection and characterization. In *2017 15th Annual conference on privacy, security and trust (PST)* (pp. 233-23309). IEEE. 10.1109/PST.2017.00035

Lazarevic, A., Kumar, V., & Srivastava, J. (2005). *Intrusion detection: "A survey, Managing cyber threats: issues, approaches, and challenges*. Springer Verlag.

Le, D., Kumar, R., Mishra, B. K., & Chatterjee, J. (2019). Cyber security in parallel and distributed computing: Concepts, techniques, applications and case studies. John Wiley & Sons.

Lee, I. (2020). Internet of Things (IoT) cybersecurity: Literature review and IoT cyber risk management. *Future Internet*, *12*, 157.

Lee, W., & Stolfo, S. J. (2000). A framework for constructing features and models for intrusion detection systems. *ACM Transactions on Information and System Security*, *3*(4), 227–261. doi:10.1145/382912.382914

Levin, D. (2021). *Strace - linux syscall tracer*. Strace. https://strace.io.

Li, H. D. Z. (2019). Using Deep-Learning-based Memory Analysis for Malware Detection in Cloud. *IEEE 16th International Conference on Mobile Ad Hoc and Sensor Systems Workshops (MASSW)*. IEEE.

Li, Z., Zhang, A., Lei, J., & Wang, L. (2007). Real-time correlation of network security alerts. In: *e-Business Engineering*. IEEE. 10.1109/ICEBE.2007.69

Liao, H., & Chen, M. (2021). Fraud detection using clustering algorithms: A systematic literature review. *Journal of King Saud University - Computer and Information Sciences, 33*(2), 209-220.

Liew, H. P., & Eidem, N. (2020). Assessing the spatial-temporal clustering and health implications of fine particulate matter (PM2. 5). *Journal of Public Health*, 1–11.

Li, J., Li, Y., Li, Z., & Li, L. (2021). Blockchain-based solutions for securing Internet of Things: A survey. *IEEE Internet of Things Journal*, *8*(2), 763–782. doi:10.1109/JIOT.2020.3025069

Li, J., Sun, L., Yan, Q., Li, Z., Srisaan, W., & Heng, Y. (2018). Significant permission identification for machine-learning-based android malware detection. *IEEE Transactions on Industrial Informatics*, *14*(7), 3216–3225. doi:10.1109/TII.2017.2789219

Li, K., Guo, Y., Wang, Z., Xie, X., & Wang, B. (2020). A novel algorithm for credit card fraud detection using transaction data. *International Journal of Information Management*, *52*, 102062. doi:10.1016/j.ijinfomgt.2019.09.011

Lippmann, R. P., & Cunningham, R. K. (2000). Improving intrusion detection performance using keyword selection and neural networks. *Computer Networks*, *34*(4), 597–603. doi:10.1016/S1389-1286(00)00140-7

Liu, X. & Zhang, D. (2021). Path planning method based on the particle swarm optimization trained fuzzy neural network algorithm. *Cluster Computing*, Springer.

Liu, C., Cao, Y., Yang, C., Zhou, Y., & Ai, M. (2020). Pattern identification and analysis for the traditional village using low altitude UAV-borne remote sensing: Multifeatured geospatial data to support rural landscape investigation, documentation and management. *Journal of Cultural Heritage*, *44*, 185–195. doi:10.1016/j.culher.2019.12.013

Liu, X., Zhang, Y., Wang, B., & Yang, J. (2013). Mona: Secure multi owner data sharing for dynamic groups in the cloud. *IEEE Transactions on Parallel and Distributed Systems*, *24*(6), 1182–1191. doi:10.1109/TPDS.2012.331

Li, W. (2004). *Using genetic algorithm for network intrusion detection.* C.S.G. Department of Energy.

Li, Y., Xia, J., Zhang, S., Yan, J., Ai, X., & Dai, K. (2012). An efficient intrusion detection system based on support vector machines and gradually feature removal method. *Expert Systems with Applications*, *39*(1), 424–430. doi:10.1016/j.eswa.2011.07.032

Li, Y., Zhang, S., Ye, F., Jiang, T., & Li, Y. (2020). A UAV Path Planning Method Based on Deep Reinforcement Learning. *2020 IEEE USNC-CNC-URSI North American Radio Science Meeting (Joint with AP-S Symposium)*, (pp. 93-94). IEEE. 10.23919/USNC/URSI49741.2020.9321625

Liyanage, C. R., & Premarathne, S. C. (2019). *A Walkthrough on Clone Profile Resolution in Social Networks. 10*(9), 1334–1337.

Liyanage, C. R., & Premarathne, S. C. (2021a). *Clustered Approach for Clone Detection in Social Media. 11*(1).

Liyanage, C. R., & Premarathne, S. C. (2019). A Walkthrough on Clone Profile Resolution in Social Networks. *International Journal of Scientific and Engineering Research*, *10*(9). http://www.ijser.org

Liyanage, C. R., & Premarathne, S. C. (2021b). Clustered Approach for Clone Detection in Social Media. *International Journal on Advanced Science, Engineering and Information Technology*, *11*(1), 99–104. doi:10.18517/ijaseit.11.1.9272

Loh, W. Y. (2014). Classification and regression tree methods. *Wiley StatsRef: Statistics Reference. Online (Bergheim)*. doi:10.1002/9781118445112.stat03886

Losada, S. F., & Holik, F. (2018, February). Classical Limit and Quantum Logic. *International Journal of Theoretical Physics*, *57*(2), 465–475. doi:10.100710773-017-3579-0

Lunt, T., & Traore, I. (2008, May). Unsupervised Anomaly Detection Using an Evolutionary Extension of K-means Algorithm, International Journal on Information and computer Science, *2*, 107–139.

Lu, T., Du, Y., Ouyang, L., Chen, Q., & Wang, X. (2020). Android malware detection based on a hybrid deep learning model. *Security and Communication Networks*, *2020*, 2020. doi:10.1155/2020/8863617

Lu, W., & Traore, I. (2004). Detecting new forms of network intrusion using genetic programming. *Computational Intelligence*, *20*(3), 475–494. doi:10.1111/j.0824-7935.2004.00247.x

MacKay, D. J., & Mac Kay, D. J. (2003). *Information theory, inference and learning algorithms.* Cambridge university press.

Maclaurin, G. J., Grue, N. W., Lopez, A. J., & Heimiller, D. M. (2019). *The Renewable Energy Potential (reV) Model: A Geospatial Platform for Technical Potential and Supply Curve Modeling (No. NREL/TP-6A20-73067).* National Renewable Energy Lab. doi:10.2172/1563140

Mahdavifar, S., Kadir, A. F. A., Fatemi, R., Alhadidi, D., & Ghorbani, A. A. (2020). Dynamic android malware category classification using semi-supervised deep learning. In *2020 IEEE Intl Conf on Dependable, Autonomic and Secure Computing,* (DASC/PiCom/CBDCom/CyberSciTech). (pp. 515-522). IEEE.

Mahmoud Abdelsalam, R. K. (2018). Malware Detection in Cloud Infrastructures using Convolutional Neural Networks. *IEEE 11th International Conference on Cloud Computing.* IEEE. 10.1109/CLOUD.2018.00028

Mahmoud Kalash, M. R. (2018). *Malware Classification with Deep Convolutional Neural Networks.* IEEE.

Makris, D. (2018). Review of Video-Based Threat Detection Approaches for Public Safety.

MaldonadoS. B.BielickiJ. M.MirandaM.Ogland-HandJ. D.HowardC.AdamsB.SaarM. O. (2020). Geospatial Estimation of the Electric Power Potential in Sedimentary Basin Geothermal Resources Using Geologically Stored Carbon Dioxide. In *World Geothermal Congress.* doi:10.3929/ethz-b-000449699

Malhotra, D. S. (2016). Cyber Crime-Its Types, Analysis and Prevention Techniques. *International Journal of Advanced Research in Computer Science and Software Engineering, 6*(5), 145–150.

Malik, A. J., & Khan, F. A. (2018). A hybrid technique using binary particle swarm optimization and decision tree pruning for network intrusion detection. *Cluster Computing, 21*(1), 667–680. doi:10.100710586-017-0971-8

Malik, V., & Singh, S. (2019). Security risk management in IoT environment. *J. Discret. Math. Sci. Cryptogr., 22*(4), 697–709. doi:10.1080/09720529.2019.1642628

Maloof, J. Z. (2006). Learning to detect and classify malicious executables in the wild. *Machine Learning.*

Marchi, R. (2012). With Facebook, Blogs, and Fake News, Teens Reject Journalistic "objectivity". *Journal of Communication Inquiry.* doi:10.1177/0196859912458700

Marek, L., Campbell, M., Epton, M., Kingham, S., & Storer, M. (2018). Winter Is Coming: A Socio-Environmental Monitoring and Spatiotemporal Modelling Approach for Better Understanding a Respiratory Disease. *ISPRS International Journal of Geo-Information, 7*(11), 432. doi:10.3390/ijgi7110432

MarketsandMarkets. IoT Security Market Worth $35.2 Billion by 2023. 2019. Available online: https: //www.marketsandmarkets.com/PressReleases/iot-security.asp (accessed on 17 September 2020).

Martinelli, F., Mercaldo, F., & Saracino, A. (2017, April). Bridemaid: An hybrid tool for accurate detection of android malware. In *Proceedings of the 2017 ACM on Asia conference on computer and communications security* (pp. 899-901). ACM. 10.1145/3052973.3055156

Masehian, E., & Sedighizadeh, D. (2010). A Multi-Objective PSO-based Algorithm for Robot Path Planning. *IEEE Xplore,* (April), 465–470. doi:10.1109/ICIT.2010.5472755

Masri, R., & Aldwairi, M. (2017). Automated Malicious Advertisement Detection using virustotal, urlvoid, and trendmicro. *8th International Conference on Information and Communication Systems (ICICS).* IEEE. .10.1109/IACS.2017.7921994

Mateen, M., Aleem, M., & Iqbal, M. A. (2017). A Hybrid Approach for Spam Detection for Twitter. *International Conference on Applied Sciences and Technology.* IEEE. 10.1109/IBCAST.2017.7868095

Mayukha S, Vadivel R. 2021. *Various Possible Attacks and Mitigations of the OSI Model Layers Through Pentesting – An Overview.* New Frontiers in Communication and Intelligent Systems, 799–809. Computing & Intelligent Systems, SCRS, India. doi:10.52458/978-81-95502-00-4-78

Mayukha, S., & Vadivel, R. (2023). Reconnaissance for Penetration Testing Using Active Scanning of MITRE ATT&CK. In M. S. Kaiser, J. Xie, & V. S. Rathore (Eds.), *Information and Communication Technology for Competitive Strategies (ICTCS 2021). Lecture Notes in Networks and Systems.* Springer., doi:10.1007/978-981-19-0098-3_66

Mazini, M., Shirazi, B., & Mahdavi, I. (2019). Anomaly network-based intrusion detection system using a reliable hybrid artificial bee colony and AdaBoost algorithms. *Journal of King Saud University-Computer and Information Sciences, 31*(4), 541–553. doi:10.1016/j.jksuci.2018.03.011

Mazzoncini, F., Cavina, V., Andolina, G. M., Erdman, P. A., & Giovannetti, V. (2023). Optimal control methods for quantum batteries. *Physical Review. A, 107*(3), 032218. doi:10.1103/PhysRevA.107.032218

Meligy, A. M., Ibrahim, H. M., & Torky, M. F. (2015). A Framework for Detecting Cloning Attacks in OSN Based on a Novel Social Graph Topology. *International Journal of Intelligent Systems and Applications, 7*(3), 13–20. doi:10.5815/ijisa.2015.03.02

Mell, P., & Scarfone, K. (2011). Vulnerability assessment: The state of the art. *IEEE Security and Privacy, 9*(4), 80–83.

Melvin, A. (2021). *The Practicality of using Virtual Machine Introspection Technique with Machine Learning Algorithms for the Detection of Intrusions in Cloud.* EUDL.

Mendonca, R. R. D., Brito, D. F. D., Rosa, F. D. F., Reis, J. C. D., & Bonacin, R. (2020). A Framework for Detecting Intentions of Criminal Acts in Social Media: A Case Study on Twitter. *International Conference on Information Technology-New Generations, 11*(3). IEEE.

Menezes, A., Van Oorschot, P., & Vanstone, S. (1996). Handbook of Applied Cryptography. CRC Press.

Mesquita, R., & Gaspar, P. D. (2020). A Path Planning Optimization Algorithm Based on Particle Swarm Optimization for UAVs for Bird Monitoring and Repelling – Simulation Results. *2020 International Conference on Decision Aid Sciences and Application (DASA),* (ppl 1144-1148). IEEE. 10.1109/DASA51403.2020.9317271

Meyer, C., & Matyas, S. M. (1982). *Cryptography-A New Dimension in Computer Data Security.* John Wiley & Sons.

Michael, R. Watson, N.-u.-h. S. (2015). Malware Detection in Cloud Computing Infrastructures. *IEEE Transactions on Dependable and Secure Computing.*

Milenkoski, A., Vieira, M., Kounev, S., Avritzer, A., & Payne, B. D. (2015). Evaluating computer intrusion detection systems: A survey of common practices. [CSUR]. *ACM Computing Surveys, 48*(1), 1–41. doi:10.1145/2808691

Minhas, HAhmad, R. (2021). A Reinforcement Learning Routing Protocol for UAV Aided Public Safety Networks. *Sensors, MDPI,* (June), 1–22.

Mishra, P., Varadharajan, V., Tupakula, U., & Pilli, E. S. (2019). A detailed investigation and analysis of using machine learning techniques for intrusion detection. *IEEE Communications Surveys and Tutorials, 21*(1), 686–728. doi:10.1109/COMST.2018.2847722

Mohammadi, S. (2019). Cyber intrusion detection by combined feature selection algorithm. *Journal of information security and applications, 44,* 80-88.

Mohammadi, S., de Vries, B., Rafiee, A., Esfandiari, M., & Dias, E. (2021). An exploratory study on the impact of physical and geospatial characteristics of the urban built environment on the buildings annual electricity usage. *Journal of Building Engineering, 102359,* 102359. Advance online publication. doi:10.1016/j.jobe.2021.102359

Mohammadrezaei, M., Shiri, M. E., & Rahmani, A. M. (2018). Identifying Fake Accounts on Social Networks Based on Graph Analysis and Classification Algorithms. *Security and Communication Networks, 2018,* 1–8. doi:10.1155/2018/5923156

Mollah, M. B., Azad, M. A., & Vasilakos, A. (2017). Security and privacy challenges in mobile cloud computing: Survey and way ahead. *Journal of Network and Computer Applications, 84,* 38–54. doi:10.1016/j.jnca.2017.02.001

Mollin, R. (2002RSA and Public-Key Cryptography. CRC Press.

Moon, D., Im, H., Kim, I., & Park, J. H. (2017). Im, H.; Kim, I.; Park, J.H. DTB-IDS: An intrusion detection system based on decision tree using behavior analysis for preventing APT attacks. *The Journal of Supercomputing, 73*(7), 2881–2895. doi:10.100711227-015-1604-8

Morgan, S. (2019). *Cybersecurity almanac: 100 facts, figures, predictions and statistics.* Cybercrime Magazine Cisco and Cybersecurity Ventures.

Moskovitch, R., Elovici, Y., & Rokach, L. (2008). Detection of unknown computer worms based on behavioral classification of the host. *Computational Statistics & Data Analysis, 52*(9), 4544–4566. doi:10.1016/j.csda.2008.01.028

Moskovitch, R., Nissim, N., Stopel, D., Feher, C., Englert, R., & Elovici, Y. (2007). *Improving the detection of unknown computer worms activity using active learning. In Proceedings of the Annual Conference on Artificial Intelligence,* Osnabrück, Germany. 10.1007/978-3-540-74565-5_47

Mostafa, M., Abdelwahab, A., & Sayed, H. M. (2020). Detecting spam campaign in twitter with semantic similarity. *Journal of Physics: Conference Series, 1447*(2), 455–472. doi:10.1088/1742-6596/1447/1/012044

Moudgil, V., Hewage, K., Hussain, S. A., & Sadiq, R. (2023). Integration of IoT in building energy infrastructure: A critical review on challenges and solutions. *Renewable & Sustainable Energy Reviews, 174,* 113121. doi:10.1016/j.rser.2022.113121

Mukkamala, S., Sung, A., Abraham, A. (2005). *Cyber security challenges: Designing efficient intrusion detection systems and antivirus tools.* Vemuri, V.

Muntasha, G., Karna, N., & Shin, S. Y. (2021). Performance Analysis on Artificial Bee Colony Algorithm for Path Planning and Collision Avoidance in Swarm Unmanned Aerial Vehicle. *2021 International Conference on Artificial Intelligence and Mechatronics Systems (AIMS).* IEEE. 10.1109/AIMS52415.2021.9466085

Murali, A., & Rao, M. (2005). A Survey on Intrusion Detection Approaches. *Information and Communication Technologies.* IEEE. , 10.1109/ICICT.2005.1598592

Murugan, N. S., & Devi, G. U. (2019). Detecting Streaming of Twitter Spam Using Hybrid Method. *Wireless Personal Communications, 103*(2), 1353–1374. doi:10.100711277-018-5513-z

Mushtaq, J. (2016). Different Requirements Gathering Techniques and Issues. *International Journal of Scientific and Engineering Research, 7*(9), 835–840.

Nair, M. M., Tyagi, A. K., & Goyal, R. (2019). Amit KumarTyagi, RichaGoyal, Medical Cyber Physical Systems and Its Issues. *Procedia Computer Science, 165,* 647–665. doi:10.1016/j.procs.2020.01.059

Nanda, S. K., Mohanty, S., Pattnaik, P. K., & Sain, M. (2022). Throughput Optimized Reversible Cellular Automata Based Security Algorithm. *Electronics (Basel), 11*(19), 3190. doi:10.3390/electronics11193190

Nasir, J., Khan, O., & Varlamis, K. (2021). Fake News Detection: A Hybrid CNN-RNN based Deep Learning Approach. International Journal of Management Data Insights. *International Journal of Information Management Data Insights.* Elsevier.

National Cyber Security Centre. (2021). *The Cyber Threat to UK Business.* National Cyber Security Centre.

National Institute of Standards and Technology (NIST). (2018). *NIST Cybersecurity Framework.* NIST. https://www.nist.gov/cyberframework

Navarro, J. C., & Higgins, G. E. (2017). Familial Identity Theft. *American Journal of Criminal Justice, 42*(1), 218–230. doi:10.100712103-016-9357-3

Nayyar, A., Nguyen, N., Kumari, R., & Kumar, S. (2019). Robot Path Planning Using Modified Artificial Bee Colony Algorithm. *Advances in Intelligent Systems and Computing.* Springer.

Nazir, S., Ahmad, F., & Ali, M. (2022). A survey of cyber threat intelligence: Techniques, challenges, and future directions. *Journal of Network and Computer Applications, 200,* 103147. doi:10.1016/j.jnca.2021.103147

Nersesian, R. (2014). Energy for the 21st century: a comprehensive guide to conventional and alternative sources. Routledge

NewComer, E. (2022). Understanding Web Services. Addison-Wesley Professional.

Nicholas, K., & Shiaeles, S. (Eds.). (2021). *Cyber-Security Threats, Actors, and Dynamic Mitigation.* CRC Press.

NIST. (2018). *Risk Management Framework for Information Systems and Organizations.* National Institute of Standards and Technology.

Nordbotten, N. A. (2009). XML and Web Services Security Standards. IEEE Communications Surveys & Tutorials. IEEE. doi:10.1109/SURV.2009.090302

Nurse, J. R. C., Creese, S., & de Roure, D. (2017). Security risk assessment in Internet of Things systems. *IT Professional, 19*(5), 20–26. doi:10.1109/MITP.2017.3680959

Nyandongo, K. M., & Khoza, L. (2018). Assessing the performance of agile methodology: A customer perspective. *Towards Sustainable Technologies and Innovation - Proceedings of the 27th Annual Conference of the International Association for Management of Technology, IAMOT 2018,* (pp. 1–17). IEEE.

OASIS. (n.d.). *Oasis security services (SAML) TC.* OASIS. https://www.oasis-open.org/committees/tc/home.php/wg abbrev=security.

O'Grady, N. P., Alexander, M., Dellinger, E. P., Gerberding, J. L., Heard, S. O., Maki, D. G., & Raad, I. I. (2002). Guidelines for the prevention of intravascular catheter-related infections. Centers for Disease Control and Prevention. MMWR. Recommendations and reports: Morbidity and mortality weekly report. *Recommendations and reports, 51*(RR-10), 1-29.

Okesola, O. J., Okokpujie, K., Goddy-Worlu, R., Ogunbanwo, A., & Iheanetu, O. (2019). Qualitative comparisons of elicitation techniques in requirement engineering. *Journal of Engineering and Applied Sciences (Asian Research Publishing Network), 14*(2), 565–570.

Okoroafor, U. C., Chi, H., Smith, A. N., & Assessment, C. R. (2018). Moving Beyond Vulnerability Scanning. *IEEE Security & Privacy, 16*(3). DOI: .2701204 doi:10.1109/MSP.2018

Olabi, A. G. (2017). Renewable energy and energy storage systems. *Energy, 136,* 1–6. doi:10.1016/j.energy.2017.07.054

Ömer Aslan, R. S. (2020). Using a Subtractive Center Behavioral Model to Detect Malware. *Security and Communication Networks,* 2020.

Onah, J. O., Shafi'i, M. A., Abdullahi, M., Hassan, I. H., & Al-Ghusham, A. (2021). Genetic Algorithm based feature selection and Naïve Bayes for anomaly detection in fog computing environment. *Machine Learning with Applications, 6.*

Oney, Lineberry, & Dampier. (2018). Effective Measures for Preventing and Responding to Insider Cyber Attacks. *International Journal of Critical Infrastructure Protection, 21.* DOI: . 2018.08.002 doi:10.1016/j.ijcip

Ouahouah, S., Bagaa, M., Prados-Garzon, J., & Taleb, T. (2022). Deep-Reinforcement-Learning-Based Collision Avoidance in UAV Environment. IEEE Internet of Things Journal, 9(6), 4015-4030. doi:10.1109/JIOT.2021.3118949

Owais, S., Snášel, P., & Krömer, A. (2008). Survey: Using Genetic Algorithm Approach in Intrusion Detection Systems Techniques. *Computer Information Systems and Industrial Management Applications.* IEEE.

P, S., & Chatterjee, M. (2019). Detection of Fake and Cloned Profiles in Online Social Networks. SSRN *Electronic Journal*, 1–5. doi:10.2139/ssrn.3349673

Palagiri, C. (2002). Network-based intrusion detection using neural networks. Rensselaer Polytechnic Institute Troy.

Paliwal, (2016). *Cyber Crime*. Nations Congress on the Prevention of Crime and Treatment of Offenders.

Pal, M. (2005). Random forest classifier for remote sensing classification. *International Journal of Remote Sensing*, 26(1), 217–222. doi:10.1080/01431160412331269698

Panda, M., & Patra, M. R. (2007). Network intrusion detection using naive bayes. *Int. J. Comput. Sci. Netw. Secur.*, 7, 258–263.

Parenty, T. J., & Domet, J. J. (2014). The Art of Cyber Risk Oversight: CISOs and Boards. *MIS Quarterly Executive*, 13(4), 197–213. doi:10.17705/2msqe.00012

Parker, G. (2021). *Building an Intelligent, Automated Tiered Phishing System: Matching the Message Level to User Ability*. SANAS Institute.

Parvin, M., Yousefi, H., & Noorollahi, Y. (2023). Techno-economic optimization of a renewable micro grid using multi-objective particle swarm optimization algorithm. *Energy Conversion and Management*, 277, 116639. doi:10.1016/j.enconman.2022.116639

Parwej, F., Akhtar, N., & Perwej, Y. (2018). A Close-Up View About Spark in Big Data Jurisdiction. International Journal of Engineering Research and Application (IJERA) 8(1). doi:10.9790/9622-0801022641

Paulose, B., Sabitha, S., Punhani, R., & Sahani, I. (2018). Identification of Regions and Probable Health Risks Due to Air Pollution Using K-Mean Clustering Techniques. *In 2018 4th International Conference on Computational Intelligence & Communication Technology (CICT)* (pp. 1-6). IEEE.

Pawar, S. & Chiplunkar, N. (2018). *Populating Parameters of Web Services by Automatic Composition Using Search Precision and WSDL Weight Matrix*. InderScience Publishers – Scopus indexed.

Pehlivanoglu, Y. (2021, November). PerihanPehlivanoglu, "An enhanced genetic algorithm for path planning of autonomous UAV in target coverage problems". *Applied Soft Computing, 112.*

Pei, J., & Zhong, K. (2022). Personalized federated learning framework for network traffic anomaly detection. *Computer Networks, 209.*

Pervez, M. S., & Farid, D. M. (2014). *Feature selection and intrusion classification in NSL-KDD cup 99 dataset employing SVMs. In Proceedings of the 8th International Conference on Software, Knowledge, Information Management and Applications (SKIMA 2014)*, Dhaka, Bangladesh. 10.1109/SKIMA.2014.7083539

Perwej, Y. (2019). The Hadoop Security in Big Data: A Technological Viewpoint and Analysis. *International Journal of Scientific Research in Computer Science and Engineering (IJSRCSE), 7*(3). doi:10.26438/ijsrcse/v7i3.1014

Perwej, Y. (2021). A systematic literature review on the cyber security. *International Journal of scientific research and management, 9,* 669-710.

Perwej, Y. (2017). An Experiential Study of the Big Data. International Transaction of Electrical and Computer Engineers System. *Science and Education Publishing, 4*(1), 14–25. doi:10.12691/iteces-4-1-3

Peter Mell, T. G. (2011). *The NIST Definition of cloud computing.*

Philip, C. L., Chen, Q., & Zhang, C. Y. (2014). Data-intensive applications challenges techniques and technologies: A survey on big data. *Information Sciences, 275,* 314–347. doi:10.1016/j.ins.2014.01.015

Pierri, F., Piccardi, C., & Ceri, S. (2020). A multi-layer approach to disinformation detection on Twitter. *EPJ Data Science, 9*(35), 525–531.

Pinto, T., & Sebastian, Y. (2021). Detecting DDoS attacks using a cascade of machine learning classifiers based on Random Forest and MLP-ANN. *2021 IEEE Madras Section Conference (MASCON),* (pp. 1-6). IEEE. 10.1109/MASCON51689.2021.9563266

Policy, P. (2020). *Got It ! Got It !* 1–6.

Prakash, S. D., & Gunjal. B. L. (2020). New Approach for Detecting Spammers on Twitter using Machine Learning Framework. *International journal of Research and Analytical reviews, 7*(3), 794-798.

Preeti Mishra, A. G. (2022). vServiceInspector: Introspection-assisted evolutionary bag-of-ngram approach to detect malware in cloud servers. *Ad Hoc Networks, 131.*

Preeti Mishra, E. S. (2016). NvCloudIDS: A Security Architecture to Detect Intrusions at Network and Virtualization Layer in Cloud Environment. *Intl. Conference on Advances in Computing, Communications and Informatics (ICACCI).*

Purba, K. R., Asirvatham, D., & Murugesan, R. K. (2020). Classification of instagram fake users using supervised machine learning algorithms. *Iranian Journal of Electrical and Computer Engineering, 10*(3), 2763–2772. doi:10.11591/ijece.v10i3.pp2763-2772

Puthran, S., & Shah, K. (2016). *Intrusion detection using improved decision tree algorithm with binary and quad split. In Proceedings of the International Symposium on Security in Computing and Communication,* Jaipur, India. 10.1007/978-981-10-2738-3_37

PwC. (2016). *Managing Emerging Risks from the Internet of Things.* PwC. https://www.pwc.com/ us/en/services/consulting/cybersecurity/library/broader-perspectives/managing-iot-risks.html

Quinlan, J. R. (1986). Induction of decision trees. *Machine Learning, 1*(1), 81–106. doi:10.1007/BF00116251

Quinlan, J. R. (1993). *C4.5: Programs for Machine Learning.* Morgan Kaufmann Publishers, Inc.

Qu, X., Yang, L., Guo, K., Ma, L., Sun, M., Ke, M., & Li, M. (2019). A Survey on the Development of Self-Organizing Maps for Unsupervised Intrusion Detection. *Mobile Networks and Applications.*

Rachmadi, S., Mandala, S., & Oktaria, D. (2021). Detection of DoS attack using AdaBoost algorithm on IoT system. *2021 International Conference on Data Science and Its Applications (ICoDSA),* (pp. 28-33). 10.1109/ICoDSA53588.2021.9617545

Rahul Kumar, K. S. (2020). *Machine Learning based Malware Detection in Cloud Environment using Clustering Approach.* IEEE.

Rai, K., Devi, M. S., & Guleria, A. (2016). Decision tree based algorithm for intrusion detection. *Int. J. Adv. Netw. Appl.*, *7*, 2828.

Rajarajan, M., Zisman, A., & Dimitrakos, T. (2013). A Survey of Cyber security Threats and Defenses. *Journal of Network and Computer Applications*, *36*(1), 1–11. doi:10.1016/j.jnca.2012.08.005

Rajendra Patil, H. D. (2019). *Designing in-VM-assisted lightweight agent-based malware detection framework for securing virtual machines in cloud computing.* Springer.

Raju, A. S., Sathappan, S., & Srinivasan, U. (2021). Machine Learning for Cybersecurity Risk Management: A Survey. *Journal of Ambient Intelligence and Humanized Computing*, *12*(8), 7941–7962. doi:10.100712652-021-03517-6

Ramesh, R. & Khandelwal, S. (2013). A Comprehensive Analysis Of Xml Digital Signature, Xml Encryption And Xkms, *International Journal Of Engineering Research & Technology (Ijert)*, 02.

Ransbotham, S., & Kiron, D. (2017). Cybersecurity's Human Factor: Lessons from the Pentagon. *MIT Sloan Management Review*, *58*(4), 41–48.

Rao, S., Verma, A. K., & Bhatia, T. (2020a). *Evolving Cyber Threats, Combating Techniques, and Open Issues in Online Social Networks*, 219–235. IGI Global. doi:10.4018/978-1-7998-5728-0.ch012

Rao, A., Carreón, N., Lysecky, R., & Rozenblit, J. (2018). Probabilistic threat detection for risk management in cyber-physical medical systems. *IEEE Software*, *35*(1), 38–43. doi:10.1109/MS.2017.4541031

Ratna, S. R., & Ravi, R. (2016). Securing jammed network using reliability behavior value through neuro-fuzzy analysis. *Sadhana Academy Proceedings in Engineering Science*, *40*(4), 1139–1153.

Ratna, S. R., Ravi, R., & Shekhar, B. (2015). An intelligent approach based on neuro-fuzzy detachment scheme for preventing jamming attack in wireless networks. *Journal of Intelligent & Fuzzy Systems*, *28*(2), 801–820. doi:10.3233/IFS-141363

Raza, S., & Kavitha, C. (2020). Vulnerability assessment techniques for internet of things (IoT) devices: A review. *Journal of Ambient Intelligence and Humanized Computing*, *11*(5), 1895–1910.

Reddy, G. N., & Reddy, G. (2014). A study of cybersecurity challenges and its emerging trends on latest technologies. arXiv, arXiv:1402.1842.

Relan, N. G., & Patil, D. R. (2015). Implementation of network intrusion detection system using variant of decision tree algorithm. In *Proceedings of the 2015 International Conference on Nascent Technologies in the Engineering Field (ICNTE)*, Navi Mumbai, India. 10.1109/ICNTE.2015.7029925

Renjith, G., & Aji, S. (2022). On-device Resilient Android Malware Detection using Incremental Learning. *Procedia Computer Science*, *215*, 929–936. doi:10.1016/j.procs.2022.12.095

Resch, B., Sagl, G., Törnros, T., Bachmaier, A., Eggers, J. B., Herkel, S., Narmsara, S., & Gündra, H. (2014). GIS-based planning and modeling for renewable energy: Challenges and future research avenues. *ISPRS International Journal of Geo-Information*, *3*(2), 662–692. doi:10.3390/ijgi3020662

Revathi, S., & Suriakala, M. (2018). Profile Similarity Communication Matching Approaches for Detection of Duplicate Profiles in Online Social Network. *Proceedings 2018 3rd International Conference on Computational Systems and Information Technology for Sustainable Solutions, CSITSS 2018*, (pp. 174–182). IEEE. 10.1109/CSITSS.2018.8768751

Rid, T., & Buchanan, B. (2015). Attributing cyber-attacks. *The Journal of Strategic Studies*, *38*(1-2), 4–37. doi:10.1080/01402390.2014.977382

Riswanto, & Sensuse, D. I. (2021). Knowledge management systems development and implementation: A systematic literature review. *IOP Conference Series: Earth and Environmental Science, 704*(1). doi:10.1088/1755-1315/704/1/012015

Rizi, F. S., Khayyambashi, M. R., & Kharaji, M. Y. (2014). A New Approach for Finding Cloned Profiles in Online Social Networks. In *Int* (Vol. 6). J. of Network Security.

Rizvi, S. T. (2018). A comprehensive survey on cloud security attacks and defense mechanisms. *Journal of Network and Computer Applications, 107*, 57–82.

Roberge, V., & Tarbouchi, M. (2020). Parallel Algorithm for the Path Planning of Multiple Unmanned Aerial Vehicles. *2020 Fourth International Conference On Intelligent Computing in Data Sciences (ICDS)*, (pp. 1-6). 10.1109/ICDS50568.2020.9268775

Rohmani, K., & Goyal, A. K., & Mudgal, M. (2015). Study of Cryptography and Steganography System. *International Journal of Engineering and Computer Science, 4*(8), 2319-7342

Romanov, A., Semenov, A., Mazhelis, O., & Veijalainen, J. (2017). Detection of fake profiles in social media: Literature review. *WEBIST 2017 - Proceedings of the 13th International Conference on Web Information Systems and Technologies, Webist*, (pp. 363–369). 10.5220/0006362103630369

Rossouw, S., & Johan, N. (2013). From information security to cyber security. *Computers & Security, 38*, 97–102. doi:10.1016/j.cose.2013.04.004

Royce, W. W. (2021). Managing the Development of Large Software Systems (1970). *Ideas That Created the Future*, (August), 321–332. doi:10.7551/mitpress/12274.003.0035

Roy, P. K., & Chahar, S. (2021). Fake Profile Detection on Social Networking Websites: A Comprehensive Review. *IEEE Transactions on Artificial Intelligence, 1*(3), 271–285. doi:10.1109/TAI.2021.3064901

Russo, D., & Miketa, A. (2019). Benefits, challenges, and analytical approaches to scaling up renewables through regional planning and coordination of power systems in Africa. Current *Sustainable/Renewable. Energy Reports, 6*(1), 5–12. doi:10.100740518-019-00125-4

Şahın, D. Ö., Akleylek, S., & Kiliç, E. (2022). LinRegDroid: Detection of Android malware using multiple linear regression models-based classifiers. *IEEE Access : Practical Innovations, Open Solutions, 10*, 14246–14259. doi:10.1109/ACCESS.2022.3146363

Saleh, M., Ismail, R., & Al-Maashri, A. (2017). Vulnerability assessment in the internet of things: A review. In *Proceedings of the 2017 3rd International Conference on Cloud Computing Technologies and Applications (CloudTech)* (pp. 1-6). IEEE

Samet, Ö. A. (2020). A comprehensive review on malware detection approaches. *IEEE Access : Practical Innovations, Open Solutions*, 8.

Sangkatsanee, P., Wattanapongsakorn, N., & Charnsripinyo, C. (2011). Practical real-time intrusion detection using machine learning approaches. *Computer Communications, 34*(18), 2227–2235. doi:10.1016/j.comcom.2011.07.001

Saranya Shree, S., Subhiksha, C., & Subhashini, R. (2021). Prediction of Fake Instagram Profiles Using Machine Learning. SSRN *Electronic Journal, 25*(5), 4490–4497. doi:10.2139/ssrn.3802584

Sarker, C. (2019). I.H. Context-aware rule learning from smartphone data: Survey, challenges and future directions. *Journal of Big Data, 6*(1), 95. doi:10.118640537-019-0258-4

Sarker, I. H. (2019). A machine learning based robust prediction model for real-life mobile phone data. *Internet Things*, 5, 180–193. doi:10.1016/j.iot.2019.01.007

Sarker, I. H. (2019). Cybersecurity Data Science: An Overview from Machine Learning Perspective. *Journal of Big Data*, 6.

Sarker, I. H., Colman, A., Han, J., Khan, A. I., Abushark, Y. B., Salah, K., & Behav, D. T. (2019). A Behavioral Decision Tree Learning to Build User-Centric Context-Aware Predictive Model. *Mobile Networks and Applications*.

Sarker, I. H., Kayes, A. S. M., Badsha, S., Alqahtani, H., Watters, P., & Ng, A. (2020). Cybersecurity data science: An overview from machine learning perspective. *Journal of Big Data*, 7(1), 1–29. doi:10.118640537-020-00318-5

Sarker, I. H., Kayes, A., & Watters, P. (2019). Effectiveness Analysis of Machine Learning Classification Models for Predicting Personalized Context-Aware Smartphone Usage. *Journal of Big Data*, 6(1), 57. doi:10.118640537-019-0219-y

Sarker, I. H., & Salim, F. D. (2018). *Mining User Behavioral Rules from Smartphone Data through Association Analysis.* In *Proceedings of the 22nd Pacific-Asia Conference on Knowledge Discovery and Data Mining (PAKDD)*, Melbourne, Australia. 10.1007/978-3-319-93034-3_36

Sarma, A., Chatterjee, R., Gili, K., & Yu, T. (2019). *Quantum Unsupervised and Supervised Learning on Superconducting Processors.* arXiv preprint arXiv:1909.04226.

Sarode, A. J., & Mishra, A. (2015). Audit and analysis of impostors: An experimental approach to detect fake profile in online social network. *ACM International Conference Proceeding Series, 25-27-Sept*, 1–8. 10.1145/2818567.2818568

Saxena, H., & Richariya, V. (2014). Intrusion detection in KDD99 dataset using SVM-PSO and feature reduction with information gain. *International Journal of Computer Applications*, 98(6), 25–29. doi:10.5120/17188-7369

Schibilia, J. (2023). *Really, How Bad Do Routers Have It?* SANS Institute.

Seager, T. P., Miller, S. A., & Kohn, J. (2009, May). Land use and geospatial aspects in life cycle assessment of renewable energy. *In 2009 Ieee International Symposium on Sustainable Systems and Technology* (pp. 1-6). IEEE. 10.1109/ISSST.2009.5156724

Sedeh, O. M., Ostadi, B., & Zagia, F. (2021). A novel hybrid GA-PSO optimization technique for multi-location facility maintenance scheduling problem. *Journal of Building Engineering*, 40(August), 102348. doi:10.1016/j.jobe.2021.102348

Senthil Kumar, N., Saravanakumar, K., & Deepa, K. (2016). On Privacy and Security in Social Media - A Comprehensive Study. *Physics Procedia*, 78(December 2015), 114–119. doi:10.1016/j.procs.2016.02.019

Sequeira, K., & Zaki, M. (2002). Admit: anomaly-based data mining for intrusions. In *Proceedings of the eighth ACM SIGKDD international conference on Knowledge discovery and data mining.* ACM. 10.1145/775047.775103

Seufert, S., & O'Brien, D. (2007). Machine learning for automatic defence against distributed denial of service attacks. In *Proceedings of the 2007 IEEE International Conference on Communications*, Glasgow, UK. 10.1109/ICC.2007.206

Shabtai, A. (2012). A survey of machine learning methods for detecting malicious executables. *Information Security Technical Report*, 16(1), 2–14.

Shabtai, A., Moskovitch, R., Elovici, Y., & Glezer, C. (2009). Detection of malicious code by applying machine learning classifiers on static features: A state-of-the-art. *Information Security Technical Report*, 14(1), 16–29. doi:10.1016/j.istr.2009.03.003

Sha, K., Wei, W., Yang, T. A., Wang, Z., & Shi, W. (2018). On security challenges and open issues in Internet of Things. *Future Generation Computer Systems*, 83, 326–337. doi:10.1016/j.future.2018.01.059

Shanmuganathan, C., & Raviraj, P. (2012, April). Performance Measures of Wireless Protocols for ATM Networks. *International Journal of Mobile Network Communications & Telematics, 2*(2), 31–44. doi:10.5121/ijmnct.2012.2203

Shao, S., Peng, Y., He, C., & Du, Y. (2020). *Efficient path planning for UAV formation via comprehensively improved particle swarm optimization.* Elsevier.

Shao, M., Zhao, Y., Sun, J., Han, Z., & Shao, Z. (2023). A decision framework for tidal current power plant site selection based on GIS-MCDM: A case study in China. *Energy, 262,* 125476. doi:10.1016/j.energy.2022.125476

Shapoorifard, H., & Shamsinejad, P. (2017). Intrusion detection using a novel hybrid method incorporating an improved KNN. *International Journal of Computer Applications, 173*(1), 5–9. doi:10.5120/ijca2017914340

Sharifi, A. M., Amirgholipour, S. K., & Pourebrahimi, A. (2015). Intrusion detection based on joint of K-means and KNN. *J. Converg. Inf. Technol., 10,* 42.

Sharma, T. K., Pant, M., & Abraham, A. (2013). Blend of local and global variant of PSO in ABC. *2013 World Congress on Nature and Biologically Inspired Computing*, Fargo, ND, USA. 10.1109/NaBIC.2013.6617848

ShaydulinR.SybrandtJ. (2017). *To Agile, or not to Agile: A Comparison of Software Development Methodologies.* 1–11. https://arxiv.org/abs/1704.07469

Shelke, F., Dongre, A., Soni, P. (2014). Comparison of Different techniques for steganography in images. *International Journal of Application or Innovation in Engineering And Management, 3*(2).

Sheng, N. G., Sun, R., & Chen, S. (2019). 6-DOF Robotic Obstacle Avoidance Path Planning Based on Artificial Potential Field Method. *16th International Conference on Ubiquitous Robots (UR).* IEEE.

Shon, T., Kim, Y., Lee, C., & Moon, J. (2005). *A machine learning framework for network anomaly detection using SVM and GA.* In *Proceedings of the Sixth Annual IEEE SMC Information Assurance Workshop*, West Point, NY, USA. 10.1109/IAW.2005.1495950

Shon, T., & Moon, J. (2007). A hybrid machine learning approach to network anomaly detection. *Information Sciences, 177*(18), 3799–3821. doi:10.1016/j.ins.2007.03.025

Shrivastava, A., Tiwari, V., Kumar, R., & Khanna, A. (2018). A comprehensive survey on vulnerability assessment techniques for cloud computing. *Future Generation Computer Systems, 89,* 79–109.

Sihag, V., Vardhan, M., Singh, P., Choudhary, G., & Son, S. (2021). De-LADY: Deep learning based Android malware detection using Dynamic features. *J. Internet Serv. Inf. Secur., 11*(2), 34–45.

Simpson, A., & Sachs, M. (2018). Cyber security Risk Management: A Review of Current Approaches. *Computers & Security, 78,* 398–416. doi:10.1016/j.cose.2018.07.006

Sinclair, C., Pierce, L., & Matzner, S. (1999). An application of machine learning to network intrusion detection. In *Proceedings of the 15th Annual Computer Security Applications Conference (ACSAC'99)*, Phoenix, AZ, USA. 10.1109/CSAC.1999.816048

Singh, A. & Malik, S. (2013). Securing Data by Cryptography with Steganography", *International Journal of Advanced Research in Computer Science and Software Engineering, 3*(5).

Singh, G., Singla, ASandha, K. (2011). Cryptography Algorithm Comparison forSecurity Enhancement in Wireless Intrusion DetectionSystem. *International Journal of MultidisciplinaryResearch, 1*(4), 143-151, August.

Smid, M. E. & Branstad, D. K. (1992). Response to comments on the NIST proposed Digital Signature Standard. *Crypto '92.*

Sommer, R., & Paxson, V. (2010). Outside the closed world: On using machine learning for network intrusion detection. In *Proceedings of the 2010 IEEE Symposium on Security and Privacy*, Berkeley/Oakland, CA, USA. 10.1109/SP.2010.25

Sommestad, T., Ekstedt, M., & Johnson, P. (2009). Cyber Security Risks Assessment with Bayesian Defense Graphs and Architectural Models. *42nd Hawaii International Conference on System Sciences*. IEEE. 10.1109/HICSS.2009.141

Sonmez, A., Kocyigit, E., & Kugu, E. (2015). Optimal path planning for UAVs using Genetic Algorithm. *2015 International Conference on Unmanned Aircraft Systems (ICUAS)*. IEEE. 10.1109/ICUAS.2015.7152274

Sood, S. S., Kaur, S., & Singh, A. J. (2021). The Role of Social Engineering in Cybersecurity: A Systematic Literature Review. *Journal of Cybersecurity, 103*.

Spoorthy, A. S., & sinha, S. (2021). Trust Based Fake Node Identification in Social Networking Sites. *IOP Conference Series. Materials Science and Engineering, 1123*(1), 012036. doi:10.1088/1757-899X/1123/1/012036

Sravanthi, R. M. (2019). Cyber Physical Systems: The Role of Machine Learning and Cyber Security in Present and Future. Computer Reviews Journal, 5. PURKH.

Stallings, W. (2020). *Cryptography and Network Security Principles and practices*. Pearson Education.

Stokes, W. H. (2016). MtNet: a multi-task neural network for dynamic malware classification. Detection of Intrusions and Malware, and Vulnerability Assessment. Springer.

Stokes, B. A. (2017). *Malware classification with LSTM and GRU language models and a character-level cnn*. IEEE.

Stone, E. (2016). Detecting Clinical Deterioration in Hospital Patients: A Survey of Methods.

Store, J. (2023). *Living Off the land as a defender: Detecting Attacks with Flexible Baselines*. SANS Institute.

Stubblefield, A. (2005). *Managing the Performance Impact of Web Security*. Kluwer Academic Publishers.

Sumathi, N. (2015). Necessity of Dynamic Composition for Web Services. *IEEE Int. Conference on Applied and Theoretical Computing and Communication Technology*. IEEE.

Sun, N., Lin, G., Qiu, J., & Rimba, P. (2020). Near real-time twitter spam detection with Machine learning techniques. *International Journal of Computers and Applications, 44*(4), 1–11.

Sun, N., Zhang, J., Rimba, P., Gao, S., Zhang, L. Y., & Xiang, Y. (2018). Data-driven cybersecurity incident prediction: A survey. *IEEE Communications Surveys and Tutorials, 21*(2), 1744–1772. doi:10.1109/COMST.2018.2885561

Supporting Digital Signature by Brenda Coulson. (n.d.). *About*. DEVX. www.devx.com

Surendran, R., Thomas, T., & Emmanuel, S. (2018). *Detection of malware applications in an- droid smartphones*. World Sci Book Chapter.

Surendran, R., Thomas, T., & Emmanuel, S. (2020). A TAN based hybrid model for android malware detection. *Journal of Information Security and Applications, 54*, 102483. doi:10.1016/j.jisa.2020.102483

Svadasu, G., & Adimoolam, M. (2022). Spam Detection in Social Media using Artificial Neural Network Algorithm and comparing Accuracy with Support Vector Machine Algorithm. *International Conference on Business Analytics for Technology and Security*. IEEE Xplore.

Szabo, B., & Hercegfi, K. (2017). Research questions on integrating user experience approaches into software development processes. *8th IEEE International Conference on Cognitive Infocommunications, CogInfoCom 2017 - Proceedings, 2018-Janua*(CogInfoCom), (pp. 243–246). IEEE. 10.1109/CogInfoCom.2017.8268250

Tahan, G., L. R. (2012). Mal-ID: Automatic malware detection using common segment analysis and meta-features. *Journal of Machine Learning Research.*

Tajalizadeh, H., & Boostani, R. (2019). A Novel Stream Clustering Framework for Spam Detection in Twitter. *IEEE Transactions on Computational Social Systems, 6*(3), 525–534. doi:10.1109/TCSS.2019.2910818

Tajbakhsh, A., Rahmati, M., & Mirzaei, A. (2009). Intrusion detection using fuzzy association rules. *Applied Soft Computing, 9*(2), 462–469. doi:10.1016/j.asoc.2008.06.001

Taminiau, J., Byrne, J., Kim, J., Kim, M. W., & Seo, J. (2021). Infrastructure-scale sustainable energy planning in the cityscape: Transforming urban energy metabolism in East Asia. *Wiley Interdisciplinary Reviews. Energy and Environment, 397*(5), e397. doi:10.1002/wene.397

Tan, S. M., & Ewe, H. T. (2014). Network security: Intrusion detection and prevention systems. *Journal of Information Assurance and Security, 9*(2), 95–102.

Thakur, L., Qiu, M., Gai, K., & Ali, M. L. (2015). An Investigation on Cyber Security Threats and Security Models. *IEEE 2nd International Conference on Cyber Security and Cloud Computing.* IEEE. 10.1109/CSCloud.2015.71

Thomas, P. (2014). Literature Survey on Modern Image Steganographic Techniques. *International Journal of Engineering Research and Technology, Vol 2,* Issue 5, May, ISSN 2278-0181

Tobin, Zapata, & Rowe. (2017). Cyber Threat Intelligence: Analysis and Recommendations for a Mature Cybersecurity Program. *Computers & Security, 68.* doi:10.1016/j.cose.2016.10.008

Tobiyama, Y. Y. (2016). *Malware detection with deep neural network using process behavior.* COMPSAC.

Tom Landman, N. N. (2021). Deep-Hook: A trusted deep learning-based framework for unknown malware detection and classification in Linux cloud environments. *Neural Networks, 144,* 648–685. doi:10.1016/j.neunet.2021.09.019 PMID:34656885

Tomlinson, R. F. (2007). *Thinking about GIS: geographic information system planning for managers* (Vol. 1). ESRI, Inc.

Tong, F., & Yan, Z. (2017). A hybrid approach of mobile malware detection in Android. *Journal of Parallel and Distributed Computing, 103,* 22–31. doi:10.1016/j.jpdc.2016.10.012

Troester, G. (2017). Threat Detection Using Millimeter Wave Radar: A Review.

Tsai, C. F., & Hsieh, H. Y. (2018). A Review of Risk Management in Cyber Security. *Journal of Information Security, 9*(2), 115–125. doi:10.4236/jis.2018.92007

Tsiaras, E., Papadopoulos, D. N., Antonopoulos, C. N., Papadakis, V. G., & Coutelieris, F. A. (2020). Planning and assessment of an off-grid power supply system for small settlements. *Renewable Energy, 149,* 1271–1281. doi:10.1016/j.renene.2019.10.118

Tung, K. (2017). A novel hybrid PSO-ABC algorithm for effort estimation of software projects using agile methodologies. *Journal of intelligent systems.*

Türker, S., & Can, A. B. (2019). Andmfc: Android malware family classification framework. In *2019 IEEE 30th International Symposium on Personal, Indoor and Mobile Radio Communications (PIMRC Workshops)* (pp. 1-6). IEEE.

Tyagi, A. K. (2019). *Building a Smart and Sustainable Environment using Internet of Things.* International Conference on Sustainable Computing in Science, Technology and Management (SUSCOM), Amity University Rajasthan, Jaipur – India. 10.2139srn.3356500

Ullah, S., Ahmad, J., Khan, M. A., Alkhammash, E. H., Hadjouni, M., Ghadi, Y. Y., Saeed, F., & Pitropakis, N. (2022). A New Intrusion Detection System for the Internet of Things via Deep Convolutional Neural Network and Feature Engineering. *Sensors (Basel)*, 22(10), 3607. doi:10.339022103607 PMID:35632016

Uribe-Hurtado, A. L., Orozco-Alzate, M., Lopes, N., & Ribeiro, B. (2020). GPU-based fast clustering via K-Centres and k-NN mode seeking for geospatial industry applications. *Computers in Industry*, 122, 103260. doi:10.1016/j.compind.2020.103260

Vadivel, R., & Mayukha, S. (2022). Port Scanning Mitigation Strategies for Penetration Testing: Blue Team Perspective, *2022 International Conference on Engineering and Emerging Technologies (ICEET)*, Kuala Lumpur, Malaysia. 10.1109/ICEET56468.2022.10007258

Van Casteren, W. (2017). The Waterfall Model And The Agile Methodologies : A Comparison By Project Characteristics-Short The Waterfall Model and Agile Methodologies. *Academic Competences in the Bachelor.* (pp. 10–13). Research Gate. https://www.researchgate.net/publication/313768860

Venkatesha, S., Reddy, K. R., & Chandavarkar, B. R. (2021). Social Engineering Attacks During the COVID-19 Pandemic. *SN Computer Science*, 2(2), 1–9. doi:10.100742979-020-00443-1 PMID:33585823

Verma, A. K., & Dheeraj, R. (2019). Decision tree based password security system. In *Proceedings of the 3rd International Conference on Inventive Systems and Control* (pp. 1746-1749). IEEE.

Verma, M., Srivastava, M., Chack, N., Diswar, A. K., & Gupta, N. (2012). A comparative study of various clustering algorithms in data mining. [IJERA]. *International Journal of Engineering Research and Applications*, 2(3), 1379–1384.

Vishnu, S. & Babu, H. (2015). A Study on combined Cryptography and Steganography. *International Journal of Research Studies in Computer Science and Engineering, 2*(5).

Vishwakarma, S., Sharma, V., & Tiwari, A. (2017). An intrusion detection system using KNN-ACO algorithm. *International Journal of Computer Applications*, 171(10), 18–23. doi:10.5120/ijca2017914079

Vishwarupe, V., Bedekar, M., Pande, M., & Hiwale, A. (2018). Intelligent Twitter Spam Detection: A Hybrid Approach. *Smart Trends in Systems Security and Sustainability*, 15, 189–197. doi:10.1007/978-981-10-6916-1_17

Wagner, D., & Dean, R. (2001). Intrusion detection via static analysis. In: *Secur. Privacy,. S&P 2001. Proceedings.* IEEE. 10.1109/SECPRI.2001.924296

Wagner, J. & Francois, T. (2011). Machine learning approach for ipflow record anomaly detection. *International Conference on Research in Networking.* Springer.

Wagner, C., François, J., & Engel, T. (2017). Machine learning approach for ip-flow record anomaly detection. In *Proceedings of the International Conference on Research in Networking*, Valencia, Spain. 10.1007/978-3-642-20757-0_3

Wan, X. G. S. (2017). Reinforcement Learning Based Mobile Offloading for Cloud-based Malware Detection. IEEE.

Wang, W. (2017). *"liar, liar pants on fire": A New Benchmark Dataset for Fake News Detection.:* arXiv:1705.00648.

Wang, X. (2020). Deep Learning for Network Intrusion Detection: A Survey.

Wang, L., Liu, L., Qi, J., & Peng, W. (2020). *Improved Quantum Particle Swarm Optimization Algorithm for Offline Path Planning in AUVs* (Vol. 8). IEEE Access.

Wang, M., Lu, Y., & Qin, J. (2020). A dynamic MLP-based DDoS attack detection method using feature selection and feedback. *Computers & Security*, 88, 101645. doi:10.1016/j.cose.2019.101645

Wang, S. X. (2012). The Improved Dijkstra's Shortest Path Algorithm and Its Application. *Procedia Engineering, 29*, 1186–1190. doi:10.1016/j.proeng.2012.01.110

Wang, S., Chen, X., & Wu, Y. (2020). A comprehensive survey on blockchain security. *Journal of Information Security and Applications, 50*, 102447. doi:10.1016/j.jisa.2019.102447

Wang, W., Ren, C., Song, H., Zhang, S., & Liu, P. (2022). FGL_Droid: An Efficient Android Malware Detection Method Based on Hybrid Analysis. *Security and Communication Networks, 2022*, 2022. doi:10.1155/2022/8398591

Wang, X., & Xie, Y. (2019). A survey of user authentication schemes based on mouse dynamics. *Journal of Network and Computer Applications, 126*, 130–152.

Wang, Y. (2020). Survey on zero trust networks: Towards the next generation of secure network architectures. *IEEE Access : Practical Innovations, Open Solutions, 8*, 100736–100752.

Wang, Y., & Nepali, R. K. (2015). Privacy threat modeling framework for online social networks. *2015 International Conference on Collaboration Technologies and Systems, CTS 2015*, (pp. 358–363). IEEE. 10.1109/CTS.2015.7210449

Wang, Z., & Zhang, T. (2019). A Survey of Cyber Attacks and Their Classification. *Journal of Network and Computer Applications, 126*, 46–69. doi:10.1016/j.jnca.2018.11.013

Wani, M. A., Agarwal, N., Jabin, S., & Hussain, S. Z. (2019). Analyzing Real and Fake users in Facebook Network based on Emotions. *2019 11th International Conference on Communication Systems and Networks, COMSNETS 2019, 2061*, (pp. 110–117). IEEE. 10.1109/COMSNETS.2019.8711124

Watkins, C. J. C. H., & Dayan, P. (1992). Q-learning. *Machine Learning, 8*(May), 279–292. doi:10.1007/BF00992698

Wei, K., & Ren, B. (2018). A Method on Dynamic Path Planning for Robotic Manipulator Autonomous Obstacle Avoidance Based on an Improved RRT Algorithm. *Sensors (Basel), 18*(February), 571. doi:10.339018020571 PMID:29438320

Weinstein, M., Meirer, F., Hume, A., Sciau, P., Shaked, G., Hofstetter, R., & Horn, D. (2013). Analyzing big data with dynamic quantum clustering. arXiv preprint arXiv:1310.2700.

Wei, Z., & Yongquan, Y. (2016). Automated web usage data mining and recommendation system using K-Nearest Neighbor (KNN) classification method. *Applied Computing and Informatics, 12*(1), 90–108. doi:10.1016/j.aci.2014.10.001

Witten, I. H., & Frank, E. (2005). *Data Mining: Practical Machine Learning Tools and Techniques*. Morgan Kaufmann.

Wu, T., Fan, H., & Zhu, H. (2022). Intrusion detection system combined enhanced random forest with SMOTE algorithm. *J. Adv. Signal Process, 39*. doi:10.1186/s13634-022-00871-6

Wu, T., Wen, S., Liu, S., Zhang, J., & Alrubaian, M. (2017). Detecting spamming activities in twitter based on deep-learning technique. *Concurrency and Computation, 29*(19), 1–11. doi:10.1002/cpe.4209

Wu, W., Kang, R., & Li, Z. (2015). Risk assessment method for cyber security of cyber physical systems. *First International Conference on Reliability Systems Engineering (ICRSE)*. IEEE. 10.1109/ICRSE.2015.7366430

Wu, Y.-C., Tseng, H. R., Yang, W., & Jan, R. H. (2011). DDoS detection and traceback with decision tree and grey relational analysis. *International Journal of Ad Hoc and Ubiquitous Computing, 7*(2), 121–136. doi:10.1504/IJAHUC.2011.038998

Xiang, S. & Lim, L. (2005). Design of multiple-level hybrid classifier for intrusion detection system. *Workshop on Machine Learning for Signal Processing*. IEEE.

Xiangmei L. (2010). *Optimization of the Neural-NetworkBased Multiple Classifiers Intrusion Detection System*. IEEE

Xin, Y., Kong, L., Liu, Z., Chen, Y., Li, Y., Zhu, H., Gao, M., Hou, H., & Wang, C. (2018). *Machine learning and deep learning methods for cybersecurity*. IEEE Access.

XML Signature Syntax and Processing Version 1. (n.d.). W3.

Xu, Z., Harzallah, M., & Guillet, F. (2018). Comparing of term clustering frameworks for modular ontology learning. *IC3K 2018 - Proceedings of the 10th International Joint Conference on Knowledge Discovery, Knowledge Engineering and Knowledge Management*. IEEE. 10.5220/0006960401280135

Xu, J., Huang, Z., Zhang, R., & Chen, Z. (2021). Deep learning in cyber security: A review. *IEEE Transactions on Neural Networks and Learning Systems*, *32*(6), 2333–2358. doi:10.1109/TNNLS.2020.3017571

Yadav, S., & Selvakumar, S. (2015). Detection of application layer DDoS attack by modeling user behavior using logistic regression. *2015 4th International Conference on Reliability, Infocom Technologies and Optimization (ICRITO)(Trends and Future Directions)*. IEEE. 10.1109/ICRITO.2015.7359289

Yadav, R. M. (2018). Effective Analysis Of Malware Detection In Cloud Computing. *Computers & Security*.

Yan, C., & Xiang, X. (2018). A Path Planning Algorithm for UAV Based on Improved Q-Learning. *2018 2nd International Conference on Robotics and Automation Sciences*. IEEE. 10.1109/ICRAS.2018.8443226

Yan, Y. D., Tang, D., Zhan, S. J., Dai, R., Chen, J. W., & Zhu, N. B. (2019). Low-rate DoS attack detection based on improved logistic regression. *IEEE 21st International Conference on High-Performance Computing and Communications*, (pp. 468-476). IEEE. 10.1109/HPCC/SmartCity/DSS.2019.00076

Yanfang Ye, L. C. (2017). *DeepAM: a heterogeneous deep learning framework or intelligent malware detection*. Springer-Verlag London 2017.

Yang, L., Qi, J., Xiao, J., & Yong, X. (2016). *A Literature Review of UAV 3D Path Planning*.

Yang, Y., Wei, Z., Xu, Y., He, H., & Wang, W. (2018). Droidward: An effective dynamic analysis method for vetting android applications. *Cluster Computing*, *21*(1), 265–275. doi:10.100710586-016-0703-5

Yang, Y., Zhang, Z., & Wang, L. (2021). A comparative study of artificial intelligence-based phishing detection techniques. *Journal of Ambient Intelligence and Humanized Computing*, *12*(8), 8943–8953. doi:10.100712652-021-03544-4

Ye, N., Emran, S. M., Chen, Q., & Vilbert, S. (2002). Multivariate statistical analysis of audit trails for host-based intrusion detection. *IEEE Transactions on Computers*, *51*(7), 810–820. doi:10.1109/TC.2002.1017701

Yerima, S. Y., & Sezer, S. (2018). Droidfusion: A novel multilevel classifier fusion approach for android malware detection. IEEE transactions on cybernetic. IEEE.

Yim, I. Y. (2010). *Malware obfuscation techniques: A brief survey*. Wirel. Comput. Commun. Appl. BWCCA.

Yue, L., & Chen, H. (2019, May). Unmanned vehicle path planning using a novel ant colony algorithm. *EURASIP Journal on Wireless Communications and Networking*, *2019*(1), 136. doi:10.118613638-019-1474-5

Yu, R., Xue, G., Kilari, V. T., & Zhang, X. (2018). *Deploying Robust Security in Internet of Things*. In *Proceedings of the 2018 IEEE Conference on Communications and Network Security (CNS)*, Beijing, China. 10.1109/CNS.2018.8433219

Zabielski, M., Kasprzyk, R., Tarapata, Z., & Szkółka, K. (2016). Methods of Profile Cloning Detection in Online Social Networks. *MATEC Web of Conferences, 76*. IEEE. 10.1051/matecconf/20167604013

Zabielski, M., Tarapata, Z., Kasprzyk, R., & Szkółka, K. (2016). Profile Cloning Detection in Online Social Networks. *Computer Science and Mathematical Modelling*, *0*(0), 39–46. doi:10.5604/01.3001.0009.4502

Zahedi, F., Abbasi, A., & Chen, Y. (2015). Fake-Website Detection Tools: Identifying Elements that Promote Individuals use and Enhance their Performance. *Journal of the Association for Information Systems, 16,*(6). doi:10.17705/1jais.00399

Zarrineh, K., & Raza, S. (2016). Cybersecurity Challenges for Modern Computing. *Journal of Cyber Security and Mobility, 4*(2).

Zhai, Y., Ning, P., Iyer, P., & Reeves, D. S. (2004). Reasoning about complementary intrusion evidence. Proceedings of the 20th Annual Computer Security Applications Conference (ACSAC 04). IEEE. 10.1109/CSAC.2004.29

Zhang, R., Huang, S., Qi, Z., & Guan, H. (2011). Combining static and dynamic analysis to dis- cover software vulner-abilities. In: *Innov. Mob. Internet Serv. Ubiquitous Com- put. (IMIS), Fifth Int. Conf.* IEEE.

Zhang, T., Huo, X., Chen, S., Yang, B., & Zhang, G. (2018). Hybrid Path Planning of A Quadrotor UAV Based on Q-Learning Algorithm. *37th Chinese Control Conference (CCC).* IEEE Xplore.

Zhang, Q., Zhou, C., Tian, Y.-C., Xiong, N., Qin, Y., & Hu, B. (2018). A Fuzzy Probability Bayesian Network Approach for Dynamic Cybersecurity Risk Assessment in Industrial Control Systems. *IEEE Transactions on Industrial Informatics, 14*(6), 2497–2506. doi:10.1109/TII.2017.2768998

Zhang, Q., Zhou, C., Xiong, N., Qin, Y., Li, X., & Huang, S. (2016). Multimodel-Based Incident Prediction and Risk Assessment in Dynamic Cybersecurity Protection for Industrial Control Systems. *IEEE Transactions on Systems, Man, and Cybernetics. Systems, 46*(10), 1429–1444. doi:10.1109/TSMC.2015.2503399

Zhang, R., Huang, S., Qi, Z., & Guan, H. (2012). Static program analysis assisted dynamic taint tracking for software vulnerability discovery. *Computers & Mathematics with Applications (Oxford, England), 63*(2), 469–480. doi:10.1016/j.camwa.2011.08.001

Zhang, Y., Ye, Q., & Xu, Z. (2015). Cloud computing security: From single to multi-clouds. *Future Generation Computer Systems, 51*, 1–3.

Zheng, B., Yoon, S. W., & Lam, S. S. (2014). Breast cancer diagnosis based on feature extraction using a hybrid of K-means and support vector machine algorithms. *Expert Systems with Applications, 41*(4), 1476–1482. doi:10.1016/j.eswa.2013.08.044

Zhonghua, V. (2018). *Artificial bee colony constrained optimization algorithm with hybrid discrete variables and its application.* Acta Electronica Malaysia (AEM).

Zhou, Y., & Zhang, P. (2021). Quantum Machine Learning for Power System Stability Assessment. arXiv preprint arXiv:2104.04855.

Zhu, B., Joseph, A., & Sastry, S. (2011). A taxonomy of cyber-attacks on SCADA systems. *2011 International conference on internet of things and 4th international conference on cyber physical and social computing.* IEEE. 10.1109/iThings/CPSCom.2011.34

Zhu, H. J., You, Z. H., Zhu, Z. X., Shi, W. L., Chen, X., & Cheng, L. (2018). DroidDet: Effective and robust detection of android malware using static analysis along with rotation forest model. *Neurocomputing, 272*, 638–646. doi:10.1016/j.neucom.2017.07.030

Zorzetti, M., Signoretti, I., Salerno, L., Marczak, S., & Bastos, R. (2022). Improving Agile Software Development using User-Centered Design and Lean Startup. *Information and Software Technology, 141*(October 2020), 106718.

About the Contributors

Prachi Ahlawat is an accomplished Associate Professor at The NorthCap University, leading the Cyber Security & Forensics specialization within the Department of Computer Science and Engineering. Her research interests span diverse areas such as Malware Analysis and Detection, Cyber Security, Digital Forensics, Memory Forensics, and the Security Challenges of Wireless Sensor Networks. Her research has resulted in numerous publications in high-impact factor journals indexed in Scopus and Web of Science, as well as presentations at prestigious national and international conferences.

Justice Kwame Appati is a lecturer in the School of Physical and Mathematical Science (SPMS) and the Department of Computer Science. He began his teaching career at Kwame Nkrumah University of Science and Technology in Kumasi as a graduate assistant and then later moved to the University of Ghana in 2017 as a lecturer. Justice earned a PhD, in Applied Mathematics from Kwame Nkrumah University Science and Technology in 2016. He also graduated in 2010 and 2013 with a BSc. Mathematics and MPhil Applied Mathematics from the same institution. His current research includes data science, mathematical intelligence, image processing and scientific computing, He has singly and jointly supervised undergraduate and postgraduate students from Kwame Nkrumah University of Science and Technology (KNUST), National Institute of Mathematical Sciences (NIMS), African Institute of Mathematical Sciences (AIMS) and the University of Ghana. Currently, Justice handles course like Design and Analysis of Algorithm, Artificial Intelligence, Formal Methods and Computer Vision. He looks forward to working with everyone interested in his field of study more especially, Intelligence and Data Science.

Rita Chhikara is currently working as the Head and Professor with the Department of CSE. A target driven, dedicated professional with more than 22 years of experience in teaching, administration and research. She holds a B.E Degree from Pune University, M.Tech from Punjab Technical University and Ph.D. Degree from The NorthCap University in the area of Machine Learning and Information Security. She is EICT and IIT Roorkee Certified Data Science Professional. She has completed two DST sponsored projects in the area of Steganalysis and Dementia. Her dedication and commitment has contributed towards successful implementation of Specializations in emerging areas in the Department. Her current areas of research include Data Mining, Pattern Recognition, Machine Learning, Image Processing, and Deep Learning. She has been instrumental in imparting training in latest programming language for Data Science to Government officials. She has published around 65 papers in peer-reviewed International Journals with good indexing and reputed national/international conference proceedings and published a book on Intelligent Healthcare: Applications of AI in eHealth in Springer. Her belief of sharing knowledge led her to deliver talks on emerging topics of Machine Learning in various reputed conferences, FDPs and Ted-Ed events. Her administrative responsibilities as NIRF nodal officer and NAAC coordinator has contributed in improving visibility of the University. Recipient of Teaching and Research Excellence National Award, certificate of appreciation for Judge Toyacathon 2021 organized by Ministry of Education and Star performer award at NCU. She has chaired various sessions in Springer, IEEE and Elsevier conferences in India, Malaysia and Singapore. She has guided around 35 B. Tech projects, 15 M.Tech theses, 3 Ph.D Scholars and currently supervising 6 Ph.D. Scholars. She is a professional member of ISTE, ACM, IEEE, and IET.

Sangeetha Ganesan received her B.E degree in Computer Science and Engineering from Periyar University Salem, M.E degree in Computer Science and Engineering from Anna University, Chennai, and Ph.D., in Faculty of Information and Communication Engineering, Anna University, Chennai. She is currently working as an Associate Professor in R.M.K. College of Engineering and Technology, Puduvoyal. Her research interests are Distributed Computing, Cloud Computing, Security, Data Science and Machine Learning.

G. Gangadevi is Assistant Professor Department of computer science and engineering SRM Institute of Science and Technology RAMAPURAM Chennai. She received her B.E computer science and Engineering in the year 2007, M.Tech degree in 2013 and received her Ph.D in the year 2023. Her area of research and interest includes machine learning,deep learning and data science.

Sangeetha Ganesan received her B.E degree in Computer Science and Engineering from Periyar University Salem, M.E degree in Computer Science and Engineering from Anna University, Chennai, and Ph.D., in Faculty of Information and Communication Engineering, Anna University, Chennai. She is currently working as an Associate Professor in R.M.K. College of Engineering and Technology, Puduvoyal. Her research interests are Distributed Computing, Cloud Computing, Security, Data Science and Machine Learning.

Ana Hol, PhD, Winner of the University Medal, is an Associate Dean Learning and Teaching at the School of Computer, Data and Mathematical Sciences at the Western Sydney University. Her research interests are in the areas of Information Systems, Information Technology use, acceptance and adoption; eTransformation and eCollaboration across industries within developed and developing countries. Ana authored over 70 publications. She is a co-editor of the International Journal on Advances in ICT for Emerging Regions and a program committee member and the reviewer for 13 international conferences. Ana is a keen educator and innovator. She received a Vice Chancellor Excellence Award for the excellence in leadership in 2016. She is a winner of both 2018 Australian Computer Society Digital Disruptor ICT Educator of The Year Award and 2018 SEARCC Global ICT Educator of the Year Award.

Sujiban I. completed his M.Sc. degree in Cyber Forensics and Information Security from Dr. M.G.R Educational and Research Institute, in April'2023. His area of interest is Cyber Forensics and Information Security

J. Jeya is currently working as Assistant Professor in SRM Institute of Science and Technology, Ramapuram Campus. Received M.E Degree from Vel Tech Multi Tech Dr.Rangarajan Dr.Sakunthala Engineering College in Computer Science and Engineering in the year 2009 and Ph.D degree from Veltech University in the year 2017. She has teaching experience of 18+ years at Undergraduate and Postgraduate Level. She has 15+ publications . She has guided more than 25 projects for UG and PG students. She has organized many Workshops and Seminars /Webinars for students as well as faculty members.

Ankitha K. is working as Associate Professor in NMAMIT, Nitte, Karkala. 14 years teaching experience and 8 years research experience. Have published more than 30 papers in journals and conferences.

Surya Prakhash doing his M.C.A degree in SRM University, Chennai. His area of interest is Cyber Forensics and Information Security

Nguyen Thi Dieu Linh, Ph.D. is Dy. Head of Science and Technology Department, Hanoi University of Industry, Vietnam (HaUI). She has more than 20 years of academic experience in Electronics, IoT, Smart Garden and Telecommunication. She has authored or co-authored many research articles that are published in journals, books and conference proceedings. She teaches graduate & post graduate level courses at HaUI, Viet Nam. She is Editor for many Books such as: "Artificial Intelligence Trends for Data Analytics Using Machine Learning and Deep Learning Approaches" and "Distributed Artificial Intelligence: A Modern Approach" publisher by Taylor & Francis Group, LLC, USA; " Intelligent System and Networks – Selected Articles from ICISN 2021, Vietnam" publisher by Springer Singapore, index by Scopus. Author/Editor for "Data Science and Medical Informatics in Healthcare Technologies" publisher by Springer Singapore, index by Scopus. She is also board member with International Journal of Hyperconnectivity and the Internet of Things (IJHIoT) and some other reputed journal and international conferences. She has attended to many conferences as Keynote Speaker, Session Chair and Guest Honor. Apart that She has chaired many technical events in different universities in Viet Nam. She worked actively as chair in The International Conference on Intelligent Systems & Networks -ICISN 2021 and ICISN 2022, 2023 ; International Conference on Research in Management and Technovation (ICRMAT 2021, 2022, 2023). She is the organizing chair for the International Conference on Intelligent Systems & Networks, (ICISN 2024); International Conference on Research in Management and Technovation (ICRMAT 2024).

Hoang Viet Long received a Ph.D. diploma in Computer Science at Hanoi University of Science and Technology in 2011, specializing in fuzzy computing and soft computing techniques with applications to electronic engineering. He has been promoted to Associate Professor since 2018. Recently, he has been concerned with Mathematical Models, Machine Learning, and Deep Learning with applications in Cybersecurity.

Bharathi Completed her PhD in 2021 from Dr. M.G.R Educational and Research Institute, Chennai. Her publication and research areas include Networks, Machine Learning and Datamining. She is the author/coauthor of over 6 referred research papers. She has published research papers in various UGC, Scopus indexed journals. She has reviewed numerous research papers in National Conferences and International Conferences.

Uma Mageswari is an Associate Professor and Deputy Head of the Department for Big data Analytics at SRM Institute of Science and Technology, Ramapuram Campus, she is having more than 20 years of academic experience. She has completed, Ph.D in Computer Science and Engineering with Medical Image Processing and M.Tech in Sathyabama University, Chennai, B.E-CSE in Sri Venkateswara College of Engineering, Sriperumbudur, University of Madras. She is a Research Supervisor the SRM Institute of Science and Technology. She published more than 40 research papers published in SCI, Scopus and UGC Care Journals. She has already published 2 books in the Computer Science domain. She has organised and participated as a core member in numerous international and national Guest Lectue, FDP's and National and International Conferences. She has two patents. She has been a member of numerous Board of Studeis and professional organizations. He has received numerous awards, including the "Tamilnadu Chief Minister Medal". She is the active member for IEEE, ACM, ISTE, CSTA and IAENG Association. Under her leadership, the Institute has faced the 1st NBA –National Board of Accreditation cycle in the year 2018 and achieved Accreditation Status.

Suneeta Mohanty, Ph.D. (Computer Science) is working as an Associate Professor at the School of Computer Engineering, KIIT Deemed to be University, Bhubaneswar, India. She has 18 years of experience in teaching various subjects in computer science & Engineering to students of Under-graduate and Post Graduate Program. She has published several research papers in peer-reviewed international journals and conferences including IEEE and Springer. She also published many edited book volumes in Springer. Her research area includes cloud computing, Quantum Computing, Edge Computing, Network Security, big data, Internet of Things, and data analytic. She was appointed in many conferences as an organizing chair, session chair, reviewer, and track co-chair.

Chitrakala Muthuveerappan is attached to Building Science, School of Architecture at Victoria University of Wellington (VUW) since 2019. She has expertise in IT implementation on Built Environment and Facilities Management and a decade of Industry experience in assisting BIM-FM integrated solutions. At present, she is keen on innovative digital research solutions reaching the built-environment industry with increased performance in a cost-effective way, especially for SME entrepreneurs. She is currently focusing on automating BIM models using Artificial Intelligence in construction processes. In addition, on her part in Sustainability, developing a material visibility environment integrates the Material petal of Living Building Challenge (LBC) with the Construction Supply Chain for Designers. Dr. Chitrakala strongly believes that 'disseminating knowledge and experience' is one of the best ways to shape everyone.

N. Umasankari is a Research Scholar at Sathyabama Institute of Science and Technology (Deemed to be University), Chennai, TamilNadu. She received her B.E. degree in Information Technology from the erstwhile Periyar Maniammai College of Technology for Women, TamilNadu. M.Tech. degree in Information Technology from the erstwhile Sathyabama University, Chennai, TamilNadu, in 2011, and also M.B.A. degree in General, from Alagappa Unversity, in 2008. She has 17 years of teaching experience. At various times in her career, she has taught, full-time in various reputed universities from 2003 to 2016 in Tamil Nadu and Produced 100% result. She has been a life time professional membership in CSI chapter. Under her Guidance one team was selected for CSI-In-App 7th National level competition.

Prepared and Co-ordinated the DST proposal as a role of R&D In-charge in 2018 for reputed institution in Hyderabad. She acted as a technical committee member in reviewing and guiding for internal and external UG and PG projects under reputed universities in Tamil Nadu and guided UG projects in Hyderabad since 2017. She has approximately 10 conference publications and 5 international journal publications. She has published 2 National Patents. She is currently working as an Assistant Professor at School of Computing, Department of CSE, Sathyabama Institute of Science and Technology, Chennai, India. Her current research interests include Multimodal Biometrics, Image Processing, Network Security, Data Science, Cyber Security, and Secured data transmission on IoT Devices.

Nguyen Ngoc Cuong is Rector of the University of Technology - Logistics of Public Security, researched in the fields of mathematics, information, applied mathematics and information security.

Umamaheswari Purushothaman received M.Tech in Computer Science from SASTRA Deemed University, Thanjavur, Tamil Nadu, and India in 2011 and M.B.A from Alagappa University, Karaikudi, Tamil Nadu, and India in the year 2006. She is pursuing a Doctoral degree in Computer Science and Engineering from SASTRA Deemed University. She has 17 years of teaching experience for UG and PG courses in Computer Science and presently working as an Assistant Professor in the department of computer science and engineering at SASTRA University, SRC Campus, and Kumbakonam. Her research interest is in Data Mining, Machine Learning, and Deep learning. She published research papers in Book chapters, International Conferences, Scopus and Science Citation Indexed Journals.

Sumathi Pawar is working as Associate Professor in NMAMIT, Nitte, Karkala. 20 years teaching experience and 15 years research experience. Have published more than 30 papers in journals and conferences.

G. Aarthy Priscilla, MCA, M.Phil., Ph.D.,NET, working as an Assistant Professor and HoD of BCA Department in St.Annes Arts and Science College, Madhavaram, Chennai. She has 14 years of teaching experiences in Arts and Science, and Engineering Colleges. She was awarded Ph.D. on March 2019. And cleared NET (National Eligibility test) on February 2022. She has published many research papers in National/International Conferences and referred Journals. Her main area of interest are Cloud Computing, Data Mining and IoT (Internet of Things).

R. Surekha completed her PhD in 2022 at Dr. M.G.R Educational and Research Institute. She is currently working as Assistant Professor in St.Annes Arts and Science College, Madhavaram, Chennai. Her publication and research areas include Image Processing, Machine Learning and Datming. She has published many research papers in Scopus, WOS and UGC care journals.

S. Raja Ratna has completed her B.E. degree in 2000 and M.Tech. degree in 2005. She has completed her Ph.D. degree in Information and Communication Engineering at Anna University, Chennai in the year 2015. Cur- rently, she is working as Assistant Professor in the department of CSE in SRM Institute of Science and Technology, Ramapuram, Chennai. She has more than 15 years of teaching experience in Engineering colleges. Her area of interest includes cyber security, wireless network and wireless security.

S. Deepa is currently working as Assistant Professor in the Department of Computer Science and Engineering in SRM Institute of Science and Technology (Ramapuram Campus). She received her BE (CSE) from Sri Venkateswara College of Engineering and Technology, Madras University, ME (CSE) from Jaya Engineering College, Anna University and PhD from College of Engineering, Anna University. She has 14.5 years of teaching experience and she has published more than 20 papers in reputed journals and conferences. She is an active member in ISTE. Her research interest include Image processing and Pattern Recognition. She also hosted many FDP, workshop and seminar and key role in accreditation activities.

Pratheepa S. - Contributing Author| **S. Pratheepa** completed her PhD in 2021, from Mother Teresa Women's University, Kodaikanal. Her publication and research areas include Image Processing, Artificial Intelligence, Machine Learning.. She is the author/coauthor of over 3 referred research papers. She has published research papers in various UGC, Scopus indexed journals. She has reviewed numerous research papers in National Conferences

Sourav Sharma is a dedicated software developer with a bright academic background. He successfully completed his graduation from KIIT University in 2023, marking the beginning of a promising career in the world of technology. Sourav's enthusiasm for the field is evident in his strong interests in artificial intelligence (AI) and cloud computing. What sets Sourav apart is his relentless curiosity and drive to explore uncharted territories within AI and cloud computing. He doesn't merely follow established trends; instead, he actively seeks out unexplored areas, looking for innovative solutions and pushing the boundaries of what's possible. This thirst for knowledge and innovation has already led him to make significant contributions to the tech community. Sourav Sharma is a true visionary, constantly seeking new challenges and opportunities in his quest to advance the realms of AI and cloud computing. As he continues to delve deeper into these fields, there's no doubt that he will leave a lasting impact on the ever-evolving world of technology. His journey is one to watch, as he paves the way for a more advanced and interconnected digital future.

R. Shobarani completed her Ph.D. degree from Mother Teresa women's University, in Feb'2014. She is currently working as a Professor and Research guide in Department of Computer Science, Dr. M.G.R. Educational and Research Institute, Chennai, Tamilnadu. Her publication and research areas include Image Processing, Artificial Intelligence, Machine Learning and Datamining. She is the author/coauthor of over 36 referred research papers. She has published research papers in various UGC, Scopus indexed, SCI journals and patent published at International level. She has reviewed numerous research papers in National Conferences and International Conferences.

Pham Sy Nguyen has 15 years of experience in research, teaching and ensuring information security and network security.

R. Vadivel completed his B.E. in Periyar University. M.E. in Annamalai University, Chidambaram. He obtained his PhD degree from Manonmaniam Sundaranar University. At present, he is working as an Associate Professor in the Department of Information Technology, Bharathiar University, Coimbatore. He has published more than 123 research papers in National, International Journals and Conferences, Book Chapters. His research interest lies in the area of Computer Networks & Security, Mobile Computing, Mobile Ad-Hoc Networks, Wireless Sensor Networks, Data mining and Digital Signal Processing. He is a life member of CSI, ISTE, ACS, ISCA, AMIE, IACSIT and IAEN

Geetha Vasantha is working as a Associate Professor and published more that 50 papers in journals and conferences.

Teresa Matoso M. Victor studied Chemistry with Chemical Engineering at Northumbria University, United Kingdom 2001 and graduated 2004 with MSc in Sustainable Chemical Engineering, University of Newcastle upon Tyne, United Kingdom. She then joined research group of Prof. Galip Akay and Prof. Alan Ward, School of Chemical Engineering and Advanced Materials, for her PhD, during her studies, invented a micro-porous inert material. She obtained PhD in Chemical Engineering, with a multidisciplinary project encompassing the areas of Chemical Engineering and Biotechnology, defended her thesis 2008. Currently associate professor and Researcher at the Higher Polytechnic Institute of Technologies and Sciences, Luanda, Angola.

Winfred Yaokumah is a researcher and senior faculty at the Department of Computer Science of the University of Ghana. He has published several articles in highly rated journals including Information and Computer Security, Information Resources Management Journal, IEEE Xplore, International Journal of Human Capital and Information Technology, International Journal of Human Capital and Information Technology Professionals, International Journal of Technology and Human Interaction, International Journal of e-Business Research, International Journal of Enterprise Information Systems, Journal of Information Technology Research, International Journal of Information Systems in the Service Sector, and Education and Information Technologies. His research interest includes cyber security, cyber ethics, network security, and information systems security and governance. He serves as a member of the International Review Board for the International Journal of Technology Diffusion.

Index

A

Active Friend 358
Advanced Security Techniques 304, 306
aerial vehicles 24-25
Aggressive Classifier 219, 222, 227-228
Anomaly Detection 4, 53, 57-60, 62, 113, 121, 123, 163, 185, 187, 200, 209, 214, 307, 310, 312
artificial intelligence 5, 18-20, 23, 54, 61, 66-67, 109-110, 112, 116, 119, 123-125, 128, 130, 132, 135-136, 141, 147-148, 198, 208, 210, 254, 288, 302, 305, 307, 323, 390, 397
attack detection 53, 318, 323, 327-332, 352
Attribute Similarity 334, 344-345, 358-359
Attribute Similarity Measure 334, 344
Attribute Weight 334, 343-344, 349

B

banking security 1-3, 6-8, 12-13, 16-20
big data 20, 76-77, 147, 153, 195, 227, 322
Binary Classification 222, 256, 258-259
Blockchain 4-6, 18-20, 147, 246, 288, 299, 366

C

categorical variables 189-190
Classification Algorithms 64, 68, 219, 241, 243, 247, 253, 255, 258-259, 311, 318, 323-325, 327-332, 339-340
Clone Detection 334
Cloud computing 4, 80, 173-175, 181, 185, 187, 206, 211, 288, 299, 301, 306, 318-319, 321-322, 332, 399, 407, 411, 415
Cloud security 135, 288, 298, 306, 309, 319, 322, 384, 397, 411
cloud-based malware 171, 173, 175, 181, 183-184, 188, 190, 194-195
Combinational Algorithm 37-39, 44, 49

contemporary computing 297, 300, 316, 383-384, 387, 398-401, 403-411, 413-416, 418-420, 423, 425-426, 428
Convolution Neural Networks (CNN) 46
Cross-Site Profiles 359
CVSS 265, 274-277, 406
Cyber crime 87, 246
cyber security 1-6, 8, 10-11, 52-54, 64, 66-68, 75-81, 84-85, 162, 198-206, 208, 265-269, 271, 273-275, 277-280, 282, 287, 296-300, 310-312, 316, 318, 352, 380, 383, 385, 387, 390-393, 403
cyber security algorithms 311
Cyber Security Risk Assessment and Management 198-199, 201-202, 208
cyber threats 1-2, 5, 9-10, 12, 14, 16-19, 66, 76-77, 80, 85, 87, 110, 115-116, 121-125, 135-142, 199-202, 204-206, 210, 266, 272, 274, 287-288, 296-300, 302-303, 306, 313-316, 361, 383-387, 396-400, 414-415
cybersecurity 1-6, 8-11, 15, 52-54, 64, 66-68, 75-85, 109-125, 127-128, 130-142, 147, 162, 198-209, 211, 265-269, 271, 273-275, 277-280, 282, 286-288, 296-305, 308-316, 318, 352, 380, 383-394, 396-401, 403, 426
Cybersecurity risks 8-9, 207, 299, 314, 316, 387

D

Data Mining 3, 52, 54, 62, 64, 66-67, 147, 246
Decision Tree 41, 43-44, 55, 64, 189, 192-193, 219, 222, 228-229, 253, 256, 258, 324-325, 327, 392, 394
Deep Learning 3-4, 37-39, 44, 46, 49, 116, 118-119, 158, 187-189, 194, 215, 219-220, 222, 225, 237, 239, 243, 245, 259, 311, 385-386, 390, 392-393
Denial-of-service (DoS) 13, 53, 117, 127, 131, 199, 204-205, 390
digital assets 77, 84, 119, 127, 266, 271, 286-287, 298
Digital Signature 361-375, 377-379, 381
digital technology 2, 123

digital world 85, 266, 401
DSA Algorithm 372
Dynamic analysis 130, 177, 179-181, 183, 244-246

E

electronic devices 297, 300, 314, 316, 361
electronic signatures 362, 364, 370, 380-381
Elliptic curve 375
Encryption 2-4, 14-16, 18-20, 80, 92-97, 100, 103, 105, 127, 176-177, 199, 205-206, 291-294, 298, 300-302, 306-307, 314-316, 372-374, 383-386, 395-396, 401, 404, 409, 411-412, 427
engineering attack 15, 204, 283, 384, 387
Ensemble Machine Learning Model 218
exploratory data 46, 254
Extraction schemes 41-44, 46

F

Fabricated News 218
Fake News 218-222, 224, 227, 233, 237
Fake Profile 336, 339, 343, 352, 359
feature extraction 41-44, 46-47, 133, 181, 185, 192, 194, 213, 247-248
feature selection 4, 41, 67, 113, 189, 191, 214, 241, 245, 247, 249, 251-253, 256, 258-259, 311, 322, 325, 327-329, 391-392, 394
Flying robots 23-25, 27
Friends Network Similarity Measures 334

G

Geospatial data 148-149, 152-154
global economy 172, 398, 400
global optimization 24, 26, 32

H

HIDS 53
Hybrid Features 246, 248

I

Image Steganography 291-294
Information and Communication Technology 81
Intrusion detection 2-4, 13, 20, 52-63, 66-68, 113, 115, 117-118, 120-121, 123-125, 132, 175, 187, 201, 205-206, 209, 211, 214, 271, 297-299, 301, 305, 308, 310, 312, 314, 320, 383-391, 394, 396, 401

Intrusion Detection Systems 13, 20, 52, 54-55, 57, 67-68, 115, 117-118, 120, 123-125, 132, 205, 209, 211, 271, 297-299, 305, 314, 320, 383-384, 386, 394, 396, 401
intrusion prevention 55, 395

K

K-Nearest Neighbour 43-44

L

learning algorithms 4, 19, 38, 44, 46, 62, 64, 110, 113-115, 119, 121-122, 124, 129-130, 133-137, 139-140, 180-182, 187-189, 192-193, 199, 201, 213-214, 218-219, 243, 245, 248-249, 254, 256, 302-303, 305, 307, 311, 322-324, 385-387, 390-393
Learning Detection 37-39, 41, 46, 49
Learning Techniques 4, 25-26, 54, 58-59, 77, 112-113, 118, 121-122, 136-137, 141, 180-181, 184, 192, 200, 219, 299, 305, 311, 318, 385-386
local minima 24, 26, 32-33
logistic regression 54-55, 193, 219-220, 222-225, 245, 323, 339

M

Machine Learning 3-5, 18-20, 23, 26, 28, 37-39, 41-45, 47-49, 52, 54-56, 58-59, 64, 66-67, 77, 109-110, 112-113, 115-116, 118-119, 121-130, 132-142, 148, 158, 171, 179-184, 187-189, 192-195, 198-203, 206, 208, 210, 213-215, 218-222, 227, 231, 233-237, 239, 241, 243-246, 248-252, 254, 256, 258, 288, 299, 302-303, 305, 307, 318, 322-323, 325, 327, 332, 334, 339-340, 385-387, 390-394, 397
Machine learning classification algorithms 323, 325, 327, 332
malicious hackers 268-269, 287
malicious software 12, 76, 85, 118, 123, 127, 131, 172, 178, 204, 302, 385, 387, 390-391
Malware analysis 3-4, 113, 115, 133-135, 173, 177, 179-180, 187, 189, 201, 305
Malware Detection 3-4, 119-120, 122, 130-135, 171, 173, 175, 177, 181, 183-185, 187-190, 192-195, 242-246, 256, 258-259, 305, 310, 312, 385-386, 390-392
Man-in-the-Middle (MitM) 13, 16, 84, 123, 204-205, 378, 409

man-in-the-middle attacks 16, 84, 409
micro blogging 38, 49
Multiclass Classification 241, 258-259
Multilayer Perceptron (MLP) 219, 222, 225-226, 325

N

Naive Bayes 41-45, 47-48, 54-55, 60-61, 64, 192, 219, 232, 322, 324, 339, 386
natural language processing 3, 116, 119, 124, 136, 140, 219-221, 339
network bandwidth 320-321
network infrastructure 127, 267-268, 272-273, 278-281, 287, 300, 408
network traffic 55, 58, 85, 115-118, 120-122, 130, 132-133, 173, 180, 199, 209, 214, 244-245, 302-303, 305, 308, 310, 312, 322-323, 388, 390, 394, 411, 415, 428
Neural Network 41, 44, 46, 61, 63, 117, 158, 185, 187, 219, 243, 253, 325, 392-393
NIDS 53, 55, 60

O

Online banking 1-4, 6-20, 297, 408
Operating System 80, 86, 178, 242, 245, 248, 256, 407, 413, 415, 418
OSN website 359

P

particle swarm 23, 25-29, 31, 33, 43, 311, 323
path planning 23-26, 32
Penetration Testing 18, 127, 265-268, 271-272, 275, 286-288, 298, 300-301, 308, 316, 388, 397, 403, 405, 409-411, 418-419, 426
PKI 92-93, 97, 99, 105, 304
Profile Clone/Fake Profile 334-337, 339, 343, 352-353, 359
Profile Evaluation 359
Proposed model 46, 94, 188-189, 259, 334, 340-341
PSNR 293-294
PSO 23-29, 32-33, 323

Q

quantum computing 19-20, 25, 147, 158-165, 299, 395-396
quantum cryptography 18-20
Quantum Machine Learning 158

R

Random Forest 5, 41, 43-44, 47-48, 183, 187, 189, 192-193, 219-220, 222, 230-231, 252, 257, 322, 324, 327, 339, 390-392
Recurrent Neural Networks (RNN) 4, 214, 220, 311
Reinforcement learning 23-26, 28-33, 110, 115, 181, 183, 214, 311
Renewable Energy 147-148, 155-157, 163-164
reputational damage 13, 15, 205, 266, 297, 313, 387, 398, 400-401, 406
reward point 23, 26-27, 29, 31-33
risk assessment 9, 198-203, 208-209, 266, 283, 286-288, 299, 309, 312, 396, 406, 426
Risk Detection 277, 296-302, 308-312, 316, 361, 383-384, 387, 397-401
Risk Detection Algorithm 312
Risk Indexing 273-274, 279, 283
risk management 9, 81-82, 139, 198-204, 282, 302, 383-386, 396-397, 401
Risk management strategies 199-204, 386, 396
route discovery 23-24

S

Same-Site Profiles 359
security field 265-267, 275
security measures 1-2, 5, 9-10, 12-18, 94, 115, 124-125, 127, 132, 140, 173, 179, 199, 206, 209, 266, 271, 277, 297-300, 303, 306, 314, 316, 320, 386-388, 391, 396-397, 399-400, 404, 414
Security Monitoring 207-208, 309
security risk 137, 198-203, 208, 277
security software 189, 211, 314, 394
Short Term Memory 44-46
Signature Attacks 381
smart surveillance 163
SOAP messages 94
social engineering 12, 15-16, 116, 119, 123, 127, 131, 204-205, 283, 288, 298-299, 384, 387, 399, 406
Social graph 46
Social Media 37-38, 46, 49, 80, 83, 116, 119, 124, 218-220, 227, 297-298, 335-337, 361, 378, 408
Social Network 38, 87, 150, 220, 334-337, 339, 359
social networking 77, 87, 335-338, 340, 358-359
software development 288, 425-426
Spammer 38, 43-45
Spatial Data 147, 154, 161-162, 164-165
SQL injection 84, 127, 204, 308, 408, 414
Static analysis 130, 180, 183, 242-245

Support Vector Machine 41, 43-44, 47-48, 54-55, 155, 185, 253, 339
Suspicious Profiles 353, 359

T

technology security 77
threat detection 3, 109, 116, 118, 121, 123, 125-126, 135, 138-141, 209-211, 213-214, 246, 303, 305-306, 397
threat intelligence 3-4, 77, 109, 119, 124, 127-128, 130, 139-141, 201, 210-211, 283, 288, 298-301, 305, 309, 315-316, 361, 385-386, 395, 397
Twitter 37-46, 49, 218, 335-336
Types of Cyber Risks 206

U

user experience 20

V

Vulnerability assessment reporting 420
Vulnerability assessment tools 416, 420

vulnerability assessments 210, 297, 300-301, 316, 396-397, 403-404, 406-408, 410-411, 425, 427-428
Vulnerability Scanning Techniques 411

W

Web Application 92, 308, 340, 408-409, 414-415, 426-427
Web services 92, 94-95, 97, 100, 103, 105, 319, 335, 359
Word vector 45-46
WSDL 93, 95, 98

X

XKMS 92-94, 96-99, 101, 103-105
XML encryption 92, 94-97, 100, 103
XML signature 92, 94-98, 100-104

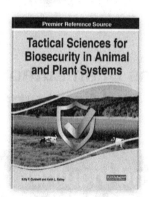

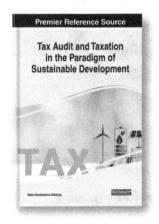

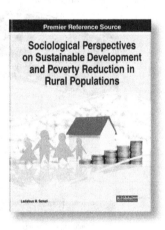

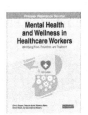